The History of
Northern Rhodesia Police

CW01083086

Frontispiece: Trumpeters of the Northern Rhodesia Police outside the High Court
Lusaka 1961 (Color Photo NRP)

The History of the
Northern Rhodesia Police

TIM WRIGHT

BECM *press*

Published in 2001 by
British Empire & Commonwealth Museum Publishing
Clock Tower Yard, Temple Meads, Bristol BS1 6QH
Design, page make-up and printing by J W Arrowsmith Ltd, Bristol

ISBN 0-9530174-4-3

Dedication

In memory of Richard Rescorla, vice president and head of security, Morgan Stanley Bank, World Trade Centre, New York, 11 September 2001 and of all members and former members of the Northern Rhodesia Police, Northern Rhodesia Police Reserve, Barotse Native Police and North-Eastern Rhodesia Constabulary of whatever race who have given their lives in the performance of their duty.

Contents

List of Maps

List of Colour Plates

(between pages 232 and 233)

List of Illustrations

Foreword

By Sir Robert Foster GCMG, KCVO, KStJ.

With the passage of time the detailed history and the stories of the Colonies, if not recorded other than in the archives, are liable to become submerged, overlaid or even lost. In the case of the Northern Rhodesia Police a book was published in 1954 (nearly fifty years ago) called the story of the Northern Rhodesia Regiment and it contained a brief account of the early days of the Northern Rhodesia Police because the Regiment owed its origins to the Police. The early history is therefore common to both Forces. However, as one would expect, the book is mainly concerned with the activities of the Regiment itself. There exists, therefore, a very large gap in the recorded history of the Police. We are indeed fortunate that Tim Wright has decided to fill this gap, and has written his book *The History of the Northern Rhodesia Police*. He has spent a very great deal of his time seeking out and researching the material resulting in a work containing extensive notes, documentation and detail and which, by any standard, can only be described as a monumental work. It becomes a very valuable addition for all who have or have had interests or connections with Northern Rhodesia. It will also be of general interest about the state of the territory up to independence in 1964.

There were two other contributions which greatly assisted towards publication. The first was that the Police Association managed to raise the funds needed for the publication and secondly The British Empire and Commonwealth Museum, which is always anxious to fill gaps in the history of the Empire, agreed to arrange publication. Tim Wright and all those concerned with the publication of this book are to be congratulated on their achievement.

The book itself covers three distinct periods. First the early history when the area was administered by the British South Africa Company, then the time of the first Great War, which very much involved this part of South Africa because of the German territories and finally the time that Northern Rhodesia was taken over by the British Government from the British South Africa Company in 1924 up to Independence in 1964. Each period is recorded with the same high regard to detail and it was during this last period in 1932 that the Police and the Regiment were separated as departments and went their own independent ways in Northern Rhodesia. There followed, from then on, an expansion of the Police and so a great need for training. Later, nearer Independence, it was to become clear that in addition to this additional expansion Africans would need to be found in the senior ranks to replace officers who would leave at Independence. There was very little time for all this to take place and the Police and others concerned with the administration would have hoped for and benefited from more time to deal with the problem but it was not to be. However great credit must go to all concerned with training that when the Northern Rhodesia Police ceased to exist as an operational force at Independence there was left behind in its place an effective Police Force, to be known as the Zambian Police Force.

The Northern Rhodesia Police have had a very remarkable history dealing with a wide variety of problems and activities in a very large part of Africa and they can be extremely proud that they can justly claim a job very well done and often in difficult conditions.

Introduction

It is now thirty seven years since the Northern Rhodesia Police passed into history when the Republic of Zambia came into existence on 24 October 1964. The *Story of the Northern Rhodesia Regiment*, published in Lusaka in 1953, did not neglect the civil side of the Force in the years up to 1 April 1932 when the old Northern Rhodesia Police split into what was to become the Regiment, and a more conventional colonial police force. The Special Edition of the Northern Rhodesia Police magazine, *Nkhwazi*, in April 1964, contained a short history written by Paul Speich. My contribution to the *Northern Rhodesia Record* in 1992, was written under the impression that it was to be annexed to a history of the Provincial Administration and highlighted links with that, the most prestigious and probably most important, part of the Government Service. My researches since then have revealed much new material so that I believe I can fairly claim that this work is not merely a consolidation of what has been previously written about the NRP, including my series of articles in the Journal of the Police History Society, but the first full history of the NRP from its roots in the last decade of the Nineteenth Century.

Some may question why so much space has been devoted to the campaigns in which the Military Branch of the Force took part between 1914 and 1918 and to military aspects over the following thirteen years. Firstly I believe I have been able to provide a more comprehensive account than that in *The Story of the Northern Rhodesia Regiment*, of the part played by the NRP in the conquest of what is now Tanzania. Secondly from 1911 until 1927 there was no direct recruitment of Africans into the Town and District police. Candidates had first to serve four years in the Military Branch. Capt Percy Wardroper, the Commissioner of Police in 1932, had himself served with the Service Battalion in the Field from 1915 until 1918 and been Adjutant of the Force for several years thereafter. Commissioned officers in the 1920s might find themselves serving a tour of duty with the Town and District police at Livingstone or Broken Hill before returning to the Military Branch. At least one Town and District constable, Ronald Howe who went on to become Chief Inspector, had a spell at the Front. The Northern Rhodesia Regiment rightly inherited the Battle Honours and colours but could claim no higher proportion of veterans in its ranks than the purely civil NRP of 1932.

In Peace the purpose of the old Military Branch was to deal with any major disturbances beyond the capabilities of the civil administrative officials and the Town and District Police. In fact the role of the Military Branch was identical with that assumed by the Northern Rhodesia Police Mobile Unit in 1949. When there was a real danger of armed incursion from Zaire in the early 1960s platoons of the Mobile Unit were deployed on the border alongside regular infantry units, as indeed, A/Insp Bernard O'Leary and a police detachment were deployed alongside the Northern Rhodesia Regiment on the same border in 1939. One cannot properly separate the military and police history of pre–1932 Northern Rhodesia.

The members of a police force serve in diverse detachments at full stretch 365 days a year in peace and war. Even on a small station the investigation of one particular crime or a public order operation will seldom involve the whole staff. Patrols and other investigations will continue though the heavens may fall. Small parties or individual police officers are engaged in separate battles and skirmishes in the war against crime, the protection of life and property and maintenance of the Sovereign's peace. To write the history of a police force is, therefore, a very different undertaking from writing that of a battalion of infantry operating as a body or in a handful of sub-units or detachments, with periods of action interspersed with peacetime routine and training, or even of a regiment with battalions serving in different theatres. Whether involved in great events or small a police force is engaged on a myriad of fronts and can never be taken out of the line to retrain, rest or reorganise. Of course major events and investigations will dominate its written history but the reader should bear in mind that in 'other corners of the Field' life was not without its dangers, frustrations and successes. It is some 15 years since a challenge in the Northern Rhodesia Police Association Newsletter led me to assemble my old Force magazines and other papers from my service with the NRP and Zambia Police, L H Gann's 'Birth of a Plural Society' and Moyse-Bartlett's definitive history of the King's African Rifles, both purchased many years before in Lusaka, and sketch out my first draft of this work. In the late 1960s I had foolishly lent out my copy of *The Story of the Northern Rhodesia Regiment*, which had not been returned. In 1990 the book was republished by Galago but this was the 1980s and I was in Germany. Happily I was able to borrow copies of that work and Colin Harding's three books from the Ministry of Defence Library (Central and Army) in Whitehall the staff of which served me well in this and other matters.

My thanks are also due to the staffs of the Public Record Office, British Library, Rhodes House Library, Oxford, Imperial War Museum, the National Police College library, Bramshill, the Commonwealth War Graves Commission, my good friends at the Prince Consort's Library, Aldershot, Dr Peter Liddle and his staff at the Liddle Collection, Leeds University and Sir Peter O'Sullevan, the son of an officer who served in the Barotse Native Police and the North-Eastern Rhodesia Constabulary and was a founder member of the Northern Rhodesia Police, Alan Walker, Peter Silk, Mike Faddy and Brian Taylor. I am grateful to the committee of the Northern Rhodesia Police Association, Michael Mylod OBE, our Chairman, Jeremy Hawkins, Chris Lyon and Priscilla Flower-Smith who read my draft, corrected errors and made helpful suggestions. I am especially grateful to Jeremy who lent me his full run of the Northern Rhodesia Journal and other publications, some of which he had previously lent me at Livingstone in 1958. I have also received assistance from many other old friends and colleagues including John Coates CPM, Bob Barkley CPM, Denis Bird MBE CPM, Don Bruce QPM, Fred Buckton, who lent me his almost full run of Nkhwazi, Wally Clarke, Roger Heckford, Nick Hulette, Joe Joseph OBE, Iain Mackintosh, Alan Marginson, John Maybank, David (Chiefie) Oliver CPM, David Deptford QPM CPM, Malcolm Flower-Smith, A St John Sugg CMG, Paul Wheeler, David Williams, the late Ross Collett CPM and 'Compol' himself, the late Col J P I Fforde CBE QPM CPM. Mention must also be made of L A Heatlie, David Mkankaulwa and B D (Chunky) Powell and Edward Deane Simmons MBE and Eddie Raubenheimer from whose contributions to Nkhwazi and the NRP Association Newsletter I have quoted or drawn material.

Every effort has been made to obtain permission to reproduce copyright material. If any proper acknowledgement has not been made, copyright holders will please accept my sincere apologies.

T B WRIGHT
Fleet, Hampshire, March 2001

CHAPTER 1

The Locus in Quo

The Territory with which we are concerned is an area of about 290,600 square miles, almost as large as France, Switzerland, Austria and Hungary together. Northern Rhodesia is now Zambia, but in 1890, when our story starts, it had no name at all and was not a political unit.

It was one of the last spoils in the 'Scramble for Africa', the major part of a political vacuum between the two Portuguese colonies of Angola or Portuguese West Africa, and Mozambique or Portuguese East Africa. If asked to whom it belonged, the Portuguese would have said it was theirs, but there had been little Portuguese penetration and no settlement or occupation.

To the south is the only major natural boundary, the Zambezi River. The late-comer to colonial expansion, Imperial Germany, had established itself south of Angola in South West Africa, now Namibia, and stretched out a finger to the east. On 28th May 1890, by treaty with the other European powers, she acquired what was to become known as the Caprivi Strip, with an eighty mile frontage on the South Bank of the Zambezi from Katima Mulilo to Kazungula[1]. From Kazungula ran the Missionary Road to the South, through Khama's[2] Country, now Botswana, but in the days of the Northern Rhodesia Police, Bechuanaland. At Germany's request the Zambezi was declared an international waterway.

East of Kazungula the South Bank of the Zambezi belonged to Lobengula, the Matabele King, who held sway over his own people and the Mashona in what was soon to become Southern Rhodesia and is now Zimbabwe.[3] The Matabele raided at will across the Zambezi against the peaceloving and unorganised Batonga.

To the North-East is now Malawi, where Harry Johnston was taking over from Lugard the task of defeating the Arab slave-traders, and was to establish the Protectorate of British Central Africa, later Nyasaland. Round the north of Lake Nyasa as far as Lake Tanganyika were the Germans again, extending German East Africa inland from the coast. In 1919 it was to become the Tanganyika Territory, now Tanzania.

In the North-West the King of the Belgians was carving out his private fiefdom, the Congo Free State.

A glance at a map of Zambia shows its strange, almost diablo, shape, with a wasp waist just over a hundred miles wide where the Katanga Province of The Congo, geologically as well as geographically part of the Zambian Copperbelt, cuts

1

in. Until November 1890 the Katanga, or Garenganze, was also nomansland as far as the European powers were concerned. Since 1875 it had been known to be rich in minerals. Cecil Rhodes wanted it. So did King Leopold of the Belgians.[4]

At Rhodes' behest Joseph Thomson and Alfred Sharpe[5] set out separately from Lake Nyasa to acquire it for him and the British flag. Thomson travelled south of Lake Bangweulu, but suffering from smallpox, and deserted by his carriers in the Watwa Swamps, had to give up. Sharpe chose a route via Lake Mweru. For a time he was held up by Chief Kazembe, but eventually, in November 1890, arrived in rags at the village of Chief Mushidi, or Msiri, who ruled over the Katanga. Mushidi had been warned by Frederick Arnot[6], a missionary friend, against speculating concession hunters. Unfortunately Arnot was away when Sharpe made his unimpressive appearance. Mushidi could not believe that a man in such a parlous state could speak for the mighty Queen Victoria. He sent Sharpe away.

That night Mushidi is said to have had a dream which caused him to change his mind. In any event he sent a message for Sharpe to return. He wanted the protection of the British rather than that of the Belgians. The message was intercepted by Captain W.G.Stairs, a Canadian-born British Army officer, temporarily in the service of the Belgian King and the Compagnie du Katanga[7]. Stairs had an impressive escort. In his conversations Stairs stressed that he was British. Eventually Mushidi signed a concession. The flag of the Congo was then raised. Mushidi realised his position and ran into his village. He was followed and, in the ensuing fracas, shot dead.

One may speculate endlessly as to the effect of this incident on the history of the Rhodesias. Whether one regards the Katangese as better or worse off for having had seventy years of Belgian rather than British rule, Stairs had done his own country a disservice.

Zambia consists geographically of a number of distinct sections. First there is the great North-Eastern Plateau which rises to an occasional altitude of 5,000 feet. In the West this is watered by the tributaries of the Luapula River and contains Laka Bangweulu. The plateau forms a watershed which separates the drainage system of the Luapula from that of the Zambezi. The Luapula Valley is fertile. In the waterways of the Bangweulu swamps and of Lake Mweru to the North, fish and waterfowl abounded.

The south-eastern section of the country includes the valley of the Luangwa River, which flows into the Zambezi. To the East, where Fort Jameson (now Chipata) was later built, was its most densely populated area. The third main region is formed by the southern portion of the central plateau with an average height of some 1,000 metres. This extends over much of what became, for a time, North-Western Rhodesia. It includes the fertile Kafue valley, merging into the tsetse infested Kasempa flat lands to the West. The northern part of this plateau, which was thinly populated, touches Angola in the West and the former Belgian Congo, in the North. To the East it merges into the north-eastern plateau.

The last main section is the Barotse valley, now the Western Province of Zambia, watered by the Central Zambezi and its confluents. Again this is fertile country. It was free from tsetse fly. Many people lived there.

Most of the country was well wooded, but with several vast open plains, and thousands of square miles under grass along parts of the Kafue and Zambezi rivers. Tall reeds covered the area south of Lake Bangweulu. In these grassy plains there is swampland where the water level fluctuates with the seasons. In the southern part of the plateau the bush is sparser and the open veldt suitable for cattle.

Until the mid-Nineteenth Century most of these regions were unknown to Europe. There were few natural lines of communication. The traveller was impeded by disease, by the uncertainties of the tropical climate, and by the vast distances of the continent. The country seemed to contain nothing to attract a white man. The natives possessed neither horses, ploughs, nor the wheel. The strength of their muscles was their only source of power. They had only hoes, axes, bows, and spears, to assist them with their agriculture, hunting, and wars. Whenever they exhausted the fertility of their gardens they moved on. Their life centred on the village, mainly composed of kinsmen. There was little incentive for trade.

Tribal chiefs controlled the allocation of land, grazing grounds, and fishing sites. The chief arbitrated disputes. He organised the defence of the tribe against outside attack. Most aspects of life were ruled by custom approved by ancestral spirits. Individual enterprise was discouraged for fear of wrecking tribal cohesion on which survival depended. Malaria, hook-worm, bilharzia, and other diseases were endemic and sapped the energy of native and visitor alike.

The country was sparsely populated by some seventy different tribes. The most powerful and politically organised were the Lozi, or Barotse. They had migrated from the Congo Basin in about 1700 and settled in the Central Zambezi valley, around their capital, Lealui. From here their Litunga, or king, Lewanika since 1878[8], claimed suzerainty over all tribes as far east as the Kafue. The language of the Barotse ruling class was Kololo, inherited from the Makololo, a Basuto horde which overran Barotseland in 1838 and held sway there until expelled in 1864. Sebituane, the Makololo chief, had crossed the Zambezi near the Victoria Falls, decimating the population, and occupied what later became the Namwala and Kalomo districts before moving west to Linyanti on the Chobe River.

Down river the remnants of the Batoka and Leya lived around the Victoria Falls ('Mosi-oa-Tunya' – 'the smoke that thunders'). They survived by taking refuge on the islands of the Zambezi whenever Matabele or Lozi impis approached.

To the East of the Falls, along the Zambezi Valley as far as the junction with the Kafue River, the Tonga people had been settled since about 1400. The Batonga had virtually no political organisation. They and their cattle were easy prey to raids by Matabele from the South, and their own Lozi overlords. The Mashukulumbwe or Ila, further from either aggressor in the Kafue Hook, remained proud and warlike.

In the far East, around present-day Chipata, the Ngoni were dominant. They were recent immigrants. Like the Matabele, the Ngoni had been driven out of Zululand by Shaka in 1821. They had fought their way north and finally settled to the South of Lake Nyasa in northern Mozambique as well as in areas which were to become parts of Northern Rhodesia and Nyasaland. Those in Northern Rhodesia were ruled by Chief Mpezeni. They had arrived in 1835. The Ngoni

3

remained highly militarised, organised in age regiments on Zulu lines, right up until 1920. They had incorporated both male and female captives into the tribe and so kept their numbers high. The Ngoni had subdued the Nsenga and Chewa who had settled in the area some two centuries earlier.

On the north-eastern plateau the Bemba were the most numerous and powerful tribe. Originating, like most of the tribes of Northern Rhodesia, in the Congo Basin, they had settled down in the Seventeenth Century and set up a strongly centralised military state under their paramount chief, Chitimukulu[9]. Their land was poor. So, instead of trading with the neighbouring Tabwa salt-makers, Tipa iron-makers or Mambwe cattle breeders, the Bemba raided them. Unlike the Ngoni, it was not Bemba policy to assimilate captives into the tribe. Instead they took to selling them to the Arab slave-traders.

The Lunda, under Chief Kazembe[10], dominated the Luapula Valley. They also originated in the Congo Basin, as part of the Lunda-Luba empire of Mwata Yamvwa. They maintained their links with the Lunda of the Congo and the 'Western Lunda' who had migrated in the mid-eighteenth century to the area around the headwaters of the Zambezi. Kazembe traded in slaves and ivory.

The Western Lunda were more oppressed than oppressors. Although they had once ruled the Kaonde to the South, with whom they still intermarried, they were themselves raided by the Lovale to the West, and by the Chokwe, who had acquired guns from the Portuguese.[11]

In 1798, Dr. F. de Lacerda, a Brazilian administrator and scholar[12], had penetrated as far as Kazembe's land. He was trying to establish an overland route to link Mozambique and Angola and bar British expansion which he foresaw as the inevitable result of the British occupation of the Cape. De Lacerda died. His expedition lost heart and returned to Tete.

In 1827 the Portuguese established a small station in the Luangwa Valley, on the route to Kazembe's land. This did not last long.

A Portuguese officer who visited Kazembe's capital in 1830, reported that it was very large, being about three kilometres across, with streets 'wide, straight, and very clean.' Strict precautions were enforced against fire. All household fires had to be extinguished each night. Kazembe IV was a despot whose laws were enforced by some thirty 'policemen' with the assistance of an army of spies and the chief executioner.

As a result of frequent clashes with the Nsenga chief, Mburuma, a fort built in 1806 at Feira, at the mouth of the Luangwa, was abandoned in 1836. At the same time a trading post at Zumbo on the Mozambique bank was evacuated. From 1845 onwards Silva Porto made a number of journeys to Barotseland and opened up that country to trade from Benguella. De Lacerda and Porto's plans for Portuguese political expansion across Africa were incapable of realisation for lack of resources and energy on the part of their government.[13]

The first Briton to reach the Territory was, of course, David Livingstone. Working north from the mission station at Kuruman in Bechuanaland, accompanied by his friend, William Cotton Oswell, Livingstone reached the Zambezi at Sesheke in 1851.[14] In 1853 he returned up the Missionary Road and went upriver to Linyanti. From there he travelled overland with a party of Makololo to reach the West Coast at Luanda. After a rest there Livingstone made his way back to Barotseland and started downriver again to become the first white man known to have seen the Victoria Falls.

In his diary the explorer wrote, 'Musioatunya bears SSE from Sekota islet after 20 minutes sail thence on 16th November 1855, saw three or five large columns of vapour rising 100 or more feet'[15]. He continued downriver to the mouth of the Zambezi, the first white man to cross Africa from west to east. The Makololo had accompanied him all the way to Quelimane, which was reached in May 1856.

Two years later Livingstone set off again from the mouth of the Zambezi. He was now 'Consul for the East Coast of Africa to the South of Zanzibar and for the Unexplored Interior'. He hoped to prove the river navigable right up to the Falls. Of course he found the Quebrabassa Rapids impassable and turned off up the Shire to Lake Nyasa. In March 1860 he set off for Barotseland to bring his faithful Makololo home.

It was in 1860 that the second European reached the Falls. The hunter, William Baldwin, offended the local chief by jumping from a boat into the river and swimming to the North Bank. The Chief told him that he would have to stay until, as Baldwin wrote: 'I had paid him for the water I drank and washed in, the wood I burned, the grass my horses ate; and it was a great offence that I had taken a plunge into the river on coming out of one of his punts; if I had been drowned or devoured by a crocodile or sea cow, Sekeletu would have blamed him, and had I lost my footing and fallen down the Falls, my nation would have said the Makololo had killed me: and altogether I had given him great uneasiness'.[16] (By sea cow Baldwin meant a hippo).

One can feel sympathy for the Chief! Luckily for Baldwin, Livingstone, his brother Charles and Dr. Kirk[17] arrived a week later, on 9th August, on their way to Barotseland. They persuaded the Chief to let Baldwin go south.

After escorting his Makololo home, Livingstone returned to the coast via Lake Nyasa. In 1865 he commenced his last great journey. He reached Lake Mweru in 1867 and Bangweulu in 1868. He then went north to Lake Tanganyika before coming back to die at Chitambo, south of Lake Bangweulu, on 1st May 1873.

The old adage, 'trade follows the flag' was not true of Northern Rhodesia. It would be more accurate to say that trade followed the Cross and the flag followed trade. Missionaries were the first Europeans to settle in Northern Rhodesia, although between 1860 and 1890 a number of hunters, traders, and sightseers visited the Victoria Falls. In 1871 George Westbeech[18] set up a permanent trading centre for ivory and rhino horn at Pandamatenga, about fifty miles south of Kazungula. From here he sent African and Coloured hunters north of the Zambezi. The young F C Selous[19] was hunting in Barotseland when he was attacked by some Mashukulumbwe and his retinue wiped out. The famous hunter escaped and walked, starving, to the sanctuary of a mission.

In 1877, inspired by Livingstone's work and reputation, the London Missionary Society sent an expedition to Lake Tanganyika. By 1889 they had established themselves among the Lunga and Mambwe, who gathered round the mission stations for protection from Bemba and Arab slavers. F S Arnot of the Plymouth

Brethren attempted to establish a mission in Barotseland, but failed. He moved north to Katanga, to become the trusted adviser of the ill-fated Mushidi.

The Paris Missionary Society was well established in Basutoland. With the support of Westbeech and of the London Missionary Society personnel among the Bamangwato, Lewanika's allies in Bechuanaland, and helped by his knowledge of the Suto tongue, Francis Coillard of the Paris Mission[20] succeeded in opening a permanent station in Barotseland in 1885. Although Lewanika once referred to the Bible as 'that rubbish heap of fables', Coillard soon became an adviser to the Lozi King's council. He also prevailed upon Lewanika to secure the acceptance of Primitive Methodists among the Mashukulumbwe.

The Roman Catholic White Fathers entered the Territory from the Belgian Congo. Chitimukulu of the Bemba would have nothing to do with any white men, but his son, Makasa, welcomed Bishop Dupont. The Plymouth Brethren also entered from the North, settling by Lake Mweru in 1891.

Inspired by Livingstone's memory the Free Church of Scotland Mission founded Livingstonia on Lake Nyasa in 1875. The Free Church did not enter Northern Rhodesia until 1895 and its influence there was never as strong as in Nyasaland. However the establishment of the Free Church of Scotland in Central Africa was to have a profound effect on the political development of Northern Rhodesia. The god-fearing Glasgow businessmen saw that support of the Mission might even bring a profit and in 1878 founded a trading concern, the Livingstonia Central Africa Company, (later known as the African Lakes Corporation), to meet the needs of the missionaries and foster trade with the Africans. In 1881 the Chairman, James Stevenson, offered a substantial sum of money towards the cost of a road to link the north of Lake Nyasa with the southern end of Lake Tanganyika. In 1883 a British Consul was appointed for the area.

In 1884 the African Lakes Corporation opened a trading station at Karonga, the starting point of the 'Stevenson Road' on Lake Nyasa. The stage was set for the confrontation with the slavers which was to end with the destruction of their power, the elimination of their trade, and the establishment of more than 70 years of British administration in Nyasaland and North-Eastern Rhodesia.

Although commonly called Arabs, the slave-traders in this area were usually coastal Swahili, only partly of arab blood. A slaver would enter a district in the role of a peaceful merchant, using all possible means to gain the confidence of the local tribes. He appeared like a powerful chief, surrounded by armed followers or 'ruga ruga'. He provided coveted trade goods, but also firearms and powder, the instruments of power. He made himself an invaluable ally in tribal battles, retaining his share of the captives following victory, which his aid virtually guaranteed. Soon he inspired his friends to embark on raids for no other reason than the acquisition of slaves who were escorted to the coast in long caravans to be shipped to Zanzibar and the Persian Gulf.

Throughout the middle years of the Nineteenth Century the operations of the Arabs steadily developed. Prosperous communities grew up at trading centres on the lakes. From Kilwa, Bagamoyo and other ports on the coast, caravans traversed well beaten tracks to the region around Lake Nyasa, and through Tabora to Ujiji and other places around Lake Tanganyika. The warlike Ngoni, Yao, Bemba, and Kazembe's Lunda were willing allies in the conduct of this trade.

A few miles from Karonga a Swahili Arab, Mlozi, and his associates, Kopakopa, Msalema and others, had built strong stockades overlooking the first section of the Stevenson Road, which ran to the mission station at Mwiniwanda's, about sixty miles north-west of the Lake. At first Mlozi professed friendship towards the African Lakes Corporation's representative at Karonga, L Monteith Fotheringham. At Karonga was merely a store, protected by a low wall open at the lakeside. The arabs traded their ivory at the store, but in July 1887 Mlozi showed signs of driving out the peaceful Ankonde tribesmen and replacing them with his native allies. Fotheringham had only 13 rifles and 34 cartridges. He tried to mediate to prevent a tribal war. Mlozi, with far greater armed strength, treated Fotheringham's efforts with contempt. Hundreds of Ankonde were massacred. In November the slavers surrounded Karonga. The siege was raised by the Mambwe from the Tanganyika plateau. The station was evacuated but soon reoccupied with the help of the Ankonde and Mambwe. In April 1888 a successful attack was made on Msalema's stockade. Kopakopa came to Msalema's aid and the Company's men and their allies had to retire to Karonga. Few of the Ankonde or Mambwe would remain in the field without the prospect of booty. It was clear that, if decisive results were to be obtained, the Company would have to produce reinforcements and supplies on an adequate scale.

Captain Frederick Dealtry Lugard of The Norfolk Regiment[21] happened to be at Blantyre, about to start on a hunting expedition. He offered his services to the Acting Consul and was accepted as commander. On 19th May 1888 Lugard left by steamer for Karonga with nearly twenty white volunteers. With Alfred Sharpe he organised a force of some 220 Atonga, 50 Yao, and 50 Mambwe, with which they enjoyed some success until Lugard was shot and paralysed in both arms, in an attack on Kopakopa's stockade. Fotheringham resumed command until, on 1st October 1889, Harry Johnston[22], arrived, having been recently appointed as Her Majesty's Commissioner and Consul-General for the Territories under British Influence North of the Zambezi. An Armstrong 7 pounder gun, supplied from the United Kingdom by the Nyasa Anti-Slavery and Defence Committee, was also now available. On 22nd October 1889 Johnston signed a treaty with Mlozi providing for the return of the Ankonde to their lands, and for peaceful co-existence between the African Lakes Corporation and Mlozi, Msalema and Kopakopa. The epicentre of the Slavers' War returned temporarily to the South end of the Lake. In May 1891 the whole of Nyasaland, or British Central Africa, was declared a Protectorate with Johnston as Commissioner. There were then 57 Europeans in Nyasaland.

Although the Arab slavers rarely penetrated into the south and west of Northern Rhodesia, slave trading existed there. Portuguese half-castes, known as Achikunda or Mambari, operated from the Zambezi Valley. Their market in Brazil was finally abolished by Government Decree in 1888, but there remained a local demand for labour in Portuguese East Africa. In 1890 Alfred Sharpe found the southern Luangwa Valley largely depopulated by the work of the Mambari. One of these,

Matakenya, owned land and trading stores from Zumbo to Tete, and was said to be able to put 12,000 men into the field.

From the West, Portuguese traders, beyond the reach of their country's administrators, worked through the Mbundu, who supplied guns and powder to Mushidi in Katanga, and Kakenge of the Lovale, in return for slaves and ivory. They were thus encouraged to make raids on their neighbours. From these wasting struggles the Bantu could only be saved by the imposition of stable government. No indigenous power possessed the resources necessary for such a task and salvation came from the European. In the case of Northern Rhodesia, it was literally one European, Cecil John Rhodes.

Contrary to popular modern belief, Queen Victoria's governments were always reluctant Empire builders. They rarely saw any advantage in it. In Nyasaland their hand was forced by the influence of the missionary societies. They had no wish to fill the vacuum to the West, either north or south of the Zambezi.

Rhodes had made a fortune in Kimberley diamonds and another in gold from the Witwatersrand. He firmly believed that the best thing for those not lucky enough to have been born British, was to be governed by the British. If Her Majesty's Government had neither the will nor the money for such philanthropy, he had plenty of both. If he could make a profit for himself and his shareholders by painting the map of Africa red, all well and good. Pure philanthropy was all very well in its way, but 'philanthropy plus five per cent', a good deal better! Using all the influence his wealth and position, as a prominent Cape politician, could bring, and after much hard bargaining, Rhodes secured a Royal Charter for his British South Africa Company on 29th October 1889. The Chartered Company was empowered, inter alia, to 'make treaties, promulgate laws, preserve the peace, maintain a police force, and acquire new concessions . . . ., to make roads, railways, harbours, undertake other public works, own or charter ships, engage in mining, or any other industry, establish banks, make land grants and carry on any lawful commerce, trade, pursuit or business'.

The area in which it was permitted to exercise these vast powers was the whole of south Africa, north of the Colony of Bechuanaland, north and west of the Transvaal and west of Portuguese East Africa. There was no northern limit.

Rhodes had already obtained a controlling interest in the financially ailing African Lakes Corporation. He met Harry Johnston before the latter took up his post in Nyasaland, and gave him a personal cheque for £2,000 to augment the parsimony of the Chancellor of the Exchequer towards the fledgling protectorate.

Johnston and Rhodes shared the dream of a Cape to Cairo railway running entirely over British territory. The Northern Rhodesia Police were to play their part in securing the last of the required land between 1914 and 1918, but by the time German East Africa became the League of Nations Mandated Territory of Tanganyika under British rule, Rhodes had been in his grave for nearly twenty years. Despite the contribution of the Peoples Republic of China by the construction of the TanZam Railway, linking Zambia to the Coast at Dar es Salaam, the dreamed of line from the Cape to Cairo remains uncompleted to this day.

Within a year of the grant of the Charter, not only had Rhodes organised and

despatched his Pioneer Column which established the beginnings of an administration between the Limpopo and the Zambezi, but Lochner, Sharpe, Thomson,
and others were at work, with varying results, to sow the seed north of the
Zambezi.

Notes

1. After Count CAPRIVI Foreign Minister, German Empire
2. KHAMA name of the hereditary ruler of the Bamangwato
3. LOBENGULA King of the Matabele d1893
4. Cecil John RHODES b1853 Bishops Stortford s/o Rev to SA'71 MP Barkly West'81 formed
   De Beers Consolidated Diamond Co'86 Goldfields Ltd'86 PM Cape'90–96 d1902
   LEOPOLD II King of the Belgians succeeded 1865 founded Comite des Etudes de Haut Congo,
   Inter African Asscn: Roi Souverain Congo Free State 8.11.84 d14.12.09
5. Joseph THOMSON b Scotland to North Eastern Zambia 1879 Explorer in East Africa, Masai
   Country'83
   Sir Alfred SHARPE KCMG'03 CB'97 b19.5.1852 Lancaster ed Haileybury, Solicitor Westmin-
   ster'76 Actg Stipendary Magistrate Fiji'85–6 Vice Consul Nyasald'91 Actg Commissioner
   BCA'94 DCommr'96 Commr'97 Gov Nyasald 1907–10 d10.12.35
6. Fredk Stanley ARNOT b'58 Hamilton Scotland, member Plymouth Brethren to SA'74 Potch-
   efstroom, Lealui, Benguella, Katanga established Garenganze Evangelical Mission Bunkya
   (M'siri's) '85 Bihe to Scotland 26.3.89 d1914
   MUSHIDI or MSIRI Chief of the Nyamwezi aka YEKE d20.12.90
7. Capt Wm Grant STAIRS RA b Canada'64 member Stanley's Emin River Expedtion'87–9 d
   Chinde, mouth of the Zambezi'92
8. LEWANIKA d6.2.16 Lealui
9. CHITIMUKULU name of the hereditary ruler of the Bemba
10. KAZEMBE name of hereditary chief of the Eastern Lunda
11. L H Gann *The Birth of a Plural Society* pp1–9
12. Dr Francisco Jose Maria de LACERDA e ALMEIDA b Brazil
13. Gann *Birth of a Plural Society* p15–16
    Antonio Francisco Ferreira da SILVA PORTO Merchant, Barotseland 1849 d'90 Belmonte
    Agila, blew himself up
14. Dr David LIVINGSTONE b Blantyre Scotland 19.3.1813 London Missionary Society Cape
    Town 14.3.41 d1.5.73 Chitambo
    Wm Cotton OSWELL Hunter & Explorer
15. Fagan *The Victoria Falls* 2nd Edn 1964 p22
16. Baldwin *African Hunting from Natal to the Zambezi*, Bentley (London) 1863) p.439 – Wm Chas
    BALDWIN b Lancashire s/o vicar Hunter Sthn Africa 1851–61
17. Dr Sir John KIRK b30 British Agent Zanzibar rtd July 1887
18. Geo WESTBEECH to Africa 1860? Natal'62 established trading centre Pandamatenga'71 d
    liver disease 17.7.88 Kalkfontein
19. Capt Fredk Courtenay SELOUS DSO b1851 ed Rugby to SA 4.9.71 visited Vic Falls'74 Guide
    Pioneer Column SR'90 Raaff's Colmn Matabele War'93 Capt Bulawayo Field Force'96 svd SA
    War'99–02; 25th (Frontiersmen's) Bn The Royal Fusiliers kia 4.1.17 East Africa
20. Francis COILLARD Paris Missionary Society NWR'78 Barotseland'85 d27.5.04
21. Moyse Bartlett *History of the King's African Rifles* pp12–17
    Frederick Dealtry LUGARD GCMG(1911 KCMG'01) CB(1895) DSO('97) PC(1920) 1st
    Baron Lugard of Abinger('28) b22.1.58 s/o Chaplain East India Co, ed Rossall & RMC Sand-
    hurst Lt 9th Foot'78 Afghan War'79 Sudan'85 Burma'86 rsgnd commission'87 Admnr Ugan-
    da'89 RNiger Co 8.94 Expedition to Kalahari'96 Commandant WAFF & Commr Nigeria'97
    High Commr Northern Nigeria 1900–6 Gov Hong Kong'07 Gov Nigeria'12 Gov Gen 1914–19
    Brit Member Permanent Mandates Comm'22 d11.4.45

22. Sir Harry Hamilton JOHNSTON GCMG 1901 K(96)CB 1890 FRGS b12.6.58 London s/o Secretary R Exchange Assce Co ed Stockwell GS King's Cllge London, R Academy of Arts, exploring N Africa '79 PEA & River Congo'82 led R Society Expedtn Kilamanjaro'84 V Consul Cameroons'85 Niger Coast Protectorate'87 Mozambique'89 Commr Nyasald'91–(& Admr NER 5.91–1.7.95) Consul Gen Tunisia'97 Commr Uganda'99–01 Adviser to President Liberia'04 d31.7.27

CHAPTER 2

The North-Eastern Rhodesia Constabulary

'In the early part of last year Her Majesty's Government extended the field of the Company's operations, so as to include the whole of the British sphere immediately North of the Zambezi, except Nyasaland. At the same time Mr H H Johnston CB, was appointed as Imperial Commissioner of Nyasaland and was permitted by Her Majesty's Government to act as Administrator of the Company's sphere of operations North of the Zambezi. The expense of administration through the entire sphere is defrayed by the Company and involves an expenditure of £10,000 per annum, which expenditure is at present almost entirely confined to Her Majesty's Protectorate of Nyasaland. Mr Johnston proceeded to Nyasaland in March 1891 and has taken up residence at Zomba in the Shire Highlands. Under his able administration great progress has been made. He has raised and equipped an Indian Police Force, has established regular postal services, and is inaugurating a scheme for the development of the resources of the territories under his administration from which a steadily increasing revenue is already accruing.' – so ran the British South Africa Company's report to its shareholders of 1892.[1]

The 'Indian Police Force' consisted of 49 Mazbi Sikh sepoys of the 23rd and 32nd (Punjab) Pioneers and 22 Mohammedan sowars from the cavalry of the Hyderabad Contingent of the Indian Army[2]. Since there was no question of the cavalrymen bringing their horses they were presumably selected because they were known to Harry Johnston's deputy, Captain C M Maguire, 2nd Hyderabad Lancers, who had gone back to India to find suitable volunteers. Maguire was killed on 15th December 1891 on the shore of Lake Nyasa in a battle with the slaver Makanjira.[3]

These 70 Indian troops and 150 Zanzibaris who supported them, are often referred to as the cadre from which grew the Northern Rhodesia Police. It must not be forgotten that despite the subsidy from the British South Africa Company, and the blandishments of Cecil Rhodes, it was with Nyasaland, British Central Africa, that Johnston was almost exclusively concerned, and on the pacification and development of which he concentrated the bulk of his resources in men and money. The main purpose and achievement of these Indian soldiers was to provide a necessary stiffening to the levies which grew to become, in 1897, the Central African Rifles, and later the Nyasaland battalions of the King's African Rifles. Nevertheless, a few of these sepoys, or of their successors, were involved in the training and organisation of the early police, both in Nyasaland and North-Eastern Rhodesia.

It has sometimes been suggested that it was to commemorate the contribution of the Mohammedan cavalrymen to the beginning of the Force that a strip of green was added to the red and white of the flash and tie of the NRP in the early nineteen thirties. It seems more likely that green was chosen because it had been the facing colour of the North-Eastern Rhodesia Constabulary immediately before amalgamation with the Barotse Native Police to form the Northern Rhodesia Police in 1911. It is true that the uniform colour of the Hyderabad Contingent Cavalry was green and this could have influenced the choice of facing colour for the North-Eastern Rhodesia Constabulary, but the majority of the Indian troops who served in the British Central African forces were not Mohammedans, but Sikhs from regiments which wore scarlet or khaki, with a variety of facing colours. What is certain is that the Indians, of whatever religion, left their mark on the Force. The Hindustani word for rifle range, 'chandamali', remained in use in the Northern Rhodesia Police until the end. At Livingstone in the nineteen fifties newly arrived assistant inspectors sometimes found themselves accommodated in the very pleasant Chandamali Government Hostel built near the site of the old Depot rifle range.

In 1893 the original Indian contingent was gradually replaced by two hundred Jat Sikhs, seconded from various regiments, under lieutenants C A Edwards, 35th Sikhs, and W H Manning, 1st Sikhs (Punjab Frontier Force)[4]. Edwards became the first commandant of the Central African Rifles, but died of blackwater fever in May 1897. Manning succeeded to the command. Brigadier-General Sir William Manning GCMG KBE CB was to be Inspector-General of the King's African Rifles from 1901 until 1907, and Governor of Nyasaland from 1910 until 1913.

Also in 1893 the original Zanzibaris, being judged neither as brave nor as reliable as the Indians, were paid off and sent home. By this time fifty Zanzibar Arabs and Makua from Mozambique, together with one hundred Ngoni had been added to the regular forces of British Central Africa. The Arabs were mostly former members of the bodyguard of the Sultan of Zanzibar. In 1895 a number of Atonga, fifty Yao, and twenty-five Marimba were recruited.

During these years irregulars, mainly Somalis, Zanzibaris, Makua, Atonga, Chewa, Bemba and Ngoni, were locally recruited and usually attached to the Civil Authority. Their pay varied between five shillings (twenty-five pence) and six shillings, a month.[5]

Meanwhile the tentacles of Empire were spreading slowly, if unsurely, into North-Eastern Rhodesia. As early as 1890 a small post had been opened at Chienji on the east shore of Lake Mweru. In 1891 Captain Richard Crawshay of the Inniskilling Dragoons[6], built a fort there which was manned by Makua police and called Rhodesia. Crawshay, known to the Africans as 'Kamukwamba', had come to Central Africa to hunt and stayed to help Johnston. In 1892 the fort was moved to Kalungkwishi, on the river of that name, about five miles up from the Lake.

It was in July 1893 that Hugh Charlie Marshall[7] was sent out by Johnston to build a station on the Stevenson Road, to be known as Abercorn (now Mbala), near the village of Zombe, chief of the Lungu. Marshall, who was accompanied by six Sikhs and some Atonga police built an impregnable stockade of poles ten foot high providing a sanctuary for refugees. In 1894 another post was established on the Road at Ikawa, Fife. Cecil Rhodes was worried that the Foreign Office might cede the area of the Stevenson Road to Germany. The name of a Royal Duke connected with the British South Africa Company was chosen for a purpose. As Rhodes said later, 'I knew they could not give up a fort named after a member of the Royal Family.'[8]

Hugh Marshall was to serve Northern Rhodesia for some thirty years, acting as Administrator of North-Eastern Rhodesia in 1911, and of Northern Rhodesia from August 1920 until March 1921.

Fort Rosebery had been marked out by Alfred Sharpe in 1892, west of Lake Bangweulu, near the Johnston Falls. In May 1894 it was reported by Harry Johnston as fortified, but it seems that this was merely a bluff to simulate occupation and deter claims by foreign powers.

At the posts that were established were placed small parties of police. They were under the orders of the local civil official, in those days known as the 'Collector', although no taxes were levied. No important tribe was subdued, indeed, Marshall was under strict instructions to leave the Bemba alone. Nothing serious was done to check the depredations of Arab slave traders in North-Eastern Rhodesia. It was impossible to do more than keep open the lines of communication until Nyasaland was secure.

Negotiations in 1894 between the British South Africa Company and the United Kingdom Government resulted in the Chartered Company becoming responsible for the direct administration of North-Eastern Rhodesia from 1st July 1895. British Central Africa, Nyasaland, remained under Imperial administration.

Major Patrick William Forbes, also formerly of the Inniskilling Dragoons, had served the British South Africa Company with distinction in Southern Rhodesia. In 1894 he was sent to Nyasaland to take charge of the Northern Section of the line being constructed by the Africa Trans-Continental Telegraph Company, another of Cecil Rhodes' projects. From this somewhat humdrum post Major Forbes was appointed Deputy Administrator responsible for North-Eastern Rhodesia. He assumed this new apointment on 1st July 1895, establishing his headquarters in Nyasaland. His escort, Sergeant Jock Drysdale and Troopers M W Barnard, 'Slick' Smith, Middleton, 'Bobo' Young and H T Harrington, had been recruited in Southern Rhodesia and attested as 'North-Eastern Rhodesia Police'[9]. At Karonga Harrington had picked up a party of Makua Police who had been trained at Zomba[10]. Drysdale being sick, Harrington was promoted sergeant and accompanied Forbes on a tour of inspection. He was then placed in charge of Choma for a few months before moving to Kalungkwishi. The troopers and most of the Makua were left at Fife which was threatened by Mlozi. On recovering his health Drysdale also joined the administrative service.

The British South Africa Company now recruited its own police from natives of Nyasaland and Mozambique. According to Sir Harry Johnston, the Imperial Government placed 'the British South Africa Company's forces in the adjoining sphere of influence under an Imperial Officer who is subordinate to the command of Lieutenant Colonel Edwards or whoever commands the forces in the British

Central Africa Protectorate.'[11] Captain J S Nicholson, 7th Hussars,[12] was seconded to command the 'Northern Zambezia Division' of the British South Africa Police from 1 July 1896 but was diverted to take charge of the Chartered Company's armaments at Salisbury and it seems unlikely that he or any other 'Imperial Officer' took command of the police in North-Eastern Rhodesia until the arrival of Captain Bright in 1903.

In order to stop the passage north to German East Africa of slaves captured by the Bemba, Forbes first strengthened the detachments at Abercorn and Fife. He then established a post further east along the Stevenson Road at Nyala. In his first annual report on 1st April 1896, Major Forbes gave, the police dispositions as:

Chambezi District, HQ Ikawa –	R.Young, 9 Makua, 40 local native police
Nyala –	40 native police under the Assistant Collector, J. Drysdale
Mirongo –	A Makua sergeant and 8 native police.
Tanganyika District, HQ Abercorn –	H C Marshall, 10 Makua and 40 native police
Mpanga –	20 native police under the Assistant Collector
Sumbu, Lake Tanganyika –	Captain C.T.Livingstone, Black Watch, and 20 native police.
Mweru District, Rhodesia, on the Kalungkwishi River –	Doctor Blair Wilson and 10 Makua, approximately.
Choma –	Hector Croad and 20 native police.
Luapula District, Fort Rosebery –	still not built.

Luangwa, a new district, Fort Jameson, near Chumulu's Kraal, Mr Worringham, assisted by Mr Colman with one Maxim, 40 Snider rifles and approximately thirty men armed with muzzle loaders assisted, if necessary, by the staff of Rhodesia Concessions with two Maxims, 100 Sniders and six or seven white men.[13] Worringham had been despatched from Zomba with 25 native police and a Maxim and established a post at Chinunda's.[14]

Robert Andrew Young and Frederick Charles Worringham had both joined the British South Africa Company's Police in 1890 and accompanied Cecil Rhodes' Pioneer Column in the occupation of Southern Rhodesia. 'Bobo' Young, a former Scots Guards private, took his discharge from the BSAP at the end of 1891 but rejoined the Matabeleland Mounted Police in 1893, before coming north with Forbes. In January 1901 he was appointed Native Commissioner at Mirongo and later served in the same capacity at Kasama and Chinsali. He was noted for his failure ever to submit returns. On leave in the United Kingdom Bobo Young married one of Harry Lauder's chorus girls.

The Jameson Raid denuded Southern Rhodesia of trained European police. The failure of the Raid was followed by the Matabele and Mashona rebellions in the south. The Chartered Company had scant resources to spare for North-Eastern Rhodesia even under direct administration. The police in the Territory remained very much irregular in organisation and training. There was no cohesive police force.

However, Major Forbes appears to have been quite satisfied with what he had. He wrote in his report, 'There are at present, I consider, quite sufficient white men and police in the different districts to keep what is practically the only open part of the country, namely from Nyasa to Tanganyika and Tanganyika to Mweru, in a quiet state, and I do not consider that there is anything to be gained by opening up a large extent of new country, into which we cannot at present offer sufficient inducement for white settlers to come, and which would entail consider-able extra expense in police posts.'[15]

Rough and ready, few and scattered, though the police of North-Eastern Rhode-sia may have been, they were engaged in a series of minor actions which resulted in the final suppression of the Arab slavers, the back of whose power had been broken in Nyasaland.

A Swahili slave-trader, Nsimba, had established himself on Kilwa Island, Lake Mweru. The Belgians had tried unsuccessfully to expel him. He displayed their heads on stakes in his stockade. In May 1894 a patrol from Rhodesia broke up a slave caravan from Kilwa killing the two leaders. This put a stop to the trade from Kilwa to the north-east. In April 1895 Dr Wilson and Hector Croad took two boats to the island with 13 Nyamwezi and 8 Mambwe police. On hearing of their approach Nsimba shot himself dead and his men then lost heart and came to terms.[16]

In April 1896 John Bell, Collector for the Chambezi District, engaged Wangani slavers who refused to lay down their arms, on the Chozi Stream near Kasama, killing two coastal Arabs and two ruga ruga, as their local followers were known, for the cost of one man wounded in the arm. Bell wrote, 'I had my Makua and Atonga police and a few natives. Keeping control of the latter was too awful. Never again will I go out with native warriors and cap guns. My insurance policy does not run to it.' He feared reprisals by the Bemba and sought reinforcements.[17]

John Drysdale, Assistant Collector at Nyala, and his police dispersed a caravan on 18 June when he captured an Arab and freed 57 slaves and another on 26 July when he scattered the slavers with a volley freeing 35 of their captives and seizing 1,000lbs of ivory[18]. On one occasion Drysdale followed a caravan into German territory and dispersed it seizing 106 tusks on which duty had not been paid. This incursion led to a claim for compensation which dragged on well into the next century.[19]

Forbes had said in his report, 'There is, however, one power that should be broken and that is the Awemba'. The Awemba, or Bemba, were allies of the Arabs, supplying them with human merchandise by preying on the weaker tribes in their neighbourhood. It was Bobo Young who broke the power of the Bemba.[20]

In September 1897 Arabs and their Bemba allies advanced against Chiwali, a Senga chief friendly to the Government. Chiwali's village on the Upper Luangwa in the Chambezi District was not far from the post at Mirongo to which Chiwali sent for help. Young immediately marched to the rescue with his ten to fifteen Makua and North Nyasa native police. With this tiny force he managed to keep the enemy in check for five days until reinforcements arrived from Fife and Nyala under the Collector, Mackinnon. The slavers were thoroughly defeated. Large numbers were killed and all their principal leaders were captured. Many slaves were liberated and the surrounding villages were freed for good from the depredations of the raiders. At one stage in the battle Young climbed a tree and from there shot and killed between twenty-five and thirty of the enemy himself.

Mackinnon, reported to the Administrator of Young, 'If he had been in the Imperial Service he would no doubt have received a Victoria Cross, but as the Company cannot give him this I would ask you to raise his pay to £250. He has always received low pay and is the lowest paid official up here.'[21]

Forbes wrote on 30th September, 'One of the most important results of this recent action is that the natives all through the territory have been brought with very little fighting or loss, to appreciate the strength of the Company in being able to overthrow the Arabs who for centuries have been their masters.' Apparently Young received his pay rise but Forbes' health had broken. He left the Territory and Captain H L Daly became Acting Administrator[22]. The last recalcitrant elements among the Bemba surrendered in 1898–9.

There was a plan to bring a force of up to fifty white police up from the South after the rains of 1897–8.[23] It was not implemented, either because of the demands of the disturbances in Matabeleland and Mashonaland or, perhaps merely because of the success of the local forces in the 'Black North'.

The local police also played their part in the suppression of the Ngoni Rebellion although the major role was taken by the Central African Rifles. By 1897 there were eight companies of Africans in the regular forces of British Central Africa. During that year two of these companies were re-organised as police, and so began the Nyasaland Police[24]. The remaining companies, three of Atonga, two of Yao, and one of Marimba were named the Central African Rifles.

Each company was commanded by a British officer assisted by a Sikh colour sergeant and three Sikh sergeants. There was an artillery battery of four 7 pounder mountain guns and two 9 pounders with African crews under Sikh instructors. The balance of about one hundred Sikhs were concentrated in a seventh company as a striking force.

By the end of 1897 the North Charterland Exploration Company was operating a concession in the Luangwa Valley and adjacent land from its headquarters at Fort Jameson in North-Eastern Rhodesia. The fort was garrisoned by twenty-five Atonga police. The old Ngoni chief, Mpezeni, had long been suspicious of British influence, but had hesitated to bring things to a head. He was now unable to control the truculence of his sons, Singu and Mlonyeni, and their followers. They had either not heard of, or were unimpressed by, Young's victory over the Bemba. The situation became so threatening in December that the Company's representative, Worringham, sent a request for assistance accross the border to Kota Kota. The Ngoni were said to number between 10,000 and 25,000 warriors. Practically the whole of the military forces of British Central Africa were mobilised to meet the threat.

After a series of forced marches the force of six officers, 118 Sikhs and five companies of Africans, a total of 650 men under Captain H E J Brake, Royal

Artillery[25], reached Fort Jameson on 18th January 1898. The handful of police had kept the flag flying.

Luangweni, a Rhodesia Concessions post with six or seven white men, about thirty miles from Fort Jameson, was already under siege. The following day, 19th January, Brake relieved Luangweni. Next morning he was at breakfast at the fort there, when he heard that six or seven hundred Ngoni warriors were massing a quarter of a mile to the East and others were on the way. Steadily the Sikhs and askaris deployed before the Ngoni who were dancing and waving their spears in defiance about three hundred yards away. 'A' and 'E' Companies, Atonga, fired one volley, fixed bayonets and advanced in line in silence. The Ngoni threw their spears at the oncoming troops, then, overawed, began to give way. When they found that other troops were turning their flank from the direction of Luangweni Village, the tribesmen broke and ran for the hills, spurred on by two rounds from the 7 pounder mountain guns. Twenty Ngoni dead were left on the field.

The troops were then threatened by a new force of at least five hundred advancing from the West. This was dispersed by four shells, a burst of Maxim fire and a charge by 'A' Company which the warriors did not wait to meet. Singu, the leader of the dissidents, was said by a prisoner to be sheltering in the hills seven miles to the South. On 22nd January Brake set out to catch him. A small herd of cattle was taken and a few villages were burnt, but Singu and his men were too wary to be caught in Brake's pincer movement. On the following day the energetic Brake set out with 'A' and 'E' Companies against Mlonyeni. The troops marched and fought for fifteen hours, capturing a great herd of cattle and destroying villages, but leaving the unripe crops standing to prevent famine. Although the Ngoni showed considerable courage, frequently coming to within thirty yards of the ranks of soldiers, they could not face the disciplined volleys.

Mpezeni sued for peace and asked for the British flag to be hoisted over his capital, Chimpingo. However on Brake's approach, the old chief fled into the bush. Mpezeni refused to come in, so Chimpingo was burnt.

On 26th January Brake with 'A' Company caught up with Mpezeni's followers. He drove them from village to village until satisfied that they had been reduced to a handful and driven into foodless country.

On 30th January Singu was surrounded and captured by troops under Lieutenant J S Brogden, Royal Marine Light Infantry. Singu was tried by drumhead court martial, and shot on 5th February 1898 in the presence of assembled headmen. Mpezeni surrendered on 9th February. He was kept at Fort Manning for a year as a prisoner before being allowed to return to North-Eastern Rhodesia and resume his chieftainship.[26]

The Ngoni Rebellion demonstrated the need for a proper garrison for North-Eastern Rhodesia. In return for an annual subsidy of £8,000 to be paid by the British South Africa Company, three new companies were raised for the Central African Rifles to meet this commitment. 'G' Company, consisting of 120 Atonga, went into training at Fort Johnston, 'H' Company, 120 Yao, at Fort Manning, and 'I', 110 Yao, at Zomba. None of these, nor any other company of the Central African Rifles, was ever stationed in North-Eastern Rhodesia. £650 was remitted from the subsidy towards the cost of the Company's police. The revenue from North-Eastern Rhodesia for the year ending 31st March 1898 was £2,065.

In early 1898 Major and Chief Inspector Colin Harding, then commanding Native Police in Mashonaland, received instructions to proceed to North-Eastern Rhodesia 'and there raise and command a native police force for its protection'. Acting on these brief instructions he set out with Sergeant-Major Greer[27] and a native orderly. They travelled via Beira and thence by water up the coast, and the Zambezi and Shire rivers, to Blantyre, which they reached on 29 May. Here Harding met Manning who informed him of the new plan to guarantee the security of North-Eastern Rhodesia by the expansion of the Central African Rifles, in which Harding was offered command of a company. Harding was naturally somewhat disconcerted at having come so far for no purpose. Having just been made a Companion of the Order of Saint Michael and Saint George for his services in the Mashonaland Rebellion, he was unwilling to accept such a subordinate position. On Harding's behalf, Sir Alfred Sharpe, now Governor of British Central Africa, wired Cecil Rhodes for instructions and it was decided that Harding should recruit and train natives from Nyasaland and North-Eastern Rhodesia for service in the police in Southern Rhodesia. Manning agreed to lend him Sikh instructors and, with a small quota of Nyasa recruits, Harding went on to Fort Jameson.

Harding seems to have ascribed the recent operations against the Ngoni to an unnecessary alarm caused by 'a highly strung official mistaking an ordinary native dance for an act of hostility'. In view of the recent slaughter of unsuspecting whites by the Matabele and Mashona in Southern Rhodesia, nervousness amongst the handful in the North was perhaps to be expected and, indeed excused, by one with Harding's experience.

Despite the loss of men and cattle, which were still being held at Fort Jameson when Harding arrived there, and the fact that Mpezeni was still in prison, or perhaps because of this, the Ngoni co-operated with Harding and a lesser chief quite happily handed over 200 of his young men as recruits.

Harding had to improvise to clothe and equip his force. He purchased white calico to make knickers (shorts), blue for smocks, and red, from which, with stiffening from the canvas in which the calico was baled, pillbox caps were manufactured. He also managed to procure enough blankets for the total of 400 recruits, who were organised into companies each commanded by a Sikh sergeant assisted by two sepoys. The senior Sikh NCO acted as battalion commander. There being no rifles for them, the recruits drilled with sticks. After a few months successive detachments were despatched overland to Southern Rhodesia. After the last draft had left, Harding handed back the instructors to Manning together with some surplus recruits and proceeded on leave to England[28]. In October 1899 he was back as Acting Resident Commissioner in North-Western Rhodesia where he was to raise and command the Barotse Native Police.

Before leaving Blantyre for Cape Town Harding met Robert Codrington who had been appointed Administrator of North-Eastern Rhodesia in July 1898 at the age of 29. Educated at Marlborough, Robert Edward Codrington was Orderly Room Sergeant-Major of the Bechuanaland Border Police in 1893, and served in Matabeleland before becoming a collector in Nyasaland in 1895. Codrington was

Colonel Colin Harding CMG First Commandant Barotse Native Police from
'In remotest Barotseland'

responsible for organising the first real administration in the North-East and instituted a regular graded civil service. During 1899 he moved the administrative
headquarters of the Government of North-Eastern Rhodesia out of Nyasaland and
established the capital at Fort Jameson.[29]

In October 1898 Mwamba, the second most powerful Bemba chief, died. In
March 1899, while claims to the succession were being considered by the Administration, a rival, Ponde, captured Mwamba's village and began to fortify it. Mackin-

19

non, the local collector, and his assistant, Bobo Young, attacked with their police and drove out Ponde and his followers.

The police had to cross open ground and a swampy stream on the far side of which was Ponde's army. Mackinnon divided his force. While Young and half the police covered their advance from the woods, Mackinnon and the rest crawled forward through the water and mire. Mackinnon then signalled Young and his men forward. Young walked upright across the plain and was said by Frank Melland in *Eastern Africa Today* (published in 1928), to have crossed the swamp and stream dryshod on the shoulders of his tallest msirikari. Mackinnon told Melland that Ponde and his warriors neither fired nor fought. 'By such means', wrote Melland, 'was this powerful and wonderfully organised tribe brought within the British Empire with hardly a shot even fired.'

Some of Ponde's men took refuge with Chief Mporokoso, who commenced to fortify his village on a rocky hill. In April 1899 H T Harrington, Assistant Collector for the Mweru-Luapula District, with about 100 African police from Abercorn and Kalungkwishi, and three other officials, Andrew Law, Hector Croad and W R Johnston, arrived at Mporokoso's[30]. Johnston had earlier been fired on by Nasoro bin Suliman an ally of Mporokoso. After a day and night of sniping, an escaped female slave pointed out a weak spot in the defences. At dawn Johnston created a diversion, while Harrington, Law and Croad led the police in a charge under heavy fire. Unable at first to gain entry, they fired through the loopholes in the stockade and drove the enemy back. The village was finally taken with little loss. Most of the resistance came, not from the Bemba, but from a number of Arabs under Nasoro. Some of these were killed. Others, including their leader, fled. Harrington and 60 police set off in pursuit and captured Nasoro within a couple of days.

The time was now ripe to bring the Eastern Lunda under control. Kazembe had always refused to enter into a treaty with the British. Codrington reported that this chief was responsible for repeated acts of aggression including having ordered the deaths of seven men. Harrington said that Kazembe sent repeated messages to him at Kalungkwishi, saying that he would like to come under British protection, but that there were so many Arabs in his country that he was powerless, and sought help against them.

Harrington offered to go with his police and clear out the Arabs, but Codrington ordered him to wait for reinforcements from Nyasaland. In September 1899 Captain E C Margesson, South Wales Borderers[31], with twelve Sikhs and sixty askari of 'E' Company, 1st Central African Regiment (as the Central African Rifles were now known) and a 7 pounder gun, set out from Karonga and marched by the Stevenson Road to Abercorn, and from there, in October, south-west to Kalungkwishi where a five barrelled Nordenfeldt gun had already arrived. A few days later Codrington himself, with police from Abercorn under W R Johnston, joined the concentration. Kazembe having failed to come to Kalungkwishi, the combined force, which was also accompanied by the Commissioner for Central Africa, Sir Alfred Sharpe, marched on Kazembe's village near Lake Mweru. The Arab slavers fled into Belgian territory, firing on a party of police from the West

Bank of the Luapula. Kazembe went with them, but returned in two weeks, and entered into an agreement. The troops marched back to Karonga.[32]

The North-Eastern Rhodesia Order in Council of 29th January 1900, promulgated in May, formalised the constitution of the Territory. The Administrator and officials were to be appointed by the British South Africa Company, subject to the approval of the Secretary of State. The Administrator was empowered to legislate for the Territory, subject to the approval of each ordinance by Her Majesty's Commissioner for British Central Africa. A High Court was established administering English Law. Previously jurisdiction had been exercised by consular courts under the African Order in Council of 1889. Now there was to be a judge at Fort Jameson and district magistrates. Judge Leicester Beaufort[33] arrived in 1901. Article 20 of the new Order in Council provided for the formation of a police force and for its organisation to be laid down in regulations. Draft regulations were prepared and sent to London for approval, but the authorities there never got round to approving them. The North-Eastern Rhodesia Constabulary was to remain in existence until 1911 on this informal basis.[34]

The first police in North-Eastern Rhodesia had been recruited and trained by each local official at his own station. In November 1898 Mr T E Tanner had been appointed Inspector of Civil Police but he left before the end of June 1899 due to ill-health.[35]

The Administrator's Report of 31st March 1900 gave the duties of the police as, 'to guard the property of the Government, to act as escorts to caravans, to carry messages from the administrative officials to native chiefs, to effect any arrests of natives that may be required, and to guard native prisons'. He listed the disposition of native police as follows:

West Luangwa District	Serenje	20
Upper Luangwa District	Nawalia	15
Chambezi District	Fife	15
	Nyala	10
	Mirongo	10
Tanganyika District	Abercorn	15
	Katwe and Mporokoso	15
	Sumbu	10
Mweru District	Kalungkwishi	10
	Choma	10
	Kazembe	20
Awemba District	Kasama	30
Eastern Luangwa District	Fort Jameson	30
Total:		210.[36]

The Government post at Nawalia had been established in September 1899 and that at Serenje did not open until April 1900.

The estimated expenditure for civil police for the year ending 31 March 1901 was £800 for pay and rations and £200 for uniforms and equipment.[37] Codrington judged an inspector unnecessary. He had originally suggested that a company of the Central African Regiment should be stationed at Fort Jameson and another at Kasama. An advance party of an officer, 3 Sikhs and 9 askari arrived at Fort Jameson in November 1899 to prepare the barracks, bringing with them, apparently unbeknown to Codrington, some convicts from Nyasaland. In the absence of the officer there was disorder in the camp and one of these prisoners was killed. Codrington had the detachment withdrawn on 2 February 1900 and resolved that North-Eastern Rhodesia should rely on its own resources.[38]

During 1900 Val Gielgud[39], a District Commissioner, dispersed slave caravans on the Kafue River, and stations were opened at Mkushi, Kapopo and Muyanga. Gielgud advocated strong patrols to prove to the indigenous population that the white officials stationed in their midst were the representatives of a powerful government. At the same time the danger was recognised that, if the administration was weak, 'every European travelling or trading will maintain, as is customary in other parts of Central Africa, a following of askari or armed natives who, either on their own account or with the concurrence of their employer will raid and intimidate the native population.' Following a murder Gielgud fined Bulibali 20 guns and detained him until his followers handed them over.

A band of Swahili, led by one Chiwala, had settled in Katanga in about 1893, trading in ivory and slaves. They had infiltrated from the coast via Nyasaland and the upper reaches of the Luapula. In 1897 they were dislodged by a Belgian force and retreated to the area of present day Ndola, the country of the Lamba tribe. By 1900 a European ivory trader, Ziehl, had joined them with his 'police' or armed retinue. C P Chesnaye and the real police brought them all to book before the end of the year.[40]

Codrington reported that traders were rapidly denuding North-Eastern Rhodesia of cattle, rubber and ivory. Chiefs Chipepo and Muyanga were extremely distrustful of white men and alarmed at their presence accompanied by armed natives. On 21st April 1900 Codrington reported an outrage by one Dana Smith against Kasanga Village.

John 'Chirupula' Stephenson had come to Fort Jameson as a telegraphist in 1899. He asked Codrington for more exciting employment and became Collector at Mkushi in 1900. He was assisted by Corporal Menzani and 9 privates. Stephenson found that the NCO was abusing his position. When occasion arose to visit another station he had Menzani arrested and brought to trial.

E D Fairbanks was recruiting labour among the Soli. Knowing that bamboo fetched a good price in the south for use as whips, he sent his recruits out to collect it. The men deserted. Fairbanks went to their village to ask for the return of the recruits or of the calico he had given as advanced payment. Obtaining no satisfactory response Fairbanks set fire to the village, whereupon he was attacked with spears and arrows. Although armed with a double barrelled shotgun he would not kill his assaillants but shot himself dead. Chirupula went to investigate and reported these facts. However to the Africans it was murder and the Administration chose to take the same view. Sergeant Masea and 12 men were sent from Fort Jameson to assist Stephenson and his police in making arrests.[41]

In 1901 a station was established by C C Sheckleton with 17 African police at Mandombe or Feira at the confluence of the Zambezi and Luangwa rivers, on the border with Mozambique opposite Zumbo. This brought to an end the unofficial reign of John Harrison Clark who had set himself up in the area maintaining order with a private army of Senga. Clark accepted three farms in exchange for the rights he had acquired.[42]

The administration now covered the whole of North-Eastern Rhodesia with 5 magistrates and 31 native commissioners. In August 1901, in the Tanganyika District, there were 27 African police at Abercorn, 16 at Katwe/Mporokoso and 13 at Sumbu. In the Mweru District were 20 at Kalungwishi and 20 at Kazembe's Kampanda. In the Luapula District there were 18 each at Fort Rosebery and Mieri Mieri. There were three stations in the Kafue District with 29 police at Kapopo, 15 at Mkushi River and 35 at Muyenye. Serenje, the only station in West Luangwa District still had 20 police. In East Luangwa which had absorbed Upper Luangwa District, were 38 at Fort Jameson, 10 at Lusangazi (Petauke) and 15 at Nawalia. In North Luangwa (formerly Chambezi) District were 18 at Fife/Nyala, 12 at Mirongo and 12 at Kokaa. Kasama and Mpija in Awemba District had 30 and 11 respectively while at Mandombe in Zumbo District were 17.

The only revenue was derived from licences, stamps, export duty on ivory and the sale of tusks given by chiefs in recognition of the sovereignty of the Chartered Company. To help finance the expansion of government influence an African hut tax at three shillings per dwelling hut per annum was introduced on 1 April 1901. Enforcement was another task for the Constabulary. Of course the new tax not only produced revenue. It also acted as a stimulus to encourage Africans to seek employment. The Silver King Coppermine had already opened in the Kafue Hook and by the end of 1901 was employing nearly 2,000 labourers and porters.

Administrative officials were now coming into contact with their colleagues from North-Western Rhodesia. These meetings on the Kafue were not always cordial. Gielgud was berated by Colin Harding, now Commandant of the Barotse Native Police, for flogging runaway labourers.

In December 1900 a mail carrier from Fort Jameson was murdered in Nyasaland. A strong patrol of the Central African Regiment was sent out from Fort Manning and discovered the dead policeman's rifle and kit in the possession of Chief Tambala in Central Ngoniland. The troops captured and destroyed several villages. Tambala was taken trying to escape through the gorge where his main stronghold was situated.[43]

So impressed had the Imperial authorities been by the performance of the Central African troops in the campaigns of the eighteen nineties in Nyasaland and North-Eastern Rhodesia that a 2nd Battalion of the Central African Regiment had been formed in January 1899 and sent to garrison Mauritius. This battalion returned to Zomba in July 1901 after seeing active service in Somaliland, Ashanti, and the Gambia. When the Board of the BSA Company heard of the departure from Chinde on 30 June 1900 of a draft of 4 officers and 340 men to join the 2nd Battalion, it had expressed concern whether sufficient troops remained to guarantee the security of North-Eastern Rhodesia[44]. In May 1901 Codrington pointed out that there were only 36 Sikhs and 400 askari in British Central Africa when 40 sikhs and 350 askari were supposed to be ready for service in North-Eastern Rhodesia at any one time. He was already in dispute with Sir Alfred Sharpe and

Col Manning concerning expenditure on the expedition against Kazembe of 1899 and now, strengthened in his view that North-Eastern Rhodesia could not, and should not, rely on outside help in an emergency, fought unsuccessfully for the subsidy towards the maintenance of the Central African Regiment to be reduced.[45]

The commitment of three companies of the 1st Battalion to North-Eastern Rhodesia was now ended. Instead the 2nd Central African Regiment was to remain at Zomba as a reserve battalion for all the East African territories. Many of the veterans chose to take their discharge. To bring the 2nd up to its authorised strength of six companies it was necessary to reduce the 1st Central African Regiment to eight and to commence a widespread recruiting campaign. Despite his dissatisfaction Codrington undertook to find one hundred recruits.[46]

On 1st January 1902 the battalions of the Central African Regiment became the 1st and 2nd (Central African) Battalions of the King's African Rifles. As such they were to serve alongside the Northern Rhodesia Police and the Northern Rhodesia Regiment in two world wars but to have very little to do with Northern Rhodesia, in peace, until 1959. From that year they were stationed in succession at Lusaka as the reserve battalion of the Army of the Federation of Rhodesia and Nyasaland. On the break up of the Federation, on 1st January 1964, the 2nd Battalion, the King's African Rifles became the 2nd Battalion, the Northern Rhodesia Regiment. The wheel had come full circle.

In 1902 the North-Eastern Rhodesia Constabulary consisted of approximately 300 men still under the command of members of the Civil Administration. Now that there was a tax to collect, these officials were no longer called collectors, but district or native commissioners. The cost of the Force was £2,650 per annum.

In August 1902 a native commissioner arrested 6 Portuguese askari for forcibly recruiting labour at Karuani's Village and sent them to Fort Jameson. On 12 October C P Chesnaye was in camp in the area when a runner appeared from Manju Wantu's Village to report that a Portuguese half-caste, Verrissimo, known to the Africans as Manawiri, had fired on the village. It transpired that four villages had been looted and destroyed, an old man flogged nearly to death and women and children carried off into Mozambique. One of these women, Ngonia, died on the march. Ptes Sabuni, Bbesa and Teramuka, staying in a village nearby had heard the commotion but remained were they were. They later explained that they had been ordered to wait there for their superior. Pte Nderremani was made of sterner stuff. He had disarmed two Portuguese askari and tied them up. Chesnaye and a colleague, Tagart, took 6 unarmed police across the border to Chimwala where they found Verrissimo and successfully demanded the release of the captives, including a party of Nyasalanders who had been en route to seek employment in Southern Rhodesia.[47]

On 31st March 1903 Captain Richard Bright, a regular officer of The Buffs (East Kent Regiment) was seconded to the British South Africa Company's service and appointed Commandant to 'organise and constitute' the North-Eastern Rhodesia Constabulary at a salary of £600 a year with £100 travelling allowance[48]. As Commandant, he was the only white member of the Force, and subject to the orders of the Officer Commanding Troops in Central Africa. Now 30 years of age, Bright had seen active service on the North-West Frontier of India. He had been seconded to the Central African Regiment from 12th June 1899 until 31st March 1902, taking part in the punitive expedition against the Yao chief, Nkwamba, on the Eastern Frontier of Nyasaland in August 1899. Bright's tenure of command of the North-Eastern Constabulary was to last exactly two years after which he returned to his regiment.

When Bright took command a company of North-Eastern Rhodesia Africans had recently been recruited for the Barotse Native Police and recruiting for another was in progress.

On 5th August 1903 instructions were issued that native constables were only to make arrests on warrant or when an offence was committed in their presence. They were to seek assistance from the local headman when effecting an arrest or serving a summons. They were not to carry arms except when accompanied by a European official or when necessary for protection from animals.[49]

In 1903 Fort Rosebery was rebuilt on its final site. A station was opened at Mwomboshi with 29 police with smaller posts at Sitanda with 10 and Chasonsa with 8. The total revenue from North-Eastern Rhodesia for the year ending 31 March 1903 was £8,640 14s 5d while the BSACo expended more than £31,960 on its administration. The cost of the Constabulary had risen to £4,461 2s 6d.

In December 1903 the establishment of the North-Eastern Rhodesia Constabulary was one officer and 385 native ranks and according to the War Office publication 'The Land Forces of the British Colonies and Protectorates' (revised 1905), the Force was recruited up to establishment. £150 was provided for a band instructor and it was hoped to recruit one of the Indian Contingent of the KAR to fill this post. £1695 was allocated for African police pay, rations, uniforms and equipment and £100 for arms and ammunition[50]. In 1904 the monthly rates of pay for the North-Eastern Rhodesia Constabulary were:

Sergeant-Major	£1 0s 0d
Sergeant	£0 17s 6d
Corporal	£0 7s 6d
Private	£0 5s 0d

In addition each man received rations (posho), a cake of soap and a length of calico. Enlistment had been for a term of two years. On re-engaging for a further term of service sergeants-major were granted an increase of 2s 6d per month, sergeants 1s 6d and corporals and privates one shilling a month. According to draft regulations prepared in 1903 engagements were thereafter to be for three years. On leaving the Force after 12 years service a sergeant-major could expect a gratuity of £20, a sergeant £10, a corporal £8 and a lance corporal or constable £6. Those who served for 21 years were to receive half as much again or land in lieu.

A disciplinary code was prepared under which a magistrate or officer commanding a detachment was empowered to award a constable imprisonment for up to 168 hours, confinement to barracks for 14 days, extra guards or piquets for offences in the performance of such duties or, in cases of drunkenness, a fine. The Commandant could award up to 84 days, or for a second or aggravated offence six months, imprisonment or 25 lashes with stoppages of pay to make good any loss or damage. Subject to the Administrator's approval he could increase the sentence to 5 years for mutiny or 2 years for desertion or disobedience to orders.

Having toured the whole Territory Bright made his report on 1 January 1904 when the North-Eastern Rhodesia Constabulary was 307 strong. He recommended a Force of a commandant, assistant commandant at £400 a year, pay & quartermaster at £250, bandmaster, an African sergeant-major, 26 sergeants, 32 corporals, 405 constables and 31 buglers. Enlistment would be for three years with subsequent re-engagements of two years. Each man would receive 2 yards of calico a week, 2lbs of flour or 3lbs of unground grain with 1lb of salt and $\frac{1}{2}$lb of soap a month, 1 full dress and 2 suits of fatigue dress a year and a blanket and jersey every two years. The sergeant-major, 6 sergeants, 9 corporals 126 constables and 9 buglers would be stationed at Fort Jameson with the remainder distributed among the 20 other Government posts. The NCOs at present in command of detachments would be brought in to Fort Jameson for a two month course and training camps of two to four weeks duration would be held in the dry season for detached personnel at suitable centres. This Force would be capable of assuming responsibility for defence as well as civil police work at a cost of £8,500 a year as against nearly £15,000 for the payment for the KAR and the cost of the existing Force. As an economy measure it was agreed that the appointment of an assistant commandant could be delayed until the Commandant was due for leave[51]. John Ebenezer Herbert Edwards was appointed Pay and Quartermaster on 4 May 1904 but died at Fort Jameson on 10 March 1905 and was not replaced[52].

The North-Eastern Rhodesia Constabulary possessed one $2\frac{1}{2}$ pounder 1·75 inch Nordenfelt Quick Firing gun, two ·303 Maxim machine guns, two ·45 Maxims, one Hotchkiss and one Nordenfelt five barrelled machine gun. No ammunition was held for the Hotchkiss or Nordenfelt machine guns. The men were armed with ·577 Snider breech loading rifles and carried their ammunition in bandoliers. In 1905 they were issued with ·451 inch Martini-Henry single shot breech loading rifles and brown leather Slade Wallace 1888 pattern or Mackenzie equipment. The Martini-Henry, used by the British regular army between 1871 and 1888, was 4 feet $1\frac{1}{2}$ inches long and weighed 8 pounds 12 ounces. The falling breech block was actuated by a lever behind the trigger guard. The weapon was sighted up to 1,450 yards and the charge was 85 grains of black powder. The rifle had a sword bayonet with a blade of eighteen and three eighths inches.[53]

The full dress uniform was a short khaki drill kurta, a shirt-like Indian style tunic or blouse with an opening in front closed by three brass buttons. The blouse had two breast pockets with pleats and flaps, each closed by a small brass button. The pointed cuffs were green, but the shoulder straps and low collar were plain khaki drill. The blouse was worn over a pair of khaki drill shorts or knickers, which had a green stripe down each side seam. In 1900 the North-Eastern Rhodesia Constabulary was reported as wearing a 'green fez cap with tassel', but this may have been merely a misdescription of the black fez with green tassel hanging to the right, which was worn in later years. The African police wore no footwear or puttees.

Photographs show men with and without the green facings on the blouse. The

Captain Richard Bright, Commandant North-Eastern Rhodesian Constabulary 1903–05
(Photo Iain Mackintosh)

blue jersies were worn under the blouse in cold weather. On duty African police wore an oval shaped brass armlet with 'NORTH-EASTERN RHODESIA' stamped round the upper edge, and 'CONSTABULARY' round the lower. In the centre was the wearer's number.[54]

In 1905 there were 252 Europeans in North-Eastern Rhodesia. 69 were Government officials, 39 missionaries, 52 traders, 68 farmers, and 24 miners and prospectors. Revenue was £18,200 towards an expenditure of £74,500. In this year the border between North-Eastern and North-Western Rhodesia was moved eastward from the Kafue River to the narrow waist separating the Katanga from Portuguese East Africa. All civil servants and members of the Constabulary in the districts concerned were transferred to the North-Western Rhodesia administration. In 1908 the white population in the reduced area of North-Eastern Rhodesia was only 243.

On 1 April 1905 Edgar Anderson Averay Jones, a civil servant, was appointed temporary commandant in place of Captain Bright. On 28 February 1906 Jones was confirmed in his appointment. He held no military or police rank. From 31 October 1906 Jones also acted as magistrate for the Eastern Luangwa District. On 1 February 1908 he reverted to the administrative service[55]. He was succeeded as commandant of the North-Eastern Rhodesia Constabulary by Lieutenant G F

Watherston seconded from the Barotse Native Police with the local rank of captain.

Supervision of the Chartered Company's administration in North-Eastern Rhodesia was about to pass from the British Commissioner in Nyasaland to the High Commissioner in South Africa who was already responsible for Barotseland/North-Western Rhodesia. Watherston's appointment was one of a number of steps towards the amalgamation of the two territories. Robert Codrington had been transferred to North-Western Rhodesia in June 1907. He arranged for a number of his old staff to follow him and some departments in the two territories, such as Posts and Telegraphs, were joined under one director.

For economy reasons not all of Captain Bright's recommendations had been implementented. The commandant was still the only European member of the North-Eastern Rhodesia Constabulary. His salary was now £450 a year. Apart from recruits under training and their instructors only sufficient African police were stationed at Fort Jameson to guard Government buildings and act as prison warders. The remainder of the Force was still scattered in detachments 11 to 15 strong under the senior offical at each Government station or boma. In the administration of his Force Watherston had the assistance of an African civilian clerk paid £44 a year. Watherston was to inspect each outlying station every year and to devote some time to recruiting for the Barotse Native Police.[56]

On 1 April 1909 Captain John Joseph O'Sullevan of the Barotse Native Police succeeded Capt Watherston as Commandant, a post he was to hold until he went on leave shortly before the amalgamation of the two forces as the Northern Rhodesia Police in 1911. Born in Athlone in 1879, O'Sullevan had enlisted in the Cape Mounted Riflemen as a trooper in 1898. When war with the Boers broke out he served as orderly to the Commanding Officer, Col Dalgety[57], who described O'Sullevan as the bravest man he had ever seen under fire. O'Sullevan later served as an officer in French's Scouts and on the staff as an intelligence officer.

In August 1903 O'Sullevan, described by Colonel Harding as 'six foot four inches of muscle and brawn', joined the Barotse Native Police. He was said to be so strong that he would pick up defaulting recruits, one in each hand, right off the ground and bang their heads together. Once, when a leopard jumped onto the horse O'Sullevan was riding, he knocked the big cat unconscious with one blow of his fist.[58]

After distinguishing himself by his defence of Saisi in 1915, O'Sullevan left Northern Rhodesia. The reputation thus established and presumably his record in the South African War led, after medical treatment, to his selection for command of a battalion in France. Colonel J J O'Sullevan DSO FRGS later became a Resident Magistrate in Killarney, but retired on the establishment of the Irish Free State.

Discipline in the North-Eastern Rhodesia Constabulary was strict despite the failure to promulgate its regulations. At Fort Rosebery in 1909 Private Chipewa (hat) was fined three months pay and awarded ten lashes for an unrecorded offence. The entry in the district notebook was endorsed 'if he does not improve he will be discharged'.

In O'Sullevan's time the North-Eastern Rhodesia Constabulary had a drum and bugle band. There was also a signal section with heliographs. In his last annual report in 1911 the Commandant, who had been granted the honorary rank of major on 1 March 1910, wrote 'These ancient instruments (helios) are not of much use and sending is somewhat slow, however, the signalling class is proficient with flags'.

He went on to complain, 'It has been impossible to prevent the inhabitants dressing up rickshaw boys and personal servants the same as the askari. It is peculiar that some employers of labour with all the varied colours of the rainbow to select from must choose almost the exact regulation pattern fez, belt, tunic and trousers, worn by the Constabulary'.[59]

Photographs show Captain O'Sullevan as Commandant of the North-Eastern Rhodesia Constabulary wearing a khaki drill service dress jacket with four pockets and an open step collar over a white shirt and black tie. His khaki breeches are worn with puttees of the same colour and brown ankle boots. His headdress was the New Wolseley pattern khaki helmet with khaki pugri. On parade he wore a Sam Browne belt with one brace and his Queen's and King's South Africa medals.

The msirikari of the North-Eastern Rhodesia Constabulary painted by Major A B Cree, wears the African General Service Medal authorised by Army Order 132 of 1902. The ribbon was yellow, with black borders and two narrow green stripes. The medal was silver, although also cast in bronze for carriers. The obverse bore a bust of King Edward VII in the uniform of a Field Marshal. The reverse showed Britannia standing holding an olive branch and scroll in her left hand and a trident in the right. Behind her appeared a lion with, in the background, the rising Sun and in the exergue the word 'AFRICA'. It was issued with a clasp 'British Central Africa 1899–1900' for the operations in Kazembe's country and Central Ngoniland between August 1899 and December 1900.

There was also the Central Africa Medal with clasp 'Central Africa 1894–1898'. This medal was authorised by Army Order 66 of 1895 and was originally issued without a clasp for operations between 1891 and 1894. The ribbon was of white, black and terracotta stripes of equal width to represent the British, African and Indian personnel engaged. The medal was silver with the head of Queen Victoria on the obverse and, on the reverse, a representation of British troops fighting Africans in the Bush, first used for the medal for the Ashanti Campaign of 1873–1874.

There appears to be no record of the issue of either of these medals to a member of the North-Eastern Rhodesia Constabulary, as such.

Notes

1. Quoted in *The Story of the Northern Rhodesia Regiment* pp2–3
2. 26 from 23rd Pioneers, 23 from 32nd, 7 from 1st Lancers, 10 from 2nd, 5 from 3rd 'The Indian Army of the Empress 1861–1903' Alan Harfield, Spellmount ISBN 10-946771-03-0 pp121–122. Moyse Bartlett gives 40 Sikhs & 30 sowars in his *History of the King's African Rifles* p17. The *Story of the NRR* p3 has 40 Sikhs & 20 cavalry
3. Cecil Montgomery MAGUIRE, 2Lt 8H 11.9.76 ISC 4.3.78 Capt 11.9.87 k15.12.91 L Nyasa
4. *History of the KAR* p19 – Brig Gen Sir Wm Henry MANNING GCMG'21 KBE'18 CB'03 b19.7.63 ed RMC Lt SWB 25.8.86 ISC 14.7.88 1Sikhs PFF 27.9.91 NWF 91 Matabeleld 93

CAR 93 Cmdt & DCommr BCA 5.97 Capt 25.8.97 IG KAR 01–07 KCMG 04 AgGov Somalild 07 Gov 10 Gov Nyasald 10 Jamaica 13 Ceylon 18 rtd 25 d1.1.32

5. *Story of the NRR* p4

6. Capt Richd CRAWSHAY 6D to North Nyasa Dist BCA 1893

7. Letter of appointment by H H Johnston, NR Journal No.5 Vol II 1955.
   Hugh Charlie MARSHALL, Collectr Chiromo BCA 1891 Abercorn 26.7.93 Civ Commr & Mag Tanganyika Dist NER 1902 Actg Admr NER May to Aug 1911, NR 8.20–3.21 rtd '21 d'49 UK

8. Alexdr Wm Geo Duff 1st Duke of FIFE'89, b1849 m.Princess Louise elder daughter of Prince of Wales'89, Liberal, Vice Chmn BSACo d1912
   Jas Hamilton 2nd Duke of ABERCORN(succeeded 1885) PC KG CB MA b24.8.38 ed Harrow Oxon MP(C) Donegal'60–'80 Marquess of Hamilton'68 Chmn BSACo'90 d3.1.13

9. Maj Patrick Wm FORBES b1861 ed Rugby RMC Lt 6D'81 BSACoP'89 Capt'90 Mag Hartley 6.91 Mag Salisby 30.10.91–1.10.92, 15.11–15.12.92 Mag Ft Vic 23.12.92–27.3.93 Maj Salisby Horse'93 Nthn Sec Af Trans–Contntl Telegraph'94 DAdmr NER 1.7.95–6.97 left BSACo Svce 1902 d'23
   NORTH-EASTERN RHODESIA POLICE, Forbes' Escort 1895.
   Sergeant-Major John Patrick Marshall 'Jock' DRYSDALE, Sgt Artillery Tp Pioneer Corps'90 Sgt Salisby Hse'93? A/Collector Nyala, d blackwater 23.4.98.
   Tpr Mostyn Wm BARNARD BSACoP'90 Salisby Hse'93 Grey's Scouts 96
   Tpr 'Slick' SMITH, BSAP 1895.
   Tpr MIDDLETON, Fife, Nyala'95 Chinunda'97
   Tpr Robert 'Bobo' Andrew YOUNG b30.9.66 Newburgh Fife; baker, Pte Scots Gds, BBP 22.2.90 BSACoP'90–1, MashonaldMP Matabeleld MP'93, NC Mirongo 1.01, Kasama, Chinsali 14.8.04, wrote *History of the Bemba* Rtd'16 Lab rctg Nyasald, to Harrietsham Kent d2.8.32.
   Tpr Hubert Tyler 'Chiana' HARRINGTON MBE'33, b Hertford, clerk Market Lane Corn Exchange; SA'90, Rhod'91 prospector, hotelier, Tpr Victoria Colm 93 Tpr BSAP, NERP'95 i/ c Choma, Kalungkwisi, A/Collector Mweru–Luapula'99 NC Mkushi Rtd 1916, T/Lt Nthn Frontier Unit East Africa Police'16 KAR GEA & PEA? ambushed on 50th birthday, Clk Ellis & Co Solrs, L'stone, d'41.

10. Article *The Taming of North-Eastern Rhodesia* Harrington, NRJ Vol II No.III 1954

11. Quoted in the *Story of the NRR* p.6

12. Brig Gen John Sanctuary NICHOLSON CB'02 CMG'05 CBE'18 DSO 8.5.97 b19.5.63 Basing Pk Hants ed Harrow, Lt 7Hrs 6.2.84 Capt 23.1.91 LLtCol OC NZambezia Div BSAP 1.7.96 OC Tps Rhodesia'96 OC Matabeleld Div BSAP 28.1.97 Cmdt Gen BSAP 28.9.98 COS SAC 1.10.01 IG SAC 4.03–8.05 Cmdt Calais Base BEF 24.5.15 BG Cmdt Le Havre Base 2.12.16 MP Westmnstr'21 d21.2.24

13. Capt Chas Patrick LIVINGSTON 'Capiteni' Lt BW 10.5.82 d4.11.96
    Dr Andrew Blair WILSON, BCA Adm 1.11.91 BSACo NER 1.1.94 Commr & Mag Mweru Dist dismissed, morphia addiction 3.03, ANC Shaloba NWR 4.04 shot himself 9.9.1904
    Hector C CROAD OBE b Londn 1865 ed Chtrhse to Canada CPR Const NWMP; Trader Blantyre'90 NC Serenje'98 Mag WLuangwa'03 DC Kasama L30.11.23–rtd 5.24 Mngr Shiwa Ngandu re–employed NRG Labour & Food Dept'30 Fmr Chiswa d23.3.49 A'corn
    Fredk Chas WORRINGHAM Tpr BSACP'90 Guide Vic Colm'93 Gifford's Hse'96 Collctr Chinunda
    A J COLMAN NER '95 ACollctr Chinunda

14. NRJ Vol VI p323

15. Quoted in *Story of the NRR* p7

16. Letter Blair Watson 18.5.95 NRJ Vol III p70

17. Bell to Honey, Forbes' Sec 20.4.96 NRJ Vol I No.1 p9
    John M BELL i/c Ikawa '95 Collctr Chambezi Dist resigned 12.96

18. Drysdale to Admr 25.6.96,21.8.96 NRJ Vol.I No.1 p9

19. PRO CO417/363

20. *Story of the NRR* p8

21. Mackinnon to Admr NRJ Vol.I No.1 p13

Chas MACKINNON Cllctr NER 1.11.96 Civ Commr & Mag NLuangwa 6.03 RM Barotseld 09 Kafue 14 rtd 9.12.17

22. Henry Lawrence DALY SLt 49Ft 28.2.74 56Ft 8.4.74 Lt 15Hrs 9.2.76 Capt hp by'92 OC Mtd Tp RHV '96
23. Forbes' report quoted in *Story of the NRR* p9
24. *History of the KAR* p24
25. Brig Gen Herbt Edwd John BRAKE CB'01 CMG'18 DSO'99 'Bwana Chiparapata' b9.2.66 ed USC Lt RA'86 Capt'96 2i/c CAR '97 T/Maj CO 2CAR 1.1.99–25.9.00 Cmdt Local Fces & IG Constby Trinidad & Tobago 02–7 LtCol 24 Hy Bty RGA 2.15 T/BG CHA XVIII Cps 15.1.17–27.3.18 OC Hy Arty Gnry Sch Winchstr rtd'20
26. *History of the KAR* pp25,6
27. John Lawrence GREER 319 Tpr BSAP 96 ACollctr NER 2.9.99 NC 1.1.01 sick lve 5.9.04
28. Harding *Far Bugles*
29. Robt Edwd CODRINGTON b6.1.69 ed Marlborough, in Virginia USA 90 ORSM BBP 90 w93 Collctr Centrel Ngonild BCA 95 Admr NER'98 Admr NWR d16.12.08 London
30. PONDE became CHITIMUKULU '16 d'23
    Frank Hulme MELLAND BA Oxon NERCS 4.7.01 Fife ANC Mpika'03 AgDC Kasempa'16 Mag 31.10.17 Solwezi '18 rtd '27?
    Andrew LAW b Canada svd RA, Afrcn Lakes Corpn NER'94 BSACo'98 Collctr Mbala'99 drnd LKilwa 14.4.99
    Walter Riddell JOHNSTON NER 98 killed by lions 15.10.00 Kambole
31. Maj Edwd Cunningham MARGESSON b Worthing 13.12.77 s/o Lt Col ed Wellngtn RMC 2Lt SWB 12.91 Niger 11.96–4.97 Capt 3.98 CAR 11.97–11.03 WAFF 1.05–9.09 Maj 2.11 2SWB k Gallipoli 25.4.15
    KAZEMBE d19.1.04 bronchitis
32. *History of the KAR* p28 *Story of the NRR* pp10–11
33. Sir Leicester Paul BEAUFORT MA BCL Gov & CJ Labuan & BNBorneo; Judge NER'01 Ag Admr 6.05–1.06,1.11–5.11 Judge NR
34. *Story of the NRR* p13
35. Codrington letter fm Ikawa 21.6.99 PRO CO417/276
    Thomas Errington TANNER Galloper Salisby Hse'93?
36. Quoted in *Story of the NRR* p13
37. PRO CO/417/283
38. Codrington 5.12.01 PRO CO 417/363
39. Valdemar GIELGUD bUSA Tpr Grey's Scouts'96 NC Gwelo'96 Sebungwe to NER 7.00 Mngr RNLB NC Bulawyo'08 d'16?
40. Maj Christian Purefoy CHESNAYE CBE b1869 s/o Col IMS; Tpr BBP'91 Tpr Gwelo V'96 Insp MMP'96 NC NER'99 Sec to Ag Admr'01 Ch Commr & Mag ELuangwa'03 A'corn'11 T/Capt NRP 24.6.16 for duty with OETA, Political Offr Bismarcksburg 7.16 PO Dar es Salaam returned to NRCS lve pdg rtmt 11.5.23
41. John Edwd 'Chirupula' STEPHENSON bNthumbrld, Clk GPO'90–Cape '96–7 Telegraphist NER '99 A/Collctr Mkushi 1.7.00 NC Ndola '04 rsgnd 22.3.07 farmer Chifwefwe, Int Cpl NRRifles'14 d15.8.57 Kapiri Muwendika, wrote *Chirupula's Tale*
42. Cecil Courtney SHECKLETON Afrcn Trans Contntl Telegraph Co 97 NERCS 11.00 NC Feira 01 Mag 4.06 BH 10.08
    Jas Harrison CLARK 'Changa Changa' NER '87 ltr Beer Hall Mngr BH Mine
43. *History of the KAR* p28
44. FO letter 13.7.00 PRO CO417/311
45. Minutes BSACo Bd 26.11.02 PRO CO417/365
46. *History KAR* p125
47. PRO CO417/371
    Edwd Saml Bourn TAGART BA Cantab ACollctr 11.00
48. Estimates yr ending 31.3.04 PRO CO417/383
    Richard BRIGHT b26.12.1872, 2lt Buffs 7.3.94 Chitral Relief Force'95 Malakand FF'97–8

CAR 12.6.99–31.3.02 Cmdt NERC 1.4.03–31.3.05 Asst to C/Insp Inspctn Staff WO 20.4.11 Maj 7.2.15 GSO3 9.5.15 GSO2 Gibraltar, Bvt Lt Col 1.1.18.
49. Memo 5.8.03 PRO CO/417/386
50. PRO CO/417/383
51. PRO CO/417/398
52. NERGov Gazette PRO
53. *Story NRR* Ch VII
54. *Story NRR* p107
55. Edgar Anderson Averay JONES MBE, NERCS 4.7.01 Cmdt NERC 1.4.05–1.2.08 A/Mag ELuangwa 31.10.06 Kalingkwisi'07 NC 4.08 Kawambwa Mpika'10 Ag DC Mweru-Luapula 14 NC Kawambwa Mag 20.4.16 Kasama 12.18 Mweru Luapula Dist 1.1.21 FJ Rtd '27 d'64
56. PRO CO/417/461
57. Col Edmund Henry DALGETY CB 1900 b17.5.47 s/o Lt Col ed Wellngtn RMC Ensign RSF 67–76 CMR 77 d5.7.14.
58. *Early Days in Kalomo and Livingstone* E Knowles Jordan, NRJ Vol I No.IV p20
59. *Nkhwazi* Vol 12 No.1 Apr 64 p21

CHAPTER 3

The British South Africa Police in North-Western Rhodesia

In March 1890 Frank Elliott Lochner[1] arrived at Lealui on behalf of Cecil Rhodes. Fearful of the advance of Arab slavers and their allies from the North-East, the ambitions of the King of the Belgians to the North, the Portuguese from Angola to the West, and Mozambique to the East, the Germans from the South-West and of invasion by Matabele impis from the South, Lewanika was anxious to obtain the protection of the British Crown. His fears were not groundless. In February 1890 a force of Portuguese African troops under Captain Conceiro had been despatched from Angola to Barotseland, but was defeated by the Bihe while en route. In 1893 6,000 Matabele were on their way to Lealui when recalled by Lobengula to fight the Rhodesian settlers.

After negotiations, and despite opposition from some of his indunas, Lewanika agreed to the 'Lochner Concession' on 24 May 1890, the birthday of Queen Victoria. Inter alia he conceded mining and commercial rights to the British South Africa Company in return for £2,000 per annum and agreed to welcome a British Resident at his capital and to suppress witchcraft and slavery. Most menial work in Barotseland was done by slaves.

Rhodes tried to persuade Francis Coillard of the Paris Missionary Society, Lewanika's friend and counsellor, to accept the post of Resident. Coillard declined although he remained well disposed towards the Chartered Company. Harry Johnston was also approached, but he was pre-occupied with Nyasaland. The post was offered to one of Rhodes' young disciples, Hubert Hervey, but he was mortally wounded in the Matabele Rebellion of 1896.[2]

Lewanika became much concerned at the failure to supply even the token of a Resident as evidence of British protection, but the Chartered Company was too pre-occupied with problems south of the Zambezi to give much attention to the requirements of the Litunga of Barotseland. However, in October 1896 Major H Goold-Adams of the Bechuanaland Border Police[3], arrived at Lealui to survey the Western Boundary of Barotseland and, at last, in April 1897 Major Robert Thorne Coryndon was appointed Resident Commissioner in Barotseland. Coryndon was also given a judicial warrant under the African Order in Council of 1889.

In September 1897 Coryndon arrived at Kazungula, accompanied by Frank Worthington as Secretary, and an escort of the British South Africa Police consisting of Sergeant Dobson, Corporal Macaulay and troopers Aitkens, Leake and

Bird. On crossing the Zambezi the party was met by Lewanika's son Letia who lived at Sesheke.[4]

Escorted up the Zambezi by Letia, Coryndon arrived at Lealui on 20 October and the Protectorate of Barotseland was formally proclaimed. Coryndon, born at the Cape but educated at Cheltenham was twenty seven years of age. He had come to Rhodesia with the Pioneer Column in 1890 and on arrival at Salisbury (Harare) obtained employment in the office of the Surveyor General. He served in the Matabele War of 1893 and in the 1896 Rebellion. During the Jameson Raid inquiry Coryndon became Cecil Rhodes' private secretary. Impressed by the young man's skill as a diplomatist, Rhodes chose him as the first Resident in Barotseland. The future Sir Robert Coryndon KCMG remained as Resident Commissioner, except for absence on leave, until September 1900, when he became the first Administrator of North-Western Rhodesia.

Frank Vigers Worthington was a former bank clerk who had left Johannesburg in April 1896 to join the Matabeleland Relief Force as a trooper. He was an accounts officer at Bulawayo when appointed Coryndon's confidential secretary in May 1897. He remained as such until appointed District Commissioner, Batokaland, in April 1901. From 1904 until his retirement in 1914 Worthington was Secretary for Native Affairs for North-Western Rhodesia and, from August 1911, Northern Rhodesia.

Sgt J Dobson became the first postmaster in North-Western Rhodesia, a post which included acting as Quartermaster for the nascent Barotse Native Police. F C Macaulay was to be a founder member of that force but transferred to the Civil Administration in October 1903 serving as a native commissioner until leaving in 1914 to join King Edward's Horse and meet his death in France. Ferdinand Aitkens, a veteran of the Riell Rebellion in Canada, had given up a commission in the Rhodesia Horse Volunteers to join Coryndon's party as a trooper. He became Coryndon's personal assistant and from 1900 until retiring through ill-health in 1907, was District Commissioner for Barotseland. Troopers Robert Henry Bird and Robert Leake were soon to be invalided back to Southern Rhodesia.[5]

Starting in April 1898 Sub Insp A P L Cazalet BSAP[6] with an NCO and twelve troopers of the Matabeleland Division made a very extensive patrol north and south of the Zambezi to put a stop to reported dealing in firearms, cattle stealing etc by Europeans. In September Captain Gordon Vallency Drury was sent up from Bulawayo with 13 men for 'the purpose of establishing the authority of the Government'[7] and built a fort at Monze some miles from the present town of that name. The troopers patrolled on horseback over the Batoka Valley and the Ila country of the Kafue Flats. Later a post was established by Lieutenant Jameson, at Kasungu at the head of the Kaleya Valley, east of Mazabuka. Tpr Alfred William Welch died at Fort Monze on 4 January 1899 aged 32. Of his comrades, only the names of Tprs Andrew Robert Ayres, William Beale and Arthur Brakspear Timms, are known[8]. According to the BSAP half yearly report of 30 September 1898 there were then eight members of that Force stationed with Robert Coryndon at Lealui.

In April 1899 Captain John Carden led his troop across the Zambezi at Walker's Drift or Sjoba's, opposite Sebungwe nearly a hundred miles downstream from the

Falls, to take over from Drury and his men. Drury went with a BSAP detachment to serve in the South African War and finished his police career as Acting Commissioner of the British South Africa Police.

We can identify less than half of Carden's men, but substantially more than their predecessors. His Second in Command was Lieutenant W P E Murray, like Drury a veteran of the Jameson Raid. The troop was accompanied by a medical officer, Surgeon Captain Lunan. Nevertheless three of the men joined Tpr Welch in the cemetery at Fort Monze. Corporal Montague George Hare died on 3 July 1899 aged 23, Sergeant-Major Josiah Norris, another Jameson raider, died of fever aged 30, on 1 December and Trooper F Rice on 14 February 1900.

Captain Carden had joined the BSAP as a trooper in 1890 and been commissioned in July 1892. He left the police shortly before the Matabele War in which he served as a scout and then a remount officer before rejoining the police as a captain. Captain Carden, Sergeant-Major F A Hodson, Hospital Sergeant H L Byas, Sergeant E J Toulson and Trooper H O Worringham were all to join the Barotse Native Police after resuming duty in Southern Rhodesia. Tprs Franklyn, Lucas and Martin remained with the Barotse Native Police after the rest of the troop returned south. Other members of the troop were Sgt Joseph Ford, Cpl Magnus Spence, Cpl Bootland and Tpr Samuel Peter Stopforth.[9]

Cecil Rhodes, concerned for economy, was firmly of the view that the police force north of the Zambezi should be African. In a letter to Lord Grey, dated 8 February 1898, he wrote of the suggestion of a white police force in North-Western Rhodesia: 'Their day's work would be – eating three meat meals, lying on stretchers for the balance, reading *Tit Bits* and devoting their conversation to cursing the country and the Chartered Company.'

The British South Africa Company was, of course, a commercial concern. It had financed the occupation of Southern Rhodesia and the extension of its interests and administration to the North, not merely to fulfil Rhodes' dreams, but to make a profit for its shareholders. White police were expensive and Rhodes and Jameson had been concerned for some years to reduce expenditure by cutting the number of European police in Southern Rhodesia. When they did, trouble broke out, which caused even greater expense. The mineral resources of Southern Rhodesia had proved less than anticipated and those north of the Zambezi were either not yet discovered or still untapped. In fact the administration of its territories was to be a drain on the Company's resources right up until it surrendered its responsibiliy for the government of Southern and Northern Rhodesia in 1924.

The main duties of the police at Monze were to ensure the safety of European traders and prospectors, coming up from the South and to prevent tribal fighting. There was little unrest. Once Sankamonia, a Mashukulumbwe (Ila) chief, stole a bale of blankets from a Jewish trader, who complained at the Fort. A patrol went out to Sankamonia's village on the bank of the Kafue. The chief was fined six head of cattle and some of his indunas (councillors) were detained for a month at Monze. On another occasion Chief Umgailla made an allegation against his rival, Mgala. A few troopers rode out and charged Mgala's village, scattering the inhabitants. The news reached Lewanika at Lealui. The Litunga complained that the police were attacking his friends. An official apology followed and Umgailla was compelled to surrender five cattle to his enemy.

In his annual report of 1899, Coryndon wrote: 'White police do not prove to be suitable for this territory. Under circumstances which necessitate frequent prolonged patrols at all seasons, and often on very limited or unsuitable rations, I have found them subject to a very large amount of general sickness and fever, and the difficulty of providing transport for white police, the expense of mounting them, and their natural inability to perform the duties required among natives quite unaccustomed to white men, have convinced me that it is necessary to police the territory with natives controlled efficiently by responsible white officers and instructors.'[10] The Colonial Office, who did not have to pay for them, favoured leaving the BSAP in place, one official referring to the proposed Barotse Native Police as, 'this dangerous force'.[11]

Notes

1. Frank Elliott LOCHNER Lt Salisbury Horse 1893
2. Lt Hubert John Anthony HERVEY Tpr Salisbury Horse'93 Lt Matabeleland Relief Force k'96 Sikombi's
3. Lt Col Sir Hamilton John GOOLD-ADAMS G(1907)CMG(1894 KCMG'02) CB'98 b27.6.58 RN RMC Lt R Scots'78 Bechuanald'84 Capt BBP'85 OC Field Force'88 Maj CO L/Lt Col 5.93 OC Sthn Colm Matabele War'93 Lt Col 9.93 lve 15.11.94–resigned 13.3.95 Res Commr Bechuanald'97 Lt Gov ORC 1901 Gov'07 HCommr Cyprus'11 Gov Qnsld '14–d'20
4. LETIA succeeded father as Litunga 1915
5. Maj Sir Robt Thorne CORYNDON K('19)CMG'11 b Qnstn SA 2.4.70 s/o Solr Kimberley, ed Cheltnhm Grahamstn, BSACo Svce 29.10.89 Tpr att BBP 9.11.89 BSACP 4.90 Pioneer Corps 4.90, Svyr Gen's Offce Salisby'90 Sgt Salisby H'93 Lt Rhodesia Hse'96 PS to Rhodes'96 Res Commr Baroteld 5.97 Admr B/NWR 9.00 Res Commr Swazild'07 Basutold'16–17 Gov Uganda'18 Gov Kenya'22 d Cape 10.2.25
   Frank Vigers WORTHINGTON CBE(1920) b1876? ed Repton, Bank of Africa, Natal, Jo'burg, Tpr MRF'96, Taylor's Scouts, Accts Offr Bulawayo'96 Sec to Coryndon 5.97 DC Batoka 4.01 Sec Native Affairs NWR'04 rtd'14 20 Monpelier Sq SW7; Deputy Chief Censor (Postal) WO'15 DDG Awards Min Pensions'19 Yellow Chimneys, Angmering Sx.
   Sgt DOBSON, Cpl MACAULAY see Chap 4 BNP
   Tpr Ferdinand V W AITKENS ed Bedford, Farmed Canada svd Riell Rebellion '85, OFS, Lt RHV'96 Tpr BSAP 8.97 Asst to Coryndon 10.98 DC Mongu 9.00 lve3.07–rsgnd ill hlth 22.11.07 Stanstead Rectory Glemsford Suffolk
   Tpr Robt Henry BIRD Tpr Vic Colm'93 Cpl D Tp Bulawayo Field Force '96 Tpr BSAP'97 invalided to Bulawayo'99
   Tpr Robt LEAKE Tpr MRF'96 BSAP'97 invalided to Bulawayo'99
6. Lt Alexander Philip Louis CAZALET, No.1994 Tpr BBP LCpl'93 Sub Insp MMP Jameson Rd, Lt MRF'96 BSAP'96
7. BSAP half yearly report 30.9.98 in possessn Iain Mackintosh
8. Maj Gordon Vallency DRURY Lt BBP Tuli 1893 att MMP Insp D Tp Jameson Rd 12.95 Capt MRF'96 Lt Col Ag Commr BSAP 1.4.11–28.1.13 Oxfordshire LI Maj MID 5.17, 35 Trg Res Bn d on parade Salisby Plain Wilts 19.11.17
   Tpr Wm BEALE MMP'96
   818 Tpr Arthur Brakspear TIMMS d self inflicted wounds Bulawayo 26.1.01
9. Capt CARDEN, SM HODSON. TOULSON, Hosp–Sgt BYAS, Sgt DOBSON, Tprs FRAN- KLYN, LUCAS, WORRINGHAM, MARTIN see Chap 4 BNP
   Lt Walter/Wm? Pringle Erskine MURRAY S/Insp D Tp MMP Jameson Rd Lt MRF'96

Dr Wm Smith LUNAN No.1863 Tpr BBP'93 MO MRF'96 Sgn Capt BSAP'96
SM Chas Josiah NORRIS Tpr A Tp MMP JRd'95 MRF'96 d1.12.99 age 30
10. Quoted in *Story of the NRR* p.17
11. PRO CO/417/283

CHAPTER 4

The Barotse Native Police

In August 1899 Major Colin Harding returned to Africa from leave in the United Kingdom. There he had had discussions with Rhodes about the replacement of white police by Africans. Harding had suggested a strength of two white Troop Sergeants-Major and 292 Ngoni from North-Eastern Rhodesia due discharge from the Mashonaland Native Police in July 1900, who should be invited to transfer after three months leave[1]. Harding was now sent up to Barotseland as Acting Resident Commissioner to relieve Robert Coryndon who left on leave in November 1899. Major Harding had orders, dated 31 August 1899, from the Commandant General in Southern Rhodesia, to take over command of the police detachment at Lealui, consult with Coryndon concerning the enlistment of native police and to enlist twenty-five to thirty, and to communicate with the troop commander at Monze who for administration and police-work would be under his orders[2]. Colin Harding was accompanied by his brother, William, a newcomer to Southern Africa, as private secretary, and by Sergeant F C Macaulay. Having reached Kazungula well ahead of his wagons, Harding made use of the time to make a brief inspection of the police stations at Kalomo and Monze. The Northern Rhodesia Police magazine, *Nkhwazi*, of September 1959, contained a report of the receipt, from the Archives Section of East Africa Command at Nairobi, of a volume of Barotse Native Police attestation forms. The first recruit, No.1 Constable Chinlele, was said to have been attested at Kalomo on 1st September 1899 but Harding did not leave Bulawayo until that day[3]. Back at Kazungula on 12 November 1899 Harding reported he had completed the 450 miles inspection trip in 14 days. The station at Kalomo was under construction and Sergeant-Major Dobson and two BSAP troopers were to be posted there. Harding had in mind a post with 50 African police in the Mashukulumbwe country, 6 under a European at Kalomo, and 6 at Walker's Drift on the Zambezi. He had sufficient arms, uniforms and equipment in his wagons.

The Hardings travelled up the Zambezi by canoe escorted by Letia, while Macaulay brought up the horses and mules by land. Colin Harding had been entrusted by the Foreign Office with an intelligence mission to ascertain the extent of Lewanika's sphere of influence to the North and West and the limits of the advance of Portuguese administration.

Major Edwin Colin Harding CMG was thirty six years of age. The son of a gentleman farmer, he seems to have devoted his life to hunting and shooting in England until the age of thirty one, when his father died leaving little but debts. In early 1894 Colin Harding arrived in Bulawayo with ten pounds in his pocket. He worked as a builder's labourer and then as a solicitor's clerk before turning to working, and dealing in, gold claims. In this he had some success and he was able to return to the United Kingdom on holiday in 1896. While he was away the Matabele and Mashona Rebellions broke out. Harding hurried back to Cape Town. He assisted with the transport of a batch of remounts by sea to Beira and overland to Umtali. Harding's previous military experience seems to have been limited to part-time service in the Rhodesia Horse in which he had held the rank of corporal when in Matabeleland. He now managed to attach himself to the staff of Lt Col E A H Alderson as a galloper or ADC. Alderson was a regular British Army officer who had been sent to Salisbury in command of the mounted infantry from Aldershot. He described Harding as having particularly distinguished himself at the action at Simbanoota's Kraal, paying no more attention to the Mashona bullets than if they were snowballs[4]. Harding was soon commissioned as a sub-inspector in the Mashonaland Mounted Police. He rose rapidly to 'Captain or Inspector' in early 1897, and 'Major or Chief Inspector' in November that year when he was appointed to command the native police in Mashonaland. From this post he was sent, as previously related, to North-Eastern Rhodesia in 1898.

The South African War broke in October 1899 while Harding was en route from Bulawayo. His request to return south to take part was refused. Whilst he was travelling up the Zambezi or soon after his arrival at Lealui, an event of more significance to the history of Northern Rhodesia occurred. On 28th November 1899 the constitution of North-Western Rhodesia was laid down in the Barotse-land/North-Western Rhodesia Order in Council. The Administrator and officials were to be appointed by Her Majesty's High Commissioner at the Cape after nomination by the Chartered Company. Article Eight of the Order provided for the formation of a police force. On 23 May 1900 the High Commissioner signed a letter authorising the formation of the Barotse Native Police. This was promulgated by Proclamation No.19 of 1901 but the Force was then already in being.

At Lealui in December 1899 Harding approached Lewanika for help with recruiting police. The Litunga was reluctant. He feared that the police would undermine his authority. Harding argued that they would only be trained at Mongu-Lealui and would then be posted to Batokaland, an area so far away that Lewanika could not maintain order there himself. He explained that the police would at any time enforce the Chief's authority if required, always, of course, under the Administration's orders and instructions.

Harding reported 'With these assurances he was content, and he promised to get forty or fifty recruits, but I am convinced that his consent was not given spontaneously. With that view before me and the likelihood of Angonis relieving the white police in the Batoka (an arrangement which I strongly recommend, and which I discussed more fully with Major Coryndon), I did not press the subject further.'

'The gist of the whole indaba was that the King, whilst only too pleased for native police, Barotse or others, to relieve the white police in the Batoka country, disliked the suggestion of having any force in the Barotse Valley, except under his control. Under the present arrangements the Queen, Letia, and the King, have from six to ten men each at their beck and call, who act as their bodyguards; these are clad in uniform and designated as police.'[5]

The first 25 recruits for the Barotse Native Police were attested at Lealui on 2 January 1900. Their terms of service were explained to them by the Ngambela, Lewanika's prime minister. The engagement was for 12 months at 10/- a month for privates, 12/6 for corporals and 15/- for native sergeants. Each man was to be issued with a free uniform and a blanket.[6]

On 19th January 1900 Harding, accompanied by his brother and a party of Lewanika's indunas with their retinues, left Lealui by canoe to follow the Zambezi to its source. Sergeant Macaulay was left in charge at Lealui where he continued training the recruits. Harding had brought with him a phonograph with a recorded message to Lewanika from the Administrator of Matabeleland, the Hon Arthur Lawley[7]. At Lealui Harding made a recording of Lewanika's voice with a message to his vassals calling on them, amongst other things, to send to the Litunga all arrears of tribute without further delay, or 'the Great White Man who now visits you will mete out the punishment you deserve.' Harding played this message to the various Lovale, Lunda and other chiefs he met and recorded their messages in reply, acknowledging the Litunga's suzerainty and pledging their loyalty. These messages were played to the boundary commission in 1903, but with little benefit to Lewanika as it awarded most of the territory through which Harding passed, to Portugal, which already had forts at Kakenge and Nyakatoro. Harding was unimpressed by the efficiency of the commandants and garrisons of these places, each of about thirty native troops.

Harding reported many deserted villages in the Lunda country where the people lived in fear of raids by the Lovale and Mambari slavers. On his return to Nyaka-toro, after reaching the source of the Zambezi, Colin Harding sent his brother back to Lealui with the boats on 1st April 1900. After a delay of some days while his horses and mules came up from the capital, Colin Harding set off overland to Chisamba in the Bihe country of Portuguese West Africa. He reported, 'Every day I am seeing traces of the slave trade. The wayside trees are simply hung with disused shackles, some to hold one, some two, three, and even six slaves. Skulls and bones bleached by the sun lie where the victims fell, gape with helpless grin on those who pass, a damning evidence of a horrible traffic. . . yesterday we met two caravans and today one, all proceeding to the Lunda country for their living merchandise. Some were carrying spare guns, some calico, others powder'[8]. The Mambari exchanged calico, guns and powder for slaves and rubber. On 9th May 1900 Harding met a caravan eighty four strong on its way to the Lunda country. Harding was in no position to take any action. He was without any force of his own and in Portuguese territory where the garrisons of the various forts appeared to ignore the passing trade.

From Chisamba Harding journeyed south-east back to Lealui. He was met by Sergeant Macaulay about two hundred miles west of the Zambezi near the Kwando River. Leaving Lealui on 5 May, Macaulay had made a forced march of 250 miles from Lealui with a few African police. They all arrived back at Lealui

PROCLAMATION

No. 19 of 1901.

By His Excellency the Right Honourable Alfred, Baron Milner, of St. James's in the County of London, and of Cape Town, in the Colony of the Cape of Good Hope, in the Peerage of the United Kingdom; a Member of His Majesty's Most Honourable Privy Council, Knight Grand Cross of the Most Honourable Order of the Bath, Knight Grand Cross of the Most Distinguished Order of St. Michael and St. George, Administrator of the Orange River Colony and of the Transvaal, and His Majesty's High Commissioner for South Africa.

WHEREAS it is expedient to establish and maintain within the limits of the Barotziland-North Western Rhodesia Order in Council, 1899, a force of police to be known as the Barotse Native Police, and to appoint for the proper discipline and control of such force such officers as may from time to time be necessary, and whereas it is expedient to make provision for maintaining discipline and good order in the said force: Now, therefore, under and by virtue of the power in me vested, I do hereby proclaim and make known as follows:—

1. There shall be established and maintained within the limits of the said Order a force of Police to be known as the Barotse Native Police, of such strength and so constituted and organised as the High Commissioner may from time to time direct. The High Commissioner shall also direct as he may see fit the employment and distribution of the said force.

2. The High Commissioner may by notice in the *Gazette* appoint to or remove from the said force a Commandant, Inspectors and such other officers as he may consider necessary, and may assign to such officers such powers, duties and functions as he may see fit.

3. Any member of the said force charged with the commission of any crime or offence, or with the breach of any Regulations that may be promulgated by the Administrator, with the consent of the High Commissioner, as applicable to members of the said force, shall be tried by an officer or by a board of officers of the said force having jurisdiction.

4. The High Commissioner may, by notice in the *Gazette*, approve Regulations framed by the Administrator, conferring upon an officer or board of officers of the said force respectively, such powers and jurisdiction as the Administrator may see fit to try members of the said force charged with the commission of crimes and offences, and specifying the sentences, fines and penalties that may be inflicted or imposed by the said officer or board of officers.

5. Officers of the said force may adopt such measures as may be necessary for the safe custody and conveyance to the central prison at Lialui, or at such other place as may be directed by the Administrator with the approval of the High Commissioner, of all prisoners whom it may be necessary to transport to the said prison.

GOD SAVE THE KING!

Given under my Hand and Seal this 31st day of August, 1901.

MILNER,
High Commissioner.

By Command of His Excellency the High Commissioner,

F. PERRY,
Imperial Secretary.

Proclamation No. 19 of 1901 31st August 1901 (PRO)

on 19 June 1900. Harding had travelled a total of 2,235 miles since leaving Kazungula in the previous October. He suggested a station be established 150 miles upriver from Lealui to stop the slave trade and Portuguese encroachment.

On Coryndon's return from leave Harding was appointed Commandant of the Barotse Native Police. There were six Company posts, Mongu, Victoria Falls, Kalomo, Fort Monze (BSAP), Kazangula and Sesheke, the last two having no permanent buildings, but being frequently visited. Kalomo was selected by Coryndon as Government Headquarters.

After his return from Portuguese West Africa, Harding did not rest for long at Mongu-Lealui. Leaving his brother in charge there, he set out with Sergeant Macaulay for Batokaland, via the Victoria Falls. By the time they reached Kalomo they had found thirty or forty recruits who were despatched to Mongu for training. Harding and Macaulay spent two days at Kalomo inspecting the new camp site, before leaving for Monze where they arrived on 3 August.

Captain Drury, according to Harding, had selected the site for this fort with 'more haste than consideration'. In the early part of 1900 Captain Carden's men had been going down with fever at the rate of four a day. A few days before Harding's arrival, fourteen troopers were invalided back to Bulawayo.

Harding wrote, 'My two days at Monze were completely employed in taking over the station, and making arrangements for Captain Carden and his garrison to leave the country. By this time they are on their way, and Macaulay and his native police are fairly established in a more healthy spot, where he is deputed to carry out the duties of the late troop.' The camp was a temporary one for 25 native police, until a new fort could be built further north in Mashukulumbwe country. Carden handed over a Maxim gun, 4 horses, a Scotch cart and 7 oxen for use by the new force.[9]

Harding and Carden had selected what they judged to be a better site for the fort, on a hill, but with a good water supply. Chief Monza expressed resentment at having to pay tribute to Lewanika, now that they were both under the protection of Queen Victoria, but he provided labour for the building of the new police quarters and brought in twenty recruits for the Force.

Colin left Monze on 5th August 1900 with ten members of his force, four of Lewanika's Indunas who had accompanied him from Lealui, and thirty carriers provided by Monza. Captain Carden left for Bulawayo shortly afterwards with the remnant of his troop, except for Trooper Lucas, who was seconded to the Barotse Native Police to assist Macaulay at Monze.

Harding had instructions to rendezvous with Mr C L Carbutt, the District Commissioner of Sebungwe, Southern Rhodesia[10]. While the latter patrolled south of the Zambezi, Harding was to patrol the North Bank sending back to the South natives who had left Southern Rhodesia to evade payment of tax. Since these were Tonga who had migrated south some years before, he could see little wrong in their return home and did not pursue the hunt with great determination. In any case, it was no easy task to establish who belonged where.

Soon after he arrived in the Zambezi Valley, Harding received a plea for assistance from Chief Mwamba. Six Matabele from Bulawayo, calling themselves 'native police', had arrived demanding food and shelter and assistance in recruiting labour. Colonel Harding found these impostors armed and wearing uniform and despatched them back south. He considered their employers to blame for sending men in this guise and without money or supplies to carry out their mission by intimidation and deceit.[11]

Harding patrolled east, past the Kariba Gorge, to the junction of the Kafue with the Zambezi. The Kafue River, which he reached on 30th August, was then the boundary between North-Western and North-Eastern Rhodesia. Although Lewanika claimed that his territory stretched far to the east of the Kafue, Harding was of the opinion that the people on the East Bank had never heard this, and certainly did not care. He continued up the Kafue, through the Balengwe Gorge, and on to the Kafue Flats, before returning to the new Fort Monze. Here he found Macaulay had made great progress.

Harding was now required to return to Mongu-Lealui. During his brief stay at Monze, Chief Monza happily produced skins to be conveyed, as his tribute, to Lewanika, and requested help in disciplining one of his own sub-chiefs, Fufa, who had declined to assist with the provision of labour for the new fort. Three native police were sent with Monza's emissary to summon this recalcitrant to a meeting with Harding. Fufa came in immediately and all was resolved to Monza's satisfaction.

Harding left for Lealui with Lewanika's indunas, fifteen Barotse Native Police recruits, armed with sticks, and the necessary train of carriers and personal servants. On arrival at the village of Samosonta of the Mashukulumbwe, a policeman was sent to call the chief in from the fields for interview. The policeman was threatened with spears and an armed crowd gathered round Harding's entourage. Luckily he was accompanied at this stage of the journey by Trooper Lucas, as the sticks of the recruits were hardly sufficient to set against the spears and bows of the Mashukulumbwe.

Eventually Samosonta came forward and the villager who had threatened the policeman was produced. Samosonta was fined two cattle. He then failed to produce carriers to relieve those provided by Monza. Harding's solution to this impasse was to divide the loads between the police, except for one. This the Commandant personally placed on Chief Samosonta. After their leader had staggered three or four hundred yards under this burden, an ample number of his people came forward to volunteer their services to carry all the loads.

Harding trekked on north-westwards to the Kafue River, calling on Umgailla and Mgala en route. He visited the mission stations at Nanzela and Nkala, where on 25 September he met his brother, who had come from Lealui by arrangement. William Harding was deputed to visit the copper workings across the Kafue while Colin pressed on to meet Coryndon at Mongu-Lealui. He arrived in time to witness the Lewanika Concession on 17th October 1900. Coryndon left to convey the new concession to England and Harding became Acting Administrator for North-Western Rhodesia.

Lewanika expressed great concern about rumours of the activities of Mambari slave traders to the north, in the Bamashasha and Balunda areas. On 21 October, Colin Harding was on the move again, to patrol the Kabompo River to its source. He took fifteen Barotse Native Police, this time trained and armed, and the necessary carriers, together with the usual group of indunas detailed by the Litunga to accompany and guide him. An American prospector, Bricker, whom Harding had met on his earlier journey up the Zambezi, volunteered to come along for their mutual protection. Harding related that as they went up river they were joined by several hundred natives, looking for lost relations.

At Kasempa Harding sent a demand that Kachakala release the slaves he held. Some old men and women were handed over. Harding sent for Kachakala but received an insolent reply. After a night march, Harding stormed the slaver's two stockaded kraals and burnt them. There was no serious opposition. Kachakala escaped but 20 slaves were liberated. Bricker was nearly drowned while helping to disperse another caravan. Again Harding found villages deserted because of the depredations of the slavers, but managed to reunite a number of men, women, and children, with their families and friends.[12]

The patrol returned to Lealui in January 1901. After a few weeks rest there, Harding left down the Zambezi for a tour of Batokaland. Between Kazungula and Victoria Falls he received news that his brother, then in charge at Monze, was down with blackwater fever. Colin Harding reached Monze to find that William had died on 11th April. Corporal B C Franklyn had come from Kalomo to nurse William Harding and Trooper Lucas, who was down with the same disease. Franklyn also contracted blackwater and died two days after the Commandant's arrival. Lucas recovered and was able to take command of the firing party at his comrade's funeral. Sgt Macaulay was on leave after four years in the Territory. Harding decided to close down the fort and left with Lucas for Victoria Falls. He wrote that fever had struck so hard throughout the Territory that rainy season that there were only four white government officials, including police, left alive to administer it.

According to Val Gielgud, Native Commissioner on the North-Eastern Rhodesia side of the Kafue Hook, Umgailla and Mgala were still feuding. Mgala refused to stop raiding Umgailla. In June 1901 Gielgud brought over 23 Matabele police for a combined operation. Harding was accompanied by Tpr Lucas with a Maxim, 70 partially trained Barotse Native Police and some 600 friendly tribesmen. They planned a surprise attack at dawn on Mgala's stockade, but surprise was lost because the friendlies could not be dissuaded from lighting fires. Mgala was arrested on 28 June and taken to Kalomo from where he was released on 1 December 1901 to live at Lealui under Lewanika's eye. The contracts of the Matabele had expired and Gielgud had to borrow four Barotse Native Police for the journey back to his headquarters.[13]

Shortly afterwards Coryndon returned to resume his mantle as Administrator and other reinforcements arrived. Harding, at Coryndon's suggestion was granted the local rank of colonel. During his travels the Commandant had selected sites for two new forts. They were to provide bases in the outlying areas from which patrols could operate to rid the country of the slavers. Sgt Macaulay and Sergeant-Major T Harris were commissioned as sub-inspectors to command the new detachments.

On 25th September 1901 Captain John Carden, the former commander of the BSAP troop at Monze, was seconded for two years as Second-in-Command of the

Barotse Native Police. When Colonel Harding left on leave on 20 January 1902 Carden, with the local rank of major, became Acting Commandant of the Force which had grown considerably in strength and influence.

The establishment of the Barotse Native Police at about this time was:

> The Commandant.
> One Inspector,
> Two Sub-Inspectors,
> One Regimental Sergeant-Major,
> Two Company Sergeant-Majors,
> Three European Corporals,
> Five European Troopers,
> Eight Native Sergeants,
> Sixteen Native Corporals,
> 224 Privates.

The disciplinary regulations promulgated in Cape Government Notice 15/01 provided for a Superior Court of Officers to consist of 5, or if necessary 3 officers, with a president of at least the rank of captain but normally a major, with power to impose the death penalty, imprisonment for 25 years or a fine of £100. An Ordinary Court of Officers, 3 officers or, if no officers were available within a

HIGH COMMISSIONER'S NOTICE.

No. 16 OF 1901.

IT is hereby notified, for public information, that under and by virtue of the powers conferred upon him by the Barotziland-North-Western Rhodesia Order in Council, 1899, His Excellency the High Commissioner has been pleased to make the following appointments:—Major Colin Harding, C.M.G., to be Commandant of the Barotse Native Police with the local rank of Colonel; Sergeant-Major T. Harris, of the British South Africa Police, to be Sub-Inspector in the Barotse Native Police; Sergeant F. C. Macaulay, of the British South Africa Police, to be Sub-Inspector in the Barotse Native Police; and Frank W. Sykes, Esquire, to be District Commissioner of the Falls District, North-Western Rhodesia.

By Command of His Excellency the High Commissioner,

F PERRY,
Imperial Secretary.

7th September, 1901.

High Commissioner's Notice No. 16 of 1901 7 September 1901 (PRO)

reasonable distance, sergeants-major, presided over by, if possible, a captain, could sentence to imprisonment up to six months or a fine of £15 but could not try an officer. An officer or British NCO in command of a detachment could award imprisonment for 7 days or a fine of £1.

The Force was to be organised into a Headquarters and two companies. Each company was to be commanded by a sub-inspector assisted by a European company sergeant-major, and was to consist of four sections each of one sergeant, two corporals and 28 men. One company was to be based at Lealui with detachments on the Kabompo River and at Sesheke. The other was to have stations at Victoria Falls, Kalomo, Monze, and on the Kafue. The European corporals and troopers were for employment as clerks, farriers etc and to effect any necessary arrests of Europeans[14]. Of course actual strength lagged behind that provided for in the establishment and actual dispositions differed from those originally proposed.

In late 1901 Sergeant-Major Mobbs, Trooper Lucas and a small party of native police pitched camp on what was later to become the football pitch at Kasempa[15]. Sub Insp Macaulay took command. A system of patrols was instituted and in February 1903 Macaulay with 9 men, after a long pursuit, surprised a Mambari slave caravan releasing two shackled women left behind when the slavers fled. On 31 March he broke up a slavers' camp at Mushime's Village capturing 15 firearms and a large quantity of gunpowder.[16]

By 1902 there were only nine European officers and non-commissioned officers actually serving in the Barotse Native Police and 240 natives, out of an establishment which had grown to three hundred. At Headquarters, at Kalomo, were the Commanding Officer, Regimental Sergeant-Major E J Toulson, Hospital Sergeant-Major H L Byas, an Orderly Room Sergeant-Major, a Company Sergeant-Major and 156 native non-commissioned officers and men. At Monze, part of the Kalomo District, were stationed only three native police. At Nkala Sub-Inspector T Harris was in command with Cpl H O Worringham and twenty one native NCOs and men. At Kasempa was Macaulay, assisted by a European CSM and thirty native police. At Lealui were twenty native police under the District Commissioner, and at Victoria Falls ten, under the District Commissioner there. The Territory was divided into five civil administrative districts. Harris and Macaulay acted as assistant district commissioners until Harris resigned from the Service in January 1903 and Macaulay transferred from the Force to the Administration that July.

Coryndon in his annual report wrote: 'The corps has made rapid strides and is now almost at full strength and is fully equipped with arms, uniforms, kit and accoutrements.'

'The corps is recruited chiefly from the Batoka natives who take to the routine and discipline at once and who make smart and reliable soldiers; a few Mashukulumbwe who contrary to expectation are amenable and obedient; and a few Barotse, who, though more intelligent, do not seem to take to the military life at all.'

'Major Carden has since his arrival in December worked up the internal discipline of the corps to a high pitch of excellence and Regimental Sergeant-Major Toulson's wide experience of native police work will always ensure a very high standard of discipline and smartness at the Headquarters Station. The native corporals and sergeants are especially good and assume and exercise their authority in the right spirit.'

Carden in his report as Acting Commandant wrote: 'The behaviour of the police has so far been excellent; they take readily to discipline, and no serious complaints have been received from native kraals to which they are occasionally sent alone.'

Because of the requirement for police detachments consequent on the development of the northern areas of the Territory, Carden recommended an increase in the establishment of the Force to 350, 'though this may, I think, stand over till the arrival of Lieutenant Harte-Barry and recruits from North-Eastern Rhodesia. The health of the white non-commissioned officers has been fair, so far there being only one case of blackwater, though a good deal of simple malaria. The health of the native police is good, except that after the rains they seem to get bad ulcers on the feet and legs from patrolling in the wet long grass.'[17]

Lt A M Harte-Barry BSAP left Salisbury towards the end of April 1902 to commence a two year secondment to the Barotse Native Police in the rank of Captain. He travelled first to Nyasaland for a two month attachment to 2nd King's African Rifles. The plan was that he should then recruit in the vicinity of Lake Mweru, the area suggested by Robert Codrington, the Administrator of North-Eastern Rhodesia. In the mean time Codrington complained that the Ngoni recruited by Colin Harding for the Mashonaland Native Police had not been brought home on completion of their engagement as promised. He was also dissatisfied with the treatment of other North-Eastern Rhodesia natives recruited to work in Southern Rhodesia. Harte-Barry arrived at Fort Jameson to find that Codrington had rescinded his agreement and had to travel to Kalomo to report for duty without the hoped for recruits. By then it had been established that the majority of the Ngoni police in Southern Rhodesia had re-engaged for further service or were otherwise accounted for. Robert Codrington relented and Harte-Barry retraced his steps to return with seventy five recruits in July 1903.[18]

Colonel Harding, mindful of his experience at Fort Jameson, proposed that twenty five Sikhs be recruited to replace the white NCOs in the Barotse Native Police. He believed that African police, noting the difference in status between officers and white NCOs, were inclined to treat the latter with insufficient respect. His proposal was approved by the High Commissioner in 1903 but was never implemented. Coryndon had thought the plan an excellent one and also considered it important that the native police should not be entirely recruited in the country in which they were to serve. He later came to the view that Africans were likely to show even less deference to Indian than to European NCOs.[19]

The original uniform of the Barotse Native Police was a blue unlined serge frock or jacket as worn by the European troopers of the British South Africa Police. This had two patch pockets fastened with brass buttons and five brass buttons down the front. The blue shoulder straps were also secured by brass buttons. White cotton knickerbockers reaching just below the knee were worn by native police with no puttees or footwear. Photographs in Colonel Harding's book *In Remotest Barotseland* of native police with Macaulay and Lucas at Fort Monze, and with Harding's patrol up the Kabompo, show them wearing blue field service caps. Later photographs, including one of a parade at Kalomo under Major

**Major John Carden, second in command (later Commandant) Barotse Native Police
with RSM Toulson, Hospital Sergeant-Major (later Major) Byas and other British
Non-Commissioned Officers (Far Bugles)**

Carden, show the black or blue pillbox cap depicted in a water colour by Major
A B Cree, but with a black tassel reaching to the right shoulder. Another photograph in *In Remotest Barotseland* shows native police at a kit inspection wearing
light khaki smocks and long shorts with field service caps of the same shade and
material. According to the War Office publication *The Land Forces of the British
Colonies and Protectorates* (revised 1905), drill order consisted of a khaki drill tunic
or jumper of the Zululand Police pattern, khaki knickerbockers and a red fez.
Ammunition was carried in a brown leather bandolier and native police wore
brown leather waist belts and bayonet frogs. They were armed with the Martini-
Henry rifle. For marching order, a cavalry pattern mess tin, canvas haversack, a
water bottle, clothes brush and waterproof cape were issued.

Sergeant Macaulay and Trooper Lucas are shown at Monze in 1900 wearing
blue patrol jackets with no buttons visible, and blue field service caps. Macaulay
wears white breeches and khaki puttees. Lucas has dark khaki breeches and either
dark puttees or leather gaiters. Both wear ankle boots and spurs. Photographs
taken at Kalomo in about 1902 show European non-commissioned ranks wearing
khaki slouch hats with the brim turned up on the left and what is probably a blue
pugree, blue serge frocks like those of the native police, and brown leather Sam
Browne belts with one brace over the right shoulder. One sergeant-major wears
white breeches and the others khaki. All wear blue puttees with ankle boots and

spurs. Rank badges, in what appears to be gold lace, are worn on the right arm only. Two have a crown on the right forearm, one a four bar chevron point upwards on the forearm, and one a three bar chevron point downwards on the upper arm surmounted by crown. In fact they appear to wear the uniform of the British South Africa Police from which they were seconded. All European members of the Barotse Native Police were mounted and had blue cavalry cloaks.

Major Carden is shown in two photographs wearing light khaki breeches and leather gaiters with spiral strapping, ankle boots and spurs. He wears a khaki drill frock with turn-down collar and very small buttons. He has the same slouch hat as the NCOs and a Sam Browne belt with sword. He appears to be wearing collar badges, the only one to do so. None wear shoulder titles. The first badge of the Barotse native Police was the lion with a tusk in its right paw from the arms of the British South Africa Company. This badge was stamped on the buttons over the letters B N P.[20]

The Barotse Native Police had two .303 Maxim machine guns with pack saddles and tripods. The tripods were manufactured at the Railway Workshops at Umtali in Southern Rhodesia. For transport there were five horses, two mules, eight donkeys and three large 'American' wagons with 54 oxen[21]. During 1902 thirty two camels were sent up to North-Western Rhodesia by the British South Africa Company for use as transport by the police and administration.

The salary of the Commandant was £650 per annum. Maj Carden received £455 or £500 when acting as Commandant. All European personnel received free rations, uniform, equipment, horse, saddlery and forage, together with pay as follows:

Inspector (Captain)	25 Shillings a day,
Sub-Inspector (Lieutenant)	17 Shillings a day,
Regimental Sergeant-Major	10 Shillings a day,
Company Sergeant-Major	9 Shillings a day,
Sergeant	8 Shillings a day,
Corporal	7 Shillings a day,
Trooper	6 Shillings a day.

Of this one shilling a day was withheld from NCOs and troopers as deferred pay, giving a man £36.10s on completion of his two year engagement. European NCOs and troopers who re-engaged for a further two years service were paid an additional shilling a day. Pay in the Barotse Native Police was between a shilling a day, for a trooper, and five shillings a day, for an inspector, higher than for the British South Africa Police in Southern Rhodesia.

Native police received free uniform and equipment. Their pay was:

Sergeants	15s 0d a month in the first year of service,
Corporals	12s 6d a month in the first year of service,
Privates	10s 0d a month in the first year of service.

Two weeks' leave on full pay was granted on completion of twelve months service. In the second year of service pay for all native ranks was increased by two shillings

49

and sixpence a month. On re-engagement for a further two years the increment was five shillings a month. Each man received free rations of 2lbs of beef each week, meal and salt.[22]

Lewanika was concerned over the delay in settling his borders with Angola. Slavers were still operating with impunity to the north of Lealui and the Bakwengari, well armed with Martini-Henry rifles were said to be raiding on the Kwando River to the west. Coryndon could see that the value of British protection must be in doubt. He pointed out to the British Government that if the Administration did not take some action the Lozi would, which would increase the likelihood of a clash with the Portuguese. On 10 August 1902 Major Carden with RSM Toulson, Hospital Sergeant-Major Byas, Sgt Worringham, 105 native police and 250 carriers left Lealui. Accompanied by 1,500 Lozi warriors they marched 175 miles west to the Kwando. Hampered by swamps and unsatisfactory guides, they passed burnt villages from which the people had fled. Finally they reached a kraal erected by the Bakwengari Chief. 600 rounds of ammunition were found within the stockade which Carden burnt. Shortage of food compelled him to return to Lealui which was reached on 20 October after an 800 mile round trip. It was planned to complete the operation during the next dry season without the mass of friendly warriors which had delayed the march, eaten up the little remaining food in the countryside and, it was thought, discouraged the local inhabitants from emerging from their hiding places.[23]

In May 1902 Harding had been required to interrupt his leave to return to Cape Town to meet Lewanika and his entourage and escort them back to England, where the Litunga was to attend the Coronation of King Edward VII. Harding clearly enjoyed this task. He and Lewanika arrived back in Barotseland on 26 November 1902, being met at Kazungula by Robert Coryndon and a guard of honour of police. The Administrator expressed his entire satisfaction at the smart and soldierlike appearance of men on parade. He said he 'thoroughly appreciated the great amount of work which it has entailed to bring the Corps to this state of efficiency.' In London, Joseph Chamberlain, Secretary of State for the Colonies, had expressed regret to Lewanika that no detachment of the Barotse Native Police had been included in the Coronation contingents, which is ironic as the Colonial Office had turned down Coryndon's suggestion that Lewanika be accompanied by 20 members of the Force.[24]

After accompanying Lewanika back to Lealui, Harding returned to headquarters at Kalomo and resumed command of his force. He brought with him lieutenants H M Stennett, who had served in South Africa with the Imperial Yeomanry, and G H Hamilton, late Imperial Light Horse, Troop Sergeant-Major Bowley and sergeants H C Ingles and H Nicholls from the BSAP to reinforce the 5 officers, 3 white NCOs and 222 native police. The Commandant was impressed by the advances made in his absence and found, 'They were now a well disciplined body of men and their drill and general appearance were everything that could be desired.' It appears from a photograph that the Barotse Native Police, although not mounted, drilled like cavalry in single rank. No doubt their white instructors from the British South Africa Police were responsible for this custom. Harding related that when he assumed command of a British infantry battalion in 1915, he knew only cavalry drill.[25]

There had been complaints that African members of the Force were inclined to be overbearing towards the local population when travelling unaccompanied by an officer or white NCO. On 23 February 1903 Col Harding issued Regimental Order No.1 stating that personnel going on leave should go in uniform but unarmed.[26]

On 26 February Harding, Carden, 2 other officers and 100 African police left Kalomo for the Mashukulumbwe country where Chief Sachekalomo complained of raiding by Mininya. Mininya having been fined a number of cattle, Carden continued to patrol the area while Harding with Lt Hamilton and police from Nkala crossed the Kafue with some of Lewanika's indunas and marched due East for 10 days visiting the North-Eastern Rhodesia administrative post at Sitanda. Although Harding appeared to be well received with a smart guard of North-Eastern Rhodesia Constabulary turned out for his inspection, Codrington later complained of an incursion which had caused the local inhabitants to become unsettled. Harding maintained that he was entitled to patrol an area claimed by Lewanika and that the local chiefs acknowledged Lewanika's overlordship.

Harding arrived back at Kalomo on 7 May 1903 having covered 900 miles and visited 150 chiefs. Mr Lewis, manager of the Northern Copper Co's Silver King Mine had asked for a police station to be opened nearby and Lt Hamilton moved his headquarters to a new fort at Linungwe. When Harte-Barry returned from the north-east he confirmed that all was calm in the area through which Harding had passed.[27]

In his annual report in April 1903 Coryndon wrote that the corps had been maintained at nearly the authorised strength of three hundred and that there had been great progress in its training in drill and routine duties, musketry, signalling, improving physique by gymnastic exercises etc. A bugle band had been formed. He reported that the Barotse Native Police was thoroughly well grounded and, 'an exceedingly smart and soldierly force, of great service in supporting the authority of civil officials, most of whom are situated at scattered and isolated stations throughout the country.'[28]

In July 1903 Robert Coryndon and Colonel Harding had to return to England to assist the Anglo-Portuguese Boundary Commission. In the event the boundaries were settled in Europe by the King of Italy who merely drew straight lines on the map. The Portuguese were confirmed in their occupation of much land over which Lewanika, rightly in Harding's opinion, claimed suzerainty. A further expedition against the Bakwengari was now out of the question, although the King of Italy's decision opened the way for the establishment of administrative posts at Balovale and Mwinilunga in 1907–08. Plans to station an officer and 25 African police at Kabompo were shelved for economy reasons.[29]

Maj Carden was due for leave in October 1903 and it was planned that Capt Harte-Barry should then act as Commandant until Col Harding's return. However on 4 September Carden found Harte-Barry drunk at Mala, the local natives unsettled and the camp in a disgraceful state. Harte-Barry chose to resign rather than face disciplinary action. Due to a shortage of grain around Kalomo the main body of the Force had been temporarily moved to Mala in May leaving only the Pay and Quartermaster, Lieutenant Byas, now commissioned after doing the job since November 1902, a white sergeant and a few African police at Kalomo. On 1 August 1903 Sub-Inspector F A Hodson BSAP had been seconded to the Barotse Native Police as Captain and Adjutant. Hodson, Byas and RSM Toulson had all served under Carden at Monze, as had Quartermaster Sergeant Worringham. Hodson being judged by Harding to have insufficient experience, Captain C L D Monro BSAP was sent up to act as Commandant when Carden left.[30]

By 12 November 1903 the main body was back at Kalomo and the Force was distributed as follows:

> Kalomo: Maj Monro, Capt Hodson, Lt Byas, RSM Toulson, QMS Worringham, Orderly Room Sergeant Watherston, C/Sgt Nicholls, drill instructor, 5 native sergeants, 12 corporals, 82 privates, 10 buglers and 3 prison warders.
> Linungwe: Lt Hamilton, a native sergeant, 3 corporals, 36 privates and a bugler;
> Nkala: Lt O'Sullevan, 2 native corporals, 22 privates and a bugler;
> Kasempa: Lt Stennett, C/Sgt Ingles, a native sergeant, 6 corporals, 27 privates and a bugler;
> Kaunga: Lt Jameson, a native sergeant, 3 corporals, 22 privates and a bugler;
> Lealui: 1 native sergeant and 9 privates;
> Tshete (Sesheke): 1 native corporal and 5 privates;
> Sejoba's (Walker's Drift) on the Zambezi: 1 N/Cpl and 4 ptes;
> Victoria Falls: Sgt Valentine Johnson, 1 N/Cpl and 6 ptes.[31]

Lt J J O'Sullevan had joined the Barotse Native Police on 12 August 1903. J W Dale Jameson had served as an officer in the Imperial Yeomanry and came to North-Western Rhodesia as Clerk Controller in July 1902, being lent to the BNP in mid-July 1903. Quarter-Master Sergeant Worringham was about to be commissioned and by 1 January 1904 had taken over from O'Sullevan at Nkala where he also acted as District Commissioner. By 16 July 2Lt Worringham had transferred to the Civil Administration but continued in charge of the police at Nkala assisted by C/Sgt Nicholls. Lt Stennett acted as DC at Kasempa when Macaulay was posted to Lealui in January 1904. Lt O'Sullevan was posted to Kaunga when Lt Jameson was invalided to Kalomo where he died of dysentery on 7 July.[32]

The estimates for 1903/4 provided for civilian staff for the Force of 11 interpreters at £6 a year each, 3 wagon drivers at £22 each, 3 wagon leaders at £8, and 40 camp hands and 16 horse and herd boys at £3 a year each.[33]

On 22 May 1904 Edward Davies, foreman at a quarry near Kalomo, got drunk and fired at African workers with his revolver mortally wounding one Samazonga who was trying to retrieve his blankets thrown close to the fire by the white man. Davies was still drunk when arrested by RSM Toulson and Sgt Lethbridge. On 8 July Davies was convicted of manslaughter and sentenced to two years imprisonment after claiming to have acted in self defence.[34]

Harding arrived back at Kalomo on 26 June 1904 and Monro left for Southern Rhodesia two days later. Carden came back from leave and left on 6 July to recruit in North-Eastern Rhodesia. Coryndon had returned in May and, on 18 July left to visit Lewanika escorted by Capt Hodson and 25 African police. They returned by river arriving at Kalomo on 8 October. While acting as Administrator Hugh

Marshall Hole had suggested that an officer be stationed at Mongu and the detachment increased to 25 men which would be more impressive at the Litunga's capital. Lewanika had been ill with heart trouble and Hole was concerned should he die and there be a dispute as to the succession.[35]

Early in 1904 the Native Commissioner for the Kafue District, A C Anderson, sent a messenger to call a man to give evidence at a trial. The messenger was assaulted at Malimbeka. Anderson called for assistance from Lieutenants Hamilton and Fowler and their detachment at Linungwe. The village was surrounded at dawn and the headman and several suspects arrested. A fine of 1,600lbs of grain was imposed on the village. On delivery of the grain the headman was released.

On 21 August Colonel Harding set out from Kalomo on a tour of inspection. On 14 September 1904 he left Linungwe to meet Field Marshal Lord Roberts at Victoria Falls. Only two miles from the fort Harding got himself mauled by a lion and was laid up for six weeks. He was initially treated by a doctor from a nearby mission station, while Sgt John Norton, his 'Cape Boy' orderly, was sent to Kalomo to fetch the Government Medical Officer.[36]

Lord Roberts was greeted at Victoria Falls on 21st September by Coryndon and a guard of honour and the bugle band of the Barotse Native Police under the command of Lt O'Sullevan. Roberts went on to inspect the police camp and watch the detachment being put through its paces at drill by Sgt Ramanzera. The Field Marshal wrote to O'Sullevan, 'I congratulate you heartily on the efficient condition of your men. Their turnout, steadiness and precision on parade excited my admiration'. A photograph of the event shows the police wearing khaki drill short sleeved jumpers and shorts with a black fez and tassel and O'Sullevan in khaki with a Wolseley helmet.[37]

Maj Carden reached Kalomo from Fort Jameson on 21 November with 123 recruits and the wives of 95 of them. Of the North-Western Rhodesia Africans, it was said, while the Lozi did not take to military discipline, the Batoka, once a slave race, were not respected by their fellow Africans and were troublesome.[38]

The Railway had reached Victoria Falls on 24th April 1904, reducing the journey time from Bulawayo to twelve hours. On the wagon road the same journey had taken ten to twelve days by Doel Zeederberg's coach service. Zeederberg now moved this service north to run between the Falls and Kalomo.

F J 'Mopani' Clarke had set up a store and hotel at the 'Old Drift', on the North Bank of the Zambezi, at some time between 1896 and 1898, and become the first settler in the Victoria Falls area. By the end of 1902 the European population of the district was nineteen, including four children. The first white woman, Mrs Tulloch, had arrived in 1901. Most lived at the Old Drift. Frank Sykes, the District Commissioner, considered the site unhealthy, as is witnessed by the cemetery there. He moved his office some five miles away to where the town of Livingstone still stands, and built himself a brick house there. The police station remained at the Old Drift. It was there that Henry Rangely, the first magistrate in North-Western Rhodesia, held his court when visiting the district.

In November 1904 Livingstone Township was marked out. On 23rd February 1905 the first sale of stands was held. The settlers were reluctant to move up from the Old Drift, but its means of livelihood as the landing place for all stores from the South, was lost with the completion on 1st April 1905 of the Falls Railway Bridge over the Zambezi. Construction took only nine weeks and cost the lives of one European and one African workman. To celebrate the completion of the bridge a grand regatta was held on the river in which Lt O'Sullevan rowed in the North-Western Rhodesia crew.[39]

O'Sullevan handed over command of the new 25 man detachment at Livingstone to 2/Lt T A G Budgen. Sgt Johnson had left the Falls by July 1904. His duties were assumed in June 1904 by Constable W T T B G Foley who was appointed Gaoler, Magistrate's Clerk and Sanitary Superintendent in October. Sgt H A Burdett had arrived from the Southern Rhodesia Constabulary in September and was made responsible, under Foley, for the policework at the Falls and process serving throughout the Territory. Unlike Johnson these two were not members of the Barotse Native Police but came under the Law Department as the North-Western Rhodesia Constabulary. In September 1905 Constable Thomas Cathcart was posted to Kalomo for civil police duties, to act as Magistrate's Clerk there and superintend sanitation.[40]

In 1905 there were 71 European officials in North-Western Rhodesia – 31 in the District Administration, 18 police, 4 judicial, 2 medical officers, 12 technical (accounts, mines and lands officers) and the balance higher administrative. The strength of the Barotse Native Police was 11 Officers, 7 British NCOs and 300 natives. The Administrator reported, 'The natives are agricultural people, particularly tractable and law abiding. A bigger police force is not necessary, especially because of the Railway.'[41]

The establishment was now the Commandant, Major, 2 captains, QM, 3 lieutenants, 3 sub-lieutenants, RSM, QMS, ORSM, a Drill instructor, 4 white sergeants, 2 native sergeants-major, 3 native sergeants, 35 corporals and 200 privates, a substantial reduction on that suggested in the original estimate. £50 was allowed for bicycles and 7 grain traders were added to the civilian staff. Col Harding pointed out that expenditure on the Force in the year ending 31 March 1905 was more than £3,000 under budget. At Kalomo four new barrack rooms, 4 stores, a stable, carpenters shop and regimental office had all been built by native artisans under the supervision of the HQ officers.[42]

There were rumours of plots against Lewanika in Barotseland. Maj Carden left for Lealui on 10 March 1905 with S/Lt Watherston and 25 men made available by the closure of Kaunga. If the situation allowed, Carden was to leave Watherston and the detachment at Lealui and go on to Kasempa to relieve Lt Stennett who was due for leave. This is what occurred as all was quiet at Lealui. On 7 March a white NCO had left to conduct 23 time expired police to Mwomboshi for repatriation to their homes in North-Eastern Rhodesia. So many of the first men recruited from there were now time expired that the troops at Kalomo were almost all untrained or half trained recruits. At Harding's suggestion Coryndon got the High Commissioner to agree that up to 60 recruits under training at any one time should not count against the establishment. This did not solve the immediate problem and the men sent to Lealui and those involved in the operation next described were almost all raw recruits. As Harding pointed out it was as well that their steadiness was not put to the test.[43]

An African Poll Tax had been authorised by Government Notice No.9 of 31st December 1900 with the consent of the Litunga, who was to receive a percentage of the money collected in the area under his suzerainty. Collection did not commence until 1904 and then in Batokaland only. Following reports that one of Umgailla's headmen had refused to come in to Shaloba when summoned by the District Commissioner, A M Dale, and of refusal to pay tax in Chief Robompo's area, Capt Hodson was sent out on 7 March 1905 with RSM Toulson, 75 men and a Maxim. Col Harding followed four days later. On hearing that the column had left Kalomo the recalcitrant headman had hurried to report to Andrew Dale so the troops went on to Kaunga where G A MacGregor was Assistant District Commissioner.[44]

In his last book, *Far Bugles*, Harding quoted from his diary of this time:

'Arrived at Robompo's Kraal at 4.30 p.m., distance 22 miles. We found the cattle grazing close at hand and the natives sitting grimly at their kraals. On pitching Camp, Robompo, the Chief, was sent for, and eventually arrived with some of his people, bringing with them several baskets of grain as presents. Robompo was asked if he had his hut tax ready, but he replied in the negative and said he had no money to pay. He was told that if he did not pay the money his kraal would be burnt and cattle sent to Kohunga till the tax due to the Government was paid. A guard was put over the cattle and the Chief slept (without irons) with the main guard.'

'I am of the opinion that the people here have no money and, therefore, cannot pay the tax due. The women and men all wear skins and you hardly see a piece of calico amongst them.'

'I again saw Robompo this morning early, with the Assistant District Commissioner. Apparently "Robompo" himself and a few others had already paid their tax levy on a former occasion. Robompo still adhered to his statement of last night that the people had no money, and that when traders bought his cattle they gave blankets for them and no money.'

After searching the huts and securing all assegais and guns, I, acting on the wish of the Assistant District Commissioner, proceeded to burn the kraal and three other smaller kraals under this chief close by.

The hut of the chief was pointed out and as he had paid his tax I did not burn it, but eventually it was ignited by sparks from the neighbouring huts. However I secured another man's hut which was handed over to the chief. The people offered no resistance, in fact, a more friendly lot of natives I have not seen for a long time. The cattle (about 15 in number) were collected and eventually sent to Kohunga. A lot of assegais and fowls were found.' Kohunga was Kaunga north-east of Mazabuka, MacGregor's headquarters.

'Received a despatch from Captain Hodson, dated April 5th. He is well and still burning kraals. The natives offer no resistance, but still say they have no money.'

Harding had arrived back at Kalomo on 4 April and the following day Hodson sent Toulson back with 35 men. Capt Hodson with Cpl Pilkington, the Maxim and 40 African police remained out until 19 May. In all 620 huts were destroyed.

Harding had already contacted the High Commissioner in South Africa direct to obtain instructions concerning hut burning. A wire was now received back from Lord Selborne ruling against such punitive action against tax defaulters. The Chartered Company, which had the problem of financing the administration, and

Coryndon, the Administrator, were not at all pleased with the result, or method, of Harding's appeal which should have been sent through Coryndon. One has the impression that Harding and Coryndon never got on particularly well and that, after his long periods of standing in for Coryndon, Harding did not find it easy to readjust to his subordinate position. He must have found it particularly galling to have to take instructions from such a junior representative of the Civil Power as an assistant district commissioner. In fact the huts destroyed were merely structures of branches and grass and Harding's concern was as much that the sanction was ineffective as that it was inhumane. MacGregor went so far as to claim that Harding had suggested his men should fire on the defaulters, but this the Commandant strongly refuted. MacGregor's later behaviour belies his reliability as a witness.[45]

Lewanika was suspicious of the BSA Company. Since accepting protection he had lost land and subjects to the Portuguese and, as he saw it, the Company's administration in North-Eastern Rhodesia, and was losing influence in Batokaland. He trusted Harding who had looked after him well in England. Coryndon and the Company felt they were too close. In September 1903 Harding's salary had been raised to £800 a year. On his way back to North-Western Rhodesia in June 1904 he had been informed of a reduction to £600 although no one had voiced any criticism to him in the many months he was in London. The Acting Administrator, Marshall Hole, had reported that Lewanika had told him that he knew Coryndon and Worthington, Secretary for Native Affairs, were trying to take his country from him and added 'Colonel Harding is my only friend'. Long before the hut burning controversy the Company and Coryndon were resolved to get rid of Harding.[46]

Meanwhile Harding got on with his job. On 23 June 1905 he set out from Kalomo with Lt Seymour, on a tour of inspection. First visiting Lt O'Sullevan at Shaloba, 90 miles north-north-west of Kalomo and 5 miles from the Kafue, where the 25 man garrison had been moved from Nkala in 1904, they went on to Lealui. From there Harding took Lt Watherston and 20 of his 25 men to Shelenda to give them a change from garrison life. Shelenda was on the Mombesi River, 330 miles north-east of Lealui, north-west of Kasempa from where Maj Carden had moved all but four of the garrison so as to be in a better position to put down the trade in guns and powder from Angola for slaves and rubber from North-Western Rhodesia, and to protect the mine at Kansanshi 60 miles to the North-West. Harding and Seymour went back to Lealui with Watherston before returning to Kalomo via Victoria Falls.[47]

Having completed two years as ADC to the High Commissioner in South Africa, Lieutenant Lord Henry Seymour, Grenadier Guards, was seconded to the Barotse Native Police from 1st May until 29th October 1905. He obviously liked Africa. The outbreak of war in 1914 found him commanding the Mounted Infantry Company of the Nigeria Regiment. After serving in the Cameroons Campaign, Seymour returned to the Grenadiers in France and by the end of 1916 was a Brigadier-General.

The railway would soon reach Broken Hill (now Kabwe). Coryndon drew up a scheme to reduce the Barotse Native Police to a tiny administrative headquarters at Kalomo with detachments, each of 2 officers, a white sergeant and 75 African police, at Shelenda and Kabompo in the far North-West. Elsewhere, he reasoned. the Peace could be maintained by district messengers who would be given some firearms training. The white male population would be encouraged to join the Rifle Association he established on 25 September 1905. In the event of serious disturbances reinforcements could be sent up by rail from Southern Rhodesia. Two officers and two white NCOs would be employed as 'inspectors of civil messengers' and most of the remainder offered civil employment. In March 1906 the Pay & Quartermaster, Capt Byas was given the additional appointment of Ordnance Officer for the Territory with responsibility, not only for the arms and equipment of the police and rifle association, but all Government Stores.

Clearly the reduced Barotse Native Police would not merit a lieutenant colonel as Commandant and Colin Harding submitted his resignation on 27 October 1905 although he assisted with the reorganisation until leaving on 31st March 1906. He always mistakenly maintained that the proposed economies were merely window dressing to justify getting rid of him. After his return to England there were questions in Parliament about Harding's treatment, but these seem to have been designed to secure him fresh employment rather than to highlight mistreatment of the native population by the British South Africa Company's Administration.[48]

In 1909 Colin Harding became a district commissioner on the Gold Coast (now Ghana). In August 1914 he was on leave and helped to raise the 2nd King Edward's Horse from colonials in London. He accompanied the regiment to France becoming Second in Command before, at the age of 52, being appointed to the command of the 15th (2nd Birmingham) Battalion, The Royal Warwickshire Regiment. Colonel Harding commanded this battalion at the Front until appendicitis caused him to be invalided home. In 1917 Harding was back on the Gold Coast as a Provincial Commissioner and a member of the Legislative Council. Colonel Colin Harding CMG DSO returned home finally in 1921.

For reasons unknown Harding had suggested Hodson as more suitable than Major Carden to be Commandant of the reduced Force and the High Commissioner made the appointment, in the rank of major, at the Company's request. Carden had gone on leave prior to Harding's departure and was due to return to the BSAP. The Southern Rhodesian authorities would give no guarantee of reinforcements in an emergency. The BSAP had also been cut for reasons of economy and any assistance would depend on the situation in their own Territory. At the instance of Lord Elgin, Secretary of State for the Colonies, the High Commissioner ordered on 12 May 1906 that the Barotse Native Police be restored to its previous strength. Lord Selborne complained that Coryndon had made cuts prematurely. Chastened, Coryndon arranged with Codrington for recruiting to recommence in North-Eastern Rhodesia, some time expired Africans re-engaged and a few recruits were found locally.[49]

In the area which passed from the administration of North-Eastern Rhodesia to North-Western Rhodesia in 1905 were 40 members of the North-Eastern Constabulary under Sergeant-Major David at Mwomboshi and 10 each at Ndola, Sitanda and Mkushi. These men had been left at their Bomas and Coryndon had intended that they should form part of his new force of armed messengers. In the interim they were to be designated North-Western Rhodesia Constabulary like the civil police. On 24 January 1906 when Lt Budgen left for Mwomboshi to return a draft of time expired Barotse Native Police he had instructions to train the Constabulary there for their new role. These men were now absorbed into the BNP.[50]

Hodson loyally agreed to stand down, and, on return from leave on 1 November 1906, John Carden was appointed Commandant of the Barotse Native Police, with the rank of lieutenant colonel at a salary of £600 a year. Major Hodson was formally appointed Second in Command on 27th November 1906.

On 17 July 1906 Lewanika formally announced the abolition of slavery in Barotseland in the presence of a huge crowd together with 40 white officials, missionaries and traders. The police detachment at Lealui had been reinforced. Capt O'Sullevan, Lt Ingles and 45 men marched through the Khotla to a bugle march, formed up in front of the Litunga and gave the 'General Salute' before taking up position behind the spectators, while the proclamation was read. Most labour in Barotseland had been performed by slaves although the Lozi had ceased acquiring slaves some ten years earlier. It was some consolation to the masters that they would not have to pay hut tax for their former slaves.[51]

On 27 September 1906, 69 Bemba recruits arrived at Kalomo from North-Eastern Rhodesia although 13 proved unsuitable and were discharged. The bugle band was to have been abolished under Coryndon's reductions but in November 1906 was converted to a drum and fife band with 13 fifes, 1 bass drum, 4 side drums, cymbals and a triangle. On 12th March 1907 the strength of the Force was 11 officers, 6 white non-commissioned officers and 294 Native NCOs and men, almost entirely recruited from North-Eastern Rhodesia. The Commandant reported, 'The force is at present a military one, maintained for the purpose of defence and the occasional escort of civil officials. Headquarters are at Kalomo, and garrisons are also maintained at Shelenda, Mumbwa and Lealui. At Mumbwa they perform a few duties as civil police'. An increase in the live ammunition allowed for annual musketry training from 60 to 120 rounds per man produced 10 marksmen. A satisfactory number of time expired men had reengaged for further service. Sgts Chenungu and Chipangwazi were each granted four months leave on re-engaging for a fifth year.[52]

The construction of the railway bridge over the Kafue involved 50 whites and attracted a floating European population including women. A white mounted constable and 4 native constables were posted there. Native constables were recruited for the North-Western Rhodesia Constabulary from the Barotse Native Police. They worked unarmed except when being drilled by their white superiors. There were 5 native constables at Livingstone and 4 at Kalomo. In the year ending 12 July 1907 12 whites, 2 Asians and 44 Africans appeared before the magistrate at Kalomo and all but 6 were convicted. At Kafue 2 whites and 33 Africans were prosecuted and at Livingstone 17 whites, 1 Asian and 12 Africans. There was said to be a rough white element which made its headquarters at Livingstone prone to the meaner type of crime and requiring constant supervision. A gaol had been completed at Livingstone to accommodate 4 Europeans and 20 Africans. Strict enforcement of the Alien Natives Proclamation was required because of thefts in towns by Africans from Blantyre, Nyasaland and the West Coast of Africa. On 24 September 1906 two Mashukulumbwe were hanged for separate murders. These were the first executions in North-Western Rhodesia under the Company's administration. The magistrate at Kasempa only had to try 4 cases, all of witchcraft.[53]

Coryndon now left the Territory on appointment as Resident Commissioner in Swaziland. On 1st June 1907 the new Administrator, Robert Codrington, arrived overland on transfer from North-Eastern Rhodesia. He was on the train south to meet the High Commissioner in South Africa when he received reports at Livingstone of two incidents which caused him to delay his journey.

On 8 June 1907, C J McNamara, Collector for Buni-Kariba, heard that a number of young tax defaulters were living high in the hills on the Musua River, raiding law-abiding villages to steal stock and grain. He sent 6 messengers to investigate. They were driven off, one being stabbed in the leg. MacGregor, the District Commissioner, took out more messengers who were met with shouts of defiance, arrows, assegais and gunfire. MacGregor fired twice and the enemy withdrew. A patrol of 25 police under Lieutenant F S James was sent by rail to Magoye and marched to join MacGregor who had raised a force of 100 tribesmen. James patrolled the hills until 14 August. 14 tax defaulters were arrested and each sentenced to a month's imprisonment with hard labour and a witchdoctor was brought back to Kalomo for trial. One man was shot dead by a policeman he had wounded with an assegai. 24 women and 58 children were found abandoned and fed and cared for. The punishment for tax evasion was now a fine of £5 or three months' imprisonment with hard labour.[54]

In early June Lt Fowler had returned to Mumbwa from a posting at Shelenda. On the night of 22 June he left his quarters, 150 yards from the African police lines, informing Sergeant-Major Newitt that he would fire a shot for a practice alarm. Newitt advised him that the normal procedure was to fire two shots, but Fowler persisted in firing only one. When he reached the guard house Fowler found the sentry, 787 Pte Chandalala, had not called out the guard although some off duty men had turned out and appeared uncertain what to do. Fowler snatched Chandalala's rifle and struck him on the arm with it, while berating him in front of his comrades. In the morning Chandalala attempted suicide by shooting himself in the neck. Sgt-Maj Newitt attended to the injured man, a Mswaka from Mwomboshi, as his fellow tribesmen would not let Fowler near him. On the advice of N/Sgt Mwachandi, Fowler returned to his quarters. Three Mswaka tried to obtain ammunition but were prevented by the guard. They then advanced on Fowler's house with their bayonets but were disarmed by Ngoni comrades.[55]

Heaton Nicholls was Collector at Mumbwa, although overdue for leave. He reported on 6 July that he had heard Mashukulumbwe discussing a plot to refuse to pay tax and murder all the whites in the Territory. He had alerted Lt Fowler who had informed him that his troops were unreliable. Lt Col Carden left Kalomo on 7 July with 50 men to replace the garrison at Mumbwa. On arrival he found no sign of unrest in the area and the garrison manning the fort in good order. Lt Fowler resigned and, after an inquiry, left the Territory with Nicholls on 14 August. The Mswaka were discharged. It was later established that Lewanika's representative among the Mushukulumbe, Motimosuana, was the source of the subversive talk and he was sent back to Lealui. Heaton Nicholls obtained a Government post in Papua but soon returned to Natal to farm and pursue a successful political career, being South African High Commissioner in London from 1944 to 1947.[56]

Kalomo had a reputation for being unhealthy. A medical inspection of the Government township ascribed the high incidence of disease to carelessness and want of sensible sanitary and anti-malarial precautions. The police camp, some 2 $\frac{1}{2}$ miles away, was reported to be perfectly clean and well laid out, apart from the white NCOs' quarters being judged to be too close to the native police lines. On 3 June 1907 Codrington reported that Kalomo had been condemned. He decided that the seat of government should be moved to Livingstone with effect from 31st August. The Headquarters and main body of the Barotse Native Police, under Lieutenant Colonel Carden, followed the Government to Livingstone. Carden was appointed Acting Administrator of the Territory from October 1907 until February 1908 while Codrington was on leave.[57]

The site of the new police camp at Livingstone was where it remains to this day. The pole and dagga barracks with earth floors and tin roofs, built by the Barotse Native Police, remained in use by the Depot of the Northern Rhodesia Police until it moved to Lilayi in 1955, leaving Livingstone Police Camp in the exclusive possession of those responsible for policing the town, and the headquarters of the Southern Division.

On 13 September 1907 Codrington issued a proposed distribution for 13 officers, 4 British NCOs and 347 Africans of the Barotse Native Police with stations at Livingstone, Lealui, Kasempa and Mumbwa controlling out-stations of from 5 to 15 African police at each Government post. The Force was now to perform constabulary duty. The largest number of out-stations, 11, came directly under Headquarters at Livingstone, including that at Broken Hill with 6 Africans and a British NCO. Sgt Kenneth Ferguson was at Broken Hill in 1907. The other British NCOs were to be at Livingstone. A warrant of expulsion issued at Livingstone on 26 March 1908 was addressed to Sgt Taylor BNP. Clearly the North-Western Rhodesia Constabulary had been absorbed into the Barotse Native Police. Whether Coryndon had wished to limit Harding's responsibilities and prestige, or had kept the civil police separate because a non-military force was not subject to the fiat of the High Commissioner, Codrington, who found fault with much of Coryndon's work, saw no point in two forces.[58]

Codrington had two Maxims sent from Fort Jameson, where he knew they were surplus to the requirements of the North-Eastern Rhodesia Constabulary. The Barotse Native Police now had two machine guns at Headquarters and one each at Mumbwa, Lealui and Kasempa, where the garrison now returned from Shelenda.

The uniform for native police was still the khaki drill short-sleeved jumper with khaki shorts, and the black fez and tassel, as worn for full dress by the Northern Rhodesia Police throughout its history. European officers wore khaki jackets and breeches with khaki puttees and brown ankle boots. They wore white shirts with a black tie except in marching or drill order when a khaki patrol shirt was worn with the same tie. A khaki service dress cap could be worn after sundown in place of the khaki New Wolseley helmet with khaki pugree. While still at Kalomo the badge of a crested crane had been adopted.[59]

The Caprivi Strip, German territory, was unpoliced and provided a safe haven for white criminals from all over Southern Africa. There was a move among the Europeans at Livingstone to form a force to clean them out. Instructions were issued that such self-help would not be tolerated. It was agreed that the Bechuana-land Police should establish a post at Kazungula while an officer and 20 BNP were stationed at Sesheke. Finally, in February 1909, Hauptmann Streitwolf, with 3 German NCOs and 14 Hottentot police, established an administrative post, soon to be named Schuckmannsberg, across the Zambezi from Sesheke.[60]

The King of Italy's award of 1906 had clarified the border in the North-West where Mambari slavers were operating undisturbed. To deter them and to keep an eye on the mining developments an administrative post was established at Mwinilunga in 1907 with C H Bellis as Native Commissioner. Some years before a headman, Kasanga, had impeded George Grey's prospecting expedition. When summoned to appear before the District Commissioner at Kasempa, Kasanga had assaulted the district messenger and sent him back to say that Kasanga would kill the next one who came. Before any action could be taken, Kasanga had burnt his village and retreated across the Kabompo River into, then, disputed territory.

Bellis now located his new village and sent messengers who returned to Mwini-lunga, saying that Kasanga had refused to accompany them and would have nothing to do with the Government. Bellis set out to reason with him but was fired on from an ambush. Bellis and three messengers were wounded. Bellis's right arm was shattered above the elbow and he was also wounded in the neck. One messenger was shot in the chest. The head messenger covered the withdrawal with Bellis's rifle.

Bellis managed to write a note to A E Copeman, District Commissioner at Kasempa, where the police detachment was commanded by Lt Salmon. On 8 February 1908 Copeman and Salmon left with 25 police covering the 240 miles to Kasanga's village in 10 days. The village was well stockaded and concealed among thorn bushes. The party split up to find a way in. Copeman came to a gate which could only be approached in single file. He was met with a volley and 544 Corporal M'dala received a bullet in the shoulder. The police opened fire and while the defenders were reloading their muzzleloaders, a messenger scaled the stockade and opened the gate. By the time the attackers got in Kasanga and his men had fled. He took refuge in Portuguese territory. The force remained at the village for ten days during which a number of women and children came in who had been carried off as slaves. Copeman burnt the village and crops before returning to Kasempa.[61]

To further Government control in the North-West G A McGregor was sent up in April 1908 to establish a new Balunda District, west of the Kabompo River. In February 1909 all but three of his 24 police deserted him and made their way to report to Lt Salmon at Kasempa. Maj Hodson was sent to enquire into the matter. He found McGregor and his white assistant washing their own clothes in a stream, their messengers and personal servants having also deserted. It turned out that McGregor, who was suffering from piles, had indulged in harsh and injudicious treatment of police, messengers, servants and the public. Three prisoners had been shot trying to escape and others flogged or forced to do hard labour without trial. McGregor was removed.[62]

In 1902 a prospector named Davis had discovered lead and zinc deposits at a place he named Broken Hill. He had previously worked at Broken Hill in Australia. Davis staked out a claim and the Rhodesia Broken Hill Development Corporation was formed in 1904. The railway reached Broken Hill (now Kabwe) on 11 January 1906, and then stopped. In April 1909 His Royal Highness the Crown Prince of the Belgians travelled by train from Victoria Falls to Broken Hill, from where he was escorted to the Congo Border by Capt Stennett and 20 Barotse Native Police. In the same year work on the railway recommenced which brought it to Sakania in the Belgian Congo on 11 December 1909.

After the completion of this escort duty, for which he was made a Chevalier of the Order of Leopold, Stennett was appointed Acting Assistant Magistrate at Kansanshi for six months to replace McGregor. The copper mine at Kansanshi owed its existence to a mining engineer from Aberdeen, Robert Williams, who had been convinced that there were valuable mineral deposits to be found north of the Zambezi. With Cecil Rhodes he formed the Zambezia Exploration Company and Tanganyika Concessions Ltd. On 12 January 1900 he had written to Rhodes, 'It is with much pleasure that I have to inform you that my expedition has discovered a new gold field in Northern Rhodesia. . . In this particular old working the natives seem to have worked for copper. . . I believe you will now have to reconsider the direction in which your railway will be extended'. The Railway never reached Kansanshi but, since the building of the stretch from Broken Hill to Sakania, and of the Benguela Railway from Katanga to the West Coast, was financed by Robert Williams, one can assume that if he had still thought it should go via Kansanshi, it would have done so![63]

The Balunda District was merged back into the Kasempa District with a total staff of a District Commissioner, 5 other administrative officers, and an officer, a British NCO and 48 Africans of the Barotse Native Police. At the end of 1909 an elephant poacher, T Richardson, was murdered on the Shambila Stream in the Balovale Sub-District, by Bemba hunters he had formerly employed. Mr Bishop, the Assistant Native Commissioner, set out with his seven African police to track them down. One, Chiwala, was himself murdered by his accomplices in a quarrel over Richardson's African concubine. The others escaped over the border and were never brought to justice.[64]

On 29 May 1911 there was another murder of a European in the district. Wilhelm Frykberg, a Swede, had joined the Barotse Native Police in December 1905. He left in 1907 to become a labour recruiter and trader. Some Kaonde he had sent down to work in Southern Rhodesia died there in a smallpox epidemic. Their relatives sought compensation from Frykberg without success. Dissension spread among a party of recruits about to go South. Three of them, Tumila, Topeka and Kungwana, all from Makabula's village, decided not to go and to kill Frykberg. He was away, so they chose another Swede, Ohlund, formerly in business with Fryberg. Ohlund worked a small gold claim at Shudanvwa. The three Africans went to his house one evening and, through the window, shot him three times in the back as he worked at his typewriter. The killers then fled into the bush.

On 11 June four police and messengers came up with the gang and Pte Chasaya was severely wounded in both hands. Some forty sympathisers and wanted persons joined the murderers in the forest. On the night of 17 June Lt F G de Satge set out with 15 police and 3 messengers to make a dawn attack. The attempt at surprise failed. Tumila, Topeka and Kungwana had fled leaving only five or six men and 15 women and children to fall into the hands of the police. Two men wanted for armed robbery gave themselves up. De Satge returned to Kasempa on 27 June. The murderers went north-east towards Solwezi, and then doubled back into Kapeshi's area near the Busanga Swamp. From there they went north across the Kabompo. Here they quarrelled with their associates and two or three were killed. Crossing the West Lunga another man and some women and children were drowned. The three murderers and their remaining followers reached Katetandimbo's village in country which was later designated as part of Portuguese West Africa, but was then more or less nomansland between the two territories.

Here they settled down, believing themselves safe from pursuit. However word of their whereabouts reached Kasempa. Katetandimbo was offered a reward of £20, enormous wealth when the usual wage of an African was five or ten shillings a month. In order to maintain surprise no white man or police went near. Head Messenger Kanyakala and eight other messengers went to the village. With Katetandimbo's co-operation they took the three murderers without resistance. Tumila confessed to an earlier murder. A few years before, when himself a district messenger, he had robbed and killed an African hawker near Kasempa.

After trial and conviction Tumila, Topeka and Kungwana were hanged outside Kasempa Prison on 11 November 1912, in the presence of a crowd which included all the chiefs of the District and a large number of headmen who were called in from their villages to witness the execution. Chief Ingwe and Sub-Chief Kapeshi had previously been sentenced to long terms of imprisonment for failing to come forward with information about the whereabouts of the killers.[65]

Life was more civilised on the line of rail where civil police work was now being performed on a permanent basis. At Livingstone eight native NCOs and men were employed as town police by 1910, under Sergeant-Major Coote, who also acted as prosecutor. A European sergeant in charge of a detachment at Broken Hill was also 'responsible for patrolling the town'. It was intended to place a similar detachment at Ndola the following year. The Bwana Mkubwa Mine was now in operation there.[66]

The following circular was issued from the Public Prosecutor's office at Livingstone in 1909:

Prisoners' Escort – Removal Warrant – Prisoner's Property
  it is most essential that any prisoners (white or black) sent down country should be in charge of a proper escort throughout the whole journey to their destination. An instance occurred sometime back of a prisoner being put on a train with no escort at all: there was nothing to prevent him slipping off at the first convenient halt or slowing down and escaping into the bush. With the escort must also go the Removal Warrant, so that the jail authorities at prisoner's place of destination may

Lieutenant Colonel Carden leads the march past for the Duke of Connaught,
Livingstone 1910 – Photo from a postcard sent by Lieutenant Sillitoe to his mother in
1911 now in possession of Brian Cooper

have the necessary knowledge as to why he has been sent thither and the necessary authority to detain him.

Prisoner's property, if of a portable character, should also be sent with the escort. It will be handed over to the jail authorities with the prisoner and a receipt therefor given to the escort. When a prisoner is released, his portable property should be handed over to him and this cannot be done if it is not at the place where the prisoner obtains his release. Also it may be that the prisoner has been given the option of a fine. Then if he decides to pay that fine, or if his friends come forward to pay the difference, the fact that some property of his is lying with the jailer will expedite the payment of fine and consequent release.[67]

The Prisoners' Removal Proclamation (High Commissioner's Proclamation No 19 of 1907) permitted the transfer of prisoners to serve their sentences in Southern Rhodesia in accordance with The Colonial Prisoners Removal Act 1884. Prior to the move of the capital to Livingstone there had been no central prison in North-Western Rhodesia and prisoners were merely left in the charge of the Barotse Native Police.[68]

On 14 November 1910, 168 men of the Force were on parade at Livingstone for inspection by Field Marshal His Royal Highness The Duke of Connaught who had come to Africa to open the first parliament of the Union of South Africa at Cape Town. The Duke and Duchess were visiting the Victoria Falls accompanied by their daughter, Princess Patricia. The Duke complimented the men on their steadiness on parade and the manner in which they went through their drill movements. A brass band had been formed in 1909 and was, of course, on parade. The Duke, as Colonel of the Corps of Royal Engineers, gave the Barotse Native Police permission to adopt as their own quick march *Wings*, the march of the Royal

Engineers. *Wings* remained the march of the Northern Rhodesia Police until Bandmaster F L Wood composed a new march, *The Crested Crane* in 1931. This was to become the march of the Northern Rhodesia Regiment. The formation of the Band had been aided by a donation of £20 to purchase instruments made by Herr Dernburg, the German Colonial Secretary, and his staff when visiting Victoria Falls on 4 July 1908 in connexion with the negotiations for the policing of the Caprivi Strip.[69]

The British South Africa Company's report for the year ending 31 March 1910 included the following statement: 'The policing and defence of Northern Rhodesia will in future be carried out by the force stationed within the Territory. The Barotse Native Police is being adequately strengthened with this objective.'[70]

By 31 March 1911 the strength of the Force was 17 officers, 7 British NCOs and 366 native NCOs and men. At Livingstone were 5 officers, 3 British NCOs and 158 native police with a further 83 at outstations under the local native commissioners or the British NCOs at Broken Hill and Ndola. At Mongu were 2 officers and 60 men while the detachment commander was also responsible for the subaltern and 20 men at Sesheke and a further 45 at outstations. There were 2 officers and 60 men at Kasempa with 9 at Mwinilunga and a British NCO and 14 native police at Kansanshi. At Mumbwa was a British NCO and 12 native police with 9 at Namwala under the Native Commissioner. The detachments at outlying Bomas had been increased from 5 to 9 police to provide for 24 hour guards on prisoners in local jails. Capts O'Sullevan and Byas and Lt Ingles were on leave in UK and rode with the Rhodesian Contingent in the Coronation Procession of King George V that June.[71]

On 10 June 1911 Lt Col Carden visited the North-Eastern Rhodesia Constabulary station at Fort Rosebery. Although he was recorded as visiting as Commandant of the Barotse Native Police, his visit was obviously connected with the amalgamation of the two forces which was about to be effected as a consequence of the unification of North-Eastern and North-Western Rhodesia[72].

Annex to Chapter 4

OFFICERS AND BRITISH OTHER RANKS BAROTSE NATIVE POLICE & NORTH-WESTERN RHODESIA CONSTABULARY

HARDING Col Edwin Colin CMG'98 DSO'16 *Sciatalamatanga* b15.8.63 s/o Chas H, Abbey Farm, Montacute Somerset to B'wayo 94 to UK 1.96 to SA 6.96 Mashonald FF, S/Insp MMP 11.96 Capt 3.97 Maj i/c Native Police 11.97 Ag Commr Barotseld 2.9.99–2.00 Cmdt BNP 7.9.01–31.3.06 DC NT Gold Coast'09 Maj 2KEdH 8.14 CO 15RWarwick 9.15–1.9.16 PC Gold Coast'17 rtd 8.21 Caversham Reading d1.39

MACAULAY Fredc Chas bIndia Tpr MMP 1.9.96 BSAP 9.12.96 S/Insp BNP Kasempa 7.9.01 & AgDC 8.6.02 DC 1.7.03 NWRCS 10.03 AgDC Barotseld 1.1–8.04 Kasempa 3.05 Sesheke, NC & Mag Mumbwa 11–28.10.14 1KEdH Sgt C Sqn kia 14.1.16 of Skelmoe Ayrshire

DOBSON J BSAP Sgt SM i/c Kalomo 8.00 PostMr Falls & QM Civ 01 Lstone 11.02

LUCAS Tpr BSAP Ft Monze 5.99 Att BNP 8.00 Kasempa'01

FRANKLYN Cpl Benjamin Chas Tpr MMP'96 BSAP Monze 5.99 att BNP Kalomo 00 d Blackwater Monze 30.4.01 age 28

MARTIN Tpr Kalomo'01

MOBBS Geo bHoughton Norf; Vic Colm 93 BSAP SM NWR'99 BNP 01–03

HARRIS T Sgt Arty Tp BFF'96 BSAP'97 SM BNP S/Insp 7.9.01–rsgnd16.1.03

CARDEN Lt Col John CMG'10 b Kineton 13.5.70 s/o Capt 36Ft ed RNS New Cross, Tpr BSACoP 13.7.90 Sgt 1.11.91 Umtali Municipal P S/Insp 7.92 Scout Salisby H, Rmnt Offr'93 Capt 12.93 Ag CofP Matabeleld'94 Adjt & CSO RHV, Adjt BFF'96 BSAP Monze 5.99–8.00 svd SA, BNP 2i/c 25.9.01 LMaj 20.1.02 L/Lt Col Cmdt 1.11.06 Ag Admr NWR 10.07–4.08 11.08–2.09 Cmdt NRP'11 rtd 18.12.12 Russell Cottage W Lavington Wilts T/Maj 5Wilts 30.9.14 CO kia Chunuk Bair 10.8.15

TUDHOPE Robt Hoblane/Holland? Tpr BSAP'96 BNP SM d Kalomo'02

WORRINGHAM Harold Ogilvie Tpr BSAP Monze 5.99 Cpl BNP Nkala'01 Sgt'02 QMS S/Lt 12.03 i/c Nkala & agA/DC Kafue by 1.1.04 NWRCS by 16.7.04 ANC Shaloba 05 rsgnd 13.3.07 Natal

TOULSON Elijah John Sgt BSAP'97 Monze 5.99 RSM BNP'02 Hd Gaoler Lstone rsgnd 1.08 3 Harcourt Terr Lamentine Rd Nottghm

BYAS Maj Henry Louis b31.7.69 ed Cheltenhm BSAP 1.99 Hosp Sgt Monze 5.99 HSM BNP 9.01 AgQM 17.1.03 Lt CP&QM, Capt 7.04 & Ordnce Offr NWR 1.4.06 Maj P&QM NRP 10.11 SO Supplies Fife rtd 23.3.17 d by 1921

HARTE-BARRY Alfd Martin 1Coldm Gds Sgt, SM BSAP'96 S/Insp C Tp'99 OC Enkeldoorn, Capt BNP 4.02–9.03 Sgt 11SAI dWW1

NEWITT W Tpr BNP 9..02 Cpl Kaunga by 1.1.04 Sgt by 16.7.04 i/c Shaloba by 5.5.05 SM Mumbwa'06

HAMILTON Granville Howard Tpr BBP Tpr MRF'96 Secy Lugard, Lt ILH Lt BNP 1.10.02–18.4.06 BH Mine; Built BH to Kansanshi Rd for traction engines'06

STENNETT Harry March CBE'24 DSO LG14.1.16 b2.8.77 Nottghm, Lt 11IY(Mx&Kent) 29.8.01 pw Tweefontein 11.12.01 S/Insp BNP 1.10.02 Capt by 12.3.06 Maj NRP 18.12.12 L/LtCol 23.9.14–10.12.14 lve 23.2–16.6.17 A/LtCol Svce Bn 12.17–s5.18 Lt Col Cmdt 10.19 T/Col 3.10.22 Col 1.4.23 L1.10.24–rtd31.3.25

BOWLEY/S Chas Edwd BSAP 99 att Customs SR TSM BNP 10.02 Mines Dept sec'd Estabs to 31.12.10

INGLES Maj Harry Clement s/o Rear Adml ed Wellngtn, BSAP 28.11.96 Sgt, SM BNP 10.02 S/Insp by 12.3.06 Capt NRP 12.2.13 OC Kasama lve 16.6–10.9.14 L4.9.17–rtd3.3.18 T/Capt 2Hants 2.18 jnd Bn OC Y Coy 7.8.18 w4.9.18; Portchester Fm Kalomo No.11 Rfn NRRifles Dist Cmdt'21

NICHOLLS Rt Hon Geo Heaton PC SA 48 *Kalapukila* b1876 ed Rotherham GS Pte DLI'93 Tirah'97 Sgt SA, BSAP Sgt; SM BNP 7.10.02 NWRCS DC's Clk 24.1.05 Compiler Census Baluba 1.10.05 A/DC by 20.9.05? Collctr Kafue 1.4.06 left NR 14.8.07 Papua ARM Lakekamu Goldflds'10 RM Mambare Div'11 left'12 Sugar Fmr Umfolozi MP 20 Sen 39 Admr Natal 42–SA HCommr UK 44–7 Hd SA Delegation UN 46 Senator'48 of Mtubatuba d25.9.59

JAMESON J W Dale Lt 89(Montgomerys) Coy 9IY 5.7.01 Clk Cntrllr NWR'02 Lt BNP by 7.03 d dysentery Kalomo 7.7.04

HODSON Col Fredc Arthur CBE 19 b Yorks 1866 pte 2Y&L SA'92 with 1/2 Coy Umtali 7.96 BSAP QMS 11.96 S/Insp AgSO BSAP by 25.6.02 Capt & Adjt BNP 1.8.03 Maj 4.06 2i/c 1.11.06 L/LtCol Cmdt NRP 18.12.12 L/Col 10.12.14 L31.3.19 Hon Col rtd 31.9.19 The Cottage Fulford d Lstone 31.1.25

O'SULLEVAN John Joseph DSO(LG14.1.16) FRGS b Mt Florence Athlone 3.79 ed Black Rock Cllge RUIMed Sch Tpr CMR'98 2Lt Northants 12.3–10.01 did not jn rsgnd because of expnse, French's Scouts Int Offr Gen Doran's Staff Tpt Offr w12.3.01 pw Ermelo 10.8.01 rlsd, S/Insp BNP 12.8.03 Capt 1.4.06 Cmdt NERC 1.4.09 Hon Maj 1.3.10–Capt NRP'11 L/Maj 15.2.15 Maj 7.9.15 inv 15.10.15 Hosp Millbank 6wks ALtCol CO 19Lab Cheshire 1.5.16 CO 11N&DR 28.7.16–s30.8,16 Cmdt Ballykinler Cmd Depot'17 relinq comm HonLtCol 8.3.18 Irish Rctg Cttee i/c Galway & Mayo Area RM Killarney rtd 10.22 to Antigua d'36 f/o Sir Peter O'S racing commentator

MONRO Chas Lloyd Doveton b23.7.68 s/o Lady M of Allan 2Lt 3 Seafth Hldrs Capt'91 BBP Lt 7.11.91 Capt K Tp J Rd 12.95 S/Insp BSAP 5.97 Capt 10.8.97 OC C Tp'99 & AgNC

Lomagundi 1.11.99 A/Maj OC SRV Eastn 6.5–17.12.02 Ag Cmdt BNP 11.03–BSAP 28.7.04 Adjt/SO 20.12.07 rtd 09

WATHERSTON Geoffrey Fell s/o Rev Alex Law W HM HinkleyGS? ORS BNP by1.10.03 S/Insp 1.10.04 LCapt Cmdt NERC 1.2.08–31.3.09 Capt 1.10.10 Adjt NRP left 16.12.13 Pemba Isld? svd MGs WWI?

FOWLER Wm Edwd Nesfield b77 Pte 11(YD)Coy 3IY Lt 27IY 17.1.02 SLt BNP 11.03 arr 1.04 rsgnd 14.8.07 Woodthorpe Hall Chesterfield to Aust? Lt YksDgns 8.14 Southgate House Chown

REILLY Jas J, Law Dept Congstd Dists Bd Ireld, Pte SIrish IY 2Lt 3.1.02 AgQM Beaconsfld Camp Kimberley 2.02 HLt16.8.02 Repat Dept, QM Mil Stock Fm nr Pretoria 9.02 Audit Br SA Customs 12.02 S/Lt BNP Nov–Dec'03

JOHNSON Valentine Sgt Falls by 1.1.04 gne by 7.04 d.27.8.08 Mongu?

WEBB Percy Edwd BSAP 00 QMS BNP 1.04 Shaloba by 1.9.05 NWRCS T/Clk Batoka 10.12.05 Clk i/c Senkobo 1.4.06 agCollctr Senkobo '07 retrenched Lve 1.12.07–1.6.08 Agent RNLB?

LETHBRIDGE John Acland Musgrave Sgt Kalomo by 22.5.04 Cattle Insp Batoka'04 rsgnd 2.05

SKEET Roland Geo Tpr BSAP 21.6.02 BNP 20.6.04 Kaunga/Kaleya

FOLEY Wm Thos Thompson Barron Galway; Const Old Drift 6.04 Gaoler 10.04 T/Clk NWRCS i/c Sjobas 12.05 d11.5.06 age 26

BURDETT Henry Aylmer MC b28.11.81 s/o Rev Jerome B 2nd s/o 6th Bart, SRC Const NWRC 9.04 2/Sgt, 2Lt Essex Regt 14–18 Capt. 10th Bart 1940 d Kenya 23.8.43

EAREE Robt Clarence Westall b12.8.80 s/o Rev at Belchamp Walter Ex to Miserden Glos ed Kg's Sch Glos, Gnr Cinque PtsAV 99 Tpr SAC 10.2.01–19.4.02 ORS BNP by 17.8.04 NWRCS Clk to DC Kafue 13.1.05 Ag Collctr Malamba'07 ANC'07 NC'08 AMag Namwala 30.11.14 Feira 3.16–1.9.16 No.10136 28London 1.1.17 Cdt No.15 (Artists Rifles) OCdtCps, 2Lt 7London 30.5.17 BEF–18.2.19

SCHOMBURGK H Sgt Kasempa 9.04 dschge 10.5.06

BUDGEN Thos Alexdr Geo Lt PoWLH 12.00 WPMR 1.02–28.8.02 S/ Insp BNP 11.04 lve 11.07 rsgnd 23.3.08 Sion Hill Bath

PILKINGTON Richd Rfn 20LondRV'96 Tpr CMR Arty Tp, Cpl BNP 1.05 Sgt by 1.9.05 AgRSM, to NWRCS Clk Barotse Dist 8.5.06

GREAVES G M ORS 1.05

SEYMOUR Ld Henry Chas DSO 16 b18.5.78 s/o Marquess of Hertfd 2Lt Militia 2lt Gren Gds'99 SA'00 ADC HCommrSA 1.1.03–1.4.05 att'd BNP 1.5.05–29.10.05 Capt GGds'07 T/Maj OC MI Coy Nigeria Regt Maj'14 BEF'15 CO 4GGds'16 TBG 2Gds Bde 19.11.16 3Gds Bde 21.3.17–2.4.18 LtCol'19 Col'21 Cmd 144Bde TA'26 Cmd GGds & Regtl Dist'27–9 rtd30

JAMES Francis Stafford b20.12.78 Clifton BSAP'03 Pay Cpl BNP 5.05 Sgt 12.05 QMS 3.06 Lt 19.6.06 Capt NRP 12.2.13 OC Mongu lve May–10.9.14 OC B Coy w3.17 lve5.6.17–6.3.18 MID 5.3.18 Hon Maj'20 L15.1.23–rtd 14.6.23 CC Chesterfield 19.2.25 Sheffield 31.12.31–12.41 dCheltnhm 17.1.55

CATHCART Thos; Civ Clk ASC SA; SRC 8.02 Pros Salisby, Immigration Umtali; Const NWRC Kalomo Clk to Mag 1.9.05 NWRCS Clk to DC Mwomboshi 22.5.07 retrenched 1.4.08

FRYKBERG Wilhelm bSweden CMR? BSAP SM BNP 12.05 Shelenda'06 Mwinilunga'07 rsgnd'07 Strekpr Lab rctr Kasempa Dist, MD Anglo–Scandinavian Tdg Co SA'15–25 Gd Duty SA WW2

TAYLOR Edwin b22.12.79 Tpr BSAP 26.11.02 SRC Immigratn 28.2.06 Const Lstone 1.3.06 Sgt BNP by 26.3.08 SM, Mags Clk BH 14.4.09 rtd post'24 Tobacco Pltr

BRUCE-MILLER Fredk Vernon BSAP ORCpl, ORS BNP 3.06 NWRCS Clk Accts'06 NC Kasempa'15 Ag Mag Mwinilunga'16 rtd post 1920

FAIR Chas Henry DSO(LG12.9.17) 12L BSAP 10.02 Sgt BNP 28.5.06 C/Sgt 1.1.07 S/Lt 8.07 Lt NRP Adjt Capt 28.10.14 No.2 Mob Colm 12.14 Adjt NEBdr OC A Coy'16 T/Maj 14.1.17 A/LtCol'17 Lve 9.4.18 Maj 2i/c 1.10.20 lve 1.11.23 rtd 31.3.24

McCARTHY Jas Joseph CBE DSO 17 MC(LG14.1.16) 33833 Tpr Scottish Hse Cpl sev w Brakenlaagte 30.10.01 2Lt ScH Lt Natal Bdr Police 30.6.02–30.6.03 Tpr BSAP, Cpl BNP 25.6.06 Sgt 1.8.06 2/Lt 4.08 Lt NRP Lve 2.14–7.8.14 L/Capt 23.9.14 Capt 1.4.15 T/Maj

14.1.17 dep 5.3.18 A/LtCol Dunsterforce Caucasas: NRP 14.2.20 Hon Maj 20 Rtd'24 planter d16.10.45

SALMON Ernest Harry Lindsell Tpr MRF'96 Cpl BSAP 96–7 Rinderpest Sp Police OFS OC Mtd Det 6mths, Nthn Rly Svy Tpt Offr 5.99–5.03 Compound Mgr Falls, Cleveld Bridge Co 3.04 Insp Natives Pauling & Co Ry Constr Falls to BH 12.05 S/Insp BNP 21.7.06 Lt NRP Capt OC B Coy to Sesheke 26.9.14 Hosp 12.14 dep NR 12.1.15 rtd ill health 11.10.15

RAMSAY Percy Robt b19.5.79 New Cross SE; 15498 Tpr75 Coy IY 22.3.00–24.6.01 Barrister's Clk London, Tpr BSAP 31.7.02 Sgt 4.04 SM 8.04 1/Cl StaffSM Pay, QMS BNP 23.7.06 NWRCS Clk Accts 10.4.07–9.08

SHERRIFF T W Hd Wdr inv 30.9.07

ALLEN 'Maudie' Const Kalomo by 1.07 BH SM dschge 12.3.10

FERGUSON Kenneth b Gawler Aust, SRC'02 2/Sgt NWRC 25.11.06 BNP BH'07 1/Sgt 25.11.08 WO 1.4.11 RSM Oi/c CID S/Insp WO1 1.4.14 T/Lt 1.4.16 d Flu Lstone 19.10.18 age 37

HILLIER Stanley Tpr BSAP 25.9.07 BNP 25.3.08 ANC Mweru Luapula 1912

EVANS Harold J de Courcy MC DCM(LG31.5.16) 818 Tpr BSAP'06 BNP 31.3.08 NRCS rsgnd 3.12 Pte 2RR 2Lt 16 KAR Lt w17

CRAIG Geo Saml Dovon Tpr BSAP 3.1.06 BNP 28.8.08

JENKINS Ernest Malcolm Tpr BSAP 12.1.07 BNP 28.8.08

REARDON P J C Tpr BSAP 2.8.06 BNP 11.9.08 NRCS NC 25.11.14 inv15.8.17 rjnd NRGS 12.19–rtd20

COOTE Arthur PC Met, Sgt BNP by 25.9.08 SM i/c Town Police L'stone & Pros'10 SM Lka–17

de SATGE Fredk Gordon b'84 s/o Cdr RN, Mdshpmn RN'98 China'00 S/Lt rsgnd'03 Tpr CMR, CMP, BSAP'07 2Lt BNP 10.4.09 Lt 1.10.10 NRP rsgnd 9.12.13 Lt 1RR'14 Lt 6KRRC 11.6.15 4KRRC by 9.15 1KRRC T/Capt 7KRRC kia Flers 15.9.16

SARGEANT Wm Heggaton Tpr BSAP 30.5.06 S/Insp BNP 17.5.09 Kasempa 6.09

MILLS F R Sgt 09 SM Solwezi Lstone 1.15 NBdr in 7.16 RSM

WARREN Sgt'09

TAYLOR W B Sgt Bandmaster rsgnd 22.4.19

SAUNDERS H J SM Mongu'11

CUSSANS Arthur Chas de Cussance MC(LG14.1.16) b St Pancras 80, 68Coy IY(Paget's H)'00 w Lichtenburg'01 BSAP'07 2Lt BNP 10.6.10 ADC HCommr'11 Lt NRP MID LG13.7.17 lve 6.11.17–6.3.18 Capt L.20.11.27–rtd 3.5.28 JP Devon'28 Lt Col CO 3KentHG d'45 Kerch Hill Tenterden

SILLITOE Sir Percy Joseph KBE b London 25.4.88 BSAP 25.4.08 Cpl VFalls 10.10 Lt BNP 8.2.11 NRP T/Capt OC E Coy 2.4.16 s1.17 OETA Bismarcksburg 15.8.17 Political Offr Dodoma 11.18 relinq comm NRP 26.5.20 Tfr to Tanganyika Svce wef 15.8.17 rtd ill-hlth'22, student Bar, CC Chesterfield 3.23 ERdg'25 Sheffield'26 Glasgow'31 Kent 3.43 DG Sy Svce'46 rtd'53 Ch Investgator De Beers'53

DICKINSON Edwd Griffith MC(30.8.17) b83 ed Kg's Cantby; Natal Police'01 Lt BNP 20.2.11 NRP T/Capt C Coy 2.4.16 T/LtCol Svce Bn 5.6.18–19 Maj 2i/c NRP 1.10.24 Lt Col Cmdt & Ch Commr Police & Prsns 20.4.30 Cmdt NRMilP 1.4.32 L5.2–rtd 2.9.33

BREMNER Alastair Bruce s/o Wm 3 Kent's Terr Torquay, Tpr BSAP'07 2Lt BNP 3.11 NRP Lt T/Capt OC Coy 2.4.16 sick lve 15.3.17–8.17 Lstone T/Capt OC Depot 9.10.17 d 1.1.18 thrown by horse, age 33

HORNSBY Chas Cooper s/o Lt Col H F Oakwd Ct Kensgtn BSAP 09 2Lt BNP11 T/Capt F Coy Hosp 3.17 d.enteric Lupembe GEA 12.5.17 age 31

WITHERS Geo Montague 2Lt 3VB Glos'00 Capt'05 6Glos TF'08 6mths att Bristol Constabulary, 2Lt BNP 1.4.11 NRP Lt'14 T/Capt OC E Coy'17 Capt 1.4.20 rtd'33

Notes

1. Harding to Coryndon 13.11.99 PRO CO/417/309
2. H/75/1904 3.8.04 PRO CO/417/423
3. PRO CO/417/276

4. *With the Mounted Infantry and the Mashonaland Field Force 1896* Methuen 1898 reprint by Books of Rhodesia 1971 p161
   Lt Gen Sir Edwin Alfrd Harvey ALDERSON K(16)CB'00 b1859 Lt QORWK'78 Adjt MI'88 Staff Cllge'94 CO MI Bn 4.96 CO Mashonald FF July–Dec 96 GOC 2Inf Bde 03–6 Maj Gen GOC Poona Div 08–12 GOC Mtd Div 5.8.14 Lt Gen GOC Cdn Div 29.9.14 Cdn Corps 14.9.15 IG Cdn Forces 28.5.16 d14.12.27

5. Harding to Sec to Admr Matabeleld 22.12.99 PRO CO/417/309 & *In Remotest Barotseland* quoted in *Story of the NRR* p17

6. Cmdt Gen to HC 9.4.00 PRO CO/417/283. Harding in a report of 5.7.00 says only 20 were enlisted PRO CO/417/311. Perhaps 5 dropped out during training.

7. Capt Hon Sir Arthur LAWLEY GCSI'11 GCIE'08 KCMG'01 b12.11.60 s/o 2nd Baron WEN-LOCK, 10Hrs PS to Duke of Westmnstr 92–6 Admnr Matabeleland'97–Gov W Australia'01 Lt Gov Tvl'02 Gov Madras 06–11 succ bro as 6th Baron'31 d14.6.32

8. Harding *In Remotest Barotseland*

9. Harding report 3.8.00 PRO CO/417/311

10. Clive Lancaster CARBUTT Croix de Guerre, NC Bube NC Sebungwe 7.00 Maj RNR'16 CO 1.4.17 Lt Col 26.1.18

11. This is presumably why Harding wrote in a report to Lawley of 26.8.00 'The natives are rather unsettled' PRO CO/417/284

12. Harding report 5.3.01 PRO CO/417/337

13. Coryndon 1.12.01 CO/417/343 & Gielgud's account in NRJ

14. CO/417/337

15. Short *African Sunset* p26

16. Coryndon 18.5.03 PRO CO/417/385

17. *Story of the NRR* pp19–20

18. PRO CO/417/343,344 Admr 2.5.02, 417/373, Harding 17.2.03 417/383 *Story of the NRR* pp20–1

19. Coryndon 25.5.03 CO/417/373 Harding 17.2.03 417/383, *Story NRR* p20

20. *Story NRR* pp108–9, Photos of white NCOs at Kalomo in *Story NRR* & Harding *Far Bugles*, all others in *In Remotest Barotseland*.

21. Coryndon report 1902 *Story NRR* p20

22. Coryndon to Rhodes 27.11.01 Coryndon 30.11.01 PRO CO/417/343

23. Telegram 1.02 PRO CO/417/343,344 Coryndon 15.9.02 417/345 Carden Report 12.11.02 417/371

24. Coryndon to HC 1.12.01 CO/417/363,343, Harding to Imp Sec 10.10.02 417/345
   Joseph CHAMBERLAIN b1836 Highbury, to uncle's firm Nettleford(& Chamberlain) screw manfctrs Birmnghm'54 Mayor B'ham MP Lib B'hm'76 SofS Colonies 25.6.95–1903 d1914

25. *Far Bugles*, photo in *In Remotest Barotseland*, Harding report 17.2.03 PRO CO/417/383

26. 23.2.03 PRO CO/417/374

27. Harding report 16.5.03 CO/417/372, 386
   Frank R LEWIS Prospector Nthn Copper Co to NR 1896

28. Quoted in *Story NRR* p21

29. PRO CO/417/372 Hole 12.7.03 417/386

30. CO/417/383, Harding 22.5.03 417/385 Carden 23.7.03 417/386, 387 Monro 8.1.04 CO/417/391

31. 8.1.04 PRO CO/417/396

32. PR CO/417/387,397,401

33. PRO CO/417/383

34. PRO CO/417/393

35. CO/417/402 Harding to HC 16.7.04 /407 Hole 26.11.03 /396
   Lt Col Hugh Marshall HOLE CMG'24 BA b16.5.65 ed Blundell's Balliol BSACo'90 Secy to Admr Mashonald'91 Lt Adjt Salisby FF'96 Lt SRV 18.8.99 Capt 1900 Civ Commr Bulawayo, Military Svce'15 Secy BSACo'19 d18.5.41

36. *Far Bugles* PRO CO/417/402
   Alexdr Collie ANDERSON Tpr MRF'96 A/DC Kafue 1.11.02 DC 9.03 suicide BH 7.7.11

F-M('95) Earl ROBERTS of Kandahar VC'58 KG, Fredk Sleigh b Cawnpore 1832 ed Eton Addiscombe 2Lt Bengal Arty'51 Capt Bvt Maj'60 AQMG 2Div Abysinnia'67 Lt Col'68 DQMG Bngal'72 QMG Bngl'78 GOC PunjabFF Maj Gen'78 GOC Madras'81 Lt Gen'83 CinC India'85 Gen'90 CinC Ireld'94 SA 1.00–11.12.00 CinC British Army 1901–4 d15

37. Report 23.11.04 PRO CO/417/407 letter & photo in possessn Sir Peter O'Sullevan
38. AgSec 15.3.04 PRO CO/417/399, 402
39. Fagan *The Victoria Falls* 1964 pp33–7 *Story NRR* p22
   F J 'Mopani' CLARKE MLC founded Zambezi Tdg Co
   Frank Wm SYKES Tpr E Sqn MRF'96 author *With Plumer to Matabeleland*; DC Falls'01 Conservator Falls rsgnd'07 to NZ
   Harry RANGELY ed Chesterfield Sch, Tpr BBP 5.96 Kimberley Scouts 11.96 Municipal Police B'wayo 11.5.97 Court Sgt'98 Solr Gen's Offce B'wayo 9.00 Mag NWR 2.7.02 (HCN69/02 30.7.02 PRO CO/417/365) Sec Legal Dept 6.06 Sec Admn NWR 12.06 & i/c Legal Dept 6.07 Sec Admn NER 1.9.08 Cotton Plntr & i/c Govt Herd'11 Tobacco Fmr'12 Sgt Nyasalnd VR'16 RNLB'18 Prospctor Russo-Asiatic Co'28 Elephant Contrl Offr'30 Supt Tea Plntn Nyasald 7.36–38 Lab Offr FJ 1.43 d'53
40. Legal Dept Report PRO CO/417/420 Rangely NRJ
41. *Story NRR* p21
42. PRO CO/417/398
43. Harding 14.3.05 CO/417/407 10.3.05 417/408
44. Andrew Murray DALE SRCS 4.01 ANC Wankie; NWRCS DC Mashukulumbwe 1.1.05 Civ Commr & Mag Lstone 5.4.09 rsgnd 23.9.10 Fmr Namwala Capt 10KOYLI w25.9.15 T/Capt NRP 13.6.17 NC Mwengwa dBlackwater Mumbwa 5.19
   Geo Alexdr 'One Eye' MacGREGOR b Australia, Cattle Tdr NWR 1900 ADC Monze SDist 4.04 NC Mwinilunga'08 Kasempa'09 Elephnt hunter Consul E'ville? Pte NRRifles '14–16 dJo'burg 1919?
45. Harding reports 14.4.05,29.5.05 PRO CO/417/408 AgSec NA 21.3.06 CO/417/423
46. Harding 11.6.04 PRO CO/417/392 Coryndon to HC 20.10.04 417/393, BSACo to Coryndon 4.2.05 417/408
47. Harding report 19.9.05 PRO CO/417/418
48. Reorganisation Coryndon 23.8.05 CO/417/409 Harding resignation 27.10.05 CO/417/418 *Far Bugles* p143
49. SofS to HC No.90 21.2.06 CO/417/432 HC 12.5.06 CO/417/423
   Wm Waldegrave Palmer 2nd Earl SELBORNE('95) KG'09 PC'00 GCMG'05 b17.10.59 s/o 1st Earl ed Winchstr Oxon MP(L) EHants'85 MP WEdinburgh 92–5 USofS Colonies'95 1st Ld Admiralty'00 HCommr in SA'05–10 Pres Bd of Agricultue'15–16 d26.2.42
   The Rt Hon Victor Alexdr Bruce 2nd EARL OF ELGIN & KINCARDINE '63 KG'99 GCSI GCIE PC b 16.5.49 Montreal s/o 1st Earl ed Eton Balliol; Treasr & 1st Commr Wks'86 Viceroy India'94–9 SofS Colonies 05–8 d18.1.17
50. PRO CO/417/418,419,423
51. Ag Admr 9.8.06 CO/417/427
52. BNP Annual Report 1907 quoted in *Story of the NRR* p22 PRO 417/446.
53. CO/417/420,423,432, Law Dept report 12.7.06 433
54. Chas Joseph McNAMARA ANC 1908
55. HC Telegram 18.7.07 Codrington reports 9.7.07,18.9.07 PRO CO/417/437 NRJ No V Vol II p63
56. Lewanika 11.12.07 PRO CO/417/451,452, Who Was Who, NRJ
57. Codrington 14175 3.6.09 PRO CO/417/446
58. PRO CO/417/438
59. *Story of the NRR* p104
60. GN No.2 9.1.08, HC No.875 16.11.08 PRO CO/417/451,465
61. Chas Halzlett Swinley BELLIS Clk NDept Mashonald; Clk NDept NWR Kasempa'04 ANC Mwinilunga'08 Ndola inv sleeping sickness'14 d'17
   Edwd Arden COPEMAN MBE'19 BA b2.1.65 s/o Canon Norwich ed Norwich GS & Cambridge, Sch Mr, PS & Tutor finally fr Geo Pauling N Borneo, Kenya to NWR 24.2.04 A/DC

Shaloba'05 DC rtd'22 Lilanda Fm Lka VConsul E'ville'27 Belge Consul Lka'30 d'60 Lka
PRO CO/417/438,452 Acct Copeman NRJ

62. PRO CO/417/467
63. CO/417/466 *Story NRR* p23
Sir Robt WILLIAMS Bt'28 DL JP AMICE MinstME b Aberdn 1860 Kimberley'81 with
Rhodes fmd Zambezia Explrg Co, Tanganyika Concsns (MD), Rhod–Katanga Co, Dir Benguela
Ry Co, VPres Union Miniere d'38
64. PRO CO/417/481
65. Hazell 20.6.11 PRO CO/417/498 Wallace to HC 18.6.12 /512, Short *African Sunset* pp27–9,
OHLUND b Ornskoldvik
66. Annual report quoted in *Story of the NRR* p23
67. *Nkhwazi* Vol 10 No.1 Aug 62 p11
68. *A History of the NR Prison Service* NRJ Vol V p549
69. PRO CO/417/462,492 *Story NRR* p23
F-M HRH Arthur Wm Patrick Albt DUKE OF CONNAUGHT b1.5.50 Lt RE '68 RA'68
RB'69 Capt'71 7H'74 Maj'75 Lt Col RB'76 m.Princess Louise Margaret of Prussia 13.3.79 Maj
Gen'80 GOC Egypt'82 Bengal'83–6 Lt Gen'89 GOC SDist'90 Gen A'shot'93 Ireld 1900 F–
M'02 IG'04 HCommr & CinC Med'07–9 Gov Gen Canada'11 d'41?
70. *Story of the NRR* p23
71. Carden report 12.4.11 PRO CO/417/496,507
72. District Diary quoted in *Nkhwazi* Vol 12 No.1 Apr'64 p16.

CHAPTER 5

The Northern Rhodesia Police

By an Order in Council dated 4th May 1911 Barotseland/North-Western Rhodesia and North-Eastern Rhodesia were joined as one territory, Northern Rhodesia. Lawrence Aubrey Wallace had become Administrator of Barotseland/North-Western Rhodesia following the death of Robert Codrington in December 1908. Wallace assumed the enlarged responsibility as the first Administrator of Northern Rhodesia on 17 August 1911. The payment by the British South Africa Company of a subsidy to the Government of Nyasaland, in return for the right (never exercised) to call for the assistance of the King's African Rifles in the suppression of serious disorder in North-Eastern Rhodesia or for its defence, had ceased from 31st March.[1]

By Proclamation No.17 of 1912, dated 18th December, the North-Eastern Rhodesia Constabulary and the Barotse Native Police were officially amalgamated to form the Northern Rhodesia Police.

Although the new force was described in the Proclamation as a Civil Police Force, Section 7 stated that, 'In the case of war or other emergency members of the force are liable to be employed for police or military purposes either within the limits of the Northern Rhodesia Order in Council of 1911, or within the limits of the Southern Rhodesia Order in Council of 1898, and when so employed, shall be subject to such terms and regulations as the High Commissioner shall determine'. When on active service this civil police force was automatically to become a 'military police force' together with any other defence units raised in the Territory.

The limits of the Northern Rhodesia Order in Council of 1911 were set out in Section 4 thereof as, 'the parts of Africa bounded by Southern Rhodesia, German South West Africa, Portuguese West Africa, the Congo Free State, German East Africa, Nyasaland, and Portuguese East Africa. The territory within the limits of this order shall be known as Northern Rhodesia.'

Under the Proclamation discipline in the Northern Rhodesia Police was to be enforced by tribunals which could be either:

a Special Board of Officers which could award imprisonment for five years, a fine of £100 or 12 strokes of the whip,
an Ordinary Board which could award imprisonment for 6 months, a fine of £15 or 3 months imprisonment, or 6 strokes,

the Commandant who could award imprisonment for 30 days, or a fine of £3, or 6
strokes, and deductions of up to five days pay to make good any loss or damage,
a Commanding Officer (of a detachment) who could award imprisonment for 14
days, or a fine of £1, deductions of up to 3 days pay, and could also recommend
reduction in rank, subject to a right to elect trial by Ordinary Board,
or a District Officer (Civil Official) who could award imprisonment for 7 days, a
fine of 5/-, 14 days confinement to barracks or extra guards and pickets.[2]

The High Commissioner, to whom the British South Africa Company's forces
were answerable, was still based at Pretoria. Most of the time of the High Commissioner and his staff was taken up with the affairs of South Africa, soon to
become a Dominion, and of the High Commission Territories, Bechuanaland,
Basutoland and Swaziland. He was represented in Salisbury by a Resident
Commissioner who was now to be responsible for Northern as well as Southern
Rhodesia.

According to a census taken on 7 May 1911 the African population of
Northern Rhodesia was then 890,985, giving a population density of a little
over three persons per square mile. There were 1,497 Europeans in the
Territory including visitors and persons in transit, 270 adult females and 287
children. Some three hundred Whites, one third of them women, were resident
in the capital, Livingstone. There were only thirty nine Asians then in Northern Rhodesia. For 1911 the revenue of North-Eastern Rhodesia was £24,500,
of which £17,000 was provided by native tax. Expenditure was £40,500. For
North-Western Rhodesia in the same year revenue was £98,000 against an
expenditure of £148,000. In the year ending 31 March 1912 exports of copper
ore were worth £33,989.[3]

Apart from a few extensions built later between the Copperbelt towns, the line
of rail was complete as it was to remain until Northern Rhodesia became the
Republic of Zambia in 1964. The mining industry had been established. By 1912
the last slave caravans had disappeared from the Territory. In 1913 the collection
of native tax was to be extended to Mwinilunga District, the last 'tax haven' in
the whole of Northern Rhodesia. Despite problems with sleeping sickness on the
Luapula, cattle disease in Barotseland and food shortages due to poor harvests, all
seemed set fair for the continued steady development of the Territory. Few could
have foreseen the coming of the Great War, and even fewer the setback it would
cause to the peaceful development of Northern Rhodesia.

In fact the amalgamation of the two police forces in Northern Rhodesia had
taken place on 17 August 1911, the effective date of the Northern Rhodesia Order
in Council. On the 20th of that month when Second-Lieutenant Dickinson visited
Fort Rosebery, he was described as an officer of the Northern Rhodesia Police.
Edward Dickinson was en route from Kasama to Ndola to join the Anglo-Belgian
Boundary Commission as escort commander[4]. He had joined the Barotse Native
Police from the Natal Police six months earlier.

Since the only officer of the North-Eastern Rhodesia Constabulary for the past
three and a half years had been a member of the Barotse Native Police on
secondment, and most of the African members of both forces were natives of

North-Eastern Rhodesia and accordingly both used the same African language, Cinyanja, the amalgamation can not have caused many problems of morale. In effect the members of the North-Eastern Rhodesia Constabulary were absorbed into the Barotse Native Police, which force adopted a new title and an enlarged area of responsibility. The regulations for the organisation and discipline of the North-Eastern Rhodesia Constabulary never having been formally approved, the Barotse Native Police was the only properly constituted force.

On 29th August 1911 the Northern Rhodesia Police were inspected at Livingstone by General Sir Ian Hamilton GCB DSO, Inspector General of Overseas Forces. Four officers and 90 men were on parade with the Band, 32 strong under Bandmaster W B Taylor. Hamilton was impressed by the soldierly appearance of the men, whom he described as 'smaller and slighter than Sudanese, but just as steady'. They handled their arms very smartly and 'the stamp of their naked feet gives more cohesion than I should have thought possible.'! After the parade the General set a short exercise. He found the officers had something to learn in the tactical handing of troops and the troops had difficulty in comprehending the niceties of the preliminary moves, but quite understood what was required of them in making a charge with bayonets fixed. They rushed forward, 'howling like wolves', several clearing a wire fence at one bound. The camp was particularly clean and neat. The wives and children of the African police paraded outside their homes, dressed in their best and scrupulously clean.

The Force consisted of 17 officers, 8 British NCOs and 760 Africans and was organised in five companies:

Sergeant Bandmaster W. B. Taylor & the band Livingstone circa 1914
(Photo Greg Koll, Kamloops)

'A' with 5 officers, 4 BNCOs, and 150 men at Livingstone, a British NCO and 10 men at Broken Hill and the same at Ndola, a British NCO and 12 at Mumbwa and 9 African police each at Kalomo, Magoye, Chilanga, Namwala, Buni-Kariba, Mkushi and Feira.

'B' with 2 officers and 60 men at Mongu, an officer and 20 men at Sesheke, and 9 African police each at Balovale, Nalolo, Mankoya, Lukona, and Mkwangwa.

'C' with 2 officers and 58 men at Kasempa, a British NCO and 12 at Kansanshi and 9 at Baluba.

'D' with 3 officers and 106 men at Kasama (perhaps this includes the escort to the Anglo-Belgian Boundary Commission), 20 African police at Abercorn, 15 at Kawambwa and 9 each at Fort Rosebery, Mpika, Luwingu, Fife, Chinsali, Mporokoso, Katwe, Chienji and Serenje

& 'E' with one officer and 60 men at Fort Jameson and 9 each at Lundazi and Petauke.

Most of the men were Ngoni or Bemba with a few Wakunda and Yao.

The old Barotse Native Police in 'A', 'B' and 'C' coys were paid 10 shillings a month during their first year of service, 12/6d in their second year and 15/- a month thereafter with rations of $2\frac{1}{2}$lbs of grain ($4\frac{1}{2}$lbs if married with a wife in station) and $\frac{1}{2}$ ounce of salt a day. Those at Livingstone were given 3lbs of meat each week while elsewhere an allowance was paid for meat. The Sergeant-Major received an extra 15/- a month, colour sergeants 10/-, sergeants 5/- and corporals 2/6d. The former North-Eastern Rhodesia Constabulary of 'D' and 'E' companies were still on five shillings a month with increments of 1/- a month for each additional year after completing their initial engagement which had been three years in both forces. The re-engagement rate was 57 per cent but Hamilton recommended that the initial engagement should in future be for four years which it was to remain for the whole history of the Northern Rhodesia Police.

The Force was armed with 763 of the single shot ·303 Martini-Metford rifle, a shortened version of the Martini-Henry, dating from 1890, with the triangular bayonet. 491 of the old Martini-Henrys were still held. Some mules were held at Livingstone for transport in areas free of tetse fly. Elsewhere carriers were employed when required and, apparently, convicts from the local gaols would be used in emergencies. Hamilton recommended that all Government owned mules should pass through police hands to be trained to carry packs and three or four extra should be acquired to provide for mounted scouts. He also suggested bicycles for reconnaissance and communications.

For signalling the NRP had 5-inch heliographs, but Hamilton was concerned about longer range communication. The only means of communication between Livingstone and Mongu was by runner which took at least nine days. A message for Kasempa could be telegraphed to Makola siding in the Belgian Congo but then had to be taken by runner via Kansanshi, six days. Fort Jameson was on the telegraph network, providing instant communication, as were Fife and Abercorn from where a runner could reach Kasama in four days although in September 1914 Maj Stennett with 100 men was to cover the distance in less than three. Hamilton reported that heliograph signalling was soon to be introduced between Abercorn and Kasama which would dramatically reduce the delay in suitable weather conditions. He suggested that consideration should be given to the introduction of wireless telegraphy but this had to wait for more than another 20 years. At the outbreak of war in August 1914 the Board of the British South Africa Company, mindful of the vulnerability of the telegraph line between Abercorn, Fife and Nyasaland, did make inquiries with the Marconi Co for the purchase of mobile wireless sets. Those available were for transport in limbered wagons and could not be broken down into loads light enough for porter transport. They had insufficient range to allow communication between Abercorn and Broken Hill without stations being set up in between.[5]

Under the Order in Council the Resident Comissioner was to have chief command of the Force on Active Service and was empowered to inspect it at any time. On 9 September 1911 Col Robert Burns-Begg KC carried out his first inspection at Livingstone. Five officers were on parade with the Native Sergeant-Major, 80 men of 'A' Company and the Band. The Resident Commissioner reported that the men were smart, well set-up and soldierly. They performed the march past and advance in review order with great steadiness and precision. Burns-Begg then selected an objective and ordered Lt Col Carden to stage an attack thereon. Burns-Begg was not only a lawyer, he had been an officer in the Volunteers in Scotland, served in Kitchener's Horse in the South African War and afterwards commanded a regiment of the Transvaal Volunteers. He complained that the attack was made in too close order with too little attention to the use of cover and too much to alignment and precision. Bearing in mind that some 30 of the men were recruits with less than 6 months service who were not expected to come up against regular troops or Boer sharpshooters, his criticism seems a little unfair. Not even Burns-Begg could have foreseen that in two years time the NRP would be in action against the Schutztruppe of German East Africa. He also pointed out that there was no provision for medical services on active service and the Force held no medical equipment whatsoever, not even a stretcher! He found the barracks and officers' quarters admirable and to compare most favourably with those provided for the BSAP in Southern Rhodesia. As the former Commissioner of the Transvaal Police his observations on the Town Police might have been of value, but if he made any they are not recorded.[6]

The normal uniform was a khaki drill tunic and shorts but blue jerseys were worn on active service and for guard duty. Personal equipment was of the Mackenzie pattern with a blanket or greatcoat carried on active service and upto 5 days rations in the haversack. It is not clear when the Force adopted Infantry Drill but in a memorandum by Lt Col Carden dated 7 October 1910 for applicants for commissions in the future NRP they were informed of the requirement for a knowledge of Infantry Drill, the Maxim machine gun and the heliograph. The training of African police on the heliograph ceased in early 1913, a measure regretted when the telegraph on the Northern Border was destroyed during the War. The badge was the Crested Crane over a scroll inscribed 'NORTHERN RHODESIA POLICE'. The Force retained the Maxim machine guns of the Barotse Native Police and the varied collection of ordnance of the North-Eastern Rhodesia Constabulary.[7]

On return from leave Capt O'Sullevan was posted to Mongu where the past year had seen some drama. In October 1910 on the Portuguese Border in a dispute over fish and a lost gun, a man and a woman had been shot dead in Kapini Village and two other persons wounded. Followers of one Mukweni were responsible and when the Assistant Native Commissioner, Mr R H Palmer, went to investigate he met with defiance from Mukweni. A proposal to send a police detachment was postponed due to doubts whether Mukweni's village was on the Rhodesian side of the border.[8]

On 6 March 1911 there had been great alarm at Lealui over a rumoured plot to overthrow or murder Lewanika. R V Roach, the Native Commissioner, immediately went over with Sgt-Maj H J Saunders and seven African police. Two arrests were made. When the first report reached Livingstone, Capt Watherston, 2Lt Bremner and 50 men with a Maxim were despatched to reinforce the 20 man detachment at Sesheke and to be ready to move further upriver if required. They were at Sesheke from 28 March until 18 April. A headman was imprisoned and Lewanika's cousin, Mbau, temporarily removed from Lealui.[9]

On 2 November 1911 2Lt Bremner, now at Mongu, was sent with 20 men 112 miles west where a Portuguese, J T Ferreira, had set up camp on the Northern Rhodesia side of the Border. He was found to have returned to Angola but 10 of his Mambari were arrested and 23 guns and a quantity of powder destroyed.[10]

Further north, in August 1911 two African policemen and a messenger, sent to arrest a Lovale for selling a woman as a slave, were fired on and beaten up and their belongings smashed. On 7 October Jack Venning, Assistant Native Commissioner, was threatened on the Kapaku River. A Lunda chief, Sinde, was murdered in Portuguese territory. Kamoche, a contender for the succession, led his followers into Northern Rhodesia to prevent the installation of Kasanda, a district messenger, as Sinde's successor. On the night 19/20 March 1912 O'Sullevan left Mongu by canoe with 28 men to reinforce Mr Palmer, now Native Commissioner at Balovale. On arrival O'Sullevan went down with fever but Palmer went out with 20 police and Kamoche fled over the Border on his approach.[11]

In the Mwinilunga Sub-District Pte Kachikamba was robbed of his rifle which was later recovered. Lt J J McCarthy reinforced Mwinilunga with 13 police from Kasempa. Privates 470 Ndalajani and 623 Mbenjere were ordered to escort four prisoners from Mwinilunga to Kasempa. The prisoners escaped. The two policemen were determined not to fail in their mission. One escapee was recaptured in Northern Rhodesia but the others got over the border into the Congo. Ndalajani and Mbenjere followed them and had retaken two more and located the fourth when they themselves were arrested by the Belgian authorities on 15 January 1912. The prisoners were set free but the two policemen were allowed to return to Mwinilunga and their arms and equipment sent back via Ndola. On 19 February J F Kenny Dillon, the Native Commissioner at Kansanshi, was shot at on his way back from the Mine to the Boma. The Boundary Commission was about to enter the district and an officer and 45 police were sent to patrol the area through which it would pass. The Administrator, Mr Wallace, arranged to leave Livingstone on 20 July 1912 with an escort of 50 men to interview the chiefs at Kasempa before going on to Lealui.[12]

Lieutenant Colonel John Carden CMG acted as Commandant for the first few months and then retired at the age of 42, perhaps because he had married in 1909! He was not to enjoy his retirement or married life for long. Soon after the outbreak of war he was appointed Second in Command of the newly raised 5th (Service) Battalion of the Wiltshire Regiment. Having succeeded to the command Lieutenant Colonel Carden took his battalion to Gallipoli where he was killed on 10th August 1915.

The officers of the Northern Rhodesia Police were listed in a Government Notice dated 12th February 1913, as follows:

> To be Chief Inspector with the rank of Major and Acting Commandant:
>> Frederic Arthur Hodson
> To be Paymaster and Quartermaster with the rank of Major:
>> Henry Louis Byas
> To be Inspectors with the rank of Captain:
>> Harry March Stennett
>> John Joseph O'Sullevan
>> Geoffrey Fell Watherston
>> Harry Clement Ingles
>> Francis Stafford James
> To be Sub-Inspectors with the rank of Lieutenant:
>> Ernest Harry Lindsell Salmon
>> Charles Henry Fair
>> James Joseph McCarthy
>> Frederick Gordon De Satge
>> Arthur Charles de Cussance Cussans
>> Percy Joseph Sillitoe
>> Edward Griffin Dickinson
> To be Sub-Inspectors with the rank of 2nd Lieutenant:
>> Alastair Bruce Bremner
>> Charles Cooper Hornsby
>> George Montague Withers
>> Edgar Collins Castle.[13]

The more senior officers had been appointed justices of the peace by Government Notice 6/11. Lieutenant Cussans and the rest were appointed JP on 4th November 1912. Second lieutenants were paid 15/- a day with Ration Allowance at 3/6d a day. They were required to pass an examination in the Cinyanja language to qualify for promotion to Lieutenant.

By Government Notice 31/13 dated 10th May Hodson was confirmed in his appointment as Commandant, with the local rank of Lieutenant Colonel from 18th December 1912. Hodson being on leave, Stennett's promotion to major, second-in-command, and acting Commandant was published at the same time. A Yorkshireman, Hodson had enlisted in the York and Lancaster Regiment in 1889. In 1896 he was with a half company of his battalion en route from Durban to Mauritius when it was commandeered at Beira by Lt Col Alderson to guard his line of communication in Mashonaland[14]. In Rhodesia Hodson took his discharge from the Army and joined the British South Africa Police.

Stennett and Dickinson were future commandants of the Northern Rhodesia Police. O'Sullevan has been mentioned earlier and will be again. Watherston,

Colonel F. A. Hodson, C.B.E., Commandant, 1912–19 (Nkhwazi)

Ingles, James, Fair and McCarthy had joined the Barotse Native Police as NCOs after service in the BSAP. Salmon had come to Rhodesia with the Matabeleland Relief Force in 1896. He had managed native labour for the builders of the Falls Bridge and the railway to Broken Hill before being commissioned in the BNP in 1906. De Satge, Cussans, Bremner, Hornsby and Castle had also served in the BSAP before being commissioned in the BNP. Withers and Castle had reached the rank of Captain in UK in the Territorial Force and Special Reserve respectively. De Satge and Watherston both left in 1913. The vacancies created by the retirement of Lt Col Carden and the departure of these two officers were filled by Sub-Inspector (Second Lieutenant) G P Burton on 14 December 1912, B J Graham on 3 June 1913, and Herbert Allport BA on 10th February 1914.

Sillitoe, the future Sir Percy Sillitoe, was to become the most renowned former officer of the Northern Rhodesia Police. He was a BSAP corporal in charge at Victoria Falls. Like many other members of the Southern Rhodesia force before and after him, he had his eye on the better prospects north of the Zambezi. Sillitoe applied for and was granted a commission in February 1911, becoming a second lieutenant in the last days of the Barotse Native Police. His service with the NRP finished for all practical purposes in early 1917, when he was invalided to Johannesburg with enteric fever.

On returning to duty, Captain Sillitoe was seconded to the administration of the occupied territory in German East Africa from 15th August 1917. In 1922 Sillitoe left Tanganyika because of ill health and began studies at the Bar in London. In March 1923 he applied for and obtained the post of Chief Constable of Chesterfield. As Chief Constable of Sheffield Sillitoe gained fame by breaking up the city's gangs. In 1931 he was appointed Chief Constable of Glasgow, where his men became known as 'Sillitoe's Guards' after he introduced the chequered cap band, based on that of the Scots Guards, which was soon adopted by police forces throughout Scotland and is now worn by police all over Great Britain. In March 1943 Sillitoe was appointed Chief Constable of Kent, when the various police forces of that County were amalgamated so as to be better able to cope with the traffic and other problems created by the preparations for the liberation of Europe. In 1946 he reached the peak of his career on becoming Director General of the Security Service, MI5. As Chief Constable of both Chesterfield and Sheffield Captain Sillitoe was succeeded by his former NRP superior, Maj James.

In his autobiography, *Cloak without Dagger*, Sillitoe showed that as early as 1911 officers of the Northern Rhodesia Police, stationed at Livingstone, were spending much of their free time south of the Zambezi, at the Victoria Falls Hotel. In those days the bridge only took rail traffic, so the evening out started with a three or four mile drive by muledrawn Cape-cart, followed by a canoe crossing to a landing stage on the South Bank above the Falls, about a mile from the Hotel. On well planned and executed expeditions the return journey was made on the northbound train, which ran two or three times a week. One night Sillitoe and three friends miscalculated the time of the train. They had to paddle back upstream against the current, not reaching the Mess until after dawn. Needless to say, they were present, properly dressed, on first parade. Apart from modes of transport nothing really changed in fifty years!

Lieutenant Sillitoe was not to remain long in the fleshpots of Livingstone. Records at Fort Rosebery showed he visited that station on 13th November 1911[15]. He would then have been on his way to join the Anglo–Belgian Boundary Commission to which he acted as escort officer until the end of 1912. On his return to Livingstone Sillitoe went down with blackwater fever which would almost certainly have killed him had it manifested itself while he was still in the bush. As it was he was fit enough to go on leave to England early in 1913[16].

One officer and 25 men formed the escort for the main party of the Boundary Commission but in April 1913 a separate section commenced work on the stretch between Lakes Mweru and Tanganyika requiring a further officer and 20 NRP as escort. The British members of the Commission were officers of the Regular Army assisted by NCOs of the Royal Engineers. In March 1913, Major H W Gordon RE arrived and the Anglo-Portuguese Boundary Commission commenced work marking the border with Angola and requiring yet another escort.[17]

The police sports day on 1 January 1913 started with a competition to find the best turned out African policeman. Among more conventional athletic events that followed was a wives water carrying race and a band walking race during which the competitors had to play their instruments.[18]

Gen Sir Ian Hamilton had criticised the provision under which the Resident Commissioner was to have command of all and any Rhodesian forces on 'active service'. He pointed out that the qualifications for appointment as Resident Commissioner did not necessarily include appropriate military experience. Accordingly when, in January 1913, Colonel A H M Edwards CB MVO arrived in Salisbury as the new Commissioner of the British South Africa Police he also held the new appointment of Chief Commandant of Police and Volunteers, with overall responsibility for the forces in both Southern and Northern Rhodesia. A regular cavalry officer, Edwards had commanded the Imperial Light Horse in South Africa until 1901 when he took command of 'A' Division of the newly formed South African Constabulary. From 1903 until 1905 he was Commandant of the Transvaal Volunteers. He then returned to conventional military employment in India. In 1906 Colonel Edwards was appointed a chief constable in the London Metropolitan Police, in which post he remained until coming to Rhodesia.

Edwards was therefore qualified by experience in all aspects of his new job. One of his tasks was to submit recommendations for the reorganisation of the Northern Rhodesia Police. This he did on 8 September 1913. His recommendations were accepted by the Administrator of the Territory, Mr Wallace, and by the Board of the British South Africa Company in London, whereupon the Force was divided into a military branch and a civil police branch, known as the Town and District Police.[19]

Anglo–Belgian boundary commission 1912, carrier transport preparing to move under a 'first rate native police sergeant' (PRO CO417/525)

The Town and District Police was further sub-divided into:

The Criminal Investigation Department and Fingerprint Bureau;
The Town Police;
The Gaol Establishment;
and The District Police.

Twelve Europeans and 328 Africans were employed as civil police. Africans were to serve three years in the Military Branch before being accepted for police duties. Since 1908 Europeans for civil police duty had been recruited direct from the Metropolitan Police in London and given the rank of sergeant or constable. Col Edwards found them not always able to adapt to conditions in Africa and recommended a return to recruiting from the BSAP. Constables were paid eight shillings a day, sergeants third class, nine shillings, second class 10/6d and sergeants first class eleven shillings and sixpence. In all cases pay was increased by 6d a day after one year and an additional 1/- a day after two years in rank. Quarters and rations were provided free of charge or ration allowance paid at 3/6d a day in lieu.

The new Criminal Investigation Department and Fingerprint Bureau came into being early in 1914 under Regimental Sergeant-Major Kenneth Ferguson, who had completed a six week fingerprint course at New Scotland Yard while on leave. During his absence from 22nd September 1913 to 23rd January 1914 Segeant-Major Coote acted in Ferguson's place, in charge of Immigration Restrictions. Ferguson was appointed Sub-Inspector without commissioned rank, and JP on 15th June 1914. In the CID he was to be assisted by one other European, Detective Sergeant R H Kirk, formerly of the CID at Bulawayo, who arrived on first appointment on 3rd July 1914, five African detectives and an African clerk. These detectives were to be posted at various stations throughout the Territory. Sub-Inspector Ferguson was responsible for the uniformed Town Police in Livingstone as well as for the whole of the CID and Fingerprint Bureau and immigration control throughout the Territory. Superintendent C J Brundell, in charge of the CID in Southern Rhodesia with his headquarters at Bulawayo, was given a watching brief over the infant CID in Northern Rhodesia. The former British Sergeant's Mess at Livingstone was converted into the Police Station and CID Headquarters.[20]

During 1914, 971 persons were prosecuted as a result of police investigations and 869 convicted, 48 whites and 269 Africans for offences against Common Law and 55 whites and 497 Africans for breaches of local ordinances. By the outbreak of War the European population had risen to some 2,250.[21]

There were now central prisons at Abercorn, Broken Hill, Fort Jameson, Fort Rosebery, Kasama, Kasempa, Kawambwa, Livingstone, Mongu, Mumbwa and Solwezi. All Africans sentenced to 6 months or more and all European prisoners served their sentences at central prisons. Although the Prisons Department was administered by the Attorney General, the officers of the NRP in command of the detachments at Fort Jameson, Kasama and Mongu were ex officio superintendents of the central prisons at those stations. A senior officer at Headquarters was appointed Superintendent of the Central Prison at Livingstone where Sergeant-

Major S J Boyd was Head Gaoler. Elsewhere the senior administrative officer acted as superintendent of any central prison. Each native commissioner was superintendent of the local prison at his station where Africans were held on remand or served sentences of less than six months. Some 75 African police were employed in the Gaol Establishment. Edwards was not in favour of warders being members of the Police Force on a permanent basis but accepted that the time was not yet ripe to form a completely separate disciplined body.[22]

Ronald Arthur Howe had been one of nine Metropolitan Police officers recruited into the British South Africa Police in 1911. After two years in Southern Rhodesia he obtained his discharge, but Colonel Edwards persuaded him to go North. Howe attested as a constable on 23 May 1913 and worked under Ferguson on town police work at Livingstone. Howe was allocated a pole and dagga hut in which he was soon joined by another recruit. The hut was so small that all washing, shaving and eating had to be done in the open air. There was not even room in the hut for their belongings which had to be kept outside. Howe must have been quite pleased to hear that he was posted to Mumbwa, but there he found that his quarters consisted of four walls only. He had to enlist the help of some Africans to construct a grass roof. Chief Inspector R A Howe MSM retired from the Northern Rhodesia Police in August 1934. He settled at Broadstairs in Kent, where he died on 9th March 1984, at the age of 98. His life spanned the whole history of the Rhodesias.[23]

Another early member of the Town Police was Paul William Mashawila, a Musenga from Mbakalungu Village under Chief Mwanjawantu in the Petauke District. Mashawila attested in 1911 and was transfered to the Town Police at Livingstone in 1914. In 1917 Mashawila was appointed to the Criminal Investigation Department as a detective at Broken Hill. He retired in the rank of Detective Sergeant-Major in 1945 after 32 years service, during which he was awarded numerous commendations. He was still alive in 1962 when one of his five sons, Assistant Inspector John Mashawila, was serving in the Force at his father's old station, Broken Hill.[24]

In 1914 there were Town Police detachments at Livingstone with 26 African police, Ndola with 14, Solwezi 13, Fort Jameson 17, Lusaka 6, Mumbwa 11 and Broken Hill with 15[25]. The only commissioned officer serving with the Town Police was Lieutenant Percy Sillitoe. His home leave had ended in June 1913 and soon after his return to duty he was sent to open the first police station at Lusaka. Col Edwards had recommended that an officer be appointed to cover the Lusaka, Kafue and Magoye areas. Some 200 Boers had settled around Chalimbana in the second half of 1911 and there was some concern about their ability to maintain themselves. The Town Police at other stations were commanded by European non-commissioned officers, answerable to the officer commanding the nearest detachment of the Military Branch.

Lusaka grew up around one of the sidings established every twenty miles on the railway line in 1905. From 1906 white farmers began to settle in the area. John Marropodi, an Italian, set up his lime kiln not far from the siding, and in 1907 Goodman's store opened in a tiny pole and dagga thatch roofed hut. By 1914 the store had doubled in size and boasted a corrugated iron roof and a verandah. In

1912 Mr L J Marston obtained a licence for an hotel, which later became known as Counsell's, and later still the Lusaka Hotel. By this time growth had been such that there was agitation for the establishment of a local authority to control sanitation. On 31st July 1913 the Lusaka Village Management Board came officially into being. The European population was eighty nine. Lusaka, described by Sillitoe as 'little more than a cluster of huts round a tiny hotel and a blacksmith's shop for the repair of trek wagons', was part of the Chilanga Sub-district of the Luangwa District. The administrative headquarters remained ten miles south at Chilanga, but Sillitoe built his police station in the village of Lusaka, on the Livingstone Road site where it was to remain until 1958. The officer in charge and his two European sergeants lived in pole and dagga rondavels across the road where the police camp for station African personnel was also to remain for many years.

At Lusaka Sillitoe's career was nearly brought to an abrupt end when his sleeping quarters were struck by lightning. Luckily he was in his living room, a nearby hut, entertaining the Assistant Magistrate from Chilanga to tea.

Percy Sillitoe wrote that his main task was to prevent game poaching by Boers. They were reported to spend more time hunting than farming. His ex-Metropolitan Police assistants did not have the experience for this type of work and so Sillitoe undertook most of the patrolling while they remained in camp at Lusaka. Rhodes' old friend and associate, 'Dr Jim', leader of the disastrous Jameson Raid, was now Sir Leander Starr Jameson, Prime Minister of the Cape and a director of the British South Africa Company. He visited Lusaka and, according to Sillitoe, authorised the secondment of two mounted troopers of the BSAP to assist with the patrol work.

Even in those early days accounts had to be kept. The Lusaka Police Station cash book for 1913 showed the following expenditure: 'Travelling duty. Purchase of 10 paddles at 3d each – 2s 6d.' Another item was: 'Public Works. Pay for 20 thatchers repairing roof, 20 days at 6s. a month – £4.'[26]

Fauna conservation was already taken seriously in Northern Rhodesia. The Ostrich Export Prohibition Ordinance of 16th March 1912 (Chapter 115 of the Laws), made it an offence for any person, except in certain circumstances, to export any ostrich or ostrich egg to any place beyond the limits of the Territory. The punishment for this offence was imprisonment, with or without hard labour, for any term not less than twelve months or more than two years.

The 205 District Police were entirely African, posted at thirty Bomas, or Administrative District Headquarters, under the Native Commissioner or District Officer. In 1912 the detachment at Fort Rosebery consisted of one corporal, seven privates and one bugler. The corporal was paid fifteen shillings and six pence, and the lowest paid, eleven shillings a month[27]. Col Edwards recommended that from 1 April 1914 the District Police should be paid 1/- a month more than their comrades in the Military Branch.

An African convicted of burglary of a European's house at Fort Rosebery was sentenced to one and a half years imprisonment, with hard labour, and 20 lashes. At an Indaba held there in 1913 Mr L A Wallace CMG, the Administrator of Northern Rhodesia, gave a warning about road robberies and the theft of carriers' loads. He said that if those responsible could not be found he would have to punish a whole village. Collective fines could be imposed under the Collective Punishments Proclamation, No.9 of 1912.

At a similar assembly in 1914 the chiefs were told of the impending arrival of the first aeroplanes from the North. Village headmen on the route were instructed to prepare large beacons of wood which were to be lit when the word was given. They were asked to give all necessary assistance to the aviators.

There was no Fire Brigade anywhere in Northern Rhodesia until the mid-1950s. One night at Livingstone in 1913 D Barnett's store caught fire. The duty bugler at the police Camp guardroom sounded the alarm and the Town police on night duty did what they could. Roused from their beds, sergeants-major Ferguson and Coote took charge and the Military Company doubled up from the camp. Most of Barnett's stock was saved and the fire prevented from spreading but the incident revealed the complete lack of fire fighting equipment.[28]

On New Year's Eve 1913 an Argyll motor car, driven by Captain R N Kelsey, and a motor cycle, ridden by a Mr Pickersgill-Cunliffe had roared into Lusaka. With Kelsey's co-driver and a newspaper reporter they comprised the 'Cape to Cairo Motor Expedition', sponsored by the Daily Telegraph. These were the first motor vehicles to be seen in Northern Rhodesia. Kelsey was killed by a lion at Serenje shortly after the expedition left Lusaka.

Captains Salmon and Ingles and Lt Castle all applied for permission to marry during their coming leave. Married quarters were rare, especially at outstations. On 27 May 1914 Col Edwards issued an order making it clear that marriage allowance and married quarters would not be granted to officers with less than three years service or who had not qualified for promotion and passed the native language examination. There was no guarantee that those who were qualified and obtained the Commandant's permission to marry would be posted to a station where suitable quarters were available either when first married or when subsequently required to move from one station to another.[29]

The possibility of war in the not too distant future cannot have been entirely absent from the minds of those in authority such as Colonel Edwards. In his report dealing with 1914, the Chief Commandant of Police and Volunteers wrote, 'Early in the year the question of forming a reserve composed of ex-members of the Northern Rhodesia Police, or King's African Rifles who resided in the North-Eastern territory, was raised. The commandant on his tour of inspection was instructed to make, and made, inquiries into the subject while in north-eastern territory, but came across very few ex-police, and reported that he did not consider the plan feasible[30].' On 16 June 1914 the Admistrator wrote to the Secretary to the British South Africa Company concerning draft legislation for a part-time European defence force. On 28 July the High Commissioner issued Proclamation No.10 of 1914 for the enforcement of the Official Secrets Act 1911 in the Territory.[31]

Col Edwards' recommendations of September 1913 had not been confined to civil police matters. 'A' Company at Livingstone then had a paper strength of 274 but, he pointed out 24 were required for guards, 6 were on leave, 3 sick, 8 were recruits, 11 band boys, 11 prison warders, 15 Town Police and 98 District Police

Ex-Sergeant Malalo in 1962 (Nkhwazi)

at out-stations. No less than 84 officers and men, mainly from Livingstone and Kasama, were employed with the boundary commissions. There were insufficient left to send out to deal with an emergency. Edwards recommended that not only should the Town and District Police and warders be separated from the Military but a separate Headquarters and Depot formed at Livingstone leaving 'A' Coy as an independent mobile column which should ultimately be based at Broken Hill. Officers on home leave should be required to serve an attachment with a regular infantry battalion at Aldershot or attend a course at the School of Musketry at Hythe. Subalterns should be sent down to the Union School of Musketry at Bloemfontein.

He was pleased to note that arrangements had been made for the collection and dissemination of Intelligence. A European civilian clerk should be employed at Headquarters to give the Adjutant, then Capt Watherston, time to act as staff officer both for the police and the part-time defence force to be formed in place of the Rifle Association and placed under command of the Commandant of the NRP. The Director of Medical Services for the Territory, Dr Aylmer May, was approached and arranged for the preparation and supply of medical panniers suitable for use in the Field.[32]

One recruit at about this time was Private Malalo from Kabwibwi Village, Chief Nkolemfumu's area, Kasama District. he already had some experience of the World, having worked from 1911 until 1913 in Salisbury, Southern Rhodesia. Malalo served in the Military Branch throughout the war and was wounded in German East Africa. After the war he served with the main body of the Military Branch at Livingstone and with the detachment at Fort Jameson. At some time he transferred to the Civil Police in which his Force number was 3. In 1936 he was at Lusaka where he was promoted from corporal to sergeant. During the Second World War Sergeant Malalo served with a party of troops and police guarding Government House. In 1942 he was awarded the Colonial Police and Fire Brigades Long Service and Good Conduct Medal. In 1946 Sergeant Malalo retired on pension and settled at Chisapa Village near Mungwi. In 1962 when a new African Police Club was opened at Kasama, it was named after Sergeant Malalo, whose son was then serving in the Force, as a sergeant at Ndola.[33]

According to Northern Rhodesia's entry in *The Empire at War* the strength of the Force in August 1914 was 19 officers, two warrant officers, five British non-commissioned officers, five British constables, and 786 native NCOs and men[34]. Ferguson's fellow warrant officer was Bandmaster Taylor. In addition to sergeants-major Coote and Boyd, and sergeants Howe and Kirk, there were sergeants-major Mills and John Taylor, and constables R E Camfield, J R Sawtell, H Robinson,and R Brown. Robinson, a regular army reservist, was recalled to the colours on the outbreak of War.

The Military Branch was organised into five companies. 'A' Company was still with Force Headquarters at Livingstone, where there was a total of 11 British (including the three officers on leave) and 179 African personnel. 'B' Company, two officers and 71 Africans, was stationed at Mongu, 'C', two officers and 76 Africans, at Kasempa, 'D', two officers and 99 Africans, at Kasama, and 'E' Company, two officers and 77 African other ranks, was at Fort Jameson. The Officer Commanding 'D' Company had overall responsibility for the detachments of District Police at Abercorn, Fife, Luwingu, Mporokoso, and Fort Rosebery. 'A' Company, at Livingstone, was capable of providing a mobile column at short notice for duty anywhere in Northern Rhodesia. It was soon to be required to take the field and to remain away from Livingstone for more than four years.[35]

Annex to Chapter 5

OFFICERS & BRITISH OTHER RANKS OF THE NORTHERN RHODESIA POLICE joined 17 AUG 1911–5.8.14

BOYD Sydney John b9.6.80 Pte Gren Guards'98 PC Met 17.11.02–Sgt NRP 19.8.11 Gaoler Lstone 1.12.11 1/Sgt SM by 7.10.14 Sec'd Prisons Dept Hd Gaoler 1.4.22 d.25.6.26 Livingstone
CASTLE Edgar Collins ed Wellngton 2Lt 6LF 7.04 Capt 4LF(SR) 14.8.08 Tpr BSAP'10 2Lt NRP 12.9.11 Lt 1.1.14 lve 16.6–10.9.14 T/Capt by 5.18 Capt 1.4.24 lve pendg retirement 3.7.31 d.59
TAYLOR John Sgt NRP Kansanshi by 19.2.12 T&D 1/Sgt'17 SM by'22

ROBERTS Sydney Thos BSAP 10.2.12 Const NRP 31.8.12

LEANEY H PC Met'09 Const NRP 12.10.12 dischgd 6.14.

BURTON Granville Pierrepoint b'86 Tpr BSAP'10 2Lt NRP 14.12.12 Lt 1.4.15 NBdr by 24.4.15 T/Capt B Coy 20.3.17 lve 26.7–6.11.18 Capt 1.10.21 A/Maj 10.27 Maj 22.8.30 NRR 1.4.32 Ag Cmdt 6.2.33 lve pdg retiremnt 31.5.33

ROBINSON H Const by 1.13 Army Reserve recalled by 18.1.15

HOWE Robt Arthur MSM'34 b23.8.85 PC 483Y Met'08 611A Met Tpr BSAP'11 Const NRP 23.5.13 3/Sgt'14 2/Sgt by 3.3.17 SM by 9.9.21 WO1 1.4.24 C/I rtd 18.8.34 DC's Clk'40 d9.3.84 Broadstairs

GRAHAM Bernard Jas b'83 SA'02 CGA 09–10 2Lt NRP 3.6.13 Lt 1.4.15 fm lve 17.4.18 T/Maj 5.6.18 Hon Capt'20 Capt 1.7.24 NRR T/Maj AgCmdt 1.6.33 Cmdt 3.9.33 rtd Hon LtCol 15.1.37.

CAMFIELD Reuben Edwin MSM'33 b London 28.6.84 PC Met 24.9.06 BSAP 21.10.11 Const NRP 25.7.13 1/Sgt 1.4.19 Insp 1.4.28 rtd 23.5.33.

READ John Gordon CMG BSAP 4.9.09 Const NRP 19.12.13 d58

ALLPORT Herbert BA BSAP'09 2Lt NRP 10.2.14(GN92/14) Lt 1.4.15 MID lve 18.4–18.10.16 T/Capt'18 A/Maj 6.11.18 Hon Capt 1.9.19 Capt 1.1.27 Maj rtd 25.4.32.

BROWN R BSAP'09 Const NRP 31.3.14 Sgt resigned 9.21

CHAMBERS Henry Herbt Tpr BSAP 7.7.12 Const NRP 31.3.14

KIRK Robt Howard b WCroydon 30.3.89 ed Whitgift emp City Merchnts Herring Dewick & Cripps'04 CityoL RFA TF'08 BSAP 8.10.10 Cpl 1.13 Sgt NRP 3.7.14 T/Sub-Insp 14.2.17 C/D/Insp equ Lt 1.11.18–3.1.21 Farmer & No.24 Rfn NRRifles Dist Cmdt Chisamba'21 T/Clk Vet & Ag 22.7.25

SAWTELL J R Tpr BSAP 3.6.12 Const NRP 28.7.14 lve 13.7.17–3.18 1/Sgt 10.10.21 i/c Lka resgnd 28.7.24 dep 10.8.24 The Laurels Bapton Codford Wilts T/AgHd Gaoler Lstone 27.7.25–8.1.26?

Notes

1. PRO CO/417/507
   Sir Lawrence Aubrey WALLACE KBE'18 CMG'10 b2.2.57 to SA Civil Engr Rly Constrn'79 Hunting NER'96 Ch Svyr NER'01 m Margaret–Marie (CBE) d/o Prof Henri Dubec of Le Havre'07 Admr NER 7.07 NWR 1.09 NR 8.11–rtd 3.21 to Calvados d26.1.42
2. NR Govt Gazette British Library & PRO
3. Annual Report 1911/12 PRO CO/417/532
4. *Nkhwazi* Vol 12 No.1 Apr 64 p16
5. Hamilton report 13.10.11 PRO CO/417/518 Exec Ctee BSACo 13.8.14 CO/417/554
   Gen Sir Ian Standish Monteith HAMILTON GCB'10 GCMG'19 DSO'91 b Corfu 16.1.53 s/o Col ed Wellingtn Lt Gordon Hldrs'73 Afghan War'78–80 SA'81 Nile'84–5 Burma'86–7 Col'91 Chitral Relief Fce'95 CB'96 Bde Cmd Tirah'97 Cmdt Musktry Sch Hythe'98 SA'99 KCB'00 Maj Gen Mil Sec SAEF'01 COS SAEF'01–2 Lt Gen QMG WO'03 with Jap Army Manchuria'04 GOC Sthn Cmd UK'05 AG'09 CinC Med & IG Overseas Fces'10 Gen'14 CinC Central Force UK 5.8.14 MEF 11.3–10.15 d'45
6. Burns-Begg 22.9.11 PRO CO/417/499
   Col Robt BURNS-BEGG KC(Tvl'06) b10.3.73 ed Ed U 2Lt Instr Musketry 7VB A&SH 17.12.92 Scots Bar'95 SR Bar'98 Lt Cape Forces 10.99 T/DAAG Int WO 6.02–Legal Advsr Tvl Govt'03 & CO Northn MR'04–7 CofP Tvl'08–10 Res Commr S&NR 11–15 d1.1.18
7. PRO CO/417/506,572
8. CO/417/498 R H PALMER ANC Mongu NC Balovale AMag Lealui'21
9. CO/417/496,507 R V ROACH ANC Mongu
10. CO/417/510
11. CO/417/499,511 – John Henry VENNING Clk RNLB NERCS 24.6.07 NC Sesheke 1.4.13 AgMag Batoka 6.5.21 Mag & DC BH 2.8.24 Kasama 11.24 PC rtd 2.30 d post 1953

12. CO/417/511,525 Wallace to HC 18.6.12 CO/417/512
    J F KENNY DILLON NWRCS 6.06 Ag Collectr 4.07 NC 4.08 inv 8.5.15
13. NR Govt Gazette
14. Alderson *With the Mounted Infantry & the MFF 1896* pp27–31
15. *Nkhwazi* Vol 12 No.1 Apr 64 p16
16. Sillitoe *Cloak without Dagger* Chaps 2,3
17. PRO CO417/532
    Brig Gen H W GORDON DSO; OC 128 Fd Coy 8.15 CRE 56Div 2.16 CE I Corps 31.10.17
18. Programme PRO CAB/45/9
19. Edwards' report 8.9.13 PRO CO/417/526
    Maj Gen Sir Alfd Hamilton Mackenzie EDWARDS KBE'20 CB'00 MVO 04 bIndia 22.9.62
    s/o W E BengalCS ed Tonbridge Lt 3Seafth Hldrs; Lt KDG'83 Maj'96 5DG'97 CO ILH'00
    A Div SAC'01 Cmdt Tvl Vols'03 MS to Viceroy, Col AAG Nthn Cmd India'05 CC Met'06
    Commr BSAP & CCmdt Police & Vols S&NR arr 28.1.13 Cmdt Gen BG 1.2.16 Hon Maj
    Gen'19 L2.10.22–rtd 31.1.23
20. Joseph Cyrill BRUNDELL pd £60pa by NR Administration
21. Annual Report
22. GN64/1912 NRGovt Gaz, NRJ Vol V p549
23. Howe letter Rhodes House Library
24. *Nkhwazi* Vol.9 No.1 Oct'61 p19
25. PRO CO/417/570
26. *Cloak without Dagger* Ch 3, Sampson *So this was Lusakaas*, Central African Post Lusaka Jubillee
    Edn 31.7.63
    Sir Leander Starr JAMESON Bt(11) MB BS(L0nd) MRCS(Eng) LSA(Eng) b Scotld 53 to
    SA'78 Matabeleld'89 Ch Mag Mashonald 18.9.91–7.10.93,5.94 Admr SR 10.9.94 led raid into
    Tvl 12.95 imprisoned 15mths'96 PM Cape'04–8 Pres BSACo'13 d26.11.17
27. *Nkhwazi* Vol12 No.1 Apr 64 p16
28. PRO CO/417/526
29. Minutes BSACo Bd mtg 28.5.14 PRO CO/417/552
30. Quoted in *Story of the NRR* p33
31. 28.7.14 PRO CO/417/542
32. Edwards' report see note 19 above
33. *Nkhwazi* Vol 10 No.2 Dec 62 p33
34. Lucas *The Empire at War* OUP Vol IV
35. Official History, Military Operations East Africa Vol 1 p169

CHAPTER 6

On Active Service

The Strategic Situation

The threat to Northern Rhodesia in a war between the British Empire and Imperial Germany was clear. To the South West was German South West Africa, with a European population of about 15,000 and a garrison of nearly 2,000 regular German troops. These 'Schutztruppe' could be reinforced by 483 armed police and 1,723 reservists and other settlers, between 17 and 45 years of age, liable for call up.

To the North was German East Africa with a European population of 5,336, of whom some 3,500 were male adults, and a garrison of fourteen field companies of Schutztruppe, a total of 216 German officers and NCOs and 2,472 native askari. Each field company was a self sufficient unit, with two to four machine guns, and 250 carriers permanently attached. In addition there were 67 German police officers and 2,140 armed native police. At around seven million the native population of German East Africa was more or less equal to the combined populations of Northern Rhodesia, Nyasaland, British East Africa (Kenya), and Uganda.[1]

In Nyasaland were only four companies of the 1st King's African Rifles, just over 300 men, half of whom were on vacation leave. 2nd King's African Rifles had been disbanded for reasons of economy in 1911. Many of the discharged askari had enlisted in the German forces. No.5 Field Company at Massoko near Neu Langenburg, used British bugle calls and words of command.

The total strength of the King's African Rifles was 73 British officers and 2,175 askari. Its remaining seventeen companies were scattered from Zanzibar, just off the German coast, through Kenya to Uganda, with the greater part in the far north of those two territories, in Jubaland and Turkana, where operations against dissidents and interlopers were in progress or preparation.[2]

A German occupied Northern Rhodesia would have provided a valuable axis, including more than two hundred miles of rail, to link the two German territories. The threat must have appeared more theoretical than real, for in South Africa there was still a British garrison with four battalions of regular infantry with field artillery and two regiments of cavalry. South Africa had its own permanent force of five regiments of mounted riflemen with artillery, as well as the part-time Active Citizen Force. German South West Africa was hardly in a position to take the offensive and Britain's weakness in East Africa could soon be made up by reinforcements from India. The war might well, for all practical purposes, have passed Northern Rhodesia by.

However, all the British regulars, except coast artillery and engineers, sailed for Europe at the end of August 1914. The Union of South Africa had only come into being in 1912, ten short years after what was really a bitter civil war. Many of the Active Citizen Force units were newly raised and consisted of very young untrained volunteers and conscripts, with few officers or NCOs with any experience of formal military organisation. Some units consisted largely of Afrikaners with little love for Britain.

A few weeks after the outbreak of war Lieutenant Colonel S G Maritz, commanding a force under training in the Northern Cape, led his men willy nilly into German hands, to captivity or collaboration. On 15 September 1914, C F Beyers, Commandant General of the Active Citizen Force, resigned his commission. On 25 September a rebellion broke out amongst disaffected Boers along the Vaal River. This lasted until the end of the year, delaying the planned invasion of South West Africa. The threat to Livingstone from the South West thus became, and remained for nearly a year, a very real one.[3]

It was soon apparent that the war in the north would not be over by Christmas. On 20 September 1914 the cruiser Konigsberg sank HMS Pegasus in Zanzibar harbour, giving the Germans temporary naval superiority on the East Coast. The Konigsberg was soon bottled up in the Rufiji River never to emerge, but it was to provide the Schutztruppe with a welcome reinforcement in guns, machine guns, gunners, artificers and medical staff as well as riflemen of sorts.

In early November two brigades from India made an unsuccessful seaborne assault on Tanga. It was to take more than India could supply in men and leaders to conquer German East Africa. Although the governor, Dr Schnee, was all for peace, the German Army had the right man in the right place in the commander of the Schutztruppe, Lieutenant Colonel von Lettow Vorbeck. An officer of outstanding energy and ability, he was determined to divert the greatest possible part of the military resources of the British Empire from the main theatre of war, for as long as possible, and so make his contribution to final victory.[4]

Thus the Northern Rhodesia Police were to be no mere spectators in the Great War. They were to be among the first British Empire troops to enter German territory, and, thanks to von Lettow, to be among the last in action more than four years later, after a long and arduous campaign.

Preparations for War

On 30 July 1914 the Colonial Office in London sent out a warning telegram concerning the possibility of war with Germany. The Chief Commandant of Rhodesian Forces, Colonel Edwards, had contingency plans ready:

(a) A detachment, consisting of two officers, ten European rank and file from the British South Africa Police and fifty armed native police from Southern and

Northern Rhodesia, with two Maxims, was to be placed at the Victoria Falls Bridge.

(b) The strength of the Northern Rhodesia Police at Sesheke was to be brought up to one officer and twenty native non-commissioned officers and men. At Sesheke, across the Zambezi from the German post at Schuckmannsberg, there were, in peace, only an African corporal and five other district police.

(c) The mobile column of the Military Branch of the Northern Rhodesia Police at Livingstone was to be brought up to establishment.

(d) There was to be made available for concentration in Southern Rhodesia at forty-eight hours' notice, 200 European officers, non-commissioned officers and men of the British South Africa Police, 100 at Salisbury, and 100 at Bulawayo.

(e) The service companies of the Northern Rhodesia Police were to be brought up to establishment, and all discharges and leave stopped.

(f) The border of Northern Rhodesia between Abercorn and Fife was to be patrolled with a view to obtaining adequate intelligence – an officer and 20 men from Kasama were on patrol by 13 August.[5]

On 6 August A P Millar, Assistant Secretary of the British South Africa Company in London, wrote to the Secretary of State for the Colonies:

> I am desired by the Directors of the British South Africa Company to enquire whether, in view of the existence of a state of war between Great Britain and the German Empire, there are any special measures which the Secretary of State desires the Administrators of Southern and Northern Rhodesia to take with regard to enemy subjects or enemy property in the territories under their administration. My Directors would be glad to learn whether there are any special defensive steps which His Majesty's Government would desire to have taken in Rhodesia. Any instructions which the Secretary of State may have to give on the matter will be punctually complied with to the best of my Directors' ability.

The officers on leave in the UK, Captains James and Ingles and Lt Castle were ordered to return by a ship sailing on 15 August. They arrived at Livingstone on 10 September. Ingles had only been home for ten days.

On 9 August 1914 the Mobile Column, Northern Rhodesia Police, 3 officers and 80 men, left Livingstone for Kasama. Major H M Stennett, the Second in Command of the Force, who had been away on a tour of inspection in Barotseland hurried back and set out after them on 15 August to take command.[6]

On 10 August the members of the Northern Rhodesia Police guarding the Victoria Falls Bridge were joined by No.1 Troop, British South Africa Police, from Salisbury, under Lieutenant F T Stephens, No.4 Troop, from Bulawayo, under Lieutenant George Parson, a machine gun section, from the Depot at Salisbury, under Lieutenant A L Tribe, and forty native members of the BSAP. The combined force under the command of Major A E Capell DSO BSAP, later to command the 2nd Rhodesia Regiment in East Africa, patrolled both banks of the Zambezi and erected blockhouses for the defence of the bridge where a searchlight was installed. A few days after its arrival No.4 Troop BSAP was recalled to Bulawayo.[7]

On 11 August, by proclamation published in the Government Gazette, the Northern Rhodesia Police Force was declared to be 'On Active Service'. Guards were placed on all other bridges in the Territory. District Police were withdrawn from some stations to swell the ranks of the Military Branch. The export of food and warlike stores was made subject to control. 62 suspected enemy aliens were investigated. Nine Germans and two Austrians were sent to South Africa for internment. Four other Germans, five Austrians and eight German and Austrian Poles were also arrested, but were released after interrogation on giving money security for their good behaviour.[8]

On 25 August the High Commissioner telegraphed from South Africa that it was not the intention of His Majesty's Government to assume the offensive against the Caprivi Zipfel. The German post at Schuckmannsberg should only be occupied if, in the opinion of the local civil and military authorities, it was essential to do so in order to protect British interests in the neighbourhood. Both settlers and Africans were anxious to see some action taken. Lewanika hoped to be able to reassert his influence over the tribes in the Caprivi.[9]

On 26 August No.1 Troop BSAP was ordered some forty miles upstream to Kazungula. Here a fort was erected on the South Bank of the Zambezi and manned by Sergeant Duncombe[10] with two other NCOs and eight troopers. About forty miles further upstream at Sesheke, on the North Bank, were lieutenants Hornsby and Castle with a detachment of 25 Northern Rhodesia Police, only about three miles across the river from Schuckmannsberg.

South West Africa 1914–15

There were reports of a German force approaching from the South-West. On 13th September 1914 the High Commissioner gave permission for the entry into German territory. At 9 am on the 15th, four officers, 41 European and 37 native other ranks of the British South Africa Police, with three maxims, left camp at Victoria Falls and marched to Livingstone where they picked up wagons and supplies. They bivouacced for the night seven miles upstream on the Zambezi.[11]

On 21 September 1914 they reached Sesheke, having been joined en route by the garrison of Kazungula. At 9 am Lieutenant Stephens was sent across the river as a parlementaire, with Corporal J H L Vaughan BSAP as flag bearer, and Native Corporal-Bugler Kapambue BSANP. The party was met on the South Bank by a German native sentry and escorted to the fort at Schuckmannsberg. Here, after an hour's discussion, the German Resident, Herr von Frankenberg, agreed to surrender. By 2 pm Stephens and his companions were back at Sesheke.[12]

At 3 pm the 'Fall in' was sounded. A section was left to guard the camp while the rest of the British force marched to Susmann's Drift where boats had been assembled by the Northern Rhodesia Police. Lieutenant Hornsby led the way across the Zambezi. On landing he had to forcibly disarm a native sentry who refused to hand over his rifle. By 5 pm the whole force was ashore and began a two mile march down a very sandy path, arriving at Schuckmannsberg at sundown.

The troops were drawn up on the square to receive the German surrender. Sergeant Onyett BSAP[13] arrested Unteroffizier Fischer. This NCO and von Frankenberg were released on giving their parole. 28 native police, nearly all Subia by tribe, were placed under guard. Some mules, arms, ammunition, and other warlike stores and supplies were captured.

At 8am on 22 September the detachments of BSAP and NRP paraded facing the flagstaff in the presence of Mr Venning, the District Commissioner, Sesheke. Lieutenant Castle broke the Union Flag at the staff while Major Capell called for three cheers for His Majesty King George V. A few days later von Frankenberg and Fischer were sent via Livingstone to Bulawayo escorted by Corporal Cecil Gardiner BSAP (later Captain NRP), and Trooper A C Davey BSAP[14]. The native prisoners were allowed to return to their homes.

In October 1914 Captain E H L Salmon and Lieutenant G P Burton NRP reached Schuckmannsberg with the main body of B Company having left Mongu by barge on 26 September. They were followed by Captain J J O'Sullevan with most of C Company who had marched from Kasempa to entrain at Broken Hill.

In view of these reinforcements, bringing the NRP strength up to 5 officers, 4 white volunteers and 134 men with 2 Maxims, it was considered safe to withdraw the British South Africa Police, and wise to do so before the rains set in. They left Sesheke on 3 November, and, leaving Sergeant Duncombe and six men back at Kazungula, reached Livingstone on the eighth. On 10 November the BSAP detachment entrained for Bulawayo.

European scouts had been sent forward towards the Okavango River. They reported no cause to fear an enemy advance from the West. The enemy force reported earlier had raided into neutral Angola and captured and burnt the Portuguese fort at Libebe on 26 November. The telegraph had now been extended to Sesheke. It was decided that there was no need to continue to occupy Schuckmannsberg. It was deemed sufficient to man Sesheke with 30 African police under

Captain J. J. O'Sullevan with No. 2 Mobile Column, NRP, Caprivi Strip 1914
(Photo Imperial War Museum Q52373)

Lt Hornsby, as an observation post and intelligence base, together with the police post at Sioma Falls, a hundred miles to the North-West. O'Sullevan described the Caprivi Strip as, 'not of much use to anyone. It breeds the largest and most vindictive, venomous mosquitoes I have seen in a long experience of tropical Africa. In the wet season it is a swamp and unhealthy; in the dry weather the heat is terrific, whilst the sand is deep and uncomfortable to walk in.'[15]

The British Government wished there to be no suggestion that the Caprivi Strip might come under the administration of the BSA Company and Captain G V Eason of the Bechuanaland Police was appointed Special Commissioner with his headquarters at Kazungula. Sgt Legge of the Bechuanaland Police was to represent the occupying power at Schuckmannsberg. In the event the Administrator of Northern Rhodesia was quite relieved as this arrangement made it easier to insist that the Lozi should not revert to grazing their cattle south of the Zambezi which would have created an animal health problem.[16]

On 17 November Captain James and 30 men left Livingstone for Abercorn with 50,000 rounds of ammunition. On 25 November Lieutenant Colonel Hodson left Broken Hill to take command on the Northern Border. At Noon on 5th December 1914 Captain O'Sullevan received telegraphic instructions from the Chief Commandant of Rhodesian Forces, Colonel Edwards, to report as quickly as possible to Livingstone from where O'Sullevan was to lead his force, now known as the 2nd Mobile Column, to the border with German East Africa: 'The same day at 3 p.m. I left in a dug out paddled by natives. We did sixty miles on the Zambezi in a blinding thunderstorm, for the rains were on. We walked (two native soldiers and I) most of the other thirty miles through heavy mud and reported to Livingstone at 3 p.m. on the 6th. The column arrived ten days later, having had difficulty with the wagon transport'. At Livingstone the 2nd Mobile Column, 2 officers and 110 men with the 2 Maxims rested and refitted, receiving reinforcements of officers and 30 men, before entraining with the captured German mules for Sakania in the Belgian Congo, from where they were to march to Abercorn. The Military Branch presence at Livingstone was now only Major Byas, Captain Salmon and 30 men, mainly bandsmen. Recruits were now to be trained at Kasama.

A European defence force, the Northern Rhodesia Volunteer Force, had been authorised by a proclamation dated 24th October 1914. Part-time local defence units of approximately twenty five volunteers with one officer were formed at Livingstone, Mongu, Fort Jameson, Kafue and Lusaka. They assisted in guarding vulnerable points. On 13th November an order was gazetted for the inspection by the police of rifles held by the various rifle associations in the Territory. A mobile column of four officers and 120 white volunteers, the Northern Rhodesia Rifles, was mobilised at Broken Hill under Major Boyd A Cunninghame, and left to reinforce the police on the Northern Border on 22nd December 1914.[17]

By 11 December 1914 it was deemed safe to remove the guards from all bridges other than that at Victoria Falls and over the Kafue which remained until October 1916. In March 1915 there were further fears of an attack from South West Africa. The South African invasion of this German territory was now well under way and it was thought that some of the enemy might attempt to break out and make for East Africa.

Having been relieved on the Northern Border by Lieutenant Colonel Hodson, Major (Local Lieutenant Colonel) Stennett was now in command at Livingstone. The detachments of the Northern Rhodesia Police at Livingstone and Mongu were each strengthened by fifty men. On 4 February Capt James had been ordered back from Abercorn to command the Depot as Capt Salmon had been invalided to England. James was now sent to Barotseland. Supply depots were established between Livingstone and the Sioma Falls in order to expedite the despatch of a possible mobile column to prevent the enemy entering the Barotse Valley. Training of recruits at Livingstone recommenced and efforts were made for the first time for some years to recruit Africans from North-Western Rhodesia. Lewanika was asked to find 60 recruits. On 18 June the Commandant General ordered an officer and 60 men to be sent from Livingstone to reinforce the 20 at Sesheke. He recommended to the High Commissioner that the company at Mongu be sent down river to Sioma Falls and replaced at Mongu by the last officer and 30 men of 'C' Coy remaining at Kasempa.[18]

On 8 July 1915 news was received that the rebel, Maritz, and his men were moving along the Okavango River in the direction of Livingstone. Five officers and one hundred men of the British South Africa Police under Major A J Tomlinson, were sent up from Southern Rhodesia, with two Maxims and a $12\frac{1}{2}$ pounder field gun. The combined force was concentrated under Lieutenant Colonel Stennett at Sesheke until 9th August, when it was learnt that Maritz had entered Angola and given himself up. On 17 September eight Germans and one rebel Boer were captured by scouts of the Rhodesian Intelligence Department under Major Robert Gordon DSO, Commandant of the Northern Rhodesia Rifles. They had trailed them for eight days over 135 miles of wilderness and brought them in 700 miles to Livingstone. The main German forces in South West Africa had surrendered to General Botha at Tsumeb on 9 July and the south of Northern Rhodesia was to remain quiet for the rest of the war.[19]

The majority of the British South Africa Police detachment returned to Bulawayo but a few remained at Livingstone to join 'A' Special Reserve Company BSAP which was raised from whites in Southern Rhodesia on a cadre of regular police. Half this company left Livingstone for the north on 18 August 1915 via Broken Hill while the remainder left on 31 August to travel via Ndola. Staggered departures by different routes were essential to ensure sufficient carriers and food supplies after leaving the railhead.

Percy Wardroper, a former BSAP trooper working as clerk in the headquarters of the Northern Rhodesia Veterinary Department, was attached to the NRP as a temporary second lieutenant together with F G Smith of the Legal Department, who, as an NRVF sergeant had been with Stennett at Sesheke. They were ordered north by forced marches with Maj Byas and 75 African police now available at Livingstone, and detrained at Ndola on 27 August. For Wardroper this was the start of a career of nearly 21 years in the Force. Capt James, Lts B J Graham and L A Russell and another 75 men marched in from Barotseland to leave for the Northern Border on 3 September. On 23 August 1915 there were 1,103 Africans serving in the NRP.[20]

The British South Africa Company's report for the year ending 31 March 1915 gave the strength of the Northern Rhodesia Police then as 24 officers (including 4 temporary), 2 warrant officers, 6 British non-commissioned officers, 19 European volunteers, 4 British constables, 813 native NCOs and men, and 93 special native police i.e. men who had served in the NRP or its forerunners or the KAR who had come forward for war service. As the Commandant General wrote, the recent organisation into two divisions, Military and Civil Police, had undergone a severe test. The necessity for an adequate reserve for the Military Branch was much felt:

> On the outbreak of war, an experienced officer was specially detailed and despatched to Abercorn to endeavour to obtain the services of ex-police and get them to rejoin the corps for the period of the war. The result was that the services of some 125 ex-native police were obtained. The Awemba provided thirty-two, the remainder were from the districts around and the north-west of Kasama. Endeavours to obtain ex-police from the Angoni tribe failed entirely. . . To keep up the military portion to the strength required owing to the war, it has been necessary to denude the districts of civil police to an undesirable extent and to a degree almost incompatible with safety.

The military police could not undertake prolonged operations, with the consequent considerable wastage, without an adequate reserve. If this was to be the District police, arrangements would need to be made to replace those transferred. These recruits would have to be trained at the relevant district headquarters – for instance, Fort Jameson and Mongu – and not at Livingstone.

> Whether it is due to the low rate of pay in the police, and the ability of the Awemba and the Angoni to secure a higher rate elsewhere, it is clear that they are not coming forward in the same way as they did in the past. It is also clear by the results given above that the martial instincts of the latter are dying out. In these circumstances, it would appear desirable either to raise the pay of the police and so increase the inducement for these tribes to serve, or to tap other and so far untried sources of supply. . .
>
> The training of the military police has, thanks to the officers of the corps, proved the force equal to, if not better than, the native troops of the Germans. The officers are rewarded for their endeavours by the fact that their men have never failed to answer the demands made on them.
>
> The training of the district police, as a civil police force, is only just commencing, and has no doubt had a serious set-back owing to the war. There is no reason why this branch of the force should not with time and careful and patient training be as efficient as civil police, as their brothers have proved themselves to be useful and reliable soldiers.
>
> The branch of the Criminal Investigation Department, which was inaugurated early in the year, has clearly proved its value and, now that initial misunderstandings and misapprehensions connected with the scope of the duties of its officers and members have been removed, should increase in efficiency and importance year by year.[21]

Sub-Inspector Ferguson was still at Livingstone as Chief Immigration Officer and in charge of the CID and local town police. He was assisted there by D/Sgt Kirk. Sergeant-Major Mills had been withdrawn from Solwezi to Livingstone in January. Sergeant-Major Coote returned from leave on 7 September 1915 to take charge of the Town and District Police at Lusaka. Sergeant-Major Taylor was in charge at Broken Hill and another NCO was in charge of the civil police and responsible for immigration control at Ndola.

Despite the drain on civil police manpower there was no great reduction in prosecutions. 945 persons were brought before the courts by the police in 1915 and 844 convicted. Only 26 Europeans were convicted for Common Law offences compared with 48 in 1914. This may have been due to the high proportion of white males on active service inside and outside Northern Rhodesia, although the number of whites convicted for offences against local ordinances was 55, exactly the same as in 1914. Not included in police statistics was the conviction of the Force at the instance of the Veterinary Department for allowing transport oxen at Livingstone to stray in contravention of new regulations to prevent the spread of pleuro-pneumonia found in cattle from Barotseland. Apparently this was the first such summons. The fine was £25. For 25 years from 1922 the Force was to assist with the control of this disease by manning a cordon from Sesheke to the Kafue. 1916 was to show a marked increase in police work proper with 1203 prosecutions and 1085 convictions.[22]

Defensive in the North

At Bismarcksburg (Kasanga), on Lake Tanganyika, only thirty eight miles from Abercorn, the Germans had a strong fort which could easily be reinforced and supplied by steamer from Ujiji, the terminus of the newly completed Central Railway from Dar es Salaam, or from Usumbara at the northern end of the Lake. Usumbara, four hundred miles away from Bismarksburg, was the peace station of the 9th Field Company, and Ujiji, one hundred miles closer, the headquarters of the 6th. At the outbreak of war the Germans mounted guns on their steamers, giving them complete superiority on Lake Tanganyika.

Since 1912 there had been concern to prevent the spread of rinderpest from German East Africa. Fears that the enemy would use diseased cattle as a weapon of war proved groundless, however at the time of the outbreak of war there had been consternation in the Fife District over a proposal to increase hut tax there from 3/- to 5/- a year, which was thought unfair when trading in cattle was forbidden. The Anamwanga living in Northern Rhodesia were regarded as disloyal as the larger part of the tribe resided in German territory.[23]

The garrison of Abercorn was a mere 12 district police under the District Commissioner, C P Chesnaye. On hearing of the outbreak of war, Mr Chesnaye promptly arranged the evacuation of European women and children, and sent out patrols of settler volunteers and natives to watch the movements of the enemy. The news of the war took several days to reach the German posts near the border. There was no enemy action until late August 1914 when sporadic raids were commenced by native auxiliaries who cut the telegraph line between Abercorn and Fife. On 1 September a telegraphist went out escorted by 6 African police but found the line intact as far as Saisi.

At this time the main effort of the enemy's 5th Field Company from Neu Langenburg (Tukuyu) was against the King's African Rifles at Karonga. During

September 1914 Neu Langenburg was reinforced by elements of 2nd Field Company from Iringa and Ubena under Oberleutnant Falkenstein. Falkenstein with a small detachment based himself at Itaka from where he operated against Fife which was already threatened by Wahehe irregulars. The normal garrison at Fife was seven district police but eleven of the Native Commissioner's 16 messengers were former policemen who now rejoined for duty and a detachment of E Company was on the march from Fort Jameson.[24]

Ober-Arzt Westhofen, a medical officer, led a force of four Germans, 52 askari and 60 armed carriers, with a light gun, from Bismarksburg towards Abercorn. They were accompanied by some 250 irregulars who ravaged the countryside, looting, raping and again cutting the telegraph[25]. On 2 September two African civilians were killed and one wounded.

At Noon that day Lieutenant J J McCarthy had arrived from Kasama with reinforcements from D Company, Northern Rhodesia Police, bringing the garrison of Abercorn up to forty. McCarthy had only returned to the Territory from leave on 7 August 1914 and may have been the 'experienced officer' referred to in the annual report as having been despatched to Abercorn on the outbreak of war to persuade former policemen to rejoin. The gaol, the only suitable building, was put in a state of defence. On 3 September the piquet came in from the Kalambo River and reported having seen the enemy at Mwanga's Village, only 10 miles from Abercorn. On 5th September at 1030am the enemy was seen near the District Commissioner's house on the ridge a mile north of the prison. The next day an attack through thick bush was repulsed but sniping continued. On 7 September the enemy withdrew.

On 8 September a patrol ran into the enemy advanced guard returning to the hill. An urgent request for reinforcements had been sent to Kasama. Few of D Company remained there, but Major Stennett had just marched in with the Mobile Column from Livingstone. Though they were tired after their four week trek from Broken Hill, Stennett at once pushed on with 100 men, covering the ninety nine miles in sixty six hours to reach Abercorn at 3.30am on 9th September. At 6 am the enemy began to shell the town from the ridge to the north, hitting a corner of the gaol. 40 shells were fired killing privates Chasesa and Madi and somewhat demoralising their comrades. Nevertheless when the enemy attacked later in the day they were driven off.

On the 10th the enemy withdrew to the Lumi River. Lt McCarthy was sent out from Abercorn with 5 white volunteers, 80 African police and a Maxim. He attacked the enemy camp at dawn on 11th September and drove them back across the Border. The Germans admitted to 3 killed and 4 wounded in this operation[26]. One of McCarthy's party was 'One Eye' McGregor, the former native commissioner, disgraced in 1909, who had walked in from Elizabethville in the Belgian Congo to offer his services.

While Abercorn was under attack the prisoners evicted from the gaol had fetched water for the garrison by night. They volunteered, and were allowed, to carry McCarthy's machine gun to the Lumi and remained with it throughout the action. Afterwards they were told that at the end of the War the balance of their sentences would be remitted.[27]

Maxim & crew at Abercorn September 1914 with Dr. R. R. Murray NRMS &
the Postmaster (Photo Imperial War Museum Q17059)

During the rest of September patrolling by both sides continued. The telegraph
from Lake Tanganyika to Lake Nyasa was constantly cut. 100 Bemba tribesmen
were employed to protect it. It took seven to ten days for messages, carried by
runner and bicycle to the line of rail, to reach Livingstone until a new telegraph
line was completed to Abercorn from the South via Kasama.

On 19 September 20 former police and KAR came in from Kasama, but with
only seven rifles between them. On 22nd September a company of African troops
from the Belgian Congo, arrived at Abercorn under the command of Lieutenant
Leleux. He had set out on the 13th from Mpweto on Lake Mweru, and marched
via Mporokoso. Early in August the Belgians had offered a force of seven officers
and 225 askari. However no agreement had been reached by 9th September when
Mr G G P Lyons, the District Commissioner at Kawambwa, heard of the first
attack on Abercorn. On his own initiative Lyons sent a request for help to
Mpweto, the nearest Belgian post. On 26th September the rest of the 500 strong
Belgian 1st Battalion reached Abercorn under Major Olsen. On the march the
Belgians were hampered by a shortage of water. On hearing of their advance the
Northern Rhodesia natives took to the Bush, leaving the villages bare of supplies.
It is not known whether this was because of a particular fear of the Belgians or
the general uncertainty of war.[28]

Meanwhile the High Commissioner informed the Belgian Vice Governor-

General that he could not authorise offensive operations and suggested that the Belgians be withdrawn. However Stennett pointed out that Bismarcksburg had been reinforced and at his request the withdrawal was deferred. Major Stennett now assumed command of the combined Anglo–Belgian forces with the local rank of lieutenant colonel.

The attack on Abercorn had demonstrated the disadvantage to the Northern Rhodesia Police of their complete lack of artillery. The Belgians brought two guns with them, but steps were already being taken to make good the deficiency to the NRP. An old seven pounder mountain gun had been found in Southern Rhodesia. It was sent up by rail to Broken Hill with Corporal Jack Horton and three troopers of the British South Africa Police, all trained gunners, and 6 BSANP as ammunition numbers. Lieutenant Percy Sillitoe received a message to leave his civil police duties at Lusaka, meet the gun and crew at Broken Hill and bring them north. With the help of the District Commissioner, Sillitoe assembled 600 carriers with supplies for the 520 mile march to Abercorn. They were ready to set out when the train arrived and completed the trek in thirty days without a break, averaging 18 miles a day. The gun, when assembled, weighed 1,000 pounds. The barrel, its heaviest component, weighed 200lbs, requiring four porters with frequent reliefs. There were 600 rounds of black powder ammunition to be carried as well as kit, blankets, and food for the whole caravan. A carrier normally averaged 15 miles a day with a 60lb load and needed 2½lbs of meal a day.[29]

Sergeant Howe had joined Sillitoe at Lusaka from Mumbwa shortly before the war. He was also sent to the Front, marching up in charge of some 30 Africans who carried boxes of ·303 rifle ammunition on their heads. After a short time in the Field, Howe returned to civil police duty at Broken Hill.[30]

One Belgian officer and 40 native soldiers took post at Sumbu in Northern Rhodesia on the west shore of Lake Tanganyika. Orders were issued for the concentration of a second Belgian battalion at Mporokoso. Since it appeared that the forces already in place were sufficient for the defence of the Territory, the Vice Governor-General was informed that this new battalion would not be required. This led to a misunderstanding and he gave instructions for the Belgians at Abercorn to return to the Congo. The advance party had left when on 17 November 1914 German troops from Bismarcksburg under Leutnant Hasslacher, landed from two lake steamers at Kituta Bay, fourteen miles west of Abercorn. The enemy destroyed a small steamer laid up there, the Cecil Rhodes, and burnt the stores of the African Lakes Corporation. By this time Percy Sillitoe had arrived at Abercorn. He was sent in command of 50 Northern Rhodesia Police to link up with the departing Belgian company and engage the Germans at Kituta. They found the enemy gone and Sillitoe returned to Abercorn while the Belgians went on their way.

However the enemy had steamed on to Kasakalawe, another fourteen miles down the Lake. Here they had landed on 19th November and destroyed or removed a large quantity of telegraphic material. An allied force from Abercorn came up on the 20th and engaged the enemy. But the Germans were able to re-embark under cover of the guns of their steamers, one of which was armed with two 10 centimetre pieces. Corporal Horton and his gunners did not manage

Mr. C. J. Thorne, assistant superintendent, Mr. J. Thomson O.B.E., chairman of the museum sub-committee, the governor, Sir Evelyn Hone, & a captain of the Northern Rhodesia Regiment at the opening of the Military & Police Museum, Lusaka 2nd April 1962; 'Cpl Horton's seven pounder' in the foreground (Nkhwazi)

to catch up in time to bring their seven pounder into action. The enemy reported one German NCO and 2 askari wounded. 2 Belgian askari were killed and 10 wounded.[31]

On 26 November Major Olsen and his troops completed their departure from Abercorn, but the Battalion was ordered to halt at Mporokoso where it remained for fifty four days.

On 27 November Mr L A Wallace CMG, the Administrator of Northern Rhodesia, and Colonel Edwards, the Chief Commandant, arrived at Elisabethville, where they agreed the following arrangements with M Tombeur, Acting Vice Governor-General for Katanga:

1. That while Belgian troops were in Northern Rhodesia they would remain under the orders of the senior British officer.
2. That the British and Belgian troops would co-operate.

3. That the British guard the border from Abercorn to Fife, while the Belgians, based at Abercorn, watch and guard the southern shores of Lake Tanganyika.[32]

However until the return of the Belgian troops to Abercorn on 26 January 1915, Stennett was too weak to undertake more than the defence of Abercorn and Fife. The King's African Rifles at Karonga were in no better state. They had had to send a double company south to the Shire Highlands because of the rising of John Chilembwe and his 'Watchtower' disciples. The Germans had been reinforced and were able to raid freely, carrying off or destroying large quantities of telegraph wire and completely isolating Abercorn. With the captured wire the enemy were able to construct a line from Neu Langenburg to Iringa. The Bemba levies with 14 old rifles between them were ineffective and unpopular with local villagers and were paid off at the end of December.[33]

On 6 December 1914 Fife was attacked by a force of 200 to 300, with a 3 pdr gun and three machine guns. 80 shells were fired at 2,000 yards range, half of which hit the fort or fell inside. 102 Private Ndarama was killed by a shell which hit him in the back when he was going through a door. Captain Ingles, in command, was impressed by the steadiness of the African police under fire. The enemy retired in the evening.[34]

On 13 December the Commandant, Lieutenant Colonel F A Hodson arrived at Abercorn to take over command on the Northern Border. There were now 6 officers, and 14 white volunteers on the Border with 105 regular and 51 special police at Abercorn and 111 regulars and 41 specials at Fife. At Kasama were Lt Bremner and 26 African police including 9 District policemen and one special.[35]

On the evening of 27 December the night piquet at Fife reported that the enemy were returning. At 10 pm Lieutenant Cussans and Temporary Second Lieutenant R M Smith led a half company out to the old German position on the West Ridge. They made contact on the crest. After a 15 minute fire fight, Cussans saw he was about to be outflanked. He ordered his men to fix bayonets and charge. Under a hail of bullets at 30 yards range they cleared the ridge although Smith was seriously wounded in the back and Pte Kanyanla in the shoulder. One enemy askari was found dead and another was captured, wounded. The enemy withdrew in disorder and also evacuated a position on Tunduma Hill a mile north-east of Fife. Cussans was awarded the Military Cross. Captain Ingles praised the conduct of Lance Serjeant Dandalika and Lance Corporal Mpepera who were each promoted to full rank, and of Sjt Mitiminji. 329 Sjt Mitiminji was to be killed in action at Likassa in 1917.

On the morning of 27 January 1915 Cpl Bwanali arrived to relieve the night piquet on Tunduma Hill. He went forward alone to reconnoitre the crest and was shot through the spleen and killed by enemy scouts.

In the interests of British prestige among the tribes in the north-east it was imperative that the Germans should not be permitted to penetrate into Northern Rhodesia. The garrisons of Abercorn and Fife, some one hundred miles apart, were insufficient for the purpose. The return of the Belgians and the arrival of other reinforcements in February, enabled a new post to be established at Saisi, or Jericho Farm, about thirty miles east of Abercorn, where the valley of the River

Saisi offered the enemy a favourable line of approach. The post was sited on a rocky knoll in the angle between the Saisi and its tributary, the Mambala, overlooking the bridge by which the Stevenson Road crossed the Saisi a mile south of the Border.

On 3 February 1915 Major J J O'Sullevan marched into Abercorn with the 2nd Mobile Column. Northern Rhodesia Police. In his lecture to the African Society, O'Sullevan described how they had arrived by train at Sakania to be met by the Belgian Administrator, who provided 700 African porters to carry the column's supplies and rifle ammunition. The machine-guns and machine-gun ammunition were transported by the mules captured at Schuckmannsberg. Belgian officials accompanied the troops through Katanga to the Luapula River where the were met by a Northern Rhodesia native commissioner with fresh porters. Fresh relays of carriers took over the loads at Fort Rosebery and Luwingu. Rations were supplemented by an elephant and a few buck shot by Captain Fair but there was little time for hunting and the game was sheltered by the long grass of the rainy season.

> The journey from Sakania was a 430-mile walk, and it was done without a single officer or man falling out. This march was accomplished in heavy rains; swamps had to be corduroyed, and several bridges had to be erected daily to get the mules over the swollen rivers. The 430 miles were done in twenty days, averaging about twenty-one miles per day. After a few days at Abercorn, Colonel Hodson, who commanded the forces on the border, sent my column to Saisi, which is on the frontier.
>
> Here we occupied and fortified the farm buildings. We made a fort and trenches, and removed the long grass, trees, and other cover useful to the enemy. Then we proceeded to patrol, and were practically in touch with the Germans daily. The fact cannot be disguised that the enemy were considerably stronger than we were along the border line, and the same applies to the Nyasaland frontier.[36]

According to the Official History the ground at Saisi was mostly solid rock which, for lack of explosives, was broken by lighting fires on it and cooling it suddenly with water. Thus the outer ring of trenches was made round the central fort.[37]

On 2 February the Northern Rhodesia Rifles arrived at Kasama, under Major Boyd Cunninghame. After travelling fifty miles by rail north from Broken Hill to Kashitu, they had marched from there 320 miles in six weeks through the bush. With 16 ox-wagons and 30,000 lbs of supplies, they had cut the first wagon road, despite tsetse fly and exceptionally heavy rains, and with virtually no native assistance. At Kasama the column rested for two days. On 4 February they set out again to cover the last 100 miles to Abercorn, arriving on the 12th, to find the 17 man detachment from Fort Jameson waiting for them. The wagons were left behind and each volunteer now had a native porter to carry his kit. All 200 oxen died at Kasama.[38]

The main body of the Northern Rhodesia Rifles marched to Fife where Maj Cunninghame took over command from Capt H C Ingles NRP. The British were now in a position to act more offensively. Captain McCarthy with 35 NRP and a Belgian company was responsible for a 35 mile front on the Kalambo and Samfu rivers north of Abercorn. His police manned piquets at Muto, Mwangwa and Zombe and he was greatly assisted with information by Chief Zombe and his

Lungu. On 26th February McCarthy led a patrol which captured eleven Ruga Ruga, as the enemy's irregulars were known, having killed one. On 17th March he was camped 1½ miles from the Border near the headwaters of the Samfu with volunteers Jack Merry and R R Bacon, four African Police, a Belgian NCO and 60 Belgian askari, when they were attacked at dawn by five Europeans and 150 native Schutztruppe. The enemy were beaten off and driven back over the Border for the loss of Private Bacon and 3 Belgian askari killed. The Germans also lost one European and three Africans killed. Two Belgian natives were wounded and a German officer captured.[39]

In his reminiscences of the campaign von Lettow wrote that in the middle of March a force from the Bismarcksburg detachment was surprised in camp at Mount Kito by an Anglo-Belgian force. Its commander Reserve Lieutenant Haun was severely wounded and taken prisoner and several askari killed. Oberleutnant Aumann of the 2nd Field Company was detached from Falkenstein's command and based at Mbozi thirty miles from Fife. This detachment was expanded to company strength. The 5th Field Company remained at Ipyana at the head of Lake Nyasa. The detachment at Bismarcksburg was expanded to about company strength and in June 1915 was to become the 29th Field Company. In April three field companies were brought from Dar es Salaam and Kigoma.[40]

A German patrol was captured near Fife on 10 April and on 16 April, after a five and a half hour march from Fife, a section of 20 Northern Rhodesia Police under Lieutenant A B Bremner and 40 Rifles under Major Boyd Cunninghame took up a position on the escarpment thirty miles to the east from which they could observe an enemy position at Mwanengombe 2,000 feet below. At 3.a.m. a loyal headman guided the force down to the fort which was half a mile from the foot of the escarpment and 400 yards from the Songwe River, near the point where Northern Rhodesia, Nyasaland and German East Africa met. Lieutenant Stannus Irvine of the Rifles was first into the stockade at the head of his section and fell mortally wounded. Forty German askari and irregulars were killed or captured.[41]

On 24 April, 82 NRP and 50 Belgian troops under Lieutenant G P Burton NRP penetrated thirty four miles into German territory. They attacked a transport column near Mwazye, dispersing the escort and capturing many carriers and loads. Tracking the escort Burton found the path crossed some high hills. He sent out Cpls Geza and Mbenjere with 8 men each as flankers and advanced slowly. About 100 yards from the top of the pass heavy fire was opened from three sides and a scout, 1117 Private Fungulu was killed. Burton ordered his men to fix bayonets and charge and went forward with Lieutenant Maurice Daffarn NRP, a former officer of the 16th Lancers, who was mortally wounded by a bullet in the neck. Cpl Geza and LCpl Chikusi were promoted for their behaviour in this engagement. In the action some of the old NRP rifles jammed and one Martini Henry burst. This and similar incidents led the Commandant to request that the Force be rearmed as a matter of urgency.[42]

On the evening of 20 May Cpl Pondani reported to Capt McCarthy at Zombe that Germans were camped on the Samfu River 9 miles away. At 8pm McCarthy left camp with 12 NRP and 130 Belgian askari with 2 officers and Sous-Officier

Verscheuren. They bivouacced after seven miles and moved on at 4am to meet the piquet on the Samfu who reported that the enemy had left at 2.30am in the direction of Nondo on the Kalambo. On the march back to Zombe the column was fired on and the enemy charged within 20 yards before being driven off. Verscheuren was mortally wounded. 790 Sjt Mwombera NRP stood over him firing until joined by SSgt Borazi, the senior Belgian askari, when they carried the European out of action under heavy fire. Private Kambowe, and 2 Belgian askari were killed and 13 wounded, one of whom later died. The British South Africa Company awarded Sjt Mwombera £10, half to be paid on his return from the Front and half on discharge from the Force. In another engagement that month a 40 man patrol of the NRRifles was surprised at night and lost two killed and three wounded.[43]

Shortly before the outbreak of war a retired officer of the German Army, Major General Wahle, had arrived in German East Africa to visit his settler son. When war broke out the General offered his services to Colonel von Lettow Vorbeck who put him in command of the Lines of Communication. On 25th May 1915 Major General Wahle arrived at Bismarcksburg to take command of the troops on the Rhodesian and Nyasaland Border, bringing with him the 24th Field Company and half the 10th Schutzen Company of white settlers.

At Manika's Village in June a Belgian officer was in command of 25 of his askari and 5 NRP. Cpl Koza NRP, on piquet, found himself practically surrounded but successfully extricated his men to warn the officer. The enemy, three Germans and about 40 askari fled. Koza was promoted to Serjeant.[44]

On 20 June at Mwanakatwe, in German territory five miles north-east of Saisi, Major O'Sullevan scattered an enemy patrol, killing one German and wounding another together with 9 of their askari. Having received information that an enemy force was entrenched on Mosi Hill, 13 miles north-east of Saisi, he telegraphed to Colonel Hodson at Abercorn. At 10pm that night, Hodson set out with about 120 NRP and Belgians and the BSAP gun detachment. O'Sullevan took out a slightly smaller column from Saisi. Reaching the hill soon after dawn he found the Germans had also gone out on patrol. O'Sullevan drove out the enemy rear party and occupied their entrenchments which were well stocked with supplies. Later in the day he captured a supply convoy and 5 Ruga Ruga, 'some excellent wine, officers' kits, plans and maps.'

O'Sullevan and his men returned to the enemy position for the night. In his lecture to the African Society he said:

> Before daybreak we burnt and destroyed the camp. The enemy had laid an ambush on the road we came by, and also on two other roads; but we marched north into their territory, and away from the roads they suspected we should take, and by a circuitous route through the bush got home to Saisi, our rearguard only being attacked.

On 24 June Colonel Hodson had attempted to surprise a party of the enemy which retreated at his approach but later managed to capture another before returning to Saisi.[45]

Early on 28 June about 500 enemy troops, the 24th and 29th Field Companies and the half company of whites, together with more than 100 Ruga Ruga, surrounded Saisi in the early morning mist They woke the garrison by bombarding them with a field gun. Privates Wood and Holt were sent with a section to reinforce the piquet at the Saisi Bridge where Wood was killed. During most of the morning and part of the afternoon there was confused fighting over the open ground south and west of the fort. The allies' two small guns were put to good use. One of the BSAP troopers, John Farrar, is said to have signalled inners and outers to the Germans in contempt of their shooting! Cpl Africa NRP did good work by spotting enemy snipers. At 11 am the next day the enemy withdrew, their artillery having made no impression. Private Mulundi NRP was killed and LCpl Uleya and ptes Tamani and Buleya were dangerously wounded. Buleya died of his wounds. Pte Pemberton was slightly wounded in the hand and Maj O'Sullevan's leg was scraped by a ricochet. Six Belgian askari were wounded, while three Germans and four of their askari were killed, and two Germans and 22 askari wounded.

O'Sullevan described the aftermath of the battle:

> In the morning we opened some graves in German territory, but found only ammunition concealed and no bodies. The graves were neatly made, but the fact of some ammunition being found near them led to an order that they should be opened. Ammunition is heavy to carry about without carriers, so if one can hide it for use on another occasion in a grave, or anywhere else, the plan is worth trying.
>
> About this time we also captured large quantities of ammunition, camp equipment, tents, tables, rifles, and other things, which we made use of against the enemy. After this latter attack, in which Lieutenants Dickinson and Allport did extremely good work, it was considered that the enemy would make more serious attempts to occupy Rhodesia. Therefore my little garrison, consisting of Belgians and British native troops trenched hard daily, and I had some 300 native carriers working at the forts and entrenchments for three weeks.
>
> Some of these carriers were not satisfied with our design in trenches, and dug themselves in so thoroughly when the shelling started that the earth fell in and buried them. Along the border, engagements were usual almost daily, but most of it was fair open fighting, and not that disagreeable trench warfare.[46]

5,000 rounds of ammunition were found buried. On 2 July Col Hodson left Saisi for Fife with Lt Dickinson and 30 African police. Maj O'Sullevan's garrison was now lieutenants Burton and Allport, ptes Holt, Pemberton and Beattie, and 160 Africans of the Northern Rhodesia Police with 2 machine guns, Dr Harold and the BSAP mountain gun and crew of 10, and six Belgian officers, two Belgian NCOs, and 280 native other ranks of the Force Publique, with a 4.7 cm Nordenfelt gun and one machine gun.[47]

About 0330hrs on 25 July the enemy were reported by the piquet on the Saisi Bridge to be digging in west of the River. They opened fire on Pte Holt and his 20 African police and when this was returned abandoned an uncompleted trench. Before Dawn they had occupied Lobb's Farm about $1\frac{1}{2}$ miles west of O'Sullevan's position. By 0740 when the mist lifted and an enemy gun opened fire, they had pushed across the Saisi and the Mambala River investing Saisi.

In his lecture Maj O'Sullevan went on to describe the second siege:

Firing continued night and day for four days, and all our mules and oxen, besides the sheep and goats, upon which we depended for food, were killed by shrapnel.

On the fifth day the German officer in command sent in a parlementaire with a note asking me to surrender, and requesting that a fully qualified officer should be sent to discuss terms at the Saisi bridge, which was 900 yards from my position. He stated that he had captured a large convoy of supplies, and had also beaten back our relief forces, that he knew we had no water, and so on.

I replied that under no conditions whatever would we surrender, and also suggested that the next time he sent to us his soldiers might be instructed not to fire on the flag of truce as they had done on this occasion. He replied appologising for his men firing on the flag of truce, and giving as a reason the fact that a certain part of the field had failed to receive his orders to cease fire.

The officer who brought the note was quite au fait with what was going on. We told him of the German South-West African surrender, having heard of it but a few days before; but he knew all about it, and before we did. That night they attacked in force by the light of a fairly bright moon, and came on bravely, but they could not get actually to our trenches. The attacking force was about 1,500, a large majority being Europeans, but though we heard them encouraging the Arabs and native troops to charge, they could not get them to do so.

The attack lasted an hour and a half. Various ruses were adopted. They blew the Belgian 'cease fire' and ours also. Firing ceased for a few minutes on our side, but was resumed, and we afterwards ceased bugle calls.

My force had considerable difficulty to get water. It is a hot country, and you want a drink sometimes, and when you want it you want it badly; but they had trenched all round and close to the water supplies at Saisi, 900 yards away, and at the Molembo, 500 yards off. We therefore had to tie some water bottles together, pack them in grass, and steal down to the river at night a few yards at a time. When they started firing the water parties lay down, for firing at night is invariably high, and when firing ceased the water party stole water, but sometimes we could not get any, despite trying in both directions, and so we remained thirsty until the next night, for it was absolutely impossible to get any in the daytime.

Fighting went on until 3rd August, when the enemy had eaten up all their supplies and all ours. They then retired to Lake Tanganyika, embarked for Ujiji, and also marched off by road to Bismarcksburg and New Langenburg. We were too done up to go after them, and were relieved by a battalion of Belgian troops after a few days.

Major O'Sullevan was most appreciative of the assistance of the Belgians. The High Commissioner in his despatch said the enemy were believed to have been the 18th, 23rd, 24th and 29th Field Companies, four other companies and the Tabora and Rukwa contingents of 400 Europeans and 200 Arabs. German sources give Wahle's force at Saisi as being the four field companies identified in the High Commissioner's despatch, strengthened by whites of the 10th Schutzen Company, giving a total strength, exclusive of irregulars and armed carriers, of 89 Germans and 680 askari, with two 1873 pattern field guns and six machine guns – nearly half of his total strength on this front. General Northey in a report to the Secretary of State dated 19 June 1916 wrote that he had established that the attack on 28 June was by 120 Germans and 600 askari while for the siege from 23 July to 3 August the enemy deployed 150 Germans and 800 African troops of the 22nd,

23rd, 24th and 29th field companies. In his report O'Sullevan stated that in the assault on the fifth night the enemy never got nearer than the outer thorn hedge fron 200 to 60 yards from the allied trenches.

Casualties among the garrison were nineteen, all Africans, including five Belgian askari and four carriers killed, one native servant died of wounds, one Belgian soldier missing, and one Northern Rhodesia Police and three Belgian soldiers wounded. O'Sullevan reported enemy casualties as five whites and 28 askari killed. The German gun was put out of action by a direct hit on its muzzle from the BSAP 7pdr.[48]

On hearing that the telegraph line from Saisi was cut Col Hodson sent out a relief force from Abercorn under Maj de Koninck consisting of the rest of the Belgian 1st Battalion, 270 askari, with Captain C H Fair, Lts Dickinson and Ingpen and 50 Northern Rhodesia Police. They came into action against the investing force on 28 July. On the 29 July 34 of them broke through to join the beleaguered garrison losing Pte Malizani, killed. The Germans succeeded in holding off the remainder, but the threat of their presence must have contributed to Wahle's decision to lift the siege. He gave his reasons as the little effect produced by his artillery and his reluctance to risk an assault with the bayonet 'in view of the present situation in the Protectorate.' The general returned to Dar es Salaam with the 18th, 23rd and 24th Field Companies, leaving his artillery at Kigoma at the Lake Tanganyika end of the Central Railway.[49]

In *Gen Smuts' Campaign in East Africa* Brig-Gen J H V Crowe CB quoted captured German documents giving the strength and location of relevant units in August 1915 as:

18 FK Bismarcksburg	18 whites	152 Askari
23 FK Bismarcksburg	15 whites	178 Askari
24 FK Bismarcksburg	19 whites	222 Askari
29 FK Dar es Salaam	?	?
5 FK Neu Langenburg	57 whites	599 Askari
22 FK Neu Langenburg	16 whites	207 Askari
10 Schutzen K	65 whites	
2 FK Iringa	7 whites	171 askari
Bismarcksburg reserve staff & L of C post	12 whites	
Kigoma Detachment under Moewe	130 whites	

C W G Stuart MBE, then a corporal in the Northern Rhodesia Rifles working in the Orderly Room at Colonel Hodson's headquarters at Abercorn, wrote of these times:

> Our best intelligence border scout was Charlie Sell, who had a deep hole in his forehead caused by a Matabele bullet during the rebellion. He had been carried out of that fight by Captain Chesnaye of the Bechuanaland Border Police. Several years later, when Chesnaye was District Commissioner at Abercorn, he gave Sell six months for poaching elephant!

On 26 May 1917 Scout Sergeant-Major Sell of the Northern Rhodesia Police was to be awarded the Distinguished Conduct Medal for performing many dangerous reconnaissances. On one occasion, with a small party of scouts, he held up and inflicted many casualties on an enemy advance guard, himself bringing a wounded man out of action. His adventurous life ended when he died of wounds on 29 May 1918.

Stuart went on to say that Capt Fair was the crack shot of the force. He would lie on top of an anthill while a dozen or more askari would hand him their Martini-Enfields to fire, meanwhile struggling to eject the cartridge cases by hooking the trigger guard on a tree stump. Some of the former district police were still armed with the .450 Martini-Henry, but soon all those at the front were to be re-armed with the Long Magazine Lee Enfield, and before the end of the war with the SMLE, mainly the converted Mark IV, a cut down Long Lee Enfield.

With the telegraph frequently out of action, communications were much dependent on the heliograph, which only Jack Bisset, the postmaster at Abercorn, Tpr Farrar BSAP at Saisi, and Corporal Kituta and his African signallers of the NRP, could operate.[50]

Stuart suggests that Corporal Africa won the DCM in 1915 for handcuffing a German, tieing up several enemy askari with his blanket, and marching them all in as prisoners. The award of the Military Medal to 106 Sergeant Africa was announced in the London Gazette of 12 March 1918. During the siege 452 Colour Sergeant Zidana of 'C' Coy carried orders under fire. It was 399 Cpl Chikusi and 545 Piyo of the same company who crept down to the river and filled 20 water bottles each at a time under fire. All three were mentioned in despatches for their conduct at Saisi as were Lieutenant E G Dickinson, Second Lieutenant H Allport, and 53 Sergeant Geza. 367 Sgt Gwiranipakamwa, described by Col Hodson as a splendid NCO, and 126 Pte Malinguka were also commended. O'Sullevan was promoted to the substantive rank of Major and awarded the DSO in recognition of his conduct at Saisi. Prior to the action in June he had been suffering from Periostitis. The injury to his leg failed to heal. O'Sullevan was invalided in September 1915, his career in Northern Rhodesia at an end.

The successful defence of Saisi did much to enhance allied prestige in the area and is said to have stimulated recruiting in Rhodesia and South Africa, especially among troops returning from South West Africa for demobilisation. The border was now undoubtedly secure. When news that the Belgian 1st Battalion had left Abercorn for the relief of Saisi reached Major Olsen on 1 August, he immediately set out from Mpweto with the 3rd Battalion to replace it. At the end of August the 3rd Battalion took over at Saisi from the 1st which returned to Abercorn.

On 4 October 1915 'A' Special Reserve Company of the British South Africa Police marched into Abercorn 160 strong under Major J S Ingham. A $12\frac{1}{2}$ pounder gun followed via Kashitu. On 18 October 'B' Special Reserve Company BSAP marched into Fife from Karonga, having evaded an enemy ambush at Mwembe. Formed at Salisbury, 131 strong, under Captain Walter Baxendale, Southern Rhodesia Volunteers, this company had travelled by rail and water via Beira and Zomba. Major R E Murray DCM BSAP arrived as overall commander of both BSAP companies, The Southern Rhodesia Column. Having been Col Edwards' staff officer since 1913, Murray had acted as staff officer to Lt Col Stennett on the South-Western Border in July and was now appointed Col Hodson's Chief Staff Officer.[51]

On 19 October a party of scouts was fired on $7\frac{1}{2}$ miles from Fife and one wounded. Capt Ingles left at 7pm with 50 NRP under Lt Sillitoe, 25 NRRifles under Capt Molyneux and 25 BSAP under Lt Hendrie SRV. They could not find the enemy but as a result of further information Maj Baxendale was sent out at 10.30 am on 20 October along the Stephenson Road. Ingles now located the enemy, 200–300 strong with 2 machine guns, north of Mbesima Village. Unfortunately Baxendale got lost and by the time Murray came up with another 50 NRP and machine guns from Fife the enemy had gone.[52]

On 22 October a German patrol attacked Lundula's Village, killing three men and two women and wounding a child. A patrol of six African police and three scouts under the gallant Sjt Mwombera engaged the enemy four of whose askari were killed, two by Pte Ndawani, but LCpl Bwanamakoa was shot dead.[53]

The Belgians now required the return of their troops to the Congo. They planned to launch an offensive north of Lake Tanganyika to take Ruanda-Urundi. Despite the arrival of the two BSAP companies, it was decided that Saisi could not be held without the Belgians. 'A' Company BSAP covered the withdrawal from Saisi on 29 October. The Belgian 3rd Battalion then left Northern Rhodesia. The 1st Battalion followed on 3 November. A detachment of the Northern Rhodesia Police replaced the Belgians at Sumbu, but some Belgian troops remained in reserve at Mporokoso. The NRP at Abercorn were now reorganised as 'A' and 'S' companies and those at Fife as 'D' and 'Q'.[54]

At 5.15am on 6 November the outlyng piquet was forced to retire on Zombe. This post, 9 miles north-east of Abercorn was garrisoned by 7 whites and 90 African police with one machine gun. Two enemy Maxim guns opened fire from the ridge to the west from where a skirmishing line tried to advance while another party worked round to the North-East. After $1\frac{1}{2}$ hours the enemy, some 200 strong, gave up and withdrew. On 21 December a patrol from Abercorn of 80 BSAP and 108 NRP under Maj Ingham, met a patrol from Fife and they remained together until 28 December. While returning Ingham became aware on 29 December of a force of some 200 of the enemy at Saisi. Being short of rations Ingham avoided an engagement. The enemy burnt Saisi.[55]

On 22 December a German force took up position at Sinyanta Hill, Nakonde, some $32\frac{1}{2}$ miles from Fife, to intercept a convoy. Captain Baxendale went out to engage them with 28 Northern Rhodesia Police, 36 BSAP and a machine gun. After two hours he was joined by Lieutenant C E Mills NRRifles with 21 Europeans and 16 African police from the convoy escort. On learning that the convoy was safely into Fife, the enemy withdrew. Seven pools of blood were found in their position. The British returned to Fife having suffered two BSAP wounded.[56]

As a Christmas gift the Queen Mary's Needlework Guild in the United Kingdom sent out 800 warm vests for the British South Africa Company's native troops.[57]

On 28 January 1916 Captain Harry Ingles with a half company of the Northern Rhodesia Police, fifty British South Africa Police, and two machine guns drove off a patrol of two Germans and 20 askari and Ruga Ruga near Ikomba, 70 miles south east of Abercorn. On 29th January Lieutenant G A Debenham NRP with his advance party of 15 men, following the enemy spoor, caught up with them crossing a dambo 1,000 yards wide and immediately engaged them, killing seven and pinning down the rest. After Ingles and the main force had come up five unwounded enemy surrendered with three badly wounded. On the British side Sergeant Anderson was slightly wounded. Ingles went on to meet Maj Murray with a patrol from Abercorn. L/Sgt Changamasase distinguished himself in this action.[58]

Debenham, a pre-war BSAP trooper, was awarded the Military Cross. By 9 April 1918 he was a captain commanding a company of Northern Rhodesian Bemba in the 2nd Battalion, 1st King's African Rifles and won the DSO for routing an enemy force on the Lureko River in Portuguese East Africa. On 5 May 1918 Debenham and his company surprised the 21st Field Company in camp bayoneting four and setting fire to their huts. Counter-attacked by four companies led by von Lettow himself, Debenham retired supported by the company commanded by Maj J H L Vaughan, who as a BSAP corporal had carried the flag of truce at Schuckmannsburg. Together they drew the enemy onto the position where the rest of the battalion was entrenched. Vaughan was killed in desperate fighting before the enemy withdrew.[59]

Annex to Chapter 6

OFFICERS & BRITISH OTHER RANKS OF THE NORTHERN RHODESIA POLICE WHO JOINED BETWEEN 6 AUGUST 1914 & MAY 1916

LANCASTER Duncan Gordon MBE FRZS b.Clifton 24.5.93 ed Shoreham GS, Rfn 16London TF'09 Tpr BSAP 10.10 Const NRP 10.14 rsgnd'21 Labour recruiter BH Mine, Elephant Hunter, Sp Const NRP Cattle Cordon 24.4.24 Ag3/Sgt 1.4.25 3/Sgt 1.11.26 Insp'31 seconded Elephant Control Offr'35 Game Dept'42, pub *A Check List of Mammals in NR* Rtd'52 d.15.10.58

INGPEN Ernest/Ed? Lucien s/o KC ed City & Guilds Cllge ULOTC Tpr BSAP'12 2Lt NRP 6.10.14 Lt 6.8.15 dow Bismarcksburg 11.6.16

OSBORNE Ronald Alexdr PS to Admr NER'03 NC, Int Offr Abercorn att'd NRP as Capt 10.14(GN84/14)

SMITH Capt Ronald Maskelyne OBE'19; NR'08 Tpt Rdr Farmr Mpanda Rcruitg fr Mines att as 2Lt 10.14 T/Lt 1.3.15 Sick Lve 20.4–20.7.15 Int, Tpt, Fmr Sunsu Mtn, Tpt Contractor, Prop Crested Crane, Mpika d Kasulu 1.2.54

SMITH Lionel Ross bro of abve NR'11 Cattle Fmr Saisi Vol NRP by 14.9.14 T/2Lt 10.14 Wagon Tpt released by 18 guided 1/4 KAR to Kasama 11.18 d Abercorn 2.57

NORTON Michael Vol A'corn by 8.9.14

BARNSHAW A L Telegraphist A'corn

EDWARDS F A i/c Bemba levy 19.11.14

BACON W R vol'14 kia 17.3.15

DAFFARN Maurice b.16.2.88 s/o W G D 14 Campden Hill Sq Ken & Valewood Haslemere ed Winchstr Trinity 2Lt 16L 3.11.09 rsgnd 7.2.12 NRGS 9.12 ANC 14 T/2Lt NRP 17.12.14 dow24.4.15

DEBENHAM Gerald Anthony DSO MC(12.9.17) BSAP 27.5.13 Instr NRVF Lstone T/2Lt NRP 1.2.15 Adjt 6.16 Capt Norfolk R 2/1KAR'18 NRP'19

SELL Chas Wm DCM(26.5.17) b'77 s/o J H S Jo'bg Tpr BFF'96 No.1 Div BSAP Mafekg
    w27.3.00 NRP Scout Sgt-Maj dow29.5.18
SINCLAIR Scout Norman k by lion he killed with Bowie knife Angola 9.5.15
KEYS W F Scout
HARVEYSON Thos Cecil 1442 BSAP'10 Const NRP 4.4–6.9.15
RUSSELL Lawrence Arnold NRGS 14.9.12 ANC T/2Lt 17.6.15 T/Capt OC F Coy'17 NC
    15.7.18 OC B Coy'18 AgMag Kafue 13.3.22 Sesheke'24 PC Eastn'33 rtd'39
LATHAM Geoffrey Chitty CdeG b Shanghai 15.3.87 s/o barrister Folkestne ed Winchstr
    Magdalen NRGS 14.10.10 Ag PS to Admr 11.10 Nat Dept 5.11 ANC Mweu-Luapula att NRP
    T/2Lt 18.8.15 AMag 8.7.16 OC A Coy'17 DCensus 21 NC AgInsp Edn'24 Ag Ch Sec rtd
    DDAfrican Educational Films'36
HENNIKER-GOTLEY Anthony Lefroy b87 ed Tonbridge, Oxfd Capt Rugby Engld, probtnr
    SRCS 11.10 West Ashby Vicarage Lincs NRCS ANC Kanunda Petauke 26.11.14 A'corn
    11.5.15 NRP T/2Lt 18.8.15 Political Offr Kasanga 11.1.17 Tanganyika CS
SMITH Frederic Gordon (ltr GORDON-SMITH) KC(Trin'33) b23.4.86 s/o Solr, Dudley Worcs,
    ed Bromsgrove, Solr 09 Legal Dept NR'13 NRVF Sgt att NRP 7.15 T/2Lt NRP 18.8.15 inv
    30.8.17 Bar Innr Temple'21 Asst Legal Advsr & PP NR 10.12.20 AsstAG'24 Solr Gen
    Kenya'26 AG NR 27 AG Trinidad'32 Judge Malaya'35 CJ Pal'41 rtd'44 Chmn Appeals
    Tribunal Eng & Wales'45 T/Judge S'pore'48
WARDROPER Percy Redesdale OBE(Civ 34) KPM(LG30.4.29) b92 BSAP'12 Clk NR Vet Dept
    26.11.14 NRP T/2Lt 18.8.15 Lt 12.1.17 Adjt T/Capt 1.2.18 Hon Capt MBE(Mil) 19 Adjt'20–
    A/Capt OC T&DP 1.12.26 Capt 1.1.27 & C/Insp Prisons 1.4.27 CofP'29 Capt NR Cricket v
    MCC 12.30 L26.2–rtd6.4.36
CASTOR Brian Kenneth 1RR NRGS 7.8.15 Lt NRP Adjt NRVF 27.8.15 T/Capt OC D Coy
    10.18 OC T&D BH 22.8.24–5.1.25 lve7.8–rtd 12.10.25 Sec Essex CCC
GRIFFIN Arthur Wilfrid Michael Stewart 'Chilli' MC'19 ed Harrow Camb, Cricket fr Mx:
    NWRGS 4.6.06 NC Gwembe 8.10 Rfn NRRifles 12.14 Att NRP T/2Lt 8.9.15 NC Gwembe
    19 A/Legal Advsr & PP 10.1.21 Ag Mag Barotse Dist 9.21 A/Mag 1.4.21 PC rtd'35
PRESTON W V L 1592 BSAP'12 Armr Sgt NRP 20.9.15
HUSBANDS Wm T s/o John 6 Waldeck Rd Carringtn Notts, Tpr BSAP'11 Cpl AgWO T/2Lt
    NRP Oi/c Sups NBdr Kasama Base Depot 1.2.16 T/Capt MID* d flu Kasama 24.12.18 age 31
MARTIN Harold Fredk 1612 Tpr BSAP 8.12 Cpl 12.14 att NRRif 12.14 T/2Lt NRP Lstone to
    Front 23.2.16 s lve11.16–relinq comm 18.3.17 rtnd to duty BSAP Bwayo

Notes

1. Haupt, *Die Deutsche Schutztruppe 1889–1918* p76,96, Offical History East Africa Vol 1 pp10–
    11, precise figures vary.
2. *History KAR* p262,265 Appendix E gives 62 Offrs, 2 BNCOs, 2,319 askari
3. Gen Salomon Gerhardus MARITZ to Madagascar'02 GSWA tk German citizenshp svd Herero
    Rebelln'06 Butcher Braamfontein'10 Tvl Police Jo'burg SAPermanent Force Lt Col Dist Staff
    Offr NWCape 11.11.12 OC Force B deserted 9.10.14 rtnd SA'23 3Yrs imprsnmnt relsd'24
    d1940 RTA
    Gen Christian Fredk BEYERS b Cape'79 Lawyer Pretoria'99 Chair Peace Conf'02 Spkr Tvl
    Parlt'06 Comdt Gen ACF 4.12 rsgnd 15.9.14 Rebel drnd Vaal 9.12.14
4. Paul von LETTOW VORBECK b20.3.70 Lt Arty China'00 SWA Herero Campaign'04 CO 2
    Marine Inf Bn Wilhelmshafen OC Schutztruppe Cameroon to GEA 1.14 Oberst, Gen-Maj'18
    rtd 5.20 d9.3.64
5. Telegram Wallace PRO CO/417/554, *Story NRR* p27
6. Exec Cttee BSACo minutes 13.8.14 PRO CO/417/554
7. Maj Francis Trant STEPHENS OBE(LG30.5.19) MC(LG4.6.17) BSAP 30.10.03 A Coy BSAP
    15 SO SRC 4.16–inv 11.16 Capt att KAR T/Maj, Ch Commr Police & Prisons Nyasald 20
    Lt Col Geo PARSON DSO*(LG26.4.& 28.12.17) BSAP OC A Coy BSAP'15 SO SRC, SO
    BSAP post war

Capt Alden Lewis TRIBE BSAP 2RR'15 att 2/3 KAR kia 17.11.17

Col Algernon Essex CAPELL CBE'24 DSO'00 CdeG b Tenenhall nr Wolverhamptn 1.11.69 ed Felsted Tpr CMR 7.89 Lt Bethune's MI 10.99 Capt'00 SAC 12.00 Dist Cmdt Swazild Maj 6.02 Deputy Div Cmdt'04 CSO'04 2i/c ORC 3.07 Cmdt ORC 3.08 A/DC Dagoretti BEA 12.08 Ch of Police Grenada 9.10 Maj BSAP 26.7.13 Lt Col CO 2 RR'15 Commr BSAP & Cmdt SRFces 1.4.23–rtd 11.2.26

8. NC reports CO/417/603, *Story NRR* p27.

9. Wallace 22.9.14 PRO CO/417/555

10. No.667 Sgt Geo Fredk DUNCOMBE BSAP

11. The occupation of Schuckmannsberg was described in the SR Defence Journal quoted by Harding in *Frontier Patrols* and *Story NRR* pp49–51. Bruce Cazel's article 'The BSAP Issue of the "1914–1915 Star"' in *The Miscellany of Honours* (Orders & Medals Research Society) 1987 includes a roll of (white) BSAP involved

12. Jas Henry Lionel VAUGHAN CdeG Tpr BSAP 13 Cpl Lt 1RR 12.11.14–31.7.15 NRRifles; 2/1 KAR T/Maj kia 5.5.18 PEA

13. Harry Thos ONYETT MC'17 Tpr BSAP'09 Lt A Coy BSAP'16 Capt Int Offr SR'19 Maj i/c B'wayo Dist by 39 d60

14. 1669 Sgt Albt Chas DAVEY Tpr BSAP'13 SRC MID(LG25.9.17) inv to Salisby 22.12.17

15. Lecture R African Soc 17.2.16 quoted in *Story of the NRR* pp53–4

16. PRO CO/417/443
Harry Vernon EASON BP S/Insp L/Capt Sp Commr Caprivi 11.14 Acct Bechuanald'15 Financial Sec d Simonstown 19.10.20

17. PRO CO/417/542
Boyd Alex CUNNINGHAME Capt Hon Maj 4A&SH Tpt rider Benguela–Kambove, bred cattle Makeni, Maj NRRifles 14.12.14 (GN12/14) inv24.9.15 d Typhoid Elizabethville 16.3.17

18. Admr 15.3.15 PRO CO/417/570 Cmdt Gen to HC 18.6.15 417/571

19. *Story NRR* p29
Lt Col Alfd Jas TOMLINSON, MMP'94 S/Insp Jameson Rd Lt MRF'96 BSAP to Front SA 4.00 Maj Lt Col CO RNR 5.16–31.3.17 Ag Commr BSAP 12.2–12.5.26
Maj Robt GORDON CMG'19 DSO'00 OBE'18 b22.12.66 ed Brisbane GS Hobart HS Lt QnsldMI att 1Gordons Tirah 97–8 1Qnsld Contgt SA tfrd 1 Gordons'00 OC MI Coy w1.01 Hon Capt Fmr Kafue OC NRRifles 14.12.14 (GN112/14) Remnt Offr EA 2.16 Chmn B'wayo Club 33–5 d9.9.44 B'wayo
Gen Louis BOTHA bNatal 27.6.62 to Vryheid Tvl'84 Feld Kornet'94 Volksraad'98 Cmdt Gen Tvl 00–2 Ch MinstrTvl'06 PM SA 31.5.10 d27.8.19

20. Admr 23.8.15 PRO CO/417/572

21. Quoted *Story NRR* pp33–4

22. Annual Report 9.5.24 PRO CO/799/1 gives figures 1914–23, Smith *Vet in Africa* p222

23. PRO CO/417/543

24. NC's reports PRO CO/417/603
Hauptmann FALKENSTEIN OberLeutnt Schutztruppe 16.6.11 2i/c 2FK Iringa by 31.7.14 OC Neu Langenburg 5FK & L FK by 5.3.16 OC $\frac{1}{2}$12FK & Songea Det by 1.9.16 kia Songea 12.11.16

25. Official History p176 Annual Report PRO CO/417/583
Ober-Arzt Dr WESTHOFEN Asst Arzt Schutztruppe 22.4.12

26. Ge Telegram, papers Col G F Philips, Liddle Collection.

27. Stennett 20.9.14 PRO CO/417/555, Chesnaye 31.12.14 417/570

28. Official History p178, Chesnaye 31.12.14 PRO CO/417/570 indicates adequate supplies provided by NR Native Commrs, HC Tel 11.11.14 CO/417/543
Geo Graham Percy LYONS MBE Tpr BSAP 96 NERGS 1.8.98 A/Mag Mweru 05 Kalunkwishi 07 Mag 23.10.11 NC Kawambwa DC Mweru-Luapula RM Barotseld 16–24
Brig Gen F V OLSEN b Denmark Maj COS & OC Tps Katanga

29. *Cloak without Dagger* pp29–31, Porters PRO CAB/45/14
1711 Jack HORTON MSM(LG4.2.19) Tpr BSAP'13 MG Sgt A/CSM RNR
1866 Tpr John FARRAR BSAP 7.14 inv Salisby 17.3.16

2Lt Edwin HADATH MSM(LG15.2.18) 1709 Tpr BSAP'13 Cpl MID LG13.7,25.9.17 T/2Lt 1710 Sgt John Matthew HENNESSEY MSM(24.2.19) Tpr BSAP'13

30. Howe Rhodes House Library
31. GE Telegram Philips papers Liddle Collection, Stennett 19.11.14 PRO CO/417/555 Chesnaye 31.12.14 417/570 Annual Rpt 417/583
32. *Story NRR* p31
33. KAR p288 PRO CO/417/570
34. Ingles 10.12.14 PRO CO/417/555 28.12.14 417/570
35. Cmdt 18.1.15 CO/417/570
36. African Society Journal Apr'16 quoted in *Story NRR* pp54–537
37. Official History p183
38. Article re NRRifles NRJ, Cmdt Gen Annual rpt PRO CO/417/583
39. Wallace 30.3.15 PRO CO/417/570,571
40. Hauptmann AUMANN Oberleut Schutztruppe 19.6.12 2FK Cmd Ubena Det 8.14 Hauptmn OC L Coy by 5.16 Cdg Abteilung Aumann (22 & L coys) 17
41. Cunninghame 19.4.15 PRO CO/417/571 NRRifles NRJ
Chas E Stannus IRVINE s/o Col Irvine DL of Killedeas Co Fermanagh ed TCD Engr svd SA emp Rhod Rys
42. Hodson 30.4.15 PRO CO/417/571
43. Hodson 28.5.15 CO/417/571,576,583
44. General-Major WAHLE Saxon Army arr GEA 2.8.14 OC LofC GEA 8.14 Sthn & Westn areas 25.5.15 Westbefehlshaber s pw Songea 18.10.18 PRO CO/417/572
45. Hodson 5.7.15 PRO CO/417/572 Official History p184 n.1
46. O'Sullevan lecture, Hodson 5.7.15 CO/417/572,571.561
No.121 D A WOOD NRRifles fm Katanga previously a volunteer with Belgian forces; 122 E C HOLT; 103 L PEMBERTON fm Ft Jameson mentioned in despatches by HCommr 10.3.17 for 'setting a fine example to native troops' to SRC
47. Official Hist p183 n.2 PRO CO/417/572
Dr James Murphy HAROLD BA MB BCH BAO b29.10.82 Kerry s/o Surgn ed TCD, Ships Sgn'06 P&O'07 Leicester Poor Law Infirmy 10.08 Hse Sgn Grimsby Hosp 11.4.10–SA 9.11 MO Union Miniere Katanga'14 Sgt NRRifles 15.2.15 Sgn Capt 22.7.15 Capt NRMC 8.10.17–31.3.25 NRMS'19 MO FJ d Cape Town 6.11.25
48. Official History p185 PRO CO/417/562,572 Norforce War Diary PRO WO/95/5229; HC's despatch *Nkhwazi* Vol 12 No.1 Apr 64 pp22–6
49. Official History p186 n.2
50. *Story NRR* pp51–3 – Chas Wm Geo STUART MBE ed Bancroft's Sch & Aberdn GS, Fm Asst SA; 8 yrs Westminster Estates NR; NRRif'14 ORCpl A'corn'15 2Lt Carrier Tpt Murray's Colm 4.16 Lt relinq commission 24.4.19
Jack BISSET NR Post & Telegraphs Postmr Abercorn rsgnd 10.12.23
51. PRO CO/417/562 Murray 22.10.15 417/583
Maj John Seagar INGHAM b70 2Lt 4Glos Militia 11.89 Depot Glos 5.90–93 MMP 14.5.94 Cpl D Tp Jameson Rd Lt BSAP svd SA 01–2 Capt Dist Supt Gwelo SR 9.17
Maj Walter BAXENDALE Lt SRV 18.8.99 Mayor Bwayo'12 Lt Col SRV Westn Div Capt BSAP'15 Maj kia22.10.16
Col Ronald Ernest MURRAY DSO*17 DCM'00 CdeG bGrahamstown Tpr CMR'94 BSAP 7.99 Cpl'00 RSM Matabeleld Div 5.01 Lt 12.01 Dist Supt Bwayo Capt SO to Ch Cmdt'13 inv 27.1.18 d NHayling 29.6.20
52. Murray 23.10.15 PRO CO/417/563
Capt Cyril Frank MOLYNEUX SALH Capt'02 NC Magoye Lt NRRif'14 Capt OC Mob Colm 11.15 NC Kasempa'16 Feira'17 DC Namwala 11.7.19 NC Ndola & Dist Cmdt NRVF 21 PC rtd 32
HENDRIE, Two brothers, Andrew Geo 'Acid Guts' Capt MC(LG4.6.17) & John Boyse Hendrie MID(LG25.9.17) joined B Coy BSAP as lts fm the SRV in 1915 & svd at the Front until 16.6.17

53. PRO CO/417/563
54. PRO CO/417/563
55. Int Summary 17.1.16 PRO CO/417/574,583
56. PRO CO/417/574,583 Norforce War Diary PRO WO/95/2229
57. CO/417/583
58. Int Summary 6.3.16 Cmdt 12.2.16 PRO CO/417/574,583
    A144 Capt Geo ANDERSON MC(LG4.2.19) SRC
59. War Diary NORFORCE PRO WO/95/5334

CHAPTER 7

A Long, Long Trail A'Winding

On Boxing Day 1915 German naval superiority on Lake Tanganyika ended. In October, after an epic journey overland from the Cape, 27 naval officers and ratings had reached Kalemie, halfway up the Western Shore of the Lake, at the mouth of the Lukuga River. Led by Commander G B Spicer-Simpson RN they had brought with them two motor launches, HMS Mimi and HMS Toutou, each armed with a six pounder gun. They now sallied out and disabled and captured the Kingani. On 9 February 1916 the Hedwig von Weissmann was sunk. By March the destruction of the German lake fleet was complete.[1]

On 6 February 1916 Lieutenant General Jan Christian Smuts was appointed Commander-in-Chief of the British Forces in East Africa. On 19 February he landed at Mombasa to take up his appointment. By 31 March, 18,700 South Africans had joined the British, Indian and African troops on the Northern Front. With these reinforcements the complete conquest of German East Africa was confidently expected within the year.[2]

There had been no significant expansion of the King's African Rifles, although 2 KAR was to be reformed on 1 April 1916. It was already appreciated that the most suitable troops for bush warfare in this country were Africans, with strong cadres of white leaders and specialists. Nevertheless it was considered that victory would be obtained in less time than it would take to train sufficient African recruits, and before the climate and the mosquito destroyed the European and Indian units. Von Lettow, on the other hand, had had to make do with local resources, supplemented by the crews and cargoes of two successful blockade runners. By 1 January 1916, despite casualties, he had managed to more than quadruple his original force to a strength of 2,712 Europeans, 11,367 askari, and 2,531 irregulars and armed porters, with 50 guns and 95 machine guns. By 5 March these were organised into the equivalent of 60 field companies.[3]

On the Southern Front there were also changes. On 29 January 1916 Brevet Colonel (Temporary Brigadier-General) Edward Northey ADC arrived at Zomba to take command of the Nyasaland-Rhodesia Field Force, in which all the troops at the front in Northern Rhodesia and Nyasaland came under unified command for the first time. Northey's instructions were clear, 'You will ensure the safety of the Rhodesia Nyasaland borders.'[4]

Northey, an officer of the King's Royal Rifle Corps, had been wounded in June

1915 while commanding a brigade in France. He had sailed from England on 4 December 1915 with three staff officers. He landed at Cape Town on 24 December and commenced consultations with local commanders and governments. From 7 to 11 January 1916 he was at Livingstone accompanied by the Commandant-General Rhodesian Forces, Brigadier-General Edwards.

After working on the reorganisation of transport, supply and medical arrangements, Northey reached Karonga on 16 February and set out on a tour of the 250 mile front from Lake Nyasa to Lake Tanganyika, reorganising defences, and planning roads, carrier services and supplies.

In Nyasaland there had been a modest reinforcement from South Africa, in the form of the 5th Field Battery, South African Mounted Riflemen, armed with German 75 millimetre mountain guns captured in South West Africa, and the newly raised 1st and 2nd Regiments of South African Rifles, each of four squadrons, or companies, of 110 men. Northey now had 1,100 European and 1,500 African troops. Facing him the enemy had about 1,500, mainly the 29th Field Company from Bismarcksburg and two field companies based at Neu Langenburg.

On 4 March 1916 Northey reached Fife where he found Major Baxendale BSAP in command with two fortified posts 800 yards apart with a valley and water in between. One company of Northern Rhodesia Police garrisoned the Old Boma with B Company BSAP and a company of NRP at Mandala Camp, the old African Lakes Corporation compound.

On 10 March Colonel Hodson and Murray, his staff officer, joined General Northey at Fife and accompanied him to Abercorn which was reached on 18 March. Northey found A Company BSAP manning Abercorn North, one company of the Northern Rhodesia Police with two machine guns and a 2.5 inch mountain gun at Zombe, nine miles away, while the rest of the NRP held the area of Abercorn Prison, the District Commissioner's house and Mandala's stores by a series of posts. Northey regarded this perimeter as too long and criticised the defence works on the frontier for being built up too high off the ground. He judged the Northern Rhodesia Police to be good material but practically untried. The ration, down to $1\frac{1}{2}$ pounds of meal a day for the past two months, was insufficient. Northey noted a requirement for 4.5 inch howitzers, never met, and rifle grenades.

On 23 March Northey left Abercorn for Fort Hill and Karonga, where he established his headquarters. His immediate plan was an operation to clear the enemy's advanced posts as soon as the unusually heavy rains had ceased. He divided his force into three columns:

No.1 under Lt Col R E Murray DCM BSAP, consisting of the two companies of British South Africa Police and four companies of Northern Rhodesia Police, based on Abercorn, was to take Namema 26 miles to the North-East. The strength of about 260 whites and 540 Africans was reduced by the requirement to leave a garrison of half of 'B' Coy NRP and some BSAP at Abercorn. Northey put the effective strength of No.1 Column at about 200 whites and 400 Africans.

No.2 Column under Lt Col E Rodger, 2nd South African Rifles, consisting of his own regiment (less one squadron), 300 men, and 'E' Company, Northern Rhodesia Police, 138 men under Captain P J Sillitoe, based on Fife, was to take Luwiwa, thirteen miles to the North-East. H G Jones, Native Commissioner at Fife and L E Hickson Wood, Assistant Native Commissioner, were commissioned into the NRP as intelligence officers for this column.

No.3 Column, under the Commandant of 1st King's African Rifles, Lt Col G M P Hawthorn, King's Liverpool Regiment, consisting of 350 men of the KAR, the 1st South African Rifles, and 150 Nyasaland Volunteers, operating from Karonga and Fort Hill, was to take Igamba and Ipiana.[5]

2,000 first line carriers recruited in Northern Rhodesia were to follow Nos 1 and 2 Columns. Colonel Hodson, owing to ill health, had to give up command in the field and take charge of the Lines of Communication in Northern Rhodesia. Warrant Officer W Husbands BSAP was commissioned as a Temporary Second Lieutenant NRP on 1 February as Officer Commanding Supplies, Northern Border at the Kasama Base Depot. Mr Briggs of the Southern Rhodesia Public Works Department was supervising the building of the Great North Road from Broken Hill, upon which Major Charles Duly DSO, the founder of the famous Rhodesian garage chain, was soon to be ferrying supplies by motor transport. Those of the Northern Rhodesia Rifles who remained at the front were absorbed into the Northern Rhodesia Police, the two BSAP companies or the administrative services.[6]

Murray divided his column into four sub-units:

'A Force' under Captain C H Fair NRP – 'A' Company Northern Rhodesia Police, and half 'A' Company British South Africa Police, with two machine guns.
'B Force' under Captain G Parson BSAP – 'D' Company NRP, half 'A' Company BSAP, with two machine guns.
'C Force' under Captain H C Ingles NRP – 'C' Company NRP, half 'B' Company BSAP, with two machine guns.
'Reserve' under Captain F S James NRP – Half 'B' Company NRP, a section of 'B' Company BSAP, with two machine guns, a $12\frac{1}{2}$ pounder breech loading field gun and two mountain guns of the South African Mounted Riflemen battery.

At 2pm on 23 May Murray's column marched out of Abercorn by the Stevenson Road. They crossed the Lumi River by portable boats and established an advanced base camp $5\frac{1}{4}$ miles west of Namema to be garrisoned by a section of 'B' Coy NRP with a machine gun. At 2pm on 24 May 'A' and 'C' forces marched out of camp to the South-West. An hour later 'B' Force left marching north-east through the Liambi Hills. By the morning of 25 May 'A' and 'B' forces were in position with scouts within 200 yards of an enemy post. 'C' Force had lost direction in the bush and only arrived on the following day. Namema was a strong position consisting of two forts about 40 yards apart, on high ground, well provisioned with underground stores. There was no question of carrying it by assault. The guns were placed on a height to the north west and the lines were closed up to about four hundred yards from the fort. On 28 May the garrison, 29 Field Company, made a sortie against 'C' Force but were driven back with the loss of their commander, Oberleutnant von Francken, captured mortally wounded. With one man for every twenty yards of thick bush it was impossible to maintain an escape proof cordon especially on the swampy ground to the North. Seeing the danger Murray called up 'Reserve' Force but on the night 1/2 June the enemy, 30 Germans and 200 askari, managed to slip away. Three whites, two of them wounded, and three Africans were captured together with 50 loads of supplies. Murray had lost four BSAP killed and three men wounded.[7]

In the morning Capt McCarthy and his scouts set off in pursuit while the rest of the force concentrated before following in the afternoon with Capt Fair's men in the lead, chasing the enemy beyond Mwazie Mission, some 25 to 30 miles. The enemy then turned west towards Bismarcksburg, breaking the bridge over the Kalambo River and lining the far bank. The Rhodesians came up and a fire fight followed for two or three hours, during which Pte Hampson BSAP crossed the bridge by the one remaining timber followed, despite heavy fire, by 2/Lt H F Martin and No.1 Section 'A' Coy NRP, for the loss of 603 Pte Wazia, killed. At about 4pm the Germans evacuated their strong position. The bridge was partially repaired with planks left lying around by the enemy but most men had to complete the crossing by crawling on hands and knees along the wooden runners. Leaving Maj Parson to follow with the rest in the morning Murray pushed on immediately with 20 or 30 men.[8]

Bismarcksburg was a strongly designed fort on a promontory. Murray's men had covered 75 miles since leaving Namema. On 7 June he called on the German commandant to surrender or, 'as soon as my guns arrive I will blow you into the Lake.' In fact the guns had been unable to keep pace with the advance and had been sent back to Abercorn. The Commandant, Leutnant Hasslacher, replied that having been reinforced by the garrison of Namema, he had no intention of surrendering.

From a hill Dr J M Harold and Lieutenant E L Ingpen NRP watched the parliamentaire enter and leave the fort. They asked a passing msikari if the Germans had surrendered. 'Yes' he replied, not having understood, but anxious to please. The intrepid doctor led Ingpen and a few BSAP through the narrow gap in the abatis right to the gate of the fort, on which they knocked. The red cross on the pugri on the doctor's helmet had enabled them to get so far without being fired on. The commandant himself opened the door and, according to Captain R W M Langham MC NRP, then a BSAP trooper, asked, in English, the reason for their call. When told that the enemy had not surrendered, Dr Harold, with a total disregard for the Geneva Convention, pulled Hasslacher out of the doorway where the German was grabbed by two troopers. Under fire from three sides, both troopers were wounded as they hustled him back through the gap in the abatis. By luck or the careful shooting of his men, Hasslacher remained unscathed. Ingpen, mortally wounded in the groin cleared the abatis in one desperate leap. Harold appears to have had the luck of the Irish, but the party was pinned down in dead ground in noman's land. Eventually, at Hasslacher's suggestion, Harold agreed to a truce. Hasslacher blew his whistle and waved his handkerchief and both sides ceased fire. The wounded were carried back to the British lines and Hasslacher returned to his command.[9]

Next morning no sign of movement could be observed in the fort. A party of troops advanced towards it in open order. They met no fire. Finally they entered, to find the birds had flown. Three dhows and a fleet of canoes had been concealed on the lake side of the fort, out of sight of the besiegers. In these Hasslacher had silently embarked his troops, their machine guns, ammunition and what stores he could, and sailed away in the darkness. Captain Fair set off up the shoreline in pursuit, but could not find them. Commander Spicer-Simpson and his flotilla had been off Bismarcksburg at dawn on 5 June. He had seen the enemy's boats but, having ascertained that the fort was manned, had taken no action. Having then withdrawn to Kituta, he now reappeared, too late to be of any assistance.

'Kaffir' Murray, as he was known in the BSAP on account of his black hair and swarthy appearance, now had to wait for supplies and new orders. Lt Graham was attached to Spicer-Simpson's flotilla in command of a landing party which took part in four operations in June.[10]

Meanwhile Lt Col Rodger with No 2 Column had left Fife on 24 May, leaving half of 'E' Coy NRP under Lt Withers to garrison the fort. By the 26th he had established a ring of widely separated small posts around Luwiwa. Here the enemy 'L' Company of 20 Germans and 180 Africans, mainly policemen, with three machine guns, held two strongly built redoubts about 1,200 yards apart. During the 26th and 27th Rodger's men closed in to within two hundred yards of the enemy positions, reducing the cordon from 8,000 to 4,000 yards, but it was still far to long to be held by only 500 men. During the night 27/28 May the enemy, having used up their rations and water, slipped away in small parties between the British posts to the south, where they were most spread out. Captain Sillitoe was left with his remaining half-company to occupy the Luwiwa District, round up a party of the enemy at Mbozi Mission and organise the collection of food into depots. Rodger set out after the Luwiwa garrison on the morning of 29 May. He pursued them over the Igale Pass, through Neu Langenburg, north-eastward through Pakalele and across the Rungwe River without firing a shot. On 6 June he came up against the enemy rearguard in the Poroto Hills, sixteen miles north of the Rungwe. Four Germans were captured together with a gun, ammunition and camp equipment. The enemy once more vanished and retired to reorganise on the line Madibira-Malangali.[11]

On 9 June Rodger was at Ilongo and Hawthorn's No 3 Column at Neu Uteng-ele. In two weeks the Nyasaland Rhodesia Field Force had occupied 20,000 square miles of German territory. The enemy dislodged in the Bismarcksburg-Namema area was estimated at 600 and the total which had retired before Rodger, 300, not including Ruga Ruga. For the start of the offensive General Northey had set up his headquarters at Fife. He now moved up to Neu Langenburg. It was decided that his next objective should be Iringa to intercept the enemy retreating before Smuts' advance from the North. Accordingly, on 11 June, Northey sent for Lt Col Murray to bring his Rhodesians two hundred miles eastwards to Rungwe.

'B' and 'D' companies Northern Rhodesia Police, Capts James and Hornsby, and 30 BSAP details were left at Bismarcksburg under Major Baxendale, to round up enemy stragglers and help Captain Chesnaye to establish British administration in the area. As Political Officer, Chesnaye was assisted by Lt E H K Jordan also commissioned into the NRP from the Northern Rhodesia Native Affairs Department. With 'A' and 'C' companies NRP and the rest of the British South Africa Police, Murray marched through Fife on 23 June and reached Rungwe on 29

June. From Rungwe he marched north-east another fifty miles, joining Rodger at Buhora on 9 July. Sillitoe with 'E' Company NRP still on the Lines of Communication now had his HQ at Neu Utengele.

On this front the enemy 2nd, 5th, 22nd and 'L' field companies had been reinforced by 10th Field Company and the crew of the Konigsberg. Rodger was ordered to march on Malangali, while Murray, on the left, was to work towards Madibira where the enemy were entrenching, 40 miles north-east of Buhora. He was to pin them down there while Rodger and Hawthorn took Malangali. On 11 July a Rhodesian patrol drove a party of the enemy out of Kawere, fifteen miles north-east of Buhora. On 25 July Murray was at Madibira from where the enemy had withdrawn on the fall of Malangali. On 28 July Capt E G Dickinson NRP drove the Germans out of Lutege, halfway from Madibira to Waussa. Murray sent Captain Fair's 'A' Company NRP a further thirty miles north to the crossing on the Great Ruaha River at Kiganga, where it remained for about a week, intercepting the enemy's mails between Iringa and Tabora and gaining much valuable information. On 9 August Fair's men captured a German naval petty officer and four askari. An attempt to bridge the Ruaha was stopped and canoes collected by the enemy destroyed.[12]

The advance was now held to await developments in the North, until on 22 August Murray entered Waussa unopposed. On 25 August three enemy askari were captured. On 26 August Murray's forward troops located the retiring Konigsberg detachment of sailors, 2, 5, 10 and 'L' field companies, 120 Germans and 640 askari with 12 machine guns, all under Hauptmann Braunschweig, at Weru, 23 miles from Waussa and 15 miles short of Iringa. Two more askari were captured together with despatches and 1,000 cattle. At 11 am on 29 August 1916 'C' Company, Northern Rhodesia Police, now under Captain Dickinson, entered Iringa, liberating 16 Indian prisoners of war and 42 civilian internees, British Asians. Three wounded Germans and 4 askari were found in the hospital and 50 German women and children in the town.[13]

Murray's Rhodesians were now only about a hundred miles from Smuts' 2nd Division, which had crossed the Central Railway at Kilosa, but it was clear that von Lettow was not to be trapped between the two forces. His troops, retreating from north and south, were heading off east for Mahenge. The plan was now to trap them between Lake Nyasa to the west, the Sea to the east, and the Rovuma River, the Portuguese border, to the south. Portugal had entered the war on the allied side in March.

Rodger was near Waussa exploiting to the east. Hawthorn was still further south and east at Lupembe. He was ordered to make for Makua, fifty five miles to his north-east. Murray, leaving a garrison at Iringa, was to march south-east on Muhanga. They would then both make for Mahenge.

Murray left Iringa on 3 September. His route was across ranges of steep hills with narrow valleys and bush so thick men had to cut their way through it. Reconnaissance showed that the enemy rearguard was well dug in at Boma Himbu on the Little Ruaha. As Murray and Rodger closed in on this position, Hauptmann Braunschweig vacated it. This was to be the pattern of the advance, the enemy occupying strong positions, forcing their opponents to deploy to outflank them, then slipping away without a fight. The rains set in, cold and depressing.

On 6 September at Lukegeta (Dabaga) the advance was checked by the fire of cleverly concealed machine guns and ptes Pandavipa and Tebulo were killed. Murray dug in within some 400 yards of the northern and western faces of the enemy position, while Rodger hacked a way round to the South-East. The investment was completed by 7pm but three hours later bombers found the enemy trenches empty. The bush was so thick that on the night 7–8 September it took 'A' Coy NRP and 'A' Coy BSAP ten hours to hack their way through five miles.[14]

On 11 September a patrol of BSAP entered Muhanga Mission in the plain. Here 13 Germans and 36 askari were found, left behind by the enemy, sick or wounded. To lighten their load the enemy had destroyed 200 rifles and a quantity of ammunition. Of the six men in the patrol three, R W M Langham, A L Messum and C F Schronen were to serve in the NRP post war. Two of the others, Bradbury and Hampson were, to be killed in action at Mkapira.[15]

On 14 September Murray reached Hange, with his advanced guard seven miles further east at Boma Dwangire. His ox-drawn guns were a day's march or more behind, escorted by 'A' Company NRP, who spent most of their time from 11 to 15 September helping to haul the guns uphill and holding them back on the downward slope, but managing to laugh and sing as they did it.

Murray's Column was now ordered to march south to link up with Hawthorn. On 24 September Rhodesian patrols ambushed two parties of the enemy, killing two officers and several askari and capturing one German, one askari and 19 cattle. On 29th September Murray reached Mkapira. The men had been on short rations for many days as they marched further and further from their supply base at Iringa. Hawthorn had little to spare, being 60 miles from his own base at Lupembe. The two columns took up a strong position on high ground between the Mnyera and Ruhuje rivers, while posts were established on the lines of communication and supplies built up. Capt Fair with 'A' Coy NRP and most of 'B' Coy BSAP was posted at Kiwanga an important crossing on the Mpanga River 20 miles to the North-West.[16]

Debilitated by sickness, Smuts' troops had been unable to reach Iringa. The German concentration to the East was such that for Northey's troops alone to press on to Mahenge would be to court disaster. Major Kraut was estimated to have available 200 Germans, 1,500 askari and 18 machine guns to the east of the Ruhuje. On 28 September he had unsuccessfully attacked Hawthorn with five companies.[17]

Meanwhile, Lieutenant Colonel H M Stennett NRP had been placed in administrative charge of the border area from Bismarcksburg to Fife. Between 26 and 31 July 'B' and 'D' companies, NRP, working north from Bismarcksburg occupied Kirando Island, where, on 30 June Capt James' 30 men impressed Cdr Spicer-Simpson by disembarking in 4 minutes, at Kala and were gradually securing the Ufipa country. Assisted for a time in August by Lt Withers' half of 'E' Company from Fife, they cleared the enemy from the area between Lake Tanganyika and Lake Rukwa to about eighty miles north of Bismarcksburg. Some 40 Germans and 300 askari remained around Mpimbwe and Kalema until, on 20 August, elements of the Northern Rhodesia Police under Major Walter Baxendale BSAP gained touch with the Belgians north-east of Mpimbwe. The Belgian advance on Tabora from the North and across Lake Tanganyika compelled the remaining enemy to withdraw.[18]

British troops from Lake Victoria were also advancing on Tabora on the Belgian left flank. Major General Wahle, in command at Tabora, was forced to fall back with his force of up to 2,500 men, to rejoin the main German concentration around Mahenge. He thus posed a serious threat to General Northey's thin line from Fife to Iringa. On 9 September Northey signalled to Baxendale to bring one of his companies to Rungwe. He arrived with 'D' Company and 35 men of 'E' Coy NRP on 29 September while the other half of 'E' Company reached Malangali the following day.[19]

On 30 September 1916 the five companies of the Northern Rhodesia Police serving with the Rhodesia Nyasaland Field Force totalled 23 officers, and 24 white, and 872 African, other ranks.[20]

One of Wahle's columns was threatening Iringa held by Lt Col Rodger and his 2nd South African Rifles. On 7 October Northey gave orders for two 12 pdr naval guns to be withdrawn from Iringa to Ngominji, as he considered these would hamper Rodger if he had to evacuate Iringa. 50 Northern Rhodesia Police were to garrison Ngominji. Maj Baxendale was to march to Iringa with two companies, escorting the 5th Field Battery, South African Mounted Riflemen. On the arrival, on 9 October, of the SAMR mountain guns and 180 NRP with four machine guns, the enemy moved off to the south-west. Sgt J F Simpson was sent north with 30 NRP and on 24 October met the advance guard of the South African Motor Cyclist Corps at Salimu. Lt Henniker-Gotley with 50 men was posted to the West near Alt Iringa.[21]

On 22 October in accordance with further telegraphic instructions from General Northey, Baxendale left Old Iringa with another officer, 4 white other ranks and 56 African police with a machine-gun, to patrol south east towards Ngominji. On 23 October, only 6 miles from Ngominji, this force was ambushed by Leutnant Zingel of 26 Field Company with 200 men. Walter Baxendale, was shot through the heart. Sergeant G C de W Taylor BSAP and four Africans were also killed. The other 4 whites were wounded and three of them captured with a number of Africans. 23 of the patrol escaped including Cpl E A Green, a medical orderly.[22]

Meanwhile on 22 October the enemy, 8 Field Company and three levy companies under Hauptmann Wintgens, had occupied the heights north of Ngominji with 3 guns and 8 machine guns. They overlooked the defensive position taken up by the garrison commander, Captain C H B Clarke SAMR, on a ridge above the supply depot. The Germans had cut the telegraph wire running north to Iringa and dispersed a convoy of porters marching from Ngominji to Iringa. When a wounded survivor brought the news of the defeat of Baxendale's patrol, it was found that the telegraph wire to the south had also been cut. Over the following days six German machine-guns on the heights beat down the fire of Clarke's 60 rifles. On 28 October the defenders repulsed an assault. Some South African engineers at the depot had improvised some hand grenades which were put to good use. However that night it was clear that the position was hopeless. Clarke gave permission for those who wished to try to escape to do so. 30 of the garrison crept out. On the morning of 29 October the remainder were overwhelmed by an attack by 8 and 29 Field Companies. Clarke and Lieutenant A M Bones SAMR were killed. The Germans were commanded by Oberleutnant Bauer who was severely wounded.[23]

Cpl Green reached Iringa with the news of Baxendale's death and Lt Col Rodger took out 100 men reaching the scene of the ambush on 24 October. Attempting to relieve Ngominji he ran into an enemy force in difficult mountainous country and withdrew to await reinforcements. At last troops of General Smuts' main army had reached Iringa which was garrisoned by 40 of Rodger's South African Rifles and 30 NRP. Lt Col Freeth's 7th South African Infantry were immediately ordered to march on to assist Rodger but by then it was to late to save Ngominji. On 30 October Capt Sillitoe was placed in command of the area from Alt Iringa to Salimu. Lt Bremner was sent from Alt Iringa to Dabaga to reinforce a detachment of 2nd South African Rifles. 2 Officers, 4 British other ranks, and 123 Africans of the NRP were with Rodger when he and Freeth were surrounded in the Muhange Hills on the night 30–31 October. Sgt Sell crept through the enemy lines to bring the news, but the enemy drew off next day having bitten off more than they could chew.[24]

On the Ruhuje, Major Kraut was reported to have at his disposal 2, 5, 10, 15, 16, 19, and 25 Field Companies, 5 Schutzen Company, 'L' Company of police askari and 8 Schutzen Company, a mounted unit of 50 whites and 60 askari. On 15 October 1916 he had begun to close in on Mkapira (Kapira's). Mkapira was held by Murray and Hawthorn with 'C' Company, Northern Rhodesia Police, facing west, 'A' Company , British South Africa Police facing south and east, and five single companies of 1st King's African Rifles, four facing north and north-east and one between the NRP and the BSAP. On 21 October patrols made contact. On 22 October the Germans rushed a KAR post on Piquet Hill 2,500 yards west of the main position. From here they opened fire with a field gun. On 23 October the enemy completely invested the British position establishing a post five miles down the Lupembe Road. The Western defences came under close range machine-gun fire. But the garrison had less than a week's rations and would soon be needed elsewhere.

Hawthorn remained in contact with Lupembe by means of a field wireless set and was able to co-ordinate arrangements for a counter-attack. Careful reconnaissance found the swamps along the Mnyera River drying up. A covered approach was found to the north flank of the German position west of Mkapira and Rhodesian scouts under Capt Jones found an approach to the South-East. On the night 29–30 October the Rhodesians and Nyasalanders enveloped the German lines. Before dawn Lieutenant Harry Onyett led 36 BSAP in a silent assault at a deliberate trot with orders not to return enemy fire. The German forward pickets immediately retired. Then from their rifle pits the enemy askari broke and ran. The German officers and NCOs in machine-gun emplacements went on firing to the last. At the same time two KAR companies successfully stormed Piquet Hill. Captain Galbraith with 'D' Company 1 KAR had been posted at Risinga west of the German block on the Lupembe Road. Joined by Capt Fair on 20 October, he now attacked along the Mnyera River. In the centre the Germans held out until 8.30am when resistance collapsed and Krauts's troops scattered into the bush in small parties making for the river crossings on the Ruhuje.

By noon the fighting was ended. Five Germans and 37 of their askari had been killed and six Germans and 76 native troops captured, together with a six centimetre gun, three machine guns, and a quantity of stores and ammunition. Most of the enemy casualties were from 10th and 25th field companies and 5th Schutzen Company but personnel of the 2nd, 5th, 19th and 'L' field companies were also identified. Kraut's offensive power was, for the time being, crippled, at a cost of one KAR officer, 2 askari and 4 BSAP troopers killed and 14 all ranks wounded.[25]

On 1 November Murray's Column marched away from Mkapira up the Mnyera Valley and climbed the escarpment to reach Lupembe on 4 November. On 6 November Captain Fair NRP was ordered to march with his company to Malangali, some sixty miles to the North-West. Here the supply depot was defended by a raw company of about 80 of the Rhodesia Native Regiment and 38 KAR, all under Captain Marriott SAR. On 7 November German scouts were on the surrounding hills and when Fair came up on 8 November the telegraph had been cut and the place was invested by General Wahle with Hauptmann Langen's 7th and 26th field companies. Shells set the food store alight but the spirits of the garrison had been raised by the sight of General Northey's first and only aircraft which dropped a bomb on the German bivouacs. Being in insufficient strength to break through, let alone raise the siege, Fair took up a concealed position about six miles south on the Njombe road.

Thanks to the efforts of the South African Engineers and native labour, the road between Neu Langenburg, Iringa and Lupembe had been declared fit for motor transport on 1 November. Northey had had 50 light lorries, Hupmobiles and Fords, assembled at Neu Langenburg and despatched to Lupembe where they arrived on the evening of 8 November. On the morning of 9 November Murray embussed 100 BSAP and 30 NRP with four machine guns and moved off at the highest possible speed via Njombe and Muawindi. By nightfall having driven 120 miles over very rough roads they were 5 miles short of Malangali when firing was heard. The troops de-bussed and bivouacced under cover. The vehicles returned to Buhora for supplies. In the morning reconnaissance showed the enemy too strong for an attack without Charles Fair's company the location of which was unknown to Murray. He had to be content with harassing the enemy. The two police forces made contact on the night 11–12 November but Wahle had by then made touch with Kraut and the greater part of the General's troops had been observed marching off south to join his compatriot. In the morning Murray and Fair closed in on the rearguard, 26th and 'D' field companies, and made a surprise attack from the south-west. By then the Rhodesia Native Regiment had suffered two killed and four wounded. The BSAP and NRP had four men wounded. Two Germans and nine of their askari were killed. Seven Germans and 10 askari were made prisoner. Dr Schnee, the Governor of German East Africa recorded that the abortive siege cost them 38 casualties. One machine-gun, 39 cattle, 15 donkeys and mules and 72 porters were also captured.[26]

On 10 November Lieutenant Percy Wardroper NRP had been sent from Lupembe with the remainder of Murray's Column, 110 NRP and 25 BSAP, to reinforce Njombe. Wahle was now heading for Njombe, Langen for Lupembe. Lupembe was now only garrisoned by some 50 whites and 200 Northern Rhodesian Bemba recruits in training for the expansion of 1 KAR. Lt Col Hawthorn and 1 KAR had been ordered on 9 November to withdraw from Mkapira to Lupembe. Murray left Malangali by motor vehicle on 13 November reaching Njombe the following day. On 12 November Hauptmann Wintgens column had invested Lupembe. Before dawn on 13 November an assault on the main position was repulsed although it was pressed hard, five of the Bemba being bayoneted in their trenches. On 16 November Murray set out marching east on Lupembe without waiting for Fair's men who arrived near Njombe later. At 11am at Hawanga Murray encountered OberstLeutnant Huebner with 200 men and 2 machine-guns. At 2.45 the Rhodesian attack was driven home. The Germans dispersed into the bush leaving three whites and 10 Africans dead. 3 Germans and 4 askari were captured while Murray lost one man killed and 4 wounded. On 19 November Murray was within 10 miles of Lupembe and in touch with Hawthorn who had relieved the garrison.

The German built post was a strong one on a high ridge with steep slopes to north and south and a deep gully on the west. The garrison had four machine-guns and three muzzle-loading 7 pounder mountain guns. The recruits had their women and children with them and the garrison was also encumbered with 50 enemy prisoners of war. In the first assault the Germans had captured an outpost and manned it with snipers. Shellfire brought down the wireless masts cutting communications with the outside. At 4am on 14 November the enemy attacked up the gradual eastern slope but were halted by intense fire from the trenches. Then a determined assault on the north face brought them right up to the barbed wire defences but no further. The garrison was subjected to galling machine gun and sniper fire that night and the following day but despite their inexperience the Bemba had won. Over the next few days they saw Wahle's columns with their carriers and cattle withdrawing across the hills to the north-east. The enemy abandoned a 12 pdr gun they had captured at Ngominji. Among the garrison was Sergeant Cecil Barton Northern Rhodesia Rifles attached to the NRP who was reported to have mown down 40 of the enemy with his machine guns and to have commanded several small parties of men with great coolness and ability. He was awarded the DCM and commissioned as machine gun officer in the 1st Battalion, 1st King's African Rifles. In all 6 Germans and 42 enemy askari were killed.[27]

Murray's force was moved back to Njombe by motor vehicle. 'A' and 'B' companies, British South Africa Police, 110 rifles and 6 machine guns now took post at Emmaburg under Captain Hendry SRV. Major Carbutt's company of the Rhodesia Native Regiment, 120 men with three maxims was at Buhora. Captain Charles Fair with 'A' and 'C' companies, 240 Northern Rhodesia Police, with six machine guns was at Njombe. By the morning of 25 November all three of these forces had closed in on Ilembule, twenty miles north-west of Njombe. They engaged the troops of Oberstleutnant Huebner who had established himself there. Capt Fair's men opened fire from maxims from trenches dug in the night within 1200 yards of the mission buildings. The next night two sections of 'A' Company

NRP under Lt G C Latham pushed right into the enemy position and gained control of his water supply in the bed of the Halali River. On 26 November the Germans tried to shell Latham's men out of the riverbed but they had dug in deep and Sgt Lochner BSAP silenced the enemy gun with his Maxim. Huebner was thus compelled to surrender unconditionally that afternoon with 6 other officers 48 German other ranks, and 249 askari of the 8th and 22nd field companies, 3 maxims and a 10.2cm howitzer, the largest the NRP had encountered. For once the fish had been netted! Rhodesian casualties were six wounded.[28]

The Rhodesia Native Regiment had been raised at Salisbury in April 1916. Its officers and European NCOs had all been drawn from the British South Africa Police and the Southern Rhodesia Native Affairs Department. To a cadre of fifty native policemen of the BSAP were added 408 African recruits, 290 being migrant workers from Northern Rhodesia and Nyasaland and the remainder natives of Southern Rhodesia. On 18th July the half trained regiment had left for the North with a view to completing its training at Neu Langenburg. Its Commanding Officer was Lieutenant Colonel A J Tomlinson who had commanded the BSAP detachment at Sesheke in July 1915.[29]

Back in the Bismarcksburg District Capt James and 'B' Company NRP had also had success. They had tracked down and, on 22 November 1916, captured 7 German officers, 47 other whites and 249 askari. Enemy morale was beginning to crumble.[30]

After their success at Ilembule 'A' and 'C' companies were joined at rest at Njombe by 'D' and 'E' and a draft under Lt Allport, back from UK leave. Here the companies were reorganised on a tribal basis. The Ngoni were separated into a new 'F' Company under Capt Hornsby. On 10 December one company with two machine guns was sent to Mbejera, thirty miles south-east of Ubena, to watch the right flank and cover the collection of food supplies in the country to the west.[31]

On 23 December all five companies and the BSAP, some 900 rifles with 8 machine guns, marched out eastwards from Lupembe under Murray, who had been awarded the DSO. The plan was for Hawthorn and Murray, in conjunction with a force from Iringa under Major General Van Deventer, to drive the enemy behind the line of the Kilombero River, which was to be held until the end of the rains. Brigadier General Northey hoped his two columns would surround and destroy the enemy force immediately opposed to them, under Major Langen. Struggling through the wet bush the Rhodesians were foiled in three successive attempts to outflank and surround their opponents. On 2 January 1917 at Mfirika, there was, as described by Northey, a spectacular fight. While Hawthorn worked round to the North, Capt Fair was to go round to the South to get astride the Sylvester Falls Road in the enemy's rear. Being unable to force a passage Fair attacked Road Hill from the South-West. The supports came up and under cover of machine gun fire overhead from ridge to ridge, 'E' Coy Northern Rhodesia Police, supported by British South Africa Police, 120 men, crept down the wooded gullies and up a spur held by the enemy. At 5 pm the charge was sounded and they went in cheering with the bayonet. The enemy fled into dense bush. Four of the attackers were wounded including Sgt Messum, shot in the groin. For three days he was carried in a machila to the field hospital at Njombe.[32]

On 3 January Murray found Langen reinforced by Major Kraut in a new position at Mtaramgunda Hill between Kirefi and Kafeke on the Mahenge road. On 4 January 'F' Coy forced an enemy piquet to retire and attacked his left flank at dusk, meeting furious fire. On the 5th 'E' and 'F' coys continued the attack in intense heat and heavy rain, supported by mountain guns of the SAMR. The enemy front and right flank were located but the wily Germans did not wait to be surrounded and on 7 January Capt Withers found the position empty.[33]

On 11 January Major Kraut turned off the Mahenge Road near Njama. Murray's Column was diverted to Ifinga with instructions to drive Kraut out of the upper Ruhuje Valley which he was using as a foraging ground. After a skirmish at Malawi's on 13 January the Rhodesians reached the river to find the bridge severely damaged. On 15 January Capt Fair's advanced troops rushed the bridge, brushing aside a piquet. He occupied a hill on the South Bank holding off an attack from the East. 'C' and 'F' coys under Capt Hornsby came up to the West of Ifinga which was strongly held. On 17 January Fair attacked and Kraut retired 1,500 yards to the hills to the South. By repeated actions in incessant rain the NRP and BSAP drove the enemy north-eastward down the valley. On 22 January Murray advanced from Ifinga to encircle Kraut's four companies but on the night 23–24 January they slipped away south-east towards Mputa, destroying the bridge at Muesa. Encountering a 50 man rearguard at a ford on the River 'F' Coy lost 4 men killed, including Sgt J F Simpson, and Lt R D N Latimer and 4 men wounded, dislodging it. By 28 January Kraut was at Mputa. On 2 February Capt Hornsby's advance was checked by outposts on the Pitu River. The advance had been over boggy tracks and swollen streams with scant food. Murray's supplies were now exhausted. He had been unable to make touch with Col Byron who was operating from Songea. The direction of the enemy's position was uncertain. Kraut had retired to Mpepo and having found scant food in the wild hills and dense bush his force had broken up into foraging parties among the scattered villages. On 5 February Murray's Columnn was ordered back to relieve 1/1 KAR garrisoning posts east and south of Lupembe.[34]

On 20 January 1917 Major General A R Hoskins[35] had succeeded General

10.2 cm Howitzer captured at Ilembule in November 1916 being conveyed to the line of rail (Photo Imperial War Museum Q17111)

Smuts as Commander-in-Chief. His army in the north was crippled by fever among the white and Indian troops and unable to resume offensive operations until the rains ended. The King's African Rifles were in the process of expansion and reorganisation; the first four regiments each forming second, and later third and fourth battalions. The Nyasaland-Rhodesia Field Force therefore had to bear the burden of keeping the enemy on the run and gradually wearing him down.

The 5th South African Infantry, reduced by battle casualties and sickness to 150 men, had been shipped from Dar es Salaam to Durban where 600 raw recruits were embarked. The battalion was landed at Beira in Mozambique and travelled via Fort Johnston, Nyasaland, to Songea where it completed its concentration by the end of November 1916. Here the Commanding Officer, Col Byron was also given command of half the Rhodesia Native Regiment and a band of irregulars raised and commanded by Captain J J McCarthy MC NRP. On 15 December Byron was ordered to take the offensive towards Kitanda. On 20 December the enemy evacuated Nyamabengo and retreated towards Likuyu pursued for two days by McCarthy with his own men and 'A' Coy 5 SAI. He had great difficulty in crossing the swollen Luwegu River. On 24 December, having received information of German reinforcements, Byron recalled McCarthy to Songea. On 5 January 1917 the South Africans took Gumbiro, 50 miles north of Songea, capturing 12,000lbs of corn which the Germans had been using female forced labour to grind. On 7 January the RNR occupied Kitanda.[36]

Byron placed McCarthy in command of two companies of 5 SAI and one of the Rhodesian Native Regiment giving him 10 officers, 461 other ranks and 5 machine guns in addition his Ruga Ruga. By 16 January McCarthy, now with the rank of major, had skillfully encircled the 7th and 12th field companies at Likuyu, cutting the road two miles to the north-east. Despite heavy rain and the lack of training of the troops under his command, McCarthy closed in, seizing successive points of vantage, until on 24 January the German commander Major von Grawert surrendered with 3 other officers, 37 white other ranks and 202 askari, having destroyed his 2 machine guns and an 88 millimetre gun. Described as the most gratifying success yet achieved in the area, McCarthy's victory had been achieved at a cost of 9 South Africans killed and 8 wounded and one African of the RNR killed.[37]

He sent back his prisoners to Songea and immediately marched to Kitanda where 230 men of the Rhodesia Native Regiment under Lt Col Tomlinson were battling to hold off Hauptmann Wintgens reinforced by some of Kraut's troops, a total of seven field companies. Crossing the still swollen River Luwegu McCarthy arrived on 28 January. On 29th January he sent in a patrol but his main attack was driven back. On 30 January, after dark, McCarthy advanced through the enemy lines to join Tomlinson and dug in in an adjoining position. On 4 February, having no more food, the Germans marched away. Total British casualties were 2 officers and 23 other ranks killed, 2 officers and 44 O.R.s wounded and 18 missing.

Max Wintgens had 500 to 700 combatant troops, 13 machine guns and three small guns. His askari were all from around Tabora. They were becoming demoralised and mutinous. While Kraut moved south and east along the Rovuma to find sanctuary at Tunduru, Wintgens set out north-west to break through

Northey's sparse cordon and make for Tabora, the only direction in which his askari would follow him.

His move came to Northey's attention on 14 February when a 35 strong foraging party appeared at Milow Mission, halfway between Wiedhafen and Tandala on the road over the mountains from Njombe, Northey's HQ, to Alt Langenburg. Tandala and Alt Langenburg were each garrisoned by about 100 convalescents, Njombe by the Headquarters staff and details. On 16 January 'B' Company Northern Rhodesia Police under Captain F S James had been ordered forward from Bismarcksburg to garrison Neu Langenburg where it arrived on 21 February, detaching a section to Mwaya on Lake Nyasa. Murray's Column had reached Ifinga. HQ 1/1 KAR was still at Lupembe with companies deployed to the east. Northey ordered 1/1 KAR to Tandala via Njombe. Murray was to detach 'E' and 'F' companies NRP to garrison Lupembe, send two companies under Captain Dickinson cross country in pursuit of Wintgens, and follow 1/1 KAR with the rest of his troops.

On 16 February a patrol from Northey's HQ encountered a German detachment at Malangali, 10 miles north-west of Milow Mission. The following day the patrol attacked but was driven off with 50 per cent casualties. Its withdrawal was covered by members of the South African Motor Cyclists Corps which had just joined Northey's command. It was in this action that the motor-cyclists' commanding officer, Lt Col J M Fairweather DSO, was shot dead. On 18 February a half company of 1/1 KAR reached Tandala by motor transport and was soon involved in desperate fighting until reinforced by two more companies on 20 February. The rest of the battalion arrived on 21 February followed by Murray the next day. When Dickinson marched in on the 25th the enemy were known to have gone off to the north-west. On 27 February two companies of KAR and Dickinson's detachment set off in pursuit up the Magoje Road, but were recalled to Tandala next day. Murray crossed Lake Nyasa from Alt Langenburg to Mwaya in order to cut Wintgens off at Old Utengele.[38]

The Rhodesian Native Regiment had been shipped up the Lake on 28 February and was placed under Murray's command giving him some 830 rifles and 20 machine guns. The RNR under Lt Col Tomlinson reached Neu Langenburg on 6 March to find that Captain James with 'B' Coy NRP had advanced to the Igale Pass half way to Utengele. Tomlinson joined him there the next day. However Murray was concerned that Wintgens would raid into Northern Rhodesia and ordered James to march to Fife on 8 March. Northey now had two aircraft at his disposal but they were grounded by bad weather. Murray had no information on the enemy's whereabouts but he was believed to be marching from Magoje via Neu Utengele to Utengele. Leaving Captain Graham's company at Neu Langenburg, Murray, with the BSAP and the remaining company of the NRP, joined Tomlinson at Igale Pass on 10 March. On 9 and 10 March patrols on the Igale-Utengele Road dispersed two enemy foraging parties and learnt that Wintgens was bridging rivers north and north-east of Utengele and that he had promised to disband his askari at Tabora. James had just arrived at Fife. Murray ordered him to march immediately to Mbosi to watch the Bismarcksburg road at the crossing over the Songwe River, destroy the bridge at St Moritz and watch the road to Fife.

Knowing this to be too much to ask of 150 men, Murray also ordered the RNR, 250 men with 6 machine guns, to Mbosi. Marching through heavy rain and swamps Tomlinson arrived on the morning of 14 March to find that James had moved on to the Utengele-Bismarcksburg road. On 15 March Tomlinson despatched Major Carbutt's company to Panda Hill where the Bismarcksburg road crossed the Songwe. That afternoon Tomlinson followed with the rest of the Rhodesia Native Regiment on short rations. In the evening Murray entered Utengele driving out the German rearguard. That night he ordered Tomlinson back to Mbosi and to march on St Moritz Mission, Galula, where the enemy appeared to be heading. On 17 March Tomlinson routed an enemy foraging party at Ndolesi on the Bismarcksburg Road capturing 8,000 rounds of ammunition and some machine gun spares but losing one officer and two other ranks wounded. During the engagement all Tomlinson's carriers fled which was not a good omen. At Ndolesi he was joined by Capt. James who had captured Leutnant Wahle, son of the major general. Tomlinson and James marched on together towards St Moritz.

General Northey's instructions were for Murray to concentrate with the Rhodesia Native Regiment to the west of the enemy position. He was not to risk an attack in detail but to close in to restrict the area in which Wintgens could forage. Meanwhile 1/1 KAR now under Major G L Baxter[39], Cameron Highlanders, was being sent to bar the German from returning east. The only route the enemy could take to the North was the bridge over the flooded Songwe at St Moritz. This was also to be blocked by 1/1 KAR.

Things did not go according to plan! Delayed by a bridge washed away Murray on 19 March was fifteen miles behind down the Itaka-St Moritz track when Tomlinson was within a few miles of the Mission. Murray sent Lieutenant Wardroper NRP to warn Tomlinson not to commit his force to a premature engagement. He was too late. While Lieutenant Baker RNR and Sergeant Bainbridge NRP were reconnoitring towards St Moritz, Wintgens was out stalking Tomlinson. On the afternoon of 20 March Maj Addison RNR's advance guard was attacked on the Itaka-St Moritz Track, a few miles short of the mission[40]. Capt James led 'B' Coy NRP forward to reinforce him. There followed a hot fight in which the German troops, boldly and skillfully handled, worked round Tomlinson's flanks. James was severely wounded and Lt Burton took command of the NRP with Sgt Bainbridge holding off an attack on the left. Tomlinson decided to withdraw for the night but being too far from the hills to the South, dug in on the plain behind a stream. Here he was quickly surrounded after having been severely harassed and charged repeatedly during the withdrawal. Two machine guns fell into enemy hands and a third was cut off and taken the next day. Outfought and considerably shaken Tomlinson's force retired a further short distance on 21 March but found the road to Itaka cut. Recconaissance at dawn on 22 March showed that the dressing station was in enemy hands. A parley in the morning led to the return of the wounded and medical staff in the afternoon. The enemy provided stretchers but retained most of the medical stores.

Hampered by his wounded whom he could not evacuate, with supplies low and carriers unreliable under fire, his men exhausted and dispirited, Tomlinson determined to remain on the defensive to await Murray. On the 22nd his troops repulsed an attack from the south-west. They were subjected to harassing fire throughout the 22nd and 23rd while the shortage of food became acute. Happily there was ample water. On 24 March firing was heard on the Itaka road and the enemy made an especially determined attack which was driven off. On the night of 25 March Tomlinson sent out a patrol under Lieutenant Booth who reached Murray on 26 March when signal communication was also effected. On the morning of 27th March the ordeal ended, Lt Langham NRP with his half-company being the first of the relieving force to arrive. They occupied the enemy trench across the stream[41]. Wintgens fell back to St Moritz. Baxter came up on 28th March. Tomlinson's force had suffered heavy casualties. As well as Capt James, 'B' Company NRP had lost LCpl Ulaya, who had been wounded at Saisi in 1915, killed, Gunner Holloway wounded and 19 African police wounded or missing. Lt Col Tomlinson had been suffering from blood poisoning for some days and was evacuated.

Murray, held up by bad weather, had received a signal on 21 March from the C-in-C, Hoskins, via Northey, telling him that 'The rounding up of Wintgens is now of greater importance than anything else in the campaign. . . you have ample troops and must even live off the country if necessary.' This overlooked the fact that the pursuing force had no option but to pass over land denuded of food by the pursued. On 23 March Capt Fair with 'A' Coy NRP and BSAP had encountered the enemy detachment blocking the road in Tomlinson's rear killing two Germans and recapturing 70 of the RNR's cattle for the loss of a splendid NCO, Sgt Gwiranipakamwa, killed. Murray telegraphed Baxter to hasten forward from Utengele with 1/1 KAR. On 24 March Murray made an unsuccessful attempt to work round the flank of the road block in very broken country, with thick bush and deep ravines.[42]

On 28 March scouts reported that Wintgens had moved the missionaries from St Moritz west to St Bonifaz. The bridge at St Moritz was almost completely demolished and strongly defended. The river was in flood. On 29 and 30 March Murray felt his way forward on a wide front to envelop St Moritz from the South-West. He bridged rivers on his right so as to be able to prevent escape to the South-East but was also ready to march back to Itaka, the driest and best route to St Bonifaz. Meanwhile Wintgens had already transfered his HQ to Iwunga on the Southern Shore of Lake Rukwa. On 29 March the Germans made a final raid on 1/1 KAR's rear echelon at Utengele. On 30 March Maj Fair encountered a piquet dug in on the left bank of the river 2,000 yards south of the Mission and drove it in. The NRP, under Fair, supported by the BSAP advanced on the enemy main position. Wintgens made an unsuccessful attack on Murray's left flank which was extended by 'A' Coy 1/1 KAR. Sgt S N Whyte BSAP in command of a section of NRP held an isolated position about 300 yards from the enemy under heavy fire. Though forced back he later regained his ground. He was awarded the Italian Bronze Medal for this action. On 31 March the RNR came up freeing Baxter's troops to further extend the left flank. The NRP again drove in an enemy piquet. Seven African police died in those two days.

On 1 April a patrol of 1/1 KAR found the Mission evacuated. Wintgens had slipped away over the St Moritz Bridge. That evening he was 30 miles away towards the Sira River. The bridge having been repaired the NRP and BSAP led the advance across the Songwe next day and came up with the enemy reaguards on 3 April in the swampy area near the junction of the Sira and Lupa rivers. The Lupa, in high flood, was bridged and crossed on 5 April but difficulties over supplies and carriers increased with every step. 600 extra carriers were required for each 50 miles advanced. Murray was never again able to close with Wintgens. On 8 April, when Murray was at Iwungu, Wintgens was 45 miles ahead at Panzi. On 1 May Murray was on the Kondo River with one company of NRP 25 miles ahead towards Kawere. On 7 May Capt Burton's 'B' Coy was on the Kawere Road, 8 miles west of the main force. On 10 May these detachments were recalled, Burton being ordered to join 1/1 KAR at Nkindu. On 16 May contact was made with the South African Cape Corps Battalion based on the Central Railway. On 21 May 1/1 KAR left Kitundu having been ordered to return to Njombe. On 28 May the Rhodesians reached the Ngluva River some 35 miles south of Sikonge, and only three days march from Tabora. Having no prospect of closing with the enemy, they were then recalled south. A force formed on the Central Railway was to take up the chase. On 21 May, racked with fever and exhaustion, Hauptmann Wintgens handed over his command and gave himself up to a Belgian unit. His successor, Oberleutnant Heinrich Naumann, remained active in the north until finally surrendering with nearly 200 men on 2 October 1917.[43]

On the return march Murray's Column covered the 150 miles to Rungwe at an average of 17 miles a day arriving on 14 June. Here they were permitted a weeks rest. On 16 June 55 African police left for Fife to commence three months leave, the first in the Campaign. On 18 June 1917 the strength of the NRP companies under Murray's command was 11 officers 13 white NCOs, and 515 African police with 24 followers, personal servants etc, and 337 carriers. The Force was also represented in the Machine Gun Company of 5 officers, 26 white and 53 African other ranks with 7 followers and 265 carriers. The rains had ended. The plan was now to drive the enemy's main force across the Mahenge plateau south-east into the arms of a British force working inland from the Coast at Lindi.[44]

On 26 April 1917 the London Gazette announced the award of the Distinguished Conduct Medal to 575 Corporal Mambo NRP. Corporal Mambo, in command of a patrol, had been severely wounded in the knee, but maintained his position and drove off a strong force of the enemy.[45]

On 25 June 1917 Murray's Column embarked at Mwaya for Wiedhafen. On 3 July Murray established his Headquarters at Songea with the BSAP, now only 56 strong, and three companies of NRP giving a total of 400 men with 8 machine guns as his reserve. On 27 June Major Fair assumed command of the NRP in the Field. The Rhodesia Native Regiment, now under Major Carbutt, Murray posted at Kitanda. Lewis light machine guns were now becoming available in East Africa. Northey decided that the BSAP remaining fit for duty should be trained as Lewis gunners and attached to the NRP and RNR, each company of which would have two machine guns and two Lewis guns.[46]

'C' Company of the Northern Rhodesia Police joined 'E' and 'F' at Lupembe making 350 men and 6 machine guns all under Captain E G Dickinson. Dickinson was ordered to drive Hauptmann Aumann's detachment, 'A', 'L' and 5th field companies with an artillery detachment, a total of some 450 men, eastward across the Ruhuje. By activity on the left bank he was to contain the enemy on the Mpepo to Mkapira front and prevent them reinforcing Ruipa. On 27 June he arrived at Nalugombe. On 7 July he commenced his attack. By the 25th 'E' Coy had driven Aumann across the Ruhuje at Mkapira Drift. On 29 July Aumann drove in our piquet, recrossed the river and occupied the old Rhodesian trenches at Mkapira. Scouts and one section forced him to disclose his position and after a 30 minute fire fight Capt Russell and half 'F' Coy drove him out at the point of the bayonet. The enemy escaped into the thick grass and reeds of the river bed. Enemy fire prevented Capt Russell crossing in pursuit. He left a strong piquet at the crossing and reoccupied the hill.

On 7 August Acting Lieutenant Colonel Fair with 'A' Company NRP from Songea, joined 1st Rhodesia Native Regiment which had moved up from Kitanda to attack Aumann from the South. On 9 August 1917 Capt Latham, now in command of 'A' Coy, drove in 2 pickets before assaulting an enemy post at Tuturu, between Kitanda and Mpepo. Lieutenant Henry William Tarbutt, a pre-War BSAP trooper commissioned into the NRP from the BSAP service compan- ies, was bayoneted in the throat and fell into the enemy trench. Two African police were killed within five yards of the German trenches and two Africans reported missing were later confirmed as dead. The enemy later retired but not before burying Tarbutt. On his grave marker a German wrote 'Lt Tarbutt, "A" Coy N.R.Police. In honour of a brave man'.[47]

On 10 August while 'F' Coy demonstrated at Mkapira Drift, Dickinson crossed the Ruhuje with 'C' and 'E' coys by canoe, 5 miles upstream despite opposition from a troop of hippo. On 13th August 'A' Coy NRP and the Rhodesia Native Regiment joined Dickinson's three companies west of Mpepo. Lt Col Fair took command of the combined force.[48]

Aumann was strongly entrenched on a ridge one mile north-west of Mpepo. On 17 August 'C', 'E' and 'F' coys dug in within 600 yards of his position with 'A' Coy in reserve while the RNR closed in from the South. 479 Corporal Samsoni and 835 Private Moto came into action with their machine gun under automatic fire 400 yards from the enemy position. Both were wounded but remained at their posts, bringing the gun out of action when the line retired. In 1919 Samsoni and Moto were awarded the DCM for this action and their conduct at the front from August 1915 to June 1918.[49]

A combined attack from three directions at 6am on 19 August was stopped by machine gun fire which killed 4873 Machine Gun Porter Gwalia and wounded 3 others and 3 African police. On 26th August from within 100 yards of the enemy trenches 'E' and half 'F' Coy NRP, under Captains Withers and Russell, rushed an outlying post, Single Hill, north of Aumann's main postion. They took it, and consolidated in time to beat off a vigorous counterattack by 'L' Field Company. It was police against police again as the enemy charged upto, and at one point, actually penetrated, the NRP's trenches. A German was heard shouting 'Retire! Retire!' in the hope of confusing the NRP. A German NCO, an African sergeant-major and an askari were killed. Six enemy askari were taken prisoner together with their Company Commander, Oberleutnant Bauer, who died of wounds. The enemy were seen to carry off ten wounded askari. The NRP suffered 14 wounded.

Hauptmann Aumann obviously considered Single Hill to be the key to his position. After subjecting Withers' men to heavy machine gun fire all through the day of the 27 August, he abandoned Mpepo that night and broke out north-east to Likassa. Here Dickinson found him on the 29th entrenched on a wooded height near the Litete River. There was heavy fighting at close quarters. The enemy counterattacked and the RNR fell back exposing the flank of 'E' Coy NRP who withdrew on the local reserve. The Germans continued their desperate attack for 2 hours with great courage right into the lines of the NRP whose ammunition was almost exhausted. The medical staff were swamped. A/36 Pte P F M Roelke BSAP was killed while clearing a jam in his machine gun under heavy fire. General Northey recorded that Captain Dickinson handled his men very gallantly. Night fell with both sides dug in. Next morning Aumann had gone The fight had been one of the fiercest yet experienced by the Northern Rhodesia Police who lost six Africans killed, and Sgt Bainbridge and two other Europeans and 14 Africans wounded, including Sgt Changamasase who with Sgt Africa was awarded the Military Medal. Two Germans were killed with 25 enemy askari and 73 wounded and unwounded prisoners were taken, at least 20 from each of Aumann's three companies. He also left behind a damaged revolver gun.[50]

On 1 September the four companies of NRP with Lt Col Fair totalled 500 rifles and the 1st Rhodesia Native Regiment, 300. Aumann was retreating rapidly north-east towards Mahenge. Fair pursued him as far as supplies would allow and on 1 October was near Liheta, twenty five miles south-west of Mahenge. A few days later Belgian troops occupied Mahenge. Aumann turned south with his 'L' and 22nd Field Companies. On 14 October Cpl Songandewo and his 'C' Coy scouts attacked an enemy magazine, captured a German and marched him back cross country wearing only one boot. On 18 October Cpl Chakanga and 10 men of 'A' Coy rushed a piquet east of Ngombere held by a German and 10 Africans and captured 4 askari for the loss of Pte Chimai, killed. On 25 October the Northern Rhodesia Police joined the Belgians in an attack on two enemy companies found to be holding a hill at Sali Mission on the Ruaha. Pte Zalile was killed and Lt Latimer and two African police wounded. On 6 November 3 German officers,

Convalescent Asirikari of the NRP (in fezzes) & RNR (slouch hats) with lioness they shot (Photo Imperial War Museum Q17101)

142 white other ranks and 189 askari, all sick or convalescent, surrendered to Lt Col Fair at Kabati Moto. By the middle of November there were no German troops within reach. Fair was ordered to withdraw and take over Mahenge from the Belgians. This he did with much ceremony on 25 November.[51]

Meanwhile on 4 September 1917 civil police elements around Neu Langenburg had been dealing with roving bands of enemy stragglers. On 15 September Fair had been ordered to send 160 of the Rhodesia Native Regiment back to Neu Langenburg to assist. Capt Graham with 'B' and 'D' companies NRP was watching the Songea Liwale Road with a detachment at Njenje. Major J J McCarthy DSO MC NRP with his well trained Ruga Ruga, in cooperation with the 5th South African Infantry under Lt Col Fulton, was holding a portion of Portuguese East Africa west of the Luchenda River, from which they had chased von Steumer. In October 54 men of the BSAP service companies had been invalided back to Southern Rhodesia. On 29 October Lt Col Stennett arrived at Mpurukasese to resume command of the NRP. He left there on 15 November with 105 men of the Depot Company and leaving garrisons of 20 men each at Mburugande, Njenje and Mirola, joined Murray on 21 November at Jumbe Faume. There were still detachments of NRP at Ubena, Lupembe, and Muhanga on garrison and police duty.[52]

On 26 November Murray with 'B' and 'D' coys NRP, and 1/4 and 2/4 King's African Rifles, was around Tunduru with patrols on the Rovuma. Fair remained with 'A' Company to garrison Mahenge while his other three companies were ordered South to rejoin Murray. Murray's task was to prevent Major Tafel, who commanded a group of 13 companies, from joining with von Lettow, who was now in the angle formed by the Rovuma and the Indian Ocean. Murray never managed to close with Tafel, but his patrols captured every runner sent by one German commander to the other. Consequently neither knew the other's position or intentions. Tafel continued south-east through waterless and foodless country. By the time he realised that von Lettow had crossed his path, making south-west towards Ngomano on the Rovuma, it was too late to avoid Van Deventer's columns pursuing von Lettow from Lindi. On 29 November 1917 Major Tafel gave himself up, together with 111 Europeans, over 1,200 askari and about 2,200 carriers. Over 200 of his troops, with about 1,100 porters had already surrendered to 1/3 KAR on 27th November.[53]

On 25 November von Lettow forded the Rovuma at Ngomano near its confluence with the Liyenda River. With him were 300 Germans, 1,700 askari and 3,000 porters. The river was 1,200 yards wide and chest high. The Portuguese guarding the frontier were scattered by a sudden attack. Hauptmann Goering, with three field companies, also crossed successfully further downstream.[54]

Murray's task, with the NRP, 1st and 2nd Rhodesia Native Regiments, and the Ugandans of 1/4 and 2/4 KAR, was to hold the Songea and Tunduru districts and prevent the enemy doubling back into German East Africa. Posts were established on the Rovuma and patrols roved far to the South of the river as well as through the occupied territory. On 15 December Murray set up his headquarters at Songea. The greater part of the Northern Rhodesia Police concentrated at Lipumbi. Few of the original British officers were still at duty with the battalion, which was now over 1,000 strong including headquarters staff and the base organisation although Lts Latimer, Neame and Jobling, Sgts Robertson and Sinclair and 142 African police were sick in hospital. After up to three years in the Field living mainly on corned beef and rice few of either race were regarded by the medical staff as in really good health. There were 24 African Police at Fife. Many of the 19 officers at the front were from the BSAP service companies, as were almost all the 14 European other ranks. The troops in the Field were now reorganised into a conventional 'Service Battalion' of four double companies, with a machine gun company of 5 officers, 2 British NCOs and 65 African police under Captain A W M S 'Chilli' Griffin, a Stokes mortar company under Captain C E 'Anzac' Mills, Lewis gun sections totalling 49 men with one officer, signallers, scouts, medical and supply and transport sections. The men of 'E' and 'F' companies were split up among the other companies. The whole battalion was issued with 1908 web equipment less entrenching tools. The belt proved too large for most Africans. They suffered in wet weather due to a lack of groundsheets which were awaited from South Africa. By 19 December the reorganisation was complete and two patrols left for the Luchinga River. On 26 January 1918 Maj Fair and Capt Latham arrived at Lipumbi with 89 of the old 'A' Coy while Lt Gardiner left with 30 men to patrol to the Rovuma and remain at Mitomini with a platoon of the RNR.[55]

Murray had developed serious heart trouble and been admitted to hospital in December. He was invalided south on 27 January 1918. Lt Col Stennett assumed command of the RNR and 3/4 KAR as well as the NRP until Colonel Clayton arrived to take Murray's place. Colonel Ronald Ernest Murray DSO and bar DCM never recovered his health and died in England on 29 June 1920.

On 11 February 1918 the Northern Rhodesia Police Service Battalion left Kigonsera for Mbamba Bay on Lake Nyasa for a well earned rest. 165 African police were granted three month's leave. The remainder trained on the new weapons and a number of patrols were sent out. The NRP were the lowest paid African troops so the announcement of a 'War Bonus' was well received.

Back in Northern Rhodesia law and order were being maintained by the 120 remaining police, the district commissioners and their messengers. During 1917, 1,545 persons were prosecuted as a result of the work of the CID and Town and District Police and 1,427 convicted. From the BSAP had come three reinforcements. Constable J B Parkin attested on 1 October 1916, followed by D/Sgt E Rochard in January 1917, both had been with No.1 Mobile Column BSAP in 1914. Parkin was posted to Lusaka to relieve Const Lancaster for home leave. The detachment there under Sgt Maj Coote had 5 African police, two detectives and an interpreter. Each European farm in the District was visited every 6 weeks. 31 Europeans were prosecuted in 1917 and 29 convicted. Parkin was to serve with the Force for many years together with F J Willson who joined in February. There was a British sergeant at Magoye with 5 African police and a constable with an African detective at Kalomo. Sgt Maj Taylor was still at Broken Hill with a native detective, a sergeant, corporal, lance corporal and 14 privates, his detachment having been increased by three in February 1916. There were seven African police at Mumbwa and a corporal and 12 men at Ndola.

There was still a small military detachment at Mongu in early 1917 but the only police elsewhere in Barotseland were the District Police at Balovale. There were District Police detachments of a sergeant, a corporal and 14 men at Fort Jameson, a corporal, bugler and 5 privates at Petauke and a lance corporal and 6 at Lundazi, but only the NCOs and bugler had any experience. The Bemba privates at these stations in 1914 had ben sent to the Front in June 1916 and replaced by recruits.[56]

In May 1917 Capt Ingles arrived in the Namwala District to recruit among the Mashukulumbwe. He met with little success before leaving for Livingstone in July prior to retirement from the Force and service in France. Ingles was relieved by the Mashukulumbwe's old District Commissioner, Capt Andrew Dale, crippled at Loos in 1915. Dale fared little better and advised that the attempt be abandoned. This was the first attempt to recruit members of this tribe since the early days of the Barotse Native Police. In later years the Ila proved themselves efficient soldiers and policemen.[57]

In March 1917 a rebellion had broken out in the Tete Province of Portuguese East Africa. On 5 April 1917 the Portuguese administrator from Zumbo fled across the Zambezi to Feira from where the District Police detachment of a corporal and 8 men had been withdrawn in November 1916. The Native Commissioner at Feira was Captain C F Molyneux who had served at the Front with the NRRifles. Molyneux crossed the river and recovered a large quantity of arms which his guest had abandoned at Zumbo and organised a defence force on the Northern Rhodesia side. On 26 July 1917 Lieut B K Castor arrived from Livingstone with Sgt Francis, 43 African police and a Maxim. Leaving Francis at Feira, Castor with the machine gun and 32 men took post at Matambwa 36 miles up-river. There were no serious incursions but some 5,000 African refugees sought shelter in Northern Rhodesia where food was already short.[58]

On 8 March 1918 Northern Rhodesia agreed to provide a platoon of NRP to police the Bismarcksburg District of the occupied German territory, at the expense of the United Kingdom Government.[59]

In May 1918 Lieutenant Colonel H M Stennett DSO was invalided to Zomba with dysentery. Major Fair having departed on long leave on 9 April, Major E G Dickinson MC assumed command of the Service Battalion. On 6 May Lt Castor arrived at Mbamba Bay with 72 recruits from Livingstone followed shortly thereafter by Capt Castle with 106 men returning from leave, which was just as well, as on 27 May 1918 the NRP Service Battalion was ordered to join Colonel Hawthorn's column with the Rhodesia Native Regiment and 3/1 and 1/4 KAR to prevent von Lettow coming west into Nyasaland. By 1 June the whole Battalion had left Mbamba Bay by steamer for Fort Johnston where it completed its concentration on 6 June. On the 10th they were rushed by motor vehicle to Limbe and from there marched past Mount Malanje into Portuguese territory in order to intercept the enemy commander at Alto Mulocque. The country was very difficult. They arrived to find that von Lettow had passed by and was already far to the South.[60]

In July Major General Sir Edward Northey KCMG CB left on appointment as Governor of British East Africa. Hawthorn succeeded him in command of Norforce, as the Nyasaland Rhodesia Field Force was known in 'signalese', with the temporary rank of Brigadier General. The NRP Service Battalion now joined the pursuit of von Lettow through Portuguese East Africa to the coast near Quelimane. The enemy doubled back north-east, cutting up 3/3 KAR at Namirrue on 22–23 July, and moving on to Chalaua He crossed the Mulocque above Tipe and headed west into the area Ilee-Munevalia. On 8 August the Northern Rhodesia Police joined 1/3 KAR in a column under the command of Lt Col C G Durham, called Durcol.[61]

Durcol marched via Namezeze, Nametil and Calipo to Alto Ligonha. The situation was confused, but the enemy was apparently moving towards Regone to the West. At one stage the NRP were stranded by lack of food due to a transport breakdown and chicken pox among the carriers. Durcol was ordered to march parallel to his northern flank, to head off any attempt to make for the Rovuma. The NRP marched through the Inagu Hills and at the end of August was near Maloketera. On 24 August the enemy successfully engaged half of 2/4 KAR at Namarroe. On the 31 August he was repulsed by 1 and 2 KAR at Lioma, but cut through the Inagu Hills at Muanhupa. 1/4 KAR and the Rhodesia Native Regiment attempted to bar his passage of the Lurio River and all three battalions of 2 KAR (KARTUCOL) were in hot pursuit. On 11 September the NRP Service Battalion was ordered to march back to Fort Johnston. In three months they had marched 900 miles, without supply columns, living as best they could, and for much of the time in the sweltering coastal lowlands. On one occasion the NRP marched forty eight miles in thirty eight hours with only four hours sleep and no stragglers. At the end, when asked whether they could move on again that night, Lt Col Dickinson felt able to say that they could.[62]

On 23 September 1918 the Battalion was moved across Lake Nyasa by steamer back to Mbamba Bay in the Songea District of German East Africa where 700 local carriers joined. As Hawthorn had realised, Von Lettow was heading north for his home territory. 'D' Coy was first to land and set off for Songea under 2/4 KAR. At 1am on 4 October the weakened NRP battalion, led by Capt Langham's 'B' Coy, was approaching Fusi, fifteen miles west of Songea on the Songea-Wiedhafen Road, near Perimiho Mission when Sgt Sinclair, on patrol, reported that four hours earlier the enemy had been two hours march to the South. Shortly after being overtaken by a Ford vanette, Langham heard machine gun fire. Lt Col Dickinson tapped into the telephone line and ascertained that the vehicle had arrived at Songea riddled with bullets. Extra flankers and scouts were sent out and the advance continued for a mile before the line was tapped again and found to have been cut. The battalion formed hollow square with the hospital, in a gravel pit, and stores and carriers in the centre though most of the local carriers soon decamped. Sgt Greenspan was sent forward with a patrol while the rest of 'B' Coy, extended each side of the road at three pace intervals and lay down in the long grass with bayonets fixed. Greenspan's patrol soon made contact and was driven back hotly pursued by the enemy who were repulsed by 'B' Coy with rapid fire and the bayonet. The enemy main force soon came up and his attack continued for five and a half hours, but von Lettow was unable to break through or outflank the NRP. Firing from another gravel pit Capt Mills' mortars put their bombs down just in front of the forward positions. While under heavy machine gun fire 640 Colour Sergeant Tegete set an outstanding example to all present, showing complete disregard of danger by walking up and down the line giving the men targets and controlling their fire. 399 Sergeant Chikusi set a fine example to his section under heavy machine gun and rifle fire and, according to the citation for his DCM, by encouraging the young askari, was largely instrumental in beating off the enemy attack. 451 C/Sgt Yasi, Langham's CSM, was awarded the Military Medal for carrying orders under fire and 421 Pte Kunenga for carrying ammunition. A/205 Sgt J Kohr BSAP attached NRP won the same award. Lieutenant L J Champion, commanding 'A' Coy, another pre-war BSAP trooper commissioned from the ranks of the service companies, died of wounds after this action. Privates 1699 Siyeya and S/33 Mwanabamba were killed and 12 African police wounded with one British NCO and two first line carriers. One man was missing believed killed.[63]

After dark the Battalion withdrew to a stronger position on high ground, but von Lettow was not going to continue the action or await the arrival of British reinforcements. He marched by night round to the west of the NRP position and made for Peramiho Mission. According to Langham, the NRP's ammunition was so low that when Lt Gardiner was sent out with half 'C' Coy to find and follow the enemy spoor only sufficient ammunition could be got together for them for 50 rounds per man. The bodies of 4 enemy askari were found and two Germans, nine of their askari and 51 porters captured. Stragglers captured later said that 3 Germans and 9 askari had been killed and 4 Germans and 20 askari wounded.

2/4 KAR, Ugandans, had now closed up from Songea and set off in pursuit still with 'D' Company NRP under command. The remainder of the NRP marched back to the lake shore immobilised by the desertion of the local carriers. It was impossible to supply more than one battalion moving overland and the lake steamers gave mobility. Unfortunately one of the three steamers chose this crucial time to break down. The Northern Rhodesia Police had to wait for the last of 1/4 KAR to be ferried north, but on 20 October they were on board ship bound for Mwaya at the head of the Lake.

Meanwhile on 17 October, 2/4 KAR had engaged the enemy rearguard south of Ubena. Entering the town on the 18th they found Major General Wahle and other enemy sick and wounded left behind in the hospital. Von Lettow had made remarkable time up the Songea-Njombe Road. He still had his hard core of 1,600 German East African porters, mainly from the Wanyamwezi tribe, renowned as the best porters in Africa. They were also brave fighters, providing a mobile recruiting depot from which to make good casualties among his askari. Other carriers the German commander conscripted as he went along. But where was he going? Tabora seemed the most likely destination. The troops on the Central Railway were strengthened. The Nyasalanders of 1/2 KAR had been shipped up the coast from Porto Amelia to Dar es Salaam, and railed west. They were now shipped down Lake Tanganyika to Bismarcksburg. The route to Elizabethville was watched by a Belgian Brigade west of Lake Tanganyika. An invasion of Northern Rhodesia seemed unlikely, but the Territory was completely devoid of fighting troops. Accordingly two King's African Rifles battalions were withdrawn to Lindi, to take ship for Beira and entrain for Broken Hill. Whatever the enemy's destination it was judged that he might first wish to raid the supply depot at Fife. This was therefore to be the destination of the Northern Rhodesia Police Service Battalion.[64]

On 24 October the first company, 'C' under Capt Allport, landed at Mwaya and marched off immediately. The race was almost neck and neck. Finding a party of the enemy across the Stevenson Road, Allport took to the bush. He reached Fife at 8 p.m. on 31 October. Major B J Graham's company, which had come overland with 2/4 KAR, left that battalion at Neu Langenburg and reached Fife at 2.40 p.m. on 1 November 1918. Von Lettow attacked at 5.30 that afternoon from three sides, driving in the police pickets. Graham and Allport had made good use of the time available for entrenching. Reconnaissance showed the German commander that an assault on Fife would be too costly. He decided to merely shell the position in the hope of killing a large proportion of the garrison. He opened fire next morning with a Portuguese field gun, a trench mortar, which happily blew up on its second discharge, and ten machine guns. The defenders gave as good as they got. Private A G Charters BSAP handled his machine gun with great ability and coolness and although under heavy machine gun fire continued to search the enemy position, and succeeded in temporarily silencing the enemy's fire. When Acting Sergeant A J Moffat BSAP's emplacement was destroyed by machine gun fire, he moved his machine gun to an adjacent fire bay, and continued to search the enemy's position, eventually silencing the machine gun opposite him.[65]

Charters and Moffat were later awarded the Distinguished Conduct Medal for their part in the defence of Fife as was a third member of the BSAP, a telegraphist at Fife. Pte G S Bouwer had been manning an advanced post on 30 October. When this had to be evacuated he remained close by, tapping out information with a vibrator until he saw an enemy patrol approaching. He then retired three miles to a position overlooking Fife and, although his carriers deserted he remained, passing back valuable information. For his conspicious gallantry and devotion to duty at Fife together with that already described at Fusi Village C/Sgt Tegete was also awarded the DCM.

According to the Battalion war diary, Major General von Lettow-Vorbeck later said that during this action he had his narrowest escape from death. He lay on the ground for half an hour while machine gun fire almost parted the hair on the back of his head.[66]

At midnight the wily enemy commander led his faithful troops off south-west for Kasama via Kayambi Mission. As General Van Deventer wrote in his final despatch, quoting von Moltke, 'There are always three courses of action open to the enemy, and he usually takes the fourth'. Northern Rhodesia was still virtually defenceless.

On 4 November Lt Col Dickinson was making for Fife from Mwaya with a third company of the Service Battalion when a telegraphist told him that the Germans had taken Fife and were en route for Kasama. Dickinson had started south to intercept them when he met an old headman who told him that Fife had not fallen. Dickinson turned north again in the hope of catching the enemy at Fife. Of course they had already gone.

On 2 November Captain Russell with 'B' Company NRP had joined 1/4 KAR near Mbosi. They now led that battalion into Fife. Here the two battalion commanders agreed that Captain Castor's company of the NRP should also join 1/4 KAR. By nightfall 1/4 KAR had covered 11 miles to Mandala, where the body of an African policeman was found. CO 1/4 KAR was confident that with six companies he could engage the enemy decisively but on 5 November higher authority ordered the return of Captain Castor's company to the NRP Service Battalion which had been ordered to march to Abercorn. Thus weakened 1/4 KAR caught up with the German rearguard at Tumba on 6th November, capturing two machine guns. The enemy held the water. 'B' Coy NRP had been in reserve but made a successful attack enabling the KAR to camp over the water.

Lt Col E B B Hawkins, CO 1/4 KAR was lucky to have an NRP company with him as he had no map of the area other than in a small world atlas. At 1255hrs on 7 November Russell's company ran into the enemy rearguard in a thunderstorm. By 1500hrs they had driven them out of Kayambi Mission and secured the ridge beyond. On 8th November at the Mpanda River Lionel Smith, a cattle farmer from Saisi, offered his services as a guide. Smith had served as a temporary 2Lt in the NRP in 1915. He was able to lead the KAR down the old mail path, 14 miles shorter than the motor road followed to Kasama by von Lettow.[67]

At Kasama there was only a supply officer, Lieutenant E J Leslie, with three lorries used to ferry supplies from the Chiwutuwutu Depot on the Lukulu River, eleven NRP African convalescents and some soldiers serving sentences. Captain F S James, also recovering from wounds, had left for Abercorn on 31 October with all those fit for service. Permission to release military prisoners from Kasama gaol was obtained by telegraph.[68]

On 1 November the European women evacuated from Abercorn reached Kasama. On 2nd November Lieutenant Sibbold 2/1 KAR came in from Chinsali with some KAR recruits. The convalescents and askari from the gaol were added to his command giving him 50-60 men. On 4 November a motor reconnaissance reported that the Germans were at Luchinda which was burning. On the 5th the enemy were reported advancing on the White Fathers' Mission at Kayambi. Orders were received by wire to evacuate stores from Kasama.[69]

The Native Commissioner, Hector Croad, sent the white women south by lorry to the Chambezi Rubber Factory on their way to Mpika. He backloaded all cash and what ammunition there was, 30 miles to the Chiwutuwutu Depot. From there much of it was removed by canoe to an island in the Bangweulu Swamps, well out of enemy reach. Having evacuated all military and European personnel and such warlike stores and supplies as he could by motor vehicle or porter, Croad obeyed telegraphic instructions to employ himself and his staff on intelligence work.

On Wednesday 6 November von Lettow was reported at Kayambi. On the 8th a scouting patrol of askari under Driver Weitz of the BSAP Motor Transport engaged the enemy on the Kalungu Stream, 20 miles north of Kasama. Weitz and

Mr R Thornton, a farmer who had volunteered and been given command of a patrol on the Abercorn Road, withdrew on Lieutenant Sibbold's main position on the Milima Stream, six miles out, where he had a machine gun. Sibbold sent word to Leslie to burn all remaining stores in Kasama. At 5 pm Croad and Leslie left for the Lukulu Depot by motor car driven by Sergeant F Rumsey. During the night Sibbold's motley band on the Milima lost their nerve and faded away. During the next day he managed to get most of them back together at Nkolenfu-mu's village. Having regard to the composition of this force, not much could have been expected of it. Most of those from the gaol had been put there for desertion. The NRP convalescents behaved well when under fire on 11 November.[70]

Von Lettow arrived at Kasama on 9 November. On the 10th Hector Croad drove up in a lorry with Rumsey. They were halted by trees felled across the road just outside the town. Reconnoitring, Croad at first thought the khaki clad troops he could see were KAR and nearly walked in. Just in time he and Rumsey noticed a gang of African women being taken to draw water under guard. The two Britons returned to Chiwutuwutu by the new motor road while the enemy advance guard was moving in the same direction by the older shorter track.

On 9, 10 and 11 November 1918, as much as possible of the supplies at Chi-wutuwutu were sent by lorry or canoe another 24 miles to the Chambezi Rubber Factory.[71]

Croad wrote in September 1937: 'At dusk on 11th November Mr Thornton, who had taken charge of the invalided Northern Rhodesia Police, fell back on Chiwutuwutu, and the natives in the rest of the canoes, who could hear the German guns to the north, cleared off down the river. At about 8 o'clock, having sent off the last lorry with loads, we poured what petrol was left over the rest and set fire to the stores. We walked off to the south as the first Germans came in from the north! At about 1 o'clock we were met on the road by Rumsey with one of the lorries. He brought me a wire from the Administrator in Livingstone informing me of the Armistice, but saying that we were to carry on till General van Deventer wired me instructions. On reaching the Chambezi we found they had managed to get two Maxims placed on the south of the river, but were wondering if they would work. On the morning of 13th November the German advance patrol started firing into the factory with Lewis guns, and very nearly bagged the late Mr Charles Simpson of the rubber factory. They were met by a quite good rattle from the south side, but as the Germans were quite concealed in the trees on the far side, nothing happened, and after a quarter of an hour firing ceased. About noon I got a wire from van Deventer for Von Lettow, with instructions to get in touch with him and deliver it. Spangenberg, in charge of the advance, received this. On the morning of the 14th I met General Von Lettow on the Chambezi. He asked me if I would assure him that van Deventer's wire was authentic, and then said he would carry out the instructions contained in it, i.e. to march his men back to Abercorn and lay down his arms there. The King's African Rifles were to follow him to Abercorn. Von Lettow wrote out, and asked me to arrange to have sent for him, a wire to the Kaiser in Berlin. I told him that Germany was declared a Republic and that the Kaiser had fled to Holland. He looked upset at this, but said his government would get it in any case. As he says in his book, he did not believe it. His original wire is now in the museum at Livingstone. The white prisoners were to be released in Kasama, and in the afternoon Spangenberg brought it in and handed over their native prisoners. I then returned to Kasama. The main body of the Germans was spread along the road from Chiwutuwutu to Kasama, and their rearguard had come in from Milima, six miles to the north of Kasama. Mr Russell, who was attached to the Northern Rhodesia Police (later Provincial Commissioner, Fort Jameson) had been in advance of the King's African Rifles and had had a scrap on the Milima with the German rearguard. The King's African Rifles did not reach Kasama and were camped out near Milima. The Germans told me they were upset at the loss of their best native gunner. Hauptmann Kohl and others told me they thought they were making for Broken Hill, and that if they had reached the railway line they would have destroyed it and followed it north into the Congo, or if they had met a force north of Broken Hill, they might have turned east to Fort Jameson and Nyasaland. I said they would have had trouble to get food in the Serenje country for their men, but they replied that they had information that they could find plenty in the villages near the Bangweulu Swamps. Their information as to the country was wonderfully accurate. Most of the native carriers were armed and could have been put into the firing line. Numbers of guns and much ammunition thrown away along the road between the Chambezi and Kasama were brought into Kasama by our own natives. I found three Maxims in the stream below my house in Kasama. Plenty of other weapons were, I think, found and never brought in. These consisted of Portuguese rifles, .303s, and the old German Mausers. The Germans were well equipped with Portuguese and .303 ammunition. The next dry season, when the grass fires started, was like a small battle round Kasama as the cartridges exploded. Von Lettow's book on the campaign, as far as I was able to check it, seemed very accurate. "The African Lakes" buildings in Kasama were destroyed by the Germans, who thought they were Government buildings. They had burnt part of the gaol and had made ready to burn the police camp buildings. The Government offices were burnt by some of our people before the Germans arrived.'[72]

1/4 KAR had reached the Milima Stream on 12 November with 'B' Coy NRP as its right forward company. Lieutenant Colonel Hawkins had heard nothing of the Armistice and was deploying his troops to surround Kasama when at 11.30 am on 13 November a patrol of askari posted on the main road reported that two motorcyclists carrying white flags had come from the direction of Abercorn, and, in spite of their warning shouts, had gone forward towards the enemy at Kasama. At 2.42 pm the advance point of the battalion, then four miles north of Kasama, met two German askari with a large white flag, bearing the telegram that von Lettow had received from the motorcyclists, announcing the Armistice.[73]

Von Lettow wrote that he was met by one of the motorcyclists, when exploring the Chambezi River and Broken Hill road by himself. The telegram was dated 12 November and read:

Send following to Colonel Von Lettow Vorbeck under white flag. The Prime Minister of England has announced that an armistice was signed at 5 hours on November

11th, and that hostilities on all fronts cease at 11 hours on November 11th. I am ordering my troops to cease hostilities forthwith unless attacked and, of course I conclude that you will do the same. Conditions of armistice will be forwarded to you immediately I receive them. Meanwhile I suggest you should remain in your present vicinity in order to facilitate communication – General Van Deventer.

Von Lettow wrote: 'Our feelings were very mixed. Personally, as I had no knowledge of the real state of affairs in Germany, I felt convinced that the conclusion of hostilities must have been favourable, or at least not unfavourable to Germany. Spangenberg's detachment, which was on ahead, had to be told as soon as possible, and I immediately set out on my bicycle after it, taking with me Haouter, a Landsturm soldier, as my sole companion. About half-way, Weissmann's cyclist patrol of Spangenberg's detachment met me and reported that Captain Spangenberg had arrived at the Chambezi. Although I had no doubts about the correctness of the English news, our position was very uncomfortable. We were in a district where there was little food, and were therefore compelled to move on from place to place. This circumstance had already compelled us to reconnoitre and secure for ourselves the crossings of the Chambezi. If hostilities were resumed we must be certain of a safe crossing. This was a burning question, as the rainy season, meaning a great rise of this river, was near at hand. We had already encountered heavy storms. I had, therefore, much to discuss with Captain Spangenberg and the English officer who would presumably be on the far bank of the river. In any case, we must continue to devote our energies to buying or getting food. Full of that idea, I sent my companion back and cycled myself with Weissmann's patrol to Spangenberg's detachment. We arrived about eight o'clock when it was quite dark. Captain Spangenberg was away on a reconnaissance, but Assistant Paymaster Dohmen and other Europeans looked after me well as soon as they learnt of my arrival. I was able to convince myself that the supply depot of Kasama really existed. I tasted jam and other good things which had been unknown to me hitherto. When Captain Spangenberg came back he told me that he had already heard of the armistice through the English. After I had gone to bed in his tent, he brought me about midnight a telegram from General Van Deventer which had been brought in by the English.'

This telegram ran as follows:

13.11.18 To Norforce. Karwunfor via Fife. Send following to Colonel Von Lettow Vorbeck under white flag: War Office London telegraphs that clause seventeen of the armistice signed by the German Govt. provides for unconditional surrender of all German forces operating in East Africa within one month from Nov. 11th.

My conditions are: First: hand over all allied prisoners in your hands, Europeans and natives, to the nearest body of British troops forthwith. Second: that you bring your forces to Abercorn without delay, as Abercorn is the nearest place at which I can supply you with food. Third: that you hand over all arms and ammunition to my representative at Abercorn. I will, however allow you and your officers and European ranks to retain their personal weapons for the present in consideration of the gallant fight you have made, provided that you bring your force to Abercorn without delay. Arrangements will be made at Abercorn to send all Germans to Morogoro and to repatriate German Askari. Kindly send an early answer giving probable date of arival at Abercorn and numbers of German officers and men, Askari and followers.[74]

Von Lettow's acceptance of the terms was handed to Lt Col Hawkins on the morning of 16 November. A few hours later the German column marched through the KAR camp for Abercorn.

1/4 KAR and 'B' Coy NRP set out for Abercorn at dawn on the 17th and arrived there on the 24th. The rest of the Northern Rhodesia Police Service Battalion had been at Abercorn since 9 November. Brigadier General W F S Edwards CMG DSO had also arrived to deputise for Lieutenant General Van Deventer at the formal surrender. General Edwards had been commanding the British troops on the Central Railway in German East Africa. He had been Inspector General of Police in British East Africa and Uganda since 1908, and should not be confused with Brigadier General A H M Edwards, the Commandant General of Rhodesian Forces.[75]

At 10.30 am on 25 November 1918 General Edwards inspected a guard of honour formed by 25 men from each battalion on the Boma tennis court. At 11 am Major General von Lettow Vorbeck appeared at the head of his troops. He read out the terms of surrender in German to his officers and European non-commissioned officers and then repeated them in English. The German commander then offered his sword to General Edwards, who refused it, saying he had much pleasure in allowing the officers to retain their personal arms in view of the very gallant fight which they had made. Lt Col Dickinson and his adjutant, Capt Wardroper, accompanied General Edwards during the ceremony.[76]

NRP at the German Surrender Abercorn 25 November 1918, Captain Griffin nearest the camera (Alan Walker)

The enemy troops then grounded their arms and equipment and stacked their machine guns and ammunition before being marched off to their camp. With von Lettow at the surrender were Doctor Schnee, the Governor General of German East Africa, 20 combatant officers, six medical officers, a veterinary officer, a pharmacist, a field telegraph officer, 125 white other ranks, 1,168 askari, 1,522 native carriers and 819 women. The force was organised in nine field companies, three schutzen companies, a battery, five medical units, a field telegraph station, four ammunition columns, and a prisoner of war camp. The arms handed over were one Portuguese gun, 24 machine guns, 14 Lewis guns and 1,071 rifles, with 40 rounds of artillery ammunition and 208,000 rounds of small arms ammunition. Although the African troops appeared to be glad that the rigours of the campaign were over, the Germans themselves felt the surrender keenly.[77]

On 26 November the NRP played 1/4 KAR at football. Neither team scored. On 16 December Lt Col Stennett arrived and demobilization commenced.[78]

Von Lettow embarked for Europe on 17 January 1919. The German commander had spoken highly of the fighting qualities of the Northern Rhodesia Police, or as his native troops had described them to distinguish them from the Rhodesia Native Regiment, 'The Old Askari.'[79]

Annex to Chapter 7

OFFICERS & BRITISH OTHER RANKS NORTHERN RHODESIA POLICE JOINED OR ATTACHED 1 MAY 1916–DECEMBER 1918

JONES Hugh Gerald MC(12.9.17) Tpr Salisby Rifles '96 BSAP '97 SR Customs 4.02 Collctr Customs NWR 21.9.05 NC 2.4.08 Insp Rhod Natives Katanga 1910–12.11 NC Fife 28.9.13 T/Capt NRP 13.5.16 Political Offr Iringa 15.12.16 T/Hon Maj 1.5.17 rtd '24

WOOD Lionel Evelyn Hickson ANC Fife T/Lt 22.5.16–1.5.17 Asst to H G Jones

SIMPSON Jas Finerty 1RR SWA'14 A225 B Coy BSAP att NRP S/Sgt kia25.1.17 age 21

CHESNAYE Maj Christian Purefoy CBE see Notes Ch2 note 40

JORDAN Edwin Henry Knowles, Post & Tel Cape 97 Clk to Civ Commr Bwayo 8.03 Clk to DC Batoka 6.5.05 ANC 13.5.06 NC 15.9.11 T/Lt NRP Asst Political Offr Kasanga GEA 24.6.16 T/Hon Capt 1.5.17 NC Chinsali'21

BAINBRIDGE Frederick 1804 Tpr BSAP'14 SRC 15 att NRP Sgt B Coy 16 w30.8.17 invalided Salisby 17

THOMAS Brian Jas b Bmghm 16.3.92 Tpr RD 1.7.09 BSAP 13.10.13 SRC att NRP Sgt'16 MID 2/Sgt MGs NRP 1.1.19 CSM 6.2.24 RSM 25.9.26 rtd 33 father of F A Thomas NRP 56 B B Thomas NRP 4.51

BARTON Cecil Algernon Bruce DCM(LG26.4.17) b Londn 12.3.91 Fm Asst Lomagundi SR 10 FJ 106 NRRifles 14 SRC 15 Sgt att NRP CSgt T/Lt MGO 1/1KAR 17 Nyasald 19 Life Pres BESL Nyasald to SA 62 d5.1.73

PARKIN John Bingley MSM 33 b26.12.82 BSAP 29.7.10 Cpl No1 Mob Colm 14 Const NRP 1.10.16 2/Sgt 10.10.21 1/Sgt 12.8.24 SM WO2 1.1.25 Insp 1.4.28 rtd4.33

MESSUM Alfd Leslie bUK 93 Tpr BSAP 12 SRC 11.15 Sgt E Coy NRP w2.1.17 Pay Offce Salisby T/2lt NRP 12.17 T/Lt 18.7.18 Lt 1.4.19 Capt 26.5.28 NRR rtd 33 SR d post 73

LANGHAM Robt Wm Marsh MC(LG5.6.19) 1459 Tpr BSAP'11 SRC'15 Cpl T/2Lt NRP 4.1.17 T/Lt 4.9.17 Lt 1.1.19 rsgnd 7.10.22 Hunter, Elephant Contrl Offr'34–47

LACEY John A38 A Coy BSAP Sgt T/2Lt NRP 10.1.17

LATIMER Roydon Digby Neville 1654 Tpr BSAP'12 SRC'15 Sgt T/2Lt NRP 10.1.17 w1.17 inv14.10.18 Clk Secretariat NR 19 ANC Tanganyika Dist'21

ROCHARD Everard 1489 BSAP'11 Cpl No.1 Mob Colm'14 Sgt NRP CID 22.1.17 D/Insp'19 rsgnd 10.8.21 Fmr Chisamba with Kirk

WILLSON Ferdinand John b Londn 20.12.88 BSAP 27.7.14 Sgt NRP 7.2.17 WO2 D/Insp 1.1.23 A/WO1 1.12.26 C/Insp CID'27 rtd'32

WHYTE Stuart Norman A250 SRC Sgt att NRP 3.17 Italian Bronze Medal LG13.8.17 dschge 5.2.18

FRANCIS H (V?) A371 SRC Sgt att NRP 17 CClk Secretariat NR?

HICKS Jas Bracher Grenfell BSAP 9.12.11 NRP 1.4.17?

CHAMPION Leonard John b84 s/o J I Burnhm–on–Sea 1412 BSAP'11 SRC'15 Sgt T/2Lt NRP 5.4.17 FrMM(LG31.8.17) dow Songea 4.10.18

GARDINER Cecil Senior 1494 BSAP'11 Cpl No.1 Mob Colm 14 Depot BSAP T/2Lt NRP 5.4.17 Lt 1.1.19 MID 5.6.19 Capt FJ 25.1.27 Salisby Hosp 8.27 appdx/gastric ulcer d brain abcess 18.10.27

TARBUTT Henry Wm s/o Henry Fison T 'Wayside' Onslow Cres Woking 1521 BSAP'11 SRC'15 Sgt T/2Lt NRP 5.4.17 kia9.8.17 Tuturu age 26

NEAME Arthur Langley 1557 BSAP'12 SRC Sgt T/2Lt NRP 6.6.17

DALE Andrew Murray T/Capt NRP 13.6.17 see Chap 4 note 44

STEVENS Edward William 1257 BSAP'10 Sgt SRC T/2Lt NRP 9.7.17

FUTTER A138 SRC MGs att NRP sl w16.8.17

ROELKE Philip Frank Max s/o M R of Raylton Bwayo A62 Pte A Coy BSAP kia 30.8.17 Likassa age 21

BROOKES Chas MM(LG12.3.18) A277 pte SRC 1.16 w30.8.17 Likassa dschge 21.2.18

WINGHAM F 1692 Tpr BSAP'13 SRC Sgt w hand Likassa 30.8.17 to UK fthr trtmnt age 27

FAIRBAIRN Aubrey John 1413 Tpr BSAP'11 Cpl SRC Sgt att NRP MID(25.9.17)

HENDERSON Walter John MSM(LG4.2.19) ed Kg Edwd's Sch Wantage, 1843 BSAP'14 SRC 12 $\frac{1}{2}$ pdr gnr'15 att NRP Sgt MID 25.9.17 Lt Carrier Tpt 18–19 ANC NR? Africa Star WW2

JOBLING Kenneth B NRGS 8.4.13 T/Lt NRP s28.2.18? ACommr Income Tax 22.3.21 Registrar Gen 21.5.22

FOSTER Sydney le Neve 1493 BSAP'11 rft SRC 3/Sgt att NRP

FRASER Andrew Wm 1622 BSAP'12 Sgt Staff Clk SRC sev w 10.16 T/Lt 7.11.17 MGO NRP– 22.5.19 age 28

GOSLING Chas Henry Tpr BSAP 19.9.13 NRP 7.11.17

HIGH A66 SRC lve 3 mths 13.11.17

ROBERTSON John, Rlys 1RR A97 A Coy SRC 15 T/Sgt att NRP s31.12.17 MID LG2.8.18

THOMSON John b Inverurie A149 SRC ASgt att NRP ddse10.11.17 age 38

SINCLAIR John Keir, Salisby 1RR A161 SRC Sgt inv31.12.17 MID LG3.6.19

McADAMS L B J A163 SRC T/2Lt NRP 18

DUNKLEY C C A191 SRC

KOHR John MM(4,10,18 LG28.3.19) A207 SRC Sgt Lewis guns

LAPRAIK Jas 1RR A210 SRC Sig Sgt MID LG25.9.17 SM att NRP T/2Lt Sig Offr 13.5.18

HALL Hugh Lumley 'Harry' A257 SRC T/Lt C Coy NRP MID25.9.17'19 Elephant Control Offr'34–k by elephant'36

WALKER Wm Henry Joshua MSM b82 Sheffield to SR'10 Mng Matabeleld SRV Pte B Coy BSAP 1.16 Medical Sect 4.17 SM att NRP '18 PWD NR '19 Insp PWD Mongu rtd '32 d'55

HAUPT A299 SRC

SMITH A310 SRC s Zomba 7.12.17

BAXTER A312 SRC NRP Fwd Depot

CRIPWELL Henry Archer MID3.6.19 A313 A Coy BSAP 16 Sgt att NRP NC SR ltr PC

GREENSPAN Max OBE A317 SRC Sgt NRP B Coy by 10.18 WAFF WW2

MILNE D NRRifles 14 A319 SRC 16

MAHER Thos Lane MM(LG3.7.19) Lstone NRRIfles A320 SRC 2/Sgt att NRP

BOUWER Gerhardus Schoeman DCM(LG11.3.20) A325 SRC 16 att NRP

CHARTERS Alfd Graham DCM(LG11.3.20) A327 SRC LGs A/3/Sgt att NRP Const NRP 25.8.21–9.9.24

MOFFAT Alexdr Jeffries DCM(LG11.3.20) A330 SRC ASgt LGs NRP 18

SAUNDERS John Thos Hollinshead b6.7.94 2RR 16.7.15 A331 SRC 1.8.17–att NRP–2/Sgt NRP 1.1.19 Kasama d20.5.28 RTA

SCHRONEN Christian Frederic 'Pop' MSM (LG4.2.19) 1457 Tpr BSAP 11 SRC att NRP Sgt MID (LG2.8.18) CSM NRP 21.3.19 RSM 15.9.23 Hd Gaoler 1.9.26 rtd 39 f-in-law of L M Clark NRP'38

WHITEHEAD John Cyril 1903 Tpr BSAP'14 SRC Sgt att NRP

WRIGHT Wm s/o Chas of Chester 1864 BSAP 14 1RR 14 SRC Sgt att NRP drnd at Sea Kenilwth Castle 4.6.18 age 28

SMITH Albert Augustus SMITH OBE20, 1623 BSAP 12 Ag/S/Insp SRC 15 Lt SO Sups Murray's Colm 17 QM SBn NRP 18 Lt P&QM 1.6.19 Capt QM & Cntrllr Govt Stores & Tpt 1.10.25 Cntrllr PWD 1.4.32 rtd 33 Pres Kitwe Chmbr of Commerce MLC 39

MILLS Chas Egerton 'ANZAC' MBE19 Mgr Leopard's Hill Estate Lka Sgt NRRif T/Lt 27.4.15 SRC MGs; OC Mor Coy NRP 18–9 Capt JP 13.11.21 NRVF rsgnd 31.3.25 hunter farmer cattle drover prospectr, Kanona GNRd dBH 46

DAWES Wm Henry 1RR A243 SRC w15 2Sgt MID(LG25.9.17) Lt NRP'18 inv 11.18

SANDFORD Thos Fredk CMG MBE BA, NERGS 7.11.08 ANC 26.9.10 AMag 1.4.13 NRVF Capt OC B Coy FJ T/Capt NRP fr Repat duty 25.2.18 NC Lundazi'21 DC Ndola'27 PC Lka'34 Ndola'37 Lka'37 Sec NA; Ag Ch Sec'40

MACKENZIE-KENNEDY Sir Henry Chas Donald Cleveland KCMG 39 BA b89 s/o Maj Gen ed Marlborough Cam, Cdt NR 7.12.12 ANC'15 NC 15.7.18 T/Lt NRP'18 NC Chilanga'24 Prin Asst to Ch Sec'27 Ch Sec'30 CMG 32 Ch Sec Tanganyika'35 Gov Nyasald'39 & Ch Political Offr EA Forces'39–40 Gov Mauritius'42 rtd'49

ALGAR Hugh Stanley b31.8.89 Tpr BSAP 10.12–Civ Clk NRP 4.10.15 T/Lt Ag P&QM 1.4.18–9.5.19 Mag's Clk Kasama 27.6.20 rtd'37

COPEMAN 2Lt 2i/c B Coy 11.18

CRAXTON Mark Wm MM 959 BSAP'08 Sgt Town Police CQMS RNR CSM T/2Lt att NRP 25.10.18 A Coy

HARPER Bertram 1391 BSAP'10 RNR Sgt ACSM T/2Lt att NRP 25.10 ddse Salisby 26.10.18 never joined

COOKE Arthur Mark 1665 BSAP'13 RNR 3/Sgt T/2Lt att NRP 6.11 18

OLIVE Clifford Frank 1897 BSAP'14 D/Sgt NRP 1.11.18 dshge own req 31.3.24

Notes

1. Official History pp192–4
   Cdr Geoffrey Basil SPICER-SIMPSON DSO RN FRGS b Hobart'76 Cdt RN'88 Midshpmn'91 SLt'96 Lt'98 Bdy Comm NBorneo'01 Svy Uppr Yangtse'05–8 LtCdr'06 DSvy Gambia'10–14 SNO Downs'14 Admiralty Cdr'15 SNO Lke Tanganyika'15 Admiralty'16 A/Capt ADNavalInt'18 Gen Sec International Hydrographic Bureau'21
2. FM Jan Christian SMUTS PC 17 CH(30) FRS KC b24.5.70 ed Stellenbosch Cambdge State Attorney SAR'98 Cmd Republcn Forces Cape 01 Colonial Sec Tvl'07 Min Interior & Mines'10 Min Dfce SA 12–20 Finance 12–13 GOC Sthn Army GSWA 14.4.15 Lt Gen CinC EA 16–War Cabinet'17 PM SA 19–24,39–48 d50
3. Official Hist p333,154, Haupt *Die Deutsche Schutztruppe* p86
4. Northey Papers IWM, Official Hist p190
   Maj Gen Edwd NORTHEY GCMG'22 CB'17 FRGS FZS b28.5,68 s/o Rev ed Eton RMC Lt KRRC India NWF 91–92 SA'99 CO 1KRRC Bvt Col T/BG 15Bde 2.3–w22.6.15 GOC Nyasald-Rhodesia FF 29.1.16 Gov Kenya'18 GOC 43Div'22 rtd'26 d25.12.53
5. Lt Col E RODGER DSO CO 2SAR 9.15
   BG Geo Montague Philip HAWTHORN CBE 23 DSO 16 b16.12.73 ed Harrow 2Lt King's'94 Ashanti'00 Somalild'02–4 IG KAR'19 rtd 23
6. C W BRIGGS SR PWD 8.99 Engr i/c Rds 12.02 d pneumonia Bournemouth 30.6.21
   Maj Chas DULY DSO 1900 b Hastings 1.1.70 Tpr BFF'96 OC Cyclists Rhod Contgt SA, Garage Proptr, OC MT BSAP'15

7. Murray's Colmn War Diary PRO WO/95/5334 CAB/45/9, Langham NRJ No.IV Vol II p85
   pw U/O Nicholas Mauser w Schutze Fredk Stiegert w, August Garnow PRO CO/417/574
8. PRO CAB/45/20 CO/417/585, Messum papers Liddle Collection
9. *Story NRR* pp57–60
10. Report Spicer-Simpson PRO CO/417/576
11. Official History p465
12. Northey IWM
13. Official Hist p484 n.2, NRP PRO CAB/45/9
    Hauptmann BRAUNSCHWEIG Hptmn Schutztruppe EA 1.10.13 OC 14FK Mwansa in 8.14
14. Parson PRO CAB/45/20 NRP CAB/45/9
15. Messum, Liddle Collection
    No.1656 Tpr Arthur Leonard BRADBURY BSAP s/o Arthur B of Wandswth kia30.10.16 age
    24, A272 Pte Felix Joseph HAMPSON bKg Wm's Town CP s/o Christina H of Pt Elisabeth
    kia30.10.16
16. Parson PRO CAB/45/20
17. Norforce War Diary PRO
    Maj Georg KRAUT Hptmn Schutztruppe EA 27.1.06 S/Capt & OC Ger/Brit Bdy Comm in
    8.14 Maj OC Bn BEA Bdr, OC Abteilung Kraut 2i/c at surrender 11.18
18. PRO CAB/45/9
19. Draft Offical Hist PRO CAB/44/4 gives Wahle 2,000–2,500 with as many carriers, History
    KAR says 2,000 men or more
20. Official Hist p505 n.3
21. War Diary Iringa Colm PRO WO/95/5334, CAB/44/4
22. Lt ZINGEL OC 26FK; Cmd three coys Wahle's Force 9.16 with Wintgens'17
    No.963 Sgt Geo Chas de Willis TAYLOR BSAP s/o Geo Hutton T of Wallingtn Sy
    kia23.10.16 age 30
    A197 Cpl Ernest Arthur GREEN lte 1RR & Lennon's Ltd Chemists
23. CAB/44/4 45/9
    Hauptmann Max WINTGENS Lt Schutztruppe EA'05 Hptmn 1.10.13 seconded to Govt GEA
    in 8.14 OC Bn Ruanda pw 21.5.17
    Lt Colpoys H Brodie CLARKE SAMR kia29.10.16
    Oberleutnt BAUER Lt Schutztruppe EA 8.9.05 Lt 8FK in 8.14 w29.10.16 OC L Coy
    dow26.8.17
24. War Diary Iringa Colm
    Lt Col C FREETH RandLI DSO(LG31.5.16)
25. Capt J E E GALBRAITH RF
    History KAR pp347,8 PRO CAB/44/4 Parson 45/20 NRP 45/9, Messum Liddle Collection,
    Norforce War Diary
26. PRO CAB/44/4, 45/9 Norforce War Diary
    Capt Thos MARRIOTT MC(LG2.3.17) 2SAR w Malangali'16 d3.5.20
    Dr Heinrich SCHNEE LLD b71 s/o Judge ed Heidelberg, Kiel, Berlin ResLt'94 Rabaul Neu
    Pommern Samoa Gov GEA'12 d'47
27. *History KAR* p349 Northey IWM Norforce War Diary
28. PRO CAB/44/4,45/9; CARBUTT see Ch4 n.10
    A3 John T Albert LOCHNER lte 1RR to Political Dept Neu Langenburg MID LG25.9.17
29. Cmdt Gen 14.1.18 PRO CO/417/640
30. PRO CAB/45/9
31. CAB/45/9 Norforce War Diary
32. Messum Liddle Collection, PRO/CAB/44/7, 45/9, Northey IWM
    Lt Gen Sir Jacob Louis Van DEVENTER KCB 17 KBE 19 CMG b77 Col Cmd Fce B
    GSWA'14 Sthn Fce 1.15 4Mtd Bde 14.4.15 Maj Gen 2 SA Div 3.16 CinC EAF 29.5.17
    d22.8.22
    Maj von LANGENN-STEINKELLER Hptmn Schutztruppe EA 27.1.06 OC 5FK Massoko
    in 8.14 w Karonga 9.9.14 Maj OC Bn'15 or Lt LANGEN Schutztruppe 17.9.06 13FK Kondoa–
    Irangi in 8.14

33. Parson PRO CAB/45/20 NRP CAB/45/9
34. PRO CAB/44/7, Parson CAB/45/20 NRP CAB/45/9
    BG Hon John Joseph BYRON CMG DSO(LG1.2.17) CO Qnsld Arty '95 Attache USArmy
    Philipines'99 ADC to Roberts SA, AAG Arty Aust 01–3 MLC ORC'07 Senator SA 10–20 CO
    5SAI'15 2i/c Dunsterforce Caucasas 12.17 d1935
35. Maj Gen Arthur Regld HOSKINS CMG DSO b1871 ed Westmnstr RMC 2Lt NStaff'91
    Dongola'96 Nile'99 Capt'00 EA'03 LtCol Instr Staff Cllge'09 IG KAR 15.8.13 AA&QMG 8Div
    22.9.14 T/Col GSO1 7 Div 12.11.14 BG 8Bde 25.3.15 BGGS VCps 3.10.15 Maj Gen 1EA
    Div 1.4.16 CinC 20.1–29.5.17 3Ind Div Mespot 18.8.17 46Div'19 rtd23 Prin Philip Stott Cllge
    Overstone'28 Bonar Law Cllge'29
36. PRO CAB/44/7
37. Norforce War Diary PRO CAB/44/7
    von GRAWERT Hptmn Schutztruppe EA 27.1.06 OC 12FK Mahenge in 8.14 OC Mahenge/
    Songea 15/16
38. PRO CAB/44/7
    Lt Col J McI FAIRWEATHER DSO(LG31.10.02) CO Kaffrarian Rif SA War, CO RandLI,
    CO Ry Bn SWA 24.4.15 CO SAMCC 3.16 kia 18.2.17
39. Lt Col Geo Lewis BAXTER DSO 16 b18.1.83 ed Eton 2Lt QOCH'05 Maj CO 1/1 KAR'17
    rtd 1920
40. Capt Wm Jas BAKER ANC SR dow26.3.17
    Maj Francis Hallowes ADDISON BSAP Cpl'96 Lt'97 CO 2RNR 10.4.17–25.1.18 Dist Supt
    Salisby'19
41. Langham NRJ Vol III p256 other accts say it was Latham but Langham must have known.
    Capt Fredk Chas BOOTH VC Johannesbruck Songea 12.2.17 LG8.6.17 DCM LG26.5.17 b
    Uppr Holloway 6.3.90 ed Cheltnhm, 1630 BSAP'12 No.1 Mob Colm 8.14 RNR Sgt 5.16 Lt
    3.17 Capt to UK 11.17 Capt 6Mx d Brighton 14.9.60
42. PRO CAB/44/8 Murray CAB/45/49 War Diary 1/1KAR
43. History KAR pp355–8
    Oberleutnant Heinrich NAUMANN Lt Schutztruppe EA 17.11.06 Lt 8FK Tabora in 8.14
44. Murray PRO CAB/45/50
45. MAMBO, a Bemba, was awarded a war pension 3.9.17
46. PRO CAB/44/9
47. .Harding Frontier Patrols
48. PRO CAB/45/9
49. LG3.9.19,22.12.19, 2431 Sgt SAMSONI DCM awarded LS&GCM 14.11.30, Pte MOTO
    DCM rejoined as 2878
50. Murray PRO CAB/45, Roelke CWGC roll, MMs LG12.3.18
51. Story NRR pp43–4
52. Northey IWM
    Lt Col F M FULTON DSO LG31.5.16 MC LG31.5.16 2i/c 5SAI'15
53. History KAR pp387–8
    Maj Theodor TAFEL Hptmn Schutztruppe EA 1.10.13 Mit Wahrnehmung der Geshafte
    Beauftragt in 8.14 10FK w Longido 25.9.14 Cmd Abteilung Tafel 1.17 surr 29.11.17
54. Hauptmann GOERING Oblt Schutztruppe EA 18.8.13 Adjt to von Lettow in 8.14 OC 4FK
    Cmd 5 coys'17 w & pw 8.9.18
55. Northey IWM, Stennett 31.12.17 PRO CO/417/611 CAB/45/9 Fair & A Coy had been on
    famine relief at Mahenge, MG Coy & BSAP LGs jnd 2.2.18 Songea Fce War Diary CAB/45/55
56. PRO CO/417/597,602,603 report 31.3.17
57. PRO CO/417/617–619
58. PRO CO/417/589,603,613 Hobson 'The Feira Affair' NRJ Vol IV p54
59. Northey IWM
60. PRO CAB/45/9 Northey IWM
61. History KAR p405 Col C G DURHAM DSO Spec List, Maj SAEF 13.1.16 CO 1/3KAR
62. Story NRR p46

63. Langham NRJ Vol IV p166 PRO CAB/45/9 No.399 CHIKUSI NRGov Gaz No.229 CHICH-ASI in LG2.12.19, TEGETE DCM LG11.3.20
64. *History KAR* p410
65. PRO CAB/45/9
66. *Hist KAR* p411 n.1 PRO CAB/45/9
67. War Diary 1/4KAR, War Diary Norforce, Hist KAR p411
    Lt Col Edwd Brian Barkley HAWKINS DSO 18 OBE 31 ed Winchstr RMC 2Lt WYks'09 KAR'12 Capt'14 T/Maj'16 CO 1/4KAR T/LtCol 18–19 Consul SWEthiopia'20–2 Maj'26 L/LtCol CO 1KAR 26–31 OC Depot WYks 35
68. Croad report 24.11.18 PRO CO/417/628
    Lt E J LESLIE A240 Pte SRC 15 Sups Fife, Salisby 1.18
69. Lt G M SIBBOLD 1799 Tpr BSAP 13 SRC Lt 2/1KAR 1.7.17
70. Alexander NRJ Vol IV p440
    A309 WEITZ SRC to BSAP MT
    Richd E THORNTON s/o BG Sir Ed AMS svd Norf IY SA, Fmr Kasama Lua Lua Mbesuma'21 partner with Rumsey d12.34
    Frank Edwin RUMSEY DCM b Hants 1880 s/o prop cycle shop, SAC'00 Durban Fire Bde, ran Launch Trips V Falls Hotel, 3/Sgt BSAP MT. Mbesuma Ranch, Chambeshi Ranch d27.5.60
71. Croad quoted in *Story NRR* pp60–2
72. Govt offices said to have been burnt by Sgt Jack Merry, Rd Overseer, in drink; d50.
    Chas SIMPSON Mgr Chambeshi Rubber Factory
    SPANGENBERG Lt Schutztruppe 18.9.07 Lt 10FK Dar in 8.14 Olt 10 FK raided Uganda Ry 6&7.15 OC 10FK twice w OC 6&10FK d18.12.18
    Hauptmann Franz KOHL Bavarian Arty OLt Schutztruppe 1.10.13 11FK Kisenji in 8.14 Hptmn OC Abteilg Kohl by 10.17 twice w
73. War Diary 1/4KAR
74. Von Lettow Reminiscences
    Unterzahlmeister DOHMEN twice w cdg 10FK at surrender
75. BG Wm Fredk Savery EDWARDS CB(19) CMG(17) DSO(01) KPM(11) FRGS b27.7.72 s/o Rev ed Christs Hosp 2Lt 3Devon Sierra Leone Frontier Police 99–01 Ashanti'00 SAC'01–6 i/c Kioga Punitive Fce Uganda'07 IG Police & Prisons Ugda'06 BEA & Ugda '08 T/BG IG Line of Communication EAF 1915–2.18
76. War Diary 1/4KAR
77. *Die Deutsche Schutztruppe* p95 *Story NRR* p47
78. War Diary 1/4KAR
79. *Story NRR* p48

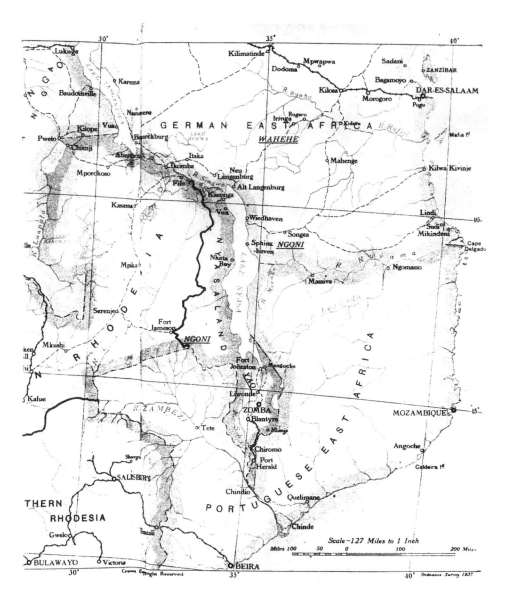

MAP 3   MOZAMBIQUE & SOUTH-EASTERN TANGANYIKA 1914–18

CHAPTER 8

Soldiers from The Wars Returning

On 20 June 1919 the Northern Rhodesia Police ceased officially to be 'On Active Service'. On 31 March that year the Commandant, Colonel F A Hodson CBE, had left for York on leave pending retirement. However he was out on a visit when he suffered an acute intestinal obstruction and died in Livingstone hospital on 21 January 1925 at the age of 59, a bachelor to the end. Hodson had been granted the honorary rank of full Colonel and made a Commander of the newly established 'Most Excellent Order of the British Empire', for his services in the Great War. Col Hodson was buried in Livingstone with full military honours.

Lieutenant Colonel H M Stennett DSO, the Second in Command since 1912, who had commanded the troops in the field for much of the war, succeeded Col Hodson as Commandant.

The return to peace conditions, although aided by the fact that the end of hostilites found the Service Battalion back on the northern border, was hampered by the influenza epidemic that swept through Northern Rhodesia as it did the rest of the World. Nine African police died between the end of hostilities and 13 January 1919. The battalion was also well positioned to send a platoon to assist the District Commissioner, C R B Draper, in dealing with disturbances in the Fife District led by Shadrach, a fanatical preacher of the Watch Tower movement. At Chunga on 30 December 1918 some 400 disciples had reacted with contempt, threatening messengers and chiefs, when told by Draper that preaching must stop. Shadrach was arrested but went down with flu and was admitted to Fife hospital from where he was rescued by his supporters. The troops under Capt Castle arrived at Chunga on 16 January and, largely due to the work of Detective Robert Simpelwe, 138 arrests were made leading to trials before Mr Justice MacDonnell in the High Court sitting at Kasama. The preacher was removed from the area. There were too many prisoners to be held in Kasama Central Prison and some 100 convicted persons were escorted to Livingstone to serve their sentences. The CID obtained a warrant under wartime regulations to censor mail and telegrams. A Nyasa telegraphist at Ndola was identified as spreading Watchtower propaganda.[1]

Watchtower was the African emanation of the Jehovah's Witnesses whose missionaries, well endowed with funds from the United States of America, had set themselves up in Nyasaland some years before the war. John Chilembwe's rising in the Shire Highlands of Nyasaland in December 1914 has been referred to in a previous chapter. The message brought to Northern Rhodesia was, in essence, that the whites had been sent by God to pass on the gift of their knowledge and wealth to the Africans, but had failed in that duty. The end of the world being at hand there was no need to obey anyone in authority nor even to cultivate crops. This led to the first prosecution of Watchtower followers in the Tanganyika District in September 1918. The uncertainty caused by the German incursion in October exacerbated the situation and there were some 1,000 incidents of assault and resistance to arrest in the Fife and Chinsali districts. In the 1920s the movement was to spread into the Belgian Congo where it was soon banned at the instance of the Roman Catholic Church, and further into Northern Rhodesia. Despite a series of ritual murders in 1926, to be described in the next chapter, Watch Tower was to remain a lawful organisation in Northern Rhodesia until 1940, when the Government decided it was harmful to the Territory's war effort.[2]

1839 Africans had served with the Northern Rhodesia Police during the War, of whom at least 100 died. In addition Northern Rhodesia had supplied 1,340 recruits for the King's African Rifles and 258 for the Rhodesia Native Regiment. But the fighting troops could not have operated without the carriers, the faithful 'Tenga Tenga'. According to British South Africa Company reports, Northern Rhodesia supplied nearly 200,000. One third of its able bodied men were away in 1918. 24,000 served as first line transport, and 40,732 served in German East Africa and Mozambique. 152,000 including 11,000 women, served within the Territory. North-Western Rhodesia provided 8,822 for work on the Ndola-Kabunda route. As far as possible no man was kept away from his home village for more than six months at a time. Some 2,000 lost their lives and 121 first line carriers were wounded in action. Enlisted first line carriers were rewarded with war medals in bronze while those of the troops were in silver.[3]

Post war honours lists, in addition to the appointment of a number of officers to various grades in the Order of the British Empire, included the award of the Distinguished Conduct Medal to S/5 Corporal Jeremani and 1179 Corporal Songandewo both for having on numerous occasions undertaken scouting missions of exceptional danger with marked success and for consistent good work during operations in German East Africa from August 1915 to June 1918. In all 47 decorations or mentions in despatches were awarded to Europeans serving with the Force and 52 to African Police for service between 1914 and 1918. In a broadcast in 1950, C W G Stuart MBE, late of the Northern Rhodesia Rifles, described the wartime Regimental Sergeant-Major, Kambondona, as having run the NRP under the strictest discipline as no white man could have done. 413 RSM Kambondona was rewarded with the Meritorious Service Medal.[4]

Government Notice 11/17 had announced the institution of a Northern Rhodesia Meritorious Service Medal, carrying a bounty of £50, Distinguished Conduct Medal, £25, and a Long Service and Good Conduct Medal with a £15 bounty. No award of any of these local medals appears in the Government Gazettes of the Great War period although the BSA Company paid bounties to Africans who were decorated. It is noteworthy that the Company's African troops were eligible for the Distinguished Conduct Medal as awarded to Imperial Troops and not the African DCM awarded to members of the KAR and West African Frontier Force.[5]

Brigadier General A H M Edwards was still Commandant General and had not lost his interest in the development of civil policing in Northern Rhodesia. In his report for the twelve months ending 31st March 1920, he wrote:

> In a military police force the members of which have to perform the double duty of a soldier and policeman, it is extremely difficult to attain and maintain efficiency on both sides.
>
> To perform both equally well would be an ideal, but one that from my past experience is rarely attained. It is possible to overdo one at the expense of the other, and when military subjects predominate, are taken up and efficiency insisted on, civil police duties are liable to be neglected and vice-versa.
>
> This is demonstrated very clearly in the Northern Rhodesia Police where owing to the past organisation and training and the war, the members, while well up and instructed in military work and duties, are with a few exceptions, totally ignorant of the requirements etc of civil police work.
>
> As far as one can foresee at the present moment, the military portion of the force will, for some considerable time to come, be greater and have more responsibilities than the civil division in respect of maintaining law and order. This, however, would be no excuse for neglecting to build up the latter, the value of which will each year become more marked as the territory becomes more civilised, and the number of European residents and settlers increases. As a matter of fact, the work it has done and is doing already proves its raison d'etre.
>
> It must be recognised and appreciated that each portion of the force has its distinct functions and role and is equally necessary for the maintenance of peace and good order in the territory. This being so any attempt to make invidious distinctions between the one and the other, or to make uncharitable comparisons, must be carefully guarded against and any dereliction of this order must, I have instructed the commandant, be severely dealt with.
>
> The gradual elimination of military ranks in the civil police and the substitution of civil police titles and grading is a subject which requires consideration. It would neither be desirable nor fair to ask those now serving in it to cease holding military ranks, but on the other hand, all who in future may be promoted officers should only be given the civil police title and grade, and in order to enable them to maintain a social status, have an equivalent military rank, for instance – in the same way as a ship's carpenter in His Majesty's Navy ranks with a field officer in the land forces; an inspector in the Northern Rhodesia civil police would rank with a captain or lieutenant in the military portion.[6]

At one stage it had been assumed that the NRP would have to continue to provide the platoon at Kasanga (Bismarcksburg) but with the establishment of a regular British administration in Tanganyika this commitment soon ended. Gen Edwards suggested that the Military Branch should be trained, equipped and employed like an Indian Army pioneer battalion. It would thus be able to contribute to the development of Northern Rhodesia by road building etc whilst remaining capable of taking the Field as infantry. While this proposal does not appear to have been formally accepted, detachments were, as will be seen, employed on 'pioneer' tasks over the next 15 years to the detriment of infantry training. The proposed post-war establishment for the Military Branch was for double companies, each 250 strong, at Kasama and Broken Hill, platoons of 60 at Mongu and Fort Jameson, and a Headquarters and Depot at Livingstone, 130 strong including recruits. The demand for economy and the realisation that intervention in Tanganyika was not a potential concern of the BSA Company led to a speedy revision.[7]

As at 31 March 1920 there were fifteen officers and European non-commissioned officers stationed with the headquarters at Livingstone, together with 300 native other ranks, including a machine gun company. Detachments of military personnel about sixty strong, consisting of a platoon (two Lewis light machine gun sections and two rifle sections) and a Vickers machine gun sub-section (one gun), were stationed at Kasama, Mongu and Fort Jameson. These detachments were permanent and personnel were only rotated to and from Livingstone to replace casualties proceeding on vacation leave or discharge. There was a firm policy that Ngoni would be posted to Kasama, and Bemba to Fort Jameson. This was to ensure that other ranks were never called upon to fire on their fellow tribesmen. The officer commanding each of these three military detachments also commanded all civil police and gaol warders on the same station and was superintendent of the central prison there. In fact, there were no civil police at Kasama.[8]

The officers in charge of the Town and District police at Livingstone and Broken Hill were also appointed superintendents of the central prisons there. The senior district official acted as superintendent at the three central prisons where no NRP officer was stationed. African police were employed as warders at the central prisons at Livingstone, Broken Hill, Mongu, Kasama and, until 1923, Fort Jameson, and at the local prisons at Lusaka, Kalomo, Mazabuka and Ndola. Sergeant-Major Boyd was seconded to the Legal and Prisons Department and was still Head Gaoler at Livingstone in which post he died in 1926. The European gaolers at Mongu and Fort Jameson, O T Wells and W Knowles, were attested into the NRP for disciplinary purposes. Sentences of up to six months could be served at the 24 local prisons, Those sentenced to longer terms of imprisonment were sent to the central prison for the district. A Prisons Board was established in 1923 consisting of the Commandant, Attorney General, Secretary for Native Affairs and Treasurer.[9]

In 1918 prosecutions as a result of police work had dropped slightly but in 1919 they rose to 1863 with 1660 convictions nearly twice the 1914 figures. The conviction of a 16 year old white youth for manslaughter led to arrangements being made for such offenders to be sent to suitable institutions outside the Territory under The Reformatories and Prisons and Juvenile Offenders Proclamation 1921. The boy who had shot an African on a farm in the Lusaka District was sentenced to 8 strokes of the cane.[10]

Under a system implemented by General Edwards, the Staff Officer of the BSAP at Salisbury kept a waiting list of suitable troopers who had expressed an interest in transfer to the NRP. When a vacancy for a constable arose a volunteer could thus be provided without delay. Constables were accepted on three months probation for a three year engagement. At the end of the initial engagement six months leave with £55 for a passage to UK was granted to those who signed on to return for a further three years. The first three months leave was on full pay but the remainder on half pay although personnel on leave were apparently paid quartering and ration allowances.[11]

African recruits attested for a four year engagement. It appears that, even at Livingstone, the Force did not have its own guardroom with cells for offenders against discipline. Defaulters could be sent to the ordinary civil prisons or awarded corporal punishment for disciplinary offences. The following entries appeared in Regimental Orders during 1920:

> 15th January 1920 – Pay (Livingstone):
> No.1997 Bugler Zeni having been discharged from Livingstone jail on 13th January 1920, returned to duty and will draw full pay from that date.'
> '2nd February 1920 – Punishments (Livingstone Jail):
> No.1974 Pte. Mijoni was on 4th February 1920, fined 5s. and awarded six lashes by the Commandant for 'Conduct to the prejudice of good order and discipline.'
> 13th February 1920 – Punishments (Livingstone):
> No.2132 Pte. Alefeyu was on 11th February 1920, fined 2s.6d. by Officer Commanding, Town Police, for 'Making away with or losing by neglect one pair of khaki knickers, the property of the B.S.A.Coy.'
> 27th July 1920 – Punishments:
> No.2066 Pte James Abanda was on 23rd July 1920, awarded one month's I.H.L. by the Officer Commanding and discharged from the Corps by order of the Acting Commandant for 'Asleep on his beat on duty.'[12]

The Kasama Detachment maintained its own herd of cattle. Regimental Orders for 2 February 1920 recorded that Herd Boy Joni had been discharged on 31 December 1919 and was struck off strength from that date. The Orders of 3 May 1920 announced the birth and taking on strength of a calf at Kasama on 5 April. The death of a grey horse there on 5 February 1920 was also published in Orders. One would not have expected a horse to be maintained so far north, but it seems a field officer commanded at Kasama and in an infantry force a field officer would be entitled to a charger. Temporary Major C H Fair DSO, who was Acting Commandant at Livingstone in May 1920, was in command at Kasama by 20 December that year when he fined 2093 Private Noah 15 shillings for 'striking a carrier.'

Captain J J McCarthy CBE DSO MC returned to duty with the Force by 31 March 1920. Early in 1918, with the rank of Lieutenant Colonel, McCarthy had been one of the picked body of officers and sergeants from all over the Empire known as 'Dunsterforce'. Under Major General L C Dunsterville they had operated in Persia and the Caucasas trying to fill the vacuum left by the collapse of Imperial Russia by organising local forces. In August 1918 McCarthy had been sent to Bijar to raise a brigade of local Christians to retake Urmia in Persian Kurdistan. Unfortunately these Assyrians did not come down like wolves on the fold but behaved more like sheep.[13]

McCarthy's pay as a captain with five years service in that rank, was now £540 per annum with ration allowance of four shillings a day. On 7 May 1920 his services in the two campaigns were recognised by the High Commissioner by the grant of the honorary rank of major. McCarthy soon retired to take up farming.

As lieutenants with five years in rank, Lieutenant G P Burton and Honorary

Captains B J Graham and H Allport were paid £381 a year, also with four shillings a day ration allowance. Children's allowance at £24 a year was drawn by Captain (Honorary Major) F S James and Lieutenants E C Castle and A A Smith OBE. Captain Graham appears to have married a widow with two children on 30 October 1920 whilst on leave in the United Kingdom, as on 28 January 1921 his entitlement was published to draw Step-children's allowance at £48 a year, with effect from the earlier date.

Constable H G Hart, a future Commissioner of Police, joined the Force on 1 October 1919 after War service. He was granted one shilling a day Extra Duty Pay from 10th April 1920 for performing the duties of Immigration Officer at Ndola.

As a 1st Class Warrant Officer, Chief Detective Inspector Thomas Hamilton, who was to become the first Assistant Commissioner, CID, drew the following pay and allowances from 19 December 1920, on first appointment:

Pensionable Pay	£450 – per annum
Marriage Allowance	£50 – per annum
Children's Allowance	£24 – per annum
Supplementary Ration Allowance	£15 – per annum
Fuel Allowance	£6 – per annum
Plain Clothes Allowance	1s per diem

Presumably he was also entitled to basic ration allowance! Mr Hamilton's son followed him into the Force and attained the rank of Superintendent. The founder of the CID, Lieutenant Kenneth Ferguson had died at Livingstone on 19 October 1918. On 1 November 1918 Sub-Inspector R H Kirk was promoted Chief Detective Inspector with the status of lieutenant. Kirk went on leave on 3 January 1921 and left the Force to farm at Chisamba. Thomas Hamilton was commissioned lieutenant on 3 July 1921 to succeed him in command of the CID. The rise in prosecutions due to the work of the police continued in 1920 with 2,131 persons prosecuted and 1,952 convicted. Of those convicted 181 were whites.

Three horses purchased on 20 December 1920 for the use of senior officers at Livingstone were numbered 3, 4 and 5. Number 3 died on 15 January 1921 and later that month, the previously acquired Horse No.2 also died. Northern Rhodesia was not horse country.

On 21 December 1920 a Board of Inquiry convened to examine some of the Force's venerable armament. It reported its opinion that the Nordenfelt gun and ship's gun, inherited from the North-Eastern Rhodesia Constabulary, 'being old and of an entirely obsolete pattern are now quite useless'. The guns were struck off strength accordingly, as was the Maxim carriage which had been 'partially destroyed by ants and borers'. The Board also found that 60 Mills bombs left over from the War, 1,310 rounds of .303 ammunition dated 1892, and 3,003 rounds dated 1903, had 'deteriorated through age and exposure', and should be struck off strength as unserviceable.[14]

During 1920 nine selected members of the British South Africa Police were brought up north to strengthen the European staff of the Military Branch during

159

the annual training period. This experiment was not a success, mainly because of language difficulties. It was not repeated.[15]

On 1 January 1921 it was announced in Regimental Orders that 'His Royal Highness, the High Commissioner, has approved the appointment of Mr William Tysoe DSO MC as 2nd Lieutenant in the N.R.Police on 6 month's probation'. Tysoe had won his decorations in France in 1918 as a second lieutenant with the Bedfordshire Regiment. He successfully completed his probationary period and was confirmed in his commission on 1 June 1921. Tysoe was one of the officers who passed into the Northern Rhodesia Regiment in 1932. His Royal Highness, the High Commissioner, was Lieutenant Colonel Prince Arthur of Connaught KG GCMG GCVO CB, Governor General of the Union of South Africa and High Commissioner from 1920 until 1923.

Also with effect from 1 January No.207 Corporal Chipwande and No.408 Corporal Ezeke, both old soldiers of the band, were each awarded one Good Conduct Badge with Good Conduct Pay at 6d. a month for having completed four years without regimental entries on their conduct sheets. Good Conduct badges were chevrons of red worsted on black backing worn point upwards on the left forearm of the longsleeved khaki jumper. Chevrons showing an NCO's rank were in khaki worsted on scarlet backing worn point downwards on the right upperarm. The European Regimental Sergeant-Major and other 1st Class Warrant Officers of all branches were ordered to wear the coat of arms of the British South Africa Company as their badge of rank, with effect from 21 February 1921.

On 1 February 1921 another old soldier, No.62 Private Jim, was promoted Transport Sergeant with pay at the rate of 37s 6d, a month.[16]

On 17 March 1921 a special Regimental Order was issued as follows:

The following is published for the information of all officers, BNCOs, Constables and Native Rank and File of the N.R.Police:

On Saturday, the 12th of March at Headquarters Livingstone, in the presence of the whole of the Headquarters Military Company, the Colours presented by His Majesty the King to the Regiment were consecrated by His Lordship the Bishop of Northern Rhodesia and formally presented by His Honour the Administrator, Sir Drummond Chaplin KCMG.

His Honour delivered the following speech:

'Colonel Stennett, Officers, Non-Commissioned Officers and Men of the Northern Rhodesia Police: It is my duty to present to the Regiment these Colours which have just been consecrated and which are presented by His Majesty the King to the Regiment as a mark of his appreciation of the service you have rendered in the Great War.

I could have wished that this presentation might have been so arranged that Mr Marshall could have performed the ceremony; Mr Marshall has had much to do in all matters connected with the Regiment, he is also known to all of you and I consider it would have been more fitting if he could have addressed you today.

I feel sure that the Regiment recognises that the presentation of these Colours by His Majesty the King is not merely as a mark of appreciation of what has been done, but is also in the nature of a sacred trust which I know the Regiment will accept wholeheartedly.

The Native members of the Regiment will not fail to let their friends and Chiefs know of the honour which has been conferred upon them: I feel sure that these Chiefs and Natives throughout the country will feel great gratification for the signal mark of His Majesty's favour, and will take it as a recognition of their help in sending their young men to the War.

The Regiment, I feel assured, will maintain the good name which it has won in the past, and will serve His Majesty the King in peace and war with all fidelity.'

The Commanding Officer in reply said:

'Your Honour, I wish to thank you on behalf of the Regiment for presenting these Colours, and for the kind words you have spoken this morning.

We look upon the Colours as a token of His Majesty the King's appreciation of the work done in the War and we will do everything in our power to protect these Colours and see that the honour of possession is not in any way soiled.'

Note – The significance of being in possession of King's Colours must be explained to all Native Rank and File at all stations.

By Order,
(Sgd.) P. R. WARDROPER
Capt.Adjt.[17]

The Bishop of Northern Rhodesia was the Right Reverend Alston May DD MA. Mr Marshall, referred to by the Administrator, was H C Marshall who had founded Abercorn nearly thirty years before, and who had just completed six months as Acting Administrator of Northern Rhodesia. The colour was one of the King's Colours authorised by King George V to be provided for every infantry unit of the Empire which had seen service in the War and was not already in possession of colours. The colours, as supplied, were plain, silk, gold fringed Union Flags, but units were permitted to have their title, in a gold circle surmounted by a crown, embroidered on at their own expense. The Northern Rhodesia Police had had this done, as did most service battalions. Similar King's Colours can be seen laid up in cathedrals and churches all over the United Kingdom.[18]

When Prince Arthur arrived at Livingstone on 23 August 1921 he was met by a guard of honour of 100 men under Capt Withers with Capt Burton, carrying the new colour, and 2Lt Tysoe. The High Commissioner remarked that this was the first such guard he had inspected in Africa in which every man wore war medal ribbons. On the following day Burton again bore the NRP colour at a parade in the Police Camp during which the royal visitor presented the Military Cross to Lt Langham, the Meritorious Service Medal to 1418 Cpl (later Sergeant-Major) Kambwamba and the King's Colour of the Northern Rhodesia Rifles which was received by Capt Molyneux. Another native commissioner, Capt Griffin who had served at the Front in the ranks of the Rifles before being temporarily commissioned in the NRP, commanded the detachment of the Rifles on parade. Of the NRP Lt Col Stennett was on parade with Maj James, the Second in Command, Capt Wardroper, Lt Smith, the Quartermaster, Capt Dickinson, Officer Commanding Service Company, and Capt Withers. No.1 Platoon was commanded by 2Lt Bagshaw, No.2 by 2Lt Tysoe, No.3 by Lt Langham and No.4 by Lt Arundell, the Machine Gun Officer. Bagshaw, like Tysoe, had served in France and joined the BSAP as a trooper in 1919. Francis Arundell MC, like

161

Langham, was a pre-war trooper and member of the Southern Rhodesia Column who was soon to leave the NRP.[19]

The Northern Rhodesia Police had no Regimental Colour until 3 July 1924 when, at another parade at Livingstone, the new Governor of Northern Rhodesia, Sir Herbert Stanley, handed over a colour which was the gift of the European ladies of the Territory. Although made at the Royal School of Needlework in London, and approved by the Inspector of Regimental Colours, the design of this colour was unconventional. It was of plain scarlet silk with, in the centre, the crested crane badge within a lozenge shaped scroll bearing the motto *Diversi generi fide pares* (different races, the same loyalty). On each side was a scroll bearing a battle honour, 'South-West Africa 1914' and 'East Africa 1914–18'. Underneath was a scroll bearing the title of the corps 'Northern Rhodesia Police'. The motto had been adopted after the War and was worn on a scroll below the crested crane on all badges and buttons in place of the title of the Force which had previously appeared there. On the cap badge and buttons the crane faced to the right of the wearer. On the collar badges the bird faced inwards.[20]

Both colours were carried on parade for the first time in July 1925 for the visit of the Prince of Wales, later King Edward VIII. These colours were laid up in All Saints Church, Lusaka, on 10 June 1938 after the Northern Rhodesia Regiment had received a new pair of colours of conventional design.

During 1921 the Force was re-armed with 1,000 Short Magazine Lee Enfield Rifles Mark III*, supplied by the British War Office at £1 5s each, said to be the cost of repairs and shipment, with bayonets and scabbards at 7/2d. Further supplies were available at £2 each with ammunition at £1 per 1,000 rounds.[21]

In 1921 new regulations were promulgated for the Northern Rhodesia Volunteer Force, the part-time European defence force consisting of the Northern Rhodesia Rifles and the Northern Rhodesia Medical Corps. At the end of the year the Northern Rhodesia Rifles were reorganised. The officers commanding the detachments of the Northern Rhodesia Police at Fort Jameson, Kasama, Mongu and Broken Hill were appointed district commandants of the Rifles for those places. Two former officers of the NRP were now members of the Rifles. No.11 Rifleman H C Ingles was appointed District Commandant for Kalomo where he now farmed, while No.24 Rifleman R H Kirk became District Commandant, Chisamba. The police cared for the weapons and stores of the NRVF and controlled the issue of ammunition. One of the duties of Sgt J D Giddings was to inspect the arms of the volunteers from Livingstone as far as Pemba. While there were many wartime soldiers among the white population most had had enough of military life and the Rifles were not well recruited. A similar attitude existed towards Territorial and other part-time forces throughout the Empire. According to the Commandant, Lt Col Arthur Stephenson CMG DSO MC, recruits only joined to obtain a free rifle. Since the rifles were obsolete Long Lee Enfields with ammunition limited to 50 rounds a year, the attraction was limited. He suggested that the NRVF be either disbanded or reduced to one officer and 62 other ranks to be known as the Northern Rhodesia Police Reserve. With two weeks annual training and modern infantry weapons this force, at an annual cost of £614, would be able to supply the necessary additional white NCOs to reinforce the NRP in an emergency together with an all white platoon as a striking force. It was to be nearly 30 years before a Northern Rhodesia Police Reserve was formed and on 1 April 1925 the Northern Rhodesia Volunteer Force was formally disbanded.[22]

In 1921 or 1922 Constable A E 'George' Berwick was the victor in a very brief encounter in the boxing ring with Lusaka's blacksmith, Laurie Thomas. News of the forthcoming match had caused much local interest. Rival training camps had been set up and large bets laid. The fight was held in the dining room of the Lusaka Hotel. Spectators came from miles around and ringside seats were at a premium. The referee, Mr Campbell Young, properly dressed in a dinner jacket, called the contestants to the middle of the ring. The gong sounded. Three or four blows were struck in as many seconds and the mighty blacksmith fell to his knees and then slid to the prone position to be counted out. According to the Lusaka Jubilee edition of the Central African Post, a number of the audience then gave a few exhibition bouts to give the crowd its moneysworth. Some of these turned into grudge fights, far more exciting than the big match. We are not told whether the evening ended with the police being called![23]

In 1921 the Post Office in Lusaka announced that it was handling mail for Lusaka Township, Mumbwa, Solwezi, Kasempa, Mwinilungu, Kalene Hill and other stations in that general direction. Mail was mostly carried by runners armed with spears. They sometimes took several weeks to complete their rounds and often returned with hair-raising accounts of battles with wild animals in defence of the Royal Mail. In January 1923 the African kapitao, foreman, at Lusaka was convicted for larceny by public servant having stolen four postal orders to the value of £1 2s 3d, and sentenced to nine months imprisonment. The orders were traced to a mail order firm in Bristol where the assistance of the local CID was obtained. An easier case to investigate occurred in 1925 when the European post-master at Fort Jameson, who turned out to have been a secret drinker, wrote to his superiors to report that he had stolen £348 6s 0d to clear his debts. He was sentenced to six months in prison.[24]

A census on 3 May 1921 had found 2,263 European males and 1,371 females in Northern Rhodesia with 56 Asians, 145 coloureds (Afro-Europeans) and 979,704 Africans. 243 whites lived in Lusaka Village and another 701 elsewhere in the Chilanga District. The European population of Livingstone was now 774 and of Broken Hill, 396. In 1922 the office of the Assistant Magistrate and Clerk of the Court moved to Lusaka from Chilanga, but the District Commissioner did not follow until 1931.[25]

Cattle in Barotseland suffered from endemic pleuro-pneumonia a disease which had spread from Angola shortly before the War. To prevent the spread of this desease into the rest of Northern Rhodesia the Barotse Cattle Cordon was established. In May 1922 a company of the Military Branch, under Captain Burton and Lieutenant Bagshaw, completed the field line from Sesheke, on the Zambezi, to Mwengwa, on the Kafue. The southern stretch followed the course of the Machili River, but the next 186 miles, a hoed road nine feet wide, went straight through uninhabited bush up to Musa, from where it followed the Kafue north. Near Meshi Teshi Regimental Sergeant-Major Yasi MM shot and killed a wounded buffalo, just in time to save the life of Major Fair, who was inspecting the operation. Fair's scalp was opened from forehead to crown. He was carried 25 miles to the Rev'd Shaw's Mission at Nanghila. Major Fair recovered but left Northern Rhodesia on retirement on 1 November 1923.[26]

The cordon was initially manned by 100 rank and file of the Military Branch with 24 posts. The line was divided into two sectors, each supervised by an officer and one British NCO. In 1924 the trained troops, one officer, a warrant officer, and 65 Africans, were withdrawn and replaced by specially recruited natives, on a lower rate of pay, under Duncan Lancaster who rejoined as a 'special constable' on 24 April 1924 and was appointed acting sergeant third class on 1 April 1925. 80 per cent of the first special African police recruited had served with the Force or KAR during the War. By 1932 the Cordon only ran as far north as Musa and was thereafter known as the Barotse Namwala Cattle Cordon until it was finally removed in 1947 and its personnel absorbed into the rest of the Force.[27]

In 1913 there had been famine in Bechuanaland creating a lucrative market for the diseased cattle from Barotseland. The British South Africa Police had then established a cordon along the Zambezi from the Victoria Falls to Kazungula. Trooper A T Tate had been placed in charge, although he had only joined the BSAP in 1912. Three camps were established with Tate and two other troopers each assisted by two native police and three or four local Africans appointed special constables. The other two troopers were withdrawn after some months and Tate ran the cordon alone until the outbreak of war in 1914. Having served in the War with the Rhodesia Native Regiment, Tate joined the Northern Rhodesia Police in 1919. In 1928 he transferred to the Nyasaland Police becoming Assistant Commissioner of that force.[28]

In 1922 the Northern Rhodesia Police War Memorial was erected at the entrance to the Police Camp at Livingstone. The cost of £760 was contributed by members of the Force and friends. The memorial was a pillar topped by the figure of a crested crane. The pillar bore the names of all members of the Force, European and African, who gave their lives during the Great War between 1914 and 1918. The memorial was flanked by two German 0815 Maxim machine guns. These guns together with two Minenwerfers, or trench mortars, and a field gun were the gift of the Imperial Government to commemorate the services of Northern Rhodesia during the War. Similar gifts of booty were made to all countries and territories in the Empire and to a number of towns and cities in the British Isles. The two mortars were still to be seen outside Livingstone Police Club in 1958. The German field gun was placed to mark the scene of the final hostilities on the Chambezi River.[29]

On 3 October 1922 Major-General Sir Alfred Edwards KBE CB CVO stood down as Commandant General of Rhodesian Forces. He was not replaced and the chief command of the Northern Rhodesia police was now vested in its Commandant. This change may well have been connected with the pending constitutional changes. Lt Col Stennett was granted the temporary rank of colonel and made substantive on 1 April 1923 with chief command of all police and military forces in the Territory. However at the same time the establishment of the Military

Branch was reduced by 2 subalterns, 2 British NCOs and 100 native ranks to 8 lieutenants, 9 BNCOs and 451 Africans. The Town and District Police was increased by 2 Africans to 2 officers, 17 British NCOs and constables and 127 native ranks.[30]

Major F S James had been Superintendent of Livingstone Prison since March 1921 and Registrar of Alien Natives since 26 January 1922. On 15 January 1923 he went on leave pending retirement. In his place Lieutenant Hamilton was appointed Chief Immigration Officer and Registrar of Alien Natives while Captain Graham became Superintendent of Livingstone Prison. James had also been in charge of the Town and District Police. The Town and District Police detachments throughout the Territory were now divided into two areas of responsibility. Captain Graham, at Livingstone became responsible for the policing of the capital, and the detachments at Kalomo, Mazabuka, and Fort Jameson, while Lieutenant E C Castle, at Broken Hill since 22 August 1921, was responsible for that town and the detachments at Lusaka and Ndola. Castle went on leave on 6 June 1923 handing over to Lieutenant Messum. Holding only the honorary rank of captain, Graham was junior to Castle who, prior to January 1923 was answerable to Major James. On return to Livingstone from leave on 10 December 1923 Castle took the post vacated in August by Captain Graham (see below) which had been temporarily filled by D/Insp Willson while the Adjutant, Captain Wardroper, acted as superintendent of Livingstone Gaol. Castle was promoted captain on 1 April 1924. On 22 April he was placed in command of all the Town and District Police detachments with Messum as his deputy at Broken Hill. In Livingstone District there were 2,416 convictions in 1923, although 1,640 of these were for non payment of native tax, in which the police were not involved. The police were involved in 3,678 prosecutions throughout the Territory which resulted in 3,412 convictions.[31]

In the CID, with which was combined the Immigration and Alien Natives Registration departments, Lt Hamilton was assisted by D/Insp Willson, D/Sgts Olive and Boyle, an African clerk and 21 native detectives, 4 at Livingstone, 2 at Kalomo, 3 at Mazabuka, 3 at Lusaka, 3 at Broken Hill, 2 at Ndola and 4 at Fort Jameson. D/Sgt Boyle was stationed at Lusaka and responsible for all CID work north of Kafue. There were 15 appointed immigration officers in the Territory. Apart from the Assistant Magistrate at Feira and the Native Commissioner at Abercorn, all were European police officers. When D/Sgt Olive resigned on 31 March 1923, D/Sgt Boyle was withdrawn to Livingstone where Const C R Arnott MC joined CID on probation.

On 31 March 1924 two British sergeants, two constables and 31 Africans were employed in the Town and District Police at Livingstone while 30 African police acted as prison warders there under Sergeant-Major Boyd. At Broken Hill were Sergeant-Major Howe, two constables and 26 Africans, including a bugler, in the Town and District Police, and a further 8 African police as prison warders. A sergeant and a constable were at Ndola with 19 Africans. There were two sergeants, a constable and 15 African police at Lusaka. There was a British sergeant and 17 Africans at Mazabuka, another at Kalomo with 9 and a sergeant, a constable and 16 African police at Fort Jameson. 18 African police were employed as warders at Mongu and 8 at Broken Hill.[32]

Company Sergeant-Major C F Schronen returned from leave on 6 July 1923 and acted as RSM when Regimental Sergeant-Major T N J Usher went on leave on 6 August. Mr Usher died in England on 14 September 1923 and Mr Schronen became European RSM. His future son-in-law, L M Clark, became a senior superintendent in the Northern Rhodesia Police. Sergeant B J Thomas had joined the British South Africa Police as a trooper in 1913. His association with the Northern Rhodesia Police also began during the East African Campaign in 1916. Thomas was mentioned in despatches for recovering a machine gun under fire and remained with the Northern Rhodesia Police Service Battalion until after the German surrender at Abercorn. After the war he transfered to the NRP as Machine Gun Sergeant. He, Sergeant-Major Schronen and Sergeants 'Porky' Taylor and Dawson, had to build their own pole and dagga huts at Livingstone. Thomas became Regimental Sergeant-Major in 1926, being the last RSM of the Northern Rhodesia Police and the first RSM of the Northern Rhodesia Regiment before he retired in 1933. His two sons joined the Northern Rhodesia Police in the 1950s. Constable A G Charters DCM, who had distinguished himself at the defence of Fife in 1918 joined the Force on 25 August 1921, but clearly his career did not prosper. He was discharged on 8 September 1924.[33]

On 15 August 1923, Captain Graham, Lieutenant H Ockendon MC and sixty rank and file of the Military Branch, with two Lewis guns, left Livingstone for the Kasempa District on the orders of the Administrator to arrest members of the Lubangu tribe, in the Jiundu Swamps, who refused to pay tax. Graham's patrol covered 1,180 miles before returning to Livingstone on 16 November. A number of arrests were made and muzzle loading guns seized. These were stored at Solwezi to be returned to their owners at the discretion of the District Commissioner. Firepower demonstrations were given with the Lewis guns. The private possession of firearms had been regulated for the first time by the Firearms Proclamation No.21 of 1922, gazetted on 6th January 1923. The patrol had been drawn from men being trained to relieve the company on the Cattle Cordon who had not fired a musketry course since before the cordon was set up. This served to support the argument for raising 'special police' to man the Cordon.[34]

During 1923 38 African police were discharged from the Force 'time expired', 8 died, 18 were discharged for medical reasons and 36 as being unsatisfactory. They were replaced by 84 recruits most of whom had previous service in the NRP or the King's African Rifles as had nearly all of the 97 who joined in 1924. This was reported as an advantage although the long term effect must have been to create an ageing Force. Recruiting was hampered by the fact that higher pay was available in Southern Rhodesia. There was a higher incidence of disciplinary offences among Africans of the Town and District Police than in the Military Branch. This was ascribed to the closer supervision of the military personnel. In 1924 a night school was started at Livingstone which was attended by 50 per cent of the Africans serving there.[35]

At this time the following Government stations were declared 'less healthy stations' at which a tour of duty of only two and a half years was to be served before a European official proceeded on vacation leave:

Petauke –	East Luangwa District
Livingstone –	Batoka District
Feira –	Luangwa District
All Stations –	Barotse District.

No doubt the declaration of the capital of the Territory as a less healthy station prompted the search for a new capital. The normal tour of duty for a European official was, and remained until 1964, three years. Malaria was prevalent throughout Northern Rhodesia. All white residents took 5 grains of quinine daily. In 1998 St John Sugg wrote in the NRP Association newsletter that despite this regular dosage he contracted malaria at Livingstone in 1936 and that since quinine tended to suppress rather than prevent the disease most Europeans were 'a bit under the weather all the time.'[36]

Annex to Chapter 8

OFFICERS & BRITISH OTHER RANKS OF THE NORTHERN RHODESIA POLICE WHO JOINED BETWEEN 1 JANUARY 1919 & 31 MARCH 1924

ARUNDELL Francis Douglas MC(LG 1.2.18) 1629 Tpr BSAP 7.12 SRC 15 Lt relinq comm 14.12.18 Lt NRP 1.1.19 rsgnd 26.2.22.

TAYLOR Alfd Ernest BSAP 10.13 SRC A/Sgt MGs MiD Sgt NRP 1.1.19

DAWSON H E 1890 Tpr BSAP 8.14 Sgt NRP 1.1.19

SCHWARTZ Const Lusaka 1919

BALL John Tpr BSAP 8.7.14 Clerical Staff 20.3.16 S/Cpl 1.5.16 3/S/Sgt 1.7.16 Sgt RNR 14.2.17 T/2Lt 7.11.17 T/Lt 15.10.18–11.2.19 Sgt NRP 25.2.19 dschge own request 30.6.19

TATE Allan Thos b Birmghm 23.6.93 1566 BSAP 5.12 RNR Sgt Lt 2/Sgt NRP Mil 6.5.19 T&D 1.10.23 to NyasaldP 28 ACP Nyasld.

UPTON Geo Robt Edwd b1.7.93 BSAP 12.5.14 SRC MGs MID LG 28.1.19 2/Sgt NRP 22.5.19 CSM WO2 1.1.20 RQMS'29 dischge 5.32

HOPKINS Maj Francis Arthur OBE 12.5.37 1684 BSAP 6.13 Cpl SRC 15 2Lt MBE LG4.2.19 Lt HQ SRC, Lt NRP 1.6.19 Capt by 1.4.32 NRR Ag Cmdt 1.10.36–22.1.37 Staff Paymr KAR 8.8.37 Rtd'39.

BLISS John Pilling BSAP 3.9.10 NRP 1.7.19?

HART Henry Geo 'Kangongolo' b17.1.94 Rfn 3SAMR 2.10.13 Gnr RFA 16.10.16 Cpl B/157 RFA 3.17–19.7.19 Const NRP 1.10.19 3/Sgt'21 2/Sgt 1.10.23 1/Sgt 24.2.27 Lt 1.8.27 ACP'28 DCP'36 CofP 12.36 rtd 47 Donegal

CLIFF Ernest b11.2.88 Boy 2Lincolns 22.9.02 Irish Gds 2.9.07–BM NRP 3/Sgt 1.11.19 2/Sgt 26.5.21 WO2 16.9.24 RTA 7.28 inv 11.28

JOHNSON Geo Guthrie Stephen SAP 13–16 EA 4.16–2.17 Const NRP 5.11.19 3/Sgt by 28.2.23 2/Sgt 12.8.24 Insp 1.8.28 C/I 35 rtd 36

DICKINSON Fredk Albert 2036 BSAP 19 NRP 1.12.19 Sgt CQMS 31.5.23 RQMS 1.9.23 WO1 1.4.26 PWD'29

USHER Thos Nicholas Joseph Tpr BSAP 2.10.09 2Lt RNR Instr NRR RSM, RSM NRP 29.2.20 lve 6.8.23 d UK cerebral tumour 14.9.23

BOYLE Wm Edmund Const 27.4.20 3/D/Sgt 1.12.21 2/D/Sgt 19.8.24 Ag Ct Clk Lstone 16.10.25 3/D/Sgt 1.8.27

HUBBARD Wm John b London 18.1.97 RH&FA'14–19 Tpr BSAP'19–Const NRP 4.5.20 3/Sgt 1.8.22 2/Sgt 20.8.26 lve 12.7–31.12.26

WILSON Alexander b12.10.98 Essex RFA TF'15 Cav'17–19 2138 BSAP 11.19 ORS NRP 11.6.20 Clk Native Affairs Dept 16.6.27 C/Clk 30 Asst Estab Offr NR'45 rtd'51 SA d'59

SMITH Frank Roland BSAP 26.4.19 NRP 16.7.20?

PARKIN Fredk Wm b Yks 25.5.95 bro of J B War Svce 24.8.14–21.5.18 Const NRP 17.9.20 3/Sgt by 31.3 dschge own req 30.6.25

HAMILTON Thos MBE 30; 1550 BSAP 12 CID WO1 i/c CID NRP 19.12.20 Lt 3.7.21 Capt ACP 1.4.32 rtd 11.32 f/o Supt

TYSOE Wm DSO 25.4.18 OBE 36 MC 18 b N'hamptn 24.6.93 T/2Lt 7Beds 18 NRussia 19; 2240 Tpr BSAP 20 2Lt NRP 1.1.21 Lt 1.10.21 Capt 1.12.30 NRR 1.4.32–37 NR Lab Offr SR 21.6.38 Hon Maj 12.3.38 rtd Salisby SR d post 30.6.79

THOMLINSON Alfd b Letchwth 21.10.93 BSAP 15.10.13–Const NRP 6.2.21 3/Sgt by 27.2.25 dschge own req 31.10.26

GIDDINGS Lt Col J D War Svce15–8, 2030 BSAP 19 Const NRP 10.6.21 2/Sgt 17.3.24 CSM 25.9.26 2Lt 11.3.31 NRR Lt 15.11.34 Maj OC D Coy Somalild'40 RSupt Div Cmdt NRPR Westn'57

BAGSHAW Lt Col Arthur Norman MBE b31.5.95 ed Elstow Sch Bedford, bank clk, pte Lincs 15.1.15 Instr SArms Sch Strensall, 6Lincs Mudros 11.15 Egypt 12.15 BEF 7.16 Sgt T/2Lt 1 Leics Cambrai 11.17 w & pow 21.3–12.18 2085 BSAP'19 Cpl; 2/Sgt NRP 27.6.21 2Lt 29.6.21 Lt 1.7.22 NRR Capt Bwana Mkubwa Det'38 rsd 2NRR'40, 4NRR, Cmdt Italian Internmnt Camp 24.1.42 DWar Evacuees & Camps 43 Rtd 49 to SR.

BERWICK Albert Edwd 'George' b Burton–on–Trent 5.3.98 Staffs Y 17.3.14–2.19 BSAP 11.6.19 Const NRP 15.7.21 3/Sgt 17.3.24 Insp 1.4.29 rtd 33

PICKTHALL Joselyn Richd Murrell BSAP 22.9.19 NRP 29.10.21

DIXON Abraham 'Ginger' MC b Cumberld 26.10.96 Pte Bdr? 14 2Lt 4Cheshire 27.3.18 Tpr BSAP 20 Const NRP 6.11.21 3/Sgt 1.7.24 Insp 31.12.30 rtd 33

SKIPWORTH R G Const NRP 10.3.22 2/Sgt 12.8.24 rtd 10.3.25

ARNOTT Cecil Rhodes MC, b Stafford 22.9.97 s/o Mental Hosp Supt, ed KEVIGS, 3618 Tpr 1LG 17.11.14 Cpl 8.15 2Lt MGC 25.5.17 98Coy BEF 10.17 Tpt Offr 33Bn 10.18–4.19 Lt 25.11.18 Pal Syria 6.19–4.20 Tpr BSAP 6.7.20 S/Cpl 8.21 Const NRP 14.4.22 D/Const 1.5.24 D/3/Sgt 1.8.24 D/2/Sgt 19.7.25 D/Insp 28 A/Supt 24.6.31 Sen Offrs Cse NScotld Yd'32 i/c CID 11.32 ACommr Imm Pal'34 ACntrllr Sups'40 AFood Cntrllr'42 DFd Cntrllr'44 AC Imm'45 Dir Migration'47

MAXWELL John b Nottghm 20.7.98 F/Sub Lt RNAS 4.17 Lt RAF 1.4.18–1.12.19 Tpr BSAP 1.3.20–Const & Storemn NRP 10.5.22 T&D 3/Sgt 1.7.25 Insp 1.4.31 C/I rtd 39

OCKENDON Harold MC 2Lt 7Essex T/Lt 1Essex 7.1.18 2298 Tpr BSAP 20 2Lt NRP 25.5.22 Lt 26.5.23 Capt 25.3.32 NRR DO A/Sec Estabs NRG 11.9.35

CURNOCK Victor Colin BSAP 11.6.10 Const NRP 13.9.22?

PAGE W J Const to Customs 7.8.23

FISH Fredk b Gt Yarmth 5.3.00 RFA'17; 2322 BSAP'20 Const NRP 3.9.23 Sgt 1.7.25 Insp 1.4.31 rtd'33

McBRIDE Eric Knox Const QM's 5.3.24 3/Sgt 1.4.26 to S&T 8.10.28

Notes

1. Admr 2.2.19 PRO CO417/616–9,637 Admr 5.5.20 417/639
   Christopher Robt Burnage DRAPER MBE Ag DC A'corn AgMag Serenje 7.10.21
   Sir Philip Jas MacDONNELL BCL MA Oxon bNI 10.1.73 ed Cliftn Brasenose Bar Gray's'00
   War Correspdnt Times SA, Tvl CS 26.4.06 APros Witz HCt'07 Legal Advsr & PP NR 31.10.08
   Judge'18 CJ Trinidad & Pres WI Ct of Appeal'27–30
2. PRO CO/417/616,795
3. *Story NRR* P48 n.1 PRO CO/417/616,640
4. *Story NRR* p53

5. PRO CO/417/628
6. Quoted in *Story NRR* p64–5
7. Edwards PRO CO417/617–9
8. *Story NRR* p65
9. History of the NR Prison Svce NRJ Vol V p551
10. PRO CO/417/623, Annual Report
11. PRO CO/417/711
12. *Nkhwazi* Vol 7 No.3 Dec 59 p23
13. Maj Gen Lionel Chas DUNSTERVILLE CB 16 CSI 18 b'65 s/o Lt Gen ed Westward Ho RMC Lt'83 Waziristan 94–5 NWF 97–8 China'00 BG Peshawar Bde 25.4.15 Agra Bde 5.12.18 d46
    McCarthy, Aust Official Hist. He was presumably selected by Col Byron who became 2i/c of Dunsterforce & under whom McCarthy had served in 1917
14. *Nkhwazi* Vol 7 No.3 Dec 59 p24, PRO CO/417/655
15. *Story NRR* p65
16. *Nkhwazi* Vol 8 No.1 Apr 60 p30, chevrons *Story NRR* p112
    HRH Lt Col Prince Arthur of CONNAUGHT KG KT GCMG GCVO CB b13.1.83 o/s of Duke of Connaught ed Eton RMC 2Lt 7H 01 Maj Scots Greys 07 Gov Gen SA & High Commr 20–23 d38
17. *Nkhwazi* Vol 8 No.2 Sep 60 p20
    Sir Francis Drummond Percy CHAPLIN GBE23 KCMG17 b10.8.66 s/o Maj ed Harrow Oxfd Bar'91 Times Corres Jo'burg 97 Morning Post Corres St Petersburg'99 Mngr Consolidated Goldfields SA'00 Pres Tvl Chamber of Mines'05 MLA Tvl'07 Hse of Assembly SA'10 Admr SR 14–23 & NR 21–3 d16.11.33
18. Rt Rev Alston Jas Weller MAY DD MA b69 s/o Capt RN HM Supt of Insps of Factories, ed Leeds GS Oriel Cam, Curate All Souls Leeds'94 St Mark's Portsmth'03 Curate i/c Chertsey 10–13 Bishop NR'14
19. PRO CO/417/662
20. PRO CO/417/694CO/796/3
    Sir Herbert Jas STANLEY G(30)CMG 13 b25.7.72 s/o Sigismund Sonnenthal ltr Stanley of Manchstr, ed Eton Balliol PS to Brit Minister Dresden & Cobourg & VConsul Dresden 97–02 A/PS to 1st Ld Admiralty 06 PS to Ld Pres of the Council 08 PS to Gov Gen SA 10 Sec 13 Res Commr S&NR 15 Imp Sec SA 18 Gov NR KCMG'24 Ceylon 27 HCommr SA 31 Gov SR 35–42 d5.6.55
21. PRO CO/417/617–9
22. PRO CO/795/1 Gov Gaz GN108/21,40/25
23. Central African Post Lusaka Jubilee Edn 31.7.63
24. PRO CO/799/8
25. PRO CO/417/662
26. Bagshaw taped interview IWM
27. PRO CO/417/711
28. 'The Outpost'
29. *Story NRR* p122
30. Admr 25.10.22 PRO CO/417/689 417/700
31. Annual report PRO CO/799/1
32. Annual report 9.5.24 PRO CO/799/1
33. *Nkhwazi* Vol 7 No.3 Dec 59 p27
34. Estimates 6.1.24 PRO CO/417/711 *Story NRR* p66
35. Int Report Stephenson PRO CO/795/10
36. NRPA Newsletter No.57 p4 Summer 1998

CHAPTER 9

Police and Military under The Crown

On 1 April 1924 administration by the British South Africa Company ended and the Colonial Office took over direct responsibility for the government of Northern Rhodesia. Herbert James Stanley CMG was appointed the first Governor and Commander in Chief of the Territory. He was to be knighted later in the year. Herbert Stanley had joined the staff of the High Commissioner in South Africa in 1910 and was Resident Commissioner for Southern and Northern Rhodesia from 1915 until 1918. He had then become Imperial Secretary in South Africa. He was, therefore, well qualified for his new post.

He was received at Government House by Colonel Stennett and inspected a guard of honour 100 strong under Major Dickinson accompanied by the band. Captain Castle acted as the Governor's ADC for the swearing in ceremony. Things did not go so smoothly for Stanley's first visit to Fort Jameson on 10 July. Captain Graham dismissed the guard of honour at dusk and the Governor arrived later that evening having been delayed in the two day motor journey from Blantyre, Nyasaland. The quickest route from Livingstone to Fort Jameson was still via Southern Rhodesia and Nyasaland. On 11 July Stanley inspected the police camp, gaol and other government buildings and lunched with Captain and Mrs Graham. On 12 July he held an indaba for which the Chewa formed up on the right, the Akunda on the left and the Ngoni, still organised in regiments, held centre stage. After the speechmaking by the Governor and chiefs, there were sports for all races, organised by Captain Graham. The Great East Road from Lusaka to Fort Jameson was not opened to motor traffic until 1929 and then was a mere track of twin footpaths. It took four to six hours for a lorry and its load to cross the Luangwa by ferry powered by paddlers.[1]

The financial vote for the maintenance of the Force, for the year 1924, was £50,890, out of a total revenue for the Territory of £364,223. A census on 31 March 1924 had found 4,182 Europeans in the Territory and estimated the African population at one million.

The Chartered Company's Administrator had enjoyed the assistance of an Advisory Council with five members elected by British subjects of European descent, over twenty one years of age, and earning a salary of at least £150 a year or occupying property of not less than that value. An Order in Council in 1924 established Northern Rhodesia's first Legislative Council with nine official and five elected unofficial members. The same Order in Council established the Governor's

Executive Council composed entirely of Government officials. The Commandant of the Northern Rhodesia Police was an ex-officio member of the Legislative Council. The franchise was altered to give the vote to all British subjects over twenty one, who either, owned a house or building with a value of £250, or owned a mining claim, or had an income of £200 a year.

In 1924 the European members of the Force adopted a diamond shaped flash, top half red, bottom white, worn on the left side of the khaki Wolseley helmet. This is said to have been inspired by the patch behind the eye of the crested crane. The badge was worn on the flash with the crane facing forward. The white shirt ceased to be worn and the khaki shirt was henceforth worn in review order as well as other orders of dress. Officers and British warrant officers, NCOs and constables wore a khaki tie with all orders of dress, including the bush shirt.

From 1924 African sergeants wore the crimson infantry sash over the right shoulder. This distinction was never worn by European warrant officers and sergeants of the Northern Rhodesia Police. African police wore the blue jersey between five p.m. and nine a.m.[2]

The new regime meant that Colonial Office authority had to be obtained for the additional expenditure of £650 a year to meet the requirement for a police presence at Bwana Mkubwa Mine. On 22nd September 1924 Bwana Mkubwa Town and District Police Detachment opened with Sergeant H G Hart in charge, assisted by one corporal and six privates. One African detective each was withdrawn from Kalomo and Mazabuka and posted to Bwana Mkubwa. The first police station was a group of thatch roofed buildings near the railway station. Bwana Mkubwa was then a bustling mine township, while Ndola was a tiny Government station centred on the Boma. Also during 1924 one European and four native police from Broken Hill were detached to keep order among the workers constructing the Mulungushi Dam. They were withdrawn in 1925.[3]

The strength of the Northern Rhodesia Police was:

Headquarters: The Commandant, Second-in-Command, Adjutant, Capt P R Wardroper MBE, Pay & Quartermaster, Lt A A Smith OBE, Machine-gun Officer, Lt H Ockendon MC, Regimental Sergeant-Major C F Schronen, Regimental Quartermaster Sergeant F A Dickinson, Orderly Room Sergeant A Wilson and Constable E K McBride, QM's storeman.

Military Branch: Captains A C de C Cussans MC, G M Withers, G P Burton & B J Graham, lieutenants H Allport, B K Castor, C S Gardiner, F A Hopkins MBE, W Tysoe DSO MC & A N Bagshaw, company sergeants-major B J Thomas & E Cliff (Bandmaster), sergeants J T H Saunders, G R E Upton & J D Giddings and 459 native rank and file.

Town and District Police: Capt E C Castle, Lt A L Messum, sergeants-major S J Boyd (seconded to the Prisons Department as Head Gaoler), and R A Howe, sergeants 1st class R E Camfield & J R Sawtell, 2nd class J B Parkin, A T Tate, & H G Hart, 3rd class G G S Johnson, W J Hubbard, A Thomlinson, A E Berwick, A Dixon MC, constables F W Parkin, A G Charters DCM, R G Skipworth, F Fish, J Maxwell, N A H Blake and W F Stubbs and 133 native rank and file.

Criminal Investigation Department: Lt T Hamilton (Chief Detective Inspector), Detective Inspector F J Willson, detective sergeants W E Boyle & C R Arnott MC, and 21 African detectives.

1/Sgt Sawtell and constables (by then 3/Sgt) F W Parkin and Charters all left the Force in the second half of 1924.

On 31 March 1925 Colonel H M Stennett CBE retired at the age of 48. The new Commandant, Lieutenant Colonel Arthur Stephenson CMG DSO MC, came from outside the Force, but had long experience of Northern Rhodesia and a fine war record in France and Flanders. After the War Stephenson had returned to Northern Rhodesia to farm at Monze. In 1919 he was appointed Commandant of the Northern Rhodesia Rifles and from 14th May 1920, Chief Intelligence Officer for the Territory. Colonel Stephenson had been attached to the NRP since July 1924 acting as commandant from 1 October 1924 while Col Stennett was on leave pending retirement.

Officers & BNCOs, Livingstone September 1924 (Photo Nkhwazi)
L to R Back: Const Robinson, RQMS Dickinson, Capt Castle, Lt Hamilton, RSM Schronen, Sgt Berwick, Lt Smith, D/Sgt Boyle, Bandmaster Cliff, Const McBride, Sgt Maj Boyd.
Middle: Sgt Wilson, Capt Withers, Maj Dickinson, Col Stennett, Lt Col Stephenson, Capt Wardroper.
Front: Sgt Giddings, Lt Ockendon, Lt Bagshaw, CSM Thomas.

The salary of the Commandant was £850 a year although Stennett had received £1,100. The Second in Command, since 1 October 1924 Major E G Dickinson MC, received £750. Captains were on a salary scale of £550 to £675 after 8 years. The salary scale for lieutenants was £410 to £530 per annum after 7 years. British other ranks pay scales were even more complicated as follows:

Regimental Sergeant-Major	£414
RQMS & Company Sergeants-Major	£374–£394
ORS & Military Branch Sergeants	£329–£349
Town & District Police Sergeants-Major	£450
Detective Inspector	£410–£430
Sergeants 1st Class	£410
Sergeants 2nd Class	£365–£385
Sergeants 3rd Class	£325–£345
Constables	£250–£310

The Adjutant and Pay and Quartermaster received an allowance of five shillings a day on top of the pay of their rank. In October 1925 the P&QM, Lieutenant Smith, was given the additional responsibility of Controller of Government Stores and Transport. It was estimated that £600 a year could be saved by amalgamating that department with the police.[4]

The Kasama Detachment was put to work building bridges and improving roads in Northern Province. This work continued until 1932. In 1926 the detachment was also required to provide 13 men for a cattle cordon from Isoka to Abercorn to prevent the spread of a rinderpest outbreak in Tanganyika. They worked under stock inspectors and district officers until special police could be recruited. In August 1927 Lieutenant F A Hopkins MBE and forty other ranks from Kasama marched via Isoka to Nyasaland, marking the route for a new road. At Isoka they met a small patrol of 1st King's African Rifles led by Captain F de Guingand on similar duties. Before returning home Hopkins' platoon joined the main body body of the KAR battalion for field firing exercises on the Nyika Plateau. This was the only occasion between the wars when troops from Northern Rhodesia trained with the King's African Rifles. In November 1926 when Capt Castle was posted back to the Military Branch to make way for Capt Wardroper, he was conveyed to Kasama by lorry by a new motor transport service being established by Maj E C Dunn, Northern Motors. Capt Burton returned to the Line of Rail by the same service.[5]

In 1926 a new Northern Rhodesia Police Ordinance was promulgated. Section 111(2) read: 'In case of war or other emergency the members of the force are liable upon the order of the Governor to be employed for police or military purposes beyond the limits of Northern Rhodesia in any adjacent or neighbouring territory specified in the order and when so employed shall be subject to such terms and regulations as the Governor may determine.'

In May 1926 Capt Allport and 2Lt Fitchie marched East from Lusaka to the Luangwa and then North-East to Serenje where they were joined by Capt Graham from Fort Jameson and Lt Hopkins from Kasama to make a force totalling four officers, one British non-commissioned officer and 100 African other ranks. Under the personal command of Lt Col Stephenson they converged on Serenje to deal with unrest caused by the activities of Tom Ulwa Nyrenda, known as 'Mwanalesa' (the son of God), of the Watch Tower Sect. The troops were to be in the Field for nearly three months during which they marched a total of 2,500 miles and performed a number of demonstrations and training exercises.

Tom Nyrenda, a Henga from Nyasaland, educated at Livingstonia, started his Northern Rhodesia operation in the Lala and Lamba tribal areas. From there he expanded it, using methods which were unlawful by anyone's book. Before he was brought to justice he was officially estimated to have been responsible for 192 murders in Northern Rhodesia and the Congo.

Assistant Inspector David Mkankaulwa had personal experience of 'Mwanalesa's' methods and, in 1960, described his childhood recollections in Nkhwazi, the Force magazine. Because of famine in the Feira District Chief Mburuma, arranged for a number of his people to settle in Chief Mpanshya's area. Accordingly Mkankaulwa's family had come to live at Nguluka Village near Rufunsa.

They had been at their new home for nearly three years when one Deacon Dikola arrived to announce the coming of Tom Mwanalesa. He gathered together nearly the whole village and informed them that the day of judgement would follow before the end of the year. Dikola taught them Mwanalesa's version of the Ten Commandments. 'Thou shalt not kill' was to apply to all living creatures except snakes, witches and wizards. These were to be exterminated. The beating of children, use of insulting or abusive language, insolence and beer drinking were declared mortal sins. It seems that the audience was spellbound!

Mwanalesa accompanied by Chief Shabila was said to be coming to Mukonka village about thirty miles away. People travelled there from miles around, camping in grass shelters outside Mukonka's. Food was provided for those who came from far away as hospitality was said to be one of the keys to Heaven. Mkankaulwa and his parents were there for at least a week before the great day came. Of that night, he wrote:

> No one slept, and prayers and hymns were conducted throughout the night. There were many thousands of people staying in the shelters and they all gathered together quietly. When a hymn was sung, one felt one's hair moving. At night strange figures resembling human beings were seen in the sky. Every-one believed that Christ would descend the following morning. On the day of baptism Tom and Shaibila were draped in leopard skins and wore headdresses made of lion skin. The two great men were accompanied by about 100 experienced deacons, deaconesses, preachers and other dignitaries. These took up positions at twenty-five points surrounding the big pond to the south of Mukonka village and there were four men at each point.
>
> The local preachers then started lining up their people in queues of twenty-five. The preachers and deacons stood in the water and Tom was carried by six strong young men who walked into the water right into the middle of the pond. The six young men had three heavy sticks resting on their shoulders. Tom stood on these sticks and kept on changing his foothold from one stick to another as he changed direction in order to address the whole of the gathering. He opened a Bible and read it to the multitude; the pond was then named Jordan, a hymn was sung and the twenty-five groups of four men each nodded their heads at the end of the hymn. They then opened their eyes and looked up to the sky. Each group was holding one of those to be baptised and almost simultaneously lifted him up and plunged him into the water. Anyone who resisted either deliberately, or because of fear, and whose body did not go right into the water, was condemned and called 'mfiti' ('witch'), and was put aside to await death. The baptism lasted a full day and about thirty people, including women, were called 'mfiti' and ordered to be killed on the spot.

A stick specially pointed like a peg was prepared for each 'mfiti'. As a deterrent the 'mfitis' were put to death in the presence of the whole assembly. After being lined up, each 'mfiti' was held fast by a number of strong men. The head was thrown backwards and a long, stout stick was driven in between the collar bones, into the throat and through the stomach, and out it went through the intestines and anus into the ground. As the first 'mfiti' was being butchered a horrible noise came from the other victims and their relatives who stood watching; no attempt was made to rescue any of the victims. I did not see any of the so-called 'mfitis' escape.

Most of the victims were old people. My grandmother was saved by my father who hid her away from Nguluka village long before the day of baptism. Deacon Dikola informed Tom and Shaibila that an old woman had disappeared from Nguluka village and that he suspected her of being a witch. An order was then given that any relatives of the missing woman were to be detained until the missing woman was found. As a result of this order my father and mother were both arrested and shut up in a dark room. My two elder sisters and I returned to Nguluka village as orphans. Before our departure from the pond, and after my parents had been shut up, a hymn to condemn the 'mfitis', most of whom had already died, was sung. This hymn was taught to the Northern Rhodesia Police Band by the late Sub-Inspector Paul Wang. Members of the Force who knew him personally are always reminded of the humorous Paul Wang whenever this tune is played.

At Mukonka, when the hymn was over, the whole gathering knelt except Tom and Shaibila. The former then conducted a final prayer earnestly requesting that the 'mfitis' be thrown down into hell because they themselves had killed many innocent people. Any person who failed to appear at the pond was presumed to be 'mfiti' and the power was delegated to every deacon and preacher to kill such persons if they were ever seen in the villages.

Mkankaulwa's uncle had not accompanied the family to Chief Mpanshya's area. When he heard what had been happening, he came to Nguluka village where he found the children. This uncle managed to rescue the boy's parents by getting the guard drunk. The whole family was reunited and travelled back by a round-about route to their original tribal area in the Feira District where Chief Mburuma would not permit the Watch Tower movement to operate. After about a year they heard of the arrest of Tom Mwanalesa and Chief Shabila in Mkushi District and later of their execution.[6]

Mwanalesa had come late to religion after working as a hospital orderly in the Belgian Congo and as a cook at Broken Hill where he landed in prison for unlawful carnal knowledge of a girl under 13 years of age. On his release he had met a Watchtower preacher, Gabriel Aphiri, who 'baptized' him and made him a preacher. Soon afterwards Aphiri disappeared. Tom was arrested as an unregistered alien native and sentenced to another short period of imprisonment followed by deportation. On his way back to Nyasaland in April 1925, he was persuaded to visit Chief Shabila who stated he was troubled by witches. Mwanalesa obliged him by identifying and drowning 15 'witches' in the course of baptismal ceremonies before apparently descending to the methods described by A/Insp Mkankaulwa, although, it must be said, the evidence at the various inquests was only of drowning.

Mwanalesa then decided to move on before the authorities caught up with him and returned to the Congo where his services in getting rid of witches were also in demand. A Belgian police patrol caught up with him and there were casualties on both sides. Mwanalesa escaped back into Northern Rhodesia. He was shielded by the faithful but a district messenger traced him to a hideout in the Mkushi District. The messenger came by night pretending to be a disciple bringing food. When Mwanalesa came out of his hut the messenger seized him. When the villagers saw that the messenger, being struck on the chest with Mwanalesa's magic book, did not immediately die, the spell was broken and the villagers assisted in trussing the preacher securely with bark rope but were afraid to loosen his bonds until they had brought him safely to Broken Hill. Here it was found that both his arms had become gangrenous. They had to be surgically amputated below the shoulder.

Mwanalesa survived the operation to be charged with 32 murders alleged to have been committed in Northern Rhodesia. He was tried, convicted, and, together with Chief Shabila and another accomplice, hanged in the presence of a selected company of chiefs. The evidence was that Tom had not started to kill until after he met Shabila. 15 others were convicted of murder but their sentences commuted to imprisonment.[7]

On the morning of 3rd September 1926 Ted Raubenheimer arrived at Livingstone by train to join the Force. He was surprised to find that the station had no platform but no railway station in Northern Rhodesia had such an amenity until the new railway station was opened in Lusaka in 1960. In 1984 he described how he was met by a British NCO who was to escort him to the Adjutant's office: 'We collected my few belongings and, to my surprise, these were put in a buckboard, drawn by two mules, and we were on our way to the Police camp. On arrival I was shown into the Adjutant's office. After he had read over the conditions of service in the Northern Rhodesia Police, I took the oath to serve His Majesty the King, and duly attested as a Constable in the Police.' A former machine gunner, he had expected to join the Machine Gun Platoon of the Military Branch, but was immediately posted to the Town and District Police to commence duty at Livingstone Charge Office. First he had to report to the Quartermaster to be measured for uniforms, which were made by the regimental tailors, and to draw a Wolseley helmet, boots, puttees, leather belt, brass buttons for tunics, and blankets. As there were no quarters available at the station, Raubenheimer was allocated a room with a bathroom, attached to a house in the Government House gardens, across the street from Government House. He took his meals at the only cafe, which was near the Charge Office.

Raubenheimer only remembered three motor cars being then in use in Livingstone, one for the Governor, one owned by the Managing Director of the Zambezi Sawmills, Mr Knight, and one owned by another businessman. Otherwise road traffic consisted of carts and horses or mules, push-bikes and motor cycles, mostly 'Red Indians'. However there was one other means of transport for residents to get to the railway station, the boat house or the Falls:

> There were trolley lines running from the town to the boat house on the Zambezi, with a branch line continuing past the station to the tea-room near the War Memorial at the Falls itself. The trolleys were pushed by Africans, who ran along the line. They were paid according to the journeys undertaken. At the Falls Bridge,

only trains could cross so residents walked over the bridge to the Southern Rhodesia side, where there were trolley lines with trolleys to take people up to the Victoria Falls Hotel, with a branch line to Livingstone's statue at the Eastern Cataract, and to the landing stage for the launch which carried visitors up the river to visit the islands. When dances were held at the Falls Hotel, the only method of transport was to catch a passenger train at the station, proceeding to Bulawayo, and after the dance, to catch a Goods Train from the Victoria Falls to Livingstone, to sit or stand in the guard's van. All this in evening dress. But people appeared to thoroughly enjoy themselves in spite of all the hardship...

The detachment at Livingstone consisted of one sergeant, Sgt Hart (he became Commissioner of Police in later years), two European Constables (Birbeck, who enlisted a fortnight before me, and myself), and a number of African police plus the CID section, comprising a Warrant Officer, two sergeants and African staff, with one officer controlling the station. The two European Constables did day and night duty, night duty consisting of one week on and one off and, in spite of being on night duty, the Constable was expected to turn up at office at 8 a.m. As far as the African police were concerned, I was hampered with the language problem, as, when I attested, the Adjutant informed me that the official native language in the Regiment was 'Chinyanja'. He gave me a book on the language and advised me to endeavour to learn the language as soon as I could, but in the meanwhile, 'Kitchen kaffir' or 'Chilapalapa' would help me along. Fortunately in less than six months I was able to speak, read and write 'Chinyanja', so I had no problems as far as the language was concerned. The Warrant Officer and one sergeant in the CID were heavy pipe smokers. They always tried to outdo the other in the size of their pipes – if one produced a large pipe, the other produced a larger one the next day. The Warrant Officer was known as 'Mac' and sported a heavy moustache. He was always laughing and full of life but he apparently did not like living in England, and was to commit suicide very soon after he retired on pension from the CID. The sergeant concerned was 'Brodie', who continued to serve for a long time. There was an African sergeant in the CID, who was noted for his excellent work in solving old murder cases. He had the knack of picking up information at beer-drinks about an unsolved murder committed some time ago. By following up the 'lead' he had obtained, he seemed always to find the body and arrest the murderer.

All our patrols in town were carried out on foot, push bike and, whilst on night duty, a small paraffin lamp on the cycle with which one could not see a foot ahead of the cycle. With the sandy roads it was no joy cycling and it was better to walk. Occasionally a mounted patrol was carried out but we were never keen on the horse 'Jumbo'. His mouth was like cast iron and he only moved when he wanted to do so. I shall never forget my first and only patrol on 'Jumbo' – I received the fright of my life, and so did a young typist in the Secretariat. On arriving at the Charge Office one morning before 8 a.m. I noticed 'Jumbo' standing outside ready saddled. On entering the office the sergeant said he had a nice job for me this morning and that was a mounted patrol along the banks of the Maramba river, to check on the plot holders. When I left the Charge Office all went well and 'Jumbo' was well-behaved until we reached the junction of the roads above Government House and the High Court opposite, 'Jumbo' refused to move. I dug my spurs into him as well as whipping him, but he stood like a rock until a young typist on a small 'Francis Barnett' motor cycle was passing. 'Jumbo' decided that was the right moment to carry on and sailed over the typist's head. Never shall I forget her startled eyes and white face as I sailed over her. No harm was done and 'Jumbo' went off down the street like an express train! After that I had no more trouble with 'Jumbo' and I was able to complete my full patrol as instructed.

I had not been long in the T&D when, one morning, the sergeant gave me instructions to proceed to the Railway station with two African Constables, where I would be taken by the Railway engineer in a motor trolley to Senkobo Siding, where there had been a blasting accident. After we left Livingstone the engineer told me that the previous evening he had instructed the ganger to move part of a bank on a curve on the railway line. To move this rocky portion it was necessary to use dynamite. He was present when the sixteen holes were drilled and charges put in, and he assisted the ganger to light the charges. The engineer, ganger and boss-boy counted fifteen blasts only. They then carried out a minute inspection, to see if there had been a misfire but, after a most careful inspection, they came to the conclusion that two shots must have gone off together. Nevertheless, the engineer gave the ganger strict instructions to carry out another inspection in the morning before allowing his gang to commence work. Next morning the ganger and his boss-boy carried out another thorough inspection, which again showed no misfires. In the meantime the gang were standing in a long line, waiting for the word to commence work. On receiving the signal to commence work, each man struck the ground with his pick. The unfortunate African had put his pick straight into the misfire, with the result that we collected parts of his head and brains which were scattered about. His pick was twisted into small knots. An African on each side of him lost their eye-sight and received several injuries. We arrived back in Livingstone with the body after dark and had to carry it from the station to the hospital on a stretcher. We had an awful job finding the mortuary in the dark. The hospital was not lit up as it was in later years. How much easier could have been the conveyance of the body had their been any decent form of transport.

At the inquest on the death of the African labourer, the magistrate insisted that one of the men near the deceased should be brought into court to give evidence about the accident. The sergeant explained that both men were very seriously injured and blinded and were in hospital, but the magistrate insisted that he wanted to hear the evidence of one man. The sergeant then requested the postponement of the case whilst we made arrangements to have the patient brought from the hospital on a stretcher. When the patient arrived with the aid of the hospital orderlies, the case resumed and the patient was very carefully escorted to the witness stand. The magistrate's reaction on seeing the patient struck us speechless. He immediately demanded to know why we should bring a man in that state before him in court, and ordered that he be returned to the hospital immediately, without any further delay. The sergeant explained that the man had only been brought to court on the magistrate's instructions – he simply ignored the sergeant's explanation and ordered the case to be resumed. After hearing further evidence, the magistrate ruled that the death of the labourer was due to an accident after steps had been taken to ensure that all safety precautions had been taken. I was to meet this magistrate again many years later in another part of the country when I was an accountant in the Provincial Administration.

Within a week of the Senkobo accident, the sergeant sent me one morning to the Maramba river to investigate an accident that had occurred to an African working for a European brick-maker (Schenk). This time the two African constables and I had to walk through the camp past the Central Prison and Askari gardens to the Maramba river. It appeared that the young African was scooping out sand under the river bank and the bank had caved in, trapping him and covering him with earth. Although he was missed for only a short period – about ten minutes, according to Schenk – he was dead when taken out. As he did not appear with any sand, Schenk went to look for him. When he looked down into the river bed, all that could be seen of the youth was two feet sticking out of the sand. Mr Schenk immediately shouted for his other labourers. They dug out the youth as quickly as they could but it was too late. The young African had died from suffocation. I was a bit shaken when I realised that I had collected two dead bodies within a week and wondered how many more I would have in my Police career. Fortunately I had no more. I was lucky – my colleague Birbeck appeared to escape all these jobs.

Another incident I had whilst on night duty was the case of an old 'timer'. One night I received a report that a European was lying drunk under the trees in front of the Printing and Stationery offices. I went down to investigate. The 'old timer' had placed a circle of beer bottles round in a circle, put his blanket down in the centre, with an old tin trunk as a pillow and started on the bottles from the right, but, as he had evidently been celebrating earlier on at one of the bars, he passed out before he had completed two-thirds of his circle. I sent for a stretcher and we carried him to the Charge Office with all his belongings. As we were putting him into a cell, he opened his eyes and asked where he was. When I told him and the reason, he just remarked 'Public place – the whole of Rhodesia is a d. . . public place,' and passed out again. We put him on the bed, leaving the door open when we left, so as to enable him to leave when he was able to do so. Next morning my colleague went to see him, taking him a whiskey and milk. The sergeant nearly went through the roof when he heard about it. My colleague merely remarked he knew how it felt after a thick night. We never saw the old 'timer' again.

Another incident I had from another night duty spell, was the case of the Canadian lumberjack working at the Zambesi Saw-mills. I have never yet seen anybody to equal him. He was well over six feet tall and huge. He had grown up in the lumber camps of Canada. His arms were about the size of an average man's legs and his whole body was covered with well developed muscles. One afternoon he beat up one of the men (a very small man) employed at the Sawmills who had been continually taunting him. The small man came to the Charge Office after 8 p.m. and asked for the sergeant. I told him I was on duty and I would take down any complaints he had but he insisted that he wanted to see only the sergeant, as he wanted to lay a serious charge against another man. I 'phoned the sergeant at his friend's house, giving him the information. He came to the Charge Office and was furious when he heard the complaint and told the man he could have given his complaint to me. The sergeant told me to take a statement from the man and then go down to the Sawmills and arrest the lumberjack. If I required assistance I could call upon anybody in the King's name to assist me, but if the lumberjack was asleep, to leave him alone and we would collect him in the morning. After taking a statement I called for the three hefty Angoni constables who always accompanied me whilst I was on night duty, and we walked down to the Sawmills. When we arrived at his quarters, I looked through the window and saw the giant asleep on his bed (which was much too small for him). I was very happy to leave him alone. Next morning I was walking down the street on my way to breakfast, when I met the giant on his way to the Charge Office. He had been told the police were after him and he came on his own to report. He looked down at me and asked 'Were you after me last night?' When I told him I had come down for that purpose, he just said 'You can take me by yourself at any time, even if I am dead drunk – I will never touch a man in the King's uniform – I learnt my lesson in Canada from the Royal Canadian Mounted

Police.' He was bound over to keep the peace for the sum of £5 but, within one week he beat up the same man again for taunting him. This time the sergeant sent my colleague, Birbeck, to arrest the giant. Birbeck went down on the horse 'Jumbo' fully armed with a revolver, but the giant was over the Falls and gone before we received the report of the assault. We did not worry about him any more.

I served in the Town and District branch for one and a half months and was beginning to settle down after learning about police work and getting really interested in the work, when I was suddenly transferred and posted to the Machine Gun Company in the Military branch. This of course meant that I had to vacate my room in Government House gardens and move into the Sergeants' Mess. There were five of us in the Mess, which was controlled by a Company Sergeant Major as Mess President. The food was simple, good and plenty of it and I found that the cost was much cheaper than I had been paying at the cafe. Each of us had our own room fully furnished. There was also a tennis court attached, this was always in use especially at weekends.

After I had been a month with the Machine Gun Company I was instructed one morning to report to the Adjutant's Office, where I received instructions to proceed to the Barotse Namwala Cattle Cordon, as I had been personally selected by the Commanding Officer for the posting as I had had some 'bundu' experience. My instructions were. . . a report had been received from villagers that Sgt Lancaster (the BNCOi/c) had been killed by a buffalo. If I found that he had been killed, I was to see that he had been decently buried and to take charge of the Cordon. If he was alive, to remain on the Cordon until further instructions were issued. I was told that carriers for the journey to the Cordon had been ordered and that I would leave as soon as they arrived. In the meanwhile I should get together stores for at least six months' supply but in this matter, I was greatly assisted by the manager of the Zambesi Trading Company, as he knew from Lancaster's orders what groceries etc. I should take out with me. He told me that Lancaster used to send in carriers every three months for his stores and anything he required, and suggested that I should do the same and not take six months' supply. He informed me that there were no stores of any description on the Cordon.

The carriers allocated to me for the journey numbered twenty. They had to carry all my loads plus that of a regular corporal and his family. The corporal was to accompany me and remain with me throughout my stay on the Cordon. We left Livingstone on the 23rd November, 1926. There was no road from Livingstone so we had to walk in single file along a native path. The ground, to commence with, was very sandy but hardened as we proceeded on the journey and further away from Livingstone. To within a distance of about ten miles we passed villages and saw human life, but after that, we did not come across any villages and human beings until the last day before we arrived at Cordon. Later, when I mentioned this, I was told that the inhabitants of that part of the country had been wiped out by the raiding Matabeles sent by Lobengula and that the natives had never returned to re-occupy the country. They were still too afraid to do so.

The journey from Livingstone to No. 16 Post on the Cordon, the nearest point, was a distance of 85 miles and it took us five days to cover that distance, although we started on the march early in the morning and did not stop to camp for the night until five o'clock in the late afternoon. During the first three days we travelled through forests of large trees and then we struck the country of the 'mopani' forests. Here the countryside was dry and hot and not a leaf on the trees, but, later, when the rains came, the trees were covered in green thick leaves and the countryside was green with grass, a vast difference to the heat and flies we had to pass through. On arrival at No. 16 Post I met Sgt. Lancaster. He was on his way back to Cordon Headquarters at No.15 Post (Maranga Pool). He was alive but was feeling very depressed and still very painful from his mauling. He had a broken collar bone and all the skin removed from his face, as well as body bruises from the buffalo mauling. He had been saved from further injuries by the Cordon tailor who was with him. Lancaster was able to get up and shoot the bull. I was very relieved to find him alive and I did not have to check his grave. Sgt Lancaster – known to all his friends as 'Lanc' – gave me an outline of our duties on the Cordon. The police guarding the Cordon were specially recruited but the senior NCOs were from the Military branch and we all came directly under the control of the Adjutant. Lanc told me that, although I had had served only three months of my first tour of duty, I must be prepared to accept the fact that once we were out in the 'bundu', we were forgotten and he was right, as I remained on the Cordon for two years before I was able to get a transfer back to the line of rail, after obtaining a health certificate from the missionary doctor at Sesheke. During the two years on the Cordon, I was able to do a lot of hunting big game, especially buffalo, and I took over charge of the Cordon whilst Lanc went on six months' leave and I received the rank of Acting unpaid Third Class Sergeant. On arrival back at Livingstone I was posted to Kasama to the military company stationed there and I was confirmed in the rank of Sergeant as the various classes of rank had been withdrawn. From then onwards I remained with the military branch which later became the Northern Rhodesia Regiment.[8]

Raubenheimer's posting to Kasama had been necessitated by the death there on 20 May 1928 of Sgt Saunders following a motor cycle accident the previous day. In 1925 Officers, British NCOs and constables had become eligible for advances of pay of up to £120 to purchase a motorcycle and side-car (£80 for a motorcycle only) with a view to their use on duty for which mileage allowance was payable at four pence a mile. Sgt Lancaster had the use of a motor cycle and side-car on the cordon. An African Sergeant and two corporals of the Military Branch were employed on the Barotse Cordon to assist in the supervision of the special police who received six months training at Livingstone.[9]

From 29 October until 3 November 1926 the Military Branch was inspected for the first time by the Inspector General of the King's African Rifles, Col J Harington CMG DSO who arrived at Livingstone with his staff officer following an inspection of the KAR in Nyasaland. Col Harington praised the drill, turnout and bearing and could find no fault with the administration of the Force. However he criticised the field training and musketry, judging the accuracy below that of the KAR. He recommended that consideration should be given to the amalgamation of the Military Branch with the KAR. Training had suffered due to commitments on the Cattle Cordon and to ceremonial and the last two second lieutenants recruited had not proved satisfactory. The Force had no trained signal instructor although the Inspector General found the seven man signal section competent with the heliograph. Not surprisingly the NRP had difficulty in keeping up with the latest British Army ideas and equipment although Lt Ockendon had spent some of his leave in 1925 on attachment to the Green Howards at Dover while Sgt Giddings had passed a two month machine gun course at Netheravon with distinction and Lt Bagshaw was about to attend the Small Arms School at Hythe.[10]

At the end of 1927, 229 African police had served for between 5 and 10 years, 130 for between 10 and 15 years and 51 for more than 15 years of whom 17 had served more than 17 years in the NRP. 194 re-engaged for further service although in 102 cases this was for only one year. Again low pay was blamed for the reluctance to reengage for longer periods. 284 men fired the range course of whom 33 qualified as marksmen and 70 as first class shots. This was the first year in which the Northern Rhodesia Police took part in the East and West Africa Police shooting competition.[11]

During 1927 the Fort Jameson detachment established a cordon with 25 men on the Nyasaland border to prevent the spread of East Coast Fever. The cordon was stood down in September. In June 1927, travelling via Elizabethville in the Belgian Congo to Kipushi Camp, Captain Graham, RSM Thomas and 25 other ranks joined the Anglo-Belgian Boundary Commission as escort. Graham left for long leave in January 1928 when the other rank strength was reduced by five. CSM Giddings relieved Thomas in command on 6 April 1928. The escort was maintained until 1932.[12]

From 1927 African civilians were recruited directly into the Civil Police in the rank of private. After basic training under Military Branch NCOs they passed into a new Civil Police Training Depot for instruction in police and court duties under Sergeant-Major Howe. It was intended that such instruction should also be given to European recruits but this seldom proved practicable due to the need to keep posts manned.[13]

In the same year the Government Stores and Transport Department of which the Quartermaster was already Controller, was formally transferred to the Force as 'Transport and Supply'. Captain Smith, as he had become, was assisted by a civilian storekeeper and clerks, the Regimental Quartermaster Sergeant and two British sergeants. By 1929 there were no uniformed personnel in this branch other than Captain Smith. On 31 October 1926 Force transport at Livingstone had consisted of 2 horses, 4 mules, 2 motor cars and 1 lorry.[14]

Also in 1927, at the suggestion of the Attorney General, the Central Prison Department was transferred from the control of the Legal Department to that of the Commandant of the Northern Rhodesia Police, whose officers and men ran most prisons anyway. Paradoxically the African police employed as prison warders were now struck off strength and formally transferred to the Prisons Department. The Commandant was now responsible for Defence, Police, Immigration, Prisons, Stores and Transport. Sergeant-Major Boyd, the head gaoler died of peritonitis on 25 June 1926 and was succeeded in his post by RSM Schronen Accordingly CSM Thomas had been promoted Regimental Sergeant-Major on return from leave on 25 September. After attending a course at New Scotland Yard, on 1 December 1926 Captain Wardroper was appointed Officer Commanding, Town and District Police with, from 1 April 1927, the additional title and task of Chief Inspector of Prisons. Lieutenant Ockendon became Adjutant with 2Lt A B Cree as Assistant Adjutant and Machine Gun Officer. In 1929 Prisons again became a separate department, but remained under the control of the Commissioner of Police until 1942.[15]

Sgt Hart was commissioned on 1 August 1927 and assumed charge at Broken

Hill. The Town & District Police had expanded and four new police stations were established during the year. Distribution was now:

Livingstone: Captain Wardroper, Sergeant-Major Howe, 1 sergeant, 2 constables, Native Sergeant-Major Chapandoma and 48 other African police.

Kalomo: 1 constable, 1 corporal and 7 privates.

Choma: 1 sergeant, 1 native sergeant and 4 privates,

Mazabuka: 1 sergeant, 1 constable, 1 native sergeant and 14 privates.

Lusaka: 1 sergeant, 1 constable, 1 N/Sgt and 16 other ranks

Chisamba: 1 constable, 1 corporal and 3 privates,

Broken Hill: Lieutenant Hart, 1 sergeant, 2 constables, 1 native sergeant, 1 bugler and 28 other ranks,

Bwana Mkubwa: 1 constable, 1 corporal and 8 privates,

Ndola: 1 warrant officer, 1 constable, 1 native sergeant and 13 other ranks,

Nchanga: 1 sergeant, 1 lance corporal and 2 privates,

Roan Antelope: 1 sergeant, 3 privates,

Fort Jameson: 1 sergeant, 1 constable, 1 native sergeant and 18 other ranks,

An additional two sergeants and 3 African police were on long leave.

The Criminal Investigation Department had also been strengthened. there was now a detective sergeant at Lusaka as well as one at Broken Hill and two at Livingstone. The police had brought 4,773 offences to court resulting in 4,343 convictions. The increase of more than 1,000 prosecutions was ascribed to the development of the Territory and the new police stations. 10 whites were prosecuted for manslaughter, 3 for larceny, 58 for assaults and 4 for forgery. 11 Africans were prosecuted for murder, 9 for manslaughter, 543 for larceny, 281 for assault and 11 for forgery. Fingerprints were sent to forces in India, Egypt, Belgium, France, Italy, Greece, Argentina and Brazil as well as elsewhere in Southern and Central Africa and the United Kingdom.[16]

Leslie Arthur Heatlie attested as a constable at Livingstone in June 1927, having served as a trooper in the British South Africa Police since 1923. On his retirement he wrote some reminiscences in the Force magazine:

> Five of us then lived in the old Charge Office at Livingstone on the corner of Mainway and Princes Street. In addition these premises served as headquarters for the Town and District Police, the Officer in Charge CID, and also served as the local Police Station. Our personal servants and a few African police lived in little corrugated iron 'dog kennels' in the small back yard. These latter were not much larger than a one man patrol tent.

His first task was to visit Mandala's (the African Lakes Corporation store) to equip himself with crockery, cooking utensils and 'a large tin bath'. Heatlie described Chief Inspector John Willson of the CID as, 'a man with an enormous gastronomic capacity who ate and was charged for the food of two persons'.

> At Livingstone the Boat Club was the most popular place for relaxation. There was a track, rather than a road, as far as the Victoria Falls Bridge, but thereafter one had to walk, as there was no roadway across the Bridge until 1929. Even this track became unusable when the river rose, it flooded across the road in several places. There were still trolley lines from Livingstone to the Boat Club and certain officials

and some old residents had their own private trolleys, though these were falling into disuse.

The most noticeable feature in Livingstone at that time was the enormous number of lightweight motor cycles used by almost everyone. Most of the town roads were just sandy wastes, but they had a cinder track on one side which served as combined footpaths and motor cycle tracks. Motorcars were still rather uncommon.

European constables were issued with pedal cycles as their personal transport. Heatlie was soon transferred to Ndola to relieve a man who had 'recently written to the Commandant saying that unless he was given commissioned rank at once he would resign.' The inevitable response had been a terse telegram, 'Resignation accepted'.

Ndola then consisted of three stores (Boothe's, Thom's and Mandala), two tiny one-man garages, one hotel, about six Government houses and about six others; also Government offices comprising Boma, Police Station, Post Office and Customs. The railway station was situated more or less at the spot where the Luanshya Branch now joins the Main Line, only a few hundred yards from the Itawa railway bridge.

Only six miles from Ndola was the comparatively large town of Bwana Mkubwa with a population of 300 Europeans. At night the lights on the mine used to look like a ship at sea and this was quite a familiar view from Ndola until Bwana Mkubwa Mine was closed down in 1931. Bwana Mkubwa Mine was an open-cast working similar to a large quarry.

Apparently Ndola had been selected as the seat of Government in preference to Bwana, so as to be entirely clear of mine property and mine influence. However, there were disadvantages, as Ndola had no electricity or water supply. All our water was carried in drums from the Itawa Swamp, which was virtually a stagnant cesspool, and why we did not all go down with typhoid I do not know. The police force at Ndola consisted of a Sergeant and one European Constable; at Bwana there was only a Sergeant.

There was a good golf course at Ndola – by local standards – but I soon found golf was not my game. So I built a duck punt and spent much time shooting duck and geese on the huge swamp up at Itawa Valley. When I got a motor cycle I used to go fishing on the Kafue. I also learned that one could catch lovely bream on fly at certain spots on the Itawa during the rainy season. Natives used to catch large barbel about five feet long, in a pool below the railway bridge.

Nchanga and Roan Antelope Mines were already being developed, and there were many Kimberley brick dwellings on them. The other mines had hardly been thought of, though there was a small 'Prospect' which they were developing at Nkana. The population at Nchanga and Roan was beginning to grow, and these centres needed and asked for police stations. But the territorial revenue was then only about £300,000 (yes, only three hundred thousand pounds) and there was no money for more police stations. Stations were only opened on these two mines in 1928 after the mining companies had agreed to defray the complete cost, even the salaries of the staff.

Just when the rainy season, 1927–28, had got started, the PWD decided it was the right time to start rebuilding the causeway carrying the only road across the dambo. For some weeks they tried to hold back the rising river with sandbags, but the river won and it was months before work could be resumed. During this time a lion chased a duiker right through the PWD camp one morning.

Part of my duties was to act as Immigration Officer, and I had to examine passengers on the two weekly mail trains from Sakania. These were due at Ndola on Wednesday and Saturday at 10 p.m. but they were often hours late. There was no proper station and no staff on duty after 5 p.m. so it was impossible to find out when the trains would arrive. So on many a night the Customs Officer and I would wait all night, in the open and in the rain, waiting for a train that eventually arrived at 3 or 4 a.m. or even 6 a.m. In 1928 the station was moved to its present site but there was no usable road so we used to walk down the track with pressure lanterns (to scare the lions away!).

George Berwick, was now the sergeant at Bwana Mkubwa while Sergeant Camfield was in charge at Ndola. In 1927 an allowance of 5/- per journey at night was authorised for immigration officers, based at Ndola, working on the trains.[17] Heatlie further wrote,

About October, 1927, a very old native woman came to the Charge Office. At first we could not understand what she wanted. Eventually it transpired that she wished to be released from slavery. In her own words, 'I have been Chiwala's slave for many years but now I am too old to work and wish to be released'. Her release was subsequently arranged by Tom Sandford, the District Commissioner. I imagine this must be the last date on which any person was released from slavery in any British territory.

When trains were running to time it was the habit of some of the miners at Bwana to go up to Sakania by the Saturday afternoon train and return again that night. The main attraction was the excellent beer at Sakania, decent beer being scarce and expensive at Bwana and Ndola. Unfortunately some of these men used to get very drunk and made nuisances of themselves, assaulted the Belgian police, etc. One day when I was at Sakania on business, the Belgian equivalent of a District Commissioner asked me to convey a warning to the people at Bwana that he intended to make an example of any others who misbehaved in this fashion. He added that the Belgian system of justice was very different from ideas in British countries, he was the sole upholder of the law at Sakania and could inflict virtually any punishment from which there could be no appeal.

I duly passed on this warning through George Berwick but it had no effect. Shortly afterwards a party from Bwana went up to Sakania by car and got very drunk and behaved in an altogether disgraceful fashion. They each got fourteen days inside and their car was confiscated. This rather drastic punishment had the desired effect.

Constable Heatlie resigned on 30 September 1928. Evidently he, and others, found life in the Northern Rhodesia Police, on charge office duty or town patrol, less congenial than 'roaming the veld on a horse' as a BSAP trooper! After two years of civilian life in Southern Rhodesia in the 'Great Depression' he admitted being very glad to be allowed to rejoin the NRP at the beginning of 1931. He was accepted directly into the Criminal Investigation Department as an Assistant Inspector and was soon posted back to Ndola as a full time Immigration Officer[18]. He was to remain on immigration duties until his retirement back to the Cape in June 1958 as the Senior Superintendent commanding Immigration Division, having spent the last 24 years of his service at Livingstone.

It was in 1928 that the first Road Traffic Ordinance came into effect. Up until then motor vehicles had only been required to carry identification numbers in Livingstone the only municipality in the Territory. The Force lost a second traffic accident victim when Bandmaster Cliff was invalided out following an accident in July. A speed limit of 25 miles per hour was authorised for Livingstone in March 1927.

By 1929 the traffic problems in Lusaka were so severe that Inspector Maxwell suggested that 'ordinary traffic' should use the east side of Cairo Road (in both directions) and that 'motor traffic' should use the west, whether travelling north or south. The Lusaka Management Board accepted his suggestion and resolved to apply for a regulation to make it mandatory. Maxwell also pointed out to the Board that rules for car parking in the township would soon be required. He was asked to prepare some.[19]

The Corps of Drums had been broken up during the War and was not reformed until 1928. The drum shells, previously blue, were now to be red[20]. The new Corps of Drums beat retreat at Livingstone every Wednesday, a tradition restored by the Corps of Drums of the Northern Rhodesia Police Mobile Unit at Bwana Mkubwa in the nineteen fifties. The 'Drums' were presumably on parade for the Review of the Military Branch by Princess Marie Louise on February 1928.

Captain Tysoe with 30 men from Mongu patrolled the Mankoya District from 10 July until 8 August 1928. Major Burton with 6 rank and file from Fort Jameson patrolled the Lundazi Sub-district. He also sent out two patrols under native non-commissioned officers to search for lions said to be responsible for the deaths of 150 Africans. They were unsuccessful, receiving little or no assistance from the local inhabitants who believed the lions to be the re-incarnated spirits of their dead chiefs. Lt Hopkins, the platoon commander at Kasama had left in January 1928 on appointment as ADC to the Governor. With the death of Sgt Saunders little could be done by this detachment which was employed rebuilding bridges between Kasama and Chambesi from 4 October until 10 November.

A field training exercise was held from 20 August to 17 September 1928. The annual report considered that there should be more frequent exercises and patrols by the Military Branch as the natives should be made to realise the firepower of modern weapons. The problem was cost.

Captain Bagshaw was congratulated for translating the rifle and Lewis gun training manuals into Cinyanja as a result of which Lewis gun training had improved. The annual rifle range classification results were deemed not as good as usual due to a shortage of officers at HQ. From the 17 marksmen an VIII had been selected to compete for the East and West Africa Shooting Cup.[21]

In the Northern Rhodesia staff list of 1 July 1928 Lieutenant Colonel Stephenson was described as Commandant and Chief Commissioner of Police. The Northern Rhodesia Police was shown to comprise a headquarters and three branches, Military, Town and District Police, and Criminal Investigation Department. Captain Wardroper was described no longer as merely 'Officer Commanding, Town and District Police', but 'Commissioner of Police'. His second-in-command, Harry Hart, was now designated 'Assistant Commissioner of Police', and the warrant officers and British NCOs of the Town and District Police were no longer shown as sergeants-major (1st, 2nd, or 3rd Class) or sergeants (1st, 2nd or 3rd

Class), but as 'Inspectors' and 'Assistant Inspectors'. The annual report showed the strength of the Town and District Police as two officers, 5 inspectors, 7 assistant inspectors, 15 constables and 207 African police, 2 A/Insps and 6 Africans below establishment. No.904 Sergeant-Major Chapandoma, the senior African civil policeman was awarded the Meritorious Service Medal on retirement on pension. Four out of six awards of the Long Service and Good Conduct Medal to African members of the Force were to members of the Civil Police and one to D10 Native Detective Njakuke.[22]

Capt Hamilton still commanded the CID with one Detective Inspector and a D/A/Insp and lady clerk at Livingstone. There was a detective assistant inspector at Broken Hill covering from the Congo Border to Chisamba, one at Lusaka dealing with serious crime from Chisamba to Mazabuka and one on long leave. There were now 26 African detectives. 5,414 offences were shown as having been dealt with in the past twelve months with 5,066 convictions, a success rate of 93.5 per cent for the Civil Police and CID.

The Regimental Savings Bank was reported to be increasingly popular with 138 depositors with a total of £538 on deposit on 31 December 1928. The thatch on the roofs of the African police quarters at Livingstone was replaced by corrugated iron which was believed to have improved health although the change had been opposed by the medical officers. Cinema shows were held in the camp. A school room and canteen were to be erected and a native teacher had been employed to improve education.

In November 1928 ten constables sat the first examination for promotion to assistant inspector. Five passed in all subjects while the others passed in Criminal Law and Evidence, Statute Law, and Charge Office Routine but were required to resit the oral examination in a native language within 10 months. Constables who failed to pass in all subjects within two years were to be discharged on completing three years service.

The question of the training of European recruits was now raised. They were being placed on duty almost immediately after attestation without any period of prior instruction. Luckily the majority had previous experience in the British South Africa Police or another force. Now that the two territories were no longer administered by the Chartered Company, the Southern Rhodesia force was less willing to act as a pool of trained manpower for the NRP and at about this time, according to Deane-Simmons, placed an embargo on young troopers leaving before the end of their initial three year engagement to join the force north of the Zambesi. It was decided that Northern Rhodesia Police constables recruited in the United Kingdom should undergo a six-month training course at the Royal Ulster Constabulary Depot, Newtownards, before sailing for Africa. It was considered that RUC training was likely to be more suitable for colonial police work than the training of a constable in Great Britain. Serving officers were to attend refresher courses while in UK on leave.[23]

African railway workers struck over pay on 16 February 1929. 95 Whites were attested as special constables to assist in keeping order but the strike finished without incident on 18 March on the promise of a review of pay and conditions.[24]

Edward Deane-Simmons MBE recorded that he left the BSAP in June 1928 to seek more lucrative employment. He found it at £400 a year as 'Secretary, Lorry Driver and General Factotum' with Rhodesian Selection Trust at Mufulira Mine General Office, then a grass-walled construction with a bucksail roof at the old pumping station on the bank of the Mufulira River. One of his tasks was to assist Assistant Inspector Walter Totman to build and open Mufulira Police Station. The Charge Office, a house for Totman and quarters for some six African police were erected at a cost of £7 10s 0d, borne by the mining company. This association made Deane-Simmons unsettled and nostalgic for the life of a policeman. With a recommendation from 'Ginger' Totman, Deane-Simmons sent in his application to join the NRP. Alas, the establishment of seven constables was full and he was left for some two or three months nursing his disappointment at being rejected both by the Force and his fiancée.

At last he was notified of a vacancy and on or about 13th July 1929 attested as a constable before Lieutenant Colonel Stephenson at Livingstone. Deane-Simmons' new salary was £246 per annum (rising by increments to £300), a considerable drop from that with the Mine, but an improvement on the £16.13s.6d. a month he had enjoyed as a BSAP trooper. Promotion to Assistant Inspector could be expected after two and a half to three years service as a constable. Evidently he avoided having to take the native language examination, which was Cinyanja oral only, before Captain Wardroper as examiner. The only examination Deane-Simmons ever had to take was law set by Chief Inspector Howe, which he passed a couple of months after joining.[25]

Life at Mufulira was not easy. In September 1929, the Commissioner of Police, Captain Percy Wardroper, wrote personally to the Assistant Inspector in charge, to say that he was sending up a case of paraffin for the African police to rub on their feet several times a day as a remedy against the 'Matakenya' pest (jigger fleas) with which the camp was infested. He also recommended that the officer rub paraffin on his socks, but considered that the best precaution was to have his feet inspected daily by his personal servant as Wardroper himself had done during the war.

In December a European Constable, temporarily in charge at Mufulira, wrote to Headquarters at Livingstone pointing out that the customs officer who shared the station, was moving to Mokambo, on the Congo Border, taking the only table and strong box. Headquarters promised to send a table, but informed him that there were no funds for a new strong box until the next financial year.[26]

The 1929 staff list showed a further step towards the divorce of the Military and Civil Police. No headquarters was listed for the Northern Rhodesia Police as a whole. The two branches were shown separately with Lieutenant Colonel Stephenson's name appearing twice; described as 'Commandant' at the head of the Military Branch and as 'Chief Commissioner of Police and Prisons' at the head of the Civil Police[27]. The salary of the Commandant was now £1,400 a year. The total revenue of Northern Rhodesia for the year was £672,289. The Northern Rhodesia Police, Military and Civil, accounted for £65,820, out of a total expenditure for the Territory of £554,527.

The Annual Report for 1929 showed 1,303 persons committed to the five central prisons. However there was a slight drop in crime with 4,889 persons prosecuted and 4,597 convictions. There were 29 convictions for murder, 46 for housebreaking and burglary, 20 for rape, 337 for various assaults and 15 for indecent assault. In one case at Fort Jameson 17 Africans were charged jointly with the murder of a woman. For permitting a prisoner under penalty of death to escape, an African policeman was tried by a special board of officers and sentenced to 18 months imprisonment with hard labour and to forfeit his Long Service and Good Conduct Medal.

WO2 Cliff's replacement, Bandmaster F L Wood arrived in 1929. In 1930 Capt Graham took the band for a two week tour of Southern Rhodesia where performances in Salisbury and Bulawayo were much appreciated.[28]

In April 1930 Lieutenant Colonel Stephenson retired. He was succeeded as Commandant by Lieutenant Colonel E G Dickinson MC, one of the original officers of the Northern Rhodesia Police. Dickinson had joined the Natal Police in 1901 and served in the South African War and the Zulu Rebellion of 1906. His name appeared only once in the Staff List for 1930 as 'Commandant and Chief Commissioner of Police and Prisons'.

Stephenson remained in Northern Rhodesia as Manager of the Native Labour Association and later Manager of the Chamber of Mines at Kitwe. As Commandant he had been an ex-officio member of the Legislative Council. In 1935 he re-joined the Council as elected member for Ndola. In 1939, at the age of 58, he was recalled to military service as Sub-Area Commander for Northern Rhodesia in the rank of Colonel.

In July 1930 Mrs Una Kirby of Pretoria was visiting the Victoria Falls when she was attacked by an African. In the ensuing struggle Mrs Kirby fell into the Gorge. Her companion reported the incident. With the assistance of the Military Branch, the area was cordoned off and a strong guard placed on the Falls Bridge. That night an African wearing torn and bloodstained clothing attempted to break through the cordon at the Bridge. In his efforts to escape arrest he too fell into the Gorge but his fall was broken by a rock two hundred feet down. Constable J N Jordan had himself lowered by a rope and, assisted by 3405 Private Nyambe, brought up the injured man with him. This brave attempt to save the life of a suspected murderer was in vain. The man died on the way to hospital and thus evaded the hangman. Jordan was awarded the King's Police Medal for Gallantry. Nyambe was commended.[29]

During 1930 agreement was reached with Rhodesia Railways for a sergeant and five privates of the Civil Police, at Livingstone, Broken Hill and Ndola to be seconded for duty as railway police. In return the Railway Company was to pay £30 a year for each man to the General Revenue of the Territory. This arrangement continued until well after the Second World War.

Experiments were made with watchman's 'Tell Tale' clocks at Livingstone and Ndola. These were reported to be invaluable as a check on the systematic working of beats. It was proposed that they be issued to all Town and District Police detachments. It seems however, no doubt for the usual reasons of economy, that this proposal was not implemented. However, at a cost of £400, the khaki greatcoats of the Town and District Police were replaced by policemanlike blue ones.[30]

After about a year in the Force Deane-Simmons was granted a transfer to the

Criminal Investigation Department, which meant immediate promotion to Assistant Inspector. Two A/D/Insps resigned in 1930 to take up civil employment in the Territory. His new OC, Captain Tommy Hamilton, was known to his men as 'The Maku' (short for Bwana Mkubwa or big boss). At that time the Commissioner of Police, Captain Wardroper, still had no authority over the CID. Deane-Simmons shared an office at Livingstone with 'one of the best men I ever knew, Norman Brodie, known to the C.I.D as Tim'.[31]

Born in Worcestershire in 1895, Norman Brodie had become a part-time soldier in the county Yeomanry at the age of 16. From April 1915 he was on active service with his regiment in the Middle East, being twice mentioned in despatches and attaining the rank of Squadron Sergeant-Major. In 1919 he joined the British South Africa Police and six years later came north to join the Northern Rhodesia Police. He was to be Officer Commanding CID and Chief Immigration Officer for fifteen years before his retirement in 1951. He then served for some years as District Commandant of the Police Reserve and was also Deputy Mayor of Livingstone where he died in 1960.

Deane-Simmons told of an investigation which started when a letter was received from Constable Trevor Wright at Choma, telling how three Africans had complained that when travelling home by train from the Witwatersrand mines, they had been required by an African immigration officer at Livingstone to make a cash deposit before being allowed to proceed. They were told that the money would be refunded at their home Boma, Choma. On arrival they had applied unsuccessfully for the promised refund. In fact there were no African immigration officers.

One of the complainants was sent down to Livingstone and 'one of our top "quicks", Detective Robert Simpelwe', took him on a tour of the African township. Before the end of the day they had returned to the CID offices with a suspect the complainant had picked out from the hundreds of Africans passing and repassing on their lawful occasions. It all looked too easy, so a second complainant was sent for, and taken to Deane-Simmons' office. Another European officer organised an identification parade at which the suspect was placed among twelve other Africans. When all was ready Deane brought out his complainant who 'took a quick glance at the parade and, with a whoop of joy, picked out the suspect.' The suspect was duly charged.

> Then the last witness was brought down from Choma and was kept overnight in the Charge Office, the accused being in Livingstone Central Prison. He had absolutely no opportunity of seeing the accused but, in the identification parade, picked out the suspect after closely inspecting the members of it. The accused was duly taken before the R.M., who handed him out a sentence of three years hard labour. We all then sat back for, I think, about nine months and I happened to be listening to Tim Brodie interrogating a well known thief, named Bwalia Moffatt, who operated all over the territory on the general principle of picking up any loose money he could lay his hands on. Any kind of theft, from burglary and theft downwards, was his modus, but only money. Well, Tim had arrested Bwalia for some skulduggery or other and this extraordinary character was entertaining himself and us with an account of all his exploits since his last release from prison. You will have, by this

time, jumped to the correct solution – Bwalia Moffatt told us about how he tricked three Africans out of all their money by posing as an Immigration Officer! I hope no one who reads this has experienced the certain knowledge that he has helped in the wrongful imprisonment of an innocent man for the best part of a year. It took a little time to get the three witnesses located in Choma and a little more time to arrange another identification parade, including Bwalia Moffatt, but it was done and they all identified Bwalia Moffatt with as much certainty as they had previously done for the convicted innocent. In fact it was quite difficult to restrain Moffatt from identifying himself. More time was taken to put the wheels of justice into reverse, but the wrongfully imprisoned innocent was eventually 'pardoned'. Now, here's the unexpected ending. . . the victim was an average African of average build and average height, say about five feet four or five inches – Bwalia Moffatt was a vast man of six feet seven inches and proportionate build. What inference can you draw and how much faith do you think I placed afterwards in identification parades?

In 1959 Mr C N Halse QPM, Senior Assistant Commissioner, contributed the following story to *Nkhwazi*:

In 1930 an American named Marshall Barnes was arrested at Roan Antelope and charged with breaking into an office at the Mulungushi dam site near Broken Hill and stealing labourers' wages in the sum of several hundred pounds from the safe.

Barnes had actually worked on the Mulungushi project as an engineer, but had left and obtained employment with the Rhodesian Selection Trust at Roan Antelope. His arrest was the culmination of a painstaking investigation by Detective Inspector C.R. Arnott, who later became Chief Immigration Officer in Palestine. The accused was shown to have left the Roan on a Saturday evening and, travelling by car, had during the night reached Mulungushi, where he had broken into the office, opened the safe with a key (which he had been seen fabricating some time before), and was back with the labourers' pay at Roan Antelope before dawn the following morning.

In due course Barnes was committed for trial before the High Court at Ndola, with Sir Euan Logan as the trial judge and Constable C.N. Halse as court orderly!

Judgment was to be delivered at 2 p.m. on the second day of the trial, but at about 11 a.m. defence counsel requested the judge to allow his client to go under escort to Roan Antelope to attend to a private matter.

The application was granted and a few minutes later Barnes, his wife (whose right thumb was missing) and I were on our way in a car driven by Barnes, with his wife beside him and myself in the back. I had not expected my prisoner to give me any trouble and so had not thought it necessary to carry my revolver. However, as we went along, Barnes said to me: 'Why don't you police carry revolvers when you escort prisoners?' I replied that I did not think it was necessary in this instance, whereupon Barnes laughed and said: 'What would you do if I stopped the car now and simply walked away into the bush?'. I suddenly became very conscious of my missing revolver and the fact that my prisoner was about twice my size. I adopted a most conciliatory tone, pointing out that in my view he would be found not guilty at 2 p.m. and that he would jeopardise everything should he give me any trouble. 'Do you really think I'll get off?' said Barnes. 'My dear fellow, I am sure of it', I replied. On we went to Roan, where Mrs Barnes gave me an excellent omelette, and at 2 p.m. we were back in court at Ndola where Sir Euan Logan sentenced Barnes to two years' I.H.L. You should have seen the savage look on Barnes' face when he was sentenced! In due course he was lodged in Livingstone prison.

A few days later his wife was allowed to see him and the following morning it was discovered that Barnes had cut his way through the brick wall and made good his escape, evidently by using an instrument brought in by his wife. Despite the hue and cry he made his way down to Cape Town and was next heard of in America. Later the Federal police there informed us that Barnes was a notorious gangster and added that his wife had lost her thumb while helping him to 'crack' a safe some years before!

V M Barnes had stolen £200 from the Roads Department Camp near the Lunsemfwa River, where he had previously been employed. D/Insp Arnott and D5 Detective Nyrenda were commended for zeal and ability in their work in this case. Benjamin Nyrenda, who died in 1931, was awarded £1. In 1930, he, Detective Mashawila and Sgt Samsoni DCM were among 14 Africans awarded the Long Service and Good Conduct Medal. D6 Mashawila was commended and awarded £1 for the arrest of an escaped convict.[32]

C Neville Halse was the elder of two brothers who served with distinction in the Northern Rhodesia Police. They came from a police family and claimed that their father, Captain Harry Halse, South African Police, killed in the Rand Revolt of 1922, and his three brothers had 120 years police service between them. A Captain Halse of the Cape Police was mentioned in despatches by Lord Roberts on 2nd April 1901. Neville and his brother, Eric, added another 66 years between them to the family record. Neville followed their father into the South African Police before coming to Northern Rhodesia in 1930. He died on 29 December 1959 while commanding Western Division.

E H Halse OBE KPM was to become Commissioner of Police in 1962. He attested as a Constable in June 1931 after serving for a year or so in the BSAP. In 1938 he transferred to British Somaliland as a superintendent. After the evacuation of British Somaliland in 1940 Eric Halse was seconded to the Army, returning to Somaliland in the rank of Lieutenant Colonel. In 1950 he was appointed Commissioner of Police for Somaliland, returning to Northern Rhodesia as Deputy Commissioner in 1953.

Evidently 1930 was a boom year in Northern Rhodesia. The expanding mining industry attracted European immigrants in increasing numbers. 3,604 Europeans entered the Territory together with 33 coloureds from the Cape and 33 Indians. John Hawkins, who was Acting Assistant Inspector in Charge at Bwana Mkubwa from 1931 to 1932, estimated that the European population there was about 800 by 1930. A new police camp had been completed that year at the enormous cost of £5,000. This time the police station was near the mining company's offices.

A J I Hawkins OBE QPM was to precede Neville Halse in command of Western Division, retiring as an Assistant Commissioner in 1956. He recorded that Bwana Mkubwa was a most unhealthy place. 'Malaria was prevalent and it seemed that about one person out of every four or five who went sick eventually died of blackwater in the hospital which, at that time, was the only Government hospital on the Copperbelt. There was a mine hospital at Luanshya about 1927. It seemed in those days that everybody (and this included many of the Africans too) had at least one, and often two days off work every week with fever. The hospital was always full and very often it was not possible to be admitted. Many died and the police were the local undertakers for both Europeans and Africans. Graves for many of these Europeans and Africans who died can still (1953) be found near Bwana Mkubwa Camp. In this graveyard a European policeman who died in Bwana Mkubwa Hospital was buried, but he had been stationed at the Sakania turnoff where there was an immigration post.'[33]

The motor search post on the Ndola to Sakania Road was only established in 1930. The police officer there also acted as customs officer. In the same year new stations opened at Nkana Mine and Mokambo, 12 miles from Mufulira. In 1929 a station had been established at Kansanshi.

In 1930 an assistant inspector nearly lost his arm and had part of his hand amputated due to injuries suffered in suppressing a faction fight which began in Mufulira as a result of a mistake over the identity of an African sergeant in plain clothes. The sergeant was killed.[34]

By 1931 there had been a considerable increase in the European strength of the Civil Police as evidenced by the number of constables mentioned in this extract from Regimental Orders:

'It is published for the information of all European Ranks, that the undermentioned Constables have passed the Civil Police Examination 1931, for promotion to Assistant-Inspector in all the written subjects. Their names are placed on the Roll of those eligible for promotion to the rank of Assistant-Inspector, subject to their being successful in passing the viva voce examination in the Chinyanja language:

No.24 G.G. BROOKS
No.27 C.N. HALSE (Sat for Paper 'B' only)
No.28 J.T. CRAWFORD (Sat for Paper 'E' only)
No.29 J.N. JORDAN
No.30 G.B.B. HESOM (Sat for Paper 'B' & 'E' only)
No.35 A.H.S. GOSLETT (Sat for Paper 'B' & 'C' only)
No.36 E. POTTER
No.37 T.A. WRIGHT (Sat for Paper 'A' & 'B' only)

No.38 H.H. KINGSHOTT
No.39 E.T. GRAINGER
No.40 C.N.BREEN*
No.41 H.S.M. HUGGINS*
No.42 A. WALLACE
No.43 E.J. PHINN*
No.47 A.J. FRANCIS
No.48 E.H. HALSE*
No.50 F.E. WELLER*
No.51 J.W. HUGHES
No.56 C.H. ROBERTS

*Passed with distinction

The undermentioned were unsuccessful in passing the examination in the papers as placed against their names. They will be required to sit again for those papers only at the next examination:

No.53 Const. S.A. WRIGHT   No.45 Const. N.W. ABBOTT
  (Papers 'A' & 'B')   (Papers 'A' & 'E')
No.54 Const. H.T. HUMPHREYS   No.49 Const. T.H. BUSH
  (Paper 'E')   (Paper 'E')

Paper 'A' is Charge Office Routine
Paper 'B' is Criminal Law and Evidence
Paper 'E' is General Knowledge

Constables E H Halse, A J Francis and J T Crawford were posted to Nkana under the command of Assistant Inspector N T Nissen, whose son Tony was to follow him into the Force. Francis later became Force Pay and Quartermaster until he retired in 1957. Like Nissen, T.A.Wright retired as an Assistant Superintendent in the early nineteen fifties, and he was followed into the Force by his son, as was S.A.Wright and, indeed, John Hawkins. Hesom, Breen, Wallace, Phinn, Tozer and Bush were all to reach senior rank before retiring.[35]

In 1931 the strength of the Military Branch was 17 Officers, 9 British Warrant Officers and NCOs and 472 African ranks. RSM Thomas and six asirikari acted as escort to the Caprivi Boundary Commission. A patrol of 2 officers, a warrant officer and 86 Africans of the Military visited the Copperbelt giving demonstrations, carrying out training exercises and generally showing the flag. Men were provided for specie and cash escorts throughout the year. Following an outbreak of foot and mouth disease in Southern Rhodesia, three British WOs and NCOs of the Military Branch were employed searching all trains entering the Territory across the Falls Bridge. The following year asirikari guards were placed on all stock trains between Southern Rhodesia and the Belgian Congo.[36]

Prior to taking up the appointment of Director of Ordnance Survey in the United Kingdom in 1930, Brigadier H St J L Winterbotham CMG DSO, late RE, had been seconded to the Colonial Office to inspect survey departments. While in Northern Rhodesia he recommended the formation of a survey platoon in the Northern Rhodesia Police. Lieutenant A N Bagshaw was selected to form the platoon and spent nearly four months on a survey course at the end of a leave in England during which he was also attached for 5 days to his old regiment and attended a refresher course at the Small Arms School.

After commissioned service in The Leicestershire Regiment on the Western Front, Bagshaw had joined the British South Africa Police, in which he reached the rank of corporal. He then transfered to the NRP as a sergeant in the Military Branch and was soon commissioned. He had nearly died of malaria while commanding No 1 Sector of the Barotse Cattle Cordon, but survived to serve many years in Northern Rhodesia. He translated the Police Ordinance into Chinyanja and was an examiner in that language, the lingua franca of the Force.

Bagshaw arrived back in Northern Rhodesia on 2 November 1930 after nearly a year away. On the return voyage he had visited the survey platoons formed in the West African Frontier Force in Sierra Leone and the Gold Coast.

He soon had his new platoon formed, largely from educated 'mission boys'. It was put to work on a chain and compass survey of Livingstone Golf Course and land surveys for African gardens on the Maramba Stream, before graduating to demarcating native reserve boundaries in Southern Province. In 1932 an African sergeant was seconded to the East African Geodetic Survey to help supervise carriers. In 1933 the survey platoon was broken up and most of the African personnel transfered to the Government Survey Department as civilians.[37]

Nkana Civil Police detachment 1931 (Nkhwazi)

The normal tour of duty for Europeans was two and a half or three years depending on the station, but vacation leave at the standard rate of five days for each completed month could be taken after a minimum of two years. Assistant Inspector Deane-Simmons left Livingstone on leave in September 1931. On his return from the United Kingdom in February 1932 he found 'There was a large encampment of recruits in tents at the northern end of the Falls Bridge.' This ties up with the following extract from Regimental Orders:

Civil Police and C.I. Dept:

CP.(DEPOT) L'STONE:

The undermentioned are attested for a period of three years (subject to the final approval of the Secretary of State) from 4–2–32 and will draw pay, pensionable, at the rate of £246 per annum, plus Uniform Allowance. They are posted to CP.(DEPOT) L'STONE from that date. Their pensionable service will count

from date of embarkation in England, viz: 7–1–32, and their residential service
will commence from date of disembarkation at Capetown viz: 1–2–32:

No.58 Constable   WILLIAM HERBERT CHARLES BROWNE
No.59 Constable   WILLIAM GEORGE WALLIS DEAN
No.60 Constable   JOHN EDMUND LONG
No.61 Constable   FRANK FREDERIC LAW
No.62 Constable   ROY JAMES RANDELL
No.63 Constable   ALDHELM St. JOHN SUGG

The undermentioned have attested for a period of four years from 3–2–32 and are
posted to CP.(DEPOT) L'STONE:

No.3964 Pte MENAN   No.3967 Pte SIANIANI
No.3965 Pte SHAPOLI   No.3968 Pte DARE
No.3966 Pte POSIANA   No.3969 Pte MAYANZI[38]

'Punch' Randell was to serve in the Force for thirty years and will be mentioned
again. John Long and St.John Sugg transferred to the Provincial Administration.
In 1959 Dare was to be one of the first Africans promoted to the rank of Assistant
Inspector. On 9th July 1958 Willie Dare watched his son pass out of the Northern
Rhodesia Police Training School, Lilayi, as one of the two best recruit constables
in his squad.

Notes

1. PRO CO795/1 Transport NRJ
2. *Story NRR* pp110–112
3. PRO CO795/1
4. Staff List Jul 1924 PRO CO795/1 Colonial Office List 1925 *Story NRR* p68
5. *Story NRR* p66–7, de Guingand *African Assignment* Guingand Hodder & Stoughton 1953 Pt 2,
   Tpt NRJ
   Maj Gen Francis Wilfrd de GUINGAND KBE 44 CB 43 DSO 42 b28.2.00 ed Ampleforth
   RMC 2Lt WYks 19 KAR 26–31 psc 36 MA to SOfS War 39–40 COS 8th Army 42 21AG 44–
   5 rtd47 Chmn Rothmans d29.6.79
6. *More than Thirty People were Murdered before my Eyes Nkhwazi* Vol 8 Nos 1 & 2 Apr & Sept
   1960
7. Stephenson *Mwanalesa* Police Journal Vol III p111, PRO CO795/11, inquest records Rhodes
   House Library
8. NRPA Newsletter Dec 1978
9. PRO CO795/1,6
10. PRO CO795/14/18020Brig Gen John HARINGTON CB 27 CMG 19 DSO15 FRGS b19.4.73
    s/o Bart 2Lt RB 95 Nile 98 SA 99–02 Capt 01 KAR 03–7 Maj 14 CO 4RB 16.4–s10.5.15 T/
    BG 139Bde 24.7.18 CO 2RB 19 3RB 20 Insp KAR 23–7 Cmd 139Bde TA 28–rtd30
11. Annual report PRO CO799/3
12. CO799/3
13. CO799/3
14. PRO CO795/10, 795/14/18020
15. Annual report PRO CO799/3, 795/8
16. Annual Report PRO CO799/3.

17. Exco 8.4.26 PRO CO799/8
18. Heatlie *The Northern Rhodesia Police Thirty Four Years Ago Nkhwazi* Vol 9 No.2 Dec 1961
19. Central African Post Jubilee Edition 31 July 1963 Exco PRO CO799/8
20. *Story NRR* p105
21. Annual Report PRO CO799/4, *Story NRR* p69
22. Annual Report PRO CO799/4.
23. Deane-Simmons NRPA Newsletter Dec 78, Annual Report
24. Annual Report PRO CO799/5
25. Deane-Simmons NRPA Newsletter Dec'78
26. *Nkhwazi* Vol 10 No.2 Dec 62 p16 *The Good Old Days*
27. *Story NRR* p69
28. Annual Report
29. PRO CO799/7
30. PRO CO796/4
31. Deane-Simmons NRPA Newsletter
32. *Nkhwazi* Vol 7 No.3 Dec 59 p14, Annual Report 1930 PRO CO799/7   Sir Ewan Regnld LOGAN Kt'28 MA b'68 ed Chtrhse, Oxfd, Bar'99 Mx & NLndn Sessions'00 2Lt IY'01 Mines Dept Tvl'01 A/RM Tvl'02 Mag EA'05 CJ Seychelles'14 Judge Gold Coast'20 CJ Bahamas'25 Judge NR'27–rtd 31.8.31
33. Hawkins *Bwana Mkubwa in the Early Days Nkhwazi* '53 & Apr'64 p84
34. Annual report 1930 PRO CO799/7
35. *Nkhwazi* Vol 7 No 3 Dec 59 p23
36. Annual report 1931 PRO CO799/9 *Story NRR* p67
37. Annual report CO799/9 Bagshaw interview IWM *Story NRR* p67
    Brig Harold St John Lloyd WINTERBOTTHAM CMG 18 DSO 16 FRGS b5.2.78 s/o Canon ed Fettes RMA 2lt RE'97 SA'99–00 St Helena 02–6 Colonial Svy OFS'08 Ordnce Svy 11 OC Ranging Sec BEF 10.14 Maps 3rd Army'15 GHQ'17 BvtLtCol Geo Sec GS WO 22 Insp Colonial Svy Depts'29–DG Ordnce Svy 30–35 Gen Sec Internatnl Geodetic & Geophysical Union, VPres Int Geographical Union
38. Deane-Simmons NRPA Newsletter, Orders *Nkhwazi* Vol 8 No.1 Apr 60 p29

CHAPTER 10

Farewell to The Military

The last Regimental Orders for the Northern Rhodesia Police read as follows[1]:

NORTHERN RHODESIA POLICE
REGIMENTAL ORDERS
BY LIEUT.-COLONEL E.G. DICKINSON MC
COMMANDING
For the week ending 24th March, 1932.
GENERAL

213. NOTICE It is published for the information of all concerned that as from 1st April, 1932, the Military and Civil Branches of the Northern Rhodesia Police will be reorganised as entirely separate departments. The Commandant will retain command of the Military Forces but will cease to hold the appointment of Chief Commissioner of Police. The Civil Police Branch, Criminal Investigation and Immigration sub-department will be reorganised as a separate department under the control of the Commissioner of Police.

The Stores and Transport sub-department will be attached to the Public Works Department. Pending the Secretary of State's approval to the renaming of the Military Force the provisional designation will be 'The Northern Rhodesia Military Police'.

214. SPECIAL NOTICE   Civil Police

Before relinquishing command of the Civil Branch, Northern Rhodesia Police, I should like to take this opportunity of expressing to the Commissioner of Police, his officers and British personnel, as also to the native rank and file my high appreciation of the loyal co-operation and ready assistance I have at all times received from them during the period it has been my privilege to command that Branch.

It is with every confidence that I hand over command of the Civil Police to Captain Wardroper and I wish them all prosperity in the future.

(Signed) E.G.DICKINSON,
Lieut.-Colonel,
Chief Commissioner of Police.

In June 1932 the Military used the occasion of the King's Birthday Parade for their formal farewell to Livingstone. At 9.30 a.m. on Wednesday, 20 July, after a ceremony at the railway station, Lieutenant Colonel Dickinson, with his headquarters and the troops from Livingstone, departed by train for their new camp, or rather the camp they were to build, at Lusaka. They took with them the Colours, the Regimental Silver, the band and corps of drums and the crested crane badge with the motto *Diversi generi fide pares*[2]. Although this may have now officially ceased to be the motto of the Northern Rhodesia Police, its words were to remain true of the Force to the end.

The Governor, in his annual report, strongly recommended that the military force 'should take the title of the Northern Rhodesia Regiment'. It was thought in London that such an apparent strengthening of the armed forces of the Empire might be regarded as a breach of the League of Nations One Year Armament Truce which did not expire until 31 October 1932. The change was accordingly delayed until 1 April 1933. In fact by the time the military left Livingstone its strength was down to fifteen officers, five British warrant officers and NCOs, and 403 African rank and file. On 1 April 1933 the strength of the Northern Rhodesia Regiment was even lower, 12 officers, 7 British WOs and NCOs, and only 376 Africans. These reductions reflected the effect on the Territory's finances,of the World Recession of 1929 to 1931, of which more will be said in the next chapter. All the East African dependencies were similarly affected. The strength of the Northern Rhodesia Regiment more or less kept pace with that of the battalions of the King's African Rifles which were all reduced to major's commands at this time.[3]

Lieutenant Colonel Dickinson left on leave pending retirement in February 1933. His Second-in-Command, Major G P Burton, acted as Commandant until he too retired on 31 May 1933. Then Captain B J Graham became Commanding Officer of the Northern Rhodesia Regiment. Graham held the post until January 1937 when he was suceeded by an officer of the British regular army, Lieutenant Colonel W A Dimoline MC Royal Signals[4]. Capt Graham had attended a Senior Police Officers' Course at New Scotland Yard in 1931 which suggests that he was keeping his career options open and may well have been a candidate for Capt Wardroper's job.[5]

The very existence of the Northern Rhodesia Regiment was in the balance for some years. In 1933–1934 Air Vice Marshal C L N Newall CB CMG CBE, Air Officer Commanding Middle East Air Force, and Brigadier C C Norman CMG DSO, Inspector of East and West African Forces, carried out a study of the requirements for the defence of East Africa in the light of modern airpower. They recommended the amalgamation of the Northern Rhodesia Regiment and 2nd King's African Rifles to form one battalion, which, with a flight of aircraft, was to be responsible for the internal security and first line defence of Northern Rhodesia and Nyasaland.[6]

The regiment may have been saved by the sentiment that if the Territory had to pay for a military unit it was going to retain a proprietory label on it! The run down of the East and Central African forces was brought to a halt by the anxiety caused by the Italian invasion of Abyssinia in 1935.

The Quartermaster, Captain Smith, was seconded to the Public Works Department in April 1932, but retired the following year to go into business as a contractor. He later became Chairman of the Kitwe Chamber of Commerce. Almost all the other officers and British ranks of the old Military Branch were replaced by British Army personnel in 1937. They either retired or, like Eddie Raubenheimer, transferred to other Government departments. Three obtained appointments in other Colonial Officer territories. Sgt N O M Burne was still serving the Northern Rhodesia Government as a principal forester in 1962. Four warrant officers and NCOs, including the Bandmaster, WO2 R P Arnold, were retained in the Regiment. Bandmaster Woods had died in 1933 after an acute attack of dysentery.

In March 1935 the military post at Mongu closed and the detachment of the Regiment there joined the main body at Lusaka, followed in April by the Fort Jameson Detachment. In November 1936 the military detachment was withdrawn from Kasama.[7]

One of the officers who served on with the Regiment was Captain Bagshaw. He commanded the Coronation Contingent in 1937. The Northern Rhodesia Regiment party was quartered in Chelsea Barracks. Regimental Sergeant-Major Chisangalumbwe was extended the privilege of drilling a party of guardsmen. He caused some consternation by giving the order 'As you were!', after one movement which he did not consider up to Northern Rhodesia Regiment standards[8]. RSM Chisangalumbwe will be familiar to collectors of cigarette cards. He was portrayed on Card No.46 of the Players 'Military Uniforms of the British Empire Overseas' series issued for the Coronation of King George VI.

When the 1st Battalion, The Northern Rhodesia Regiment saw its first action in World War Two, the only former Northern Rhodesia Police Military Branch officer with it was Major J D Giddings, commanding 'D' Company, the first to encounter the Italians at Hargeisa on 5th August 1940. He and his company fought a delaying action against 10,000 enemy troops before falling back on the main body of the Battalion at Tug Argan. Giddings had been commissioned from Company Sergeant-Major in March 1931 and was to finish his military career as a Lieutenant Colonel. He later served as Divisional Commandant of the Northern Rhodesia Police Reserve at Ndola.

Also with the Battalion in the defence of British Somaliland were four former members of the old NRP Service Battalion of 1918, RSM Chisangalumbwe, Company Sergeant-Major (later RSM) Mulenga, Sergeant Chibalili, who was killed at Tug Argan, and Sergeant Kaputula DCM.[9]

Notes

1. *Nkhwazi Vol 12 No.1 Apr 1964 p32*
2. *Story NRR p69 Nkhwazi Apr 1964 p33*
3. *Story NRR p70 History KAR Chap 16(iii) pp462–465*
4. Maj Gen W A DIMOLINE CB CBE DSO MC, RSig Cmdt NRR 1.37 Brig 26(EA) Bde 30.1.42 22(EA)Bde 1.4.42 21(EA) Bde 10.8.43–30.10.43 28(EA) Bde 15.5.44 GOC 11(EA)Div 3.3.45
5. PRO CO799/9
6. Marshal of the RAF Lord Cyril Louis Norton NEWALL CB CMG CBE AM b15.2.86 s/o Lt Col IA ed Bedfd Sch RMC 2Lt RWar 05 Zheka Kel Expdn'08 2GR'09 RFC Sitapur'13 CO 41Wg RFC 10.10.17 T/BG VIII Bde RFC 1.2.18 DDPers Air Mnsty'19–22 DOps & Int & DCAS'26 AVM AOC Wessex Bombing Area'31 AOC RAF ME'31–4 CAS & Chmn CofS Cttee 9.37 Gov Gen NZ'40–45 d'64

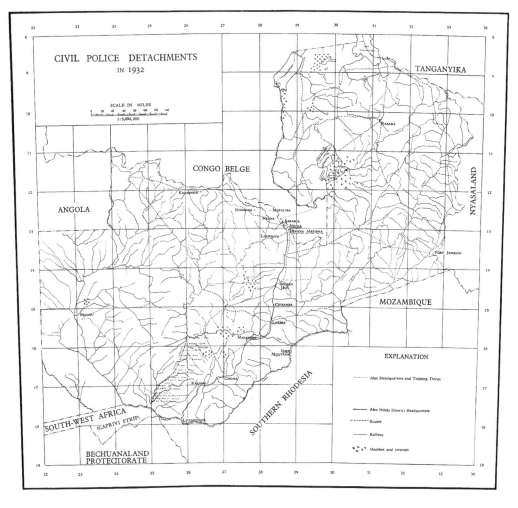

CIVIL POLICE DETACHMENTS
IN 1932

SCALE IN MILES
0   20   40   60   80   100   120   140
1:5,000,000

TANGANYIKA

CONGO BELGE

ANGOLA

NYASALAND

MOZAMBIQUE

KASAMA

KANSANSHI

NCHANGA · · MUFULIRA
NKANA · · SAKANIA
NDOLA
LUANSHYA · BWANA MKUBWA

FORT JAMESON

BROKEN
HILL

CHISAMBA

LUSAKA

MUMBU

MAZABUKA

ISOKA
MUNYAMA

EXPLANATION

KALOMO

CHOMA

SOUTHERN RHODESIA

- - - - -   Also Headquarters and Training Depot

———   Also Ndola District Headquarters

- - - - -   Routes

———   Railway

Marshes and swamps

SOUTH-WEST AFRICA
(CAPRIVI STRIP)

LIVINGSTONE

BECHUANALAND
PROTECTORATE

MAP 4   CIVIL POLICE DETACHMENTS IN 1932

Brig Compton Cardew NORMAN CMG 19 DSO 17 b'77 2Lt RWF SA'99–02 WAFF w'05 CO 2RWF Cmd 158(RWF) Bde TA'27 IG WAFF'30 & KAR'31 rtd'34

7. Exco PRO CO799/9 *Story NRR* p70
8. *Story NRR* p72 Bagshaw interview IWM
9. *Story NRR* p73

CHAPTER 11

Purely Police

The first orders for the new civil force were as follows:[1]

NORTHERN RHODESIA CIVIL POLICE
POLICE ORDERS
BY CAPTAIN P.R. WARDROPER M.B.E.
COMMISSIONER OF POLICE
for the week ending 1st April 1932

1. NOTICE It is published for general information that the separation of the Military and Civil Branches of the Northern Rhodesia Police will take effect from 1st April, 1932. The provisional designation of the Civil Police will be 'The Northern Rhodesia Civil Police' and will include the Criminal Investigation and Immigration Branches.
2. COMMAND The Northern Rhodesia Civil Police (including the B.N.C. Cordon) will be under the command of the Commissioner of Police.
3. ABOLITION OF TITLE The Title 'Officer-in-Charge Criminal Investigation Department' is hereby abolished.
4. APPOINTMENTS Captain P.R. WARDROPER, M.B.E. to be Commissioner Police whilst in command of the Northern Rhodesia Civil Police to date 1–4–32. Captain T.HAMILTON, M.B.E. to be Asst. Commissioner of Police to date 1–4–32 and ceases to act as Officer in Charge Criminal Investigation Department from that date.
   Superintendent R.J. VERRALL to be Paymaster N.R. Civil Police to date 1–4–32. Authority: Chief Secretary's Minute No. T.S.2/1/4/4 dated 15–3–32.
   Asst.Superintendent E.S. FOLD to be Staff Officer to the Commissioner of Police, to date 1–4–32. Authority: Chief Secretary's Minute No. T.S.2/1/4/4 dated 15–3–32.
5. ESTABLISHMENT The authorised Establishment of the N.R. Civil Police for the financial year 1932–33, is as follows:

Commissioner of Police	(1)
Asst. Commissioner of Police	(2)
Superintendent and Asst.Superintendent	(4)
Chief Inspector	(1)
Chief Detective Inspector	(1)
Inspectors and Detective Inspectors	(11)
Asst.Inspectors and Det.Asst.Inspectors	(22)

British Constables and Det.Constables	(40)
Native Police	(494)
Native Detectives	(42)
Native Civilian Employees	(31)
Barotse Namwala Cattle Cordon Native Police	(50)

Capt Wardroper had been awarded the King's Police Medal on 30 April 1929. His salary was to be £1,000 per annum. Assistant Commissioners, the second was Lt H G Hart, were on a salary scale of £600–£840. Mr Verrall, who after eight years in the BSAP, had only joined the NRP at the end of June 1928, had been commissioned in 1929. Andrew Pickup and Cecil Arnott were the other officers, commissioned in December 1930 and June 1931 respectively. Both attended a senior officers course at New Scotland Yard in 1932. Pickup had joined the Force in July 1925 and 'Gerry' Fold on 28 July 1924. The pay scale for assistant superintendents and superintendents was from £380 to £500 a year. Otherwise the strength on 1st April 1932 was 73 chief inspectors, inspectors, assistant inspectors and British constables, 447 African sergeants-major, sergeants, corporals, lance-corporals and privates, 41 African detectives and 45 Barotse Namwala Cattle Cordon police. Capt Hamilton and Chief Detective Inspector Willson retired before the end of the year and Arnott took command of the CID and Livingstone Police Station. Fold was Superintendent of Livingstone Gaol.[2]

The new Northern Rhodesia Police Ordinance, as drafted, still contained the stipulation that the Force could be used for police or military purposes within and without the Territory. It authorised a 'rewards and fines fund' for the first time. Disciplinary charges could be heard by boards of officers which could award a maximum punishment of six months imprisonment or by the Commissioner who could sentence a British constable or inspector to up to 20 days imprisonment and an African policeman to 30 days.

Headquarters and the Depot remained at Livingstone. There were police detachments at Livingstone, Kalomo, Choma, Mazabuka, Sakania, Ndola, Bwana Mkubwa, Luanshya, Nchanga, Mufulira, Kansanshi, Nkana, Fort Jameson, Mongu, Lusaka, Broken Hill and Chisamba. In 1930 the Victoria Falls Bridge had been widened to provide for a roadway alongside the railway track and in 1931 a post had been opened at Victoria Falls following the outbreak of Foot and Mouth disease among cattle in Southern Rhodesia. The Constable in charge made road reports for immigration and acted as customs officer. By the end of 1931, 24 out of 73 would be immigrants entering by this road had been rejected.[3]

The cattle cordon established in 1922 now only stretched as far as Musa. The remaining eighteen posts and camps on the cordon were, from north to south:

NRP Post 1,	Musa
Camp 2,	Ngoma
Camp 3,	Shakalonga
Camp 4,	Chonza
Camp 5,	Kasha
Camp 6,	Winsi-Winsi
Camp 7,	Kalumbu

Camp 8,	Mukuni
Camp 9,	Simamba
Camp 10,	Muouli
Camp 11,	Buwe
Camp 12,	
Camp 13,	Kuminyane
NRP Post 14,	(Barker's)
NRP Post 15,	(Maranga Pool) Cordon HQ
NRP Post 16,	(Beacon and grave)
NRP Post 17,	Musikili
NRP Post 18,	Kasaya.[4]

During 1932 Ibwe Munyama Police Preventive Post was opened on the Zambezi near modern Chirundu. There was still no bridge other than that at Victoria Falls but a track to the south ran near Ibwe Munyama Mission to the riverbank. Two British constables were posted here during the dry season, mainly for immigration and stock control. The post was closed during the rains as the track was then impassable. In anticipation of the removal of the military detachment there, a civil police station was opened at Kasama in November 1932 under Insp Maxwell. During 1931 the military detachment commander had prosecuted two important cases there.

Crime continued to increase steadily. 10,510 offences were reported in 1932 resulting in 9,932 convictions. There was a large increase in housebreaking, theft, fraud, theft by false pretences, forgery, affray and assault. No doubt in part because of financial difficulties due to the depression 56 Europeans committed fraud or false pretences. There were 1,918 committals with an average prison population of 544·76 persons. There were five executions. The Commissioner of Police continued to be Commissioner of Prisons and was also Officer in Charge of Aerodromes and Registrar of Aircraft. Since 1927 Northern Rhodesia had been required to maintain aerodromes at Livingstone, Ndola and Abercorn so that the Cape to Cairo route was always open for the Royal Air Force. RAF and South African Air Force planes passed to and fro each year to co-operate in exercises.[5]

As well as normal police duties, members of the Force were responsible for: service of civil process, disposal of property in deceased estates, collection of customs and hospital debts, inspection of trains under the Cattle Diseases Regulations, collection of landing fees at aerodromes, supervision of cattle dipping at Broken Hill, issue of permits to export hides and supervision of dipping prior to export, collection of dog tax in certain districts, issues to bomas of motor, dog and cycle licences, issue of film permits, issue of Governor's permits for the importation of firearms and ammunition, rabies patrols, provision of warders, normally African police, at local prisons at stations where there were police detachments and fire brigade duties at Livingstone. Police officers served 2,110 civil summonses and other civil process during 1932. A civilian had been appointed to do this work in Ndola saving much police time. It was recommended that Government make similar appointments elsewhere and that these officials should also take over the preparation of inventories of deceased's property. In 1933 civilian process servers were appointed in Luanshya, Nkana and Lusaka. During 1932 8,830 motor vehicle and 30,000 cycle licence badges were issued, together with 1,127 driving permits, 8500 dog licences, and 1,700 film permits.[6]

The police were to be responsible for the enforcement of a new Weights and Measures Ordinance and with this in mind an assistant inspector had attended an appropriate course with the Board of Trade in England in 1930.[7] Although the necessary equipment arrived in 1932 the Ordinance was still not in force.

Just as the development of the infant Town and District Police had been stunted by the outbreak of war in 1914, so fate dealt the newly independent civil police force a savage blow within a year of its inception. World recession had started in 1929 and it may be that the boom in European immigration into Northern Rhodesia in 1930 was partly due to the unemployed from the more developed parts of the English speaking world seeking to restore their fortunes in the developing colonies. Whether or not this surmise is correct, the respite was brief. The depression began to bite in Northern Rhodesia in 1931 and continued into 1933 although the effects lasted much longer. The European population of the Territory had risen to 13,846 in 1931 with 1,702 new immigrants but it now entered a period of decline. There was a net loss of over 3,000 whites in 1932 and 801 in 1933. Of 615 immigrants in 1932, 90 were deported as being unlikely to be able to support themselves in the Territory. 409 destitute white residents were repatriated as against 157 in 1931. 1,179 passports were issued and 268 renewed. The African population was put at 1,382,705. There were 176 Asians in the Territory and 425 persons of mixed race.[8]

Inspector E S Fold had taken charge of the Bwana Mkubwa detachment in 1931, but was soon recalled to Livingstone to become Paymaster, and then, as we have seen, Staff Officer on promotion to Assistant Superintendent. Acting Assistant Inspector A J I Hawkins took over command of the African sergeant, lance-corporal and eight privates who made up the detachment together with the civilian interpreter, Elias Mumba, who was for many years interpreter and clerk at Kitwe after Bwana Mkubwa closed. During 1931 production at Bwana Mkubwa Mine started to run down and equipment was moved to Nkana. The European population shrunk from about 800 to about 40 and the African workforce on the mine to around 1,000. Until 1932 Bwana Mkubwa continued to produce limestone which was sent to Nkana for processing, but during 1932 Bwana Mkubwa Mine closed altogether. The police camp, now under the command of Assistant Inspector T M Davidson, another future assistant commissioner, was closed soon afterwards.[9]

Detective Assistant Inspector Heatlie had been sent to Ndola in February 1931 for immigration duties in connection with the influx of Europeans but, as he later wrote:

A very short time after my return to Ndola, there were indications that the boom was ending. From time to time a few persons would call at the Boma seeking relief or repatriation, and they used to be turned over to me. Then in the latter part of 1931, Bwana Mkubwa mine shut down and the flood set in. Everywhere people were trying to get out of the country. Many were unable to do so having lost their 'domicile' elsewhere. Relief in the form of rations and housing was provided by the Government.

In 1932 Nchanga closed down, then Mufulira. The early beginnings of Chambishi were abandoned. All along Broadway in Ndola the road was bordered with little grass shelters accommodating European families. A large part of the Civil Service was retrenched. From the latter part of 1931 to about mid-1933, I was employed solely in investigating destitute persons and families and in making reports and recommendations as to what assistance should be given.'[10]

The Annual Report showed 428 Europeans as destitute in the Territory in January 1933, between five and ten per cent of the white population. When Mufulira Mine closed in August 1932 the officer in charge of the police detachment there became responsible for protecting property in the almost deserted mine township, issuing all forms of licences, collecting native tax and running the telephone, telegraph and postal services. He was housed in the building vacated by Barclays Bank until the police detachment itself was withdrawn in December 1932.[11]

On 31 December 1932 Force Headquarters at Livingstone comprised Captain Wardroper, Mr Verrall, Mr Fold, an acting inspector, 2 acting assistant inspectors, a constable, a lady clerk, an African sergeant-major, 15 other African police, 2 African clerks and 3 tailors. At the Depot were an inspector, a constable, a sergeant-major, a sergeant, 5 corporals, 10 lance corporals, 45 Native constables, as privates were now called, 24 recruits and an African interpreter. Under Mr Arnott at the police station were an inspector, an assistant inspector, 3 constables, a lady clerk, 43 uniformed African police, a detective inspector, a detective assistant inspector, 2 detective constables, 5 African detectives and 3 civilian interpreters. There was 1 Sgt with 6 natives constables at the Railway Station and one British constable, a lance corporal and four native constables at Victoria Falls.

The rest of the Force was distributed as follows:

Choma: 1 A/Insp 1 Cpl 1 LCpl 8 Native Consts 1 Interpreter 1 Native Detective.

Mazabuka: 1 Insp 1 A/Insp 2 Consts 1 Sgt 1 Cpl 16 N/Consts 1 Interpreter 2 detectives.

Lusaka: Mr Pickup 1 Insp 3 Consts 1 Sgt-Maj 45 other African uniformed police 1 interpreter 1 D/A/Insp 5 native detectives.

Ibwe Munyama: 1 Const 1 Cpl 2 N/Consts.

Broken Hill: 1 Insp 2 A/Insps 3 Consts 1 Sgt 34 other African uniformed police 3 interpreters 1 D/Const 4 detectives.

Broken Hill Railway: 1 Sgt 7 N/Consts.

Bwana Mkubwa: 1 A/Insp 1 Sgt 8 N/Consts 1 interpreter.

Ndola: Mr Hart 1 Insp 2 A/Insps 4 Consts 1 Sgt-Maj 41 other African uniformed police 1 interpreter 1 D/Insp 1 D/A/Insp 7 detectives.

Ndola Railway: 1 Sgt 5 N/Consts.

Ndola Motor Search Post: 1 Const 1 Cpl 3 N/Consts.

Luanshya: 1 A/Insp 2 Consts 2 Sgts 27 other uniformed African police 2 interpreters 1 D/A/Insp 3 detectives.

Chingola: 1 A/Insp 1 Sgt 7 N/Consts 1 detective.

Mongu: 1 Actg A/Insp 1 Sgt 6 N/Consts 1 interpreter 1 detective.

Kasama: 1 Insp 1 Sgt 1 Cpl 7 N/Consts 1 interpreter 1 detective.

Nkana: 1 Insp 1 A/Insp 3 Consts 1 Sgt 2 Cpls 2 LCpls 31 N/Consts 2 interpreters
   3 detectives.
Fort Jameson: 1 Insp 2 Consts 1 Sgt 1 Cpl 1 LCpl 18 N/Consts 1 interpreter 3
   detectives.
Cattle Cordon: 1 Acting A/Insp 50 African police
On long leave were one inspector, 1 A/Insp, 7 constables (pending discharge) and
15 African police.

The new Force was armed with 380 rifles and bayonets. When the new Governor, Sir Ronald Storrs arrived at Livingstone Railway Station on 1 December 1932 the civil police provided the guard of honour with the band of the military brought down from Lusaka for the occasion.[12]

The detachments of the force at Kansanshi, Chisamba, Nchanga were withdrawn before the end of 1932 and during 1933 those at Ibwe Munyama, Sakania, Kalomo and Kasama were all withdrawn. The Northern Province was left without one police station. Some police stations were never reopened. In the detachments that remained in Northern Rhodesia, station buildings fell into disrepair and even essential items could not be purchased. However Mufulira police detachment was re-established in 1933 with a constable and 10 African police.[13]

Seventeen European inspectors, assistant inspectors and constables, 42 African police, 9 African detectives and 4 interpreters were discharged 'on reduction of establishment'. Originally 23 European police were given notice. Tommy Davidson was already on the train for the south when his notice was rescinded. He was intercepted at Livingstone and told of his reinstatement. Those remaining in the service were hit by a levy on the salaries of all Government servants on a sliding scale commencing at five per cent. Five inspectors retired on pension and one constable resigned. The concession by which African police could be exempted from Native Tax on retirement was withdrawn from 1 January 1933.[14]

Northern Rhodesia suffered another heavy blow in 1933 when clouds of red locusts swept in from Tanganyika, devastating the crops. At Fort Jameson, Constable Sugg was asked by the Provincial Commissioner to try, while on patrol, to get some concerted efforts by Africans to prevent locusts settling to lay their eggs. A swarm could be made to move on by much banging of tins etc. From 26 March until 12 April four officers, three British NCOs and 182 men of the Northern Rhodesia Regiment were deployed on farms west of Lusaka to assist the civil authorities and population in trying to halt the advance of these insects. The immature 'hoppers' which could not fly were the biggest menace. Trenches were dug across their path to a depth of about two feet. As the trenches filled up with stranded hoppers, insecticide powder was added. Only a minority could be trapped in this way. The remainder moved on, leaving bare farms and bankrupt farmers behind them. At least it must have made a change for the troops whose usual duty at the time was building the Great East Road.[15]

A platoon of the Regiment took over manning posts 1 to 3 on the Barotse-Namwala Cattle Cordon from the police from September 1933 until November 1934.

In 1933 there was a slight drop in reported crime, perhaps reflecting the decline in the strength of the police force and closure of stations. There were 9,337 offences reported and 8,774 convictions, a clear up rate of 93.9 per cent. Constable Eric Halse and sergeants 86 Mwanada and 122 Yobe were commended by the Commissioner for their investigation of burglaries at Nkana. Const Goslett was commended for rescuing a lunatic at Mazabuka. In 1934 Constable Owen Mitchell and D/Const 'Punch' Randall disarmed a European homicidal lunatic at Broken Hill. Both were commended, Mitchell's bravery earning him the Governor's commendation. Randall was also commended by the Commissioner for his investigations into stock theft. Both constables were to retire as senior superintendents.[16]

Once the name of the Regiment had been settled there was no need for the retention of the word 'Civil' in the title of the police force which became the Northern Rhodesia Police under the Northern Rhodesia Police Ordinance, Chapter 44 of the Laws, passed in 1933. The question of a badge remained.

In March 1925 the need had been recognised for an emblem for the territory of Northern Rhodesia for use on flags and possible incorporation in a Public Seal. Prior to 1 April 1924 the seal of the British South Africa Company had been used on all official documents, but this could not continue under the Colonial Office. The Governor took to using his own private seal. In 1926 he appointed a committee to consider the problem. The first suggestion was to use the crested crane of the old Northern Rhodesia Police, but it was found that Uganda was already using the crane in its coat of arms. Various designs were discussed without agreement until, in 1927, Sir Richard Goode, then Acting Governor, hit on the idea of a fish eagle (nkhwazi) grasping a fish over the Victoria Falls. In heraldic language this became 'Sable six palets wavy Argent on a Chief Azure an Eagle reguardant wings expanded Or holding in the talons a Fish of the second'. This design was approved by the King in 1930. Presumably it did not take long to decide that the badge of Northern Rhodesia should be the basis of the badge of the Northern Rhodesia Police. Mr R I Hockey, of the Government Survey Department, designed the new Force badge. It was issued in brass at the beginning of 1933 and remained in use until 1949.[17]

The uniform for British ranks remained basically the same as before 1932, except for the badge which appears to have been worn only on the collar and not on the khaki helmet, which remained the 'new Wolseley' pattern. The diamond flash on the left of the helmet was now divided top half blue, bottom white. The pugri remained khaki but with the top fold blue for officers. The khaki tie and brown leather Sam Browne belt were worn with all orders of dress, including the bush shirt. In full dress the Commissioner and, like an infantry adjutant, his staff officer, wore breeches, brown field boots and spurs. All other British ranks wore khaki puttees and brown ankle boots. Revolvers were carried in working dress. The Sam Browne belts of constables, assistant inspectors and inspectors, had snake fasteners instead of buckles.

African police wore khaki shorts, or knickers as they were still officially called, and the same khaki drill long sleeved tunic that had been worn since 1911, but with dark blue or black shoulder straps with brass shoulder titles. Rank chevrons were still khaki on red cloth and good conduct badges red on black. The black fez was worn with a black tassel but no badge. The military had adopted a scarlet tassel for ceremonial in 1927, but it may never have been worn by the Town and

District Police. A brown leather waist belt with a brass snake fastener was worn with the short baton hanging from a hook on the left side. On duty a brass brassard bearing an identification number was worn on the left upper arm. African police still had no footwear. Swagger canes were carried by all African police in walking out dress.

The Commissioner wore the crown and star rank badges of a lieutenant colonel. Assistant inspectors wore one, and inspectors two blue worsted braid loops on the shoulder straps of the shirt and, like a naval officer, around the cuff of the long sleeved tunic. All metalwear was brass.

In 1930 or 1931 a green stripe had been added to the red and white tie of the old Northern Rhodesia Police. The main reason was that the original red and white striped tie soon became soiled, but the green served to commemorate the green facings of the North-Eastern Rhodesia Constabulary. It cannot have taken long to think of replacing the red stripes with blue to produce a suitable tie for the new civil force.[18]

In the Police and Military Museum, which opened in the old Boma at Lusaka in 1962, was a smart blue mess jacket with green facings, introduced for officers of the Force in 1935 but sadly not revived after the Second World War. The old white mess jacket remained in use and both were worn with blue overalls with a two inch side stripe of black oakleaf braid and a blue cap. The white jacket was to be worn with a blue cashmere kamarband and the blue with a white waistcoat.[19]

Livingstone, a mere 3,250 feet above sea level, is hot and humid. Since the completion of the railway there had been talk of finding a more suitable seat of government. Livingstone was deemed, 'to have an unsatisfactory climate and not to be sufficiently centrally placed'. Among the sites considered were Broken Hill, Bwana Mkubwa, Chilanga and Lusaka. The Legislative Council commissioned a special committee headed by Sir Stanley Adshead, Professor of Town Planning at London University, to consider the matter. The committee narrowed down the choice to three sites in the Lusaka area – Chilanga, Lusaka Village itself and a ridge three miles south of the railway station and village. The water supply at Chilanga was said to be unreliable. Lusaka Village was hot, dusty and prone to flooding. Accordingly it was announced in August 1930 that the new capital would be on the ridge. In the same year Lusaka was upgraded to a township by notice in the Government Gazette. The Township Management Board was to be responsible for an area of 4,500 acres. It was to consist of the Provincial or District Commissioner, as Chairman, the Government Medical Officer and four-non official appointed members.[20]

Harry Franklin arrived in Lusaka as a District Officer of the Provincial Administration in about 1931. He later wrote: 'At erratic intervals along Cairo Road, the corrugated iron roofs of the Boma, the Grand Hotel, two or three general stores, a butchery, a bank, Counsell's Hotel and a few offices and oddments grumbled metallically as they contracted or expanded according to the temperature. Nearby, lost in the long grass, was a hospital'.[21]

The administrative district headquarters had only moved to Lusaka from Chilanga in 1931. In 1932 the population, white and black, of the Township was about 1,000. The Management Board's annual budget had reached £1,919.

Lusaka Township Management Board did not control the new capital site. The Governor, Sir Ronald Storrs, told the members in October that they would be unwise to wish to do so. The townspeople dubbed the area 'Snob's Hill' but the Chief Secretary wrote a letter emphasizing that this name was not to be used in official correspondence! It was not until 1st January 1936 that the Management Board's responsibilities were extended to cover the area of the new capital.

On 3 April 1934 the foundation stone of the Secretariat building was laid by Prince George, later Duke of Kent. To mark the Royal Visit many prisoners were granted three months remission of their sentences.[22]

There were now five European police officers in the Lusaka Detachment, Acting Inspector N T Nissen, in charge, with Constables Sugg and Tozer, Detective Assistant Inspector Deane-Simmons and Detective Constable Goslett. The development of the new seat of government was now so advanced as to require the opening of the 'New Capital Site Police Post' with twelve African police. Their tiny camp was to gradually expand to become the main police residential area in Lusaka, Wardroper Camp, and to house Force Headquarters from 1949 until 1962.

Police methods had to keep pace with new developments as shown in the following report of Lusaka's first speeding case:

LUSAKA
24th September 1934
The Staff Officer,
to The Commissioner of Police
LIVINGSTONE.
TRAFFIC: KING GEORGE'S AVENUE

Sir,

I have the honour to refer to your 806/1a/13 of the 31st August ulto, and in accordance with your instructions beg to submit my report in terms of para.3 of your communication.

2. On 8th September I hired a motor car and accompanied by Const. Tozer proceeded to King George's Avenue with a view to trapping motorists for speed. At about 11 a.m. Mr Flutter of the P.W.D. was followed from the top of King George's Av; to the Administrative Offices and keeping a uniform distance behind Mr Flutter's car and also permitting him to GRADUALLY DRAW AWAY, it was noted that his speed was between 33 m.p.h. and 35 m.p.h. over a distance of $\frac{1}{2}$ mile. Mr Flutter was duly summoned and the case was heard by the Actg: Resident Magistrate on Friday 21st inst. Accused pleaded guilty and the Magistrate found him guilty and warned and cautioned Mr Flutter as being the first case of this nature brought before this Court. The prosecution brought up the question of costs and I attach Const. Tozer's report of the reply of the Court to the application.

3. The strongest point in favour of the prosecution in this type of case, was the fact that the police had permitted the offender to gain on the police car and that the offender had not been overtaken at the time when the distance over which accused was speeding was being recorded. The speedometer of the police car had been checked twice, once before the car was actually being used for speed trapping and immediately after accused had been caught.

4. The first attempt was completely abortive, and it was after nearly an hour of

fruitless cruising that Mr Flutter was trapped. To date over £1 approx. has been spent. The expenditure sheet of Mr Flutter's case working out as follows:

Hire at 5/- per hour: 1½ hours	7/6
@ 9d per mile 8 miles	6/-
	13/6

I have the honour to be, Sir,
Your obedient servant
Actg: Inspector.[23]

On 15th February 1935 the Commissioner of Police, Captain Wardroper, accompanied by his staff officer, moved his office from Livingstone to the new capital. At first they occupied a corrugated iron building near the Secretariat. After about eight months four rooms in the Secretariat itself were made available for occupation by the Commissioner, Staff Officer, records and a typist. The Commissioner's office was the Governor's retiring room when the Legislative Council was in session, at which times Captain Wardroper had to move in with the Staff Officer. Finance was as short as ever and the Commissioner had a long struggle to secure funds to purchase a retiring civil servant's bookcase for his office.[24]

Const J W Hughes was seconded to the Northern Rhodesia Regiment from 24 February until 4 April 1935 as the only person in the Territory qualified to overhaul the unit's ageing rifles.[25]

In June 1935 the new capital was officially opened as part of the celebrations for the Silver Jubilee of King George V.

In 1933 the first aircraft had landed on an improvised airstrip four miles east of Lusaka Railway Station. It was a light aeroplane piloted by Mr Coull, a Salisbury building contractor, on a visit in connection with the construction of the new capital. So began the Lusaka Airport which was to remain in use until after the Territory became the Republic of Zambia.

Sir Hubert Young KCMG had become Governor of Northern Rhodesia in 1934 on transfer from Nyasaland. In 1935 Lady Young and a Dr Kirby were missing for four days after taking off in an aircraft from Lusaka on 28 February. The search extended from Lusaka to Monze. The Northern Rhodesia Regiment was called out to assist until word was received that the party was safe after crash landing near Gokwe in Southern Rhodesia.[26]

On 27 May 1935 a flight of Victoria troop transports of the Royal Air Force was at Lusaka in the course of a training exercise from Cairo to Salisbury. Its presence was fortuitous. Word was received of riots on the Copperbelt. Captain Tysoe, lieutenants Hughes and Cree, Sergeant Burne, and forty-four African soldiers of the Regiment emplaned in the early morning to be flown to the Copperbelt. They reached Nkana at 8.40 a.m and immediately gave assistance with patrols there.

Lieutenant, later Major, Angus Cree produced a number of water-colours showing uniforms of the Northern Rhodesia Police and Regiment and their predecessors over the years.

On 17 and 18 May 1935 Africans on the Copperbelt had been informed of a tax increase from ten shillings to fifteen shillings a year, to offset a reduction in tax for those in rural areas. African mineworkers were paid about twenty-five shillings per 'ticket' of thirty shifts worked. There were disturbances at Mufulira where the mine had reopened. On 21 May an inspector and 24 African police were sent from Ndola as reinforcements. That evening Const Abbott with the District Officer, Mr Moffat, two NRP and two African 'Mine Police' arrested 8 men seen earlier armed and causing trouble. Later further arrests were made and twelve men were prosecuted 8 of whom were convicted. On 23 May African mineworkers began to drift back to work and on 25 May all was back to normal at Mufulira. The Commissioner of Police visited the Copperbelt by air on the weekend 25–26 May. Although all was quiet at Mufulira he arranged for 50 additional police to be sent to arrive at Ndola on the Monday morning bringing the total of reinforcements on the Copperbelt to 71. At Nkana 200 strikers ran to the concentrator and drove out the workers. That night four policemen were injured by stone throwing. Armed police were posted at the Magazine and Power House and two lorries with regular and 'mine police' patrolled the compound with a good effect. The ringleaders were arrested by a party under Insp Wilkinson. By Tuesday 28 May nearly all the miners at Nkana were back at work.

However information was received that the African miners at Roan Antelope intended to stage a protest strike the next day. Inspector Maxwell was in charge of the police at Luanshya assisted by Constable A H Pipe and one other European. Maxwell had sent off three of his 26 African policemen on 26th May to guard the pontoon crossing over the Kafue River on the road to Nkana. A telephone call for reinforcements was now put through to Nkana. At about 4.30 a.m. on 29th May Superintendent E S Fold arrived at Luanshya to take command. Fold was followed by two European and 78 African police brought from Nkana in lorries to arrive before dawn.

At about 6.15 a.m. word reached the police camp that the Bemba workers had struck, but men from other tribes were trickling in to work. The strikers had organised pickets to stop them. The police then left camp by lorry for Roan Antelope Mine. Some of the African police from Nkana had rifles but all the ammunition was left at Luanshya police camp except for a bandolier of 50 rounds carried by A/Insp Arthur. The police were to escort Africans who wished to go to work and to protect property. Parties of eight police each, with rifles, were posted at the smelter, concentrator, power house, and winding engine house, and at the bridge connecting the mine compound with the plant, all under A/Insp Arthur.

This left less than thirty African police, who arrived at the compound office shortly after 7 a.m. Several miners had assembled at the office, afraid to go to work without escort. A crowd of fifty or sixty strikers who were threatening these men, was dispersed by Superintendent Fold and about a dozen African police, but a large mob remained some way off, dancing and waving sticks.

Some of the miners who wished to work were placed in a lorry and sent off to Number 15 Shaft with Colonel Stephenson, now working for the Mines. Maxwell and Pipe each took out a patrol in a vanette and dispersed several groups of strikers who were armed with sticks. The African police had been issued with miners' helmets to protect their heads from missiles.

At about 7.30 a.m. a large mob of strikers charged the compound office, but was turned back by the police. An hour and a quarter later some 2,000 returned to the charge, hurling stones and other missiles. Several police were injured before their attackers drew off. Maxwell and Pipe, returning with their patrols, had to run the gauntlet, driving through the mob which pelted the vanettes with stones. One private was badly cut on the head, his miners' tin helmet being dented. Others received lesser injuries.

At about 9.15 a.m. Mr A W Bonfield, District Officer in charge at Luanshya, with another district officer, G S Jones[27], Mr M Spearpoint, the Mine Compound Manager, and the Assistant Manager, H H Field, went, unarmed, to talk to the main body of strikers who were then on the compound football field. The party mounted an anthill to address the men who crowded round them armed with sticks and stones, shouting. When Bonfield was able to make himself heard, he asked what the trouble was. A general cry was raised for reduced taxes and more pay. Bonfield told them that if they thought the tax was too high, they should make representations in the proper way. He promised to forward their requests if they immediately put down their weapons and returned quietly to work. He told them to approach the mine management in a proper way concerning their pay. His words were not well received and the four Europeans made their way back to the compound office through a hostile and threatening crowd.

On reaching the office, Mr Bonfield conferred with Superintendent Fold. Inspector Maxwell was despatched in a vanette with a party of police to assess the situation and collect ten rifles and ammunition from Luanshya police camp. On the way the vehicle was again heavily stoned. Part of the mob had split away to attack the smelter. On his way Maxwell picked up a number of African police who had been driven from their posts, and some of the mining company's 'police', who were with him, took advantage of these stops to dismount and fade away. The police party at the mill was strengthened, those with rifles being ordered to fix bayonets. Some white miners, who had been exchanging stones with the strikers, were told to retire into the buildings to avoid provocation.

On returning from the police camp Maxwell's vanette was again stoned. The ammunition was taken into the compound office. No cartridges were issued, but the ten rifles were distributed among the members of the Luanshya police detachment. The African police were lined up in front of the office facing the howling mob, where they were subjected to further stoning and threats. One charge was repulsed, but a second drove the thin line of police back onto the verandah. Mr Bonfield estimated the crowd at between three and four thousand, saying it advanced rapidly to envelop the offices. Most of the office windows were broken by the hail of stones, iron bars, pieces of piping and other missiles. One African policeman was rendered unconscious by a large piece of rock. Several others had been hurt. Finally the line broke and the policemen poured in through the three doors to the offices asking for ammunition, shouting 'We shall all be killed. This is war!' Maxwell said he had never seen such a threatening crowd. When he had asked whether he should issue ammunition, Fold had said 'Not yet'. Now the superintendent was beset by rioters at the back of the offices. As Maxwell, who was hit on the head by a stone, went to him, the African police appear to have helped themselves to cartridges. Several opened fire through the windows. As the crowd drew off the police advanced beyond the verandah, still firing, until Colonel Stephenson and Superintendent Fold came and knocked up their rifles, ordering them to cease fire. Some had already been disarmed by Maxwell who had rushed back when he heard the first shot. Seven rioters were killed and twenty wounded in the firing which was said to have continued for ten minutes although only forty rounds were fired. The bodies lay between 15 and 50 yards from the office.

A lull ensued during which, at 10.50 a.m., Captain Tysoe arrived with the troops flown in from Lusaka. He ordered his men to line a ditch in front of the verandah. The mob was only twenty yards away. Tysoe and his officers went forward and began to collect weapons from out of the hands of the strikers, until the surprise wore off and they encountered resistance. The crowd began to press forward again, threatening and insulting the troops and police, who were now only in support. Captain Tysoe made four arrests before it was clear that any further such action would merely spark off greater violence. The rioters were pressing the troops 'belly to belly'. Hosepipes were turned on the crowd but the pressure was insufficient. The troops had been stood there for more than two hours when some were struck in the face. This caused the soldiers to throw their rifles up into the standing load position. The crowd shrank back. Some soldiers began to load but were stopped by their officers. Tysoe ordered bayonets to be fixed, which caused the rioters to withdraw further. The captain was standing in front of his men when one fired accidently in the course of clearing a jam in unloading. The bullet

Plan of area surrounding Compound Manager's Office, Roan Antelope Mine.

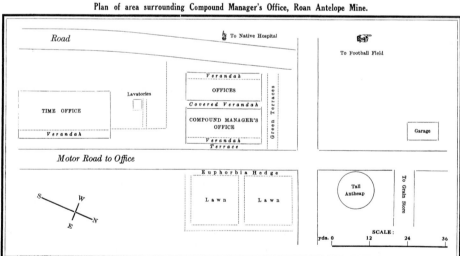

The Compound Office area shewn above is surrounded by the Compound Native Quarters, except on the east side.

Plan of area surrounding compound manager's office, Roan, Antelope Mine 1935 (PRO)

214

passed just over Tysoe's head. The mob fled a considerable distance and so calm was restored.

The troops and police were then redeployed to protect Luanshya Township as well as the mine plant and compound. At 5.50 p.m. dissidents began looting a grain store. William Tysoe went to investigate with a Lewis gun section. The looters ran off leaving some sacks behind them. That night Major Graham, Commanding Officer of the Northern Rhodesia Regiment, arrived from Lusaka by train with another 150 troops, so that in the morning the exhausted police could be withdrawn from the mine compound.

Further use was made of the RAF planes to fly Captain J E Ross and fifty Europeans of the British South Africa Police up from Salisbury to Ndola. One hundred European and African police from that Force came by train from Bulawayo. Peace quickly returned to the Copperbelt. The BSAP remained until 17 June.[28]

At the inquest into the deaths of the shot strikers, Captain Tysoe expressed the opinion that well-disciplined troops, such as those of the Regiment, accustomed to work as a body, were better qualified, as well as better equipped, to deal with unruly mobs, than civil police, used to working as individuals and amongst whom discipline could not be enforced in the same way. Captain Wardroper, the Commissioner of Police, stressed that the police were also still trained as soldiers. They were accustomed to acting under orders in a disciplined way and often acted together in groups of tens and twenties. They had considerable experience in quelling disorders. He mentioned the riot at Mufulira in 1930, when a sergeant was killed and an assistant inspector badly injured, an attempt by a mob to storm the gaol at Ndola, and faction fights at Livingstone and Broken Hill. Captain Wardroper accepted that the Roan Antelope riot was the worst which had yet occurred in Northern Rhodesia. He also acknowledged that once a policeman had left the Training Depot his duties were largely performed as an individual except for weekly parades.

Wardroper and Tysoe were in agreement that 29 police supported by a number of the mining company's 'police boys', were quite insufficient to deal with the sort of mob that they had had to face, and of that there can be no doubt. Clearly the rapid growth of the African urban population had found the new Northern Rhodesia Police with insufficient manpower, training and equipment for riot control. The Force had been starved of finance and had until recently been always under the shadow of the military. The African police appear to have shown exemplary steadiness until driven to the limit, and, had they not taken things into their own hands must almost certainly have been overrun with probably disastrous consequences. The decision to send some of them into the compound armed with rifles while leaving the ammunition back in the police camp is difficult to understand but the Provincial Commissioner, back at Ndola, had given instructions that there was to be no firing without reference to him! The situation when the ammunition did arrive would appear to have demanded the formation of an armed section to be held in reserve under the command of a European officer. Controlled volleys should have produced the required result with less casualties. Superintendent Fold, having turned down Inspector Maxwell's suggestion that ammunition be issued, appears to have allowed himself to be distracted from the main threat. As a result neither he nor Maxwell was on the spot when firing broke out. However as the Governor pointed out, Fold, at the time, had been almost without sleep for four days. The Governor did not accept the finding of a Commission of Inquiry that an 'ill-judged attempt to disperse small groups standing near the compound office' caused the strikers to attack. According to Captain Wardroper, seven of the 29 police at the Roan Antelope compound office had been drawn from cattle cordon duty and were only partially trained.

There was no suggestion that it had been unnecessary to open fire, although G S Jones, the young district officer, gave evidence of one belated shot which appeared unnecessary and scored a hit. Jones had earlier made himself useful as driver of the vanette carrying Constable Pipe's patrol. This was not to be Jones' only experience of riots on the Copperbelt. He was to be Provincial Commissioner in 1956.[29]

The strength of the Northern Rhodesia Police at the time of the riot was 475, including 50 on the cattle cordon. The establishment of the Copperbelt stations for 1935 was:

Ndola: 4 European and 42 African police,
Luanshya: 3 European and 31 African police,
Nkana: 5 European and 44 African police,
Mufulira: 3 European and 20 African police.

A total of 15 Europeans and 137 Africans, including the superintendent at Nkana. Only the 'Government townships' were routinely patrolled the 'mine townships' and compounds were left to the management of the mining companies whose 'mine police' were more of the nature of watchmen and messengers.

The Commission of Inquiry into the causes of the disturbances and the action taken, was satisfied that the detachments of the Force available for normal policing on the Copperbelt were quite insufficient to deal with such unrest, and that a reserve of manpower was required close at hand. Accordingly a detachment of the Northern Rhodesia Regiment was posted at Bwana Mkubwa, and remained there until its services were required elsewhere after the outbreak of the Second World War. The Establishment of the Northern Rhodesia Police was increased by nine Europeans and 96 African police, the majority for duty at Copperbelt stations.[30]

615 tear gas bombs, 40 respirators and 200 pairs of goggles were obtained from the Union of South Africa and distributed to be held at stations in case of riots. The gas was in liquid form, contained in glass spheres, about the size of cricket balls, which, when thrown, smashed on impact releasing the gas. A sergeant-major from the Union Defence Force came up from Pretoria to give instruction in this new device.[31]

Captain Wardroper had told the inquiry, 'There are no written instructions issued to my officers as to how to deal with a case of riot or anticipated riot'. A pamphlet 'Instructions on the Use of Armed Force for Civil, Military and Police Officers' was now issued. Amended from time to time this pamphlet was issued to all assistant inspectors on joining the Force throughout the remainder of its existence.

135 Private Katungu was commended for single handedly arresting seven rioters

in one disturbance in 1935. Three other privates, 140 Chongo, 278 Chimba and 508 Chisulu received commendations for arresting two armed burglars at Livingstone. Native Detective Machisa was commended for the single handed arrest of a triple murderer who was armed with a rifle.[32]

Not only was manpower short on the Copperbelt, accommodation left much to be desired. On 5 April 1935 the Commissioner had written to the Government to urge the need for new housing at Mufulira. During the rains water poured through the roof on the men as they worked in the office. The three European constables, who slept in one room in the same building, had to move their kit almost every day to prevent it being eaten by white ants. During Captain Wardroper's inspection a window had fallen out and a door had dropped off its hinges. As a temporary measure two tents were supplied as office accommodation. By August 1935, all the European police had abandoned their quarters because the Kimberley brick was infested with bugs and white ants. They had built themselves grass huts to live in. The officer in charge, Inspector G W Rees, lived in a grass hut right through the ensuing rains.[33]

There were six European police at Mufulira by the end of 1936, the others being, Assistant Inspector Owen Mitchell, and constables J E Long, L Mitchell, A R Collett and D B M Patten. Like Owen Mitchell, Leslie Mitchell and Alan Ross Collett were to serve for many years and reach senior rank.

Native Detective Gilbert Chakalunta, a 27 year old Nyasalander, attested in 1935 at a salary of £1 10s 0d, a month. He served with the Criminal Investigation Department for twenty-eight years receiving ten commendations. In 1959 'Chak' was to be one of the first Africans promoted to Detective Assistant Inspector.

It was in 1935 that the folowing report appeared in the local paper:

> An unusual type of patient is occupying the maternity labour ward at the Lusaka Hospital. It is a man.
> Asst Inspector R. J. (Punch) Randell of the Northern Rhodesia Police was sent down from Broken Hill with a bad bout of fever.
> As all the beds in the hospital were full, the hospital authorities did the next best thing and put him in the empty labour ward.
> The Governor's secretary, Miss Edith Kilburn, and Mr E (Gen) Sergeant have made the rounds of Lusaka's gardens and have filled the ward with flowers, to give it the gay appearance it usually has when in use.[34]

Punch Randell had been articled to the surveyor of the Royal Estates at Sandringham before going to Malaya in 1926 to plant rubber. In 1927 the foreign settlements in China were threatened in the disturbances which brought Chiang Kai Shek to power. Strong military reinforcements were despatched from the United Kingdom. As a part time soldier in the Malay States Volunteers Punch was mobilised and sent to help protect Hankow. The Great Depression put him out of a job. In 1931 he began a training course with the Royal Ulster Constabulary and, as mentioned, earlier arrived in Northern Rhodesia in February 1932.

He used to tell another story of those days in Broken Hill. He had occasion to go to Chisamba to investigate a sudden death. Having no further immediate use for the body he packed it up, attached a label addressed to 'Assistant Inpector R

J Randell, Northern Rhodesia Police, Broken Hill', put it on a northbound train, and continued his investigation. On his arrival back in Broken Hill he found the body had arrived safely, and the whole town was in mourning for 'poor old Punch'!

In 1942 Punch was to pay another visit to Lusaka Hospital when he went to visit Assistant Inspector Jack Seed. Jack introduced him to a newly arrived nursing sister and another confirmed bachelor bit the dust!

R J Randell QPM, Senior Superintendent of Police retired in March 1960. His son John returned to Lusaka in the early 1970s to practise as a solicitor. Jack Baron Seed was Senior Superintendent commanding Southern Division in 1964. In about 1960 an African constable who had just been before 'the Baron' on a disciplinary charge informed the author that he felt no bitterness about being punished by Bwana Seed, because he was a 'very gentleman', a description from which none would dissent.

In 1936 the first 'Standing Orders, General Instructions and Dress Regulations' for the Force were issued in one slim volume of 58 single sided pages, compiled by Assistant Superintendent Andrew Pickup, who was Staff Officer until going on leave at the beginning of the year. While on leave Mr Pickup and Insp Arthur attended a course at the Civilian Anti-gas School, Falfield, Gloucestershire. It was already clear, even in Northern Rhodesia, that war might come. On his return in July Pickup became Superintendent in Charge of Ndola and the Copperbelt. Supt Fold was in charge at Broken Hill, Supt Croxford had succeeded Pickup as Staff Officer and Assistant Superintendent Brodie was in charge of the CID and Chief Immigration Officer.

The Force Paymaster, Superintendent R J Verrall was also in command of the Depot. The rank of Deputy Commissioner was introduced in 1936, but the first holder, Mr H G Hart, then 42 years of age, almost immediately became Acting Comissioner of Police when Captain Percy Wardroper OBE went on leave pending retirement on 6th April. Mr Verrall became Mr Hart's deputy on 23 August 1937. Supt Pickup then took over as Paymaster and in charge of the Depot until the functions were separated on 1 November 1937. Supt Fold, returning from leave, was then appointed Force Paymaster.

In July 1936 five Africans left Solwezi and walked to the Copperbelt to find work. They camped about 2 miles from the Chambezi cross roads towards Mufulira and some 50 yards off the Nkana road. Having eaten they sat round the glowing embers of their fire and watched the cars passing. One coming from the direction of Mufulira stopped. They saw someone get out. A shot rang out. The Africans ran into the bush and four climbed trees hearing their companion shout that he was wounded and dying. The next morning the frightened men climbed down from their hiding places and found his body not far from the ashes of the fire. On the road they found a used Greener shot gun cartridge. They decided to go home and report the matter to the District Commissioner at Solwezi. It was therefore a month before the police at Nkana were informed of the case. Insp Batty went to the scene with a medical officer. The body was exhumed. An SSG pellet was found in the heart. It was established that one Sunday in July there had been a football match in Mufulira and scores of cars had used the pontoon ferry over the Kafue near the town. All such crossings were recorded in a book, which was checked. The whole station staff was employed in tracing and interviewing the drivers. Information was obtained that a man had been seen standing by a particular car but that car was not in the book. The owner was traced but was out when the police called. He later came to the police camp and explained that he had been picnicking near the ferry but had not used it. He had had his shotgun with him and fired at the river. When asked if he had fired on his return journey he admitted taking a shot at some 'eyes' in the Bush but on the Nkana side of the crossroads. His house was searched and a shotgun and Greener SSG cartridges found. He was arrested and charged with manslaughter but at his trial before a judge and assessors maintained his story and was acquitted. Nevertheless Insp Batty and all at Nkana police station were commended for tenacious investigation and good teamwork.[35]

Seven youths were attested as boy buglers, an experiment which was deemed a success. Boy buglers, usually the sons of African policemen, remained a feature of the Force.

The population of Northern Rhodesia in 1936 was estimated to be 1,378,000, of whom 9,913 were Europeans and 342 Indians. During the year 11,123 cases were taken to court by the Northern Rhodesia Police. The Native Courts Ordinance of 1936 came into force on 1st January 1937 establishing courts of chiefs and other African notables to deal with civil disputes and minor crime entirely involving Africans as both complainants and defendants.

In December 1935 the Northern Rhodesia Government, at the suggestion of Capt Wardroper, had requested that the Force be inspected by Sir Herbert Dowbiggin CMG. Sir Herbert had served as Inspector General of Police in Ceylon (Sri Lanka) for twenty years. He had carried out an inspection of the Cyprus Police in 1926 and the Palestine Police in 1930. There was at this time no Inspector General of Colonial Police. Dowbiggin was unable to come to Northern Rhodesia until March 1937 having retired from his post in Ceylon that January.[36]

He found a force 636 strong, including the Cattle Cordon and recruits, leaving some 465 trained African police. Strength on the Copperbelt, where the population had risen to 70,866, was now:

Ndola	The superintendent, 6 other Europeans and 62 African police (Including 6 employed as railway police)
Luanshya	5 European and 55 African police.
Nkana	6 European and 56 African police.
Mufulira	5 European and 55 African police.

Dowbiggin recommended that an assistant superintendent be posted to Nkana. He was to be responsible to the superintendent, for the supervision of Nkana and Mufulira, enabling his superior to concentrate on Ndola and Luanshya. Ndola and Nkana each had one European detective on strength. Dowbiggin recommended that the European CID staff on the Copperbelt be doubled by the provision of European detectives for Luanshya and Mufulira.

African police strength elsewhere was:

Broken Hill	45 plus 6 railway police.
Lusaka	60.
Mazabuka	31.
Livingstone	51 plus 6 railway police.
Fort Jameson	23.
Choma	13.
Mongu	13.

At the Depot at Livingstone there were two intakes each year of 42 recruits each for a six month training course. 25 African police attending a six or twelve week refresher course at the Depot on return from vacation leave formed the only trained reserve. Training courses were also provided for prison warders, 24 attending in 1937.

The Chief Secretary to the Government, the Hon Charles Dundas CMG OBE[37], had pointed out that in 22 districts there were neither police nor troops stationed. This was dangerous in view of the poor communications in the Territory. It took nine days to reach Balovale from Mongu by river. Chinsali was three days march from Kasama and it took three days to drive from Ndola to Mwinilunga in good weather and ten in bad weather. Various suggestions, such as giving military or police training to district messengers, stationing a detachment of the Northern Rhodesia Regiment at each Provincial Headquarters and stationing police in all districts, were considered and rejected by Dowbiggin. His solution was for landing grounds to be prepared at each district headquarters and wireless installed. Prompt reinforcement would then be possible all over Northern Rhodesia.

Sir Herbert Dowbiggin rated the 11 uniformed African police at Mongu the weakest and most inefficient body he had seen. He reported that they had nothing to do. Mongu was still a three week journey from Livingstone, although it was hoped that a new road from Lusaka would soon be completed and reduce the journey to three days. He noted that the Mongu detachment had not been visited or inspected for two years. Prosecutions there had dropped from 162 in 1935 to 81 in 1936, and 7 in the first four months of 1937. The station was only manned because of a stipulation in the Lewanika Concession that the Resident Commissioner be accompanied by 'a suitable suite and escort'.

On the other hand he considered that the prison warders at Mongu had plenty to do. Accordingly he recommended that the uniformed police and interpreter be withdrawn and replaced by a European gaoler and six additional district messengers. Dowbiggin estimated that this would result in a saving of £208 per annum. An African detective would remain as the only policeman at Mongu, security being guaranteed by air and wireless communication.[38]

This recommendation was not implemented. Instead a European police officer was posted to take charge of the Mongu detachment. A year or two later the detachment commander was reported by a visiting officer from headquarters for failing to run his detachment properly. The delinquent answered that he could hardly be be expected to have time to do so. He was also in charge of prison industries. Prisoners were the only regular labour force in Mongu. He was responsible to the district commissioner for repairs to government houses, furniture, roads and bridges, the painting of buildings, and prison sanitary and water services. He had been given the job of building a new brick runway for the aerodrome and, since there was no mechanic in Mongu, he had also to maintain all government transport![39]

Sir Herbert Dowbiggin had more general criticism. He reported that in quality the European police, seven officers and 61 inspectors and constables, compared favourably with the police in any country he had visited, but numerically they were far below the strength needed for policing the Territory. The decision to separate the civil police from the military had been sound, but the implications had not been satisfactorily followed up on the civil side. No steps had been taken to properly train African rank and file as policemen. The whole of the police work proper was being carried out by the Europeans assisted by African detectives. On grounds both of policy and expense it was essential to set about training an efficient African force. The aim was only to accept recruits with Standard IV educational certificates or more but insufficient could be found.

As a result of Dowbiggin's report the system of training African police was much improved, Training in crowd control and riot drill was introduced. African recruits now spent 30.95% of their time at Drill and Musketry, 27.8% Law and Police Duties, 11.2% education, 8.5% Baton Drill and Crowd Control, 6.8% First Aid, 8.5% Physical Training, 4.2% Methods of Arrest, with the remaining 2.1% oral tests and revision under the Officer Commanding. Dowbiggin was responsible for the requirement that every European police officer be capable of moving a squad on parade and commanding an armed section in riot drill.

Dowbiggin was very concerned about internal security. Musketry practice had been much neglected. He found one African sergeant who had not fired his rifle since the end of the Great War, and an inspector who, despite having worn his revolver every day as part of normal working dress, had not fired it since joining the Force fifteen years previously. On Sir Herbert's recommendation an annual musketry course was introduced. African police were to fire fifteen rounds with the rifle at up to one hundred yards every six months, while each European was to fire 12 rounds from his revolver every half year. New ranges were to be built for this purpose.

The Force held 324 service rifles. Dowbiggin recommended that twenty rounds be held at each station for each rifle on charge with a reserve of ammunition to be held at each district headquarters. The military 1908 pattern web equipment was to be withdrawn and replaced by a single leather pouch to be worn on the waistbelt when rifles were issued. His recommendation that 10 rifles and 500 rounds be held at each Boma, was not accepted. When in May 1939 the Commissioner of Police asked for 628 new rifles for the Force, his request was refused.[40]

Dowbiggin found riot shields already in use and the system of supply simple. They were of bamboo and each private at each station was required to make three. Tearsmoke was, of course, already available and long bamboo riot batons were in the course of issue. Section 56 of the Northern Rhodesia Police Ordinance authorised the enrolment of special constables when necessary. Dowbiggin recommended that stocks of shields, batons, whistles and armbands be held at stations ready for issue to special constables if the occasion arose.

Sir Herbert Dowbiggin presented the Force with a Sports Team Challenge Cup. This was first competed for at Ndola on 24 July 1937 when the Ndola Detachment team beat teams from Luanshya, Nkana and Mufulira.

As a result of the Dowbiggin Report, the rank of British Constable was abolished with effect from 31st December 1937. All serving constables became assistant inspectors, grade II, although their pay remained on the scale £246–£300 per annum. Bicycle allowance was payable at 2s/6d per month! Those who had already become assistant inspectors were now designated Assistant Inspector Grade I. They retained their rank badges while the humble assistant inspector grade II wore none. Africans were now to be known as 'Native Police' and not 'Askari' as before and given ranks more suitable to a police force. It will be recalled that privates became 'native constables' in 1932 but the old title was soon brought back. Now that there was no risk of confusion with a rank held by Europeans, all privates and junior NCOs became constables. The native police ranks were now:
Sergeant-Major, First, Second or Third Class;
Sergeant, First, Second or Third Class;
Constable, Merit Class, Long Service Class, First, Second or Third Class.
Merit class constables wore a two bar chevron, gold braid on blue; Long service class a two bar chevron khaki braid on blue; first class constables a one bar chevron, khaki on blue. There were three grades in each class, a most complicated system! It is said that the titles 'corporal' and 'lance corporal' continued to be used unofficially.

Constables were paid fifteen shillings a month plus rations, free quarters, uniform and medical treatment. On Dowbiggin's recommendation literacy allowance of five shillings a month was paid to those proficient in English.

Despite the shortcomings found by Dowbiggin a conviction rate of 81.47 per cent was achieved during 1937. D/Const R C Ladell was commended for the successful investigation of a burglary at Victoria Falls. He took plaster casts of footprints and followed a spoor for six miles to the Zambezi Sawmills compound arresting the two criminals concerned within 24 hours of the commission of the offence. The taking of plaster casts was a recent development in police practice. C/Insp Maxwell and Sergeant-Major Malipenga were awarded the Coronation Medal.[41]

On 22nd May 1938 the Commissioner and his headquarters staff moved from the Secretariat building to five offices on the top floor of Charter House, Lusaka.

There was now a unified Colonial Police Service. Gazetted officers were to be permitted to transfer from one colony to another, thereby widening the opportunities for promotion and widening experience by cross-fertilisation. In 1938 Inspector Eric Halse obtained a transfer to British Somaliland in the rank of superintendent. There were also plans to institute a common uniform for all forces but these had to be shelved on the outbreak of war in 1939. The only pre-war change in the uniform of the Northern Rhodesia Police as a result of these pro-

A meeting in the Zambezi Valley circa 1938; BSAP left NRP (Inspector A. J. I. Hawkins) right

posals was the adoption of black gorget patches in place of Force collar badges by the Commissioner, Deputy Commissioner and Staff Officer.

The Force now had a motor transport fleet of 12 Ford V-8 vanettes, one for each station but one on the Line of Rail. Mufulira, which now had a complement of one assistant superintendent, seven members of the inspectorate, and forty seven native police, had a motor vehicle on charge. In August 1939 the District Commissioner wrote to the Commissioner of Police complaining that twice in the last three days he had been asked to authorise the hire of motor transport for Mufulira Police Station because the station vanette was 'worn out, useless, and a danger to the driver and the general public'![42]

During 1938 no less than 36 Europeans, and 128 Africans attested in the Force. All the European recruits had previous police experience either in the BSAP or in Palestine. The net strength increase was 25 assistant inspectors at the end of the year. In January 1936 four newly joined British constables had started a twelve week course of instruction at the Training Depot and such courses for European recruits were to be held in 1946 but recruit training within the Territory for Europeans was not implemented on a permanent basis until 1955 after the opening of the new Police Training School at Lilayi, near Lusaka.

Also in 1938 promotion courses for African police were started at the Depot and the rank of sub-inspector was created for the most experienced and proficient. Mr Pickup handed over the command of the Training Depot to Assistant Superintendent H M L Wilkinson, who, in turn was succeeded in 1939 by Mr T M Davidson. Tommy Davidson was to hold the appointment for the next twelve years. In September the police returned to Kasama with a strength of 1 inspector and 7 African police.

In October 1938 a Photographic Bureau was established at the Headquarters of the Criminal Investigation Department in Livingstone, equipped to develop and enlarge spool film received from stations. The Photographic Bureau also did a considerable amount of work for the Depot for instructional purposes.

While on leave Detective Assistant Inspectors Read and Ladell attended a forensic science course at the Home Office Laboratory at Nottingham. Chief Detective Inspector Deane-Simmons attended the same course in 1939.[43]

It was in 1939, or shortly thereafter, that native police ceased to wear the brass brassard on the left arm bearing the letters NRP and their identification number. It was replaced by numerals worn above the left breast pocket. These numerals were not the same as the wearer's Force number. This caused confusion as occasionally an irate member of the public would demand a constable's number, and when given it accuse the man of lying since it was not the number on his tunic! The redundant brass brassards were cut into discs and issued to African detectives as a means of identification.[44]

With a strength of 8 gazetted officers, 5 chief inspectors, 83 inspectors and assistant inspectors, 542 African police, 32 African detectives, 3 European lady clerks and 24 African civilians the Northern Rhodesia Police was only 3 African police, 5 detectives and 2 African civilians below establishment when war broke out. There were chief inspectors in charge at Luanshya, Nkana and Mufulira and a chief detective inspector with the superintendent at Ndola. A detachment of one European and 26 African police had been established at Chingola.

Notes

1. *Nkhwazi* Vol 12 No.1 April 1964 p31
2. Annual report PRO CO/799/11
3. PRO CO799/9
4. Map *Nkhwazi* April 1964
5. Annual reports Rhodes House & PRO
6. *Nkhwazi* April 1964 p33; Annual reports
7. PRO CO799/7
8. Annual reports
9. Hawkins 'Bwana Mkubwa in the Early Days' *Nkhwazi* Apr 64 p85

10. Heatlie *Nkhwazi* Apr 64 p5
11. Annual report; *Nkhwazi* Vol 10 No.2 Dec 62 p16
12. Annual report 1932 PRO CO/799/11
    Sir Ronald STORRS K(29)CMG 16 CBE 19 b19.11.81 s/o Dean of Rochestr ed Chtrhse Camb Egyptn CS Min Fin'04 Mines Sec Customs Audit, Oriental Sec Br Agency Cairo'09 LO Mespotamia, Sec War Cabinet, Lt Col Mil Gov Jerusalem'17 Gov Jerusalem & Judea'20 Kt'24 Cyprus'26 NR'32 inv'34 d Bury St Edmunds 1.11.55
13. Annual report 1933 Rhodes House; *Nkhwazi* Dec 62 p16
14. Exco PRO CO/799/19
15. Sugg NRPA Newsletter; *Story NRR* p67; PRO CO799/12
16. Annual reports Rhodes House or PRO CO799/12,13
17. *Nkhwazi* Vol 11 No.1 May 63 p15
    Sir Richd Allmond Jeffrey GOODE Kt 28 CMG 24 CBE 18 bNewfoundld 30.4.73 s/o Rev, ed Fettes, Sec to Admr NER'00 NWR 08 Sec to Admr NR'11 DAdmr'20 Ch Sec'24 Commr for Rlys NR'27 rtd 36 SA d25.5.53
18. *Story NRR* p106
19. PRO CO/795/45002
20. Sampson *So this was Lusaaka's*; CAP Jubilee Edn;
    Sir Stanley Davenport ADSHEAD MA MArch FRIBA b68 Prof Town Planning L'pool 09 London 14 designed Ramsgate Pavilion, Carnegie Library Ramsgte, L'pool Rep Theatre, Duchy of Cornwall Estate Kenningtn, Worthing Pavilion
21. *The Flag Wagger*; Harry FRANKLIN OBE BA Oxon b06 Insp Natve Edn NR 28 PA 29 DO 31 Bar Lincoln's, Judcl Dept 36 Secretariat 40 Info Offr War Corres 43–5 DInfo 46 rtd MLC Min Tpt & Wks 62
22. Exco PRO CO799/19; HRH George Edward Alexander Edmund DUKE OF KENT b20.12.02 RAF k flying acc 8.42
23. *Nkhwazi* Vol 10 No.1 Aug 62 p23
24. *Nkhwazi* Apr 1964 pp51 & 55
25. Annual report NRR PRO CO/799/14
26. *Story NRR* p68
    Maj Sir Hubert Winthrop YOUNG K(34)CMG 23 DSO 19 b6.7.85 s/o Lt Gov Punjab ed Eton RMA 2Lt RA 04 IA 08 A/Political Offr Mespot 15 sec'd FO 19 Colonial Offce 21 Colonial Sec Gib 27 Cnsllr to HCommr Iraq 29 Min Plenipotentary Iraq 32 Gov Nyasald 32 NR 34 Trinidad & Tobago 38–42 d20.4.50
27. Arthur Wm BONFIELD BA b5.91 NRGS PS to Admr 13.8.14 ANC Mwinilunga 18 NC Solwezi 7.7.21 DO Luanshya 35
    Sir Glyn Smallwood JONES G(64K60)CMG 57 MBE 44 BA b9.1.08 ed King's Chester, Oxon, Asscn Football for Wales; Cdt NR 31 DO'33 Commr Native Developmnt'51 PC Westn'55 Sec Native Affrs'58 Ch Sec Nyasald'60 Gov'61 Gov Gen Malawi'64–6 Advsr to PM Lesotho 69–71 DChmn Pearce Comm Rhodesia'72 Obsvr Zimbabwe Elections'80
28. John Ellis ROSS b7.6.93 Forest Hill ed Kg's Worcester, Tpr BSAP 15.10.13 No.1 Mob Colm 8.14 RNR
29. *Report of the Commission of Enquiry into the Disturbances in the Copperbelt of Northern Rhodesia* Cmd 5009 PRO CO/795/45083; Annual report 1935 CO/799/14; Exco CO/799/19, *Bulawayo Chronicle* 15.6.35, *Story NRR* pp71–2
30. Annual report
31. *Nkhwazi* April 1964 p37; Annual report
32. Annual report PRO CO/799/14
33. 'The Good Old Days' *Nkhwazi* Vol 10 No.2 Dec 62 p16
34. CAP Lusaka Jubilee Edn 31.7.63
35. *Nkhwazi* Vol 5 No.1 Mar 57 p34
36. Sir Herbt Layard DOWBIGGIN Kt 31 CMG 26 KPM b80 s/o Rev ed Merchnt Taylors' Insp Ceylon P'01 ASP'01 Supt'05 IG'13 rtd 1.37
37. Sir Chas Cecil Farquharson DUNDAS K(38)CMG 34 OBE 23 b6.6.84 s/o Vsct Melville, Clk Elder Dempstr Line 03 Cdt A/DC EA 08 DC 14 Political Offr GEA 16 Sen DC Tanganyika

20 Sec Native Affrs 26 Colonial Sec Bahamas 29 DGov 31 Ch Sec NR'34 Gov Bahamas 37 Uganda 40–44 d10.2.56
38. Dowbiggin Report, National Police Cllge Library Bramshill
39. *Nkhwazi* April 1964 p37
40. Exco PRO CO/799/19
41. Annual report 1937 Rhodes Hse & PRO CO799/16
42. Annual reports'38,9 Rhodes Hse & PRO CO799/17,18
43. Annual reports 38.9.
44. *Nkhwazi* April 1964 p37

CHAPTER 12

On The Home Front

The steady progress towards modern police methods with up to date equipment, and, perhaps more importantly the general development of Northern Rhodesia, now suffered another great setback with the outbreak of the Second World War on 3 September 1939. This time the enemy's borders were far away. Nevertheless there was still a sizeable number of Germans among the European population of Tanganyika. Their reaction to the outbreak of hostilities could not be foreseen and a company of the Northern Rhodesia Regiment was immediately despatched to reinforce the King's African Rifles in that territory. There were also intelligence reports of a Nazi force assembling in Angola to threaten Katanga and the Northern Rhodesia Copperbelt. On 29 August the remainder of the Northern Rhodesia Regiment, with 80 African recruits and 50 Europeans of the newly reformed Northern Rhodesia Volunteer Force, a total of 400 men, had been deployed on the Congo Border in the Mwinilunga District, west of Chingola, to counter this threat, which never materialised. Assistant Inspector Bernard O'Leary and a party of police were also involved in this operation, setting up a post at Kansanshi. By the end of September the threat was deemed no longer to exist and the Regiment returned to Lusaka to prepare for its move north.[1]

Meanwhile the Northern Rhodesia Police had been engaged in the arrest and internment of enemy aliens. This task was completed on 4 September with the aid of special constables recruited from members of the European population whose loyalty was not called into question by their ancestry. There were 1,160 aliens in Northern Rhodesia, 9 per cent of the white population. 63 German and 39 Italian mine employees had earlier been identified and watched as potential saboteurs, although strict instructions were now given that nothing should be done to cause offence to still neutral Italy. 116 men, women and children were arrested and taken to a temporary camp at Ndola. Some were released while those who appeared to require internment were sent to Gwelo in Southern Rhodesia. Hans Rhuys, who had taken employment with Moore's Chemists in Livingstone not long before the war, was believed to be involved in a plan to blow up the Victoria Falls Bridge. While in internment he made no secret of his commitment to the Nazi cause. He killed himself before the war's end.[2]

Special constables also assisted with guarding vulnerable points, including airfields and the mines, the product of which was vital to the allied war effort.

Guards on vulnerable points on the Copperbelt were in place by 11pm on 22 August, only three hours after the alert was received from London. A similar alert during the Munich crisis of 1938 had served as a useful rehearsal. Assistant Inspector F H Letchworth of the regular force died of blackwater fever while guarding the Luangwa Bridge. He would not leave his post before his scheduled relief arrived. The burden on the Northern Rhodesia Police was eased in 1942 when the Northern Rhodesia (African) Defence Force was formed and took over the duty of providing many vulnerable point guards.[3]

At the outbreak of war air raid precautions were instituted throughout the Territory. In Fort Jameson the signal for an anticipated raid was to be the ringing of bells. Naturally the District Commissioner had to order that bells should not be rung for any other purpose. However by 12 September 1939, he felt able to announce that, owing to the manner in which the war had developed, the restriction on the ringing of bells could be lifted. Should any unforeseen emergency arise, a warning would be given by very fast and continued ringing of the Dutch Reformed Church Mission bell.

A pigeon was caught on a mine building in Kitwe with a piece of paper tied to its foot. The paper bore pencil marks which could possibly have been a plan or a map. With great secrecy the paper was sent posthaste to London to be examined by M.I.5. Some while later it was learnt that the missive appeared to emanate from a member of a religious sect, the members of which were in the habit of communicating with God by pigeon post![4]

In 1940 the total strength of the Force was 7 gazetted officers, 87 members of the inspectorate, and 578 African police. The Nkana Detachment was renamed Kitwe Detachment. There were some 10 Europeans and 42 African police serving at Luanshya under Inspector John Hawkins, soon to be promoted Chief Inspector.

Luanshya Detachment 1940 (Felix Adams)
Front Row: A sergeant, C O Gordon, N M Irvin, H A Arrigonie, C G Byrne, A St J Sugg, A J I Hawkins, G M Beal, R Gabb, C F Norton, a sergeant.

Nearly all the European members of the Northern Rhodesia Police volunteered for military service. All were conscripted under the Emergency Powers Regulations and required to remain at their police duties in the Territory, although on 1 June 1940 six were released for duty with the Armed Forces. On 12 July instructions were issued that applications for release must cease and only four more European police officers were allowed to leave the Territory for active service with H.M.Forces during the war. This caused much discontent. One assistant inspector deserted from the Force in order to enlist. He was apprehended and underwent a sentence of imprisonment for his offence. Most of those released were employed on police duties in occupied and liberated territories, although A/Insp G M Beal, who had completed a short service commission with the Royal Air Force before joining the Colonial Police, returned to flying duties, initially in Southern Rhodesia, where many RAF aircrew learnt their trade under the Empire Air Training Scheme, but later on operations with Bomber Command.[5]

3,626 offences against the Penal Code were recorded for the year 1940, and 7,695 against other ordinances, a slight increase on the 1939 total of 10,538 for all offences. Despite competition from the Army, 80 African police were recruited during the year. Of these 14 had had no formal education, and 14 had reached only Standard 1. 18 recruits had attained Standard IV but only 7 Standard VI. In the whole Territory only 3,000 African children were in their fifth year of schooling and only 35 were receiving secondary education. The first secondary school for Africans, Munali, had only opened in 1939.[6]

Early in 1940 Sitali Shilling had reported at Livingstone Police Station that his brother, Sipuku, had been taken by a crocodile while herding cattle on Long Island in the middle of the Zambezi. Others of the 20 or so Africans employed there corroborated his story. Two weeks later A/Insps Jack Seed and Geoff Bolton were enjoying an evening swim in the floating bath near the Zambezi Boat Club. There attention was drawn to the partially decomposed body of an African which had washed up against the boom which protected swimmers against crocodile. There was a jagged wound on the side of the throat which, at first sight, seemed consistent with an attack by such a beast. At the mortuary Sitali identified the body as that of Sipuku. However A/Insp C G Byrne noted that the dead man's clothing was caked in blood, which one would have expected to have dispersed in the water, had the man been seized and dragged straight in by a crocodile. The post mortem revealed that Sipuku had not died from drowning.

Sitali Shilling took Seed and Byrne in his canoe to the place where he claimed the accident had occurred, on the Northern Bank of Long Island, about a mile above the swimming bath. Experiments with a log indicated that, if the story were true, the body would have been washed over the Victoria Falls without going anywhere near the Boat Club. Detectives Kabole and Shanabwato with Const Akaliwa searched the mainland bank opposite Long Island and found a flattened patch of reeds with apparent blood stains. A log launched from here finished up against the swimming bath.

Further inquiries on the island revealed that there had been illness among the inhabitants for which the deceased had been blamed. Sitali, the capitao in charge of the herdsmen, was looked upon as a witch-doctor. He had had Sipuku taken to the mainland and held down while he cut the man's throat in such a way as to resemble the indentations of a crocodile's teeth. Sipuku had been left there overnight to bleed to death. The next day his body had been thrown into the Zambezi and the fictitious report made to the police. On 20 March 1940 Sitali Shilling was convicted of murder and sentenced to death.[7]

There were now 24,000 Africans and 2,500 Europeans employed in the Copper Industry. On 17 March 1940 the European miners at Mufulira came out on strike followed on 21 March by those at Nkana. To ensure that production continued their pay was increased and work recommenced on 27 March. The example was not lost on African mineworkers who struck two days later. There was intimidation of those who wished to go to work which extended to visits to the European Mine Townships to force out African domestic employees.

The Northern Rhodesia Regiment had recently been expanded to two battalions. The 1st Battalion had left for Active Service in the Horn of Africa, while the 2nd, under the command of Lieutenant Colonel A N Bagshaw, remained to perform internal security duties at home. A company of this battalion was now sent to Mufulira and another to Nkana, to guard the mine installations and compound offices while the Europeans of the Northern Rhodesia Defence Force patrolled the white townships. The police provided protection for Africans who wished to go to work.

Assistant Superintendent H M L Wilkinson had arrived to take command of the 17 European police and 50 Africans of the Nkana Detachment on the 29 March. At 0600 hrs on 3 April he deployed with a strong police party to the mine workers' compound to protect the loud speakers at the football field where a crowd of 5–6,000 assembled. So well behaved were the strikers that at 0815 hrs Wilkinson sent his men back to the station except for A/Inps Proust and Lindsay and 4 constables with whom he patrolled the compound in a vanette. The police wore steel helmets and carried long batons, Africans having wicker shields and Europeans their .45 revolvers and tear gas bombs. After three quarters of an hour the vehicle brakes proved defective and, rather than risk an accident the patrol returned to the compound office which was guarded by Capt R Francis Jones, two other officers, 4 British sergeants and 70 asirikari of 2 NRR with two Lewis guns.

At 1045 hrs Wilkinson was in the office when he heard a loud noise and saw a huge crowd surging down the road from the football field. The leaders swung to the left and through the compound gates. Some Africans who were lined up outside the office waiting for their pay scattered pursued by the crowd throwing stones. Some had sticks. Wilkinson who, after calling for reinforcements, had gone towards the gates, and the other 6 police were unable to stop the rush. They tried to close the gates but one was stuck fast due to lack of use. A European mineworker was asked to block the entrance with his ten ton truck but this was forced aside. In any event there was a gap in the fence only 20 yards along where a railway line entered the compound and rioters were already using this route. Police calls for them to stop were ignored. So frenzied were the strikers that some were seen gnawing at the wire fence to get in. The head of the mob stormed down the east side of the office until they came to the garage and turned west straight through a double line of soldiers knocking some over and disorganising the rest, stopping at the store where the railtrack ended. The offices were now surrounded by a mob which was enraged by the news of their colleagues drawing pay. The soldiers tried to force the crowd back by bringing the butts of their rifles down on bare feet. The police threw 5 or 6 tear gas bombs which temporarily stemmed the rush but despite repeated warnings by the police the mob rained stones on the security forces. Wilkinson went to Capt Francis Jones who was close to the side of the offices. 12 Africans were some 8 yards away advancing with bricks. The officers drew their pistols but their assailants came on. Wilkinson gave a final warning before firing 5 shots at the knees of the men nearest to him. Jones fired his automatic pistol and ordered his men to fire. An African sergeant manning a Lewis gun was laid out by a blow on the head before he could fire. The disorder had broken out so suddenly that the troops were still wearing their soft felt slouch hats. The other Lewis, manned by two British sergeants, was put out of action by a rock on the magazine after four shots had been fired. A/Insp S A Neal was felled by a brick in the act of throwing a teargas bomb which exploded among the security forces. At first the firing had little effect. Agitators had told their followers that the weapons were only loaded with paper! Finally the attackers drew off and the 'Cease Fire' was sounded on the bugle. A/Insp Hughes and two constables had appeared just before the firing commenced and further police reinforcements now arrived from the station so that when brave spirits launched a second assault it was beaten off by the police alone with 10 tear gas grenades. The dead and injured were collected by mine 'police' and first aiders. There was a first aid station close by the offices.

258 rounds of rifle and Lewis gun ammunition had been expended by the troops, one accidently. Capt Jones had fired 20 shots from his pistol and another Army officer, one. Police officers had fired 23 rounds in all from their revolvers. 17 rioters were killed and 63 wounded. None were killed by police officers although at least four were wounded by revolver shots. 20 soldiers and 11 policemen had been injured. A/Insp R E Proust was wounded in the back of the head by a rock that dented his steel helmet. A/Insp Byrne was injured in the knee and Lindsay's face had been grazed by a stone. Most of the soldiers had only a few months service and there is no doubt they were much shaken. Like the police at Roan Antelope in 1935 some took shelter in the building and fired through the windows. However the firing was kept under control by the sufficient number of officers and NCOs. Had the order to fire not been given the troops and police would undoubtedly have been overpowered and lives among them lost.

The subsequent inquest found that the 17 dead had been 'killed by unknown soldiers of the Northern Rhodesia Regiment acting in defence of life and property'. Two missionaries who were present agreed that it was necessary to open fire. Capt Jones gave evidence that the European police, at considerable danger, remained close to the crowd, giving warnings until eventually they had to retreat under a hail of stones. The Coroner described Mr Wilkinson's conduct as beyond criticism and beyond praise. He was subsequently awarded the Colonial Police Medal for Gallantry for his part in the action.

After the mob had dispersed hooliganism continued in the compound where huts were burnt and the property of compound staff damaged. There was minor rioting at Chingola after an African woman was hit by a clerk issuing rations and a European mine employee joined in the dispute. 200 white troops were brought up from Southern Rhodesia where a detachment of the BSAP was stood by. The local units of The Northern Rhodesia Defence Force were reinforced but by the time Harry Franklin and the rest of the Broken Hill Detachment arrived on the Copperbelt, all was quiet. They patrolled the silent compounds by night in lorries, with bayonets fixed. On 8 April all the strikers were back at work. Their wages were increased.[8]

In September 1940 Senior Assistant Superintendent T M Davidson, in command of the Depot at Livingstone, was having a good root round the Stores when he came across the shell of an old drum left behind on the departure of the Military in 1932. At the Depot were now ten boy buglers and Mr Davidson hit on the idea of forming a drum and bugle band. He had been a keen drummer in his school Officers Training Corps band, and was able to put the drum into a serviceable condition. He had some drum sticks made at Livingstone Central Prison and taught some of the boys to beat a 2-four or 6-eight march. By whistling some bugle marches Tommy Davidson was able to teach the buglers to play them. As a substitute bass drum he acquired a Barotse drum.

At about this time Assistant Inspector L M Clark joined the Training Depot staff as Second in Command and only other European officer. Nobby took up the new project with enthusiasm so that when, soon after, the Commissioner came from Lusaka on inspection, he was received on parade with a salute played by the embryo band. Money and all types of equipment were difficult to come by, but Mr Hart could see the value of a band for parades and enhancing morale. Knowing that Sir Stewart Gore-Brown DSO, then an active and influential member of the Governor's Council, was about to visit Livingstone, Harry Hart arranged for him to include the Depot in his itinerary. The 57 year old former Royal Artillery officer gave the band his backing, promising that if he could not persuade Government to make a grant of £100 for band equipment, he would provide the money out of his own pocket.[9]

A few months later the Government provided the money and four side drums and a proper bass drum were purchased. A spare drum-major's mace, once used by the Regiment's band was found at Lusaka, and sent down. The Deputy Commissioner, Mr R J W Verrall, presented a leopardskin for the bass-drummer. Nobby Clark painted all the drums with the Force crest and his wife, Joan, daughter of the former RSM Schronen of the Military Branch, made a drum-major's sash. Boy Bugler Sibanyati was selected as drum-major and promoted sergeant. Davidson and Clark became even more ambitious and a fife was purchased. There being no further funds available, a number of other fifes were made from steel conduit piping by Inspector J W 'Gunner' Hughes, in charge of the Police Stores. After much hard work the buglers managed to produce tunes on these instruments.

The Commissioner then proposed that there should be a Force march. His wish was Mr Davidson's command, and Tommy produced a tune with lyrics which were taught to recruits by Sergeant (later Sub-Inspector) Paul Wang. This tune was later incorporated into the march *Nkhwazi*, composed for the Northern Rho-

North-Eastern Rhodesia Constabulary

Northern Rhodesia Police 1911

Northern Rhodesia Police 1914

Northern Rhodesia Police 1932

Northern Rhodesia Police 1947

Northern Rhodesia Police 1955

desia Police by Mr George Hey ARCM, who became bandmaster in 1954. The original words were:

> We are proud of the Police Force,
> And proud of our uniforms too.
> And when you see us marching with our rifles
> You would think we are in the Army too.
>
> But we are only policemen
> and have very many things to do
> and when you see us on beat duty
> You'll know we're looking after you.
>
> Wc are all of one tribe.
> Our tribe is the N.R.P.
> And now we are together,
> Three cheers for the N.R.P.[10]

In 1941 a new Northern Rhodesia Police Ordinance was promulgated. Section 6 required that 'the Police Force shall be employed in and throughout the Territory for preserving the peace, for the prevention and detection of crime and for the apprehension of offenders against the peace'. It stated, 'The provisions of this Ordinance shall be in addition to and not in substitution for or in derogation of any of the powers, authority, privileges and advantages, nor of the duties and responsibilities of a constable at Common Law'.

The Commissioner of Police, subject to the orders and directions of the Governor, was to have 'the command, superintendence, direction and control of the Force'. The Ordinance listed 51 punishable offences against police discipline, the last one being 'any act, conduct, disorder or neglect to the prejudice of good order and discipline not hereinbefore specified'.

Although recruitment of European officers had been brought to a halt by the War, 102 Africans were recruited during 1941, of whom 7 had no educational qualifications, and 8 had only completed Standard I. The majority, 59 had reached Standard IV, but only 5 had attained Standard V or VI. Expenditure on the Force was £64,577. 13,908 offences were reported in 1941.

For the following year expenditure increased to £74,056. The number of recruits more than doubled to 263. Education was improving. While 10 of these new constables had had no formal schooling and 4 had only completed Standard I, 34 had reached Standard II, 79 Standard III, 83 Standard IV, 42 Standard V, and 11 Standard VI. In the whole Territory 86,300 African children were said to be in school. Crime had continued to rise with a total of 16.139 offences reported to the police.[11]

The European Mineworkers Union led by Frank Maybank continued to threaten production. Maybank was said to be an ardent communist who hated capitalism and regarded the war as unnecessary. Among his allies were Afrikaners who felt no loyalty to the Empire. On the other hand, mineworkers, like the police, were prevented by Emergency Powers Regulations, from leaving to join the armed forces. Some non-union members supported the drive for a closed shop in the belief that once it was implemented they would be sacked and thus free to enlist! With Government sanction the mining companies entered into a closed shop agreement in September 1941 but the Emergency Powers Regulations prevented its full enforcement while the War continued.

Intelligence indicated that on a visit to Soviet Russia, Maybank had been shaken to find that all men there were not treated as equal. Evidently the explanation he received from the Russian leadership as to why such an ideal was not yet practicable for the Russian people helped him to follow a union policy a major aim of which was to prevent African mineworkers progressing to jobs held by whites.

Neither the grant of the closed shop nor Hitler's invasion of Russia nor threats of deportation persuaded Maybank to cease agitation. Things reached a head in September 1942 when he tried to involve the European miners and railway workers in an industrial dispute at the Katanga mines in the Belgian Congo. It was decided that Maybank and two Afrikaners should be deported. The Southern Rhodesia Armoured Car Regiment was brought in to assist the police in maintaining order while the arrests and deportations were effected but all went quietly. Back in England Frank Maybank obtained employment as a seagoing storekeeper which suggests that his attitude to the War had changed to some extent. In 1945 he returned to his union activities on the Northern Rhodesia Copperbelt.[12]

On 9 July 1942 Inspector S A Wright led a party to the rescue of an injured man at Victoria Falls. A stretcher was improvised and the man was brought up 400 feet out of the gorge. In 1946 Sydney Wright was to be awarded the Life Saving Medal of the Order of St John in recognition of this exploit.[13]

Although an independent Northern Rhodesia Prisons Department came into being in 1942, four officers of the Northern Rhodesia Police were still holding additional appointments as superintendents of local prisons as late as 1946.[14]

From early in the War some 4,000 Polish refugees reached Northern Rhodesia. A camp was established for them at the disused Bwana Mkubwa Mine site under the command of Captain S 'Chops' Grills. Fifteen African police were posted for duty at this camp. In 1944 members of the Force had to be found for duty at a second Polish refugee camp at Katambora, near Livingstone. A third was subsequently required and they remained open until 1948.

In December 1941 Northern Rhodesia was asked to prepare an internment camp for 1,500 Italian civilians formerly resident in Abyssinia. This was put in hand at Kafue. In March and April ten Poles were attested as temporary assistant inspectors of police and with 128 specially recruited African guards commenced training at the Depot at Livingstone. On 7 May 1942 Lieutenant Colonel A N Bagshaw was appointed Commandant. Having raised and trained the 2nd Battalion, The Northern Rhodesia Regiment, he had been judged too old to lead it on active service overseas, and sent to form the 4th Battalion at Fort Jameson. East Africa Command sent the Italians elsewhere and the guard force was disbanded in late August. An Army Malariologist criticised the camp as being in a malarial area. The Northern Rhodesia Government's Director of Medical Services pointed out that the whole Territory was a malarial area! In 1943 Arthur Bagshaw was seconded to the Northern Rhodesia Government as Director of War Evacuees and Camps succeeding Lt Col Sir Stewart Gore-Brown DSO MLC in that post.[15]

In 1940 Superintendent Andrew Pickup had been transferred to Aden as Deputy Commissioner of Police. In September 1942 he returned as a Lieutenant Colonel and Assistant Director of Intelligence and Security for Northern Rhodesia. Assistant Superintendent Deane-Simmons and another European police officer were seconded to assist him.

14 African police were detailed for duty as Government House Guard at Lusaka under the veteran Sergeant Malalo, Number 3 in the Force. The Northern Rhodesia Police furnished this guard until 1 July 1946 when it again became a military responsibility. In 1944 the Force took over the guarding of Lusaka Airport from the Northern Rhodesia Regiment. This guard was maintained until 1 April 1946.[16]

In 1943 the number of African recruits had again increased, to 295. In 1944 the number dropped to 245. Seven of these held Standard VII certificates of education and one Standard VIII, although the vast majority continued to be Standard III or IV. During the last year of the War only 178 Africans were recruited, none holding more than a Standard VI certificate.

Assistant inspectors grade II attested before 1 January 1944, who passed the Northern Rhodesia Civil Service Examination in an African language at Lower Level, were eligible for promotion to Assistant Inspector Grade I after four years service, and to Inspector after completing seven years in the Force. Conditions of Service were now changed to require those recruited after that date to complete seven years as assistant inspectors grade II, and eleven years service for promotion to Inspector.

Early in the War the Northern Rhodesia Police had had to give up its ·303 Lee Enfield rifles to arm new units of the Northern Rhodesia Regiment and was issued with American ·300 Springfields. These were so unsatisfactory that in 1944 the annual musketry practice had to be cancelled because of the number of blowbacks.[17]

The *Standing Orders, General Instructions and Dress Regulations* issued in 1936 had become out of date and were replaced in 1944 by a loose leaf volume of *Standing Orders*, consisting of 143 single sided pages – twice as long as the original work but easier to amend!

Expenditure on the Northern Rhodesia Police had risen steadily since 1941 to reach £88,918 for 1944. Offences against the Penal Code had risen to 5,754 in 1943, while other offences reported reached a wartime peak of 10,571 in 1942. Breakings and theft markedly increased during the War, while murders averaged forty per year. Other crimes of violence had shown a tendency to decrease. The increase in breakings into African housing was ascribed to the rising cost of living and shortages in the supply of blankets, cooking pots, food and clothing caused by the War. Nevertheless 1945 showed a slight drop in all offences with 5,378 against the Penal Code and 10,408 against other laws. Expenditure on the Force was reduced by £2,000 in 1945.

During the War the powers of native courts to deal with criminal cases were increased and urban native courts established.[18]

Towards the end of the War so many categories of African in the Territory wore a khaki uniform with black fez, that it was decided that African police should wear the Force badge in front of theirs. Seven battalions and one independent garrison company of The Northern Rhodesia Regiment had been raised and most had served outside the Territory, including those who saw action in Somaliland, Ethiopia, Madagascar and Burma. The soldiers returned home wearing boots. Accordingly, after the War, the African police were issued for the first time with black ankle boots, worn with long blue puttees. 'Knickers' were henceforth to be called 'shorts'.

Mr. H. G. Hart, Commissioner of Police 1936–47 with officers circa 1943
(Photo Bob Barkley)
L to R Back Row: T H Bush, E J Phinn, T M Davidson, A Wallace, A J I Hawkins, D W Humphrey. *Front Row:* H M L Wilkinson, R J W Verrall, H G Hart, A Pickup, G Carr Smith.

The title 'Detachment Commander' for the senior officer on a police station was discontinued towards the end of the War, to be replaced by 'Officer in Charge'.[19]

Notes

1. PRO CO795/111/45237 *Story NRR* p76
2. Governor's telegram 5.9.39 PRO CO795/111/45237; *Nkhwazi* Vol 12 No.1 Apr'64 p37
   Leopold F MOORE MLC founder, proprietor & editor Livingstone Mail, proprietor Moore's Chemists Livingstone
3. Governor's telegram above, *Nkhwazi* Apr'64 p39
4. *Nkhwazi* Vol 12 No.1 Apr 1964 pp38–9
5. *Nkhwazi* Apr'64 p37; Cox report National Police College library Bramshill; NR report 1940–46 IWM
6. NR Report 1940–46 IWM, *A History of Zambia* Andrew Roberts

7. Article J B Seed *Nkhwazi* Vol 1 No.4 Apr 1953
8. PRO CO795/116/45109/7F; *Story NRR* pp83–4; *Nkhwazi* Apr'64 p39; Bagshaw taped interview IWM
   Lt Col R FRANCIS-JONES ltr CO 3NRR
9. Lt Col Sir Stewart GORE–BROWNE DSO 17 b83 s/o Sir Francis KC ed Harrow RMA RFA Lt Anglo–Belgian Bdy Comm NR'11 OC 32BAC 14 Staff Capt RA 12Div'15 BMRA 5Div 1.16 LO with Portuguese 17 GSO2 MA to CinC BAOR 10.4.19–31.5.20 Shiwa Ngandu Estate Mpika'21 MLC Kt'45 d67
10. *Nkhwazi* Vol 10 No.1 Aug'62 p4 & Vol 12 No.1 Apr'64 p58
11. NR Report 1940–46 IWM
12. PRO CO795/122/45109/7
13. Annual report 1946 Rhodes House
14. NR Report 1940–46 IWM
15. PRO CO795/133/45369
16. Annual report 1946 Rhodes House
17. *Nkhwazi* Vol 11 No.1 May 63 p13
18. NR Report 1940–46 IWM
19. *Nkhwazi* April 1964 p39, 'knickers' Vol 10 No.2 Dec 62 p31

CHAPTER 13

Post War Reconstruction

The European strength of the Force had become run down during the War when recruiting stopped. Some of those who had managed to get away on active service did not return for one reason or another. Those left behind had been unable to take vacation leave in the United Kingdom. Lord Kitchener[1] once said that 'The Front' is wherever a soldier is ordered to be. The Northern Rhodesia Police had done their duty on 'The Front' allotted to them, but many felt bitter at having been denied a more glamourous role in the war effort of the Empire. Many stations were now having to be run with less than half of their European establishment. Morale was low and on 3 January 1946 the inspectorate petitioned the Governor for a Commission of Inquiry.

This was granted and on 2 July the Cox Commission, named after its chairman, Sir Herbert Cox, Chief Justice of Northern Rhodesia, commenced taking evidence at Livingstone. The other members were Superintendent Walter Calver of the London Metropolitan Police, Mr H W Priest, a member of the Northern Rhodesia Legislative Council, Mr L F Leversedge, a district officer with the Provincial Administration, and Colonel H P Rice OBE, a district assistant. Hearings were held at various centres in the Territory and the Commission also visited the Head-quarters of the British South Africa Police in Salisbury, Southern Rhodesia, and that of their Matabeleland Division in Bulawayo. Evidence was taken from 56 European officers of the Northern Rhodesia Police, 14 other government officials, 23 white non-officials, of whom 16 represented public bodies, and 22 Africans.[2]

41 per cent of the European members of the Force and 47 per cent of the Africans were stationed on the Copperbelt at Ndola, Kitwe, Chingola, Mufulira and Luanshya. The other large police stations were at Lusaka, Livingstone and Broken Hill. There were small police stations at Mazabuka, Choma, Fort Jameson and Mongu. At Mongu were one European and 17 Africans to police Barotseland, an area of 50,000 square miles with a population of 260,000. At Mulobezi, Pemba, Monze, Kafue, Chisamba, Kasama and Fort Rosebery were sub-stations or posts, staffed entirely by African police[3]. The European officers had been withdrawn from Kasama and Fort Rosebery for duty elsewhere during the War, and not replaced, leaving 13 uniformed African police and 4 detectives to police the whole Northern Province. On urban stations African police worked six hour shifts and attended two periods of arms or riot drill and two training lectures each week.

Superintendent Brodie, in charge of the Criminal Investigation Department and Immigration, was also responsible for the uniformed branch at Livingstone and Choma, an arrangement which had lasted since the CID was first formed under Sub-Inspector Ferguson in 1914. The Superintendent at Ndola was still responsible for the supervision of all five Copperbelt stations. The officer in charge of each of the other police stations was directly responsible to the Commissioner. The Cox Commission recommended that the Territory be divided into police divisions.

African police could serve for up to 21 years when they were retired on pension. The Commission found that out of 704 serving in September 1946, 453 had completed less than five years, 159 between five and ten years, and 92 more than ten years service. Three sergeants and fifteen constables were still employed as railway police. The Commission noted that there were no members of the Northern Rhodesia Police stationed in the African mine townships and recommended that the establishment be increased to provide adequate police there. 23 African civilians were employed with the Force as clerks.

In the Criminal Investigation Department were one Chief African Detective and 43 African detectives. Eleven of the detectives had joined under the old system straight from civilian life while the remainder had been selected from men serving in the uniformed branch.

The Chief African Detective was stationed at the Depot at Livingstone which was under the command of a senior assistant superintendent. The remainder of the Depot staff comprised one assistant inspector, one African inspector, and five NCOs and constables. The recruit course consisted of 26 per cent drill and musketry, 18 per cent physical training and games, 43 per cent police duties, and 13 per cent education and first aid. Since 1932 a total of 1,645 recruits had passed through the Depot and 410 African police had attended refresher courses and 236 promotion courses there.

Europeans were attested as assistant inspectors grade II for two tours of duty of 36 months each. Those who failed to pass the examinations required for confirmation in their appointment were discharged after six years. January 1946 had seen the arrival of the first post-war European recruits, who had to be at least 5'8" tall and between 22 and 28 years of age. Training courses were instituted for them at the Depot. Relations between these young men, most of whom had seen active service, and their instructors, who had perforce had to remain in Northern Rhodesia, were not always easy. It is said that on one occasion a squad of such veteran recruits marched itself smartly off parade and into the bar of the North-Western Hotel. In November the Commissioner of Police wrote to the Officer Commanding congratulating the staff on their efforts, 'now that the last European recruit has left the Depot'[4]. 32 Europeans joined the Force in 1946.

The Annual Report for 1946 gave the strength of the Northern Rhodesia Police as 19 gazetted officers, 83 members of the inspectorate and 793 African police. The establishment was:

1 Commissioner of Police	at an annual salary of £1,350
1 Deputy Commissioner	at an annual salary of £1,000
3 Superintendents	at an annual salary of £720–840

14 Assistant Superintendents	at an annual salary of £360–720
91 A/Inspectors & Inspectors	at an annual salary of £300–600
1 Chief Detective	at an annual salary of £72–96
5 African Inspectors	at an annual salary of £42–84
45 Detectives	at an annual salary of £18–60
18 Sergeants-Major	at an annual salary of £30–42
73 Sergeants	at an annual salary of £24–27
651 Constables	at an annual salary of £12–24

Mr Hart was still Commissioner with Mr Verrall as his deputy. The three superintendents were Pickup, Brodie and Totman. The 14 assistant superintendents (including senior assistant superintendents) were Fold, Wilkinson, Carr Smith, Deane-Simmons, Davidson, Phinn, Hawkins, C N Halse, Wallace, Bush, Humphrey, Mitchell, Helliwell and Day.

A census that year showed that the European population of the Territory had grown from approximately 15,000 at the outbreak of war to 21,881, including the Polish refugees many of whom settled in Northern Rhodesia. During the year 325 Europeans were convicted of offences under the Penal Code, including 82 for crimes of dishonesty. 1,214 whites were convicted of offences against other ordinances. Juvenile crime had increased, especially among Europeans[5]. The growing white population could only effectively be policed by Europeans. Questions of racial discrimination apart, the African police of the day lacked the necessary sophistication. The Cox Commission recommended the re-introduction of the rank of European Constable, but this was one recommendation which was not implemented.

An assistant superintendent held the appointment of Force Paymaster. He was assisted by Chief Inspector A J Francis who had been employed in the pay office since 1932. Chief Inspector H H 'Bisley' Kingshott at Force Headquarters had been posted there as a constable in 1931, being unfit for ordinary police duty. Inspector H K E Dashwood was seconded as Acting Workmen's Compensation Commissioner. Insp J W 'Gunner' Hughes was employed as Force Armourer with an assistant inspector grade II to help him.

The Cox Commission recommended a new rank of senior superintendent be introduced and that the rank of senior assistant superintendent be abolished. It also recommended that in future the Paymaster should be a civil servant seconded from the Accountant General's Department, assisted by civilian clerks, with one inspector employed in the Pay Office to gain experience between normal tours of police duty. The Commission further recommended that CID Headquarters, the Pay Office and the Training Depot should be moved from Livingstone to Lusaka. Yet another recommendation which was implemented was that there should be a Police Association created by legislation.

During 1946 Force Headquarters moved from Charter House, Lusaka, to a Kimberley brick building with thatched roof and hessian ceilings on the site which was to be called Hart Road, where it was to remain until 1962. Here there was the necessary room for expansion to provide for the CID and Pay Office.[6]

The transport fleet of the Northern Rhodesia Police consisted of 22 vanettes and trucks of various makes (9 Fords, 6 Chevrolet, 2 Dodge and 1 GMC plus 4 which were useless and being cannibalised for spares), 15 motor cycles and 224 pedal cycles.[7]

For 1946 expenditure on the Northern Rhodesia Police rose 20 per cent to £108,518. The Force dealt with a total of 20,318 offences of which 6,111 were against the Penal Code. 98 criminal cases, including 49 murders, were tried in the High Court.[8]

On 1 March 1947 Mr H G Hart proceeded on leave pending retirement. Mr R J Wyndham Verrall, the Deputy Commissioner, became Acting Commissioner of Police pending the arrival in June of Colonel J E Workman, on transfer from Commissioner of Police in Fiji. Mr Verrall was, therefore, Acting Commissioner at the time of the Royal Tour of Southern Africa during which, in April 1947, His Majesty King George VI and the Royal Family visited both sides of the Victoria Falls. In recognition of the police arrangements made in connection with this visit His Majesty invested Mr Verrall as a Member of the Royal Victorian Order.

It was on the occasion of the Royal Visit that the Drums, Bugles and Fifes of the Northern Rhodesia Police Training Depot made their first major public appearance. They beat retreat at Livingstone in the presence of Their Excellencies the Governors of Northern and Southern Rhodesia and the Governor-General of the Belgian Congo. Unfortunately the Royal Party were unable to stay for this parade which made a most favourable impression on the Government and public. The Band now consisted of one sergeant and four constables, who had joined the Force as boy buglers, and 16 buglers. Five constables at stations away from Livingstone were in receipt of 'bugler allowance' at two shillings a month. Two boy buglers were also serving at out-stations. Buglers were paid 15 shillings a month.[9]

All records and duties relating to civil aviation were now transferred from the Police to a newly formed Department of Civil Aviation. These had been the responsibility of the Force under the guidance of the Director of Civil Aviation, Southern Rhodesia, since 1930.

The staff officer responsible for radio communications in the British South Africa Police made a survey with a view to the establishment of a radio communications network in Northern Rhodesia. Effective Force motor transport now amounted to 23 vehicles and 9 motor cycles.

The District Commissioner, Lundazi, requested police assistance to combat an extensive illicit trade in arms and ivory between Chief Kambombo's Area and Tanganyika and Nyasaland. An African sergeant-major was sent to investigate assisted by district messengers and kapasus. 72 elephant tusks, 20 rhinoceros horns, 94 muzzle loaders and 16 rifles and shotguns were recovered.[10]

The Veterinary Department had at last succeeded in eradicating endemic pleuro-pneumonia amongst the cattle in Barotseland. On 31 December 1947, after twenty five years of existence, the Barotse-Namwala Cattle Cordon was withdrawn. As Assistant Inspector H A Arrigonie and his sergeant-major trekked down the Cordon for the last time picking up the men from each post, one of the landmarks of the Force and the Territory lapsed into history. The personnel

The Governor with officers and inspectors Livingstone 1947 (Mrs L M Clark)

Front Row: A J Francis, H H Kingshott, T M Davidson, W Trotman, M.B.E., N. Brodie, R J W Verrall, M.V.O., J.P. (Acting Commissioner), Sir John Waddington, K.C.M.G., K.C.V.O., Lt.-Col. M Fletcher (Private Secretary), G C Smith, E Deane Simmons, O Mitchell, S A Wright. *Middle Row:* H J Hathrill, G A Pharaoh, R M Jacques, J B Attenborough, L M Clark, A W Horsfield, G T Bolton, J Dodd, P R L Lewis, H L Waters, R S Monteith, A H S Goslett, R J Read, J S Espey, G M Beal, M R Bridger. *Back Row:* L A Hicks, R J Randell, J W Hughes, P R Blyth.

from the cordon were redeployed to normal police duty throughout Northern Rhodesia.[11]

The Cox Commission's recommendation for the formation of police divisions was implemented in 1948. The Superintendent, Western Province, as the senior officer on the Copperbelt had become known, Mr H M L Wilkinson, now became Officer Commanding Western Division, which comprised all stations and posts in the Western and North-Western Provinces. Assistant Superintendent R J Randell was appointed Officer Commanding Northern Division, responsible for Northern Province, which included the area around Fort Rosebery, later to become Luapula Province. Central Division under Acting Superintendent A J I Hawkins (Bwana Kabwata), covered most of the rest of the Territory, with stations at Broken Hill (Divisional Headquarters), Lusaka, Chisamba, Fort Jameson, Mongu, Mazabuka and Monze. Arrangements for Livingstone and Choma remained unchanged. 3 gazetted officers, 14 members of the inspectorate and 56 African detectives were serving with the CID territory-wide.

CID Headquarters and the Paymaster's Office were now moved to Lusaka,

Colonel J. E. Workman, Commissioner of Police, 1947–51 (Nkhwazi)

while the Training Depot and Paymaster's Stores remained at Livingstone. The stores were redesignated 'Police Stores', and the Paymaster became 'Officer in Charge Stores and Accounts'. At the Depot were 1 superintendent, 1 inspector, 1 African inspector, 2 sergeants-major, 8 sergeants, 1 African detective inspector and 1 detective sergeant. The establishment provided for an assistant superintendent and two more inspectors. 219 African recruits were obtained. The drum and fife band led a successful recruiting drive on the Copperbelt. However a number of recruits were found to suffering from hookworm and bilharzia. Recruits' rations were increased to include 1½ lbs of meat each week with an orange every day.[12]

Orders were placed for wireless equipment to link the eight main stations with Force Headquarters. One motor vehicle at each of these stations was also to be fitted with radio. Lusaka, with a station staff of 10 Europeans and 80 African police, had two Chevrolet vanettes, one Ford vanette and a Dodge 15 hundred-weight truck, together with three or four BSA 350cc motor cycles. There was also a 'fire engine', the property of Lusaka Town Management Board, kept at the police station. This was a red three ton flat top truck with foam tanks and various pieces of elementary fire fighting equipment. There was still no Fire Brigade in the capital. European police in Lusaka were paid a retainer of £2 a month by the Town Management Board for performing fire fighting duties, which they did with much enthusiasm – if moderate skill. It is said that it was after a fire at Tarry's agricultural and hardware store in the early Nineteen Fifties an insurance assessor reported that the water damage far exceeded the fire damage and the Municipality thereupon decided that it must have a professional full-time fire brigade.

In 1948 the salary of an Assistant Inspector Grade II had increased to £490 a year, rising by annual increments of £20 to £690, and by further increments of £25 a year to £740. Promotion to Inspector could bring further annual increments of £25 to reach the top of the Inspectors' Scale at £840 a year. A uniform allowance of £12 a year was also paid.

After the United Kingdom gave up its mandate over Palestine in May 1948, the Palestine Police became for a short time an even more common source of European recruits than the British South Africa Police. Of 44 European recruits in 1949, 17 had served in Palestine, one in the Singapore Police, one in Ceylon and 6 in the BSAP.

In 1948 No.D155 Detective Sergeant Mathew Phiri was awarded the King's Police Medal for Gallantry. He had made an arrest when his prisoner speared him. Nevertheless Phiri brought the man in over many miles of bush. He later became a Detective Assistant Inspector. 499 Inspector Mkuzo became the first African member of the Force to be awarded the Colonial Police Medal for Meritorious Service. No.1978 Detective Constable Kapelanshila was awarded the Royal Humane Society's Medal for Life Saving.[13]

At the beginning of 1949 the uniform for European police officers was shorts, bush-shirt (now worn without a tie), and khaki stockings, with brown shoes and belt and brass buttons. The Wolseley helmet, now worn with a brass Force badge in front, instead of the old blue and white flash on the side, was their only headwear, except for immigration officers who wore khaki peaked caps. When two general duties assistant inspectors acted as motor cycle escort to the Governor, now Sir Gilbert Rennie, for the opening of the Kafue Road Bridge, they borrowed caps from immigration colleagues as being more likely to survive the sixty mile round trip intact.[14]

By the end of 1949 the Force had changed to the Colonial Police Service uniform. European police officers adopted the dark blue cap with black mohair band and black patent leather peak. The buttons and badges for all ranks were henceforth of white metal and all foot and other leather wear, black. The khaki stockings for Europeans now had blue tops. All in all the new uniform was more easily recognisable to British eyes as that of a policeman. The khaki helmet was retained for full dress and, if required, for hot weather, but with a blue pugri.

Before the War Mr Hart, had expressed a preference to change the Force badge to one on more conventional police lines, surmounted by a crown. Mr Martin Morris of the Livingstone Travel and Publicity Bureau made a design with the fish eagle and fish superimposed on a roundel on which appeared the title 'NORTHERN RHODESIA POLICE'. The roundel was surmounted by a Tudor Crown. The new Commissioner, Colonel Workman, favoured this design, which was similar to the badge of the Fiji Police, and the new badge was now introduced. It was used for cap, fez and collar badges, the old design being used on the new buttons.[15]

African police now wore a short sleeved open necked bush jacket in working dress, with a dark blue helmet shaped rather like a miner's safety helmet. This helmet bore the new chrome Force badge in front.

Identity cards had now been issued to both uniformed police and detectives. For a short time a chrome hexagon replaced the Bath Star in the rank badges of an assistant superintendent, but the traditional star was soon revived.[16]

In February 1949 Mr R S Crighton, a retired superintendent of the Metropolitan Police, arrived in Northern Rhodesia to advise on training. It was planned to retain him as Chief Instructor at the Depot but due to ill-health he could not take up the appointment.[17]

The Training Depot continued to occupy the old Barotse Native Police Lines at Livingstone. On Fridays, after instruction had finished for the day, squads would march to the banks of the Maramba River, a mile away, to collect mud to smear on the earth floors of the old tin roofed, pole and dagga barrack huts. Different muds were used to produce coloured patterns. When the floors had been suitably decorated the recruits would lay their kit out before retiring to the sand in front of their quarters to sleep, leaving the interior ready for Saturday morning inspection, a feature of training establishments throughout the British Commonwealth and Empire.

The Depot kitchen arrangements were by traditional 'Missionary' sized cooking pots over open fires. The African recruits paraded by squads at mealtimes, bringing with them banana leaves on which they received their maize porridge and relish, before carrying it away to eat under the trees.

European officers, including the Officer Commanding, Mr Davidson, took part in the football matches which were a regular fixture at the Maramba Location ground. It is said that, on one occasion, Mr Davidson, at centre forward, kicked off at the start by passing the ball smartly to his second in command, Tom Coton,

Motor cycle patrol circa 1950 (NRPA)

who kicked it up the field. The Officer Commanding set off in pursuit of the ball, but was unable to catch up with it. The opposition fled at this onslaught of senior officers and the ball rolled gently into the net without being played again. There were no Depot canteen facilities. Passing out parties and other celebrations were also held at Maramba Location, (now Mulamba Township).[18]

Training for African recruits lasted six months, but from August 1949 squads only remained at Livingstone for the first three months and completed their training at the newly formed Mobile Unit at Bwana Mkubwa.

The Copperbelt riots of 1935 and 1940 had demonstrated the need for a striking force which could be used to rapidly reinforce the general duties police officers should any unrest or crime waves occur in any area. The military might not always be available and the demands of training for modern war left them little time to devote to internal security training. The problem was in essence that identified by General Edwards, the Commandant-General of Rhodesian Forces, back in 1920 – training for war is not the ideal for effective police work.

It was therefore decided to form a unit within the Force for use as a mobile reserve. The sum of £2,000 was voted to establish it. The next problem was where this mobile unit should be stationed when not required to take the field. Obviously it should be on or near the Copperbelt. The Bwana Mkubwa Mine site was now again vacant as the last of the Polish refugees had been transferred to a camp near Lusaka in 1947. The Bush had, of course, crept back in, attacking the Kimberley

246

brick and thatch barracks erected for them, but it seemed to be the site which could most easily and cheaply be made ready.

In June 1949 Mr C N Breen, Assistant Superintendent, Officer in Charge at Ndola, despatched Assistant Inspector D Butcher to inspect the site. The grass had grown so tall that many of the houses could not be seen, but it was apparent that some were habitable and many others could be repaired. Under 'Danny' Breen's direction, Assistant Inspector R J Jowett took charge of clearing the Bush and repairing houses.

By July sufficient progress had been made to enable Inspector L M Clark to move in with 75 men from the Training Depot and commence training. Inspector and Mrs Clark occupied the only European married quarter, a house which remained the Commanding Officer's residence for fifteen years during which the Mobile Unit grew to a strength of 800, the equivalent of an infantry battalion, and the post of the Commanding Officer was upgraded to Senior Superintendent. In August 1949 Assistant Inspectors A D Milne and M Townley joined the Unit.

Training took place from 0600hrs until 1300hrs while, in the afternoons, all performed fatigues, building the camp round them. A high priority and the most difficult job was clearing and levelling the parade ground. The trees were cut down and their stumps dug out, but there remained a large number of ant hills.

African police recruit squad at the depot circa 1952 (Photo D. I. Oliver)
L to R Front Row: Insp M Mataka, first African Commissioner of the Zambia Police, A/Supt J B Seed, Supt T M Davidson, Supt A Wallace, Insp D I Oliver.

A local farmer helped tackle some of these, by ploughing round the bottom of each ant hill until it resembled a sphere rather than a cone. A squad would then descend on this sphere with picks and hoes, breaking it up and scattering the earth. The sites of these ant hills could be identified ten years later in patches of grass greener than the norm.

The Unit manufactured its own Kimberley bricks and cut its own thatch for building and repairing quarters. Latrines were dug. During the dry season bush fires were frequent, threatening to destroy the results of hard work. On one occasion three newly thatched huts went up in smoke while the fire party with their stirrup pumps were kept at bay by the intense heat.

The Polish priest's house, which required little repair, contained a lifesize mural of the crucifixion. This house was allocated to the senior African policeman, Inspector Mkuzo, a devout catholic.

With recruits spending their second three months of training at Bwana Mkubwa, the total intake of recruits at the Training Depot could be increased. As the additional recruits passed out and joined their stations a surplus of trained men became available. In October 1949 one hundred such NCOs and constables from stations throughout the Territory were posted to Bwana Mkubwa to form the first operational platoons of the Mobile Unit which was issued with five vehicles for their use. A number of them had been wartime soldiers and they took to the internal security training with great enthusiasm. Eventually a system of direct entry to the Mobile Unit was introduced with recruits who lacked the required educational qualifications for training for general police duties.

A Wireless Telegraphy School was also established at Bwana Mkubwa under Sergeant-Major Mukandawire, late of the Department of Posts and Telegraphs. 16 African police passed through his hands during 1949.[19]

The last building job of the year, after the completion of the African police canteen, was the Inspectors' Mess, which was formally opened by the Deputy Commissioner, Mr Verrall, on Boxing Day 1949 when the Northern Rhodesia Police Mobile Unit was considered well and truly launched.[20]

During 1949 steel helmets were issued to all ranks on the Copperbelt including, of course, the Mobile Unit, which was under the overall command of the Officer Commanding, Western Division.

The building programme for the Northern Rhodesia Police as a whole was such that a Force Building or 'Pioneer' Unit was authorised, staffed by an inspector of works and 2 European building foreman with 33 African workmen. A police inspector posted to a proposed police and immigration station at Nakonde was instructed that, on arrival, he would find the materials necessary to commence brick making, after which he was to build the station. Happily, before the building was finished an African building foreman arrived to assist him. The following year, 1950, the Pioneer Unit completed stations at Kawambwa, Lundazi and Solwezi and started work on the site for the new training school at Lilayi.[21]

In 1948 the governments of Northern Rhodesia and the Belgian Congo had become worried about the amount of fish being taken from Lake Mweru, and the effect of over-fishing on breeding. A joint commission of experts advised that, provided fishing was prohibited in certain breeding grounds, it would be safe to allow 4,000 tons a year to be taken from the Lake. The appropriate legislation was enacted in each territory. The prohibited grounds were all in the eastern or North-ern Rhodesia half of the Lake. They were clearly marked by booms constructed from empty forty-four gallon petrol drums joined together by chains.

The major commercial fishermen were Greeks working from Kasenga, in the Congo, where four shipyards were established by 1950. These had turned out about sixty vessels of a design used in the Dodecanese, each capable of carrying up to four tons of fish packed in ice. Each craft carried two or three dinghies, was equipped with about twenty nets, and was driven by fast and efficient modern diesel engines. The Greeks decided that their immediate profits were more important than even their own long term interests. They decided to ignore the new legislation.

In 1950 Assistant Inspector B D Powell was posted, as Officer in Charge, to the newly built police station at Kawambwa. The problem was referred to him and he consulted the Belgian Administrateur at Kasenga. This offical had no European police officer in his district, but agreed that if the NRP caught any Greek poachers, he would deal with them. 'Chunky' Powell's next problem was to find a boat. He consulted the District Commissioner, Kawambwa, and was provided with a twenty foot wooden launch on loan from the Development Auth-ority. Built in Durban and fitted with a suitably powerful twin cylinder diesel engine, the 'Kilwa' had been laid up for some time, but Powell managed to put it to rights, obtain fuel, and even fit a searchlight. He had kept a constable posted in the relevant area for some time to report on the movements and routine of the poachers. At about 2200hrs one night Inspector Powell finally set sail from Nchi-lenga with three constables and a large Union Flag. The unsuspecting poachers did not question the arrival of a strange craft in their midst and did not spot the flag. They assumed that they had been joined by fellow lawbreakers.

Powell stopped his engine and drifted until three vessels had spread their nets nearby. He then started his engine, switched on his searchlight and headed for the nearest boat at full speed. As he came alongside a constable leapt aboard the Greek vessel. The second offending vessel was also taken before it had time to haul in its nets. The third sped off into the night. Powell gave chase and overtook it after a mile or two, whereupon the Greek implored him not to open fire!

The three prizes came quietly into Nchilenga. The master of the last vessel taken appeared put out to find no gun mounted on the 'Kilwa'. The next day the convoy sailed to Kasenga where Inspector Powell was invited to prosecute in the Administrateur's court. The Administrateur, who had served with the United States forces during the War, acted as both interpreter and magistrate! Heavy fines served to show the Greeks the error of their ways. Poaching in the breeding areas on Lake Mweru ceased, but the Officer in Charge, Kawambwa, was able to enjoy the use of the 'Kilwa' for some less exciting patrols.[22]

Wireless sets had now been installed at Force Headquarters and main stations, and one set had been fitted in a motor vehicle for experimental purposes. The first traffic section was formed with three European officers at Ndola to cover the Copperbelt road network, although one road patrol was performed, via Kapiri Mposhi, as far as Abercorn. In its first year the Traffic Section dealt with 437 offences. Force transport now consisted of 7 cars for senior officers, 2 panel vans, 31 vanettes, 4 lorries for building works, 17 troop carrying vehicles, 1 mobile canteen (at the Mobile Unit with 9 of the troop carriers), 24 motor-cycles, 210 bicycles, 4 horses, and, undergoing trials, 4 jeeps and land rovers.[23]

In August 1950 Superintendent A Wallace was appointed to command a new Southern Division, with Headquarters at Livingstone, and responsible for the stations at Choma, Monze, Mazabuka, and Mongu, the last three having until then belonged to Central Division.

On 24 April 1950 Mr G E Jackson ARCM, formerly bandmaster of The Queen's Own Royal West Kent Regiment, took up the new appointment of Bandmaster in the Northern Rhodesia Police and the task of converting the Drums and Fifes to a full military band. Twelve brass instruments were supplied that year. In January 1951 the Band was moved from the Training Depot to join the Mobile Unit at Bwana Mkubwa. When Mr Jackson left on resignation in December 1951 the Band had thirty brass and woodwind instruments.[24]

During 1950 12,411 Penal Code and 22,502 other offences were recorded. 28,214 cases were prosecuted, resulting in 26,732 convictions. In December 1950 the strength of the Force was 1472 out of an establishment of 1799. The deficiency was made up of one gazetted officer, 25 inspectors and 301 African police. From 2nd May until 31st August 1950 three assistant inspectors were seconded to the Bechuanaland Police due to the unrest following the marriage and deportation of Chief Seretse Khama.[25]

By mid-1951 Colonel Workman was due to retire as Commissioner of Police, but had first to show his successor, Mr Fforde round his command. Fforde arrived by air at Ndola in August to be met by Workman and Mr A J I Hawkins, com-

Chevrolet Vanette (NRPA)

manding Western Division. After a three day tour of Copperbelt stations Workman and Fforde left for Lusaka. Six days later Fforde saw Workman off from
Livingstone Airport. Colonel Workman was to enjoy nearly 25 years of retirement.

John Percy Ilbert Fforde was forty one years of age. He had entered the Palestine Police in 1931. In 1941, as an assistant superintendent in the Criminal Investigation Department he was awarded the Colonial Police Medal for Gallantry after
taking part in a shoot out with members of Irgun Levi. His only companion in
this affair, Geoffrey Morton, was to become Commissioner of Police in Nyasaland[26]. Later in 1941 John Fforde was seconded for service with the British Military Government in occupied Syria. In 1946, with the military rank of colonel, he
was promoted Assistant Inspector General, commanding the Criminal Investigation Department of the Palestine Police. In 1948 Fforde became Commissioner
of Police in Sierra Leone and it was from that post that he came to Northern
Rhodesia. A man of impressive personality and energy, he was to command the
Northern Rhodesia Police for eleven years of expansion and modernisation against
a background of political unrest and uncertainty.

The new Commissioner found a force of 47 gazetted officers and 200 European
inspectors and 1,720 African police. There were 32 police stations and posts grouped in to four divisions. The annual expenditure on the Force was £506,821.
One Assistant Commissioner, 5 superintendents, 12 assistant superintendents, 83
inspectors, 12 African inspectors, 13 sergeants-major, 71 sergeants and 791 constables were stationed on the Copperbelt. The Special Branch, instituted in 1948
consisted of one superintendent, one assistant superintendent and 12 inspectors.
Five of these officers had attended courses with MI.5 in London.

Fforde had no time to settle in to the job gently. Within two and a half weeks
of his coming to the Territory, the Colonial Secretary, James Griffiths[27], arrived
for a two week visit prior to the opening of the Victoria Falls Conference to
discuss the federation of the two Rhodesias and Nyasaland. Six weeks after his
arrival the new Commissioner was required to appear before the budget sub-
committee of the Legislative Council with the Police estimates for 1952. The new
establishment was to be for a total of 2,335, including 2,039 African police.

Fforde was concerned with the problems of command and control caused by
the vast area of the Territory, now with a population of some 1,890,000. He
decided that police divisional boundaries should conform to administrative boundaries and that accordingly the number of divisions should be increased.[28]

He gave impetus to the programme of improvement in wireless communi-
cations. A Home Office expert was sent out to make a survey, and Mr A W
Rhodes was seconded from the Birmingham City Police arriving on 15 November
1951 as Force Signals Officer in the rank of assistant superintendent. Arnold
Rhodes was to remain with the Northern Rhodesia Police for the rest of its history.
In 1952 a Chevrolet 'pickup' vehicle No. NRG1838 appeared on the Copperbelt
fitted with VHF radio, a loud hailer and a siren. Driven by Assistant Inspector
Tony Kirby, it was the first vehicle in the Force to be so equipped. No.88 'Walkie
Talkie' sets were issued to stations on the line of rail.[29]

Fforde had talks with the Director of Civil Aviation, Muspratt-Williams, an
old school friend, concerning the possible use of aircraft for police communications

and the transport of reinforcements in emergencies. The talks also covered training for such eventualities and the organisation of police search parties in the event of aircrashes. Government approval was obtained for the acquisition of a Rapide aircraft, on which the Commissioner of Police was to have first call. Inspector G H Layne, a former Royal Air Force pilot, was transferred from Mazabuka to Lusaka to be available to fly this plane when required for police purposes.

The Cox Commission had recommended the introduction of the rank of Senior Superintendent. The first officer to be promoted to this rank was Mr George Carr-Smith in 1950. He was further promoted to Assistant Commissioner on 1 January 1951. A First World War veteran of the South African Scottish, he had joined the South African Police in 1924 and the NRP in January 1927. On 21st September 1951 Mr Carr-Smith was promoted to Deputy Commissioner following Mr Verrall's transfer to the Bahamas as Commissioner of Police.

Mr F A Roberts, Superintendent, took over command of the Training Depot when Mr Davidson was promoted Senior Superintendent and appointed Chief Commandant of the Northern Rhodesia Police Reserve, with the task of raising and organising this new part-time force. In the months of November and December 1951 an intensive recruiting campaign was pursued. 650 Europeans, Asians and Coloureds were recruited for the Reserve against an establishment of 1,445, and 139 Africans for an establishment of 928. Four regular officers were permanently employed with the reserve as staff officers.[30] In March 1953 the first women reservists were recruited. By 1961 there were 332, all Europeans.

The Northern Rhodesia Police Reserve included an Air Wing recruited from the flying clubs at Lusaka, Livingstone, Nkana, Ndola, Luanshya and Mufulira. Most of the pilots had flown in the armed forces. The wing used a variety of light aircraft, some belonging to members and others to the clubs. A pilot required a valid licence and either to have logged 500 hours or a minimum of 150 hours as pilot in charge, having landed at 10 different aerodromes, flown three different types of aircraft, and completed a 300 mile cross country flight. Holders of valid licences with at least 50 hours flying as pilot in charge, who had made landings at at least five different aerodromes and completed a 100 mile cross country flight were permitted to join as observers. They were not allowed to pilot a plane on operational duties unless they happened to own it![31]

The Cox Commission had concluded that the best way of patrolling the Territory's bushland was on horseback, that mounted patrols could exercise improved supervision over farming areas, and that a mounted police unit should prove extremely useful in keeping down bush fires and the illegal killing of game. Accordingly it had recommended that a small mounted detachment of European and African police should be set up at Lusaka. On 24 December 1951 three horses arrived at Lusaka from South Africa. Although several European officers had had mounted training and experience with other forces, there were no African police with any experience of horses at all. The Commissioner of the British South Africa Police, always a mounted force, offered assistance in training instructors and farriers.[32]

During 1951 three officers attended the Senior Course and five the Junior

Course at the newly established Police Staff College then at Ryton-on-Dunsmore.[33]

The rank of chief inspector had been abolished in 1945 and inspector was the highest non-gazetted rank until the rank of Senior Inspector was introduced in 1952. At the same time it was decided that all rank titles of those below assistant superintendent appointed to the Criminal Investigation Department should bear the prefix 'Detective'.

On 3 February 1952 the Lusaka Sub-Division was formed for an experimental period of six months under Mr D W Humphrey, Superintendent. The experiment was deemed a success and on 1st August 1952 all stations in the Lusaka Administrative District became part of Lusaka Division.[34]

On 27 February 1952 Mr George King, formerly of the bands of The Royal Scots and Royal Signals, Assistant Bandmaster of the British South Africa Police, was appointed to the post of Bandmaster of the Northern Rhodesia Police left vacant by Mr Jackson's departure two months before. In June 1952 Mr King took the Band on a tour of Eastern Province. This was the first tour of any of the rural areas by the Band. Such tours, of up to three months duration now became annual events, covering the whole Territory.

In May 1952 there was a strike among African railway workers. At Broken Hill on 17 May some Watch Tower members, who were also railwaymen, wanted to return to work. This angered the strikers. A platoon of the Mobile Unit was quickly flown down to deal with the situation. A crowd of 300 was dispersed with tear smoke. There were no further incidents.

The British Labour Party, at its annual conference, condemned the idea of a Central African Federation unless the African inhabitants of the two northern territories agreed to it. This coincided with a demand by African mineworkers for higher wages. There was a general strike from 20 October until 10 November without disorder. However on 1 December 1952 violence broke out at Mulobezi during a strike by Zambezi Sawmills employees. Police were flown in from Livingstone and five men were subsequently convicted for threatening violence and each sentenced to four months imprisonment.[35]

On 12 November 1952 Mr E H Halse MBE returned to the Force as Deputy Commissioner on transfer back from Somaliland where he had been Commissioner of Police since 1950. 'Uncle George' Carr-Smith, as he was affectionately known, retired from the Northern Rhodesia Police but remained living in the Woodlands suburb of Lusaka serving as Divisional Commandant of the Police Reserve, with the rank of Reserve Superintendent until his death in 1959. He was also Sergeant-at-Arms of the Legislative Council, a member of Lusaka Municipal Council and Chairman of the Lusaka Race Relations Committee.

By the end of 1952 the strength of the Northern Rhodesia Police had risen to 264 European officers and 1,943 African policemen against an establishment of 286 Europeans and 2,039 Africans. During the year the Force had dealt with 15,327 offences against the Penal Code and 14,568 against local laws, exclusive of traffic offences. 21,597 prosecutions had resulted in 20,385 convictions. A new station had been opened at Wusikili outside Kitwe under A/Supt J B Seed with A/Insp G B Bird, a sub-inspector, sergeant and 30 constables. A station had also opened at Chirundu with an assistant inspector, an immigration officer, a sergeant, a wireless constable and four other constables.

On 1 January 1953 the Central Division was further reduced when Eastern Division Headquarters opened at Fort Jameson, under Mr E A Morgan, Assistant Superintendent, with responsibility for the whole of Eastern Province. In addition to the police station at Fort Jameson there was one at Lundazi and a police post under an African NCO at Nyimba[36]. 'Tash' Morgan had joined the Northern Rhodesia Police in 1946 after service in the Uganda and Palestine forces.

During January the first issue of the Force magazine *Nkhwazi* appeared, edited by Mr Gordon Layne, Acting Superintendent. This was one of the methods of fostering esprit de corps encouraged by the new Commissioner, Mr Fforde. The cover design and title were suggested by Mr L M Clark, now an assistant superintendent.

Also in January 1953 Mr Fforde, with Mr J C Day, then commanding the CID and Special Branch, and Mr J M Helliwell, Chief Commandant of the Northern Rhodesia Police Reserve, visited Kenya to see the methods used by the Kenya Police and British Army to combat the 'Mau Mau' Rebellion there.

In February, there was an outbreak of lawlessness among the fisherfolk who inhabited the Luapula Valley south of Lake Mweru. These people were traditionally averse to the need for authority. In this instance, encouraged by the African National Congress, they were protesting against fish conservation legislation, including the imposition of closed seasons, measures introduced in their own long term interests. Their attitude was 'God gave us the fish. Who are you to stop us taking it when we like?' It was a common Congress tactic to encourage Africans to refuse to comply with measures which might be irritating, but were introduced for their own good. Later in the decade Congress organised refusals to bring cattle for dipping in the Southern Province. If compliance was enforced, resentment increased, if it was not enforced, disease would spread, leading to hardship and discontent. Either way Congress could not lose.

At the beginning of April 1953 Congress attempted to organise a two day general strike, or 'National Days of Prayer', as they described them, in protest against Federation. It was not a great success from their point of view, although 80 per cent of African mineworkers at Mufulira absented themselves from work, only 150 of the Territory's 7,000 African civil servants stayed away and there was not one absentee among the African police.

In June 1953 Mr Jack Helliwell, Senior Superintendent, Chief Commandant of the Northern Rhodesia Police Reserve, was transferred to Nyasaland as Deputy Commissioner of Police. He was soon to see old friends there.

Late on 22 August the majority of the Mobile Unit were at Kitwe celebrating victory in the Western Division Inter-Station Sports Championship. Back at Bwana Mkubwa Mr J B Seed, Assistant Superintendent, was in command of the standby party with Inspector W R Allen and Assistant Inspector Joe Grincell, when the Commissioner telephoned from Lusaka to say that a detachment was required to leave immediately for Nyasaland where serious disturbances had broken out in the Chola District, where Chief Gomani, deposed by the Government, was heading the African National Congress Council of Action. Congress had advised the people not to pay rent, not to observe rules concerning agriculture and not to take part in celebrations of the Coronation of Her Majesty Queen Elizabeth II. Trouble was sparked off at a citrus estate at Thyolo when the owner and his son caught Africans with sacks of stolen oranges. There were also incidents at Ncheu and Mangunda, the largest citrus estate in Nyasaland.

Three platoons were mobilised. Inspectors brought hurriedly back from their jollifications at Kitwe were pushed under a cold shower and bundled into troop carriers. At midnight the company of 126 officers and men was on the road, led by the Commanding Officer of the Unit, Mr C N Halse. Two and a half days later they arrived in Blantyre. The detachment remained in the Southern Province of Nyasaland on operations until 17 November. In all the disturbances cost the lives of 11 Africans and 72 persons were injured. Allen, Grincell, African Inspector Dare and Sergeant Mpezeni, a Burma veteran, earned special commendations for courage and leadership when faced with rioters at Namitambo on 28th August. This was the first award of certificates of Special Commendation, another of Mr Fforde's innovations.[37] Willie Dare was also awarded the Colonial Police Medal for Meritorious Service for his conduct during these operations.

'Big Paddy' Allen, the eldest and largest of a string of brothers who served in the Force in the Fifties and Sixties, did himself permanent injury when, single-handed, he lifted an overturned landrover to free a constable pinned under it by the arm. Happily this was not the end of Allen's career. He served on to become a superintendent.

On 30 August 1953 an accident occurred which brought to an end the useful life of the Rapide aircraft and nearly brought to an end that of Mr Fforde. He had decided to fly to visit the detachment in Nyasaland. With a civilian pilot, Ted Lenton, and two reinforcements for the detachment, assistant inspectors J G Webster and D J Crowther, he was due to spend the night at Fort Jameson. They encountered stiff crosswinds and their radio beacon equipment failed. Unable to find Fort Jameson, Lenton was finally forced by lack of fuel to crash land just after 2100hrs. He brought the Rapide down by the Munyamadzi River, a tributary of the Luangwa, opposite the small village of Lambwe in Chief Nawalya's area of the Mpika District. Thanks to the villagers a rescue party was able to find the Commissioner's party within thirty-six hours and bring them to Lundazi. From there they were flown to Lusaka by the Royal Air Force. None were seriously hurt except Mr Fforde, who suffered injury to his back which was to keep him away from his duties until December and was to cause him permanent trouble.[38]

In 1953 a new badge was issued. At the first senior officers' conference after Mr Fforde took over command, the majority view was that the Force should resume its original badge of 1933, still borne on the buttons, but with the addition of a crown. In July 1952 the Lord Chamberlain's approval was received for the use of St Edward's Crown, introduced by Her Majesty Queen Elizabeth on her accession in preference to the Tudor Crown. Headdress and collar badges as well as buttons now bore the new design in chrome. This was the final badge of the Northern Rhodesia Police.[39]

It was in 1953 that the Northern Rhodesia Police had an encounter with Holly-wood, when Associated British–Marcel Hellman Productions came to Livingstone to shoot a film entitled *Duel in the Jungle*, starring Jeanne Crain, David Farrar and Dana Andrews. The plot centred on an adventurer who, after faking his own suicide, disappeared into the African bush to prospect for diamonds financed by the proceeds of the insurance policy on his own life. His fiancee and an insurance investigator trace him and trouble ensues.

A number of members of the Force had small 'walk on' parts and training at the Depot was virtually at a halt whilst recruits, noticeable for their clean white vests and khaki drill shorts, acted as villagers and carriers. The 'Police' appeared in a number of sequences with actors and extras wearing the uniform of the Northern Rhodesia Police, with the exception of their shoulder titles which were 'CAP' for 'Central African Police' instead of 'NRP'. The film was noteworthy for the sight of an ocean-going liner docking just opposite the North-Western Hotel! Later, the hero and heroine leave Livingstone by motor vehicle and in no time are at a village in the Northern Transvaal.

Most memorable of all to members of the Force was the performance of Inspector Michael Mataka, the senior African instructor at the Training Depot, who had joined the Force in 1941. With commendable foresight the casters had not chosen an American negro actor to play the part of 'Vincent', the resourceful and faithful guide who escorts the hero and heroine through many vicissitudes to the eventual happy ending. They chose Mataka. In one scene the villain suspends him by a rope from a tree as a punishment and as a warning to his fellow Africans, his own recruits, who are forced to sit round and watch. Many recruits would have been delighted to see an instructor so treated!

Michael Mataka accompanied the makers back to England for the completion

Armoured car Mobile Unit 1953 (NRPA)

of the film[40]. He was offered a film contract, but chose to return to his duties. This was a wise decision as in 1966 Michael Mataka became the first African Commissioner of the Zambia Police.

Training was soon back to normal. 311 African recruits were attested in 1953. During the year the Force dealt with 16,721 Penal Code offences and 17,778 against other laws. Exclusive of traffic offences there were 24,695 cases prosecuted and 23,478 convictions. 2,210 road traffic accidents were reported resulting in 107 deaths. 1,160 persons were injured on the roads. On 2 March a station had opened at Mufulira Mine Township and on 23 March a post opened at Kabushi on the Kafuba River with a sergeant, a detective constable and 18 other constables. In May a police station was established at Petauke under A/Insp Nicholas with Sgt Kapondole and 4 constables. In June a police station was opened at Mindolo, Kitwe, under Inspector B G Coase with two assistant inspectors, Sub/Insp Sitaka and twenty six African police. Another new station was at Samfya on Lake Bangweulu with an assistant inspector, Sgt Lupashya and 12 constables. The establishment of the Force was increased to 344 Europeans and 2,530 African police and the estimate for the maintenance of the Force £780,000.[41]

Notes

1. F-M Ld Horatio Herbt KITCHENER KG b1850 Franco-Prussian War 70 Lt RE'71 Egypt'85 Sirdar'92 COS SA'99 CinC SA 12.00 India 02 IG Overseas Fces 09 Br Agent Egypt 11 SofS War 8.14 drnd 15
2. Cox Commission Report National Police College Library
   Sir Herbt Chas Fahie COX Kt 46 b'93 Sub Insp Br Guiana Police 13 Bar Middle Temple 15 District Insp'16 Army 17 Asst AG 20 AG Bahamas'25 AG Gib'29 Solicitor Gen Nigeria'33 AG'35 CJ NR 46 Tanganyika'52–6 Chmn Commn Inquiry Disturbances Sierra Leone 56 Mbr Dorset CC'63–9 DChmn Wilts Qtr Sessions'64–8 d21.9.73
   Col Harry P RICE OBE KPM 29, RA(V) SAC'06 Cpl SAP 1.4.13 7Bty SAA 7.9.14 Kenya Police, DCmdt CID Pal AIG CID 22.7.32–rtd 38
3. Report 1940–46 IWM
4. *Nkhwazi* Vol 12 No.1 April 1964 p71
5. Report 1940–46 IWM
6. *Nkhwazi* April 1964 p51
7. Cox Commission report Bramshill
8. NR Report 1940–46 IWM
9. Cox Commission report Bramshill
10. Annual report 1947 Rhodes House
11. *Nkhwazi* Apr'64 p39
12. Annual report 1948 Rhodes House
13. *Nkhwazi* Apr'64 p12
14. Sir Gilbert McCall RENNIE K(49)CMG 41 MC Kt 46 b95 ed Stirling HS Glasgow U 2Lt 3KOSB'15 Bde Maj, Cdt Ceylon 20 Police Mag Ceylon'23 Addtnl Dist Judge'25 Cntrllr Fin & Supplies 32 Govt Sec 34 Fin Sec Gold Coast'37 Ch Sec Kenya'39 Gov NR'48 HCommr Fedn Rhod & Nyasald Londn'54–61 Chmn UK Cttee Freedom fm Hunger Campaign & Jt Treasr Royal Soc of Arts'65
15. *Nkhwazi* Vol 11 N0.1 May 63 p15
16. *Nkhwazi* Apr'64 p39
17. Annual report 1949 Rhodes House
18. *Nkhwazi* Apr'64; letter to author fm D I Oliver
19. *Nkhwazi* Apr'64; Annual report 1949 Rhodes House

20. Milne 'Early Days at the Mobile Unit' *Nkhwazi* Vol 8 No.3 Dec 60 p8 & Apr'64 p95
21. *Nkhwazi* Apr'64; Annual report 1949, Arrigonie in *British Colonialism* Edward Gaskell publishers Bideford ISBN 1-898546-26-6 Chap 6 gives an account of Nakonde
22. Powell *A Fishy Case Nkhwazi* Vol 6 No.2 June 1958 p5
23. *Nkhwazi* Apr'64 p42; Annual report 1950 Rhodes House
24. *Nkhwazi* Apr'64 p42, 59
25. Annual report 1950
26. Geoffrey J MORTON Pal Police'30 Trinidad P'45 CofP Nyasald '48–53
27. Rt Hon Jas GRIFFITHS PC 45 CH 66 b90 MP(Lab) Llanelly'36 Min Nat Insce'45 SofS Colonies'50 Wales'64–6 d'75
28. Fforde unpublished memoir *Eleven years in Northern Rhodesia*
29. Annual report 1951 Rhodes House
30. Annual report 1951 Rhodes House, *Nkhwazi* Apr'64
31. *Nkhwazi* Apr'64; G R Sunderland *Northern Rhodesia Police Air Wing* Air Britain Digest Jul/Aug 1985
32. *Nkhwazi* Vol 7 No.1 Mar59 p18
33. Annual report Rhodes House
34. *Nkhwazi* Apr'64 p42
35. Annual report 1952 Rhodes House
36. *Nkhwazi* Apr'64 p42
37. Annual report 1953 Rhodes House; *Nkhwazi* Apr 64 p42; MPEZENI served for many years with the Mobile Unit as a sergeant-major/head constable
38. Fforde *Eleven years in Northern Rhodesia*
39. *Nkhwazi* Vol 11 No.1 May 63 p15, Apr 64 p42–4
40. *Nkhwazi* Apr'64 p55–6
41. B G Coase Rhodes House, *Nkhwazi*'53 & Apr'64

CHAPTER 14

Towards a New Dominion

On 3 September 1953 the territories of Northern Rhodesia and Nyasaland and the internally self governing colony of Southern Rhodesia were joined in the ill-fated Federation of Rhodesia and Nyasaland or Central African Federation. Ever since 1924 the whites in Northern Rhodesia had sought what they saw as the security of closer links with the south with its larger European population. In 1936 there had been a conference at the Victoria Falls Hotel between unofficials from Northern Rhodesia and members of the various political parties of Southern Rhodesia. This conference recommended amalgamation of north and south. Consequently the British Government appointed the Bledisloe Commission[1] to explore the feasibility of closer association between the two Rhodesias and Nyasaland. Thus, at an early stage, it was clear that the price that the whites of Southern Rhodesia would have to pay to share in the mineral wealth of the Copperbelt, and those north of the Zambezi for the desired link with the south, would be the inclusion of purely rural Nyasaland with at least as large an African population as Northern Rhodesia and only about one-sixth of the number of Europeans. The Bledisloe Commission duly reported in 1939 that closer association of the three territories was desirable, although the Africans in the northern territories were averse to closer links with the south.

In 1945 a Central African Council was established in Salisbury. In the same year the constitution of Northern Rhodesia was amended to provide for an enlarged Legislative Council of nine officials, eight elected white unofficials and five members nominated by the Governor. The Executive Council was to consist of five official and three unofficial members.

In 1946 there had been further constitutional changes. An African Representative Council was created. Chaired by the Secretary for Native Affairs, it was to consist of twenty-five Africans chosen by African Provincial Councils chaired by the respective Provincial Commissioners, and four sent by the Litunga of Barotseland. The African Representative Council was to advise the Governor on any matters affecting Africans and to nominate two Africans as members of the Legislative Council. In 'Legco' there were now to be ten officials, ten elected white unofficials and, in addition to the two Africans, two white unofficial members nominated by the Governor to see that African interests were not neglected. Roy Welensky[2], who had succeeded the ageing Sir Stewart Gore-Brown as leader of the unofficials, predicted that 'by 1968, if the present policy continues, there will be an elected African majority here'.

In 1948 the white politicians demanded responsible government in Northern Rhodesia without delay and threatened to paralyse the Government if they did not get it. There was a conference at Victoria Falls on amalgamation of Northern and Southern Rhodesia, which resulted in a hint from the Labour Colonial Secretary, Arthur Creech Jones[3], that the British Government would be in favour of a federation, including Nyasaland. In November 1949 Welensky made a formal proposal for Federation in the Legislative Council. Acting on instructions the official members abstained. The motion was carried against the votes of the African members.

African opposition grew. In July 1948 the Northern Rhodesia African National Congress had been formed from the Federation of African Societies, originally a grouping of African Welfare Societies from various towns, brought together by Dauti Yamba, a schoolmaster, and George Kaluwa, a Mazabuka businessman. In 1951 Harry Nkumbula, another schoolmaster, or rather ex-schoolmaster, returned to the Territory, having failed to complete a course at the London School of Economics. He took over the leadership of the African National Congress.[4] In September 1951 there was another Victoria Falls Conference and the decision was taken in London that Federation should go ahead.

In April 1952 a communist agitator and adviser to the African National Congress, Simon Ber Zukas, was deported, but continued to maintain contact with African nationalists from London. In December 1952 Donald Siwale proposed in the African Representative Council that, if the Government's policy was partnership between Africans and Europeans, there should be parity between the numbers of Africans and Europeans in the Legislative Council. In April 1953 during the 'National Days of Prayer' Harry Nkumbula burnt a copy of the White Paper on Federation in front of a crowd of nearly 800 at Ndola. In August 1953 another former teacher, Kenneth Kaunda, became Secretary General of the Northern Rhodesia African National Congress.[5]

African opposition to Federation played on fears of settler domination and seizure of African land. Many Administrative officials regarded Federation as a derogation from the trust under which they had been brought up to believe they ruled the African for his own good and not for the benefit of settlers and investors. This was the policy expressed by Lord Passfield, Sidney Webb[6], Secretary of State for the Colonies in 1930, 'That the interests of the African natives must be paramount, and that if those interests and the interests of the immigrant races should conflict, the former should prevail. His Majesty's Government regard themselves as exercising a trust on behalf of the African people, and they are unable to delegate or share this trust, the objective of which may be defined as the protection and advancement of the native races.'

Settler protests led a Joint Select Committee of the United Kingdom Parliament to explain in 1931 that this policy meant, 'No more than that the interests of the overwelming majority of the indigenous population should not be subordinated to those of a minority belonging to any other race, however important in itself'. Sir Hubert Young, on his arrival as Governor of Northern Rhodesia in 1934, had further sweetened the pill by adding that it also meant 'no less than that the interests of the non-native minority must not be subordinated to those of the native majority'.

Now, at the very onset of Federation, all officials were instructed to express only neutral views of its advantages and disadvantages. The Federal Government was now responsible for Defence, Immigration, External Trade, European Education and Communications, whilst the individual governments of the territories continued to be responsible for Law and Order and African Administration and Education. The Federal Assembly of thirty-five members was to include two Africans and one white from each territory, elected to keep watch over African interests.

On 1 February 1954 the Commissioner of Police was giving a cocktail party in honour of the visiting Inspector General of Colonial Police, W Angus Muller[7], when a telephone call was received from the Headquarters of the British South Africa Police. Coalminers had gone on strike at Wankie in Southern Rhodesia, between Bulawayo and the Victoria Falls. The Southern Rhodesia Government had called out troops, but assistance from the NRP was now requested. The cocktail party ended in a planning conference and a detachment of the Northern Rhodesia Police was soon on its way south under Mr F A Roberts, Officer Commanding the Training Depot at Livingstone. The trouble was resolved without the need to resort to force. Many of the strikers were Northern Rhodesia Africans, who were pleased to see their countrymen. Fred Roberts' excellent knowledge of African languages was put to good use. In seven days the miners were back at work and on 8 February the NRP, 6 Europeans and 66 African police, were back on their home ground. The operation helped preserve and enhance the always good relations between the two police forces. The BSAP magazine *Outpost*, reported that the Northern Rhodesia Police had not been regarded as outsiders as they included a number of former members of the Southern Rhodesia Force.[8]

By the end of 1954 the strength of the Northern Rhodesia Police was 329 European officers out of an establishment of 410, and 2,357 African police out of an establishment of 3,030. 194 African recruits had been attested during the year. 22,633 Penal Code offences and 28,235 other offences had been dealt with. Apart from traffic offences there had been 36,416 prosecutions and 34,585 convictions. 2,603 traffic accidents had resulted in 123 deaths and 1,198 persons injured. On 1 November the Federal Immigration Department came into being but a reduced Immigration Division of the NRP under Mr L A Heatlie acted as its agent in Northern Rhodesia for some years.

The dark blue helmets worn in working dress by African police were replaced by khaki covered cork 'polo' helmets of the style worn by South African troops in the early days of the Second World War. This helmet was worn with a dark blue pugri, like that on the Wolseley pattern helmet worn in full dress by European officers. It is said that the African police helmet was changed because, when wearing the plain blue helmet at night with the dark blue greatcoat or raincoat, they were invisible until they smiled! At about this time a grey shirt was issued to African police, also for working dress.

A whole new range of publications were produced under the chief editorship

Dress and equipment armed section

of the Commissioner, including Training Manual, Parts I and II for ceremonial and riot drill, the Northern Rhodesia Police Handbook, and a Cinyanja Manual, for language training. Under Mr Fforde Force Standing Orders became a comprehensive document dealing with administration and policework and were a model of their kind.

The first intermediate headquarters between station and division came into being when Lusaka Central, Woodlands, Kabwata and Matero police stations, with Chinika Post and the Mounted Section, were grouped into Lusaka Urban District under the command of Mr R J Read, Superintendent. In February 1954 a new purpose built station building opened at Woodlands with offices and armoury on the ground floor and two one bedroomed flats for European officers above. This was the first of a number of such buildings for sub-urban stations. The new station was responsible for Kabulonga, Twin Palms, Chelston, Kalingal-

Armed section drill: moving at the High Port

inga and Chilenje where its African Police were accommodated and a post was to open in 1956.[9]

Both Dowbiggin and Cox had recommended that a new site be found for the Training Depot. In 1949 consideration had been given to a site in forest reserve a few miles north of Lusaka, but it was rejected for lack of a water supply. Then Reserve Assistant Inspector P T S Miller offered a site on his farm, Lilayi, close to the railway between Lusaka and Chilanga to the south. Messrs D W Humphrey and F A Roberts, together with Inspector D I Oliver, reconnoitred the site and found it satisfactory.

Work began and, in May 1952 the Force Band moved in from Bwana Mkubwa. The Mounted Section was billeted at Lilayi until new stables were built in Ward-roper Police Camp, the headquarters camp at Lusaka, in 1955. During 1954 Police Stores moved from Livingstone to Lilayi and the new site was used as overflow accommodation for Lusaka Division personnel. In October 1954 Mr Roberts, Officer Commanding the Training Depot, took up residence at Lilayi to make sure that all was ready for the final move.

In April 1955 the Band was sent down to Livingstone to lead the Training Depot on its farewell march through the town, when the salute was taken outside the Municipal Offices by the Mayor, Mr Harry Thom.

A special goods train was made available four days before the move so that furniture, vehicles and personal kit could be loaded in advance, and on 29 April the Depot entrained under the command of Mr R S Taylor, Assistant Superintendent. The journey took 23 hours, stops being made every few hours to take on hot water for washing and making tea. The spirits of the European officers were kept up by the contents of a hamper provided by David Habershaw, proprietor of the North-Western and Fairmount Hotels and a senior member of the Police Reserve. The final break was at Kafue in the early hours of 30 April when all ranks washed, shaved and changed in to clean uniforms for their arrival at Lilayi Siding at 0930 hours. The first impression of their new home was unfortunate. The Rains had not finished and it was grey and drizzling. Nevertheless they detrained and marched into and around the new premises and finally past the saluting base where the salute was taken by Mr Davidson, who had commanded the Depot for so long, and the resident Commanding Officer, Mr Roberts. After an address of welcome by Mr Davidson, the men were dismissed to their new quarters.

The change of station brought a change of title in keeping with the policy to replace military terms with ones more appropriate to a civil police force. The training establishment of the Northern Rhodesia Police was henceforth to be called the Police Training School.[10]

At the time of the move 137 African recruits were under training, and a total of 218 were attested during the year. The improved facilities at the new school enabled more recruits to be trained and during 1956, 339 Africans were attested. There were also quarters for European recruits. Henceforth all European recruits without previous police experience in the Federation were to attend a twelve week course at Lilayi in law and police duties, foot, arms and riot drill, musketry, first aid, physical training, self defence, the Cinyanja Language, and equitation and/ or driving. The first batch of European recruits, Squad Four of 1955, joined soon after the move to Lilayi. On passing out No 557 Assistant Inspector C P T Vaughan-Johnson was adjudged the best all round recruit in the squad and became the first recipient of the 'Cane of Honour'. Since October 1947 those without previous police experience recruited in the United Kingdom had attended courses at No.4 Police District Training School first at Eynsham, Oxfordshire, and later at Mill Meece, Staffordshire. It was also possible at the new school at Lilayi to run courses for specialists and to increase the number of promotion courses for African police.

In 1954 the rank of Chief Inspector was re-authorised with an establishment of four, one for the Training Depot and one to be posted to each of the main police camps, at Lusaka, Ndola and Kitwe. The posts were to be filled by senior members of the Inspectorate who were unlikely to reach gazetted rank despite good service. Inspector D I Oliver had joined the Palestine Police on leaving the Army in 1945,

Police training school staff 1955 (Photo D. I. Oliver)
Seated L to R: Mrs J Porter, Insp F Berryman, Insp J D Dixon MTO, A/Supt R S Taylor, Supt
F A Roberts, C/Insp D I Oliver, Insp E Jones, Insp J Robertson, Insp M Mataka.

and the Northern Rhodesia Police in 1950. After some months on immigration
duties at Livingstone he had joined the Training Depot staff on 22 May 1951. In
1955 he was promoted Chief Inspector and was to be Chief Drill and Weapon
Training Instructor at Lilayi until the end, being awarded the Colonial Police
Medal for Meritorious Service in 1960 and promoted Assistant Superintendent in
1964. David Oliver was the very soul of the Police Training School.

Mr George King had resigned as Bandmaster on 27 May 1954. In August 1954
Bandmaster C W G Hey of the King's Shropshire Light Infantry retired from
the Army and on 2 September assumed the appointment of Bandmaster of the
Northern Rhodesia Police. It was George Hey who brought the Band up to it's
final high standard, in recognition of which he was to be promoted Assistant
Superintendent on 1 July 1956. One of his first innovations was the formation of
a dance band section. In February 1955 the Band President, Mr Denis Humphrey,
casually informed Hey that he had accepted a booking for the infant dance band
to play at the Catholic Hall, Lusaka, the following week. The new Bandmaster
rose to the occasion. On the night the band had a repertoire of some twenty-five
numbers and by dint of repeating them, got through the evening.

Another new venture was the training of a 28 man strong drum, bugle and fife
band for the Mobile Unit, all taught by ear. By early May 1955 the Mobile Unit

Band was ready to leave the nest and, after performing before the Commissioner at a passing out parade at Lilayi, they returned to take up their duties at Bwana Mkubwa[11]. There they were to beat retreat every Thursday evening at the parade of the standby company, and to be a great asset in making an occasion of the weekly Commanding Officer's Parade as well as parades for visiting dignataries. A constable trained as a bugler accompanied each platoon on operations or detachment. At one stage Mr Hey suggested that bagpipes be introduced in the Mobile Unit Band[12], but this proposal came to nothing.

By the end of 1955 Mr Roberts had relinquished command of the Police Training School, being succeeded by Mr T E Coton, Superintendent, who had transferred to the Force as an assistant superintendent after 13 years in the Palestine Police.

On 3 January 1955 African miners came out on strike on the Copperbelt on the issue of African advancement and a claim for a flat increase of 10s 8d a shift, to nearly double their pay. The African Mineworkers' Union received money from the Trades Union movement in the United Kingdom and elsewhere, enabling food to be supplied to the strikers and their families. Nevertheless by 24 January 2,500 were back at work. By 28 February 11,000 had returned and output was at 65 per cent of the pre-strike level. On 4 March all claims were withdrawn and the strike ended. African National Congress leaders had played an active part in encouraging the workers to stay out.

In January 1955 Harry Nkumbula, President of the Northern Rhodesia African National Congress, and Kenneth Kaunda, Secretary General, were each sentenced to imprisonment for two months for possession of prohibited literature, *Africa and the Colonial World* supplied by the Communist Party of Great Britain, the Women's International Democratic Federation of Great Britain and the Council of African Affairs, New York.[13]

On 16 January 1955 a flat was broken into at Kitwe. At 0545 hrs some 50 yards from the flat a mine worker going on shift challenged an African who was carrying a bundle. The man dropped the bundle and ran off into the darkness. Entry to the flat had been gained through the kitchen window on the sill of which an impression of the ball of a foot was found and lifted. Some 60 Africans working in the block of flats were interrogated and 120 foot impressions taken. One matched that found on the window sill and its owner was also placed on an identification parade where he was picked out by the miner as the man he had accosted.[14] Northern Rhodesia Police Force Standing Orders required all identification parades to be photographed some thirty years before the Code of Practice for the Identification of Persons Suspected of Offences made under the Police and Criminal Evidence Act 1984 required a similar procedure in England and Wales.

Ever since the earliest days fingerprints taken in Northern Rhodesia had been sent to the Criminal Record Office of the British South Africa Police in Bulawayo for search and filing with their collection. The NRP had also had its own fingerprint bureau in a small way since Sub-Inspector Ferguson set it up in 1914. In 1936 it had been decided to work towards independence by taking two sets of prints in each case, one to be sent to Bulawayo and the other to be retained. In 1950 it was agreed that all Northern Rhodesia finger prints should be extracted from the Southern Rhodesia collection and transferred to the new Criminal Investigation Department Headquarters at Lusaka, which would henceforth run its own Bureau completely independently. In 1951 it appeared possible that Federation would bring with it some form of central police authority. The BSAP accordingly suggested that it would be unwise to break up their collection, only for it to have to be reassembled a year or two later on the establishment of a Federal Criminal Record Office. By 1955 it was clear that such a federal agency was unlikely to come into existence for some years, if at all. The Northern Rhodesia Police Fingerprint Bureau was now quite self-sufficient. The practise of taking an additional set of prints to send to Bulawayo only made unnecessary work. It was therefore decided to discontinue the practise from 31 August 1955, except in cases involving Southern Rhodesians, persons believed to have a record in the south, or other special circumstances.[15]

According to the Colonial Office Report on Northern Rhodesia for 1955, the year had been 'marked by notable expansion of commerce and industry allied to higher wages for Africans', while, 'in the field of constitutional development the year was one of consolidation and political awareness, especially among the African population'. The Government became seriously concerned at the situation arising from the 'attraction offered by the towns – high wages, good housing, sport and other amenities were drawing more and more people away from the rural areas'.

The Governor, Sir Arthur Benson, who had succeeded Sir Gilbert Rennie early in 1954, announced the intention in the Legislative Council 'to provide better amenities in the rural areas and to introduce measures designed to encourage Africans to abandon their shifting system of subsistence agriculture'. Considerable sums of money were made available for spending in the rural areas, but none for new police stations there. Benson had served as a cadet and district officer in Northern Rhodesia. He believed that members of the Provincial Administration, with their district messengers, and exercising indirect rule through the chiefs and their kapasus, were well able to maintain law and order among the rural Africans. He closed down a number of police stations in the Bush. This paternalist policy was not popular with the Force, amongst whom it was felt that every community needs a properly trained police force. The number of times over the following ten years when the Mobile Unit was called out to support the administrative officials and restore order in rural areas gives support to the police view. The half finished police station building at Kawambwa was turned into a Boma store! One of the European officers was posted to the Line of Rail. The other and the 15 African police were transferred to other stations in Northern or Eastern province.[16]

In pursuance of Benson's policy the station at Kashiba, under Inspector J R Barber, was closed on 31 December 1955. Samfya Police Station, only opened in February 1953 because of the disorder among the fishing folk, was closed on 14 June 1956. Kashiba was to be reopened in April 1960 in the presence of Roger Barber, by then Superintendent commanding Luapula Division. Samfya was to reopen in May 1960.

Benson maintained his policy despite signs of increasing disrespect for the established order in rural areas. On 22 April 1955 the Acting Provincial Commissioner, Northern Province, had reported to the Secretary for Native Affairs that the African National Congress District Committee at Chinsali had decided to form six 'action groups' to precede Government officials on tour, to dissuade villagers from showing respect to Native Authority and Boma representatives, and encourage a refusal to supply them with food, water and firewood. In June an unusual amount of ANC infiltration was reported and in Mporokoso District an administrative officer on tour found villagers uncooperative and disrespectful. ANC sought to undermine the authority of the chiefs.[17]

By the end of 1955 the strength of the Northern Rhodesia Police had risen to 425 European officers against an establishment of 471 and 2,412 African police the establishment for which remained 3,030 as in 1954. 1,412 African police had attained Standard IV in education, 331 Standard VI and 6 Standard VIII. 663 African police, mainly in the Mobile Unit, had no educational qualification.

During 1955 an establishment of twelve European women police officers was authorised. There were already a number of ladies serving in the Police Reserve, so the innovation was easily effected. In fact the first three full time women officers, Mrs Prior, Mrs Carswell and Miss Prior, had been recruited as clerks in the previous year and attested as Women Reserve Assistant Inspectors, although working full time in uniform. Initially women officers were employed on charge office work at the larger stations in the daytime, thus freeing male officers for outside work.

24,203 offences against the Penal Code and 31,365 other offences, excluding traffic, came to the attention of the Force in 1955. Investigations resulted in 32,077 prosecutions and 30,370 convictions. 3,255 traffic accidents left 112 persons killed and 1,246 injured.[18]

An African, Shandano, set fire to two huts in Chief Nkana's area and shot a young boy through the thigh with an arrow. A constable was sent from Kalulushi to arrest the offender. He found the man had acquired a muzzle loading gun but nevertheless, though unarmed, gave chase through the bush. Shandano turned and fired seriously wounding the constable in the right thigh, missing the main artery by a quarter of an inch. Shandano successfully hid in the bush for many weeks until one morning he was found outside Kalulushi Police Station sitting at the base of the flagpole with his arms clasped around it. This is believed to have been the last instance of an offender giving himself up in this way which since the early days had been thought to give protection to an offender. Since it removed all question of force being necessary to effect an arrest the belief cannot be said to be unfounded.[19]

In late 1955 violence on the Copperbelt had increased with the stoning of houses and of cars, usually after traffic accidents. In October a mobile crane killed an African. A hostile crowd gathered from the mine compound and demanded that the driver be handed over. When this was refused the mob stoned Europeans and wrecked cars, machinery and buildings. After five hours they were dispersed by baton charges. Three persons were arrested and sentenced to nine years imprisonment. Disturbances such as this led to the passing of the Riot Damage Ordinance 1955 providing for compensation.

Harry Nkumbula denied Congress involvement and called on those responsible to desist. Harry Franklin, now retired from the Government Service and an unofficial member of the Legislative Council responsible for African interests, made a fact finding tour of Chingola. Thereafter he assured the public that the stonings were not politically inspired since they were aimed at both Africans and Europeans. He suggested that it was the type of hooliganism that naturally resulted from inferior housing, poor educational facilities, and the breakdown of traditional family life among urban Africans. Whatever the reason, militant ANC leaders were certainly not averse to taking advantage of any discontent.

On 16 February 1956 Nkumbula, as President of the Northern Rhodesia African National Congress, issued a circular to all branches, describing racial discrimination and the social colour bar in Northern Rhodesia as worse than in South Africa. This was followed in April by an organised attempt to boycott European and Asian shops in most places on the Line of Rail. This was called off on 23 April and ceased in May. In June there was a new outbreak organised at local branch level, starting in Ndola. This was over by the end of June except in Mufulira where picketing continued into July. There was some substance in this protest as Africans were frequently kept waiting by European shop assistants, and in some cases, forbidden entry to the shop itself and required to make their purchases through a hatch in the wall. Nevertheless there was no justification for the intimidation by which some Congress supporters tried to enforce the boycott. A positive result was that the Government established an inter-racial committee to examine the problem of race relations.

Industrial relations deteriorated in parallel with, if not in consequence of, a fall in the World price of copper which in March had reached the grossly abnormal height of £437 a ton. On 26 June a three day strike commenced on the copper mines called by the African Mineworkers Union ostensibly because of a regulation which required Africans, but not Europeans, to wear protective leg guards while working underground. This was followed by a series of so called 'rolling' strikes in July and August. By September the railwaymen were also on strike and a General Strike was threatened. Violence had increased with the stoning of houses and cars in the compounds, followed by more serious disturbances.

The Governor was away from the Territory on vacation leave. On 11 September the Acting Governor, Mr A R Williams, proclaimed a State of Emergency in the Western Province. Forty-five union leaders, including Matthew de Luxe Nkholoma, General Secretary of the African Mineworkers Union, were arrested. 30 members of the African Mineworkers Union and two officials of the African National Congress were detained in a camp at Mumbwa. The Union's president, Lawrence Katilungu, was away at a World Trades Union solidarity meeting in Brussels. Initially these arrests brought further disturbances in the Copperbelt towns especially Ndola. Troops were called out and detachments of the British South Africa Police and Nyasaland Police were brought to the Copperbelt as reinforcements, remaining for three weeks, by which time Katilungu had returned and encouraged his members to return to work. All was back to normal by 24 September.[20]

On 15 October Benson attended a meeting at the Colonial Office with the Inspector General of Colonial Police and other officials. On 29 June the closure had been announced in the Legislative Council, of the four man police posts at Namwala, Nyimba, Kabompo and Shibuyunji. The police station at Lundazi was also to be closed and Mwinilunga was only to be retained due to lack of accomodation at Solwezi. The rationale was that improvements in wireless and road communications and better transport permitted the concentration of police at provincial headquarters. In any event each district commissioner had 60 messengers at his disposal. John Gaunt MLC, a former district officer, had protested. He pointed out that the people should regard a policeman as a friend, a civilian in uniform, and not as someone they only saw with a steel helmet on his head and a riot gun in his hand. Sir Edgar Unsworth had had to concede that the Commissioner of Police was not in full agreement with this policy.[21]

At the Colonial Office meeting Benson defended his policy by pointing out that police formations on the Copperbelt were undermanned and the development of new mines was likely to create a requirement for twice as many police there within eight years. The shortage of European police officers meant that a small bush station would be commanded by an assistant inspector with less than three years service and little knowledge of the local people and language. When the adverse effect on the gathering of intelligence was raised he suggested consideration of the creation of an intelligence organisation separate from the police. It was agreed that the Special Branch and Criminal Investigation Department should be separated within the Force and each headed by an Assistant Commissioner. This should attract a high quality applicant for the senior Special Branch appointment. It was agreed in principle that a member of the Provincial Administration should be

Landrover on the Zambezi 1956 (Photo NRP)

attached to Special Branch and European police officers should serve secondments of a few months to the Provincial Administration.[22] These measures to improve liaison were introduced in the following years although few police officers were ever seconded.

The deficiency on the Copperbelt was 7 gazetted officers and 21 inspectors out of an establishment of 175 Europeans, and 228 African police from an establishment of 1,026. By the end of 1956 the total European strength of the Northern Rhodesia Police had risen to 448 out of an establishment of 512. There were 2,606 African police, still well below the establishment of 3,030 set in 1954. The increase was mainly in the Mobile Unit and there were now 910 African police substandard in education. A drop of 102 in the number who had attained Standard IV, to 1,310, was only half offset by an increase to 381 of those with Standard VI. Only five had reached Standard VIII.

During the year the Force dealt with 24,581 Penal Code offences, including 138 homicides, 13 attempted murders and 5,395 burglaries, house and storebreakings. Const Robert Nalushebo of Woodlands, who had only passed out of Training School in May was shot dead by an African on 13 December 1956. Exclusive of traffic offences, 30,628 non Penal Code offences were reported. 29,820 prosecutions resulted in 21,736 persons convicted for such offences and 7,600 for offences against the Penal Code. Those convicted were 820 Europeans, 39 Asians, 46 Eurafricans and Eurasians, and 28,431 Africans. Traffic accidents continued to increase steadily along with the number of vehicles on the road. There were 3,255 road traffic accidents in 1956 with 116 deaths and 1,246 persons injured. In March 1956 a lion started to terrorise Chief Mabumba's village. It was shot by a party of African Police from Fort Rosebery under Sgt Museba, whose claim to have fired the fatal shot was disputed by Const Banda.

A tourist spotted a body floating 360 feet down below the Knife Edge at the Eastern Cataract, Victoria Falls. The current was keeping it away from the bank and it was clear that it could only be recovered from above. This was done with a wire scoop borrowed from the Inspector of Works at Livingstone and a winch from the BSAP station on the South Bank.[23]

Recurrent expenditure on the Northern Rhodesia Police for the year 1955–56 was £1,200,090 of which £32,776 spent on the Immigration Division was recouped from the Federal Government. Capital expenditure was £133,988. For the financial year 1956–57 recurrent expenditure was to be £1,386,368 and capital expenditure £412,719. Immigration accounted for £32,824 of recurrent expenditure.

On 26 September 1956 the Officer in Charge at Mongu, the only police station in Barotseland, requested CID assistance. The body of an African male had been discovered in Kalabo District with the head partly severed. On 27 September Mr Jan Waller, Superintendent, set out from CID HQ at Lusaka, bound for Mongu. By 1 October investigations into the case had been completed and three Africans were committed for trial on a charge of murder.

On 2 October the District Commissioner, Kalabo, heard from a Roman Catholic priest at Siholi Mission, forty miles away, that two African women were believed to have been murdered. There were rumours of witchcraft. Mr Waller had boarded a plane to return to Lusaka when he heard of the report and immediately commenced inquiries assisted by Sergeant Mushemi. For four days he met with little success, but on the fifth information was received from the seven year old granddaughter of one of the missing women, Namununga of Sikambanda village, that she had seen a large hole in the back of her grandmother. This led to the discovery that two indunas had seen the body and the wound, but had failed to report the matter and allowed burial. Waller drove 45 miles along a shocking road and then 20 miles through the bush, to arrive at Sikambanda at about 2030 hours. The indunas were interrogated and alleged that the women had been shot by two witchdoctors with a 'kalalozi' gun. The bodies were exhumed. Each had been shot in the back. At post mortem examinations at Mongu eight copper slugs were removed from the body of Namununga, and four from that of the other woman, Makoi of Mutama's village.

After a further seventy mile drive and an eight mile walk to Sinonje on the Angola Border two brothers Somili Muyawa and Lice Maakoyi were arrested in Somili's enclosure. Somili confessed outright to the murder of Makoi. Both stated that they had been hired to carry out the killings by the deceased's relatives who believed the women were witches responsible for certain deaths in their villages.

The house of Somili had a hidden door leading to a small enclosure decked with chicken feathers and numerous charms, such as horns and tortoise shells, many of them encrusted with red and black 'lucky' beans, said to be used only by killer witchdoctors. At the entrance to this 'temple' four posts were sunk in the ground, ringed with various coloured paints. Parts of the skulls of two children were recovered together with the cranium of an adult. This contained a black compound in which three human bones were embedded.

Lice admitted that on hearing that the police were in the area, he had buried his kalalozi gun. He led Mr Waller to a village six miles from Siholi Mission and showed him the spot. Here the detectives unearthed a parcel containing the gun. The stock was tied on with snakeskin and the whole weapon was studded with the red and black beans. There was also a short log, studded with the beans and pieces of mirror, and a cranium with similar macabre contents to that found at Somili's house. The rim of this skull was encrusted with lucky beans.

Interrogation of witnesses in these two cases produced the names of other alleged witchdoctors and the investigation snowballed as one inquiry led to another. In December Mr E J Stephens, newly promoted Assistant Superintendent, Detective Sub-inspectors Neta and Katembo and two other African detectives, joined Waller at Kalabo, and continued the investigations after that officer returned to Lusaka. Reports of witchcraft cases came in from all parts of Barotseland except Mankoya. Kalalozi guns were also said to have been manufactured in the Mulobezi District of Southern Province.

By 18 March 1957 seven persons had been convicted and condemned to death for three murders, while nine were awaiting trial for five other murders. Six had been convicted of attempted murder and three of conspiracy to murder, while six persons were under arrest for the former and three for the latter of these offences. A further 120 persons had been convicted by the District Commissioner, Kalabo, for various offences against the Witchcraft, Arms and Ammunition and Inquest

Standard Vanguard (NRPA)

ordinances. Seven were awaiting trial for interfering with graves. By the end of 1957 this major CID investigation, in an area not normally policed, had resulted in 711 charges.

The investigation proved beyond doubt that witchcraft had been practised in the Kalabo District for a long time. The people were steeped in it. Their traditional fear of the witch-doctor, in Silozi 'Muloyi', made them extremely reluctant to give evidence. This fear was unfortunately compounded by the knowledge that it was an offence under the Witchcraft Ordinance to name a person as a witchdoctor, while they failed to realise that the offence was not committed by giving such information to a district officer or European member of the police! A number of anonymous letters were received denouncing people as wizards, and an increase in suicides during the period of the investigation was noted.

All 'fully fledged' witchdoctors questioned were found to have one or two inch long needles under the skin of their chests. These were apparently inserted during the inititiation ceremony to strengthen the bearers in the use of the kalalozi gun and to protect the witchdoctor himself from being bewitched. Detectives were told that the ceremony included the eating of human flesh. The craniums found were used as vessels in which the brain matter of a recently deceased person was mixed with crushed lucky beans. The needles were dipped in this mixture before insertion under the initiate's skin. Aspiring witchdoctors apparently paid one cow for the initiation ceremony, and another as the price of their kalalozi gun.

These guns, according to local belief, possessed magic powers, particularly for the killing of witches. In the morning the muloyi would point his gun at the Sun and later at his victim, who was supposed to die that night without leaving a trace of the cause of death. The original kalalozi guns were made of human bone. Some of this type were found during the investigation, but it was found that, since 1942, a metal barrelled model had become popular.[24]

On 28 February 1957 Mr J C Day had relinquished command of the Criminal Investigation Department and Special Branch. Mr J F Castle, Senior Superintendent, took temporary charge of the CID until the return from leave of Mr L A Hicks on 2nd September. Lawson Hicks was promoted Assistant Commissioner on 29 April 1957, on which date a new rank of Senior Assistant Commissioner of Police was created. Julian Day became Senior Assistant Commissioner, Headquarters. The other SACP was Mr C N Halse, who remained in command of Western Division in the new rank.

On 26 August Mr Eric Leighton, formerly of the Indian Police, arrived to take up the new appointment of Assistant Commissioner, Special Branch. The Special Branch, which had been steadily built up by Mr Day since 1949, then became completely independent of the Criminal Investigation Department.

In April 1957, owing to the absence of a battalion of the Federal Army on Active Service in Malaya, the Northern Rhodesia Police Mobile Unit assumed responsibility for furnishing the ceremonial guard at Government House, Lusaka. This commitment continued into 1958. The Mobile Unit also found two of the four guards for the Queen's Birthday Parade at Lusaka at which Messrs O L Mitchell, T E Coton, and R J Read and detective inspectors Gordon Chakulunta and Caution Chiluba were presented with the Colonial Police Medal for Meritorious Service.

At the beginning of 1957 the Mobile Unit, under the command of Mr J F Matheson, Senior Superintendent, consisted of a headquarters company (with the band, transport, signals, stores and training wing), and three operational companies, A, B and C, each under an assistant superintendent and comprising three platoons. With effect from 1st July the establishment was increased to allow for a fourth operational company, D. On 16 September a platoon was detached to Chingola. The increase in establishment was to provide for this and similar permanent detachments at Livingstone and Broken Hill, which were to be set up in 1958.

On 31 December 1957 the strength of the Mobile Unit was 5 superior police officers, 19 senior inspectors, inspectors and assistant inspectors, and 569 African police, against an establishment of 6 SPOs, 1 chief inspector, 30 other members of the inspectorate, and 555 African police. 223 African recruits were attested and trained within the Unit during the year, while 18 riot drill courses were held for European officers and two for African NCOs.

On 2 July 1957 an African National Congress inspired boycott of beerhalls commenced in Lusaka. Disturbances occurred in four African suburbs and cases of arson were reported. Attempts were made to intimidate members of the Force residing in the African suburbs.[25]

On 8 July Queen Elizabeth, the Queen Mother, arrived from Salisbury in the course of a tour of the Federation. She visited Ndola, Luanshya, Kitwe, Broken Hill and Lusaka. On 11 July she opened the new High Court Building in the capital and laid the foundation stone for the Cathedral of the Holy Cross. That afternoon Her Majesty attended a garden party at Government House which ended with beating retreat by the Band of the Northern Rhodesia Police. That same evening the Queen Mother presented the Force with a signed portrait photograph which was hung in the Officers' Mess at Lusaka. On 12 July Her Majesty left Northern Rhodesia.[26]

On 28 July a Congress meeting was held at Kasama. The maker of an inflamatory speech was arrested. A procession of 100 men, women and children then marched on the office of the Provincial Commissioner and had eventually to be dispersed by police using tearsmoke. Later a small crowd in an African suburb was found threatening a patrol of District Messengers. It was dispersed by police. As a result of these incidents at Kasama thirteen persons were prosecuted.

A beerhall boycott started at Chingola on 30 July 1957. During the ensuing week it spread to all centres on the Copperbelt except Bancroft and Kitwe. On 31 July Insp R A Chasemore, A/Insps N E Fletcher and J S Willett, Sergeant-Major Nabale, Sgt Treu, and Consts Bisayi, Chisambi, Chilenga and Chewa went to Nchanga Mine Beerhall to control the disorderly conduct of African National Congress pickets. On arrival the police found about fifteen Africans, mainly women, abusing all who entered. The pickets were warned, but ignored the warning to desist. An attempt was made to arrest four of the male pickets. The police party was then attacked by the others reinforced by bystanders armed with stones, sticks and bricks. The crowd grew to about 150 and the police withdrew into the beerhall enclosure, with two prisoners. After a further demonstration and the arrival of Mr B G O'Leary, Supt, with police reinforcements, the crowd dispersed. Several arrests were made for rioting and assault on police. At the close of the ensuing trial the Resident Magistrate commended Mr O'Leary and Insp Chasemore and his men for their resolute courage clearly displayed in the riot and congratulated them on retaining their prisoners in the face of determined opposition by overwelming numbers. They later received special commendations from the Commissioner of Police.[27]

In Eastern Province similar boycotts were organised by ANC in August. These too were accompanied by acts of hooliganism and arson. Seven Congress leaders in the area were arrested on charges of arson or conspiracy to injure a person in his trade or business. Two were discharged but the remainder were sentenced to imprisonment.

The Northern Rhodesia Agricultural Society's Annual Show was held at Lusaka on the 3, 4 and 5 August. In previous years the Force had added to the Show's attractions with police dog demonstrations, a physical training display, and, of course, the Band. In 1957, for the first time, a motor cycle display and musical ride were also provided by European officers from the Mounted Section and Police Training School under Insps Denis Lee and Jimmy Robertson. Some of the recruits had been riding for less than six weeks having only arived in the Territory on 9 June. 80 African recruits in green, white and blue vests gave a physical training display under Mr J Porter MM Assistant Quartermaster. In the evening they performed by torchlight. The show also saw the first use of a new mobile police station built on a Leyland Comet chassis. It was equipped with a diesel generator power supply and doubled as a mobile wireless workshop.[28] The 'Ride and Drive' was to become a regular feature of the Show and was always of a high standard.

On 7 August a car driven by a European collided with an African cyclist at Mufulira. A crowd of some 800 Africans quickly gathered and stoned the European and an African driver who came to his assistance. A woman was arrested for stone throwing. A crowd of about fifty who attempted to free her was dispersed by force.

On 24 and 25 August disorderly conduct by African National Congress pickets at Luanshya Beerhall led to serious disturbances at Mikomfwa and Roan Antelope locations. The police were compelled to use tearsmoke. Over 100 Africans, many of them women, were arrested.

On 29 August officials of the African Mine Workers' Union and African Municipal Workers' Union arrived at Chingola from Kitwe to address a meeting. They were mobbed and stoned by a large section of the assembled crowd. Two or three of the officials were injured before being rescued by the police. During the weekend 31 August–1 September the aggressive behaviour of ANC pickets at Luanshya led to disturbances and numerous cases of arson, assault, malicious damage, stoning, obstruction of roads and threatening behaviour.

On 2 September Chief Shimumbi of Luwingu District in Northern Province, attempted to arrest a Congress agitator who had been attempting to undermine the Chief's authority. A riot occurred and police and messenger reinforcements were required to arrest the rioters. Eighty-two persons were convicted in the Chief's court and seven ringleaders were brought before the Magistrate's Court, convicted and sentenced to terms of imprisonment ranging from four months to two years.

On 4 September a stoning incident occurred at Nchanga when the manager of the Mine African Cinema refused to refund money to a number of dissatisfied patrons. On 8 September a crowd endeavoured to rescue an African who had been arrested for burglary at Mufulira. The landrover carrying the prisoner was obstructed by the crowd.

On 14 September eight men were arrested for disorderly behaviour at Chifubu African Location. They had been picketing the beerhall. Subsequently twenty-five persons, mainly youths, demonstrated outside Ndola Central Police Station demanding the release of the arrested men. These twenty-five were themselves arrested. A grass fence surrounding Chifubu Beerhall was set on fire and some windows broken in revenge for these arrests.

On 17 September there was continuous rioting at Mufulira during which a Nyachusa tribesman fell from his bicycle and received injuries from which he died. The subsequent inquest recorded a verdict of accidental death. More than sixty people were arrested and prosecuted as a result of this riot.

On 18 and 19 September at Chingola disorderly crowds and an unauthorised procession had to be dispersed by force. Many arrests were made. African staff at Nchanga Mine Compound complained of ill-treatment, threats and victimisation by members of African National Congress because they refused to join the boycott. Seven persons were convicted as a result of these complaints. On 25 September 1957 Congress called off the boycotts.[29]

Federation and the high price of copper had brought a boom to the Copperbelt. Although the starting salary for an assistant inspector was now £745 a year, the Force suffered a considerable 'brain drain' of young officers tempted by high salaries to leave for jobs on the mines and in commerce. Government eventually decided that action was required. On 14 September 1957 the Governor appointed a Commission:

(i) To inquire into the causes of any wastage of personnel from the Northern Rhodesia Police Force (which term shall be deemed to include the Police Reserve) due to voluntary resignation and withdrawal from the Force of police officers;

(ii) To make recommendations as to any measures that may be necessary in order to provide inducements towards stability.

By that time the price of copper had fallen. This together with an increase in salary scales, which might have appeared the obvious answer, could well have solved the problem. Nevertheless the appointed Commissioner, Mr P A P Robertson of the Colonial Office arrived from London on 20 September and remained for five weeks, during which he visited most police stations, and interviewed a number of Government officials and members of the public, as well as police officers. His report was issued in 1958. It resulted in improvements in pay and conditions and the establishment of a Police Service Commission in place of the Police Advisory Board, but little was implemented before 1959.

On 23 October 1957 a European fisherman complained that African fishermen, camped across the Kafue River on the North Bank, Lusaka Rural District, were threatening his nets. He stated that stones had been thrown. Police investigated the complaint and made two arrests. On leaving they were attacked by the African fishermen who succeeded in freeing their arrested comrades. On 25 October police, in adequate strength, together with a district officer and district messengers, returned to the fishermen's camp and arrested thirty-nine of them.

The Lusaka Division now consisted of two districts, Lusaka Urban, under a superintendent, and Lusaka Rural District, under an assistant superintendent, and comprising Lusaka Rural, Kafue, Chilanga, and Chirundu police stations, a sub-station at Chalimbana and posts at Ngwerere, Mwembezi and Balmoral. The Mounted Section had been removed from Lusaka Urban District and, with Lusaka Traffic Section, was directly under the control of Divisional Headquarters. Mr J W E Ross, Acting Senior Superintendent, had assumed command of Lusaka Division when Mr R J 'Punch' Randell left for vacation leave on 22 June 1957.

Central Division had been upgraded to a senior superintendent's command on 1 July when Mr R J Read, who had succeeded Mr P R Blyth as Commanding Officer on 7 February, was promoted. On 25 November 1957 Broken Hill Urban District Headquarters opened under a superintendent with Broken Hill Central

Mobile police station 1957 (Nkhwazi)

and Bwacha police stations and Kapiri Mposhi Police Post under command together with Raylton Police Station which had opened on 8 March and Broken Hill Mine Police Station which opened on 16 October. The rural stations at Mkushi and Mumbwa, and posts at Kalabo and Malembwa, remained directly under command of Divisional Headquarters.[30]

In the early hours of 27 November 1957 a goods train was derailed at Chunga just north of Lusaka. Fish-plates and clips had been removed from a complete section of line, on an outside bend of the track near a small bridge over a dried up stream. A number of horses and cattle on the train were killed but there were no human casualties. An African was subsequently arrested by district messengers. He was charged with endangering the safety of persons travelling by rail and tampering with the railway line, convicted on both counts and sentenced to twenty years imprisonment.[31]

A guard of one European and one African policeman was placed on the Victoria Falls Bridge. The entire length of the railway line was patrolled, at first on foot, but later on bicycles specially modified for use on the rails. Motor rail-trolleys containing armed police were used to precede the thrice-weekly mail train on its forty-eight hour journey from Livingstone to Ndola and back. These precautions were not only a great drain on police manpower, but provided little job satisfaction or useful experience. Unfortunately they had to continue for several years. 2700 Constable Phiri of C Company of the Mobile Unit was killed by a train while on patrol at Lusaka.

The establishment and strength of the Northern Rhodesia Police on 31 December 1957 were as follows:

European	Establishment	Strength
Commissioner	1	1
Deputy Commissioner	1	1
Senior Assistant Commissioners	2	2
Assistant Commissioners	3	3
Senior Superintendents	11	10
Superintendents	19	20
Quartermaster	1	1
Assistant Superintendents	68	56
Assistant Quartermaster	1	1
Chief Inspectors	7	4
Senior Inspectors, Inspectors & Asst Inspectors	471	401
Women Assistant Inspectors	32	26
Cadets	12	9
Total	629	535

AFRICANS:

	Establishment	Strength
Inspectors and Sub-Inspectors	92	81
Sergeants-Major	57	46
Sergeants	396	351
Constables	2,540	2,519
Buglers	45	48
Total	3,130	3,045

Civilian Staff – European	Establishment	Strength
District Officer (seconded)	1	1
Principal Accountant	1	1
Secretary	1	1
Accountants	2	2
Desk Officers	2	2
Records Supervisor	1	–
Telecommunications Officers	2	2
Radio Maintenance Technicians	4	3
Armourers	2	1
Stores Officers	3	3
Photographer	1	1
Passport Officer	1	1
Assistant Passport Officer	1	1
Clerks (Male)	4	2
Clerks (Female)	93	100
Telephone Operators	3	3
Housekeepers	11	12
Inspector of Works	1	–
Building Foremen	2	3
Total	136	139

European	Establishment	Strength
Civilian Staff – African		
Welfare Assistant	1	1
Clerks and Interpreters	13	12
Teachers	2	2
Tailors	27	23
Shoemakers	12	12
Office Orderlies	20	18
Domestic Servants	31	20
Total	106	88

The increase in establishment, effective from 1 July 1957, had been 15 Superior Police Officers, 92 European subordinate officers, including 12 women, and 100 African police. The continued expansion meant that the Force was a young one. The average age of European members of the inspectorate on 31 December was $25\frac{1}{2}$ years. Only 58 European officers and 476 Africans had served more than ten years in the Force, while 175 Europeans and 1,006 Africans had less than two years service. More than half the Europeans and nearly half the African police had completed no more than four years in the Northern Rhodesia Police.

Four Superior Police Officers had retired during the year including, on 2 January 1957, Mr T M Davidson, Assistant Commissioner. Mr W H Cowham CGM, Assistant Superintendent, had been transferred to the Judicial Department as Master Interpreter on 4 December 1956. Born in Fort Jameson, 'Happy', Cowham had won his Conspicious Gallantry Medal over Germany in 1943 while serving with the Royal Air Force. Four members of the Inspectorate transferred to other government departments, two retired on pension and 24 left on resignation or termination of agreement during 1957. 285 African police were struck off strength that year, including three who died in service and nine invalided.

On the credit side, 103 European officers had been attested, 48 of whom were still undergoing their thirteen week recruit training course at the end of 1957. Extensions to the accommodation at the Police Training School had been completed to provide for 60 European and 300 African trainees at any one time. In fact 303 African recruits were in training at Lilayi on 31 December and 322 had completed the six months course of instruction during the year. 28 Africans had been recruited directly into the Band.

The Permanent Staff of the Training School, in addition to the Commanding Officer, still Mr Coton, now Senior Superintendent, was established at one superintendent, one assistant superintendent, one chief inspector (the redoubtable Oliver), 12 inspectors, one African inspector, 3 sub-inspectors, 7 sergeants-major, 28 sergeants, 30 constables and 3 buglers. In addition to the training of recruits, the School had provided promotion courses for 67 African police, driving courses for 50, riot drill courses for 68 NCOs and equitation courses for 7 constables. On 16 March 1958 twelve assistant superintendents assembled at the Police Training School at the start of the first training course for Superior Police Officers.

Lusaka Division HQ and Central Police Station 1958 (Photo NRP Nkhwazi)

Railway patrols motor trolly 1958 (Photo Jeremy Hawkins)

During 1956 an experiment had begun of recruiting local European residents between the ages of 18 and 20, as 'probationers'. These youngsters, without any police powers, were attached to the police station nearest their home to gain experience with a view to attesting as assistant inspectors on attaining the age of 21. On 1 January 1957 there had been only two probationers. During 1957 the title was changed to 'Police Cadet' to conform to United Kingdom nomenclature.

The standard of education of African police had risen markedly. 159 serving personnel passed the Government Standard VI examination in English during 1957. On 31 December 13 African police held Standard VIII certificates, 612 Standard VI and 1,628 Standard IV. At 792 the number of those with no educational qualification had declined by more than 100 despite the increase in the strength of the Mobile Unit.

The tribal composition of African police on 31 December 1957 was:

Bemba	384	Tonga	355	Lozi	266
Chewa	281	Nsenga	240	Tumbuka	137
Ngoni	126	Ila	103	Lungu	82
Bisa	64	Kaonde	80	Lenje	78
Lamba	39	Lunda	54	Kunda	53
Chisinga	10	Lala	47	Lovale	66
Ushi	57	Mambwe	32	Mbunda	47
Mwinimwamba	60	Soli	25	Henga	50
Toka	57	Mkwangwa	61	Lumbu	20
Nkonde	45	Subiya	52	Ngumbo	13
Other tribes	61				

The number of offences against the Penal Code recorded in 1957 was 26,254, an increase of 1,673 over 1956. 79 were cases of murder, 45 manslaughter and 20 attempted murder. Burglaries and other breakings totalled 5,590. Offences against other laws had also increased to 31,577 exclusive of traffic offences. Also exclusive of traffic offences, there were 28,794 prosecutions in 1957 and 27,715 convictions. 721 Europeans, 48 Asians, 43 Eurafricans and Eurasians, and 27,689 Africans were convicted of offences. 59 European juveniles between the ages of 11 and 18, and 974 Africans between 8 and 18 were convicted. There were no juvenile offenders of other races convicted. The value of property reported stolen during the year was £274,591 16s 3d of which £73,212 4s 10d worth was recovered. 2,164 bicycles were recovered out of 4,931 reported stolen.

The Criminal Investigation Department consisted of the Assistant Commissioner CID, a senior superintendent, 5 assistant superintendents, one chief inspector, 37 other European officers and 151 African detectives.

Of 12,700 sets of fingerprints received for search at the Fingerprint Bureau during the year, 24.8 per cent were identified as belonging to persons with criminal records. 23 wanted persons were identified. The fingerprints of 44,064 persons were on file in the main collection and those of 1,624 persons in the single fingerprint collection under the Battley System. 439 finger impressions lifted from scenes of crime were received in the bureau during 1957 and were of assistance in clearing up more than 100 cases. Force fingerprint experts gave evidence in court in 23 cases where impressions had been found at scenes of crime and 8 cases in which previous convictions were denied. Ballistic evidence was given in court in ten cases, and evidence on handwriting and the examination of documents on 22 occasions.

146 persons were killed on the roads of Northern Rhodesia in 1957 while 603 were seriously and, 719 slightly, injured. 3,441 traffic accidents were reported to the police. 34,676 alleged traffic offences were investigated, resulting in 1,196 warning letters, 29,815 prosecutions and 229,596 convictions.

One Senior Superintendent, Mr J Hynds, as Chief Commandant, and eight other regular officers were employed full-time in the administration and training of the Northern Rhodesia Police Reserve which increased in strength to three reserve superintendents, 12 reserve assistant superintendents, 1,483 other Europeans, Asians and Coloureds and 750 Africans.

During 1957 five district headquarters had been established in Western Division. Divisional Headquarters at Ndola now controlled:

Ndola District   with Ndola Central and Ndola Location police stations, Ndola Traffic Section, and Raylton and Sakania police posts.

Kitwe District   with Kitwe Central, Wusikili and Mindolo police stations, Kitwe Traffic Section, and Buchi Police Post.

Luanshya District   with Luanshya Central and Roan Antelope police stations, Luanshya Traffic Section, and Mikomfwa Post.

Mufulira District   with Mufulira Central and Mufulira Mine police stations, Mufulira Traffic Section and Mokambo Post.

Chingola District   with Chingola Central and Nchanga police stations, Chingola Traffic Section, and Chiwempala Post.

Each district was commanded by a superintendent. Outside the district organisation were Kalulushi, Bancroft, Solwezi and Balovale police stations, and Konkola and Kansanshi posts.[32]

Early in 1958 the Government divided the Northern Province into two. The western part now became Luapula Province with Head-quarters at Fort Rosebery. The police organisation was altered to conform. Mr G H Layne, Assistant Superintendent, took command of the new Luapula Division with his headquarters also at Fort Rosebery. The Northern Division now comprised Kasama, Abercorn, Mpika and Nakonde police stations.

On 12 February 1958 the District Chairman of the African National Congress for Kawambwa in the new Luapula Province made a speech in which he falsely alleged that people living on the shores of Lake Mweru were to be moved to make room for a new airfield. This speech led to considerable agitation in the Kambwali area. A party of police was stood by. There were no incidents until 22 February when an African surveyor and his team were obstructed by a large crowd armed with hoes, sticks and axes. Three district messengers accompanying the surveyor were assaulted. A motor vehicle driven by a cadet of the Provincial Administration was stoned after he had arrested thirteen of those responsible. Police reinforcements were sent to the area and there were no further incidents.[33]

On 20 March 1958 the District Commissioner, Choma, went to Kachenji Village to arrest some twenty Africans who had failed to pay fines imposed by Chief Mapanza for contravening cattle inoculation orders. The District Commissioner was met by about 50 men armed with knobkerries. He withdrew and called for police assistance. On arrival the police made 21 arrests and dispersed an unruly crowd. All the cattle in the area were inoculated to the benefit of the inhabitants and the disappointment of the African National Congress.

From 9 April 1958 a platoon of the Mobile Unit was stationed at Livingstone. Later in the year the district organisation was adopted in Southern Division. Livingstone District comprised Livingstone Central and Libuyu (opened on 1 February 1957) police stations, and police posts at Livingstone Airport (reduced from a sub-station), Linda (opened on 1 March 1957), Mulobezi and Victoria Falls. Choma District was composed of Choma, Kalomo and Pemba police stations. In Mazabuka District were Mazabuka, Monze, Kariba and Chirundu police stations and Magoye Police Post.

In March 1958 African National Congress officials at Ndola, where Hayden Dingiswayo Banda was District Chairman, attempted to organise a boycott of African Area Housing Board elections in protest at increases in house rents. Nkumbula intervened to stop the boycott but Congress only won three of the eighteen seats. Local party officials then urged the people to boycott the municipal beerhalls and the Housing Board, and to refuse to pay rents. Serious disturbances broke out on 8, 9 and 10 April in the Main Town and Kabushi townships. A beerhall and an African owned tearoom were set on fire, buildings were damaged, passing motor vehicles were attacked and the police heavily stoned. Order was restored after the police had opened fire, killing one rioter and wounding four others. Nkumbula denied Congress responsibility for the violence, but African traders claimed that they had been intimidated by ANC action-group members who were later seen leading the stoning of African shops. Of 28 persons arrested and convicted of various offences connected with the rioting, 23 proved to be ANC members, including 13 members of the Action Group, six women, and two party officials. The locality was declared a Riot Damage Area in accordance with the legislation and a levy imposed on the inhabitants was collected without incident.[34]

Work on the vast Kariba Dam across the Zambezi had commenced in 1956. It brought an influx of Italian construction workers as well as providing employment for many Africans. Although the Kariba Township was established on the South Bank there was a requirement for a police presence on the Northern Rhodesia side and Kariba Police Station was opened there under an assistant inspector.

Plans had to be made for the relocation of some 39,000 Northern Rhodesia Africans, mainly Valley Tonga, whose homelands would disappear under the waters of the 2,000 square mile manmade lake, which was to stretch back for 175 miles upstream at an average width of twelve miles. The lives and beliefs of these simple people were bound up with the mighty river. It was beyond their imagination that the Zambezi could be tamed, even by white men. Record floods in 1957 and 1958, which caused set-backs to construction work, including bursting over the coffer-dam on 23 February 1958, reinforced their disbelief. People were therefore receptive to the blandishments of Congress agitators that they should not allow themselves to be moved.

After a disturbance at Chief Chipepo's village early in June, a detachment of police was sent to the Gwembe area, which would commence to flood when the dam was closed in November. In Southern Rhodesia the people were moved to higher ground, but those of chiefs Chipepo and Chisamu in Northern Rhodesia made clear their intention to stay put.

More platoons of the Mobile Unit were concentrated in the area, together with one formed from personnel from stations through-out Southern Division. The Governor, Sir Arthur Benson, had served in the area as a young administrative officer. He was sure that the people would listen to him. Benson went to Chisamu's village on 6 September. He called an indaba which he attended in full ceremonial dress accompanied by the Police Band. Only one hundred tribesmen could be prevailed upon even to come to listen to him. The following day only Chisamu, two of his headmen and thirteen others appeared to hear the Queen's representative. The people were not going to move, nor would they allow their women and children, old men and sick to be taken.

Sir Arthur departed. Tribesmen from miles around began to assemble at Chisamu's armed with spears and bows. On 10 September 1958 they attacked the police who had to open fire, killing eight and injuring thirty-two. Twenty-four arrests were made. Resettlement then proceeded in an orderly manner.

The Commission of Inquiry appointed by the Northern Rhodesia Government to inquire into the incident completely exonerated the police. It laid the blame for the tragedy largely at the door of local members of African National Congress, although it found no direct evidence that they had acted on instructions from party headquarters. The lawyer representing Congress did not question the action of the police in any way.[35]

Just as consideration was being given to ceasing rail escorts, there was a derailment on 29 September 1958 near Chilanga, ten miles south of Lusaka. The train was the 14-up, mixed passenger and goods, known as the 'Mixed Mail', which left Kafue at 0445hrs with 300 African passengers. The line near Chilanga consists of bends with cuttings, culverts, embankments, and gulleys. Because of this, and in accordance with Rhodesia Railways speed limits, the train was not travelling very fast, when the locomotive gave a sudden lurch. The driver later said that, 'Immediately I was certain in my own mind that the train had become derailed'. With great skill and presence of mind he was able to pull up his 200 ton locomotive within 280 feet. It came to rest leaning against a cutting on the east side of the line.

On dismounting the driver found that the locomotive and tender had become detached from the rest of the train. Happily the passenger carriages had been at the rear. Only nine goods wagons had left the line. The first seven of these were

Officers and European Civil Staff of Southern Division HQ and Livingstone Central 1958 (Photo N. C. Hulette)

L to R Back Row: Sub Insp, D/Sub Insp, D/Sub Insp, A/Insps H G R Pope, J Hambly, M K Marron, N C Hulette, R E Dixon, J J I Hawkins, S/M Zulu. *Middle Row:* S/Insp K R Killick, Insp A V Allen, W/R/A/Insp Holzer, A/Insps P Ryan, T B Wright, Insp F G Buckton, A/Insps J D Barker, P D Taylor, K G Steer, W/A/Insp A Adams, Mrs E E Aronson, Mrs P J Burgess, A/Insp J G McLean, S/M. *Front Row:* D/A/Insp N Mason, Insp R Mbewe, Miss D M Davis, Mrs Payne, W/A/Insp M Upton, J S Cullen Supt, O L Mitchell S/Supt, I O Ward A/Supt, P. Wheeler A/Supt, G A Harris A/Supt, W/A/Insp V Dixon, Sub Insp.

piled up together in the cutting, virtually reduced to matchwood. The wagon immediately in front of the first passenger coach had come to rest with its front bogey off the line and its rear bogey on the rails. The driver, guard and conductor, all Europeans, quickly ascertained that no one had been injured other than the conductor himself, who had received a blow on the head as a result of the sudden application of the brakes.

Lying at the side of the track were found seventeen pairs of clip bolts and nuts and four pairs of fish plates, which are used to join one rail to another. Scattered about were a number of bolts, nuts, washers and clips. Obviously the derailment was the result of a deliberate act. The line had been inspected at 1600hrs the previous day and another train had passed over since then.

A State of Emergency was declared throughout the Railway Reserve, the strip of land including the line itself and 100 feet each side of it. In 1959 special police railway detachments, of two or three subordinate police officers and about 20 other ranks each, were set up at Livingstone, Monze, Lusaka, Broken Hill and Ndola. Meanwhile platoons of the Mobile Unit were employed patrolling the railway. One constable was attacked by a leopard while cycling along the line between Chilanga and Kafue.

Meanwhile investigations were proceeding into the derailment under Mr J F Harrison, Assistant Superintendent, District Criminal Investigation Officer,

Lusaka. There was, of course, a striking similarity with the derailment at Chunga in 1957. During that investigation information had been given by a former constable who had become a man of power and influence in an unauthorised shanty town near Lusaka. Jim Harrison had had the doubtful privilege of paying this character £250 after his information led to a conviction. Shortly after the Chilanga derailment the ex-constable was arrested for housebreaking and theft, convicted and sentenced to imprisonment. On the way to Broken Hill Prison he offered to provide the names of those responsible for the latest derailment. It was too much of a coincidence! The same modus operandi and the same informant knowing the identities of what must be a different party of saboteurs, for the others were safely in jail!

Inquiries were concentrated on the former constable's haunts. In his absence people became talkative. He was said to have announced at about 5.30 am on 29 September 'I am going to the police to give information about a train that has fallen off the tracks that way' and pointed towards Lusaka. His wife said that on the morning of the crash he had not returned home until after the 'second cock', i.e. about 4.30 to 5.00 am. He had washed himself thoroughly and cleaned his clothes before going to sleep.

Intensive inquiries and cross checking of statements revealed that five men had set out in the direction of Chilanga on the night 28–29 September to derail a train

Inspector F. G. Buckton, A/Inspector N. C. Hulette and A3 platoon mobile unit parade in full dress at Livingstone 1958 (Photo N. C. Hulette)

so that 'more money can be got from the Government', as the ringleader, the ex-constable, finally admitted.

The accomplices had been carefully selected. No one but their leader knew who else was to take part until they set out, five men with three cycles, on the evening in question. En route to Chilanga they stopped at a compound on the outskirts of Lusaka to fortify themselves with beer. Foolishly they quarrelled with the beer-seller over change and he remembered them, picking out the former constable at an identification parade even though the man's twin brother was included in the line-up.

After the beer drink the five moved on south past the Police Training School at Lilayi. Near Chilanga one remained with the bicycles while the others went to the cutting. Here another was posted to keep watch while the remainder unbolted the rails.

After all had been arrested, two, including the cycle watcher who claimed to have fallen asleep, turned Queen's evidence, and only the cunning ex-policeman and two others were committed for trial on 18 November. After a three week trial all three were convicted on 24 February 1959 and sentences of eight, three and one years imprisonment awarded. The motive had been pure private enterprise but the State of Emergency was not lifted.[36]

The phenomenal development of previous years slowed down in 1958 but the demand for increased police services in Northern Rhodesia did not. A major expansion plan was implemented with a view to almost doubling the strength of the Force over a four year period.

Provision was made in the 1958–59 estimates for increases in establishment of 189 Europeans, including 13 Superior Police Officers and 8 women, and 1,100 African ranks. £900,000 was allocated from the Capital Fund for the continuation of the special building programme launched in 1957 for the construction of new stations and housing. Actual capital expenditure was to be £859,737 with recurrent expenditure on the Force at £1,968,423.

By the end of 1958 there were 105 Superior Police Officers, 536 European subordinate officers, 3,470 African police, 13 police cadets and 46 buglers out of an establishment of 121 SPOs, 693 European subordinate officers, 4,084 African police, 18 cadets and 56 buglers. The problem of a shortage of experienced officers, inevitable during a period of sustained expansion, continued and was to remain with the Force permanently. 58 per cent of European subordinate officers and 62 per cent of African police had completed less than five years police service.

During 1958 reported offences against the Penal Code increased by 14 per cent with the perpetrator identified and convicted in 33 per cent of true cases. The continued increase in such cases was attributed to the steady growth of the urban population of the Territory, especially the increase in the number of urban unemployed caused by a temporary recession particularly in the building trade. Burglaries, housebreaking and thefts involving the property of Africans showed an increase by 30.1 per cent over 1957, but there was a significant decrease in cases involving Europan property. This was ascribed to the increased security-mindedness of the average white householder, modern buildings, and the use of radio controlled patrol cars and more foot patrols in European residential areas.[37]

Railway cycle patrol 1959 (Nkhwazi)

There had been a marked increase in juvenile crime. There were 114 cases involving European juvenile offenders double those in 1957. At 1,053 cases involving African juveniles were up 8.1 per cent. These increases were attributed to lack of parental control, aggravated in the case of Africans by the loosening of moral standards due to de-tribalisation brought about by urban life.

In the New Year's Honours List Mr D W Humphrey, Assistant Commissioner Headquarters, was awarded the Queen's Police Medal for Distinguished Service. Denis Humphrey was one of the original members of the purely civil Northern Rhodesia Police, joining as a constable in 1932. On 31 January 1959 he left on transfer to Tanganyika as Deputy Commissioner of Police.

In January 1959 a Central Firearms Registry was established at Force Headquarters to record details of all breech-loading firearms in the Territory.[38]

In March 1958 the British Government had issued a White Paper supposedly designed to associate Africans in greater measure with the government of Northern Rhodesia. It contained complicated proposals to widen the franchise for an enlarged Legislative Council with 22 directly elected members and an Executive

Council with a majority of unofficials. This was deplored by Welensky's United Federal Party as going too far with African advancement, and by the African National Congress for not going nearly far enough. Nevertheless Harry Nkumbula showed an inclination to take advantage of what was given and spoke of Africans not being ready for self-government for another ten years. Other Congress leaders urged a boycott of the new Constitution and a campaign to bring about majority rule by 1960. They wished to see a more militant policy, as witnessed by the acts of violent resistance to Government authority described above. In Lusaka three members of African National Congress were convicted of arson having set fire to the houses of fellow Africans.

In May Nkumbula had made himself unpopular by handing the accounts of the Western Province Branch of Congress to the CID at Ndola. The investigation went on for several months to the annoyance both of dishonest party officials and of those who wished to see a purified party, but one which had nothing to do with the police. Nkumbula's fondness for alcohol and the good life generally, alienated puritans.

In the months leading up to ANC's national conference, held at Chilenje African Township, Lusaka, on 21 October, Nkumbula tried to purge the party machine of his opponents. Kenneth Kaunda who was becoming increasingly dissatisfied with Nkumbula's leadership had left Northern Rhodesia in May for a World Assembly of Youth Conference without Nkumbula's blessing. Thereafter he remained well out of the way in India until 12 October. The ANC executive conference, and subsequent general conference, were marked by bitter quarrels and walkouts. In spite, or perhaps because, of this, Harry Nkumbula was reelected president unopposed on 26 October. On the same day Kaunda and Simon Kapwepwe resigned from ANC and announced their intention of forming a rival Zambia African Congress.

On 8 November sixty delegates attended ZANC's first conference near Broken Hill. Kaunda was elected president with Kapwepwe as treasurer. Munukuyamba Sipalo, expelled from ANC in 1957, was elected Secretary General of the new party.

Zambia African National Congress was determined to make a mockery of the Legislative Council elections on 20 March 1959. The Government was anxious that the extended franchise should be demonstrated by substantial numbers of Africans registering as voters. ZANC embarked on a campaign of intimidation to prevent this and to cause more desertions from ANC. Nkumbula stood as a candidate.[39]

The security situation was not improved by the activities of an up and coming Labour Party member of the United Kingdom Parliament, John Stonehouse. Immigration was a Federal Government concern. The Federal Prime Minister decided that enough was enough even from a British politician. On the Morning of 3 March 1959 Stonehouse was taken to Lusaka Airport by immigration officers and deported.[40]

It was decided that ZANC must be neutralised if the elections were to proceed peacefully. On 9 March plans were laid in great secrecy and on the 11 the Governor, using his powers under Section 2(1) of the Emergency Powers Ordinance, issued the Safeguard of Elections and Public Safety Regulations 1959. Before dawn on 12 March Kaunda and fifty five of his most prominent followers were arrested in a territory-wide swoop, 'Operation Longjump'. Kaunda was flown to Balovale and from there driven to Kabompo. The remainder were rusticated to other remote areas mainly in Barotseland and North-Western Province. In a broadcast the Governor described the Zambia African National Congress as akin to 'Murder Incorporated'. The elections passed off quietly. Harry Nkumbula became one of six African members of the Legislative Council. 6,821 Africans had registered as 'special' and 796 as 'ordinary' voters.

The long term results of Operation Longjump were more in Kaunda's favour. ZANC had been declared an illegal organisation, but was soon to rise again as the United National Independence Party. The restricted leaders, well supplied with Government money, led a comfortable life spreading the nationalist word in areas selected by the Government because of the previous lack of political awareness locally.[41]

Early on Sunday 15 March a district officer and three messengers went to the UNIP office on Chilubi Island, Lake Bangweulu. Faced with a group of villagers armed with spears and sticks, he withdrew to rumours of arson on all Government and Mission property. Mr G E K Walsh, District Commissioner, Luwingu, a district assistant and a party of thirty messengers arrived late on 15 March. Next morning twenty one persons were arrested for various offences but were released in a brief confrontation with hundreds of tribesmen at Muchinchi sub-boma in which the DC received a spear wound and his assistant was so seriously injured that he had to be flown to hospital in Lusaka. Four villagers were killed and ten wounded and several messengers and kapasus injured before the Government Party withdrew leaving the buildings to be burnt and looted. In accordance with Sir Arthur Benson's policy the area was without police.

C/Insp Don Bruce was serving an attachment with the Provincial Adminis-tration at Chinsali. He received a signal from the Commissioner of Police ordering him to return to CID duty and proceed to Chilubi with D/Sgt Bwalya who would reach him that night with a landrover. Bruce obtained a statement from Mr Walsh at Luwingu and embarked on a seven hour journey by boat from Nsombo to Muchinchi where he found Insp Brian McEwen had already arrived with a platoon of the Mobile Unit and set up camp. Order had been restored. More than 100 adult males were arrested. Some 50 were tried and convicted on the spot for minor thefts etc. Others were remanded for trial at Kasama where 32 were convicted of offences from riot to attempted murder receiving sentences of from five to ten years. It turned out that the manager of Booth's store had taken advantage of the turmoil to remove the contents of the safe. He readily confessed and being able to identify his usual customers provided useful evidence to corroborate that of the Boma messengers. His own sentence of six months imprisonment was suspended by Mr J W Cronin SRM.[42]

In January 1959 a mob had run riot in Limbe after Doctor Hastings Banda had held an 'Emergency Meeting' of his Nyasaland African National Congress. On 20 February serious disorder broke out in various other places in Nyasaland. On 28 February a platoon of the Northern Rhodesia Police Mobile Unit was sent to Fort

Jameson. This precaution led to a dramatic headline in the Northern News, 'N.R. Guns on Nyasa Border'. Hastings Banda said 'you have heard of the so called riots. Well things are hot here. I have the whole of Blantyre and Zomba on fire. Very soon I hope to have the whole of Nyasaland on fire'. On 3 March the Governor of Nyasaland, Sir Robert Armitage, declared a State of Emergency. Additional troops of the Rhodesia and Nyasaland Army were sent in with detachments of police from Tanganyika and Southern Rhodesia. Northern Rhodesia being now calm, Mr Fforde was able to accede to the request for reinforcements.

No.3 Platoon of the Mobile Unit left Bwana Mkubwa for Lusaka at 0530hrs 25 March, being joined en route by 4 Platoon from Broken Hill. At Lusaka the detachment picked up additional stores and reinforcements before leaving at 0500 hrs Thursday 26 March. On Easter Sunday, 29 March, the detachment reached Lilongwe and pitched camp at the old airport which had to first be cleared of grass six foot high. Additional European officers enabled each platoon to be divided into three patrols of one officer and 12 African police. Working in landrovers with attached field intelligence officers drawn from Nyasaland Government departments such as Agriculture and Veterinary, these patrols were found to be a suitable organisation for the required follow up operations and arrest of wanted persons.

There were two large operations. Ndevu's Village, some 23 miles from Lilongwe on the Fort Manning Road was said to be recalcitrant. A cordon and search operation was mounted with two platoons of the Rhodesian African Rifles, Southern Rhodesians, providing the cordon, while the two Northern Rhodesia Police platoons carried out the search of the village which was about a mile long and lay 300 yards from the road. 37 arrests were made and Congress funds and ammunition seized.

On 10 April a patrol visited Mbewa's Village in the Fort Manning District. Insp O'Neill of the Nyasaland Police and A/Insp Donald Scott, Head Constable Mpezeni and consts Seven and Mutonga of the NRP were attacked by two men armed with pangas whilst trying to effect their arrest. They secured one but the other escaped.

A night operation was mounted. The platoon from Fort Jameson under Acting Inspector Geoff Hills and A/Insp Paddy Ryan was already operating in the Fort Manning area. It was now joined by 3 and 4 platoons who travelled ninety miles from Lilongwe to the rendezvous. Mbewa's village was cordoned in darkness and search parties moved in at dawn. The wanted man was found sleeping in his garden hut some distance from the village and arrested.

In all 12 European officers and 143 African police under the command of Mr J F Matheson, S/Supt, Officer Commanding the Mobile Unit, with Mr J R Barber, A/Supt, formed the detachment in Nyasaland, supported by a civilian wireless technician, Mr Ivor Finter, and a vehicle mechanic, Mr Bill Crook. The NRP covered 46,826 miles in 41 vehicles of various types and made 72 arrests in Nyasaland. Some of those arrested had attended a secret meeting near Blantyre at which murderous attacks were reported to have been planned against Government officials and white families.[43]

Twelve assistant inspectors of the Northern Rhodesia Police were seconded to the Nyasaland Police to assist with general police duties until that force could recruit adequate European staff.

On 21 March 1959 Colonel H B Perkins OBE had arrived from England to take up the new post of Assistant Commissioner, (Special Duties). An officer with much security service experience in the Mediterranean and elsewhere, Perkins was to be responsible for advising the Northern Rhodesia Government on counter-sabotage and to organise security precautions on vital installations. Another new post, Assistant Commissioner (Training) was filled on 21 May by Colonel J D Stewart, a police officer from Scotland who had served as Deputy Inspector General of Police with the Control Commission in occupied Germany.

On 22 April 1959 the Northern Rhodesia Police provided a guard of honour at Lusaka Airport for the departure of Sir Arthur Benson on retirement. He was succeeded as Governor of Northern Rhodesia by Sir Evelyn Hone KCMG CVO OBE who had been Chief Secretary since 1957.[44]

On 27 April North-Western Division was established under Mr F D R Gray, Assistant Superintendent, with stations at Solwezi and Balovale. In May 1959 a police station was opened at Namwala in Central Division.[45]

For over a year there had been intermittent trouble in the Chinsali District of Northern Province due to the activities of members of the Lumpa Church, founded by the 'prophetess' Alice Lenshina Mulenga Lubusha of Kasomo Village. In 1953 Alice Lenshina, then about 29 years of age, had some form of religious experience during which she 'died' and came to life again. She resumed instruction with the United Church of Central Africa at Lubwa and was baptised. She then began preaching herself and exorcising 'witches'. Disciples were drawn to Kasomo by such an indigenous expression of worship which they found lacking in the existing churches. Soon Alice Lenshina found herself at the head of a truly African church. By the end of 1955 the movement was widespread in the Kasama, Isoka, Chinsali, Mpika and Lundazi districts. She encouraged her followers, known as Lumpas, to join the African National Congress, but did not welcome any interference in the running of her church.

In September 1956 a Lumpa church member was sentenced to one month's imprisonment for calling a Roman Catholic priest a wizard. There were demonstrations at Chinsali Boma during which Lenshina's husband, Petros Chitankwa, and others were arrested. Chitankwa was sentenced to two years in prison for proposing violence to an assembly. The Lumpas set up unregistered villages and held unauthorised meetings outside their churches. Early in May 1959 a platoon of the Mobile Unit was called to assist the Native Authority to restore order at a village near Lenshina's headquarters, Kasomo. On arrival the police were surrounded by a crowd of Lumpas armed with various weapons, and had to open fire. Three of the crowd were wounded but none fatally. The official report showed that, although Alice Lenshina had been unco-operative throughout, the extent of the disobedience and resistance to authority encountered was due more to the influence in the area of the Zambia African National Congress.[46]

In May 1959 the state of Northern Rhodesia was such that the Governor lifted some of the restriction orders, made in March. In July the progressive release of the remaining detainees started. Kenneth Kaunda was not yet to roam free. On

Mobile unit officers and NCOs on return from Nyasaland 1959 (Photo N. C. Hulette)
Seated L to R: H/Const Zulu, H/Const Mpezeni, A/Insp P Spring, Ag Insp G L Hills, R J Barber
A/Supt, Ag Insp N C Hulette, A/Insp M G Anketell, A/Insp P Ryan, H/Const, H/Const Bota.

20 June a Lusaka magistrate sentenced him to six months imprisonment for conspiring to effect an unlawful purpose and three months for convening a unlawful assembly. On 29 June Munu Sipalo was convicted and sentenced for similar offences committed prior to Operation Longjump.[47]

On 31 October Assistant Inspector C N Barr, Constable Mate and a driver were in a police car on patrol in Kitwe when they received a report of a disturbance in domestic servants' quarters at 14th Avenue Nkana. A gardener appeared to be running amok. On the arrival of Barr and Mate the man ran off down a sanitary lane. The police officers gave chase. As Colin Barr came up to him, the man turned and stabbed him in the stomach. He then attacked Mate with a knife but the constable managed to defend himself with his baton. Barely conscious Barr staggered away and telephoned Kitwe Central Police Station. Mate ran back to the police car and radioed for assistance. Assistant Inspector Robert Vivian Winney was on traffic patrol with Constable Peter Pensulu Kasalu. They went to the scene where they were joined by a local resident, Mr Ronald Gordon Schmidt. All three went to the servants' quarters where the man had taken refuge. Schmidt opened the door and as the man ran out Kasalu threw his greatcoat over his head,

The Commissioner of Police, Mr. J. P. I. Fforde, visiting mobile unit in 1959
(Photo P. Spring)
L to R: Mr Fforde, J F Matheson S/Supt, A/Insp P Spring, Ag Insp N C Hulette, H/Consts
Mpezeni & Bota, a sergeant.

but he threw it off. Bob Winney then attempted to take the knife and received stab wounds in the stomach. Kasalu was stabbed twice in the back and Schmidt once in the arm before the culprit was overpowered.[48]

On 1 November Winney died from his injuries in the Llewellyn Hospital Kitwe. He was posthumously awarded the Queen's Police Medal for Gallantry. Barr recovered from his serious injuries and returned to duty in 1960. He and Peter Kasalu were awarded the Colonial Police Medal for Gallantry. Mr Schmidt received the British Empire Medal. Kasalu, a 27 year old Lenje from Broken Hill District, had joined the Force in 1953 from the Department of Posts and Telegraphs. In 1965 he was serving at Lusaka Central as a sub-inspector in the Zambia Police.

Recurrent expenditure for the year ending 30 June 1959 was £1,968,423 against an estimate of £1,946,274. Capital expenditure was £859,737. In December 1959 Mr A J Austin, formerly Accountant General for Northern Rhodesia, joined Force Headquarters as Financial Adviser. His son was already serving as a police cadet.

A total of 61,599 offences of all types were recorded during 1959 and the fingerprints of 55,882 persons were filed in the main collection.

Notes

1. Rt Hon Sir Chas BATHURST 1st Baron BLEDISLOE of Lydney 18 PC 26 KCMG 30 KBE 19 FSA b21.9.67 ed Sherborne Eton Oxon R Agric Cllge Cirencestr Bar'94 MP(C) SWilts'10–18 Parlty Sec Min Food'16 RMonRE Capt, MS Salisby Trg Cntre'16 Director Sugar Distrbn'17–19 Parlty Sec Min Agric 11.24–2.28 Gov NZ'30–6
2. Sir Roland (Roy) WELENSKY PC K(53)CMG 46 b Salisby SR 20.10.07 s/o Michael b Poland, left sch age 14 Fireman Rys & boxer BH'24 Rly Wkrs U, MLC'38 UFP MP Fed Parlt'53 MinTpt & Developmnt & Deputy PM, PM Rhod & Nyasald 2.11.56–31.12.63 left Zimbabwe'81 Blandfd Forum d5.12.91
3. Arthur CREECH-JONES PC 43 b91 Nat Sec TGWU 19–29 MP(Lab) Shipley'35 PPS Lab & Nat Svce'40 PUS Colonies'45 SofS'46–50 MP(Lab) Wakefield'54 d64
4. Dauti YAMBA b Kazembe's, Teachr, Hd Mstr Luanshya Af Sch'41–Edn Cncllr Lunda NAuthy'47 Co–Founder Fedn of Welfare Socs 18.5.46 ANC MLC'51 Fed MP'53
   Geo KALUWA Tdr & Fmr Mazabuka. Co fndr Fedn of Af Societies 18.5.46 A/Treasr ANC 7.48
   Harry NKUMBULA ANC Ila b Namwala'14 ed Kafue Trg Inst Stndd VI Tchr'34 Tchr NRG'38 Hd Mstr Wusukili Af Sch'44 UCllege Makere Uganda'46 LSE BSc(Econ) failed 1.50 Pres ANC 8.51
5. Kenneth David KAUNDA s/o Sch Mstr ex Nyasald Sec Gen ANC 8.53 Pres ZANC'58 UNIP'59 Min Local Govt & Social Welfare 12.62 PM 64 Pres Zambia 24.10.64
6. Sidney James WEBB 1st Baron PASSFIELD 29 PC 24 LLB b Londn 13.7.59 Clk Colonial Brkrs Offce'75 WO'78 Svyr of Taxes'79 Class I Civ Svt Colonial Offce'81–91 Bar'85 Mbr LCC 92–1910 RComm Trade Union Law 03–6 ProfPub Admn LSE 12–1.27 MP Seaham Durham'22–29 Pres Bd of Trade Jan–Nov 24 SofS Dominion Affrs'29–30 & Colonies 29–31
7. Col Wm Angus MULLER CMG 46 KPM 44 CPM CStJ b30.7.98 ed UCS RCSc, Pte Queens'15 2Lt RGA AMaj'18 Ceylon P'20 CofP & Cmdt Loc Forces Trin & Tobago'38 OC Tps 39–40 CofP Tanganyika'48 IG Col Police'51–7 d18.1.70
8. *Nkhwazi* Vol 12 No.1 Apr'64 p44, Annual Report 1954 Rhodes Hse
9. *Nkhwazi* Apr'64 p44
10. *The Old Depot & the New Training School Nkhwazi* Apr'64 p70
11. *The Northern Rhodesia Police Band Nkhwazi* Apr'64 p58
12. Letter seen by the Author at FHQ in 1958
13. *Nkhwazi*, Mulford *Zambia, the Politics of Independence 1957–1964* p39
14. *Nkhwazi* 1955
15. *Nkhwazi* Apr'64 p45
16. Sir Arthur Trevor BENSON G(59K54)CMG 52 b21.12.07 Staffs s/o Richd A H Benson fmrly of Co Limerick & Jo'burg ed Wolverhamptn Oxon Cdt NR 32 Colonial Offce 39 War Cabinet Offce 40 Col Offce 43 Secretariat NR 44 Adm Sec Ugda 46 Ch Sec Centrl Af Councl 49 Ch Sec Nigeria 51 Gov NR 54–9
17. PRO CO/1037/28/94/3/02
18. Annual Report
19. Hamish Scott-Knight NRJ
20. Annual report 1956 Rhodes Hse
    Matthew de Luxe NKHOLOMA Gen Sec ATUC & AMWU
    Lawrence KATILUNGU Pres AMWU & ATUC until 8.55 agn Pres 56 dRTA 9.11.61
21. PRO CO/1037/28/94/3/02
22. PRO CO/1037/28/94/3/02
23. *Nkhwazi* vol 6 No.1 Mar 1956
24. 'The Mongu Trials' *Nkhwazi* 1957, *Note on Barotse Witchcraft Murders* CID HQ 18.3.57
25. Annual report 1957
26. Annual report 1957, *Nkhwazi* Apr'64 p45
27. *Nkhwazi* Vol 6 No.1 Mar 1958 p18, Annual report 1957
28. *Nkhwazi* 1957, Annual report
29. Annual Report 1957, Mulford *Zambia, the Politics of Independence* p64

30. Annual report 1957 Govt Printer Lusaka, *Nkhwazi* Apr'64
31. Annual report 1957, *Nkhwazi* Apr'64 p46
32. Annual report 1957
33. Annual report 1958
34. Annual report 1958, Mulford *Zambia, the Politics of Independence* p67
35. Annual report 1958, Mulford p72, *African Life* Jan 1959
36. Annual report, Harrison *Sabotage Or? Nkhwazi* Apr'64 p112
37. Annual report
38. *Nkhwazi* Apr'64
39. Mulford *Zambia, the Politics of Independence* pp68–76
40. Stonehouse *Prohibited Immigrant*
41. Mulford p77–106p
42. Bruce NRPA Newsletter No.51 Summer 1995 p19, Roland Hill *Father A L Boumier GM* Journal of the Orders and Medals Research Society, Winter 1989, *Nkhwazi* Apr'64
    John W Cronin b14.10.15 Solr 46 RM NR 19.8.55
43. *Nyasaland Patrol Nkhwazi* Vol 7 No.2 Sept 1959 p4
    Dr Hastings BANDA ed Edinburgh U, GP UK returned to Nyasald 58 Pres Malawi 63
44. Sir Evelyn Dennison HONE GCMG(65) CVO(54) OBE(46) b13,12,11 s/o Arthur Hone MBE Salisby SR edWellgtn RhodesU Grahamstown, Rhodes Scholar, Bar Lincoln's Inn, Cdt Tanganyika 27.7.35 A/DO'37 Sec to Govt Seychelles'44 ASec Pal'46 Colnl Sec Br Honduras'48 Ch Sec Aden'53 NR'57 Gov NR 22.4.59–24.10.64 d18.9.79
45. *Nkhwazi* Apr'64
46. Hudson *A Time to Mourn* pp12–30, *Nkhwazi*
47. Mulford *Zambia, the Politics of Independence* pp102–108
    Munu Kayambwa SIPALO, Lozi ed India to NR'57 ANC Exec expelled 12.57 Gen Sec ZANC/UNIP 11.58–62 Min Nat Resources 1.64
48. *Nkhwazi* Vol 8 No.2 Sep'60 p6, Vol 12 No.1 Apr'64 p47

CHAPTER 15

Interior Economy

The dress of the Northern Rhodesia Police reached almost its final form in 1957. There were several orders of dress:

European Officers:

Class I Full Dress: Khaki drill long sleeved jacket of service dress pattern with a flapped pouched pocket on each front skirt and a pleated and flapped patch pocket on each breast. The jacket was closed by four large Force buttons and had a step collar on each side of which was worn a small Force badge with the fish-eagle facing outwards. The initials NRP in chrome were worn on the khaki drill shoulder straps below any rank badges which were also white metal. All badges were worn over black felt backing, usually made from worn out fezzes. The pockets were fastened by medium sized Force buttons while the shoulder straps were secured by small Force buttons and three buttons of this size closed the opening behind each of the plain pointed cuffs.

The jacket was worn over a khaki-green Vantella shirt with detachable collar and a blue tie. Nether garments were khaki drill shorts reaching to one and a half inches above the knee, black ankle boots, blue woollen hosetops and green garter flashes. The puttees were light khaki for Superior Police Officers and drab for others. In later years all ranks adopted the light shade.

Full dress headdress was the khaki Wolseley helmet with blue pugri and the Force badge in front. The helmet peak was bound with black patent leather. All European officers wore a black leather Sam Browne belt with steel fittings and one shoulder brace. Superior Police Officers and Chief Inspectors carried an Infantry pattern sword with a black leather scabbard, frog and knot, while more junior officers carried a malacca cane with a silver knob embossed with the Force badge. The whistle was carried in an insert in the left breast pocket and attached to a blue lanyard worn on the left shoulder in all orders of dress.

Mounted officers wore Bedford cord breeches with black knee boots and steel spurs. In winter mounted escorts wore the blue Class II (Winter) jacket with blue breeches and a white Wolseley helmet with one blue fold in the white pugri. The helmet, whether khaki or white was embellished with a steel spike and chin chain.

298

The escort carried lances with pennons in the Force colours – blue, white and green. A blue shabraque edged with two white stripes and with the Force badge in the rear corners was placed under the saddle. Saddlery and harness was brown leather and headropes, white. Black leather gauntlets were worn.

Class II (Summer):   The same jacket shirt and tie as in full dress, worn with long khaki drill trousers with turnups, khaki socks and black leather shoes and the blue peaked cap. On less formal occasions and for office wear, a khaki drill belt with chrome buckle might be worn in place of the Sam Browne. When not wearing a sword, Superior Police Officers carried a black leather covered cane with a whistle at one end.

Class II (Winter):   A blue cloth uniform of identical cut to Class II (Summer) but with no turnups on the trousers and worn with a white shirt, black tie, blue socks and white string gloves. The blue uniform had first been introduced in 1951 but fell into disuse until revived by Mr Fforde in 1954.

Working Dress: Khaki drill shorts with a short sleeved khaki drill bush tunic with an open collar and fastened with four large Force buttons. The bush tunic had breast pockets of the same kind as the full dress jacket, but the pockets on the front skirts were not pouched. As an alternative a brown cotton patrol shirt could be worn except when attending court. This shirt, which made youthful officers look like boy scouts and others like Hitler's stormtroopers, was not popular. Officers took to having their own shirts made from khaki drill or wearing old Army shirts, until in 1958 a flannel shirt of a greenish drab was introduced. This in turn was replaced in about 1961 by the same grey shirt with miniature Force buttons as worn by African police. In working dress either boots, hosetops, garter flashes and puttees could be worn or black shoes with Colonial Police pattern blue-topped khaki stockings without garter flashes.

Prosecutors and officers employed in offices might wear the khaki drill belt, but otherwise the Sam Browne was worn in working dress. Superior Police Officers invariably carried canes and members of the inspectorate normally did so.

On the rare occasions when it was required the ·38 revolver was carried in a black leather holster on the left side of the belt. The blue revolver lanyard was worn round the right shoulder.

A V-necked khaki jersey-pullover of British Army pattern with shoulder loops could be worn with the shirt when required. In rural areas a khaki drill cover could be worn over the blue peaked cap and Superior Officers could wear a blue folding travelling cap of the type commonly called a side-cap, but more properly, a field service cap.

A khaki trenchcoat with brown leather buttons was the official wet weather wear.

Motor cyclists wore khaki breeches in working dress and blue in Class II (Winter) and all European members of traffic sections wore black leather gaiters in place of hosetops and puttees, and white cap covers. Crash helmets were white with 'POLICE' stencilled across the front in black. White traffic sleeves could also be worn.

The Staff Officer at Force Headquarters and all officers of or above the rank of Assistant Commissioner wore black gorget patches in all orders of dress. Superior Police Officers wore blue patrols on certain occasions. The patrol jacket had a closed collar and the trousers or overalls were decorated with a broad buff stripe down each outside seam. At the end of the decade a blue waist sash was adopted by Assistant Commissioners and above for wear with patrols on ceremonial occasions in place of the Sam Browne belt and on these occasions they carried their swords in steel scabbards suspended on slings.

Superior Police Officers wore blue patrols with cloth belt as Mess Dress in Winter. In warm weather the patrol jacket was replaced by a white mess jacket worn with a white shirt, wing collar, black bow tie and blue cummerbund. Miniature collar and rank badges were worn on the mess jacket.

Inspectors wore the mess jacket with wing collar, black tie and cummerbund whatever the season. This was to be worn with ordinary civilian black evening trousers, although the custom grew up of wearing blue uniform trousers with Mess Dress, since some officers were without civilian evening dress of a traditional pattern.

Badges of rank were worn on the shoulder straps in white metal as follows:

Motor cycle dispaly team 1960 (Nkhwazi)

Commissioner	Crossed tipstaves surrounded by a wreath surmounted by a crown
Deputy Commissioner	Crossed tipstaves surrounded by a wreath surmounted by two stars
Senior Assistant Commissioner	Crossed tipstaves surrounded by a wreath surmounted by one star
Assistant Commissioner	Crossed tipstaves surrounded by a wreath
Senior Superintendent	A star surmounted by a crown
Superintendent	A crown
Assistant Superintendent	Three stars
Acting A/Supt	Two stars
Chief Inspector	Three bars
Senior Inspector	Two bars
Inspector	One bar.

Assistant inspectors wore no badge of rank, but in the words of one constable in an examination paper 'just that big belt and NRP on his shoulder'.

Caps of assistant commissioners and above were decorated with silver oak leaf embroidery on the peak, while those of senior superintendents and superintendents bore a band of plain silver lace $\frac{3}{4}$ inch wide on the peak.

Badges of rank for African police were:

African Inspector	Two blue braid loops on each shoulder strap
Sub-Inspector	One braid loop as above
Sergeant-Major (from 1959 Head Constable)	A white metal crown on the right sleeve (a sergeant-major with four or more years service in that rank wore a wreath round the crown)
Sergeant	A three bar chevron worn point downward above the elbow, white tape in working dress, silver lace in full dress each on a dark blue background.

Entitled African police wore proficiency and specialist badges as follows, in white metal on black or dark blue backing on the right sleeve

Best shot in the Force	Crossed rifles surmounted by a crown surrounded by a wreath
Best shot in Division or Member of Force shooting team	Crossed rifles surmounted by a crown
Marksman	Crossed rifles
Qualified in first aid	Badge of the Order of St John
Bandsman	A lyre surmounted by a crown
Bugler	A stringed bugle
Driver	A wheel

Wireless operator	A box aerial within a circle
Armourer	Crossed pincers and hammer
Dog handler	An alsation's head within a circle
Farrier	A horseshoe
Mounted Branch	A horse's head.

At the Police Training School the orderly sergeant wore a scarlet infantry worsted sash over the right shoulder while the provost sergeant wore a similar sash in dark blue.

All ranks were issued with a steel helmet, a round metal shield and a long wooden baton, the size of a pick helve, a 1944 pattern respirator and a pair of anti-gas goggles, for use in riots. All European officers in the Force and all African police in the Mobile Unit were issued with 1937 pattern web equipment with waist belt, basic pouches, braces, haversack and straps supporting, water bottle and carrier, and, in the case of Europeans, pistol case and ammunition pouch. Web equipment was blancoed khaki-green and steel helmets were painted blue with 'POLICE' stencilled on the front in white. In the Mobile Unit, company commanders, platoon officers and sergeants-major had their steel helmets painted in the company colour for ease of recognition, for instance red for 'A' and green for 'C' Company.

Besides the ·38 revolver issued to each European officer and kept by him in his quarters, all firearms were kept in station or formation armouries. Sufficient ·303 Short Magazine Lee-Enfield Number 4 rifles with bayonets were held for issue to nearly every African policeman. For operations and drill a web sling and bayonet frog were used, but black leather slings and frogs were issued for ceremonial parades and guards of honour. Single barrelled Martini action Greener shot guns were available for use against snakes, rabid dogs etc and, during riots were normally issued to drivers to protect their vehicles. Bren light machine guns and Sterling sub-machine guns were issued on a scale of one each per Mobile Unit platoon and on a similar scale elsewhere.

An anti-riot platoon was normally organised into an armed section of six riflemen and two baton waves of approximately eleven men each. Each man in a baton wave carried a long baton, shield and a haversack of tear-smoke grenades. With the armed section the platoon commander had available two men carrying $1\frac{1}{2}$ inch riot guns and a supply of tearsmoke shells and baton rounds. In the Mobile Unit these men also carried eighteen inch bayonets which were useful to clear hard extractions. The platoon was completed by two first aid men and a bugler.

In Working Dress African police wore a grey flannel shirt with shoulder straps, two patch pockets and Force buttons. The whistle was worn in the left breast pocket on a chain hooked over the top button. Khaki shorts were worn with black ankle boots and long black puttees, which were replaced during 1958 by blue hosetops, green garter flashes and short drab puttees as worn by European inspectors. African sub-inspectors and inspectors wore their whistles on blue lanyards like European officers and might wear black shoes and Colonial Police stockings. African police headdress was the small khaki covered cork 'polo' helmet with blue pugri and Force badge. On traffic duty a white helmet was worn with a white pugri. White traffic sleeves were also worn on such duty. African police wore a divisional number prefixed by a letter indicating the division over the right breast. In chrome metal with black backing the divisional number was replaced by the man's Force number by 1959. At night and in cold weather the shirt was replaced by a blue woollen jersey with leather shoulder patches. At night in winter long khaki drill trousers were worn in place of shorts, together with a dark blue single breasted greatcoat with black horn buttons bearing the Force badge. A blue single breasted raincoat was also issued to African police.

Constables and sergeants wore a black leather waistbelt with a white metal locket fastener bearing a crown and the Force title. This was in the process of being replaced by a locket with the Force crest. The short baton was worn on the right side of the belt suspended from a white metal detachable baton hook. In later years a baton pocket was sewn into the shorts. The handcuffs were worn on the left side of the belt. Sergeants-major and above wore the black Sam Browne belt and carried malacca canes. Sergeants carried canes whangee (bamboo).

In riot dress the Force number was not displayed and the jersey was normally worn rather than the shirt.

In full dress African police wore a black fez with a black tassel falling to the right and the Force badge in front. A long sleeved bush tunic with detachable black shoulder straps replaced the shirt except for sub-inspectors and inspectors who wore a similar jacket to European officers but with a stand-up collar closed with hooks and eyes and bearing the collar badges.

Bandsmen wore the tunic with stand up collar with collar badges, black shoulder straps edged silver, black and silver wings and blue and silver dress cords. They wore white belts over blue cummerbunds and white spats in place of puttees. The fez tassel for bandsmen was black and silver.

Women officers wore blue peaked caps of the type then worn by women police officers in England, black shoes and khaki drill skirt with bush tunic or khaki drill jacket with greenish khaki shirt and blue tie. In winter women officers wore the blue Class II Winter uniform with a blue skirt. Women did not wear the Sam Browne belt. In 1959 women regular officers adopted a blue air hostess style cap and a khaki terylene Summer uniform the jacket of which had rounded skirts. The cotton shirt had patch pockets for working dress wear.

Members of the Northern Rhodesia Police Reserve wore the same Class II (Summer) and working dress as the regular Force, with shoulder titles 'NRPR'. Reserve assistant inspectors were not issued with Sam Browne belts and neither Full Dress nor Class II (Winter) were worn by members of the Northern Rhodesia Police Reserve, except those attached to the Mounted Section.

Cadets wore a light blue band round their caps and a black cloth shoulder title with 'POLICE CADET' embroidered in white. Cadets did not wear the Sam Browne. Recruitment of European assistant inspectors through the Crown Agents for Overseas Governments and Administrations in London was failing to produce sufficient numbers and new steps were taken to obtain suitable recruits in South Africa and Southern Rhodesia. The European cadet system, introduced in 1956, had been limited to youths who were locally resident. The end of conscription in the United Kingdom meant that potential recruits had already embarked on

Woman assistant inspectors Class II summer and working dress 1960

careers by the age of twenty one. Accordingly, during 1958, recruitment of United Kingdom school leavers as police cadets was commenced through an appointments board provided by the Commissioner for Northern Rhodesia in London. The age for attestation as assistant inspectors was lowered to twenty.

In September 1958 the first African policewoman, Woman Constable Veronica Changu was attested. W/Const Changu was a 24-year old Tonga from Mazabuka District and had formerly worked as a nursing assistant. On completion of the recruit training course at Lilayi she was posted to Choma. A second woman constable was recruited during the year, but the number of African women in the Force was always to be very small. Women constables wore the same grey shirt as the men, with a khaki drill skirt and a dark blue felt hat with a round crown and a brim. There was a blue ribbon round the crown of the hat which was worn with the Force badge in front.[1] By mid 1961 the hat was replaced by the blue

Riot drill 1956. Shield and baton drill: moving in extended formation
(NRP Riot Drill Manual)

peaked cap as formerly worn by European women of the regular Force and still worn by the Reserve.

In January 1959 the rank of African Inspector was abolished. Five of those who had held the rank were promoted Assistant Inspector Grade II and the remaining thirty-six, Assistant Inspector Grade III. European assistant inspectors were designated Assistant Inspector Grade I. This was the first step towards africanisation of the Force. Henceforth there were to be no references to European police or African police. Those of or below the rank of Sub-Inspector were to be known as 'Other Ranks' while holders of the ranks of Assistant Inspector Grade III up to Chief Inspector were to be known as Subordinate Police Officers, abbreviated to

Grenade drill: draw grenades, with respirator, shield and baton

s.p.o. to distinguish them from S.P.Os (Superior Police Officers) of gazetted rank. All grades of Assistant Inspector wore the same uniform without badge of rank. Rates of pay differed for each grade.

The most common police vehicle was the long or short wheel-base landrover with canvas canopy, although these were gradually replaced by the hard top variant. The Mobile Unit was equipped with the Bedford RL 3-ton troop carrier, introduced in the British Army in 1955, while until about 1960, other formations had to make do with older vehicles for troop carrying purposes. All troop carriers had the body of the vehicle protected against missiles by wire mesh. Bedford 3-ton load carrying vehicles, known as 'flat tops' were also in use, together with smaller Bedford vanettes, and closed vans for transporting prisoners to and from court.

Woman constable Changu 1958

All the above vehicles were painted blue with 'POLICE' stencilled in white on the doors. Wolseley saloons were used for traffic patrols and other work on tarred roads. By 1960 these had been replaced by Rovers.

To co-ordinate and promote sporting activities within the Force a Central Sports Committee had been formed in 1954 with Mr T M Davidson, Assistant Commissioner, as its first chairman. The expansion of the Northern Rhodesia Police brought plenty of good sportsmen into the Territory. Six members of the Force played in the Northern Rhodesia European Association Football Team which beat Bolton Wanderers three goals to nil at Broken Hill in May 1959. All three goals were scored by Assistant Inspector George Sharp, late of Darlington and Oldham Athletic. Assistant Inspector Derek Debell captained the Northern Rhodesia Team and was chosen as Lusaka's 'Sportsman of the Year'. Five members of the Lusaka European Police Football Team were selected to play for Northern Rhodesia against the Belgian Congo in August 1959.

Meanwhile multi-racial sport, in which the Force had always set an example, was not neglected. Lusaka Urban District were the 1959 winners of the Unsworth Cup with a team of four Europeans and seven African police. The cup had been presented to the Force in the early 1950s by Sir Edgar Unsworth, the then Attorney General and Minister responsible for the police. The Unsworth Cup

New Wolseley 6/90 patrol cars at force headquarters 1956

was the Force's football challenge cup, competed for annually by teams from all formations and the larger stations. To ensure a proper racial balance, each team had to contain not less than two and not more than four Europeans.

On 13 September 1959 the NRP team, consisting of Sgt Nyrenda, A/Insp Steel and Sgt Namalongo of Training School, Band Constable Shamainda of Mobile Unit, Const Mwelwa of Matero and A/Insp Durose of Ndola, beat nine other teams in the first cycle relay race from Lusaka to Broken Hill and back. Sgt Nyrenda took the lead from the start at 0900hrs but after 15 minutes his chain broke and he was 'Tail End Charlie' by the time he had replaced it. Nevertheless he was lying third when he handed over to A/Insp Steel who was soon in the lead which his team mates never lost. The police team covered the 172 miles at an average speed of 18.2 MPH despite Nyrenda's mishap with A/Insp Durose crossing the finish line at 1825 hrs.

The Northern Rhodesia Police played the British South Africa Police at rugby football each year, from 1956 until 1964, and never lost a match. In Lusaka a combined Military and Police team, Lusaka Forces, was prominent in the local league.

In each of the three years it was held, the Northern Rhodesia Police team won the Combined Services Hockey Tournament for teams from the Rhodesia and Nyasaland Army, the Royal Rhodesian Air Force, and the police forces of each territory.

In 1960 the Northern Rhodesia Police Shooting Team was to win the East and West Africa Police Cup for the first time although in 1956 a team consisting of sergeants-major Mwachiaba and Yaladi, Sgts Mwendachabe, Mumba and Mubulo and consts Sampa, Namachila and Kamala had scored 664 points out of a possible 672.

On 6 August 1961 Constable Alfred Ngoma crossed the finishing line at the new Civic Centre, Lusaka, breaking the unofficial World Record for the 110 miles walk by nearly an hour. The first of 44 contestants in a race organised by the

Lusaka African Welfare Office, Ngoma completed the distance in 25 hours and 3 minutes. There were only eight finishers. Some had given up through injury, some with blistered feet. Three gave up at the 55 mile post because they feared being eaten by a large lion they had seen on the road! Constable Ngoma was presented with two silver cups by the Mayor, Richard Sampson.[2]

On 3 January 1961 the Police Advisory Board was replaced by a Police Service Commission under the chairmanship of Sir Charles Hartwell, formerly Chief Secretary to the Uganda Government, who was also Chairman of the Northern Rhodesia Public Service Commission. The establishment of the Police Service Commission was in accordance with a recommendation in the Robertson Report. The Commission was to advise the Government on appointments, admissions to the permanent and pensionable establishment, promotions and discipline.[3]

Mr C. W. G. Hey, assistant superintendent, bandmaster, inspector D. Scott, assistant bandmaster, sub-inspector Kapape, drum major and the band Lusaka 1962 (Photo NRP)

In 1960 the Northern Rhodesia Police had celebrated the Diamond Jubilee of the raising of the Barotse Native Police. On 28th April the Force Band beat retreat at Wardroper Police Camp, Lusaka. Colonel The Lord Robins KBE DSO took the salute and, as Chairman of the British South Africa Company, presented the Force with six silver bugles and a silver statuette of the drum-major.[4]

As a mark of the common origins of the Northern Rhodesia Police and the Northern Rhodesia Regiment the police now replaced their green garter flashes with a new felt pattern showing red over green, while the regiment incorporated a strip of police blue in theirs.

On 2 April 1962 His Excellency the Governor, Sir Evelyn Hone KCMG CVO OBE, opened the Northern Rhodesia Military and Police Museum in the Old Boma building, Cairo Road, Lusaka. The museum was administered by the Trustees of the Rhodes-Livingstone Museum through a sub-committee which included the Colonel of the Northern Rhodesia Regiment, the Commissioner of Police, The Mayor of Lusaka, the Director of the Rhodes-Livingstone Museum and representatives of ex-servicemen's organisations, under the chairmanship of Mr J Thomson OBE. Pride of place among the exhibits was given to 'May Jackson', the seven pounder muzzle-loading mountain gun which first saw service with the Pioneer Column in Southern Rhodesia in 1890 and was taken north by Percy Sillitoe in 1914 for use against the Germans in East Africa.[5]

On 29 June 1962, at a ceremony at Wardroper Police Camp, Lusaka, recognising the golden jubilee of the Northern Rhodesia Police, His Excellency the Governor presented the Force with the following sterling silver band instruments, valued at some £4,000:

Six side drums, one bass drum and one drum-major's mace, with sterling silver embellishments, the gift of the Northern Rhodesia Government, three bugles and one tenor drum, the gift of the Anglo American Corporation, and three bugles and a tenor drum, the gift of the Rhodesian Selection Trust.

The final strength of the Band was:

1 Assistant Superintendent, C W G Hey, Bandmaster,
1 Inspector, Assistant Bandmaster,
1 Sub-Inspector, Drum-major,
1 Head Constable,
4 Sergeants,
54 Constables,
28 Buglers,

a total of ninety with the following instrumentation:

1 Flute,	5 Horns,	26 Bugles,
1 Piccolo,	14 B Flat Cornets,	5 Bass,
2 E Flat Clarinets,	4 Tenor Trombones,	6 Side Drums,
1 Oboe,	2 Bass Trombones,	2 Tenor Drums,
11 B Flat Clarinets,	2 Euphoniums,	1 Cymbals,
2 E Flat Saxophones,	2 B Flat Saxophone,	1 Bass Drum.[6]

Notes

1. *Nkhwazi* December 1958 p35
2. *Nkhwazi* Vol.10 No 2 Dec 62 p26
   Richd SAMPSON Mayor of Lka, author *So this was LUSAAKAS*, UNIP candidate'63
3. *Nkhwazi* Vol 12 No.1 Apr'64 p51
   Sir Chas Herbt HARTWELL Kt 60 CMG 54 b04 ed Cam CeylonCS 27 Pal 40 Ceylon 42
   DEstabs Kenya 47 DChSec 52 Ch Sec Ugda 55–7.60 Chmn NR Pub & Pol Svce Comms NR
   10.60–Min Overseas Develpmt 12.63 Advsr Govt Mauritius 66 Chmn Pub Svce CommHK 67–
   71 d31.8.82
4. *Nkhwazi* 1960
   Thomas Ellis ROBINS KBE 54 DSO 19 BA 1st Baron'58 bPhiladelphia 31.10.84 s/o Maj Robt
   P Robins US Army ed University of Pennsylvania Rhodes Scholar Oxfd, Asst Ed Everybody
   Magazine NY'07 PS to Earl Winterton & Lity Sec Anti–Socialist Union GB'09 City of London
   Yeo'14 PM EEF 2.19–1.21 Sec Conservative Club'21 OC CoLY Bty RHA TA'25–28 Res Dir
   BSACo Rhod, Lt Col Dir Int SR, CO 1RR'40 AA&QMG SR'43–5 Trustee Rhodes Livingstone
   Museum, Pres BSACo d21.7.62
5. *Nkhwazi* Vol 10 No.1 Aug 62
6. *Nkhwazi* Vol 12 No.1 Apr 64 p61

CHAPTER 16

Retreat from Federation

January 1960 brought a visit to the Territory by the British Prime Minister, Harold Macmillan[1], fresh from his 'Winds of Change' speech to the South African Parliament. The African nationalist parties staged demonstrations for his benefit. Macmillan handled the demonstrators well at Livingstone Airport, walking a little towards them and waving as if, according to one report, 'he was receiving an ovation from his constituents'. The crowd loved it and there was much cheering and good humour.

On 15 February 1960 the 26-member Advisory Commission on the future of the Federation, known after its chairman as the Monckton Commission, assembled at Victoria Falls. Lord Monckton of Brenchley[2] had been an adviser to King Edward VIII at the time of the Abdication crisis and to the Nizam of Hyderabad when that prince was attempting to avoid his state's absorption into the Republic of India. Prospects for the future of the Federation were not good! The Northern Rhodesia Police escorted members of the Commission who toured the Territory taking evidence from all who cared to approach them. The Commissioner of Police gave evidence of intimidation and violence by the African nationalist movements, particularly by the United National Independence Party, of which Kenneth Kaunda had become president on his release from prison in January. Kaunda and his followers declared that the Monckton Commission was biased in favour of Sir Roy Welensky, the Federal Prime Minister. UNIP boycotted the Commission raising the slogan 'Independence by October'. They got it in October, but four years later.

The Monckton Commission left Northern Rhodesia on 21 March and on the 27th Ian Macleod, the newly appointed Secretary of State for the Colonies, landed at Lusaka Airport[3]. His arrival in Nyasaland a few days earlier had resulted in allegations of brutality against the Nyasaland Police. A European inspector had accidently trodden on the bare foot of a woman demonstrator. In Lusaka a detachment of the Mobile Unit was positioned at the Longacres Hostel, but the police presence at the Airport was deliberately kept to a minimum. All European officers were ordered to wear shoes rather than boots! The United National Independence Party had decided that Macleod should be greeted by a major demonstration, the stars of which were to be a number of women, naked except for G-strings. Macleod tried to emulate his Prime Minister, but he was no 'Super Mac' and a

Lusaka crowd was a different proposition to a Livingstone crowd! Macleod approached too close to the barriers. An African leapt over and ran towards him shouting 'I will kill you!' A large number of yelling men and women burst through the thin police cordon. Macleod wisely withdrew to the safety of the official party and was bundled into the Governor's car and driven off down Jubilee Road. At one stage a banner was stretched over the windscreen so that the driver could not see and the vehicle had to come to a halt. The Commissioner of Police, himself, was seen plucking Africans from the front of the car so that it could proceed. Soon the reinforcements arrived from Longacres and the way was speedily cleared. Mr Fforde followed the Governor and his guest to Government House. Here a crowd of several hundred soon gathered. Several arrests were made before it dispersed peacefully.

The uncertainty following the departure of the Monckton Commission and the visits of the British ministers led to an increase in politically motivated intimidation and violence, including arson and stone throwing. The United National Independence Party applied for a permit to hold a public meeting at Ndola on Sunday 8th May. Because of the likelihood of violence, and interference with police recording teams at recent meetings, the application was refused. On the evening of 7 May the beating of drums was heard in Chifubu, accompanied by announcements that the meeting would be held the next day. An attempt was made to hold the meeting but the crowd was dispersed at 10 a.m. by two platoons of the Northern Rhodesia Police Mobile Unit. Agitators formed gangs from those leaving the scene of the meeting to set up road blocks and stone cars on the Mufulira and Kitwe roads. In Chifubu, houses, a clinic, welfare premises and beerhalls were attacked as well as police patrols. Beer was looted from the beerhalls. Attempts were made to burn two generating plants. The police had not been totally unprepared. 127 arrests were made that day and night.

At about 10 a.m on 8th May Lillian Burton was driving her children home from Ndola to Kaniki Plots on the Mufulira Road. Near the five mile peg she was forced to stop by a mob. The windows and windscreen of Mrs Burton's Morris Traveller car were smashed and petrol was splashed over her and ignited.

Mrs Burton's two daughters, aged twelve and five, managed to escape from the rear seat, although the younger girl suffered minor burns. Their mother had locked the driver's door but succeeded in rolling out of the blazing car through the nearside door. She landed on the ground with her hair and clothes alight. Lillian Burton and her daughters were brutally assaulted. Their pet spaniel was burnt alive in the car. A forest ranger found Mrs Burton in the Bush a short distance from the road. A passing motorist took her and the children to Ndola Hospital where they were admitted at 1.50 p.m. The mother was then wearing only shoes and a brassiere. She was in shock and suffering from 75 per cent burns, mostly third degree, and fairly extensive bruising.

Mr Denis Brockwell, Senior Superintendent, Divisional Criminal Investigation Officer, Western Division, received the report of Mrs Burton's admission at 3.00 p.m. Having arranged for the necessary immediate action to be taken at the scene of the crime, he went to the hospital with Mr G D Patterson, Superintendent, of Ndola CID. The two children were able to give the officers a brief description of the incident. Mrs Burton never recovered sufficiently to give her account, although women police officers were stationed at her bedside until her death a week later.

An African, Amon Nikusulumani, reported to Ndola Police Station and at 5 p.m, accompanied Brockwell and Patterson to the scene of the crime. Darkness was approaching as they examined the burnt out car. The door handles, steering wheel, dashboard, bonnet hinges and gear linkage had all melted in the intense heat. Molten solder was visible on the tarmac. A toolbox and certain articles from a vanity bag were missing from the car.

The Morris Traveller was about 350 yards from the junction of the Ndola-Mufulira Road with a dirt road from Chifubu, three miles away. On this dirt road were found three abandoned vehicles, a petrol driven Bedford lorry, a Ford Mercury saloon and a diesel Thames panel van. The Mercury had no petrol tank cap, merely a cloth bung.

Nikusulumani told the police that he had been delivering meat for his employer and was driving home from Mufulira to Chifubu in the panel van. At about 12.15 he was stopped on the dirt road by a group of Africans and forced to join them. He said he had escaped before observing any further action.

On 9 May the examination of the scene continued. A metal screw cap was found. Photographs were taken from the air to show the positions of the various vehicles. The owner of the Ford Mercury was identified as Balaboza Mutenge, who admitted running an unlicensed taxi service to Chifubu. The driver of the Bedford lorry, Fixon Mulenga, and two passengers, Banda and Kazembe, were also traced. All described being stopped and forced to join the group moving down the Chifubu Road.

It became clear that activists had recruited or press-ganged members of the crowd leaving Chifubu for Kabushi and elsewhere, and others encountered en route, and led them in two main groups. One had beset the Mufulira Road. The other had moved on to the Kitwe Road before attacking Kabushi Beerhall at 5 p.m. Twelve cars had been stoned on the two main roads, resulting in shattered windscreens and injured passengers. All except the Burtons had managed to get past. The difficulty was going to be to identify those directly responsible for the attack on the Burtons amongst so many.

There was widespread alarm and revulsion, with talk of forming vigilante groups among the Whites. Led by the United Federal Party and the European Mineworkers' Union they called for the proscription of the United National Independence Party. Riots and other disturbances had continued for several days. Swift action was taken to bring the unrest to a halt before it could be made worse by European reprisals. On 11 May the Governor, in accordance with the Preservation of Public Safety Ordinance, banned UNIP in the Western Province and declared all its Copperbelt branches unlawful. Kenneth Kaunda was away in London, but on 12 May orders were made banning him, Simon Kapwepwe, Munu Sipalo and two others from entering Western Province.[4]

Shock and indignation was not confined to Europeans. 600 people of all races attended the burial of Lillian Burton. One bouquet of flowers sent to her in hospital had borne the message 'From the Africans of Chifubu, the vast majority of us are horrified at the incident'.

Denis Brockwell and his superiors were well aware that the best way to reassure the public was by speedily bringing Mrs Burton's murderers to justice. The widespread shame at what had occurred was in his favour, but fear was against him. In 1964 he was to write in the Police Journal, 'Never during my twenty-seven years police career in Africa have I experienced such profound fear as prevailed in witnesses' minds during this investigation'.[5]

On 12 May he moved the base for the investigation from the Western Division Headquarters building to a vacant house in Wilkinson Police Camp, Ndola. Here the investigators worked in complete secrecy. Windows were blanketed and guards posted night and day. Nikusulumani and other witnesses were given police protection and initially housed under guard at the Mobile Unit Camp at Bwana Mkubwa. On 8 July 1960 they were moved to a wired enclosure built to house emergency detainees in Wilkinson Camp. Twenty-two witnesses with their wives and children were housed here until after the prosecution closed its case in January 1961. Detectives lived with them and, as far as possible, witnesses were prevented from communicating with each other. The task of cross-checking statements was thus made easier. Witnesses prevaricated for fear of implicating themselves as accomplices as well as out of fear of reprisals by African nationalists.

Information was received that a Central African Road Services bus conductor, Marko Mwansa, had mentioned being with a gang which stopped one of his company's buses. Other witnesses had described a tall man leading such a gang. Mwansa's evidence enabled this man to be identified as Cresta Ngebe, a former teacher, absent from his employment with Lafferty and Company at Ndola since 7 May.

Inquiries revealed that Ngebe had returned to Ndola after a mysterious absence, but had not returned to work. Mwansa related how Ngebe had stopped the three vehicles on the Chifubu Road and ordered the occupants to join his party. Mwansa had heard Ngebe demand petrol from Nikusulumani and Balaboza and told how Ngebe had removed a two gallon petrol tin from Nikusulumani's van. The charred remains of such a tin had been found 20 feet from Mrs Burton's car. The screw cap found earlier fitted it. Nikusulumani conceded ownership of the tin and corroborated Mwansa's account.

A suitcase and a piece of plastic tubing had been recovered from Balaboza's Ford Mercury. The owner of the suitcase, Chidule Aston, was located in Southern Rhodesia and brought back to Ndola. He had been Balaboza's passenger. Both now further corroborated Mwansa's story. They said a short man had used the tubing to syphon petrol into a two gallon tin similar to that recovered. Ngebe had commandeered the Bedford lorry to transport some of his party to the Mufulira Road junction, whilst others had been ordered there on foot.

The driver of the CARS bus was identified as Tennis David. On 8 May he had been driving a football team to Chifubu. He was now on scheduled service to Mbeya. His bus was intercepted by an aircraft of the Northern Rhodesia Police Reserve Flight before it entered Tanganyika. David was flown back to Ndola. He said he had been stopped from entering the Chifubu Road by a group which included the tall man, Ngebe, and also Mwansa and one Chanda, both of whom he recognised, and who had persuaded the crowd not to attack his bus. He had thus been able to turn back to Ndola.

On 25 May the Solicitor General was informed of the evidence collected. Plans were laid to pick up 14 suspects including Ngebe. Their homes were kept under observation and at 3 a.m. on 28 May 1960, Patterson, Brockwell and 14 teams of detectives set out to make the arrests. Cresta Ngebe was arrested in Chifubu. He claimed to have been in Elisabethville on 8 May and to have received treatment there for injuries received in tribal fighting. One Congo franc was found in his possession. An identification parade was held, with the witnesses hooded for their protection. Ngebe was identified, formally charged and remanded in custody by the court.

Brockwell flew in a Reserve Flight plane to Elisabethville. Assisted by the Katanga Judicial Police, he established that Ngebe had stayed at the Hotel Congolese there from 10 to 24 May. His accommodation had been arranged by the Conikat Party of Patrice Lumumba, who was also visiting Elisabethville at this time[6]. There was no record of any tribal fighting or of Ngebe having received medical treatment in Elisabethville. Immigration and Customs registers showed no record of Ngebe's entry into the Congo. Eventually information was received that on 9th May a man answering Ngebe's description had obtained a lift from Sakania to Elisabethville in a car belonging to a Conikat member, Symphorien Mwansa. On 11th June Symphorien and his other passenger, Kiola, also of Conikat, picked out Ngebe at an identification parade.

Marko Mwansa named the short man as Bulyo and said he had seen one Winter Kaponda on 8 May struggling for possession of the vanity bag at the scene of the murder. On 6 June Kaponda was found at Luanshya. He was intemperate and a drug addict, but after five days patient interrogation Kaponda had named the short man who syphoned petrol as Robin Kamima. Kaponda said he had seen a man called Chanda carrying a toolbox when they moved from the scene through the Forest Reserve to the Kitwe Road. He pointed out a house frequented by a youth with whom Kaponda had struggled for possession of the vanity bag.

Watch was kept on this house and after his identity had been confirmed by Kaponda, the youth was tailed to a house in Chifubu. It was searched and a black notebook, a jar of Pond's cream and a purse were found. The youth, James Paikani Phiri, was arrested. He claimed to have been in Kitwe on 8 May and refused to take part in an identification parade. Information from Phiri's room-mates led to the recovery of a Croxley notebook and a headwrap from the house of one of his relatives in Chifubu, and a powder compact which he had given to a girl friend. The two notebooks, the purse, headwrap, compact and jar were all identified by Mrs Burton's mother as originating from the vanity bag.

Kamima was finally located and arrested on 17 June. His claim to have been away from Ndola on 8th May was disproved. On the same day Bernard Chanda's house and car were searched without result. Chanda was brought in for questioning and admitted leaving the toolbox in the Bush. Next morning he took the detectives about five miles down the Ndola-Luanshya/Kitwe Road where motorists had been stoned on the afternoon of 8 May. On top of an anthill he showed them a toolbox which he said he had carried from the scene of the murder and left to collect later. Once the box had been identified as from Mrs Burton's car, Chanda was arrested and charged with murder. He admitted being with Ngebe at the Chifubu turnoff and having chased and stoned the car.

On 18 June the preliminary inquiry opened before Mr John Cronin, Resident Magistrate Ndola. By 28 June it had reached the stage for evidence from eyewitnesses. For their protection the court adjourned to Solwezi, 300 miles away. The transport, accommodation and feeding of the accused, the witnesses, their families, the press, CID and court officials was a major operation. Patrol car escorts were provided for the journey and the Mobile Unit found guards at Solwezi. 400 statements had been recorded, analysed and cross-checked. Twelve eye-witnesses from groups which had included the four accused, Ngebe, Chanda, Kamima and Phiri, had been found. Considerable effort had been required to obtain the truth from these witnesses, mainly accomplices to some degree. European and African detectives had worked round the clock to secure the evidence so quickly. Between 1 and 6 July the depositions of these witnesses were taken at Solwezi. All came up to proof.

On 13 July the inquiry resumed at Ndola. On 20 July all four accused were committed to the High Court for trial. Ngebe had been represented throughout the preliminary inquiry. The other three had declined legal aid. Chanda, Phiri and Kamima elected to give evidence. Phiri and Kamima retracted their alibis but endeavoured to shift responsibility on to certain Crown witnesses, alleging that these had coerced them into going to the scene.

On 17 August the trial opened at Ndola before Mr Justice Anthony Somerhough OBE and four assessors. Chanda, Phiri and Kamima had now accepted legal aid, being represented by Messrs David Houston-Barnes, Fin Burke and Brian Gardner. Cresta Ngebe continued to be represented by Mr Syd Pearce. All four pleaded not guilty to the joint charge of murder. Tape recorders and microphones were installed to supplement the work of a palantypist. The trial record was played back and corrected in the presence of counsel at the close of each day's proceedings. Prosecution witnesses were subjected to lengthy cross-examination. Some, as accomplices, had been granted immunity from prosecution. Two perjured themselves. Inquiries revealed that, despite all security precautions, they had received threats.

On 26 September Mr Paul Counsell, appearing for the Crown, had to withdraw through illness. The trial was adjourned until 3rd October to enable Mr Desmond O'Connor to take over the case. The Crown case was approximately three-quarters through, 11,605 pages of evidence having been recorded from 61 witnesses. On 2 October Mr Justice Somerhough died after an unexpected stroke[7]. His sudden and tragic death threatened to bring all the efforts of Brockwell and his men to nought. Witnesses were becoming more and more restless in their conditions of quarantine. They now had to undergo the ordeal of giving evidence in court for the third time.

The new trial opened on 8 November before Mr Justice John Blagden OBE TD[8] with four fresh assessors. Due to the situation in the Katanga, the attendance of five Congolese witnesses could not be secured, but statutory provisions enabled their evidence recorded at the first trial to be placed before the court.

Ngebe now retracted his alibi and all four accused tried to place the blame on Crown witnesses. The accused called no witnesses. All four were convicted of murder. On 13 March 1961 Ngebe, Chanda and Kamima were sentenced to death. Phiri tried to avoid the gallows by claiming to have been under 18 years of age at the time of the murder. There was no compulsory registration of African births in Northern Rhodesia, and therefore no relevant birth certificate, but medical evidence of bone fusion showed that he was at least 22 years old. On 5 April Phiri too was sentenced to death.

On 14 July 1961 the appeals of all four were dismissed by the Federal Supreme Court. Petitions to appeal to the Privy Council and, for clemency, to the Governor, were rejected. On 23 November 1961 Cresta Ngebe, Bernard Chanda, Robin Kamima and Paikani Phiri were hanged at Livingstone Central Prison. They were later declared martyrs of the struggle for the independence of Zambia and had streets named after them in Lusaka.

Denis Brockwell was awarded the Queen's Police Medal for Distinguished Service and 'Paddy' Patterson the Colonial Police Medal for Meritorious Service for their work on this case.

18 May 1960 had brought a welcome visitor, when Her Majesty Queen Elizabeth the Queen Mother arrived at Livingstone to be greeted by a guard of honour of 106 officers and men of the Mobile Unit under the command of Mr R S Monteith, Superintendent. On 17 May Her Majesty had officially opened the Kariba Dam from the Southern Rhodesia side, while members of the Northern Rhodesia Police, drawn from Mazabuka District, the Police Training School, Lilayi, and Lusaka Division, performed crowd control duties on the North Bank. She now paid a flying visit to Barotseland and the Copperbelt before travelling to Lusaka where she unveiled a plaque on the statue 'Physical Energy' outside the new High Court building. The erection of this statue, a duplicate of that commemorating Cecil Rhodes at Groot Schuur in the Cape, had not been without controversy. It was said to represent the Federal concept of partnership with the European as the rider and the African as the horse! The Queen Mother took advantage of the occasion to announce that Lusaka was to be granted the status of a 'city' in September. From the capital Her Majesty went on to visit Fort Jameson.

On 30 June 1960 the Belgian Congo was granted independence. On 4 July the Force Publique, the army of the new state, mutinied. Chaos ensued. Murder and rape of whites led to a mass exodus of Europeans from the Congo. Emergency refugee centres were set up by the Northern Rhodesia Government and voluntary organisations. The main aim was to pass the fleeing Belgians through to the south with all speed. The Public Works Department provided free vehicle servicing and petrol to facilitate the rapid passage of the majority who came by car. The Northern Rhodesia Police were much engaged with traffic control and giving guidance.

On 11 July Moise Tshombe[9] took the opportunity to declare the secession of the Katanga Province from the turbulent Congo. He paid the police forces of Southern and Northern Rhodesia the compliment of requesting the services of 5,000 Rhodesian police to ensure law and order and maintain the integrity of his new state. This request was politically and practically impossible to grant. Tshombe began to recruit mercenaries instead. Meanwhile a United Nations Peacekeeping Force had arrived in the Congo where it was to remain for four years with varying fortunes.

Northern Rhodesia's frontiers with the Congo and Katanga had to be watched for many months by police and troops to prevent incursions by the various official and private armies which sprang up in the former Belgian colony. The breakdown of law and order there led to an increase in car thefts in Northern Rhodesia as the vehicles disappeared into the vacuum. Rabies among household pets became a problem for the first time in many years.

In September it was announced that a conference would be held the following year to discuss constitutional changes in Northern Rhodesia. This was in spite of demands by the United Federal Party that the 1959 constitution should run its full course until 1963. Kenneth Kaunda had made good use of his overseas tour. In October the report of the Monckton Commission was published stating: 'The strength of African opposition in the Northern Territories is such that Federation

Saluting base, passing out parade at Lilayi 1960 (Nkhwazi)
L to R: Insp M W St A Campbell, Insp B C Borrodale ADC, J P I Fforde, L M Clark
Ag S/Supt, Sir Evelyn Hone, Governor of Northern Rhodesia.

cannot, in our view, be maintained in its present form'. Relations between the Federal and United Kingdom governments reached an all time low, while the African nationalists were elated.

Also in September 1960 the African National Congress leader, Harry Nkumbula, was sentenced to twelve months imprisonment on conviction for dangerous driving and leaving the scene of a road traffic accident. He had knocked down and killed a constable. Released on bail pending appeal, Nkumbula, was able to travel to London for the constitutional talks before being committed to prison in April 1961 when the Federal Supreme Court dismissed his appeal. The case further lowered Nkumbula's reputation with the African public and was another severe set-back in Congress's power struggle with the United National Independence Party.

It was not all strife on the Copperbelt. On 2 October 1960 an athletic competition was held at Nchanga Mine Sports Stadium between the Northern Rhodesia Police of Chingola District and the employees of the Mine for the 'Copperfields Trophy'. The police won the tug-of-war. Assistant Inspector Mike Beaves was the winner of the hundred yards sprint and Inspector John Lawrence won the longjump. A football match in the afternoon in front of 4,000 spectators ended in a draw, but overall the police lost the competition by 63 points to the Mine's 102. The day was brought to a conclusion by the drum and fife band of the Mobile Unit beating retreat, with Mr Gordon Layne, Officer Commanding Chingola District, taking the salute.

The end of Sir Arthur Benson's governorship and the instances of disorder in the Luapula Province had led to the reopening of Kawambwa Police Station under Inspector Les Bardwell in January 1960, Kashiba, ceremonially reopened by Senior Chief Mwata Kazembe on 30 April, with Inspector Brian Soulsby as Officer in Charge, and Samfya under Inspector Michael Mylod in May. Kashiba was to be renamed Mwense in 1963.

There were also new stations on the Line of Rail. Prospect in the farming area of Central Division opened under Assistant Inspector Jim Wilkinson in February 1960. Riverside in the Kitwe District opened on 15 August with responsibility for the Buchi, Kamitonda and Kwacha townships, a combined population of about 30,000, while Kitwe East Police Station opened in October 1960. On 1 January 1961 the post at Ngwerere in Lusaka Rural District was upgraded to a station.

It was during 1960 that Constable Tsikari, while checking for stolen bicycles, attempted to make an arrest and received fatal stab wounds.

In January 1961 there was rioting at Roan Antelope in which four people were killed and seventeen wounded. Chief Inspector A R Kirby and constables Mulumpa and Mukangwa were awarded the Colonial Police Medal for Gallantry and Assistant Inspector M Hugh-Jones received a special commendation for 'outstanding discipline and courage in the face of a riotous mob' as a result of this action.

In January the price of copper was £200 per ton. Its peak for 1961 was £242. In December 1961 it stood at £230. Economy was the watchword and from January until August all police recruiting was suspended. This was in the year that Northern Rhodesia was to experience its worst period of lawlessness and internal strife since the beginning of European administration. The year started with a constitutional crisis when the United Federal Party boycotted the review conference as did the Dominion Party, leaving only the two African nationalist parties and the liberals, led by Sir John Moffatt, at the table. Kenneth Kaunda threatened that if majority rule was not granted there would be disorder 'which by contrast would make Mau Mau look like a child's picnic'[10]. On the other side there were rumours that Sir Roy Welensky intended to unilaterally declare the Federation of Rhodesia and Nyasaland independent. During the year there was light hearted discussion between members of the Federal Army and the Northern Rhodesia Police as to which force would succeed in disarming the other in the event of a breakdown in relations between the United Kingdom and Federal governments!

Iain Macleod announced the British proposals for Northern Rhodesia's legislature – fifteen members elected by voters on the upper roll, fifteen elected by lower roll voters and fifteen elected on a proportional basis on the votes cast on both rolls. Neither side was happy. At a United National Independence Party rally at Mulungushi early in July, Kaunda accused the British Government of a breach of faith. In August serious disorders broke out centred at first in the Northern and Luapula provinces where bands of up to 300 armed men roamed at large through the Bush.

Roads were blocked, bridges destroyed, and schools and other buildings burnt. Mass destruction of Situpas (African identity certificates) was organised. Meetings were held in defiance of the Law. There were attacks on police and much intimidation. After a few days the disturbances spread to the Copperbelt. Before long few parts of the Territory were unaffected. On the Copperbelt and in Lusaka explosives were used for the first time as a means of sabotage, albeit to little effect. European special constables were enrolled and used in large numbers to patrol the residential areas in the major towns.

Between 24 July and 1 September 1961, 901 incidents were recorded resulting in total of 1,400 arrests. 38 schools were burnt down, including 34 in Northern Province. More than 60 road blocks were reported and 24 bridges destroyed or seriously damaged. 27 people were killed. By the end of October more than 3,000 persons had been arrested and 2,691 convictions obtained in the courts, 2,158 involving known supporters of UNIP.

On Tuesday 8 August 1961 at about 1800 hours the Officer Commanding, Northern Division, received a report that an American mission doctor and his family were trapped on the road about 65 miles north of Mpika. The Officer Commanding informed Chinsali Police Station from where Detective Inspector J A Coates, in charge of CID there, and Acting Inspector F K Buckingham, Head Constable Luchembe, a driver constable and 8 constables of the Mobile Unit, set out immediately down the Great North Road in two landrovers. They were armed with two pistols, a Sterling sub-machine gun, 4 rifles, a $1\frac{1}{2}$ inch riot-gun and a signal pistol also capable of firing tear smoke projectiles.

On the way the police party had to clear a number of road blocks and repair several damaged culverts. At one point a landrover tipped over and had to be righted. After 30 miles they came upon a burnt out bus. At about 0600 hours on 9 August about 8 miles south of Matumbo the patrol was approached by about 50 men armed with spears and axes. These claimed responsibility for blocking the

Senior officers conference Lusaka circa 1960 (NRPA)
L to R Back Row: R Coulthard, F D R Gray, A W Horsfield, A W Rhodes, P R Blyth, J D O
Bird, J Fowlie, D Forde, R A Ockwell, ?; *Middle Row:* B G O'Leary, J F Matheson, T E Coton,
A J Austin?, J D Stewart, J W E Ross, J S Espey, L M Clark; *Front Row:* J F Castle, F A
Roberts, E H Halse, J P I Forde, L A Hicks, E Leighton, H B Perkins.

road and announced that they were UNIP which was now the government! While
the police were attempting to persuade them to return to their villages, they were
joined by another very militant crowd of about 70 armed youths. After argument
the crowd was partially dispersed and the patrol continued on its way south.

After repairing another large culvert the police reached Phillipo School 54 miles
south of Chinsali at 0815 hours. Here they found Dr and Mrs J Foust and their
sons aged 12 and 11, together with Mr and Mrs R Wright, Mrs Wright's mother
and their children aged 5 years, 3 years and 18 months. These people had been
travelling north in a long wheel base landrover and a Chevrolet vanette. The
school had been burnt down. The African headmaster, another male teacher, his
wife, mother, brother, 5 small children, and a female teacher all asked to
accompany the police.

Phillipo School was 15 miles from Sir Stewart Gore-Brown's homestead, Shiwa
Ngandu, but John Coates knew that the Post Office telegraph there was out of
order. He had no information as to the condition of the road south to Mpika.
With 33 people and much luggage the convoy of four vehicles set off back to
Chinsali at about 0930 hours.

Five miles up the road was the large culvert the police had repaired, but their
work had now been undone. The crossing was barred by a crowd of about 150
Africans armed with spears, axes and bows and arrows. Coates halted the convoy
about 100 yards away and walked some 40 yards towards the mob accompanied

by Buckingham, Luchembe and four constables. He pronounced in a loud voice the words of the Riot Act, which all officers carried written inside the covers of their notebooks, 'All persons here assembled are commanded in the Queen's name to disperse peacefully to their homes. . .'. Head Constable Luchembe translated. The mob ignored repeated warnings and advanced slowly on the handful of police shouting and waving their weapons.

At Inspector Coates' order constables Kaluba and Silungwe fired 5 tear smoke shells from the riot-gun and signal pistol. Several men in the crowd were seen to try to cover the shells with earth to stop the smoke discharge. The crowd came on until Coates ordered Buckingham and Luchembe to fire. Frank Buckingham fired 5 rounds from his Sterling and Luchembe 2 from his rifle. Noone appeared hit but the crowd divided leaving the roadway clear. The vehicles were brought up to the broken culvert.

Most of the mob were to the east of the road. They now closed in threatening the vehicles. Others approached from the West. The police shouted repeated warnings but the crowd came on, harangued by certain ringleaders. They were about 15 yards away when Coates shouted a final warning. Jacob Kapanga, Secretary of the Muchinga Constituency Branch of UNIP, was directly in front of him and shouted back 'Shoot me then, shoot me.' Coates gave the order 'Prepare to fire' and the police raised their weapons. The crowd continued to press forward so that its leaders were only 10 yards away when John Coates shouted 'Fire', and fired one round from his ·38 revolver. As soon as he saw the crowd beginning to

Women reserve assistant inspectors in the wireless room force headquarters Lusaka circa 1960 (Nhkwazi)

323

turn round he ordered 'Cease Fire' and was immediately obeyed. He checked the ammunition expenditure finding that Buckingham had fired 6 rounds from the Sterling and the Head Constable and constables Lungu and Mahango had fired a total of 6 rounds from their rifles. The Driver Constable, armed with the fourth rifle, had been guarding the vehicles and was not engaged.

It was now 1030 hours. Guards were posted while the rest of the police and their charges set to work filling the culvert. The bulk of the crowd had fallen back into the trees and after some shouts of defiance began to drift away. Detective Inspector Coates took Dr Foust out to examine the casualties. Jacob Kapanga was lying fifteen feet from the roadway with a wound in his right thigh and another in the lower chest. He was treated by the doctor and placed in a vehicle. The same distance from the road was a man dying from a wound in the groin. There were two other casualties, both dead, one at the very edge of the road about six feet from Dr Foust's vehicle. Four spears, an axe, two bows, a club and four arrows were with the bodies.

By about 1100 hours the convoy was able to move on north. Two hours later, near Matumbo, they met another crowd of about 100 to 150 persons. Two men came forward and demanded to inspect the vehicles. This was, of course refused. The men returned to the crowd and after some argument amongst themselves the crowd moved back into the village. The convoy approached the village slowly over several roadblocks. In the village the crowd lined the road many of them armed. The police dismounted and escorted the vehicles through. Small groups of armed men detached themselves from the crowd and kept pace with the vehicles. While negotiating a roadblock the last vehicle turned over. As this vehicle was being righted the crowd closed in. They were warned to keep away but caught sight of the wounded Kapanga. Several men and a female were seen to hurry ahead, with the obvious intention of assembling a larger crowd.

At about 1320 hours approximately two miles north of Matumbo a crowd of some 250 was encountered coming down the road towards the convoy. With some difficulty they were prevailed upon to halt, while two leaders were permitted to approach. These demanded to search the vehicles for the wounded man. They were sent back to the crowd with a warning to disperse or the police would be compelled to fire. The crowd advanced in a hostile manner. Eventually they were cajoled into clearing a narrow lane down the centre of the road but refused to move off it. John Coates ordered Buckingham to fire down the cleared passage. He fired 14 rounds of Sterling in short bursts. The mob sullenly pulled back to about ten feet from each side of the road. Escorted by the police on foot the convoy drove through.

The remainder of the journey was without incident apart from the necessity to make culverts passable. At about 2000 hours, five miles south of Chinsali they met another party of police sent out to their assistance.

The question of whether the police were justified in firing is best answered by the medical missionary. Dr Foust said 'I thought John had left it too late!'[11]

On 29 August Inspector G I Walford and part of his platoon of the Mobile Unit were returning across the Zambesi at Chavuma, near Balovale in North-Western Province, after a successful dawn patrol, when their boat capsized. 'Taffy' Walford was drowned together with constables 1649 Musa, 2007 Mayengo, 3171 Tembo,

Woman constables 1961

4696 Shumbwamuntu, 5645 Muboboto, 5818 Banda and 5853 Njoru. Mr Alan Milne, Assistant Superintendent, saw the disaster, and, although not a strong swimmer, and despite the danger of crocodiles, immediately dived into the river. He succeeded in rescuing one constable and a prisoner. Mr Milne and Constable Kamboyi were subsequently awarded the Royal Humane Society's Bronze Medal. A Dean's Chair and kneeler were presented by the Force to the Cathedral of the Holy Cross at Lusaka in memory of the dead men.[12]

On 17 October 1961 *The Voice of U.N.I.P.* published a special issue – *A Grim Peep into the North* – making allegations of brutality against the security forces. In January 1962 the Government issued a 78-page reply – *An Account of the Disturbances in N.R. – July to October 1961*. Some 500 huts had been burnt by the security forces, mainly Army units, deliberately or by accident in the course of operations 'particularly in areas which were most disaffected and where violence and intimidation were rife'. About 320 of these were in the Chinsali District. Matumba Village, said by the District Commissioner to be the worst in the district, was, according to a report quoted by David G Mulford, cordoned off by the Mobile Unit and forty-four of its sixty-four huts, pointed out as belonging to troublemakers, burnt on the DC's orders. Mulenga Chenaeka Village in Mporokoso District was burnt on the orders of Chief Chitoshi, because it had been a constant source of trouble and its inhabitants had refused to obey the Native Authority laws or to acknowledge their chief.[13]

Seven complaints of rape were made against members of the security forces. All except one were found to be false on inquiry or failed to result in the identification of a suspect. In one case a soldier was convicted and sentenced to two years imprisonment, but his conviction was quashed on appeal.

As a result of the operations in Northern and Luapula provinces, Mr J D O Bird, Superintendent, a future commissioner of the Gibraltar Police, was awarded the MBE and Mr J F Fitzgerald, Superintendent, Mr J D Williams, Assistant Superintendent, Detective Inspector J A Coates, Assistant Inspector F K Buckingham, and Head Constable Luchembe were all awarded the Colonial Police Medal for Meritorious Service.

The President of the United States of America, John F Kennedy, had appointed George Mennen 'Soapy' Williams to the new post of Assistant Secretary of State for African Affairs in his 'new look' administration[14]. On 27 and 28 August 1961 Williams honoured Northern Rhodesia with his first and only visit. The Governor, Sir Evelyn Hone, accompanied the American to Lusaka Airport at the end of this flying visit. As they were saying their good-byes on the tarmac, a white resident of long standing, Stewart Finlay Bisset of Northern Fisheries, left the Airport Bar, strode towards the VIP party and punched Williams on the jaw.

Finlay Bisset, known to Africans as 'Kamamanya' from his involvement in labour recruiting, was prosecuted for assault at Lusaka Magistrate's Court. Williams was safely back home in America. The Governor, as the Queen's representative was constitutionally barred from giving evidence in the courts of Northern Rhodesia. His Aide de Camp, Senior Inspector Jeremy Hawkins, was under no such disability. Bisset was duly convicted and fined £50.

In September 1961 the United Nations troops in the Congo began an operation to end the secession of Katanga. The United Nations Secretary General, Dag Hammarskjold, decided to meet Moise Tshombe, the Katanga president, for conciliatory talks on neutral ground at Ndola. A member of the British Government, Lord Lansdowne, was acting as an intermediary. At about 1700 hours on 17 September Lansdowne took off from Ndjili Airport, Leopoldville, to fly to Salisbury via Ndola. Tshombe and Lord Alport, British High Commissioner in Rhodesia and Nyasaland, were waiting at Ndola.[15]

At 1751 hours Hammarskjold's DC-6B four engined jet chartered by the United Nations from the Swedish Transair Company, left Ndjili in conditions of great secrecy. The aircraft, designated SE-BDY, known as *The Albertina*, was piloted by Captain Halonquist, who was assisted by a crew of five other Swedes. With Hammarskjold travelled Heinrich Wieschhoff of his New York Staff, Vladimir Fabry, legal adviser to the United Nations in the Congo, Alice Lalande, a Canadian secretary, William Ramallo, the Secretary-General's personal aide and five security men – two Swedish soldiers, a Frenchman, an Irishman and an American, Sergeant Harold M Julien, Acting Chief Security Officer ONUC.

A flight plan had been filed giving the Albertina's destination as Luluabourg. The captain flew over Lake Tanganyika to avoid Katanga and maintained radio silence until two hours from Ndola when he contacted Salisbury Air Traffic Control. At 2338 hours Halonquist requested descent clearance for Ndola for 2357 hours. At 2347 hours he reported his aircraft abeam of Ndola. At 0010 hours the

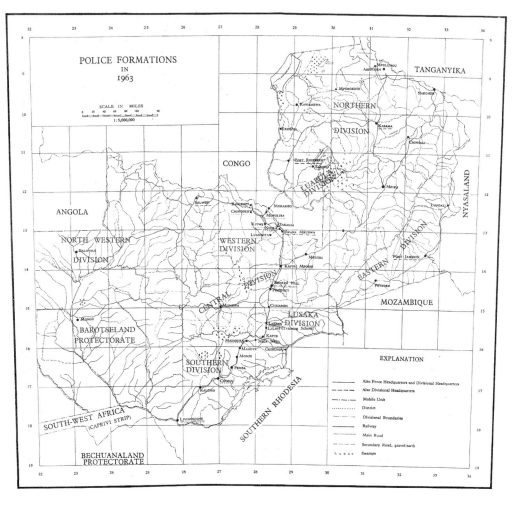

MAP 5   POLICE FORMATIONS IN 1963

pilot reported 'lights in sight' and a number of those on the ground saw and heard an aircraft. Due to the circumstances of secrecy surrounding Hammarskjold's movements there was no great concern when the aeroplane appeared to have flown off and radio communication was lost. It was assumed that the Secretary-General had merely changed his plans.

At about this time people saw flashes in the sky but assumed them to be lightning or bushfires. A number of police officers were on standby duty at the Provincial Commissioner's house. One of these, Assistant Inspector M Van Wyk, reported to Assistant Inspector Begg at Ndola Central Police Station that he had heard a large aircraft overhead and a few minutes later saw a red flash in the sky. The Ndola Airport Manager, Mr Williams, was woken at his hotel, but he advised leaving the matter until daylight. Nevertheless the police sent out patrols on their own initiative. These found nothing to report, as did patrols sent out from Mufulira Central after Assistant Inspector Vaughan had reported a sudden light in the sky and having the impression of something falling.

In the early hours of 18 September Salisbury Air Traffic Control put out an alarm and requested the Royal Rhodesian Air Force to commence a search at dawn. In the late morning the crash site was located by an RRAF pilot, and in the early afternoon a charcoal burner named Mazibisa reported having found the crashed Albertina in the forest reserve about nine and a half miles from Ndola in the direction of Mufulira. Mr M T Cary, Assistant Superintendent, Senior Inspector T E A Wright, Detective Inspector G R Lowes and Mr Nuns, a police photographer, set out for the scene immediately. Ian Colvin in his book *The Rise and Fall of Tshombe* says that he flew over at 0900 hours and saw police already there on the ground, while Colonel Ben Matlick, the United States Air Attache from Leopoldville, claimed to have been the first to have reached the scene by motor vehicle. Be that as it may the police found utter desolation. The aircraft had cut a swathe 800 feet long through the trees, tearing itself to pieces and finally bursting into flames of such intense heat that the metal of the fuselage fused together.[16]

The only survivor was Sergeant Julien. He was quickly removed to hospital, but his burns and other injuries had been aggravated by his exposure to the blazing sun. Harry Julien never recovered consciousness. He died five days later with Senior Inspector A V Allen at his bedside. All the bodies had been badly burned except that of Hammarskjold himself. A playing card, the ace of spades, was found sticking out of the Secretary-General's collar on one side of his neck. He must have been playing cards when the end came.

Not surprisingly this tragedy caused a worldwide sensation. There were suggestions of sabotage and attack from the ground or air. Those hostile to the Federation took the opportunity to try to cast the blame on Roy Welensky and the Rhodesian forces. An intensive police investigation began immediately in conjunction with the aviation authorities. The Governor-General appointed a Commission of Inquiry under the chairmanship of Mr Justice Clayden.

The report of this inquiry was published in February 1962. The time of the crash was established from the stopped watches of the victims at 0013 hours 18 September. The Albertina was found to have crashed while at the normal angle for descent with its engines running and wheels locked in the landing position. From this it was deduced that the pilot had been turning to land at Ndola, but that for some reason he had misjudged his height from the ground and the plane struck the treetops.

The Commission thoroughly investigated the other possibilities, including sabotage, error in ground/air communications, mechanical failure, defective altimeters and attack by other aircraft. All were finally dismissed. Major Delin the pilot of Katanga's only warplane, a Fougar fighter, voluntarily appeared before the Commission to give evidence that his aircraft was grounded at the relevant time.

It was suggested that Captain Halonquist might have confused the altitude of Ndola Airport, for which no approach chart was found in the wreckage, with that of Ndolo, near Leopoldville, an approach chart for which was found. However there was evidence that the captain had been heard to mention the correct altitude of Ndola some days before the fatal flight.

During the investigation all the parts of the Albertina were laid out in position in a hangar at Ndola and in due course cut into pieces about eight inches square to see whether any trace of hostile missiles could be found. Still later, during the United Nations sponsored inquiry, all parts of the fuselage were melted down with the same object. Nothing was found.

Although the United Nations' inquiry agreed with the Clayden Commission that pilot error was the most likely cause, it chose, whether or not from ulterior motives, to leave open the possibilities of a time bomb having been placed aboard at Ndjili, incomplete landing instructions and attack by the Katangese Fougar or other aircraft.[17]

A memorial was subsequently erected at the site of the crash which is now a national monument and park. A library and sports stadium at Ndola were named after the late Secretary-General.

On 10 December 1961 Assistant Inspector J W Maxwell of Chingola was off duty enjoying a swim in the Kafue River with the three sons of a farmer friend, when he spotted a large crocodile between the children and the riverbank. Maxwell shouted a warning and directed the boys to a rock in midstream. One, aged nine, managed to reach the rock and scramble to safety. The others, aged twelve and seven, were unable to scale its slippery sides. John Maxwell placed himself between the boys and the crocodile and lifted the eldest onto the rock. As he was helping the seven year old up, the policeman was seized by the legs by the reptile. Although grievously injured he hit the crocodile on the snout and gouged out one of its eyes, obtaining a temporary release. Before Maxwell could reach the safety of the rock the beast returned to the attack and dragged him down to the riverbed in deep water. Almost out of breath Maxwell managed in desperation to find the crocodile's other eye and gouge it out.

With one leg practically severed and the other badly mauled, the police officer surfaced and reached the rock. The boys dragged him up and helped him tear up a towel to make a tourniquet. The two elder boys waded ashore and ran a quarter of a mile to their home where they met Mrs Belina Maloni. Mrs Maloni hurried to the river where she saw Assistant Inspector Maxwell still on the rock while the infuriated crocodile thrashed about in the water nearby. The African woman could not swim but, regardless of the danger that the blood in the water would attract other crocodiles, waded out to the rock. She helped Maxwell onto her back and, crawling on hands and knees, bravely carried him through the water to the shore. He was then placed in the front passenger seat of his motor car. While he manipulated the gears, Dorothy Kathleen Cox, a fourteen year old who had never before driven a car, steered the vehicle until they reached Nchanga Hospital.

On 20 December a full dress parade was held at Chingola Police Camp in honour of Mrs Maloni who was presented with a bicycle purchased through donations from all ranks in the District. On 17 March 1962 Maxwell left Ndola by air for the United Kingdom where he received further treatment and was fitted with an artificial leg at Queen Mary's Hospital Rochampton. The immediate award of the George Medal to Belina Maloni and Assistant Inspector John William Maxwell was announced in the London Gazette of 10 April 1962.[18]

Also in December 1961 a man stabbed the District Commissioner, Kabompo, and several members of his staff, before fleeing into the game reserve. D4 Platoon of the Mobile Unit under Inspector Paul Moller was called in to track the man down. The police flushed him out and the offender was shot by five district messengers only 300 yards from the border with Angola.

During 1961 Detective Sergeant Bwalya was stabbed to death while making inquiries concerning a spate of burglaries. In January 1962 Reserve Constable Kacha was attacked by a mob and fatally injured while on patrol in Wusikili Township. Reserve Constable Ndiweni of Raylton, Broken Hill earned a commendation for arresting a six foot two European man who had escaped from prison earlier in the day.

Colonel J D Stewart, Assistant Commissioner (Training) resigned in 1961. The post lapsed with his departure.[19]

In 1961 new 'Local' Conditions of Service were introduced. Henceforth all admissions to the permanent and pensionable establishment were to be on these conditions. Serving officers were invited to transfer to local conditions with a higher retirement age and no entitlement to free passages to and from the United Kingdom for vacation leave.

Qualifications for promotion remained unchanged except in one respect. Under the old conditions an assistant inspector grade I who had passed the examinations in Force Standing Orders, Police Duties, and a local language at Government Lower Standard, would, if he had completed three years service in that rank and was recommended, be promoted inspector. After two years in rank an inspector who had passed the Northern Rhodesia Government examination in a local language at Higher Standard, a second language at lower standard, or in Criminal Law and Procedure and Local and Applied Law, was eligible for selection for promotion to chief inspector. Before he could be selected for promotion to assistant superintendent an officer required a pass in both law and a second or higher language. Officers serving on local conditions were not to be required to sit the language examinations. Transfer to local conditions was therefore attractive to those European officers whose careers were held back by their inability to pass these examinations.

In mid-1960 Michael Mataka became the first African to be promoted Assistant Inspector Grade I. In 1961 the rank of Assistant Inspector Grade III was abolished all holders of the rank being upgraded. On 1 December 1961 fourteen Africans were promoted Assistant Inspector Grade I. In April 1962 there were 75 Africans serving as assistant inspectors grades I or II. With the introduction of local conditions of service suitably educated young Africans became eligible for direct recruitment in the rank of Assistant Inspector Grade I.

In April 1962 Force Headquarters moved from the Hart Road site it had occupied since 1946 to an imposing new purpose-built building on the Ridgeway. On 25 April a new police station was opened at Nega Nega in Mazabuka District with Assistant Inspector R A Bull as officer in charge. The introduction of the 'Centralised Train Control' system, making the control of rail traffic far safer, developments in improved construction on the line, and the growth of the Rhodesia Railways Security Guard Unit, made it possible for the last of the Northern Rhodesia Police railway detachments to be closed during the year.

In March 1962 it was announced that elections under the 'Macleod' constitution would be held at the end of October. While, as far as public order was concerned, 1962 was a less dramatic year than 1961, political intimidation remained at a high level. Some Africans took to carrying party cards for both the United National Independence Party and the African National Congress in order to avoid attack by either. Party bully boys countered this by pretending to be from the opposing party. When the unfortunate person they had accosted produced what he had been led to believe was the required card, his tormentors revealed their true persuasion and beat him up.

Nomination day was 9 October. From mid-October sporadic violence became regular. UNIP's Youth Brigade members harrassed ANC canvassers and Congress activists reciprocated where they could.

Registration of voters had started slowly but the Northern Rhodesia Government was anxious that the elections should be meaningful and properly reflect the extension of the franchise. The combination of government encouragement and publicity, and the efforts of the nationalist parties, resulted in the registration of 37,152 upper roll voters, including 7,321 Africans, and 91,942 lower roll voters, almost all African, out of an estimated adult population of 1,275,768.

The complicated arrangements for the 'national constituencies' for which both upper and lower roll votes were cast, necessitated bye-elections on 10 December 1962. In the end no party was left with a majority in the Legislative Council. The United Federal Party had won 16 seats, the United National Independence Party, 14, and the African National Congress, 7. ANC and UFP had to a large extent worked together in the hope of neutralising UNIP, but now UNIP and Congress formed an uneasy alliance to form a ministry. Kenneth Kaunda became Minister of Local Government and Social Welfare, while Harry Nkumbula took the African Education portfolio. Responsibility for the Police remained with the Chief Secretary, and the ministries of Finance, Native Affairs and Justice remained in the hands of officials.[20]

On 3 December 1962 the Commissioner of Police, Mr J P I Fforde CBE CPM KPM, left on retirement. Mr E H Halse OBE KPM CPM succeeded him in command. Mr Fforde's departure was preceded by a series of farewell visits and parades. On his final visit to the Police Training School, Mr Fforde was presented with an engraved silver tray on behalf of all the other ranks of the Northern Rhodesia Police. In his eleven years in command he had put his personal stamp on the Force and brought it successfully through times of great constitutional and economic change. Despite the difficulties and setbacks caused by events and considerations outside his control, he had created an efficient, well founded and organised police force in pace with the development of the Territory. The Northern Rhodesia Police now consisted of 133 gazetted officers, 788 subordinate police officers and 5,126 other ranks. There were sixty-six police stations and fourteen posts in the Territory, apart from CID units, traffic sections and other supporting and specialist groups. The were 16 gazetted officers and 67 subordinate police officers, five of them African, in the Criminal Investigation Department. The estimated expenditure for the 1962-63 financial year was £4,479,000.

The population of Northern Rhodesia was said in the mid-fifties to be 60,000 Europeans, 20,000 Asians and Coloureds and $2\frac{1}{2}$ million Africans. A Census in the early sixties showed there were more than four million Africans in the Territory.

The new Deputy Commissioner was Mr J C Day QPM CPM who had been Senior Assistant Commissioner (Headquarters) since 1957. He had served in the Northern Rhodesia Police since 1938, for the first nearly twenty years mainly in the CID and Special Branch.

On 23 December 1962 A3 Platoon of the Mobile Unit, under Inspector Peter Lendrum, returned from patrol in Northern Province where it had been deployed in connexion with the elections. The platoon managed to enjoy Christmas and New Year back at Bwana Mkubwa, but on 2 January 1963 was back on the road, this time to Solwezi. Katanga was again in turmoil and refugees were fleeing into Northern Rhodesia. There was danger of incursions by Katangese, Congolese or United Nations Troops, some of whose records for humanitarianism were not too good. The platoon patrolled the Border in conjunction with units of the Army of the Federation of Rhodesia and Nyasaland. No.1818 Sergeant Banda arrested an armed mercenary, while 4109 Driver Constable Mafulo earned a Commissioner's Commendation by disarming and arresting 24 Katangese gendarmes he found in a tearoom on the Northern Rhodesia side of the Border. Mafulo was alone and unarmed. Among the weapons he seized were 22 sub-machine guns! A3 Platoon returned to Bwana Mkubwa on 29 January.[21]

The Mobile Unit now consisted of Headquarter Company, with the motor transport, corps of drums, training wing, administrative staff and stores, and four operational companies each of 150 men divided into four platoons. Permanent camps with one platoon each were maintained at Livingstone, Broken Hill and Chingola. Platoons, accompanied by their families, were detached to these stations for six months or so at a time in turn.

For some time there had been rumours that mining operations would recommence at Bwana Mkubwa, and a new site had been selected for the main Mobile Unit camp at Kamfinsa, some nine miles from Kitwe on the Ndola Road. During 1963 sufficient accommodation was completed at this new camp, named the Neville Halse Camp, for C Company to move in under Mr R M Gavin, Assistant

Superintendent. Besides more modern housing and better amenities, the new site had the advantage of a more central position on the Copperbelt.

The Dog Section had started in 1956 with tracker dogs, mainly dobermans, under S/Insp S J Dippenaar who was joined by another veteran of the South African Police, S/Insp Tom Deetlefs. In 1959 A/Insp Jeff McLean returned from leave having attended a dog handlers course in the United Kingdom. Patrols with dogs commenced. In 1960 a dog training establishment was opened at Lilayi under Insp James Ford, formerly of the Royal Air Force Police, training dogs and handlers for the police and security guards for Key Point installations such as the mines and railways. By 1962 patrol dogs and their African police handlers were regularly on the beat in Lusaka, Ndola and Chingola while new kennels were under construction at the other main centres on the line of rail. In early 1963 on the Copperbelt 5589 Const Ndemanga was on patrol with his dog Simba II when he saw a man who appeared up to no good in a sanitary lane. On being challenged the suspect fled. After the third unheeded challenge Ndemanga released his dog who quickly made an arrest. When the constable began to search the prisoner, he was stabbed and the man again fled. Without further order from his incapacitated master, Simba gave chase, re-arrested the man and held him until help arrived. Dog and handler received commendations.[22]

The Eastern Province had been one of the last areas to come under nationalist influence. Few of the prominent men in either the United National Independence Party or African National Congress came from the province so there was no natural tribal loyalty involved. Nevertheless, since 1961, UNIP had taken steps to strengthen its position in the area and the success of Dr Hastings Banda and his followers in Nyasaland had impressed those living near the Border.

In January 1963 it was suddenly announced that Kenneth Kaunda, Wesley Nyrenda, MLC for Eastern Province, Hayden Banda, UNIP's Director of Youth, and James Skinner, an Irish lawyer practising in Lusaka who had become UNIP's legal and campaign adviser, were about to visit Lundazi[23]. Lundazi had no police station. At the Provincial Headquarters, Fort Jameson, were not more than 60 police. The Officer Commanding, Eastern Division, despatched an inspector and four constables to Lundazi. There was no reason to believe that the Minister for Local Government would wish to stir up trouble, nor that his party would attract opposition. A number of political meetings were held at which party members marched in procession, some in uniform. Disrespect for the chiefs and government officials appeared to be increased if, not encouraged, by the speeches.

After two days Kaunda, Skinner and Nyrenda left for Lusaka. A meeting was scheduled for the following day at Magodi's Village. Robin Short, the District Commissioner, feared for the safety of Chief Magodi and his staff. With only three district officers, the five police, eight district messengers and a handful of kapasus, the authorities had been careful to take no action which might provoke a disturbance. Now Short decided that things had come to a head. He informed the Chief that he was cancelling the meeting. The District Commissioner sent out parties on each of the approach roads to tell the people to go home. They refused to accept that Kaunda had gone or that the meeting was not to take place. After some disorder and stone throwing Hayden Banda arrived and sensibly agreed to persuade the people to disperse. However he called a meeting for the following Thursday.

By that day the Officer Commanding, Eastern Division, Mr Harry Taylor, Superintendent, had arrived at Lundazi. The Government forces amounted to 15 police and 15 district messengers. As a crowd approaching Magodi's from one direction was stopped and turned back, another would be reported coming on a different road. Stones and knobkerries were used against the authorities and one man tried to cut the throat of a sub-inspector with a sickle. Frequent charges had to be made in order to maintain the initiative and freedom to manoeuvre. Finally the agitators appeared to lose heart, one group meekly obeying an order to sit down and later assisting to rebuild a bridge and remove tree trunks from across the road.[24]

As a result of these disturbances and a subsequent riot at Nthembwe, where an inspector and seven men were attacked by Youth Brigade members and forced to open fire with buckshot, two platoons of the Mobile Unit were sent to restore order. On 20 May 1963 the police station at Lundazi was reopened under Inspector P H Gillies assisted by Sub-Inspector Chipongoma, Detective Sub-Inspector Kazeze, sergeants William and Nyakadzino, driver constables Banda and Mbewe and constables Munganda, Mwelwa, Chiwembo, Mhango, Sambo, Tembo, Jere, Sitali, Chisenga and Kumasa, and Detective Constable Theo. Peace was brought to the district but only for a year.

The coalition of the United National Independence Party and African National Congress was never cordial and brought no improvement in relations between supporters of each party outside the Legislative Council. Between 20 March 1963 and 23 April 1963 no less than 1,366 offences attributable to political causes, were recorded in the Territory. 124 of these occurred in the Lusaka District[25]. On 21 September Assistant Inspector L A Chito was bludgeoned to death while on duty at Mikomfwa Location, Luanshya. Three men were arrested and tried for this murder.

African National Congress was still in disarray, beset by both disunity and financial problems. Creditors, now certain that ANC would not be the post independence ruling party, no longer felt inhibited from court action. A meeting on 3 August to promote party unity, ended with an assault by pro-Nkumbula youths on Job Michello, Parliamentary Secretary to the Ministry of Land and Natural Resources and ANC National Secretary. Michello resigned as National Secretary and on 5 August announced the formation of his own party, the People's Democratic Party. Pedco, as the new party soon became known, started boldly with the purchase on credit of a fleet of vehicles with talk of a subsidy from Tshombe.

On 28 August 1963 it was announced that there would be a further General Election in Northern Rhodesia in January 1964, with universal suffrage for those over 21 years of age. Federation was to end on 31 December 1963.

Nkumbula, Michello and John Roberts, the United Federal Party's territorial leader, all tried to persuade the Governor that the elections should be delayed. Each hoped that he could enhance his following given time. There was a great deal of uncertainty and unease among the white population, but heated words by

Dogs and handlers 1963 (Nhkwazi)

factions such as the short-lived Rhodesia Republican Party were not turned into deeds.

Violent clashes between supporters of the three African parties increased towards the end of the year. Immediately before nomination day, 20 December, ANC and Pedco announced that they were reunited. Nkumbula petitioned the Governor, claiming that ANC-Pedco candidates had been prevented from submitting their papers on time by UNIP thugs. An extension was granted until 28 December but UNIP candidates were left unopposed in 24 of the 64 constituencies, while in four ANC and Pedco competed against each other[26]. After the elections a number of prosecutions were launched for forgery of nomination papers.

Although much police time and effort over the years had been taken up in combatting politically motivated crime, it must be remembered that, except for brief periods, as in August 1961, such work never engaged the main effort of the majority of the Force. Normal life went on for the bulk of the population, accompanied by normal crime and death and injury on the roads. Like any other police force in the World, it was with this that members of the Northern Rhodesia Police were primarily engaged.

The police were not concerned with trying to stop any party gaining a following or coming to power, but they struggled to ensure that all parties did so peacefully and in accordance with the Law.

Notes

1. Maurice Harold MACMILLAN 1st Ld Stockton 84 OM 76 PC 42 FRS 62 ed Eton Balliol 2Lt Gren Gds ADC Gov Gen Cda 19–20 MP Stockton 24–9.31 Dir MacMillan & Co MP(C) Bromley 11.45–9.64 Parlty Sec Supply 40 Colonies 42 Min Res AlliedHQ NWAfrica 42 SofS Air 45 Minstr Housg & LGovt 51 Defnce 10.54 Foreign Sec 4.55 Chancllr Exchequr 12.55 PM 1.57–10.63 d29.12.86

2. MONCKTON of Brenchley Walter Turner Monckton 1st Viscount 57 PC 51 G(64K37)CVO KCMG 45 KC 30 MC MA b17.1.91 ed Harrow Balliol 2Lt 4QORWK, Bar Innr Temple'19 Rcdr Hythe 30–7 AG to PofW 34 AG Duchy of Cornwall 36–47,48–51 DG Press & Censorshp Bureau 39 DG Min Info 40 SolrGen 45 MP(C) Bristol W 2.51–1.57 Min Lab & NS 51 Defence 12.55 PMG 10.56–1.57 d9.1.65

3. Iain MacLEOD PC 52 BA MP(C) Enfield W'50 b11.11.13 ed Fettes Cam, Bar Innr Temple'38 enl 39 w40 DAQMG 50Div'44 Chancellor Exchequer 50 Min Health 52 Lab & NS 12.55 SofS Colonies 10.59 Chancellor Duchy of Lancaster 61–63 d20.7.70

4. Mulford, *Zambia, the Politics of Independence* p153
Simon KAPWEPWE bChinsali Dist ANC resgnd 10.58 Treasr ZANC UNIP Min Af Agriculture 12.62 Home Affrs 1.64 VPres Zambia 24.10.64
Munukuyamba SIPALO, Lozi ed India to NR'57 ANC Exec expelled 12.57 Gen Sec ZANC/UNIP 11.58–62 Min Natural Resources 1.64

5. Brockwell *The Burton Atrocity* Police Journal Feb 1965 p61 this account is largely based on his article

6. Patrice LUMUMBA b Kasai 2.7.25 emp PO BCongo fdr Mouvement National Congolaise'58 PM'60 murdered 7.1.61

7. Anthony Geo SOMERHOUGH OBE 48 b15.12.06 ed Dover Cllge, HMS Worcstr, PO RAF'27 Bar Grey's 36 Deputy to JAG'36 LegalSO RAF BEF'39 Wg Cdr DJAG MEF'40–Gp Capt Oi/c War Crimes Gp NWE 45–8 MBE'46 Crown Counsl Kenya'49 DepPP'50 Judge NR'54 d2.10.60

8. Sir John Ramsay BLAGDEN Kt 70 OBE 44 TD MA b Davos 25.7.08 s/o PhD ed Marlboro Cam 2Lt 7Essex TA'28 Bar Lincoln's 34 Capt 35 Maj'38 CO 644 HAARegt'43 Col PP Mil Govt Cts BAOR 11.45 Judge Control Comm'47 Sen Mag Sarawak 12.11.50 Judge Trinidad'56 NR 16.9.60 Appeal Judge Zambia'64 CJ'65–9 d3.6.85

9. Moise TSHOMBE Pres Katanga ltr Pres Zaire

10. Observer 12 Feb'61 quoted by Mulford *Zambia, the Politics of Independence* p183
Sir John MOFFATT MLC for African interests, Mmbr Federal Assembly & Chmn African Affrs Bd'53 fdr CAP ltr Liberal Party NR, unsuccessful UNIP candidate Ndola'64

11. Coates' report in the author's possession

12. *Nkhwazi* Vol 9 No 2 Dec 1961 p25

13. *Zambia, the Politics of Independence* p205

14. John FitzGerald KENNEDY b Mass 20.5.17 ed Harvard USN Lt'41 Corres INS'45 Congress'47 Senate'53 Pres 20.1.61 murdered 22.11.63

15. Dag Hajalmar Agne Carl HAMMARSKJOLD BL DPhil b Sweden05 ed Uppsala StockholmU AProf Stockholm 33 Sec Comm Unemploymt 30 Sec Bank of Swedn 35 USofS Fin 36 & Chmn Bk of Swedn 41 Fin Advsr FO & Swedish Delegate UN 49,51–Sec Gen 53 d17.9.61
Geo John Chas Mercer Nairne Petty-Fitzmaurice 8th Marquess of LANSDOWNE b27.11.12 edEton Christchurch 2Lt ScH, Greys 40 Maj 44 PS Ambassador Paris 44–5 PUS FO 58 Min of State Colonial Affrs 62–4 & Cmmnwlth Reltns 63
Cuthbt Jas McCall Ld ALPORT PC 60 TD MA b22.3.12 s/o Prof MD FRCS ed Haileyby Cam, Artist Rifles TA & Bar 34 Hon Lt Col MP(C) Colchstr 50 APostMG 12.55 PUS Cmmnwlth Reltns 57 Min State 10.59 HC Rhod & Nyasald 61–3 Life Peer 61 d98

16. Colvin *The Rise and Fall of Tshombe* Leslie Frewin London 1968
Heinrich WIESCHOFF UN Staff NY Deputy to Undr Sec Dept of Political & Secy Council Affrs

17. *Nkhwazi* Vol 12 No.1 Apr'64 pp48–51 – Rosalyn Higgins *United Nations Peacekeeping 1946–*

1967 Documents & Commentary 3 Africa OUP 1980 p407 says 'while not ruling out the possibility the Commission found no evidence that pilot error could have been the possible cause'
18. *Nkhwazi* Vol 10 No.1 Aug'62 p43
19. *Nkhwazi* Vol 12 No.1 Apr'64 p52
20. Mulford *Zambia, the Politics of Independence* Chap VII
21. *Nkhwazi* Vol 11 No.1 May'63 p80
22. *Nkhwazi* vol 9 No.2 Dec 61 p20, Vol 11 No.2 Oct 63 p18
23. Jas SKINNER b Dublin Solr Lka Legal Advsr & Campaign Organsr UNIP 62 MP 64 AG Zambia'64, CJ Malawi
    Wesley NYRENDA BA(Hons) ed London U, Prin Munali Secondary Sch; UNIP MLC Eastern'62 Speaker'64
    Hayden Dingiswayo BANDA b Lundazi Dist. Dist Chmn Ndola ANC 58 Pres ANC Western Province; ZANC 58 DYouth UNIP 11.61 Minister Housing & Social Development'64
24. Short *African Sunset* Chap XII
    Robin SHORT b Jersey 2.27 s/o Lt Col ed Wellgtn Rfn RB 1.45 2Lt 1.46 Pal 47 Secy Offr AHQ Pal 48 Colonial Offce Cse Qn's Cllge Cam 49 Cdt NR 50 DO Kasempa DC Ft J rtd 65 Ministry of Lab UK 65–8 Jersey Bar Innr Temple 72
25. Evidence by Oi/c Chilanga Police Station quoted in Northern News 24.4.63
26. Mulford *Zambia, the Politics of Independence* pp304–327
    Job MICHELLO Sec ANC Sthn Province 12.58 Gen Sec 59 MLC 1.62 Parlty Sec Land & Natural Resources 12.62 Pres People's Democratic Party 5.8.63 Gen Sec ANC 64

CHAPTER 17

End of Empire

The last year of the Northern Rhodesia Police opened with Mr E H Halse OBE KPM as Commissioner and Mr J C Day QPM as Deputy Commissioner. Other senior posts were held as follows:

Senior Assistant Commissioner (Headquarters) – Mr L A Hicks QPM
Senior Assistant Commissioner (Western Division) – Mr F A Roberts
Assistant Commissioner (Staff) – Mr D J Forde
Assistant Commissioner (Special Branch) – Mr E Leighton OBE
Assistant Commissioner (Special Duties) – Col H B Perkins OBE
Assistant Commissioner (Crime) – Mr D M Brockwell QPM
Assistant Commissioner (Administration) – Mr S A Neal
Assistant Commissioner (Western Division) – Mr R J Read
Officers Commanding:
Lusaka Division – Mr B G O'Leary, Senior Superintendent
Training School – Mr J T Edwards, Senior Superintendent
Mobile Unit – Mr J F P Fitzgerald, Senior Superintendent
Southern Division – Mr J B Seed, Senior Superintendent
Northern Division – Mr R S Monteith, Senior Superintendent
Central Division – Mr R A Ockwell, Senior Superintendent
Eastern Division – Mr H Taylor, Superintendent
Luapula Division – Mr B G Coase, Superintendent
North-Western Division – Mr F D R Gray, Assistant Superintendent.

Derek Gray with 11 subordinate police officers and 66 other ranks, was responsible for policing an area of 48,500 square miles, some six times the size of Wales, with a population density of just over three persons to a square mile.

There were to be many changes before the year was halfway through. On 6 January 1964 a scheme of retirement benefits for members of Her Majesty's Overseas Civil Service and other designated officers, was issued to take effect from 1 May. This enabled any of these officers to retire on giving six months notice at any time. No officer who gave notice within a month of 1 May was to be required to remain in Northern Rhodesia after independence. Those retiring before the age of 55 were to receive pensions calculated in the normal way at 1/600 of their final annual salary for each completed month of service, together with lump sum compensation on a sliding scale starting at 0.16 of annual salary for a 21 year old with three years service, and rising to a maximum of 4.32 for a 41 year old with ten or more years service, before descending again. A 54 year old officer with only three years qualifying service was to receive a gratuity of only 0.15 of his salary, but with ten or more years service he received the equivalent of half his annual salary.

Those retiring voluntarily or continuing to serve were to receive their lump sum compensation in up to six instalments. The first was to be paid on 1 May 1964 and was to be one sixth of the total due or £1,000, whichever was the greater, for those who qualified for more than £1,000. Those whose age and service qualified for £1,000 or less received the full sum. Interest was payable on outstanding balances. For those who continued to serve beyond 1 May 1964, compensation was to be recalculated each year, or at the date of retirement to take into account increases in age, length of service and salary, so long as to do so was to the officer's advantage. Those accepting promotion after 1 May 1964 were to be required to give an undertaking to serve for at least two years in the new rank.

Officers could be required to retire to facilitate the introduction of constitutional changes or to make way for the promotion of local officers. In these cases the full amount of compensation was payable in one lump sum.[1]

Annual salaries for officers serving on Overseas Aid Scheme terms were now:

> Assistant Inspector Grade I: £945 rising to £1,200 over five years,
> Inspector and Senior Inspector: £1,200 rising to £1,600 over seven years,
> Chief Inspector: £1,645 rising to £1,780 after two years,
> Assistant Superintendent: £1,780 rising to £1,995 over three years,
> Superintendent: £2,065 rising to £2,275 over three years,
> Senior Superintendent: £2,345 rising to £2,600 over four years,
> Assistant Commissioner: £2,655,
> Senior Assistant Commissioner: £2,770,
> Deputy Commissioner: £3,005,
> Commissioner: £3,235.

Even before the General Election it was announced that Northern Rhodesia would be granted independence as Zambia on 24 October. It was not known for certain until the middle of the year that the new state would be a republic, albeit remaining in the Commonwealth. 24 October 1964 was the sixth anniversary of the formation of the Zambia African National Congress.

The General Election on 20 and 21 January meant long hours of duty for all members of the Northern Rhodesia Police. The United National Independence Party secured 55 of the 75 seats in the new assembly. Kenneth Kaunda thereby became Northern Rhodesia's first and only Prime Minister. Simon Kapwepwe became Minister for Home Affairs, but the Chief Secretary remained responsible for the Northern Rhodesia Police.

From May 1964 Superior Police Officers were retired in significant numbers, starting with assistant superintendents, to facilitate the rapid promotion of Africans. Records had been reviewed and entries expurgated which might handicap the careers in Zambia of officers who had given good and faithful service to the Crown. 77 SPOs and 339 spo's left during the year. Eric Halse, the Commissioner and Julian Day, his deputy retired. Mr L A Hicks succeeded as the last Commissioner of the Northern Rhodesia Police. Lawson Hicks had joined the Force in 1939 after two years as a constable in the London Metropolitan Police. He was to be the first Commissioner of the Zambia Police.

The last months of the Northern Rhodesia Police were darkened by the bloodiest internal disturbance in its history, directed not against the Crown nor the white settler community, but against the new African regime. The growth of United National Independence Party influence and intolerance had made a clash of some kind with Alice Lenshina's Lumpa Church virtually inevitable. UNIP agitators intimidated Lumpas as they did any other African found not carrying a party card. They could not, or would not, understand the church's desire to stay aloof from politics. In some villages Lumpa churches were burnt. A mood of desperation overtook the church people who saw themselves as likely to receive even worse treatment when colonial rule ended. As intimidation, assaults, and even murders of church members increased, they concentrated more in their own villages and built stockades for their protection.

Between June 1963 and July 1964 fourteen Lumpas had been murdered by UNIP supporters, while 28 of their churches and 121 of their houses had been burnt. 66 Lumpas had been assaulted, 22 of them seriously. In the same period Lenshina's followers had responded by killing seven UNIP members and were responsible for ten assaults and the burning of two houses.

In October 1963 a serious fight had occurred in the Luangwa Valley in which six people were killed and thirty-two wounded. Towards the end of that year the newly established Chinsali Rural Council, which replaced the Native Authorities, resolved that the unauthorised Lumpa villages should be destroyed. In mid-December there was a widespread outbreak of violence, resulting in ten deaths and nearly 100 wounded. Prompt police action contained the situation. On Christmas Eve information reached the new police station at Lundazi of an impending attack on a nearby Lumpa settlement. The police went out and spent Christmas at the village to guarantee its safety. Kenneth Kaunda and Alexander Grey Zulu, Minister for Native Affairs, visited Chinsali and prevailed on Alice Lenshina to instruct her followers to return to their proper villages by 18 January 1964. Peace was temporarily restored, but the Lumpas were too wary to leave their stockades. Suspicion and fear remained undissipated.

According to the report of the Commission of Inquiry into the former Lumpa Church, the major disturbances were sparked off by a trivial incident at Kasanta Village in Chief Mubanga's area of the Chinsali District on 25 June 1964. An adult UNIP member rebuked a young Lumpa relative for not attending school and struck him. The boy reported the incident to fellow church-people at Kameko Village in the same area. Fifteen or sixteen Lumpas seized sticks and spears and attacked Kasanta, burning houses and injuring residents.

On 26 June a sergeant and three constables arrived at Kasanta in the course of a patrol. They went on to Kameko where they made 13 arrests. On the way to Mubanga's court they met a passing vehicle which took eight prisoners and three police on to Chinsali. There was no room for the others who were left with one constable at Mubanga's. A large number of Lumpas then appeared at Mubanga's Village and compelled the release of the prisoners there. When this news reached Chinsali, Senior Inspector Les Ellis, the Officer in Charge, Detective Inspector D Hopwood, assistant inspectors W E Lester and Simulopwe and ten police other ranks went to Kameko Village. They were met by a few armed men who, when ordered to put down their spears, attacked the police, forcing them to open fire in self defence. A cry of 'Jericho' went up and 200 Lumpas gathered and charged the police with spears, axes and machetes etc. Senior Inspector Ellis and one constable received minor spear wounds as the police withdrew leaving five Lumpas dead and the same number wounded.[2]

During the next two weeks police reinforcements arrived in the area, which was visited by the Commissioner of Police and other senior officers. Extensive patrolling was carried out and contact was made with the deacons of the church in an effort to persuade offenders to give themselves up. Police visited Lumpa villages, including Kameko, and prisoners and weapons were surrendered. However tension remained and threats were exchanged between UNIP supporters and Lumpa churchmen.

On 9 July 1964 the Central Security Council met in Lusaka. The Prime Minister, Kaunda, was confident that his party's supporters in the registered villages could be persuaded to receive the Lumpas back to live among them without animosity. The Council concluded that it was almost inevitable that recourse to some emergency measures would be required, but resolved that a further attempt should be made to persuade Lenshina's followers to return to their villages of origin and abandon their unauthorised settlements.

On 13 July Kenneth Kaunda visited Chinsali. He addressed separate meetings of UNIP officials and Lumpa Church deacons. The Prime Minister instructed the Lumpas that they must return to their official villages and called upon both sides to resume friendly relations. Alice Lenshina attended the meeting with Kaunda against her will and maintained that the unsatisfactory situation was entirely the fault of his party followers. Police patrols accompanied delegations sent round the Lumpa settlements to persuade them to abandon them, but the net result was increased concentrations of Lumpas who continued to strengthen their defences. They now identified the police with Government, and therefore UNIP, policy, and treated patrols as enemies at whose approach they went into hiding.

At 0820 hours on 24 July twenty men of the Northern Rhodesia Police Mobile Unit under Assistant Inspector Derek Smith, left Chinsali on a routine patrol to Mpundu, a Lumpa village, some sixty-five miles to the South. En route they met two district messengers and a kapasu who reported that they had been chased away from another Lenshina settlement, Chapaula, four miles off the Great North Road about 23 miles north of Chinsali. The police patrol was diverted to Chapaula.

Leaving their vehicles on the road, the police approached the village on foot, as the track was not motorable. On the way they met a man carrying a stick to which was attached a bicycle chain to make a flail-like weapon. On seeing the police he fled. When the police came in sight of the village which was surrounded by a stockade, a woman was seen running away. All was quiet. The village appeared deserted, Leaving the rest of his party twenty yards from the entrance, Smith went forward with one man, Constable Mpapa. As they passed through the gateway Smith was wounded in the back by a spear thrown by a man hidden just outside the gate. With the spear still lodged in his back, Smith caught his assailant. A shout of 'Jericho' was then heard and a large crowd of people, armed with spears, sticks and pangas, charged. A woman attacked Mpapa who struck her down with his rifle butt. He was about four yards from Smith who called for help. Mpapa opened fire at those attacking his officer, who reeled back through the gateway, firing his revolver, and collapsed after covering ten yards. His assailants followed shouting 'Hallelujah' and speared the assistant inspector repeatedly as he lay on the ground. Mpapa fought his way back to the main body of the patrol, which retired fighting to its vehicles, leaving Constable Chansa dead, but bringing away Driver Constable Kabiba, seriously injured.

Two platoons of the Mobile Unit were sent to Chapaula and recovered Chansa's body, which had been mutilated. Strong opposition was encountered and it was decided not to attempt to storm the village. The report of the Commission of Inquiry states that 'owing to recent events the morale of the African police had reached a low ebb'. It will be born in mind that they had already lost many of their more experienced and trusted officers and well knew that many more were about to go. They found themselves carrying out the dictates of a government formed from those who had until recently been regarded as the organisers of disorder and revolt. They knew that the Lumpa Church people had been the victims of intimidation and provocation. Neither the African police nor their remaining European officers relished the task of suppression.

Trouble became widespread. Three UNIP villages in the Siachepe area were attacked by Lenshina's adherents. Four people were killed and two wounded. Patrols to Lumpa settlements found the occupants truculent and defiant.

Further reinforcements were despatched to the Chinsali District. Mr J D O Bird MBE, who had distinguished himself in the disturbances in Northern Province in 1961 and was now an assistant commissioner of police, was placed in charge of operations. On 25 July three platoons of the Mobile Unit went to Chapaula. The villagers opened fire and attacked with great ferocity. The police fired in reply. Two other ranks received flesh wounds and Assistant Inspector Peter Standaloft was speared in the back during the action in which fourteen Lumpas were killed and fifteen wounded including a woman and child. The women appeared to have a complete disregard for bullets and exhorted their menfolk to greater efforts throughout the encounter which lasted about one and a half hours. Prior to and during the action the District Commissioner, Mr Hannah, appealed unsuccessfully to the villagers through a loud-hailer to lay down their arms and give themselves up.

The body of Assistant Inspector Smith was found about 150 yards from the village, near a river. A number of muzzle-loaders, bows and arrows, spears, axes and machetes were seized by the police, who also recovered firearms lost by their comrades on 24 July.

On 26 July 1964 a police patrol went to a Lumpa settlement known as Musanya, finding burnt houses en route and the body of a murdered man. Large numbers of refugees from the disrupted areas began to accumulate at government and mission stations.

The Central Security Committee met again and decided to send three more platoons of the Northern Rhodesia Police Mobile Unit to the Chinsali District, together with both battalions of the Northern Rhodesia Regiment. The provisions of Stage 1 of the Preservation of Public Security Regulations were applied to the whole of the Northern Province and the Lundazi District of Eastern Province, where Lenshina's influence was also strong.

On 27 July four platoons of the Mobile Unit were despatched to the Chilonga area east of Mulanga Mission. On the way a number of bridges were found to have been damaged and were repaired as the convoy went on. At one such halt the two leading landrovers were ambushed. Inspector Peter Jordan was killed and Inspector Hopwood seriously wounded as they debussed. The attackers, about a hundred strong, came on with a complete disregard for their own safety and only drew off after five of their number had been killed.

The headquarters of the Lumpa sect were at Sione, where a large church had been built. Alice Lenshina and a number of prominent deacons were believed to be there. On 29 July the Army arrived at Chinsali. The Governor and Prime Minister flew up to attend a meeting of the Northern Province Operational Committee. It was decided to take firm action to prevent further outrages by the Lumpas and retaliation by UNIP supporters or others. Sione was to be occupied in overwhelming force, if possible without violence, and the church leaders arrested. The 1st Battalion of The Northern Rhodesia Regiment was to be the Government's main instrument for this purpose.

At 0830 hours on 30 July, the battalion accompanied by police arrived outside Sione Village, which was surrounded by a strong stockade. The District Commissioner, using a loudhailer, called on the inhabitants to lay down their arms and surrender. Immediately there was an attack on the security forces who had to open fire. There was an exchange of fire for about thirty minutes, during which the troops advanced towards the village. They were then halted while the District Commissioner made a further appeal. This was ignored. The troops resumed their advance slowly towards the church which was the central feature of the village. As they moved forward they were attacked with frenzied fanaticism on both flanks, with spears, arrows and assorted firearms. The soldiers replied with automatic weapons. The opposition gradually weakened and the troops burst into the village. Here fierce resistance again erupted from men, women and children, gathered round the church. The church itself was full of women and children. When the police entered to clear it with tearsmoke, they were attacked by screaming women and had to use firearms, including Sterling sub-machine guns to protect themselves.

By 1530 hours all resistance had ceased. Fifty-nine male and seven female Lumpas were dead and 110 wounded. After receiving first aid all the wounded were taken to Chinsali Hospital, as were the government casualties, Inspector David Marnham and five African soldiers, one of whom later died of his wounds. The weapons seized, which included firearms, filled a five ton truck.

On the same day 2nd Battalion The Northern Rhodesia Regiment occupied

Chilonga which was found to be deserted. This battalion had come into being at Lusaka on 1st January 1964 by the conversion of 2nd King's African Rifles. The unit still had a strong cadre of Nyasalanders to which Northern Rhodesian recruits, many from the UNIP Youth Brigade, had been added.

On 31 July 1964 the police at Lundazi, some 150 miles south-east of Chinsali, received a report of a minor incident at Chikwa's village, the scene of lawlessness in 1963. Investigations commenced. There were also reports of disturbance in the Mpika District 120 miles south of Chinsali.

On 31 July and 1 and 2 August military and police patrols were active in all areas where there was evidence of Lumpa activity, searching for Alice Lenshina, who had not been found at Sione, and identifying strongholds where fugitives from previous actions were assembling. Leaflets were dropped from aircraft exhorting the church people to lay down their arms and return to their proper villages.

At approximately 0200 hours on 3 August a gang of about 200 Lenshina followers made a surprise attack on the tiny police station and camp at Lundazi, whose staff had given up their Christmas to protect a Lumpa settlement. The station, with only one man on night duty in the office was soon overrun and ten rifles, two Greener shotguns with 75 cartridges, a Sterling sub-machine gun with 4 full magazines and a riot gun stolen from the armoury. In the police camp a driver constable, three wives of policemen and three children were slaughtered. A Sergeant with Lumpa relatives was taken as a hostage.

Inspector Paul Gillies, still Officer in Charge, rallied five constables and obtained six shotguns and ammunition from Indian traders. At about 0330 hours he led his men towards the Government Offices to which the raiders had now turned their attention. Both the District Commissioner and District Officer were away. As soon as they saw the police, the Lumpas charged. Vastly outnumbered and with no advantage in firepower, Gillies and his men were compelled to withdraw into the Asian trading area, while the mob continued to rampage round the township, killing people and destroying buildings. At first light, having gathered a few reinforcements, Inspector Gillies again advanced on the Boma. It was deserted. The raiders had left Lundazi. The police commenced patrolling the township, finding that, in addition to their own casualties, two Asian men and one woman, and four African men and three women, had been killed and twenty people injured.

At 0630 hours Gillies was able to contact Fort Jameson to request reinforcements which arrived at 1015. At 0715 news of the attack on Lundazi was received at Chinsali. Two companies of 1st Northern Rhodesia Regiment were despatched by air to Lundazi where they commenced landing at 1030 hours. During the morning reports came in of other atrocities in the Lundazi area bringing the death toll to 50. Chief Chikwa was among the dead, together with a district messenger and nine others at his village, where the Lumpas had found firearms. That evening the remaining two companies of 1 NRR were sent by road to the Lundazi District, permission to use the Nakonde-Fort Hill road having been given by the Government of Malawi.

Information indicated that the attack on Lundazi had been mounted from Chipoma, a fortified settlement a few miles to the North. At 1230 hours on 4 August two companies of troops and a detachment of police approached the stockade. The District Commissioner called upon those inside to surrender. As the force advanced it was attacked on both flanks and in the centre. Fire was opened and the troops fought their way into the village, which was eventually cleared. In this action 81 Lumpas were killed, 43 wounded and 11 arrested. The ten rifles and the Sterling stolen from Lundazi Police Station were recovered.

On 5 August a report was received that Lenshina's followers had attacked Magodi's village, twenty miles north of Lundazi. Air reconnaissance showed a number of burnt villages. Patrolling was commenced to restore confidence and Chikwa's village, east of the Luangwa, was visited.

Meanwhile back in the Chinsali District 2 NRR and police had taken a settlement at Chasosa on 4 August. They were ambushed about 100 yards short of the stockade and suffered six minor casualties. Seven male and eight female attackers were killed and five wounded. A number of arrests were made.

On 6 August it was established that the people of Chikwa Village had fled to the west side of the Luangwa River. Gangs of Lenshina's supporters were still roving the area. Kambombo Village, 90 miles north of Lundazi was reported occupied by Lumpa forces and barricaded. A spotter plane was fired on over the village.

At Pikamalesa Village 17 people had been killed by Lenshina's followers on 3 August and 50 abducted, although some of these had since managed to escape. Armed bands of Lumpas from Chipoma were still active and terrorising the area. Unarmed Lumpas were being roughly handled when found by non-churchmen.

Paishiku, 90 miles north of Lundazi, was a known Lumpa stronghold. The Provincial Operations Committee had planned to clear it on 6 August. This operation was postponed on instructions from Lusaka. Clearance having been obtained the operation against Paishiku was finally mounted on 9 August. Paishiku was found to have been destroyed. The mutilated bodies of eleven men, eleven women and nine children were found in the ruins. A handful of survivors came forward and it was learnt that UNIP supporters from neighbouring villages had made their own attack on 7 August. Fifteen other bodies were found which were thought to be those of members of the attacking force.

On 10 August troops of 2 NRR and elements of the police Mobile Unit moved against a fortified Lumpa settlement at Chaba in the Mpika District. As they approached three men fired at the security forces with muzzleloaders and escaped into the thick bush. A little further on fire was opened from the front and left flank by up to 18 men with firearms, inflicting several casualties on the troops. A hundred yards from the stockade the force halted as the District Commissioner attempted to address the villagers through a loud-hailer. This attempt was frustrated by continued firing. After a 15 minute firefight, many of the men fled from the village into the bush and 145 persons, mainly women and children, responded to the continued appeals to give themselves up. 55 Lumpas had been killed and 28 wounded. Of the security forces 3 officers (2 superficially), and 4 other ranks (2 of whom later died of their injuries) were wounded. Nine muzzleloaders, a quantity of gunpowder and a number of bows, arrows and spears were found.

On 11 August Alice Lenshina surrendered herself in the Kasama District and was flown to Ndola. The following day, with her husband and two children the priestess was flown to Mumbwa where she was to remain in detention and later under restriction until December 1975 when she was moved to Chilenje a suburb of Lusaka where she died on 7 December 1978.[3]

On 13 August 1964 her supporters made an attack on Chikanda Matipa Village in the Isoka District, killing two people and seriously injuring two more. Leaflets were now dropped with a message from Alice Lenshina, calling on her people to lay down their arms and give themselves up. On 16 August one company of 2 NRR and half a platoon of the Mobile Unit went to Chikanda Matipa with the District Commissioner. En route they encountered an armed band of Lumpas. After a warning by the DC eight men surrendered.

The major operations described, patrols in other areas, and the leaflets with Alice Lenshina's message, gradually caused the Lumpas to abandon the struggle and give themselves up. Reports of hut burnings and disturbances declined, although on 18 August it was confirmed that Lumpa deacons at Chiwala Village, Chinsali, had fired on their own congregation, wounding eleven, because the people had shown insufficient keenness in fighting the security forces.

United National Independence Party supporters and ordinary villagers were alarmed at the return of Lumpa church people to live among them. Some Lumpas who had returned to their proper villages therefore moved out again. Numbers of Lenshina's disciples remained in hiding in the bush for fear of reprisals. There were reports of the formation of new gangs for offensive action or merely to steal food to survive.

Villagers in Chief Kambompo's area of Lundazi District adopted a very antagonistic attitude towards Lenshina's followers and threatened to kill any strangers they encountered. Lumpas in hiding to the West of the Luangwa River raided villages on the East Bank for food. On 21 August 1964, following reports that abandoned Lumpa settlements were being re-occupied, regulations were made authorising their destruction.

On 22 August troops in the Chinsali District found a large Lumpa camp which showed signs of having been hastily vacated. Thirty-two axes, two muzzleloaders and two bows were found and destroyed. Isolated bands of Lumpas surrendered to security forces.

On 31 August Lumpas made a night raid for food on a village in Chief Chikwa's area and reconnaissance aircraft spotted a large gang on the west side of the Luangwa near the Lundi River. Generally however, the situation was so improved that 2 NRR returned to Lusaka while the 1st Battalion redeployed with HQ and the main body at Chinsali and one company remaining in the Chikwa area of Lundazi District.

At about 1600 hours on 2 September three platoons of C Company 1 NRR were patrolling along the Luangwa, west of Chikwa when, one of them came across a stockaded settlement. The occupants were urged to surrender. Instead they opened fire, killing two soldiers. The platoon returned fire whereupon the Lumpas placed their women and children to the front and invited the troops to carry on shooting. The soldiers were not prepared to kill women and children and withdrew as darkness approached. B Company of the battalion was flown from Chinsali as reinforcements.

The next day a message was dropped from the air, again calling on those in the village to surrender. On 4 September the two companies of troops, a platoon of the police Mobile Unit and teams of Special Branch and CID crossed to the West Bank of the Luangwa and established a base. A second Mobile Unit platoon remained at Chikwa. The scene of the action was visited and three deserted encampments found. Escaped hostages reported that the Lumpas had no intention of surrendering and had been preparing for a raid on Chipamba Village, east of the river, when the troops arrived. The graves of four men and one young girl were found. Among the dead were one Chibanga, said to be the leader of the rebels, and Jacobi Lungu, a former Army corporal, who was said to have killed the two soldiers.

Information was received that the Lumpas would move north to regroup. Troops and police patrolled on both sides of the Luangwa but no contact was made, although, on 7 September a gang of about 100 was sighted from the air heading west to the escarpment and the Lundi River.

Between 20 and 26 September 559 Lumpas surrendered in the Chinsali District. Intelligence indicated that not more than 100 were still at large in this district. On 7 October information was received that a number of UNIP supporters had visited the Lumpa settlement at Chipepela in the northern part of the district to encourage the church people to return to Musanya Village. The male Lumpas fled into the bush leaving about thirty women and children who were removed to Musanya. On the following day UNIP men went to a settlement at Mutwalo for the same purpose. They were attacked by about twenty Lumpas armed with spears and axes. One UNIP man was killed and two injured. A Mobile Unit platoon and a CID team were sent to investigate this incident.

2 NRR had relieved the 1st Battalion on 14 September. On the afternoon of 10 October a platoon of 2 NRR located a Lumpa hideout west of the Luangwa. The occupants, about 150 persons, were instructed to assemble in one spot and surrender. A party broke away, trapped a soldier and speared him to death. Fighting then became general. Sixty Lumpas were killed, 28 wounded and a further 95 taken prisoner.

On 15 October 1964 the situation in the Chinsali and Lundazi districts was reviewed in the light of police and military commitments for the independence celebrations on 24 October. Although things had much improved there were still gangs at large. It was decided to leave two platoons of the police Mobile Unit and the greater part of a company of 1 NRR in the Northern Province and one platoon of Mobile Unit and a company of 2 NRR in the Lundazi District.

The total police casualties during the disturbances had been 4 killed and 7 wounded. The Army suffered 6 killed and 9 wounded. A total of 472 Lumpas were killed and 251 wounded by the security forces. The Commission of Inquiry

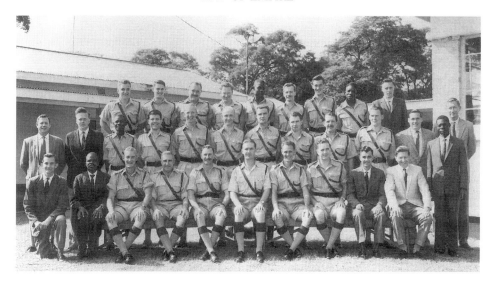

Officers of Luanshya District March 1964 (Photo N. C. Hulette)
L to R Back Row: R Roebuck, M. Needham, P B Widd, Deerden, J J B Kasaila, R A Nesbitt,
C E Britton, K J B Tembo, M J Beaves;
Middle Row: D McKenzie, I J S Russell, Siamata, N C Hulette, D C Cameron, C D N Dobson,
R F M Anderson, K J Hatcher, S L Halse, C C Heygate, R E Dixon, Chiwila, E J Pamphilon;
Front Row: P J F Fillery, J Mumba, E H Warrington, D J Anderson, R A Coppard,
I R Mackintosh, H N Nevett, G S Blythe, J Gowland, G B Bird.

found that 185 civilians had been killed by the rebels and 128 wounded while other civilians had killed 46 Lumpas and wounded three.

While mopping up operations were in progress in Northern Province and Lund-azi District, preparations were being made all over Northern Rhodesia for the independence celebrations. Plans were made for traffic and crowd control. The main ceremony was to be at Lusaka Showground on the night of 23 October, but every town and village was to celebrate in its own way.

Official delegations from sixty-four countries travelled to Lusaka for the occasion together with representatives of the United Nations Organisation, the Organisation for African Unity and other bodies. The Lusaka Division of the NRP was strongly reinforced by permanent staff and recruits from the Police Training School and by the Northern Rhodesia Police Reserve.

The Princess Royal, the daughter of King George V[4], was sent out to represent the Queen and hand over the Constitutional Instruments for the Republic of Zambia. A mounted escort was provided for her by the Northern Rhodesia Police and its reserve. Mr J F P Fitzgerald, now an Assistant Commissioner of Police, commanded the escort, but riding as his lieutenant was Major G W 'Squire' Beeston Bancroft, late Indian Army, Divisional Commandant, Northern Rhodesia Police Reserve, Lusaka. Beeston-Bancroft had landed in France with the Indian Cavalry Corps in 1914 and it was fitting that the Princess should have such a contemporary from the Imperial past in her escort.

Just before midnight on 23 October 1964 the massed bands of the Northern Rhodesia Police and Regiment played *God Save the Queen*. The lights were dimmed at the Independence Stadium and the Union Flag was slowly lowered.

At the stroke of midnight the Northern Rhodesia Police passed into history and its remaining members became the Zambia Police.

Notes

1. NR Establishment Circular No.B166 6.1.64 *Scheme of Retirement Benefits for Members of H.M.O.C.S. and for Officers Designated under the Overseas Service (Northern Rhodesia) Agreement 1961*
2. *Report of the Commission of Inquiry into the Lumpa Disturbances* Lusaka 1964
3. *A Time to Mourn* John Hudson, Bookworld Publishers, Lusaka, ISBN 9982-24-012-9
4. Princess Victoria Alexandra Alice MARY b25.4.97 m28.2.22 Vsct Lascelles ltr Earl of Harewood

APPENDIX 1

Glossary

1d = One penny (6d = 5 (new) pence or 10 ngwee)
1s = One shilling = 10 (new) pence or 20 ngwee
1/Sgt = First Class Sergeant
A'corn = Abercorn (Mbala)
ACP = Assistant Commissioner of Police
ADC = Assistant District Commissioner or Aide de Camp
Adjt = Adjutant
AG = Adjutant General (Mil) or Attorney General (Civ)
A/Insp or A/I = Assistant Inspector
ANC = Assistant Native Commissioner (pre 1924), African National Congress
Askari or Asirikari = African troops
A/Supt or ASP = Assistant Superintendent of Police
BBP = Bechuanaland Border Police
BCA = British Central Africa, Nyasaland now Malawi
BH = Broken Hill (Kabwe)
BNCO = British Non-Commissioned Officer
Boma = originally a stockade, later a district or other government administrative headquarters
BPP = Bechuanaland Protectorate Police
BSACo = British South Africa Company
BSANP = British South Africa Native Police
BSAP = British South Africa Police, the police force of Southern Rhodesia
Bwayo = Bulawayo
Cdt = Cadet
CAP = Central African Post, Lusaka'as newspaper
CAR = Central African Rifles, Central Africa Regiment
CC = Chief Constable
C/Insp C/I = Chief Inspector
Cmdt = Commandant
CofP CP = Commissioner of Police
COMPOL = Commissioner of Police (telegraphic address)
Const = Constable
Cpl = Corporal
Coy = Company
CPM = Colonial Police Medal for Meritorious Service
CPM(G) = Colonial Police Medal for Gallantry
C/Supt = Chief Superintendent
DA = District Assistant, Provincial Administration
DC = District Commissioner   "   "
DO = District Officer   "   "

District Messenger = A uniformed African with certain powers of arrest, serving in the Provincial Administration to assist a district commissioner.
DCM = Distinguished Conduct Medal
DCP = Deputy Commissioner of Police
DSO = Distinguished Service Order
FJ FtJ = Fort Jameson
FK = Feld Kompagnie (Field Company) German Forces
FR FtR = Fort Rosebery
Gazetted Officer = A police officer of or above the rank of assistant superintendent
GEA = German East Africa later Tanganyika Territory
GSWA = German South West Africa now Namibia
HKP = Hong Kong Police ltr Royal = RHKP
Insp = Inspector
IG = Inspector General
JP = Justice of the Peace, empowered to issue warrants or take oaths but not, in Northern Rhodesia, sitting as a magistrate
Kapasu = a chief's messenger or policeman
Kimberley Brick = Sun baked brick
KAR = King's African Rifles
KPM = King's Police Medal
Kraal = a village
LC = Local conditions of service
LCpl = Lance Corporal
Lka = Lusaka
Lshya = Luanshya
Lstone = Livingstone
Maz = Mazabuka
MC = Military Cross
MLC = Member of Legislative Council
MO = Medical Officer, Modus Operandi
Maxim = Machine gun designed by Hiram Maxim
MG = Machine gun
Met = London Metropolitan Police
MM = Military Medal
MID = Mentioned in Despatches
Msirikari = Soldier or policeman (Cinyanja)
MSM = Meritorious Service Medal
Muf = Mufulira
NC = Native Commissioner
NCO = Non-commissioned Officer
NER = North-Eastern Rhodesia
NERC = North-Eastern Rhodesia Constabulry
NRDF = Northern Rhodesia Defence Force (1939–45)
NRG = Northern Rhodesia Government
NRMS = Northern Rhodesia Medical Service, a Government Department not to be confused with the Northern Rhodesia Medical Corps (NRMC) of the NRVF consisting of members of the NRMS and others
NRP = Northern Rhodesia Police
NRPR = Northern Rhodesia Police Reserve
NRR = Northern Rhodesia Regiment
NRRif = Northern Rhodesia Rifles (at the time they were referred to as NRR, there being then no NR Regiment)
NRVF = Northern Rhodesia Volunteer Force (1914–25)
N/Sgt = Native sergeant
NWRC = North-Western Rhodesia Constabulry

OBE = Officer of the Order of the British Empire
OETA = Occupied Enemy Territory Administration
ORS = Orderly Room Sergeant
PA = Provincial Administration
Paymr = Paymaster
P&QM = Pay & Quartermaster
PalP = Palestine Police
PC = Provincial Commissioner
Pedco = People's Democratic Party
PNGP = Papua New Guinea Police
QM = Quartermaster
QMS = Quartermaster Sergeant
QPM = Queen's Police Medal
RAF = Royal Air Force
RAR = Rhodesian African Rifles
RIC = Royal Irish Constabulary
RM = Resident Magistrate, Royal Marines
RNR = Rhodesia Native Regiment 1914–18
RQMS = Regimental Quartermaster Sergeant
RRAF = Royal Rhodesian Air Force
RR = Rhodesia Regiment ltr Royal (RRR)
RSM = Regimental Sergeant-Major
RUC = Royal Ulster Constabulary
Ruga Ruga = Armed retainers or irregular troops
SAC = South African Constabulary
SAI = South African Infantry
SACP = Senior Assistant Commissioner of Police
Salisby = Salisbury (Harare)
SAMR = South African Mounted Riflemen
SAP = South African Police
SAR = South African Rifles
Sgt (Sjt) = Sergeant (Serjeant appears to have been in use in the early Great War period)
Section = Originally 20–35 men (a quarter of a company), after the adoption of the double company system a sub unit of a platoon, 4–12 men under a Cpl or LCpl
S/Insp S/I = Sub-Inspector pre 1924 or BSAP, Senior Inspector NRP post 1950
SM = Sergeant-Major
SPO = Superior Police Officer (see Gazetted Officer)
spo = Subordinate Police Officer, (A/Insp to C/Insp)
SR = Southern Rhodesia (Zimbabwe)
SRC = 1915–18 Southern Rhodesia Column ('A' & 'B' (Special Reserve) Companies BSAP, the service coys), pre 1908, Southern Rhodesia Constabulary
Sub/Insp = Sub Inspector
S/A/Supt = Senior Assistant Superintendent
SRM = Senior Resident Magistrate
Supt = Superintendent
S/Supt SSP = Senior Superintendent
SWA = South-West Africa now Namibia
Tpr = Trooper
QPM = Queen's Police Medal
UFP = United Federal Party
UNIP = United National Independence Party
WO = Warrant Officer
ZANC = Zambia African National Congress
ZP = Zambia Police

APPENDIX 2

Fatal African Casualties Northern Rhodesia Police 1914–18

112 Pte CHASESA kia Abercorn 9.9.14
190 Pte MADI kia Abercorn 9.9.14
102 Pte NDARAMA kia Fife 6.12.14
74 Cpl BWANALI kia Tunduma Hill Piquet 27.1.15
1117 Pte FUNGULU kia nr Mwazye 24.4.15
399 Pte KAMBOWE kia nr Zombe 21.5.15
559 Pte BULEYA dow Saisi 28.6.15
842 Pte MULUNDI kia Saisi 28.6.15
1184 Pte MSAPENDA kia Saisi? 28.6.15
1185 Pte MALIZANI kia nr Saisi 29.7.15
1077 Cpl KANGOMBE 7.10.15
1201 LCpl BWANA-MAKOA kia Lundula's Village 22.10.15
551 LCpl GABRIAL 16.11.15
1242 Pte MUMBWE kia Kalimbe Piquet 23.3.16
603 Pte WAZIA kia Kalambo River 7.6.16
70 Pte JONASI 11.6.16
717 Pte LEMBERANI 29.7.16
269 Pte THOMAS 5.8.16
888 Sjt CHEOKO 13.8.16
1365 Pte PANDAVIPA kia Lukegeta 6.9.16
1539 Pte TEBULO kia Lukegeta 6.9.16
S/96 Pte CHAMBESI 9.9.16
1573 Pte KASANTA 23.9.16
428 Pte CHIWAYA 10.10.16
948 Pte MUNDATI 18.10.16
761 Pte MIPANDO 10.11.16
1318 Pte MALAMBOKA 8.12.16
209 Pte BENJAMIN 26.12.16
576 Pte LAFWAEDI 27.12.16
535 Pte KUUMA 1.1.17
530 Pte ZACHARIA 15.1.17
346 Cpl MAKONDA kia Muesa 22.1.17
641 Bglr JOHNNY kia Muesa 22.1.17
838 Pte MALIDADI kia Muesa 22.1.17
1462 Pte LIJONYO kia Muesa 22.1.17
S/111 Pte PENSULO 24.1.17
382 Pte ULEYA 25.1.17
1537 Pte NGUNGU 26.1.17
1489 Pte CHESWENGA 3.2.17

953 Pte SUBUNI 13.2.17)
1510 Pte KAMBUI 13.2.17)
1571 Pte PONDANI 20.3.17
367 Sjt GWIRANIPAKAMWA kia St Moritz 23.3.17
566 LCpl ULAYA kia St Moritz 23.3.17
S/55 Pte JEREMANI 30.3.17
377 Pte ZINGANI 31.3.17
410 Pte MUWANGO 31.3.17
1128 Pte KACHAZ 31.3.17
1203 Pte KUNDANGWI 31.3.17
1623 Pte SHAMONGA 31.3.17
S/118 Pte SALIMU 31.3.17
1101 Pte SAMBO 15.4.17
1227 Pte SIANSINGU 8.5.17
S/119 Pte MAMADI 12.5.17
1057 LCpl CHAPONDA 26.5.17
1211 Pte MINANGU dysentry Takamali 10.6.17
514 Pte ZUZI 18.7.17
1308 Pte SHIMATANDAWILA 24.7.17
443 Cpl MASHONGA 29.7.17
1198 Pte WAZIA kia Tuturu 9.8.17)
1380 Pte KALUNGU kia Tuturu 9.8.17)
1544 Pte MUWITA kia Tuturu 9.8.17)
S/104 Pte KATAKO kia Tuturu 9.8.17)
4870 Ptr KAKILA kia 11.8.17
4873 MGPtr GWALIA kia nr Mpepo 19.8.17
0329 Sjt MITIMINGI kia Likassa 30.8.17
0416 Pte CHIPANDI kia Likassa 30.8.17
1171 Pte KAWALEZA kia Likassa 30.8.17
1421 Pte KULEYA kia Likassa 30.8.17
S/99 Pte SOLOMON kia Likassa 30.8.17
4677 Ptr KASELESELE kia Likassa 30.8.17
1017 Sjt KOZA 16.9.17
1832 Pte TONANA 18.9.17
824 Pte NDAWANI 15.10.17
287 Pte CHIMAI kia East of Ngombere 18.10.17
1474 Pte ZALILE kia Ruaha River East of Mpili 25.10.17
1199 Pte KACHIKUMBA 9.11.17
1902 Pte LIBEBE 19.11.17
S/228 Pte BULANDA 10.12.17
861 Pte FOLOMANI 16.12.17
1856 Pte TAKAMWENDO 17.12.17
1890 Pte CHOMA 18.2.18
1331 Pte MASIKINI 8.3.18
377 Pte CHIPALAMWAZANI 9.3.18
300 Cpl POTANI 28.3.18
1220 Pte MWAPI 22.4.18
1395 Pte MAKUNTA 20.7.18
1601 Pte CHIKOWI 2.8.18
1699 Pte SIYEYA kia Fusi 4.10.18
S/33 Pte MWANAWAMBA kia Fusi 4.10.18
1380 Pte KALIZA 24.10.18
2026 Pte NDANDALIKA 25.10.18
420 Pte CHINTHONA kia nr Fife 3.11.18
518 Pte KWATIWANI w30.8.17 d24.11.18

1841 Pte WHALE d29.11.18
1804 Pte LUSALE d6.12.18
251 Pte TEREKA d14.12.18
322 LCpl MPATA d16.12.18
808 Sjt WASAVILA d20.12.18
1068 Cpl NGUNGU d23.12.18
2063 Pte KUNDIKERU d24.12.18
1984 Pte DULANI d28.12.18
071 Pte CHAZINGWA d13.1.19

APPENDIX 3

Some Honours Awarded to Africans of the Northern Rhodesia Police for Service 1914–18

Distinguished Conduct Medal

229/399 Cpl CHICHASI/CHIKUSI LG2.12.19
479 Cpl SAMSONI LG3.9 & 22.12.19 LS&GCM as Sgt No.2431 14.11.30
575 Cpl MAMBO LG6.4.17
640 C/Sgt TEGETE DCM LG11.3.20
835/635? Pte MOTO LG3.9 & 22.12.19 rejoined as No.2878
1179 Cpl SONGANDEWO LG3.9 & 22.12.19
S.5 Cpl JEREMANI LG3.9 & 22.12.19

Military Medal

106 Sgt AFRICA LG23.3.18 mentioned in despatches as corporal 1915
238/0318? Sgt CHANGAMASASE LG12.3.18 wounded 30.7.17
421 Pte KUNENGA 4.10.18
456 C/Sgt YASI 4.10.18 Gaz 21.11.19 RSM by 1922 LS&GCM 1924
689 Sgt KAWERENGA 1919
1343 Pte CHIPIMINO 1919

Meritorious Service Medal

53 Sgt Maj GEZA LG1.1.19 awarded LS&GCM 1925 MID 4.15
131 Sgt KWAFIRO LG3.6.19 as 2290 Sgt Maj LS&GCM 1926
325 TIYALI rtd as RSM 1926
413 RSM KAMBANDONA 1919
690 Sgt MUSAMANGA/MUSAMANENGA? 1.1.19 CSM by 1926
900 LCpl KACHEPA 1.1.19
1418 Cpl KAMKWAMBA 1.1.19 MID as LCpl 25.9.17 ltr SM

Mentioned in Despatches

53 Cpl GEZA Sgt 4.15 SM MSM
97 LCpl LUKUBA Sept 1918
0126 Cpl MALINGUKA 1919 for Saisi 1915 rejoined as 2850
334 Pte MAMBO Sept 1918 rejoined as 2400

375 Pte SKINIBIRA 1917
452 C/Sgt ZIDANA 1915
545 Pte PIYO 1915
580 Cpl DANA
614 Cpl KUMEKA 25.9.17 rejoined as 2399
615 Sgt KOZA 10.17 d16.9.17
621 Sgt NJOMBWA 9.18
669 Sgt MWANACHIWAMBO 9.18
780 Sgt NSOFALI twice
790 Sgt MWOMBERA 1915
794 Sgt KADAWERE rejoined as 2533 LS&GCM 18.7.27
1044 Sgt ULAYA
1105 LCpl DOKOTELA ltr Cpl
1118 Cpl KAMBANI
1177 LCpl MYERE
1204 Pte SATA 9.18
1418 LCpl KAMKWAMBA 25.9.17 MSM 1.1.19

Awards to African Police below the Rank of Assistant Inspector 1932–1964

King's Police Medal for Gallantry

D.155 D/Sgt PHIRI 1948

Colonial Police Medal for Gallantry

Const P P KASALU 1960
Const MULUMPA 1961
Const MUKANKANGWA 1961

Colonial Police Medal for Meritorious Service

499 Insp MKUZO 1948
122 Insp YOBE 1949
D.26 D/SM SIKALANGWE 1949
  D/Insp WASISYA 1950
  D/Insp S APHIRI 1951
  D/Insp P D APHIRI 1951
  Insp W DARE 1952
  Insp M MATAKA 1952
D/Sub-Insp MATALIKA 1953
  Const ANDERSON 1953
  Sub-Insp TEMBO 1953
  D/Sgt KASESHYA 1954
  Insp MWAFULILWA 1955
  D/Insp CHAKALUNTA 1956
  D/Insp CHILUBA 1956
  Sub-Insp KAPITO 1958
  D/Sub-Insp SILEBELO 1958
  Insp MWALILINO 1959

   D/Sub-Insp SHIMWESHI 1960
   H/Const LUCHEMBE 1962
   D/Sub-Insp CHIPASULA 1963
218 D/H/Const MULENGA 1964

Royal Humane Society's Medal for Saving Life

1978 D/Const KAPELANSHILA 1948
   Const KAMBOYI 1962

APPENDIX 4

Alphabetical List of Officers of the Northern Rhodesia Police Appointed 1 April 1924—23 October 1964

(Including British constables to 31.12.37 & British sergeants to 1.4.32)

ABBOTT Michael W b18.8.35 A/I 17.10.59 Luanshya 62
ABBOTT Neville W b Oldham 23.12.07 BSAP'29 Const NRP 15.5.31 Insp'41 A/Supt 1.1.52 i/c Kalalushi L3.1.57 rtd NR
ABERNETHY David A/I Chingola 59
ABRAMS Charles A b15.8.31 PC Met 53 A/I NRP 21.10.56 Insp 21.10.59 PP Lusaka 15.4.60 S/I 62
ADAMS Ann T/W/A/I Lstone 57 Lusaka Traffic 61
ADAMS B A J b30.5.24 A/I 6.9.51 Imm sec'd Fed Svce 1.4.57
ADAMS John Felix C A/I'38 sec'd PA'45–1.7.48? Legal Exec Preston & Redman Solrs Bournemth d2.84
AFFLECK Ian b29.12.40 A/I 18.5.61 Riverside 61–2
AINSWORTH Tom C b4.9.30 A/I 29.5.52 Insp 13.8.56 Rd Tfc Insp Tpt & Wks 12.2.59 Kitwe 9.62
AKALILWA M CPM b15.4.12 Const 17.12.39 A/I II 11.12.60 Lstone 62
ALDEN Geoff H b9.5.11 PCMet 34 S/I NRP CIDHQ 5.3.59 lve 19.8.62
ALDHOUS Nigel F b30.4.36 A/I 14.2.57 Insp 14.4.61 Ndola 62–4
ALDRIDGE John b5.2.40 A/I 11.12.60 A/Bandmr resigned 62
ALFORD Anthony A/I Bwacha d.62
ALLAN D M BSAP'33 A/I NRP 14.2.38 CID Nkana rsgnd Mines 7.46
ALLAN James D b14.6.34 PCDundee'54 A/I 7.4.55 resigned Nchanga Mines Scy 61
ALLAN Joan Mary bMuree India W/A/I 55 mM T Cary
ALLAN Robt b16.9.31 PCDundee'52 A/I NRP 7.4.55 Kitwe 60
ALLEN Alfred Victor b15.5.28 b/o W R PC Met 49 A/I NRP 19.5.52 Insp 19.5.55 C/I 1.4.62 lve5.7.62 SA d94
ALLEN Fredk J A/I Muf'40 Kitwe'46
ALLEN Fredk W H b26.7.38 b/o A V Cdt Ndola 12.2.57 A/I 26.7.58 Insp 13.10.61 Kitwe 62 ZP AgS/Supt Lka 68
ALLEN Holt M b31.1.28 b/o A V PalP 46 PC Met 48 A/I NRP 19.2.53 Insp 19.2.56 S/I 6.59 Muf 14.8.62 A/Supt
ALLEN Wilfred R b10.3.26 b/o A V RUC 44 A/Insp NRP 2.12.48 Insp 12.53 A/Supt 15.11.55 Supt 4.3.61 Lka UDist 11.2.62
ANDERLE M L Cdt 12.5.60 A/I 16.11.61 Muf resgnd 63
ANDERSON David H b18.6.39 A/I 11.1.62 Instr PTS 63

ANDERSON Denis J b30.3.28 A/I 27.8.53 C/I 1.12.60 i/c A'corn 62 Chingola 64 d3.99
ANDERSON Derek b9.9.35 A/I 10.3.59 Muf 60 resigned 10.3.62
ANDERSON E W Const 19.4–3.8.28
ANDERSON John G b7.4.41 Cdt 1.9.59 A/I 7.4.61 Lshya 61–2
ANDERSON K N A/I 46
ANDERSON Letitia W/A/I Chingola PTS 59 Chingola
ANDERSON Margaret Gray Blair W/A/I 27.7.56 Ndola mDuffield 23.9.58
ANDERSON Robert F M b8.11.35 A/I 10.6.56 Insp 15.10.60 i/c Chingola Tfc 64
ANDERSON Thos Stewart (Paddy) KPM CPM b25.8.14 BSAP 6.36 A/I NRP'38 Mil Svce Sgt
    1/2 KAR'41? Lt OETP/BMAP It Somalia Supt Somalild Consty'46 DInt&Sy'49 Sarawak
    Consty'53 SSupt'54 ACP Brunei'57 ACP Sarawak'58 DCP'59 AgCP'62 rtd63 Co Cmdt USC
    Lt Col 4UDR'69 rtd'71 IoM
ANDERSON W B b12.1.42 Cdt 27.9.60 A/I 12.1.62 BH 62
ANDERTON Jeremy A/I 58 Kalulushi 59 NGP
ANDREWS Frank Russell, Cdt 9.4.59 A/I 20.7.60 MU 62 2Lt RMP 9.10.65 Capt RAPC 3.3.76
    Maj 30.6.79 rtd95
ANDREWS Ron G F b6.2.40 A/I 8.8.62 Kitwe 63
ANGELL Bryan Lomax (Dave) b24.1.33 2lt RA A/I NRP 4.8.60 Kitwe 11.61 Lka 62 k.Harare
    1990
ANGELL John R J b29.3.35 BSAP 55 A/I NRP 11.12.58 Insp 11.12.61 Lshya 26.6.62
ANKETELL M George b25.4.34 RUC 56 A/I NRP 11.7.57 Kitwe 62
ANNAL Peter M b17.2.34 1Queen's A/I NRP 21.10.56 Chingola Lshya
ANTHONY G A A/I.47 resgnd 48 Kees Store Lka
APPLETON David b3.6.30 PCMet'50 A/I 29.5.52 D/I 29.5.55 Maz l.58
ARCHIBALD J Norman C b13.1.38 A/I 12.5.60 Muf 62
ARKELL-HARDWICK G Const'35 Ndola'36
ARMSTRONG Gwen Mrs G E NRG9.2 T/W/A/I 20.12.55 Lka Tfc Insp 13.10.61 rgd 63
ARMSTRONG Robt A/I.51 Eastn 53 Kitwe resigned 10.55
ARNOLD John B b15.2.36 A/I 6.6.57 Ndola Location'58
ARRIGONI Henry Anthony 'Kapyanga, The Sweeper' bA'shot 9.10.13 s/oCapt ed Manch
    CentlHS LonUTutoril Cllge Pte Kg's Own 22.8.32 PCMet'34 PalP 28.2.35 2BSgt 8.38 A/I
    NRP 30.7.39 C/Insp 1.1.59 DCIO Eastn L1.4.63–rtd2.64
ARTHUR G L Const 29.8.30 AgA/I Depot 33 Insp 36
ARTHUR Helen W/A/I 6.12.56 Kitwe C 57 Tfc 59
ASHBY E S b12.6.33 A/I 1.12.57 Insp 13.4.62 Mokambo
ASHCROFT David J b4.11.35 PC L'Pool 57 A/I NRP 1.5.58 60 Muf 62 FJ SArabia
ASHCROFT K A/I 10.11.47
ASHTON Neil N, Cdt Kitwe 28.7.60 A/I 29.4.62 Kitwe CID 63
ATKISS Roy b20.1.19 A/I 17.6.52 Acct Min Fin 1.1.57 L30.3.62
ATTENBOROUGH James B 'Pendeke' b.26.4.11 A/I 23.7.46 A/Supt 30.10.54 Supt 1.7.59 AgS/
    Supt CID HQ 4.8.62 d.SA 3.78
AULD William Morton b12.10.32 PC Lanark 53 A/I NRP 10.1.58 Insp 10.1.61 Lshya 17.9.61–2
AUSTIN John L bLka 4.6.40 Cdt 8.5.59 A/I 4.6.60 Insp 4.6.63 ZP Lka Tfc

BACKHOUSE Charles Arthur b16.8.30 PCMet 52 A/I 14.1.54 Insp 14.1.54 S/I AgC/I Maz 62
    C/I
BACON H A BSAP Const NRP 13.11.28 d.Tetanus on Cattle Cordon rains 1929/30
BADCOCK A/I.48
BADENHORST Ronald J Cdt 21.2.59 A/I 28.12.60 resgnd 62 RN
BAILEY John F, Cdt 26.1.61 A/I 13.3.62 Kansenji 63 Switzerland
BAINBRIDGE A/I 57 Muf
BAKER Colin Malcolm CPM'88 bBexley 20.3.37 RSx, Int Cps A/I NRP 10.2.61 Ndola Loc HKP
    SSupt rtd 97
BAKER Gordon Cdt Lka 63 A/I BH 63 HKP 64 Insp
BAKER Norman b5.9.36 RMP A/I NRP 11.4.58 resigned 19.4.61

BAKER Wm A b1.12.34 A/I 16.7.59 Lstone Rly 60 MU'61

BALE Geo E b14.2.40 A/I 25.6.60 Ndola C Loc 62–3 Bermuda P 64

BALL C H G Const 7.5.32 Ndola 33

BALL John b27.5.35 PCLancs 51 A/I NRP 4.12.55 Lka'57

BANDA Elija A b15.10.29 Const 14.6.51 A/I II 1.4.62 A/Supt 64 ZP

BANKS Graham J b19.9.40 Cdt 13.10.59 A/I 19.9.60 Lve 10.62

BARBER Douglas Basil b07 ed Uppinghm BSAP'29 Const NRP'33 Insp Zanzibar 12.3.38 Mil Svce'40–Supt seconded PA'43 PA'46 Sen DC Zanzibar'49 OC Clove Control Sch'49–50

BARBER John Roger OBE'78 CPM'59 b19.6.26 A/I 22.6.50 A/Supt 30.10.54 Supt 1.7.59 MU 62 RAF FijiP

BARDWELL Les J b24.3.33 A/I 4.12.55 A/Supt 16.8.61 Lve 11.7.62

BARKER John Derek b23.1.30 A/I 15.10.53 L'stone Rtd ill-health 18.12.58

BARKER Les M b29.9.38 A/I 4.8.60 Div Insp NW to MU lte 62

BARKER R N b12.11.41 Cdt 6.2.60 A/I 12.11.61 Choma 62

BARKLEY Robert J CPM b28.10.23 RN FAA'42 BSAP'46 A/I NRP 14.6.49 A/Supt 30.10.54 Supt 1.7.59 Kitwe Dist 63 FCO

BARLOW Brian A/I Chingola 53 Tfc resigned 54 mines

BARNES Audrey WPCMet 52 sec'd CyprusP 57 W/A/I NRP 27.9.60 Lka 62 rgd 63

BARNES Richd Seymour bHarlech 16.8.27 A/I 21.7.49 AgInsp 53–7 AEO Establishmnt Div NRG 28.11.60 L31.3.62

BARR Colin N CPM(G)'60 b23.8.36 RAF A/I 14.2.59 P P Lka 62

BARR William G b14.1.30 A/I 13.8.53 Insp 13.8.56 S/I Kitwe CID 62 C/I Lve8.63

BARTLETT Frank A G b9.4.33 KenyaP 53 A/I NRP 10.6.56 Insp 1.7.60 Nakonde 62 L63 C/I ZP i/c Lshya C 65

BATCHELOR Ronald H b19.5.28 PCMet 50 A/I 16.5.53 Insp 16.5.56 C/I 1.3.60 Lstone CID 63

BATEMAN Wm D/I BH lve 56 Luanshya CID rsgnd Fmg Karroo 57?

BATESON F Michael b24.12.35 A/I 15.10.59 Bancroft 61–2

BATTERS Ken BSAP 46 A/I.49

BATTY Robert Const 25.11.27 A/I 1.7.30 C/I 1.1.38 rsgnd'39

BAXTER J Const'34?

BEAL Gordon Morris b19.7.12 SSC RAF'31 PalP.33 Const NRP 14.6.35 RAF Flyg Trg Cmd SR'40, Bomber Cmd, NRP'46 Tanganyika Police A/Supt 23.9.50 NRP 21.10.52 rtd'64 d.1990 SA

BEAMAN G Wm H A/I 46 dischgd 12.46 FBC Pers Lka NRPR R/A/Supt Dist Cmdt Lka Urban 60

BEARD Sam W B b24.3.35 A/I 10.6.56 Insp 10.6.59 i/c Samfya 11.63 SAAF

BEAVERSTOCK Derek M b5.3.34 PC Newport 55 A/I 17.1.59 Muf Mine CID 62

BEAVES Michael J Cdt 11.6.59 A/I 4.3.60 Chingola Insp 4.3.63–4

BEAZLEY Brian M b10.2.35 A/I 12.5.55 Lshya Tfc rsgnd 8.59 Old Mutual Ndola

BECK Terry S R b30.7.28 A/I 1.4.57

BEECH John T b13.5.38 A/I 20.4.61 FJ 61 PTS rsgnd 63

BEECROFT John Evan bSettle 6.7.31 PCMet 52 A/I 3.9.53 Insp 3.9.56 Dist Insp LkaU 12.61 rgd 12.62 Probn Offr GB Cda GB

BEGG Adrian E b9.11.40 Cdt 29.10 A/I 9.11.60 Nakonde 62 rgd63

BELL C M b11.9.01 A/I 20.2.51 Sen Imm Offr 1.7.55 Sec'd Fed Svce 1.4.57

BELL Henry b14.8.29 NRG4.1.55 A/I 1.1.57 Mindolo CID 59 Kitwe C

BELL James Leonard bArgentina 17.1.35 RN A/I 15.10.59 MU 62 ZP

BELL Katherine B W/A/I 3.12.56 Insp 3.12.59 Lka CID 61–2

BELL Richard J b17.4.32 KenyaP 53 A/I NRP 21.10.56 resigned 10.5.62

BELL T G b27.2.43 Cdt 4.4.62 A/I 27.2.63

BELLAMY Jack b/o R S S A/I 60

BELLAMY Richard Steel Somers bNCaledonia 20.2.30 A/I 12.5.55 Insp 8.4.60 S/I Lstone 22.3.62 ZP A/Supt Lka 68? Antibes

BELSON Les b4.12.25 PCNotts 47 A/I 7.1.54 Insp 12.8.58 S/I Eastern Lve 12.60 FJ 62

BENHAM Peter A/I Mindolo CID 59

BENNETT John R L b29.11.35 A/I 10.10.59 Kawambwa 62 Mngr Totalisator Bd Agency Sydney NSW 68
BENTLEY John OBE'57 b Bexleyhth 11.10.09 ed HMS Worcester Cdt Discovery Antartic'25– 9.9.27 Pal Police'3? Const NRP 7.1.36 Insp to DA PA'46 SenDC Westn 1.7.57 rtd 17.3.62 d7.99
BENTLEY P T b7.2.39 A/I 20.2.60 Lstone Tfc 62 rgd 63
BERMINGHAM Andrew P QPM 93 b11.8.41 Cdt 26.1 A/I 11.8.61 BHC 62–3 Bermuda CPM(G) 66 D/C/Supt
BERMINGHAM G H b29.4.40 Cdt 7.1 A/I 29.4.60 MU 62 resgnd 63
BERRYMAN Frank A/I 52 FJ 53 PA DA Maz 59 FJ 61
BESA J b29.7.23 Const 13.5.49 A/I II 1.4.62 Choma
BESTIC Michael J RM Sgt A/I NRP 21.9.57 Chingola SB 59 Resgnd 60 Mines
BIDDLECOMBE Bernard A/I.52 Lka C Mazabuka 54
BIELBY D S b24.9.30 PC Hull'50 A/I NRP 11.11.54 resignd 15.4.57
BIGNALL David A/I 60? d.Maz 16.1.82
BINYON Geoff A b17.4.39 A/I 8.8.62 Kafue 63
BIRD G Brian b7.4.28 A/I 17.4.52 Insp 17.4.55 C/I 1.3.60 Chingola CID 63–4
BIRD J Denis O MBE'62 CPM b23.9.24 A/I 21.7.49 A/Supt 27.5.54 Supt 13.1.59 ACP 64 CP Gib
BIRD Jo B A/I 52 BHC 12.54
BIRD Ronald L b9.9.16 BEF PalP 15.10.42 NRP 6.1.49 A/Supt 30.10.54 Supt 1.7.60 Kitwe Dist L63
BIRD Roy A b27.2.41 Cdt 1.10.59 A/I 27.2.61 Lka
BIRD Mrs W H NRG14.12.54 W/A/I 11.12.56 BH'57
BIRKBECK J Const 10.8–26.12.26
BIRMINGHAM John A/I BH 54
BIRTALL Fred b18.1.31 A/I 11.3.56 Insp 13.4.62 Kasama
BIXBY A B W/A/I 10.12.60 Kitwe 62
BLACK Gordon J b14.6.34 A/I 12.5.55 Muf Kitwe 58
BLACKWELL Clive b11.8.26 A/I 22.6.50 Insp 1.7.53 A/Supt 11.2.57 CIO Lstone 61–2 Supt AgSSupt 64
BLAKE A Indian P NRPrisons, A/Supt NRP.54
BLAKE Alan PCMet A/I Chingola 59 PCMet 60
BLAKE Norman Arthur Hampton b8.11.98 Worthing, Army'16–19 Egypt; BSAP'20 Const NRP 9.4.24 Customs 31.5.27 rtd '33
BLANDY Richd Lloyd A/I d95
BLINCOW C L 'Toni' T/W/A/I 23.1.57 Lka
BLYTH Harry G b16.3.28 PC Leeds 48 A/I 11.11.54 C/I 1.12.60 Lshya 11.3.62
BLYTH Paul Redman CPM'59 bA'corn NR 6.9.12 BSAP'34 A/I NRP 10.9.38 A/Supt'50 Supt 1.7.54 S/Supt 1.6.59 rtd17.6.62 SA d10.1.85
BLYTHE George S b20.11.26 PCNewport 48 A/I NRP 27.5.54 Insp 8.4.60 Chingola 62–C/I 64
BOFF Robt A/I Muf Kashiba 54 Chingola PP 55
BOLTER Alan W b12.12.37 A/I 23.9.60 Kitwe 62 rsgnd63
BOLTON Geoffrey T A/I'38 Insp Lstone'47 Gambia P A/Supt 16.5.49
BOLTON Noddy A/I Lshya Tfc 63
BONNELL Eric PalP A/I NRP.48 Lstone 53
BOONZAIER John W b8.7.34 A/I 20.5.60 Lka Info 62 rsgnd5.63
BORRADALE Basil C b11.2.28 A/I 10.6.54 Insp 10.6.57 S/I BH 62
BOSMAN Donovan b19.1.30 Kenya P 54 A/I NRP 17.1.58 Lshya 62 TasmaniaP 68 ACPF 70 Osaka
BOSWORTHICK Tom A/I Chingola 6.53
BOUGHTON E W b17.7.27 Mal P 50 A/I 14.2.57 Samfya 62
BOURNE John Coldm Gds A/I 10.62 Chingola 5.63 ZP Lka
BOWSKILL David C A/I Kitwe AgI 5.53 resgnd by 5.56 Kitwe
BOYD Jock D J b16.8.40 A/I 24.9.60 Lstone 62BOYD Ron L b30.4.33 A/I 15.1.59 Chirundu 61

BOYD T Paddy b30.10.35 A/I 10.6.56 Insp 8.4.60 Ndola CID 62 C/I
BOYER Ken b5.11.29 MalayaP 51 A/I NRP 14.2.59 Ndola 63 FCO
BRACEY Donald b3.6.24 PCMet 48 A/I NRP 24.7.52 Insp 26.11.56 L27.7.62
BRACKEN W Hugh b1.1.31 A/I 11.4.58 Insp 11.4.61 CIO NW 62 d.Ireland 1.84
BRANDT Drew A/I 3.59 Lka Kafue 59
BRATT Vincent A/I 49? AgInsp 5.53 Stn Insp Chingola
BREEN Charles Morris 'Danny' CPM 51 Const 29.12.30 A/Supt'47 Supt'51 OC MU lve 4.53 rtd
    17.6.54 NRPR Ndola'60
BREEN M G b1.4.37 A/I 18.5.58 Chiwempala 62
BREENE Michael J b1.12.29 A/I 28.4.55 C/I 1.4.62 Lka 4.7.62
BRENNAN John F b3.1.40 A/I 9.2.61 Maz 62 SwazildP?
BRENNAN Len J b3.4.33 A/I 15.5.55 Insp 15.10.60 BH i/c Raylton 5.63
BRENNAN W 'Paddy' b10.3.13 Malaya P A/Supt NRP 3.8.61 Tpt Offr Western 62
BRETT R Pte Sc Rifles 14 SG 23 Sgt NRP 18.2.32 NRR AgRSM 11.6.36
BRETTINGHAM Anthony W b2.10.28 A/I 30.6.50 Insp 13.8.56 S/I i/c Wusikili 59 Leave 30.6.62
BRIDGE B J b21.12.38 A/I 8.8.62
BRIDGER Michael Richd CPM 50 bDurban 27.9.11 edRondebosch BSAP 32 Const NRP 30.11.37
    A/Supt 1.1.53 Supt 1.7.58 SO FHQ rtd 10.62 Somerset West d'86
BRIGGS Barry W b16.6.36 A/I 11.7.57 Lstone 59 rsgnd60
BRIGGS Peter T G b27.4.35 RA A/I 4.12.55 Insp 8.4.60 L6.7.62 SA
BRINDLE Geoff E b25.11.41 Cdt 26.1 A/I 25.11.61 Chilenje 62
BRISTER Roger D b2.6.40 PCMet 58 A/I 10.12.60 Lshya 61–2
BRITTLE A Richd b18.5.13 Met 34 S/I NRP CIO 22.1.59 Swazild CRO
BRITTON Colin E b22.4.38 A/I 17.1.59 Chingola 27.7.62–4
BROCK Gerald D b17.10.26 A/I 13.3.52 Insp 13.3.56 S/I AgC/I i/c Lstone C 59 Lab Offr 62
    SA d.89
BROCKBANK Howard C b1.9.30 A/I 13.5.54 Insp 13.5.57 S/I i/c Bwacha 62 C/I
BROCKWELL Denis Montague QPM'62 CPM'52 bS'pore 1.6.16 ed Ellesmere BSAP'37 A/I NRP
    15.9.38 A/Supt'50 Supt 1.7.54 S/Supt 15.10.57 ACP(C) rtd'64 d91
BRODIE Norman CPM 45 'Chinakila' = patient, b Worcs 95 Worcs Yeo TF'11 Tpr BSAP'19
    Const NRP 16.10.25 CID 1.10.26 D/Sgt'27 D/I 1.4.31 A/Supt 34 OC CID Supt 13.12.37
    Rtd 20.7.51 Dist Cmdt NRPR L'stone 51–55 d.L'stone 29.7.60
BROOKS A E Const 4.4.28
BROOKS G G Const 30
BROOKS Peter A b12.11.29 A/I 10.6.54 Insp 9.10.59 S/I Mumbwa 62 C/I ZP A/Supt LkaC 66
BROWN Anthony A/I 55
BROWN Alexander S b16.7.29 2Lt RE A/I 4.12.55 PTS L58 Kitwe D
BROWN Brian G b3.9.36 A/I 19.3.59 L 20.4.62 Lshya CID
BROWN Catherine Anne T/W/A/I Kalulushi 58 Lka Tfc 59 Inld Rev
BROWN Charles Gordon Rogers b27.3.40 A/I 19.5.60 Kasama 61–2
BROWN Colin S b19.7.38 A/I 2.5.62 Saudi Arabia
BROWN Douglas Chassar b11.6.34 A/I 28.4.55 Insp 17.4.59 L1.6.62
BROWN Errol A/I Nchanga 60
BROWN J K W b20.2.28 BSAP 49 A/I NRP 1.6.52 Insp 1.6.55 A/Supt 12.1.59 Maz 24.6.62
BROWN Jas b21.8.34 RUC 53 A/I NRP 7.12.54 Insp 8.4.60 Pros Muf 62 to BSAP
BROWN Keith A/I FJ 61 L12.61
BROWN Michael A/I BH 54
BROWNE Wm Chas Const 4.2.32
BROWNRIDGE W N b22.9.19 A/I 4.7.46 Sec'dWeights & Measures'48 AfEdn SecLEA 1.1.53
    Mongu 62
BRUCE Gordon L QPM PMGM ZPM b6.10.27 SG A/I 17.9.53 Insp5.10.56 A/Supt 1.3.60 CIO
    Kitwe 62 L6.63 Supt 64 ZP DCIO Lka ACPF C/Supt 78 Cdr rtd88
BRUCE A/I 63
BRUCE Laura M WPC Abdn 56 W/A/I 7.4.60 Lstone 63 mDavidson 63
BRYAN Colin RN 43 SLt 11.44–47 SporeP 6.48 A/I NRP 7.49 SB kRTA Muf 7.10.53

BRYAN George W b1.3.33 A/I 21.10.56 Insp 21.10.59 Lshya 62
BUYALL C F A/I'49
BUCHANAN David J F b22.7.34 A/I 11.3.56 Insp 8.4.60 Ndola 62
BUCHANAN G C b26.12.38 A/I 18.2.60 BH 61
BUCKINGHAM Francis K CPM 62 b12.5.36 A/I 19.3.59 ZP A/Supt MU 68 d.90
BUCKTON Francis G b8.2.26 PC WRdg 47 A/I NRP 24.7.52 Insp 13.8.56 S/I Leave 7.6.62
BULL Reginald A b10.9.27 MalayaP 53 A/I NRP 21.9.57 Nega Nega 25.4.62 Zimbabwe d3.92
BULLARD Alan A/I Wusikili 59
BULLOCK Ian b10.12.37 A/I 16.5.59 L18.5.62 NGP Harare d91
BUNN David P b22.1.35 PCMet 56 A/I 7.9.58 Insp 7.9.61 PTS 62
BURGESS Derek S b27.4.36 A/I 17.1.59 L15.2.62 d2000
BURGHOPE Colin Arthur bGillinghm9.2.34 RN Rhine Sqn Crown Agts A/I 19.3.59 Insp 13.4.62 rtd12.64 RAF 20.7.65 P/O Sectl F/O P&SS S/Ldr 2i/c 2RMP NI OC RAFP HK 76 AgWCdr Strike Cmd W/Cdr Int SHAPE 82 rtd89 d93
BURN Jack M b14.1.29 A/I 16.7.53 Insp 16.7.56 C/I 1.3.60 i/c Kabwata 25.11.60–2
BURNE N O M Const Mil 31.8.27 Sgt by 12.5.30 NRR 32 Forestry Dept, Principal Forester 1.3.52 Mwekera 62
BURNETT David B b1.3.36 A/I 21.10.56 Insp 21.10.59 Chingola 62
BURNETT J S A/I 46
BURNEY Anthony W CPM b23.9.21 RA WO2, PalP 30.9.44 Sgt A/I NRP 9.12.48 A/Supt 15.11.55 Supt 18.12.61 SBHQ 25.3.62 S/Supt i/c Scy Lesotho rtd Portugal d29.10.93
BURNHAM Regld A A/I 2.5.38 Insp Maz'46 to Windwd IslesP'50 rtd Florida
BURNS S M b28.7.40 A/I 9.3.61 Kitwe 62
BURTON Peter C b28.12.35 BSAP 54 A/I NRP 22.8.58 Insp 22.8.61 i/c Kalomo 62–3
BURTON Peter D Cdt 2.4 A/I 8.8.59 L5.4.62 rgd 62 Insce
BUSH Thomas Herbt CPM 53 b'06 ed AliwalHS Cape, BSAP'27 Const NRP 19.6.31 A/Supt'45 S/Supt'53 Western Div Rtd 1.9.57
BUTCHER Denis W b18.4.24 A/I 26.2.48 S/I 21.3.56 A/Supt 11.2.57 Lstone Ag Supt 21.5.62 d
BUTLER Helen P Mrs R W/A/I 15.5.57 Insp 15.5.60 Chingola 59–61
BYRNE A T b12.3.15 A/I 2.5.38 Insp sec'd Rd Svces Bd 15.11.46 Rd Tfc Insp Ft J'62
BYRNE C G 'Kafupi' bPretoria 18.9.10 BSAP'32 SwazildP'35 A/I NRP 1.1.40 A/Supt'51Supt 1.7.58 rtd 12.1.62 Mngr Zambezi Boat Club Livingstone
BYRNE Jack G b9.9.36 A/I 20.4.61 MU 62 rsgnd
BYRNE J(Sean) G b9.9.36 A/I 20.4.61 Ndola 61 MU 62
BYTHEWAY A/I David Mindolo 62–3

CAINEY David J b25.7.33 A/I 11.3.56 FR'57 Lka Kitwe 60
CALDECOURT Don R A/I 4.51–5.53
CAMERON Donald C b27.2.36 RAF A/I 21.9.57 Insp 21.9.60 Nchanga 62–4
CAMERON O Michael b3.9.39 A/I 16.1.60 Lshya 61–2
CAMIDGE W David D b20.3.34 2Lt DWR A/I 10.1.58 Insp 10.1.61 Serenje 62
CAMPBELL Harry A/I Lka Rural 59
CAMPBELL Lou A/I Lka 62
CAMPBELL Michael W St A b15.2.32 RHG A/I 23.6.55 Insp 14.4.61 Muf 61 lve14.2.62
CAMPBELL Roderick McL b12.1.35 RHG A/I 24.10.57 Insp 13.10.61 Lka 62 FIPersMan 78
CAMPION William M b2.7.31 PCLincs 51 A/I NRP 7.4.55 Insp 10.4.58 S/I Bancroft 23.8.62 rtd Rhokana MineP
CANTLEY J M A/I 1946
CANTRELL A/I Lshya 47
CANTRELL Christopher H W Cdt 1.1.59 A/I 25.6.61 Kapiri 63
CANTRILL B O W A/I 51
CARELESS Hugh P b20.7.41 A/I 14.9.61 Instr PTS 63
CARLETON Anthony H b14.4.41 Cdt 6.8.59 A/I 14.4.61 Kansenji 63
CARMODY James P b16.8.36 A/I 23.7.60 Kitwe Riverside 63
CARR Peter W b11.11.40 A/I 7.1.61 Lshya 61–2

CARSON A B b19.2.43 Cdt 8.8.62 Lka A/I 19.2.63
CARSWELL Elisabeth Mrs C E NRG1.10.54 T/W/A/I 1.7.55 Lshya Tfc rsgnd 1.5.61
CARTER Frank b20.7.39 A/I 9.3.61 Wusikili 62 rsgnd3.64
CARY Michael T b20.3.27 PCMet 47 A/I NRP 3.8.50 Insp 3.8.53 mJ M Allan A/Supt 11.2.57
  CIO Kitwe 10.63 Supt
CARY Vernon b12.1.33 A/I 11.5.55 Insp 8.4.60 Kitwe 20.6.62
CASEY Terence K b17.2.33 RUC 52 A/I 21.9.57 Insp 13.4.62 MU 63
CASSELL Margaret W/A/I 3.7.56 Chingola 59 mNichol 6.60
CASTLE J Fredk CPM b15.12.17 SwazildP 1.8.37 Basutold P 47 Supt NRP 9.6.53 S/Supt 5.3.56
  CID HQ ACP 2.2.59–AgSACP 4.5.62+
CATOR David J b29.11.32 A/I 3.3.55 Insp 17.4.59 FJ 9.61–2.63 S/I
CATTON Geoffrey C A b27.10.33 A/I 23.6.55 MU 59 Monze L60
CAVE E M WPC Bristol 59 W/A/I NRP 8.6.61 Muf 62
CHAKALUNTA Gilbert CPM 56 b.Zimba Ny 1.7.O7 N/Det 17.6.35 D/Sub/Insp 52 D/A/I II
  1.3.59 I 1.11.60 Rtd 7.63 Rumpi Ny
CHAMBERLAIN Jeremy A b7.2.41 Cdt 1.10.59 A/I 7.2.61 Lka L10.62 Durban d7.4.97
CHAMBERS Richd A/I 63? to RAF
CHAMLEY T E Const 7.9–6.12.27
CHANGAOPA Max S b18.11.17 Const 28.10.40 A/I III 59 II 1.4.60 I 1.11.60 Ag Insp i/c Pemba
  6.62 A/Supt 64
CHAPLIN Syd S T Cdt 15.12.59 A/I 19.2.60 Chingola 61 rgd Cape Town U 62
CHARLES R H Const 36?
CHARLTON D 'Ginger' b21.3.24 A/I 7.7.47 S/I 10.2.55 C/I 1.1.59 Nchanga 63
CHASEMORE P Colin A/I MU 12.52
CHASEMORE Richard A b31.5.24 A/I 26.12.51 Insp 29.12.54 A/Supt 1.1.58 OC Choma Dist
  10.62 RAFP SLdr rtd79
CHAVASSE Gerald B B b20.1.37 RE A/I 14.2.59 Insp 14.2.62 L15.8.62
CHELA Fabiano b1.7.25 Const 11.9.49 A/I II 1.4.62 PTS 62 A/Supt 64 ZP CP
CHESHIRE Robt S b15.4.35 A/I 6.6.57 Insp 6.6.60 Samfya 11.61–11.63 A/Supt
CHESTER Peter D b22.11.34 A/I 29.11.57 Insp 13.10.61 Kashiba 62–3 ZP S/Supt CO Para Mil
  72 d.Lka 12.1.82
CHESTERTON David P RM A/I 10.57 Lka rgd 59 PCSx
CHIBUYE Herbert b5.6.22 Const 5.6.45 A/I II 1.1.61 Kawambwa 61–2 A/I I
CHIKOPE David Weybridge CPM 64 b4.5.24 Const 29.8.45 A/I III 59 II 1.4.60 I 1.11.60 Insp 63
  A/Supt 64 ZP DCP
CHILDS Alan A/I 5.63 Chingola
CHILUBA Caution I CPM 56 Pte 31 D/A/I II 1.59 rtd5.6.59
CHIMFWEMBE E D M b28.6.26 Const 28.12.49 A/I II 1.4.62 Kabwata
CHITO Leir Andrew bA'corn 25.8.20 Const 1.4.39 A/I III 60 II 1.1.61 murdered on duty 21.9.63
CHIWAYA D M A/I MufC 63
CHIZU E A b15.2.24 Const 18.5.49 Choma A/I II 1.1.61 C/I 64
CHONGO J B b30.8.20 Const 5.10.42 A/I III 59 II 1.4.60 A/I I 1.11.60 BHC 62
CHURCH Eric b11.6.42 Cdt 8.11.61 A/I 11.6.62 Kitwe CID 63
CILLIERS Denis J b12.12.37 A/I 10.10.59 Lka Tfc 63
CLAMP T Brian b5.8.35 A/I 3.4.58 Kashiba 59 resigned 17.4.61
CLANCY Richard RUC A/I NRP 21.9.57 Luanshya MU 59
CLARK Llewellyn Michael CPM'51 bHoupoort SA 10.11.18 BSAP'38 A/I 13.9.38 A/Supt'51
  Supt 1.7.56 S/Supt'62 OC Muf Dist'63 dOudtshoorn'87 son in law of RSM Schronen NRP
CLARKE B G b6.5.38 A/I 16.5.59 rsigned 5.6.61
CLARKE R W b21.11.42 Cdt 2.5 A/I 21.11.62 resigned'64
CLARKE Wm H Jack bBelfast 29.6.28 RUC 46 A/I NRP 11.11.54 Insp 9.10.59 S/I SB Lka 62–3
  ZP FHQTrg rtd70 Security Bnk of Engld, Schweppes, CSO Courtaulds NI, de Lorean
CLARKE Walter Allister bLndn 27.8.30 A/I 24.3.55 Insp 24.3.58 S/I L1.3.62 ZP A/Supt rtd 69
  Kitwe Interprtr Zambia Awd fr Distinguished Svce 2Cl d.Joburg 25.2.97

CLEASBY Michael b29.12.26 PalP 45 A/I NRP 31.7.48 S/I 21.1.57 C/I 1.3.59 Ndola Dist L16.2.63 Mfg Mutual Insce Sydney

CLELAND J G Cdt 27.10.60 Choma A/I 15.6.62 Chingola 9.62

CLELAND J M 'Paddy' b17.1.33 RUC 51 A/I NRP 55–6 A/I 1.11.57 Insp 1.11.60 Roan 63

CLIBBORN–DYER Ronald J CPM 91 b9.10.40 A/I 28.10.60 Lka 62 md/oR J Read HKP Supt NT Tfc 79 S/Supt rtd97

CLIFFORD J M b29.8.39 A/I 4.10.61 Lshya 62

CLIFT John W b25.9.38 A/I 28.10.60 Ndola CID 62 rgd 63

COASE Brian G CPM b5.8.28 PalP 6.11.46 A/I NRP 6.1.49 A/Supt 15.11.55 Supt 25.12.60 Muf Dist L9.62 Luapula Div rtd64 Solr Pros Thames VP Lincoln CPS WMidlds

COATES John b12.6.31 PCLincs 51 A/I 8.4.54 Insp 8.4.57 Kasama A/Supt 1.4.62

COATES John Aylmer CPM 62 bAylesby 30.11.35 RHG A/I 2l.10.56 Insp 14.4.61 C/I CIO Lshya ZP lve pdg rtd 24.6.65 BUPA AGenMgr rtd90

COBURN T C b29.6.28 A/I 18.5.61 Ndola 62

COCHRANE John G b11.11.34 A/I 10.1.58 Mporokoso 62

COCKBURN Rex b1.8.30 Gds A/I 9.11.53 C/I 60 A/Supt 12.4.61 Ndola 62

COCK Irene Mrs R T T/W/A/I 1.4.58 Chingola Tfc Insp 1.4.61 ,62

COLE M J A/I 1948

COLEMAN John M b27.6.34 A/I 15.10.59 Muf 61 rgd 62 Muf Mine Security

COLLETT Alfred Ross CPM'56 b Croydon 24.9.11 BSAP'34 Const NRP 27.8.35 A/Supt'51 Supt 1.7.54 S/Supt 1.7.60 rtd 10.62 d12.12.97 Oxfd

COLLETT John F ABIRE b7.6.26 NRG 24.7.52 Police Telecoms Offr 21.2.56 Supt NRP 21.3.60 lve30.7.62

COLLINS E H A/I'38 dschge own request 31.8.38

COLLINS Nial F b27.7.40 OCdt Irish Army Cdt NRP 28.1 A/I 27.7.60 Lka 61 Chalimbana 62 Insp ZP Lka rtd post 72

COMERFORD Duane E b3.12.30 A/I 20.4.54 Insp 20.4.57 S/I BH 62 Pers & Sfty Mgr Imp Chem Aust 69

CONCHIE Ian D PC Manch A/I 10.62 Chingola Tfc 64

CONINGHAM Richd RUC A/I NRP 21.9.57 Lshya

CONNICK Peter A/I 58 Muf rsgnd 60 underground op Muf Mine

CONNORS Terry A/I Muf 54

COOK Francis Bryan 'Wopika' b11.11.30 PCMet 51 A/I NRP 29.5.52 Insp 29.5.55 D/C/I 60 A/Supt 16.8.61 SDiv 62 Aden StateP LesothoMP R Oman P Head of SB Brig 83 d27.2.91

COOK Richard G b22.1.25 PCMet'48 A/I 19.5.52 Roan 58 ACTP S/I 78

COOK R J A/I 58COOKE Arthur J PalP A/Supt NRP 48 FHQ AgSupt Lka 53 KenyaP 54

COOKE Martin A B b8.5.40 PCMet 59 A/I NRP 28.10.60 Petauke 62

COOP A b11.7.41 A/I 28.2.62 Lstone 62

COOPER Brian O b13.5.32 PC Leics & Rtld 53 A/I NRP 25.10.58 Insp 25.10.61 Lshya 20.5.62

COOPER Edwd A V b26.2.25 BPP 47 A/I NRP 24.7.51 A/Supt 15.11.55 CIO SDiv 10.62

COOPER F A b19.8.25 BSAP 48 KenyaP 52 BSAP 56 A/I NRP 5.11.57 Insp 5.11.60 S/I Lstone 62

COOPER G S b23.8.21 CeylonP A/I NRP 22.8.48 Passport Offr 1.7.54 Lstone 57

COOPER Michael J B b28.7.31 PCMet 53 A/I NRP 3.2.55 Insp 8.4.60 Lka 12.3.62 C/I ZP CIO Lshya 24.6.65 A/Supt Ndola 68 d8.79 Hamble

COOPER Richard BSAP KenyaP A/I NRP Luanshya

COPPARD Alan Roy b6.9.25 A/I 21.7.49 Insp 12.53 S/I 1.8.57 A/Supt 1.1.58 NW Div 61 Chingola 64

COPPEN Fred L A/I Chingola 52

CORBETT F Aileen RUC W/A/I NRP 13.1.57 mA Moulds

CORBETT Maurice b1.7.35 b/o F A A/I 11.3.56 Insp 11.3.59 Pros Kitwe 61–2

CORRIGAN Norma W/A/I Ndola C 59

COTON Thomas E CPM 57 b.Stockwell 1.4.12 Pal P 35 A/Supt NRP 17.12.48 Supt 3.1.53 CO PTS.55 S/Supt 3.1.57 Ag ACP(A) 60 Rtd 12.61 d.Budleigh Salterton 12.7.75

COTTAM Terence b9.4.28 PalP'47 BSAP'48 PCKent'52 A/I 21.4.55 FJ 12.58 L61

COUCOM Cyril Lshya'52

COULSON Alan Kalomo'60
COULSON R Ian b16.1.40 A/I 10.2.60 Choma 62
COULTHARD Ralph b10.7.24 A/I 21.7.49 A/Supt 1.4.56 Supt 8.1.62 FHQ
COURT Patrick b7.3.37 A/I 18.2.60 Lka mC Eglin resgnd63 SA
COUTRIN Alec G b10.8.19 A/I 26.2.47 A/Supt 1.7.54 Supt 29.12.59 BH Dist 62
COWHAM Walter Humphrey 'Happy' CGM over Hannover 18/19.10.43 bFJ 12.5.23 RAF Sgt
    A/Gnr 657Sqn A/I NRP 26.1.46 A/Supt 54 Mstr Intprtr Judcl Dept 4.12.56 Bar Gray's 61
    RM Lka 62 Customs & Excise UK Legal Asst 78 d91
COWLING Alan D b3.9.42 Cdt 2.5 A/I 3.9.62 Kalomo 63
COWPERTHWAITE Brian D b27.9.33 A/I 10.8.55 Ndola'57
CRABBE Derek PCMet A/I NRP Chingola 7.53
CRABTREE Robert N b21.8.26 Pal P 24.11.46 A/I NRP 27.1.49 S/I 27.1.57 A/Supt 1.1.58 SO
    Southern 4.63 Supt d.8.11.78
CRAWFORD Chris E b21.1.43 Cdt 9.6.62 A/I 21.1.63 Emmasdale 63
CRAWFORD Jack T Const 9.5.30 A/I Cdt PA 40 Sen DO Luangwa 59
CREASEY H W Const 12.4.29 A/I 1.7.31 Choma 33
CREE Angus B 2Lt 19.9.26 Lt 19.10.27 NRR Capt 12.8.36 AgADC&PS to Gov 16.12.37 Maj
CREED William b24.12.15 PCMet 38–41 A/I NRP 2.1.51 S/I 12.4.56 A/Supt 1.7.57 CRO 58–62
    d.19.7.88
CRESSWELL Jo A/I 58 Kitwe
CRIBB John H b23.4.33 RN A/I 17.5.58 Insp 17.5.61 ADC 62 ZP A/Supt to Jamaica, Plessey; JP
    Dorset
CROASDELL Brian Cdt 1.10.59 A/I 11.4.61 Chingola rsgnd 10.62?
CRONIN E Mrs J W W/A/I 25.6.56 Lka 57
CRONJE Ivan A b25.2.37 A/I 16.5.60 Wdlds 3.62
CROSS Martin A/I Chingola 1.55 Nchanga 56
CROWLEY David b31.10.40 A/I 27.6.62 PP Ndola 63 Finance HK
CROWLEY Dan A/I Lshya'53 rsgnd'54 Nthn News?
CROWTHER D b14.9.26 NRG6.7.50 A/I 1.1.56 Imm sec'd Fed 1.4.57
CROWTHER Dawn B W/A/I 1.9.56 Ndola Tfc 58
CROWTHER Denis J A/I Muf'50
CROWTHER Ian A MBE'00 b21.2.37 A/I 10.1.58 Insp 10.1.61 Kitwe 62 BathU Anglo American
    Nchanga to SA Maj Tvl Scots
CROWTHER James L b4.4.28 A/I 20.4.54 Insp 29.5.58 S/I BH 62
CROWTHER M A/I 62
CROWTHER Ron b18.8.38 A/I 14.1.60 Kansenji 61–2
CROWTHER W David b2.5.37 A/I 19.3.59 BH CID Insp 19.lve20.3.62
CROWTHER Mrs W D W/A/I 13.8.59 BH61
CROXFORD Douglas Harry 'Mkwezalamba' = ready for anything, Const 15.2.29 A/Supt 1.4.33
    Supt Copperbelt'39 to Palestine 10.43
CUBITT Brian Bertram b12.3.38 A/I 17.1.59 Insp 17.1.62 MU KwaZuluP Col
CULLEN Jack S bJo'burg 10.8.09 BSAP'33 Const NRP 12.8.37 A/Supt'52 Supt 30.5.57 rtd 19.5.60
    Pte Security Svce L'stone'62
CUNNINGHAM Ray A/I Ndola 60
CURRY A Joseph b3.12.17 Gds 36 Lt Para A/I NRP 14.5.46 Judcl Dept Clk of Ct Lstone 58 SEO
    AReg Ndola 17.10.60 L20.8.62 d'92
CURTIS G F Const 13.4.31 L'shya 33
CUTBUSH Desmond K Gordon CPM b26.2.16 PalP 18.11.36 A/I NRP 3.2.49 C/I 1.10.55 Cmdt
    Wilkinson Camp 63 d.91
CUTLER W D A b5.8.37 A/I 16.5.59 D/I BH CID 16.5.62

DALE V C W/A/I 6.4.62 Ndola
DALY J b14.4.17 NRG23.7.51 Imm Offr 15.10.55 Sec'd Fed 1.4.57
DALY J Vincent b28.8.37 A/I 23.4.60 Lshya 61 rsgnd 25.4.62
DALZELL Peter Giles b6.7.37 RN A/I 25.10.58 Insp 25.10.61 Lka Tfc 29.5.62

DAMP R M H b2.7.34 A/I 5.5.55 Insp 15.10.60 Ndola 25.5.62

DANIELS John H b29.4.28 RN A/I 13.8.53 Insp 13.8.56 C/I 1.3.60 Dist I Muf 62 L63

DANIELS William A/I Pros Ndola 58

DARE Willie CPM 52 b1.7.14 Pte 3.2.32 Af Insp MU A/I II 1.3.59 I 1.11.60 L9.62

DARLASTON Keith D E b5.11.36 A/I 9.3.61 Lshya 9.63 mN Watters

DARROCK Joseph H b28.2.28 Kenya P 53 A/I NRP 10.6.56 i/c Chilanga 57

DASHWOOD H K E A/I'38 D/Insp Lka'48 A/Supt Tanganyika'50

DAVENPORT Alan b27.7.43 Cdt 4.10.61 A/I 27.7.63 BHC Pilot RAF 70Sqn 69

DAVEY L A A/I Ndola C 63

DAVIDSON A/I Mtd 54

DAVIDSON Mrs H T/W/A/I 5.3.58 L5.4.61

DAVIDSON Thomas Middleton CPM 51 'Two Engine' b'06 s/o DCP SA, ed Hilton Natal, Const
  SAP Const NRP 23.9.29 A/I 1.7.31 Insp'36 Cricket fr Rhod'39 C/I 39 A/Supt'41 S/A/
  Supt'45 Supt 30.10.46 S/Supt Ch Cmdt NRPR'51 ACP Rtd 2.1.57 NRPR Ndola d'87

DAVIDSON Wm A G b14.7.36 A/I 9.2.61 Lstone 62–3 m.L Bruce Rhod Iran 77 Saudi Arabia

DAVIES Chas T b28.2.40 A/I 21.5.60 Kitwe C 60–2 Patrol Offr NG

DAVIES Ivor b8.4.41 Cdt 1.10.59 A/I 8.4.61 BH 62

DAVIES J R CPM(G)'45 A/I'38 Mil Svce A/Supt Somalild'45 NBorneo

DAVIES Peter PCMet A/I NRP Chingola 59 Bancroft rsgnd PC Met 61

DAVIES W B b21.4.40 A/I 4.4.62

DAVIS Michael J b4.10.36 A/I 11.7.57 Insp 15.10.60 Stn I Riverside 63 L64

DAW W D A/I 49

DAWSON J E A/I 47

DAWSON John E b15.4.36 A/I 14.2.57 Insp 14.2.60 Mpika 62

DAY Julian Canning 'Jerry' OBE QPM'56 CPM'51 bSouthsea 9.12.13 ed Blundell's fmg Choma
  31 BSAP 34 Rubber Plntg Malaya 37 A/I NRP 23.6.38 A/Supt 45 Supt 50 ACP(C) 53
  SACP 29.4.57 DCP 12.62 rtd10.64 d Harare 9.90

DAY-LEWIS George A H b2.6.36 A/I 6.6.57 Lshya 58

DEAN Wm Geo Wallis Const 4.2.32 Insp to West Africa 47

DEANE-SIMMONS Edwd MBE 53 CPM 50 b'02 ed Grahamstown; Tpr BSAP'24 Rhod Selection
  Trust Muf 6.28 Const NRP 13.7.29 D/A/I 1.6.30 C/D/I 1.1.38 sec'd Int & Sy 40–45 A/
  Supt 41 S/A/Supt Kitwe 46 Supt 1.1.48 S/Supt i/c CID'50 rtd 11.3.52 d29.9.88

DEBELL Derek A/I 58 Lka rsgnd 61

de COENE V b9.11.23 Home Svce Insp NRP 21.5.62 Lka

DEERDEN A/I Chingola 64

DEETLEFS Tom W S b15.7.02 SAP 23 S/I NRP Dogs 25.4.59 L4.6.62

DELANEY Capt Miles b10.7.16 SAP 37 A/I 9.1.52 S/I 11.4.57 C/I 1.1.59 Lka 62

DENEHY R P b24.10.38 A/I 11.10.59 BH 61

DENNEHY T G b21.10.41 Cdt 1.10.59 A/I 11.10.61 Ndola 62

DENNIS M Rowenna WPC Denbigh 56 W/A/I NRP 21.4.60 Ndola 62 d15.7.96

DENNISON P D/I d94

DEPTFORD David QPM'94 CPM'91 Cdt 1.10.59 A/I 20.9.60 MU 61–2 HKP Supt HQOps Ctre
  79 SSupt 2i/c PTS 81 CSupt rtd96

de VILLIERS E P R b11.12.37 A/I 19.5.60 BHC 61 resigned6.7.62

DERBY Louise L'stone 57 mP D Taylor 58 Civ Tele Op Chingola 28.11.60–2

DEVITT John C b22.8.41 A/I 11.1.62 Bwacha 63 Booker McConnell Zambia Aust 76

DEW Reginald F E b.24.8.23 PC Met 47 A/I NRP 25.3.48 A/Supt 1.1.53 Supt 13.1.59 Ndola 62
  S/Supt 64 d.1.5.85

DIBSDALL Norman A/I Muf Mne 53 Lshya 54

DICKENSON Nigel C A b30.11.32 A/I 8.12.55 Ndola 57 resgnd58

DICKINSON John A b10.11.35 A/I 14.2.59 Lshya 63 Agric Lstone Dept Agric WAust

DICKINSON R P N b31.12.38 Probnr 1.5.57 BH

DICKINSON V D E A/I 46

DIPPENAAR S J b15.1.98 SAP17–51 NRP 28.6.56 S/I 28.6.57

DISCOMBE Michael W S b16.11.43 Cdt 2.5.62 A/I 16.11.63 HKP

DIX Maurice A/I BH 59 rsgnd 59
DIXON Anthony N b18.9.38 A/I 7.1.61 Lka C 62 rsgnd1.64
DIXON Charles D b1.5.36 b/o J D A/I 1.5.57 Insp 13.4.62 i/c Chilanga 5.64 ACPF Perth Airpt 78
DIXON John D 'Paddy' b27.3.27 PalP 46 Acct Gen's Dept NR 3.2 A/I NRP 13.6.49 Insp 8.8.55
    S/I MTO PTS 61 Lka C 62 C/I d00
DIXON Richard E b19.8.34 A/I 23.6.55 Insp 15.10.60 Chingola 64 ACPF Supt 78 rtd91 POScy
    Aust
DIXON Valery w/o R E T/W/A/I L'stone 18.3.57–8
DIXON Mrs T T/W/A/I 23.4.56 BHC 58
DOBSON C D Noel b13.12.31 RUC 51 A/I NRP 3.4.58 Insp 3.4.61 Chingola 63–4
DOCHERTY Ken b5.2.40 PCMet 58 A/I NRP 24.9.60 Roan rsgnd 63
DOCKING Tony W G b24.2.28 MalayaP 55 A/I NRP 13.12.58 Insp 13.4.62 Wusikili CID 63 ZP
    Lka, Bar London
DODD Barry W b9.11.29 PCHerts 50 Insp NRP 11.4.62 PTS d99
DODD Jack CPM 57 b6.8.21 A/I 11.8.46 A/Supt 24.11.52 S/Supt 13.6.62
DODD Michael F b28.3.42 Cdt 6.4.59 A/I 28.3.62 Lka CID 63
DODDING A/I 52
DODDS G Walter M b27.11.33 A/I 3.4.58 Lka 29.8.62 ZP
DONALD Brian b6.3.40 Cdt 2.11.59 A/I 6.3.60 D/I Muf Mine 5.63
DONALDSON Duncan Douglas b31.5.40 A/I 4.4.62 Muf Mine 62
DONALDSON-SELBY Hugh Cdt 58 k.RTA 60
DORMER Beverly A/I Chingola Lka 5.53 Roan rgd Roan mng 56 R/A/I
DOUGLAS George A b15.11.28 A/I 6.11.53 Insp 6.11.56 C/I 1.12.60 Lstone 62 A/Supt
DOVE John Beck b.Kenya 6.6.39 Cdt 3.59 A/I 6.6.59 k.RTA Lka 16.4.61
DOVEY D Michael b18.11.29 Korea A/I 24.3.55 Chingola 55–8
DOWNHAM A/I Chingola 54
DOWNS Peter H b16.3.32 A/I 6.6.57 Muf C 58
DOYLE-DAVIDSON D A A/I 1948
DREWETT Phil M b14.1.39 A/I 24.9.60 Lshya 61–2
DRONFIELD-WATTON John b30.6.39 A/I 2.5.62 Kitwe 63
DUCKFIELD Ken A/I MU Lshya 6.53 rgd54
DUFF Barry A/I MU 59
DUFFIELD Martin b5.9.32 Kenya P 53 A/I NRP 21.10.56 mM G B Anderson 23.8.58 Insp
    21.10.59 S/I Dist Insp Lshya 62
DUFFY Bernard Francis b21.12.33 A/I 10.3.55 Chingola 59 rgd 60 Sy Offr Nchanga Mine
DUGUID A John b11.8.39 A/I 22.9.60 Kitwe Tfc 63
DUGUID Peter G b25.10.37 A/I 16.6.59 L5.5.62 rgd62 Sgt SAP 63
DUNBAR Alistair F A/I 59
DUNCAN I F b9.1.37 RUC'55 A/I NRP 19.7.58 rsgnd 5.7.61
DUNCAN Ivan J b26.5.39 Cdt 8.1 A/I 26.5.59 Pros Lusaka 63
DUNKLEY Trevor J b13.10.41 A/I 8.8.62
DUNN Colin b6.7.34 A/I 8.12.55 Insp 15.10.60 lve13.8.62
DUNN Keith J G b27.1.27 Gds Pal P PCMet 48 A/I NRP 22.2.51 Insp 8.8.55 S/I Muf C 58 Lka
    C 29.10.60 Cmdt Wardroper Camp 61–2
DUROSE David b15.3.37 A/I 1.5.58 Insp 1.5.61 i/c Solwezi 63
Du TOIT Basil b8.6.37 A/I 16.6.59 Ndola Tfc 63
DYER Alan E b26.6.39 A/I 4.4.62 Kansenji 63 NGP

EADE John A b7.10.28 PalP 46 PCMet 48 BermudaP 49 A/I NRP 30.4.53 Insp 30.4.56 C/I 1.3.60
    Ndola Loc 62 A/Supt 63
EADIE D Wm b8.6.39 A/I 20.6.59 Insp 20.6 L16.7.62
EAGLE David b17.9.41 Cdt 2.11.59 A/I 17.9.61 Ndola 62 d.91
EARLE J K T Const 21.1.32
EDNEY Albert W b22.5.18 KenyaP 24.4.47 A/Supt 18.11.50 NRP 9.2.52 MU Coy Cmd 6.62
EDWARDS Garnet G b29.11.34 Para A/I 24.10.57 Insp 24.10.60 FR 62

EDWARDS J Trevor b21.12.57 PalP 25.8.46 A/I NRP 17.3.49 Insp 3.53 A/Supt 27.5.54 Supt 1.7.59 S/Supt CO PTS 31.7.63 ZP ACP
EDWARDS John Ray RN b26.8.36 A/I 8.2.57 Lka Rsgnd 8.2.60 TA Maj
EDWARDS P K T A/I 48
EGLIN Christine PCWRdg 57 W/A/I NRP 7.4.60 mP Court 60 Lka 61–2
ELLIS John b10.2.22 PCMet 47 A/I NRP 49–mng Muf 52 A/I NRP 27.1.53 Insp 27.1.56 C/I 1.3.59 i/c Nchanga 62
ELLIS Les b6.12.29 PCMet 52 A/I 9.6.55 Insp 15.10.60 S/I Div Insp Sthn 8.7.62 Chinsali 64
ELLIS P A/I 48
ELLISON Anthony Vincent b16.10.21 RB A/I 26.2.48 Secretariat 51 Min Fin SEO 15.6.57 Lka 62 Dir Zambia State Lottery d6.5.00
ELLISON Douglas T b29.6.36 A/I 3.7.58 Chingola 62 dBulawayo 14.4.98
ELLWOOD D F W b24.11.38 A/I 4.4.62 Chingola
ELS Richd II b3.2.18 SAP 37–52 A/Supt NRP 26.1.55 FHQ Supt 1.7.58 L2.5.62 FHQ S/Supt
ESPEY Joseph Stuart CPM'57 bCT 29.5.10 BSAP 33 Const NRP 36 left 37 A/I 25.2.40 A/Supt 50 Supt 1.7.54 S/Supt 1.7.59 Central Div rtd 10.62
EVANS A Eric b26.5.26 A/I 6.6.59 Armr S/I 1.9.61 Lka 62 Tchr Kabulonga Sch to Borrowdale SR
EVANS Alexander LLewellyn IA A/I 47 Lka 48 Imm Lka 49
EVANS David Vincent Cdt to HKP C/I dHK 9.10.97
EVANS W M T b4.8.37 RUC 56 A/I NRP 18.4.58 Insp 13.4.62 Kitwe
EXELBY G R A/I 2.5.38 dschge own req 2.12.38

FAIRBAIRN Duncan S b12.3.40 A/I 28.2.62 Kitwe 62–3
FALLA Paul Ainsley b21.1.40 PC Lincs 59 A/I NRP 26.8.60 Lka 61–2
FANSLAU Geo b21.10.40 A/I 7.1.61 Monze 61–2
FARRANT Basil B Const 5.11.30 D/A/I 13.10.31 D/I 37 C/I BH'46
FEATONBY Theodore b22.4.38 Cdt 14 A/I 22.4.58 Bancroft 19.5.62
FELGATE Vincent R b18.7.36 SA A/I 14.3.59 rsgnd 18.3.62
FELL M b2.3.41 A/I 9.3.61 Muf 62
FENNER Roger b28.5.42 Cdt 27.9.60 A/I 28.5.62 Choma
FERGUSON A M O'S b27.5.39 A/I 26.6.60 Kitwe 61
FERGUSON Ian A/I 26.9.60
FERNEYHOUGH Alan Duncan b18.11.30 KDG KenyaP 55 A/I NRP 21.9.57 Insp 21.9.60 BH 62 A/Supt 64 ZP United Tpt Bar DPP's Dept Engld
FERNIE R F b10.10.35 A/I 26.8.60 Ndola C 61 MU 62
FERRIS R S b2.3.34 A/I 10.6.56 Insp 15.10.60 MU 62
FETHERSTONHAUGH Tim F K b7.7.26 BSAP 48 A/I NRP 6.5.53 Insp 6.5.56 S/I Lshya 62
FfORDE Col John Percy Ilbert CBE 60 KPM CPM(G) bMargate17.3.10 ed ISC Const PalP 28.11.31 Cpl AgASupt 35 Maj BMG Syria 41 AIG(CID) Pal 46 CP SLeone 48 NRP 14.8.51–12.62 Gp Scy Advsr Rand Mnes 62–79 d93
FIDLER Millicent Home Svce W/A/I 13.8.59 Chingola C 63
FIELD Christopher C Cdt Kitwe 28.1.60 A/I 22.11.61 Chingola62–3
FIELD Francis G P PalP Insp NRP 11.9.47 rtd 1.9.57
FILLERY Paul J F b8.6.36 A/I 11.7.57 Insp 13.4.62 Chingola 63–4
FILSELL Wendy E W/A/I 6.4.62 Lka 62–3 Probn Offr UK
FINDLAY R J b20.9.40 A/I 8.8.62
FINLAY H C O'H b5.6.38 A/I 20.2.60 FJ 62
FINN Colin W b23.9.39 Probnr 7.7.57 A/I Kitwe 23.9.59
FINNIE Andrew W b3.7.25 A/I 17.7.52 Chingola 52–4 Imm Offr 6.3.56 sec'd Fed 1.4.57 UK Prisons
FISHER Douglas A b27.6.32 A/I 14.2.57 Insp 14.4.61 Ndola 62
FISHER John O b28.8.26 PC B'hm 49 A/I 27.3.52 Insp 8.8.55 C/I 1.12.60 SDiv SB 63
FISK Pete J b18.11.37 A/I 16.5.59 rsgnd29.5.62 PNGP
FITCHIE G W 2Lt 7.5.26–resigned 19.11.26

FITZGERALD J F P CPM 62 b26.9.21 A/I 14.8.46 A/Supt 30.10.54 Supt 1.7.59 CO Luapula 62 L5.63 S/Supt ACP 64

FITZPATRICK Arthur J b6.12.29 A/I 6.10.50 Insp 6.10.53 A/Supt 1.7.57 Kitwe AgSupt 62 Pers Offr Aust Aircraft Corpn Melbne 69

FLEMING Jack b10.11.31 A/I 4.7.55 Insp 14.4.61 Kitwe 63

FLETCHER Christopher A/I Chingola 58 Stn Insp Ndola C 60

FLETCHER N E b13.2.32 A/I 12.5.55 Chingola'57

FOALE Richard J b27.7.35 A/I 10.6.56 BH 61 Insp 13.4.62 Bwacha 62 LC C/I ZP A/Supt 64 d.Zambia 5.88 Award fr Dist Svce 2Cl post

FOLD Edward Stanley 'Gerry' Const NRP 28.7.24 3/Sgt 20.8.26 A/Supt 1.4.31 Supt 35 L31.3.46–rtd1.4.47

FORBES Ann W/A/I Lstone 56

FORD A/I Choma 59

FORD James Foot Moodie b7.12.33 RAFP Insp NRP Spec Dog Hdlr 28.10.60 PTS 62

FORDE Dennis Joseph CPM'57 bLondn 8.6.16 BSAP 38 A/I NRP 18.8.38 Insp 46 sec'd Secretariat 12.48–31.6.49 A/Supt 51 Supt 1.7.54 S/Supt 1.7.58 ACP(A) 12.62 DCP d92

FORDYCE-HARVEY A G b27.4.20 A/I 12.5.53 Imm Sec'd Fed 1.4.57

FOREMAN Owen C b11.1.41 A/I 18.5.61 Ndola CID 62

FORESTER-GRANVILLE-PITCHFORD D S A/I 48

FORREST Robt b7.10.24 PCLancs 47 A/I 21.2 52 Insp 21.2.55 C/I 1.4.62 Kitwe 63

FORREST Wm M b18.5.32 A/I 21.10.56 Kitwe'57

FORSHAW John A F b16.10.30 A/I 27.8.53 Insp 27.8.56 S/I Camp Cmdt Lstone 62

FOSTER Jean W/A/I 1.4.57 mW R Allen 7.1.60 T/W/A/I 2.4.62 Lka

FOWLIE Alan "Sandy" b2.11.32 RN A/I 6.12.57 Insp 13.4.62 Choma ZP A/Supt i/c Lka C 65

FOWLIE Jack b26.12.22 PC Met 46 A/I NRP 26.2.48 A/Supt 1.1.53 Supt 1.7.58 OC Kitwe 62 S/Supt

FOY Giles A/I Chingola.54 d.Newbury 18.12.84

FOY Jean Mrs H J G H W/A/I 55 Clk 17.3 T/W/A/I 11.11.58 Kitwe rsgnd 27.3.61

FRADLEY Norman b3.7.06 BSAP 30 Const NRP 1.4.35 A/Supt 1.6.53

FRANCIS A Joseph CPM 53 Const 4.6.31 Pay Office AgA/I'32 Insp 18.8.38 C/I Paymr'46 A/Supt 53 P&QM rtd 13.2.57 Woodlands Lka.

FRANCIS Wm A/I 62

FREEBORN Ronald E b30.4.33 BSAP 52 A/I 13.9.55 MU L58 Muf

FREEMAN Gordon A/I Chingola 52 rsgnd 11.53 Nchanga mng

FROST Edward T b18.6.34 A/I 10.6.56 Lshya PP'57

FRY E John M b14.10.36 A/I 6.6.57 Dvg Instr MU59

FULLER Christine A WPCWRdg 59 W/A/I NRP 27.9.60 Ndola C 61–2 m Van Zyl

FULTON Brian A b1.8.33 A/I 2.8.55 Insp 8.4.60 lve 6.7.62

GABB Ronald A/I Lshya 40

GALLIAS Geo H bMossel Bay SA 11.11.11 BSAP 35 A/I NRP 2.4.39 A/Supt 1.1.52 rtd 2.61

GALLOWAY John Cunningham b27.10.27 Musselburgh RN 1.7.47 A/I 15.5.52 Insp 15.5.55 ADC A/Supt 1.7.57 Supt 63 rtd64 Sec Brch RAF S/Ldr rp82 RO Cambs d95

GANGE R John b13.5.31 PCSom 49 Met 55 A/I NRP 6.6.57 Insp 6.6.60 Ndola CID 62 ZP A/Supt Lka CID 65

GARDNER Bernard b28.8.29 A/I 3.3.55 Insp 14.4.61 Ndola Loc 63 SA kRTA 79

GARDNER Chris b8.7.40 A/I 7.1.61 MU 62–3 rsgnd

GARLICK Malcolm RAF A/I 21.9.57 rsgnd Nchanga Mine wk study 59

GARRETT Merlin b11.4.36 A/I 21.10.56 Insp 21.10.59 Lka 62

GARSIDE Ruth de B W/A/I 13.9.61 Kansenji 62 mJ Pollitt

GARVEY Seamus b31.5.30 DMP 54 A/I 6.6.57 Mindolo PTS 58 Maz 59

GAVIN Rod M 'Chiwulu' b2.12.23 A/I 17.5.46 A/Supt1.8.56 L4.4.62

GEDDES Janet WPC Herts 59 W/A/I NRP 5.9.60 Lka 61

GEDDES Norman E bAbdn15.12.28 A/I 21.8.52 S/I Kafue 59 A/Supt 16.8.61 Mongu 62 Rtd 64 Inld Rev Surbiton to Rhodesia to Yks

GEORGE Tudor A/I BH 54 Ag Insp i/c A'corn 56 Fmg Choma 12.56
GEORGEL Roger b1.7.39 A/I 9.3.61 BHMine 63
GERRARD D J P b6.7.42 Cdt 27.10.60 BH A/I 6.7.62 Lka 62
GILL Brian W b9.12.40 A/I 4.4.62 Muf Mine 63
GILL Sheilagh W/A/I BHC 58
GILL R G b26.10.37 A/I 27.6.62
GILLETT Norman G b24.4.28 PCSom 49 A/I NRP 21.1.54 Insp 9.8.60 S/I CIO Maz 62 d Dallas
    2.11.95
GILLETT R J b19.7.41 Cdt 28.1.60 A/I 19.7.61 Bancroft 62
GILLIES John McLennan 1Queen's A/I NRP 21.9.57 Ndola Rsgnd Roan Mine 61
GILLIES Paul H CPM 64 b25.12.37 b/o J McL A/I 18.7.59 Insp 18.7.62 i/c Lundazi 20.5.63
GILPIN John E b28.6.38 A/I 20.2.60 Bancroft 60–1
GINGLES Thomas F b20.7.37 A/I 18.1.59 Chilanga left 61
GLANVILLE C Anthony b3.2.41 A/I 11.1.62 Muf Tfc 63
GLAYSHER E C F b10.3.42 Cdt 27.10.60 A/I 10.3.62 Kitwe 62 Botswana P ?
GLIMOND E WPC Cheshire 50 W/A/I 9.2.61 BH 62
GLOVER Margaret I WPC Leic Cty 48 W/A/I NRP 4.12.58 BH 19.7.62
GOBLE G W 'Gus' b6.10.39 Cdt 16.6 A/I 6.10.59 m.d/o C G Byrne D/I Kalomo 63
GODDING Peter F b27.7.25 PalP 46 MalayaP 48 A/I NRP 2.10.51 Insp 5.10.54 A/Supt 1.1.58
    Lka C 62
GOETZSCHE Anthony F b14.6.36 A/I 11.10.59 Mwinilunga 62
GOLDSACK T b8.8.41 Cdt 28.1.60 A/I 8.8.61 rsgnd 29.4.62
GONDWE Kenwood A/I Muf 63 Ny
GOOCH Roy E b18.6.15 PalP 30.4.44 A/I NRP 14.2.49 Insp 24.8.52 C/I 1.3.59 L pdg rtd 1.8.62
    Planning Offr Fidelity Gds Joburg
GOODFELLOW Geo b27.6.30 A/I 13.5.54 Insp 13.5.57 C/I 1.3.60 MU 62
GOODFELLOW John N s/o DC Cdt 28.1.60 A/I 21.1.62 Lka Mtd 62 RA Maj
GOODING Geoff J b1.5.30 A/I 24.6.54 Insp 17.4.59 S/I Lstone 62
GOODMAN V Michael b23.9.31 PC Oxfds 52 A/I NRP 4.12.55 Insp 8.4.60 Mindolo CID 63
GORDON Chas Ongley BSAP 8.4.37 A/I NRP 7.7.39 Lshya 40
GORDON Peter A/I BH Mine 63
GORDON Roy b7.2.31 A/I 21.10.56 Insp 14.4.61 i/c BH Mine 1.3.63 C/I ZP Paymr FHQ
GORNALL John M b10.6.37 A/I 10.1.58 Insp 10.1.61 PTS 63
GORST J A/I 55 Luanshya rsgnd 57
GOSLETT Arthur Houston Stanley ltr HOUSTON Const 1.9.30 Insp Lstone 47 to NR Prisons
    Dept 29.1.49
GOWLAND Daphne Mrs J WPC Herts 52–5 W/A/I NRP 1.11.58 rsgnd 30.8.61 d.84
GOWLAND John 'Jack' b21.1.27 PCHerts 50 A/I NRP 23.12.54 Insp 17.4.59 S/I Chingola CID
    62–4
GRAHAM Eric Studholme b17.8.29 PCBhm 49 A/I NRP 15.4.55 Insp 13.10.61 MU 63 Leeds 69
GRAHAM B C L b3.8.43 Cdt 27.6.62 Chilenje 62 A/I 3.8.63
GRAINGER E T Const 21.11.30 A/I by 1937
GRANT Ian A b13.4.39 PC Stoke on Trent 58 A/I NRP 7.1.61 FJ61–2
GRANT Michael M b18.4.35 A/I 29.11.57 Insp 29.11.60 Kitwe 62 rsgnd NGP
GRAVES John Christie 'Paddy' b09 ed UCS Londn BSAP 29 Const NRP 25.6.34 A/Supt
    Nigeria 47
GRAY Derick A b23.8.34 A/I 14.12.61 Kitwe 62
GRAY Francis Derek R b19.6.24 PalP 45 MalayaP 48 A/I NRP 9.8.51 S/I 12.4.56 A/Supt 1.1.58
    MU 62 CO NWDiv 64
GRAY Pam W/A/I 8.8.62 Lstone CID m.F B Cook 7.9.63
GREASLEY Wm H b14.12.36 A/I 17.12.59 Lka 62
GREEN John? A/I 46
GREEN Don K b15.10.29 BechuanaldP 51 A/I NRP 15.10.58 Petauke 61
GREENE Paddy b17.5.25 PCMet 47 A/I 29.5.52 S/I 1.3.56 A/Supt 1.7.57 BH CID d.25.11.62
GREENHALGH R S A/I 50

GREENWOOD David C G Cdt 4.12.58 A/I 17.3.60 Lstone L62 rsgnd
GREGORY D G b11.1.25 Radio Maint Tech NRP 29.4.57 A/Supt 12.4.61–4
GRIFFIN Allan A b16.7.39 A/I 17.12.59 MU 61–2
GRIFFIN Raymond C BSAP 35 A/I NRP 14.9.38 dischge own req 10.1.46
GRIFFITHS 'Bunny' Mrs H C W/A/I 25.5.57 Ndola
GRINCELL Jo b9.10.28 PalP 47 NR Acct Gen's 18.11.48 A/I NRP 10.3.50 Insp 10.8.53 C/I 1.1.59
    L5.7.62 Mine Scy Sierra Leone 68–5.69
GRINDLEY-FERRIS Michael Cdt 24.2.58 A/I 16.11.59 MU 62
GROBLER Chris J 2.60 Ndola C
GROBLER Ronald J Cdt 3.4 A/I 10.6.57 Insp 10.6.60 Balmoral 62

HAAMUPUNJI C M b30.5.24 Const 6.5.44 A/I II 1.1.61 Kitwe 63–4
HADLEY Dan b15.2.35 RAF A/I 21.9.57 Insp 13.4.62 Lstone Tfc Parks Dept Kafue Ch Rgr/
    Admr, Woodwork Business ELondon 68, Warden Botswana, Brecon Beacons NPk
HAILE Harry A/I i/c Main Town Lka 52 Mng Muf by 61
HAINES Gordon R S b23.12.32 RN A/I 29.11.57 Insp 29.11.60 Monze 62 Ch Immigration Offr
    Vanuatu
HAINES Roger A b19.7.37 A/I 19.7.58 Stn Insp Kansenji 63
HALE D Malcolm b15.1.41 A/I 8.1.61 Kansenji 62 L63
HALL Desmond P D b26.2.25 A/I 21.7.49 Insp i/c FR, Rd Tfc Insp Tpt & Wks 22.10.56 L62
HALL W/A/I Chingola 56
HALL John A/I Kafue 5?
HALL Leonard S b19.11.27 Radio Maint Tech 9.12.56 A/Supt 12.4.61 Ndola 62
HALLACK A/I 46
HALSALL Wm A/I lve Nchanga 52 Kafue 54
HALSE Capt Chas Neville QPM 57 CPM 52 b.Peddie Cape 6.07 s/o Capt SAP; Const SAP'27
    NRP 6.5.30 A/I'34 Mil Svce N Africa'41–6, C/I 42 A/Supt'45 S/Supt'52 ACP(A) 11.53
    OC Western Div 1.56 SACP 29.4.47 d.29.12.59
HALSE Lt Col Eric Harvey OBE 61 QPM 54 CPM 45 b.Peddie 12.12.08 b/o C N, BSAP'30
    Const NRP 12.6.31 A/I'36 Supt Br Somaliland'39 Mil Svce'40–48 DCP Somalild'46 CofP
    MBE'50 DCP NR 12.11.53 CofP 12.62 Rtd'64 d Somerset West Cape 17.8.82
HALSE Steven L b28.12.25 A/I 3.8.50 Insp 12.4.56 S/I Ndola C 62–3 Chingola 64
HAMBLY John b30.5.35 2lt Dorset A/I 11.3.56 Insp 15.10.60 Emmasdale C/I ZP A/Supt
HAMILTON B b22.6.05 PCMet 26–52 A/Supt NRP 1.10.60 Lka 62
HAMILTON T Antony b4.7.27 s/o T A/I 6.12.49 Insp 1.7.53 A/Supt 1.3.60 AgSupt Ndola 62
    Supt d.91
HANBRIDGE Mike A/I SA
HANBY John L b24.1.15 PalP 10.5.41 NRP 13.1.49 Insp 10.8.54 S/I Lve pdg Rtd 29.7.62
HANGLIN P T Cdt 9.4.59 A/I 12.8.60 L26.6.62 Prisons Uk
HANJASE P b1.7.32 Const 21.1.53 SubInsp 1.2.62 A/I Kansenji 63
HANKEY W A Const 11.8.26–31.5.27
HANSON Stan T b13.2.30 PCMet 50 A/I NRP 21.4.55 Insp 17.4.59 S/I Mpika 26.8.62 Kitwe
    CID 63
HARDIMAN K b14.8.39 A/I 14.1.60 Bancroft 61
HARGREAVES Donald Wm b15.7.36 A/I 14.2.57 Kitwe CID L59
HARGREAVES Warner O b5.3.34 A/I 5.5.55 Lka'57 rsgnd 59
HARINGTON David J Cdt 15.9.59 A/I 20.6.61 Kansenji rsgnd 61
HARLAND Michael F b6.8.39 A/I 10.10.59 Lshya 61–2
HARLEY C J F b19.12.40 PCMet 60 A/I NRP 18.5.61 Ndola 62
HARRIS Geoffrey A b15.8.24 A/I NRP 21.7.49 D/I 12.53 A/Supt 15.11.55 DCIO SDiv 58
    rsgnd59 C/I NRP 24.11.60 Muf 61–2
HARRIS L Nicholas b5.10.35 A/I 25.10.58 Insp 25.10.61 Wdlds 63
HARRISON James F b10.3.24 PC Birkenhd 47 A/I NRP 18.12.52 S/I 18.12.56 A/Supt 1.7.57
    CID Lka 62
HARRISON John G Cdt 28.1.60 A/I 22.4.61 Lka 61–2 Ibiza 67

HARRISON T David b21.6.38 A/I 27.6.62 Kitwe 63 rsgnd
HART J H Const 3.9–30.11.26
HART L David b23.6.30 PCManch 50 A/I 12.6.52 Insp 12.6.55 S/I L13.4.62 Lshya
HARTLEY Derek PC WRdg 49 A/I Chingola 53 Muf 53 regard Muf Mine Sy'57 pte detective
    Cheltenham 66 d23.2.01
HARVEY Arthur Patrick A/I 38 Ndola 39 inv d81
HASELDEN Michael A b18.4.36 A/I 6.6.57 Insp 6.6.60 Chinsali 62 Crown Counsel HK
HATCHER Kenneth J b14.6.32 PCMet 55 A/I NRP 10.1.58 Insp 10.1.61 Chingola Tfc 62 Stn
    Insp Chingola C S/I 64
HATHRILL H J A/I 46
HATTON Alan A/I Kitwe 53
HAWKEY M J N b11.6.38 A/I 27.6.62
HAWKINS Arthur John Inskipp OBE 56 QPM 55 CPM 49 'Bwana Kabwata' b.28.7.06 Disley ed
    St Bees, Engrg Appr Manchester; NR 26 farming Landless, Chisamba, mines, rlys, Const
    6.2.30 A/I'33 Insp i/c Maz'37 C/I 41 A/Supt'43 Supt 11.8.48 S/Supt 1.1.51 ACP 9.51
    Westn Div 55 rtd 25.1.56 i/c Rhokana Mine Police dWales 6.12.81 f/o J J I H
HAWKINS Jean W/A/I 59 BH 11.59
HAWKINS John Jeremy Inskip bLka 13.3.35 s/o A J I BSAP 53 A/I NRP 1.9.55 Insp 9.10.59 C/
    I 3.63 rtd64 Chartered Consolidated
HAYES Colin b29.5.33 PC Notts 54 A/I NRP 3.7.58 rsgnd 25.4.61 Ontario P
HAYWARD Beryl WPC Notts W/A/I NRP 7.4.60 Lka mA J K Wright
HEAPE R Colin b24.6.38 A/I 15.8.59 Bancroft L1.4.62
HEARD Richd L J b13.7.34 A/I 15.5.55 Insp 9.10.59 L30.11.61
HEATLIE Leslie Arthur 'Peter' b.Cape, BSAP'23 Const NRP 1.6.27–30.9.28 to SR, Const NRP
    3.2.31 D/A/I 3.8.31 Insp'36 C/I 41 A/Supt 47 Supt 51 S/Supt 14.7.53 Rtd Cape 6.58
HECKFORD Roger B b24.10.28 A/I 28.6.51 Insp 21.9.55 C/I 1.1.59 Kalulushi 62 A/Supt
HEDGES Tony b16.2.30 A/I 13.9.51 Insp 13.9.54 C/I 1.7.59 Ndola 62
HEELAN Michael C b12.3.40 A/I 4.10.61 rsgnd63 BermudaP 64
HELLIWELL John Meade 'Jack' CPM 49 b13 NRP A/Supt 46 S/Supt Ch Cmdt NRPR 52 DCP
    Nyasald 6.53 Chmn Rhodesian Broadcstg Corpn64–74 dSomerset West SA 2.7.64
HEMMING Terry R b2.12.38 A/I 20.4.61 Muf CID 62
HEMPHILL Robin J F B b19.9.36 RUC'55 A/I 6.6.57 Lshya 58 Roan
HENDERSON Geo A b14.6.24 RAF BSAP 46 A/I NRP 4.5.52 Insp 4.5.55 S/I 1.3.67 FHQ
    13.7.62
HENDERSON I T A/I 48
HENDERSON Wm b3.4.33 PCMet 54 A/I 17.1.59 Kansenji 61 resigned
HENDRY Reg A/I Lka Mtd 52,3
HENRY R A/I 52
HESLOP J F Const 2.12.26 AgMG Sgt 1.12.26
HESOM Geo Bernard bStaff 06 rsd FJ Const 4.8.30 A/Supt 47 Supt 54 Central Div S/Supt rtd
    3.7.57 Ndola Copper Refinery d91
HEWISON K b28.9.36 A/I 17.7.58 Muf 61
HEWITT Richd A/I Luanshya 52 Chisamba 56
HEY Cornelius Wieger Geo ARCM bBton 11.3.14 Bdsm 1Ches 23.6.30 BM KSLI 24.7.45 S/I
    NRP BM 2.9.54 A/Supt 1.7.56–rtd 64
HEYGATE Colin C b28.10.39 PCMet 58 A/I NRP 9.3.61 Chingola 62–4
HICKS H F Const 22.4.29 A/I 1.7.31 AgInsp 34
HICKS Lawson Augustine QPM 59 CPM 51 bFarnborough 29.10.13 ed BromleyGS PCMet 37
    A/I NRP 16.11.39 A/Supt 49 Supt 51 S/Supt 54 ACP 29.4.57 SACP Westn 29.12.59 CofP
    64 ZP IG 66 DOverseas Police Advsr FCO dFowey 15.8.97
HILES N M b1.12.34 KenyaP 55 RUC 59 A/I NRP 8.8.62
HILL Brian b18.2.33 A/I 23.6.55 Insp 15.10.60 L9.2.62
HILL D E F A/I 46
HILL Michael W b9.12.37 A/I 14.2.59 Insp 14.2.62 Lka Tfc 9.62
HILL Robin G b22.8.40 A/I 7.1.61 Raylton MU 62 Lka Info 62

HILLS Geoffrey Lancaster b19.9.35 A/I 27.10.56 MU rsgnd59 Tetse Cntrl Sprvsr 3.4.60 Mumbwa 62 d96

HINE Wm CPM b27.7.15 PalP'40 A/I NRP 23.12.48 Insp 53 C/I 20.1.55 L pdg rtd 13.4.57

HIRST Colin R A Cdt 11.6.59 A/I 8.2.60 D/I Lka CID 63

HOBBS Michael Francis Hampden bDundry 42 Cdt 26.1.61 A/I 25.2.62 Chingola C 62 Zambia to Rhod 78 Salisby

HODGSON Keith M B b20.9.38 A/I 16.5.59 resigned 30.4.62 West Scy Lka 68

HOFFMAN Brian W b17.7.41 Cdt 26.9.60 A/I 17.7.61 RN SAN Cdr

HOLDING John R G A/I 62 Chingola C 5.63

HOLLING Kevin REME A/I Lka 60

HOLLOWAY John P b5.8.31 A/I 9.11.53 Insp 15.10.56 A/Supt 1.12.60 Lka 62 CP Solomons Rtd 83

HOLMAN David b11.3.34 A/I 11.4.58 Muf 62

HOLMES Bruce L b16.9.35 A/I 20.2.60 MU 61

HOLT Gerald A E b10.5.37 A/I 19.3.59 Lve29.5.62

HOOD John Gordon bBristol 13.8.36 A/I 14.2.57 Insp 14.2.60 Ndola CID 62 C/I

HOOK Ann KenyaFANY W/A/I 9.3.61 Lka 61–4 ZP

HOOK D E b21.3.36 A/I 17.12.59 BH 62

HOOKHAM Ray b21.12.26 PC Lincs 47 Kent 51 A/I NRP 20.3.52 S/I 1.3.57 C/I 1.1.59 W Div 62 Lve 11.5.62

HOPWOOD Derek C b29.6.37 A/I 23.4.60 D/I Chinsali 63–4

HOPWOOD P G A/I 10.62

HORLOCK Barrie A/I 62 Lshya CID 63

HORNBY Arthur Lockyer BSAP 17.5.35 A/I NRP 31.3.37

HORNE G David b7.2.36 A/I 24.10.56 Lka 57–9

HORNER Ben H b7.2.36 A/I 21.10.56 Muf C 57–8

HORSFIELD Arnold W b5.6.18 A/I 23.7.46 APayMr 53 QM 1.7.56–64

HORTON Rosemary E WPC Som 54–9 W/A/I NRP 30.5.60 Chingola Tfc rsgnd 6.62

HOUSTON A H S see GOSLETT

HOWARD P D b16.5.31 BSAP'50–7 A/I NRP 27.6.58 Muf 61

HOWELLS Glyn T b27.4.38 A/I 16.5.59 Insp 16.5.62 L24.5.62 Mgr Sugar Estate, Fmr Lka 68

HOWELLS Rex E W BSAP 35 A/I NRP 8.3.38 D/I 46 A/Supt sec'd Fed Min Home Affrs 1.12.54 rtd 56

HOWLETT John H R b17.4.30 PCMet 50 MalayaP 51 A/I NRP 29.11.57 Insp 29.11.60 FR 62 Aust dNZ 98

HOWIE A/I Choma 59

HOWITT P J b6.10.39 Cdt 11.6 A/I 6.10.59 resigned 31.8.61

HOWSE Des J Cdt Muf 13.5.60 A/I 16.2.61 Lstone 62 resigned

HUBAND Pat J b12.3.32 A/I 10.3.55 Insp 17.4.59 Choma 62 A/Supt 64

HUDSON B W b20.5.43 Cdt 4.4.62 BH

HUGGINS H S M Const 10.1.31 Lusaka 33

HUGH-JONES Michael G b15.9.33 A/I 7.9.58 Insp 7.9.61 i/c BH Mine 5.63 SO FHQ 64 Barrister Melbourne 78

HUGHES Hugh Thos 2Lt 18.2.27 P&QM 18.4.28 NRR QM Capt 18.2.37

HUGHES Ian StClair b14.6.36 A/I 11.8.60 Muf 62 rgd 63 Scy Offr Rhod Iron & Steel 63 Mgr Gwelo Spts Club 69 Adm NT Hardwick Hall 79 d94

HUGHES J W 'Gunner' Const 4.8.31 Armr Stores L'stone, QM&MTO MU'49 rtd Mazabuka Managemnt Bd'54

HULETTE Nicholas C b16.9.34 RMP A/I NRP 11.7.57 Insp 14.4.61 Lka Pros 64 ZP A/Supt

HUMPHREY Denis William QPM 59 CPM 54 b.Windsor 8.9.10 ed Ampleforth; Const NRP 10.2.32 A/I'37 Insp'41 A/Supt'45 SO FHQ 23.4.46 A/Clk Legco 5.49–Supt 9.50 S/Supt 53 ACP 2.1.57 SACP(W) 58 DCP Tanganyika 1.59 Colnl Police Advsr Bramshill d94

HUMPHREY Oliver J s/o D W Cdt 19.6.60 A/I 18.9.61 Muf 62

HUMPHREYS H T Const 31–2

HUMPHREYS W Fred b24.10.25 PalP 45 PC Shrops 48 A/I NRP 7.1.54 Insp 7.1.57 A/Supt
    1.9.59 AgSupt Lka 62 ZP ACPTrg 68–72 d98 Zimbabwe
HUMPHRIES Mrs M T/W/A/I Lka 1.12.56
HUNGERFORD Richard A/I 50
HUNT Douglas H b15.11.31 A/I 24.10.57 Insp 24.10.60 Chingola 62 Farming Lka
HUNT J E Cdt 28.1.60 A/I 20.12.60 Chingola 62
HUNTER Jock R D b6.2.40 A/I 9.2.61 MU 62–4
HUNTER Robt L b18.7.29 PCDurham 49 A/I NRP 6.3.52 A/Supt 1.3.60 DSBO Nthn 15.8.62
    L63 Supt
HUNTER R J Cdt 28.7.60 A/I 20.4.62 Muf
HURST Cliffd Joseph PMG bLpl 1.2.36 A/I 15.10.59 Kitwe CID to 62 BasutoldMP 64 Salesman
    74 Sec Witz U 77
HUTCHESON Robt 26.3.30 A/I 25.9.52 A/Supt 1.12.60 AgSupt Lka 62
HUTCHINSON Thos BSAP 4.4.38 A/I NRP 12.9.38
HYDEN Edward J b29.6.36 A/I 20.6.59 rsgnd 30.6.61
HYNDS James b31.3.05 Pal P'30 A/Supt NRP 17.12.48 S/Supt 29.7.56 Ch Cmdt NRPR 57

IMRIE J B M Cdt 15.9.59 A/I 28.6.60 Kitwe 61
ING Chris R Cdt 27.9.60 A/I 23.5.61 Bwacha 63 d29.11.99
INGLIS B S 'Happy' b16.5.30 PC Nthmbrld 53 A/I NRP 11.3.56 Muf A'corn 57
IRELAND Jas J b8.6.36 A/I 3.4.58 Insp 3.4.61 BH 62
IRVIN N M 'Husky' PalP 35–7 A/I NRP 39 Agric Dept 13.9.46 d92
ISDELL Edwd N b6.8.07 RUC 28 Insp NRP 7.1.54 C/I 1.7.56 A/Supt 64
IVEY Charles A/I Muf Pros 6?

JACKSON Geo Edward ARCM Bdsm RInnisF 21.3.24 BM 2QORWK 8.5.38 BM NRP 24.4.50
    rsgnd12.51 DoM RAAF 53
JACKSON Leslie Rueben b94 to NR Prisons Dept d IoMan 59
JACOBS F Const 29
JACOBS R G Natal Carbineers Const SAP 20 Const NRP 18.11.26 Insp 1.4.31 i/c L'stone rsgnd
    33 Personnel Roan Mine d16.11.54
JACOBSEN Barry A/I 59 PE Scholarship Michigan U 59
JACOMELLI A I M W/A/I 58?
JAMES Geo Emlyn Const 1.4.25 3/Sgt 1.12.26 A/I BH 13.3.28
JAMESON David A/I Lka CID 63
JAMESON I b25.4.42 Cdt 28.2 A/I 25.4.62 Chingola
JAMESON Peter J b10.9.34 A/I 15.8.59 L16.8.62 d94
JAMIESON G H b26.1.25 PC BTP 46 A/I NRP 14.2.52 S/I 13.8.57 C/I 1.3.60 Chingola 21.5.62
    Dist Insp 63
JAMIESON Paddy A/I PTS dogs 63
JAQUES R M 'Jack' A/I.46
JEFFREY Elizabeth B R WPC Leeds 51 W/A/I 17.3.60 Lshya Tfc 63
JEFFEREYS Colin H A b9.11.32 BSAP'53 A/I NRP 5.2.57 BHC MU 58
JEMBO A/I Mpika 63
JENKINS F J Sgt by 4.10.29 CSM 11.3.31 NRR RSM 1.1.34
JENKINS Roger b6.3.41 A/I 8.8.62 Fawcett Scy Lka 68
JENKYN Richard A A/I 62 Ndola Loc 63 Bermuda Solr
JENNINGS Colin B b12.1.37 A/I 15.8.59 L pdg rgn 22.8.62
JESSON Ronald F b1.10.34 A/I 5.5.55 Ndola C 18.1.60 sec Ny P 60 rsgnd mining Roan 61
JEVONS Elizabeth W/A/I 11.12.60 BHC 62
JINKS D A/I 62
JOBO D M CPM b1.7.22 Const 1.6.42 A/I II 1.4.62
JOBSON Alan G PC Manch A/I NRP
JOHNSON A BSAP Const NRP 21.4.26 BSAP 18.7.26 own request
JOHNSON Alan b24.4.30 A/I 8.12.55 Insp 8.4.60 L30.6.62

JOHNSON Marjorie W/A/I Lshya CID 63
JOHNSTON D J H 'Bertie' b20.10.32 RUC 52 A/I NRP 10.8.55 Insp 15.10.60 L6.4.62
JOHNSTON Iris M WPC Bradfd 52 Hants 57 W/A/I NRP 21.5.59 Insp 21.5.62 PP Ndola 63
JOLLIFFE Leonard E b2.3.41 A/I 20.4.61 Kafue 62
JONES C Ashley b9.11.37 A/I 16.1.60 Isoka 62
JONES David J H b5.1.35 PCMet 54 A/I 11.7.57 Insp 11.7.60 Kitwe 62
JONES Edwin b2.10.17 PCFlints 39 RhodesU 47 A/I NRP 8.3.51 S/I 11.4.57 C/I 1.7.59 Ndola
    29.3.62 Justices' Clk IoM
JONES M ELizabeth WPC Denbigh 51 W/A/I NRP 25.2.60 Chingola 60–2
JONES Philip b19.7.30 PCWRdg 50 A/I NRP 2.3.55 Insp 25.9.59 S/I Lka 62 C/I
JONES Robert V b11.6.27 A/I 23.9.52 Insp 23.9.55 A/Supt 1.12.60 Luapula 63
JONES R Gwyn b1.2.41 PCMet 60 A/I NRP 9.3.61 Chirundu 9.62
JONES Stan F b8.10.27 PC Birkenhd 48 A/I NRP 7.5.53 Insp 26.8.57 S/I Choma 7.60–62
JORDAAN Rene, Mrs L H W/A/I 11.6.56 Bancroft 11.2.60–2
JORDAN James J b28.2.40 A/I 20.4.61 Muf Mine 62 L63
JORDAN John N KPM(G) 30 Const 30–1
JORDAN Peter b15.5.37 A/I 14.2.59 Lka 16.8.62 k30.7.64
JOSEPH A Neville OBE 91 b17.3.31 A/I 24.3.55 Insp 24.3.58 L4.2.62 C/I DGov Borstal Portld
    79 Gov Walton
JOWETT Ronald J b25.6.15 PalP 22.10.37 NRP 27.1.49 C/I 1.8.54 L23.3.62
JUDE R A W/A/I 9.2.61 Muf 62
JUGGINS Horace Paul b24.9.30 PC Warwicks 52 A/I NRP 7.1.54 Insp 7.1.58 Div Insp Eastn
    5.61–2
JUSTICE Derek Edwd b29.6.42 A/I 8.8.62 Lstone 63 PC Met Supt

KABAGE Gordon M CPM b15.9.26 Const 21.9.46 A/I III 59 II 1.1.61 I 1.12.61 Lka ZP D/C/I
    CIO Lka 68 rtd Malawi
KABAMBA B b15.11.19 Const 19.6.40 A/I III 59 II 1.12.60 Lka Solwezi 62
KALOLO Bernard M b25.5.28 Const 3.5.49 A/I II 1.4.62 Muf 62
KAMANGA K S A b15.7.23 Const 25.9.43 A/I II 1.1.61 I 1.12.61 L8.62
KAMBELA R J b15.1.24 Const 4.11.49 A/I II 1.4.62 A/Supt 64
KAMUKWAMBA Douglas b15.10.26 Const 10.3.50 A/I II 1.4.62 Samfya 62–3
KAPONDE F b10.2.23 Const 19.7.48 A/I II 1.4.62 Ndola C/I 64
KASAILA John Jokwe Banda A/I Chingola by 3.64
KASONDE Patrick Const 62 Sgt 64 A/I 64 ZP A/Supt 64 S/Supt 72
KASUMBA J W b1.7.30 Const 21.6.49 A/I II 1.4.62 Lka
KATAMBI Eliss b1.7.28 Const 23.1.53 SubInsp 1.4.62 Bancroft D/A/I Kitwe 63
KATEMBO David D/A/I Lstone Dist rtd 7.60 to Mankoya
KATUNDU R CPM b15.10.28 Const 19.10.50 A/I II 1.4.62 Mongu
KELLY T H A/I 49
KELSEY R Jock b27.7.33 A/I 23.4.60 Kitwe 62 Aust
KEMPTON C H b9.12.38 A/I 24.9.60 BH 62 rsgnd
KENNEDY J B A/I 51
KENNEDY R WPC L'pool 57 W/A/I NRP 29.6.60 mSpofforth Ndola 61–2
KENNY Mrs J R L T/W/A/I 19.10.56 Ndola'57
KER David E A/I Kitwe 52–L54
KER David W b31.7.37 A/I 13.12.58 Dogs Lka 22.6.62
KEW Alan b14.7.42 Cdt 17.11.60 A/I 14.7.62 BH
KHAN-REIN C A A/I 50
KIDD Desmond H b9.6.35 A/I 21.10.56 Insp 14.4.61 Kansenji CID 62
KIGGELL L S Const Ag2/Sgt 2.12.26 2/Sgt sec'd Rds Dept 14.11.27
KILGOUR David A/I Lka 52
KILLICK H T BSAP A/Supt NRP 29.11.51
KILLICK K Roy b19.2.30 A/I 14.6.50 Insp 10.8.54 C/I 1.3.60 Kitwe Riverside 5.62
KING Geo Bdsm RScots RSig BM BSAP BM NRP 27.2.52 rsgnd 27.5.54

KING G W b18.4.42 Cdt 28.2 A/I 18.4.62 Chingola 62
KING J R P b5.6.31 A/I 16.6.52 Imm sec'd Fed 1.4.57
KINGSHOTT H H 'Bisley' Const 3.10.30 AgA/I Rcds 32 Insp 1.8.38 C/I 46–7 rtd Durban
KIRBY Anthony R CPM(G) 61 b20.1.28 A/I 10.10.52 Insp 10.10.55 A/Supt 12.4.61 L18.8.62
KIRKBY E John N b7.10.35 A/I 10.6.56 mW/A/I 59 Insp 10.6.59 Kitwe 3.60–Riverside 63 C/I d94?
KIRKBY Mrs E J N W/A/I 57–9 T/W/A/I Kitwe 1.7.60–62
KNIGHT Roger b18.7.36 A/I 15.10.59 Chingola 60 PTS 61–2
KNOX Don Mck b28.5.28 A/I Lshya 24.6.54 rsgnd57 Ndola Brewery d.Botswana 2.78
KOETSEE Theuns A/I.60 Nchanga 61
KUMALO S M b2.1.21 Const 15.2.44 A/I II 1.1.61 A/I I 1.12.61 L2.6.62
KWILIKO A/I BHC 63

LADELL Dr R C H BSAP NRP'36? D/Const 37 resgnd 47 med studies Londn Bristol GP Kloof SA
LAMB Brian E b4.11.35 A/I 24.10.57 Insp 13.4.62 Lka CID 62–3
LAMBERT Barry Russell b12.4.39 A/I 18.5.61 Chingola C 62–L63 Aust
LAMBERT J R Const 1.9–20.12.28
LAMMAS Tom J J b6.11.35 A/I 12.12.58 Ndola 15.6.62
LANCASTER Paul A b22.10.41 A/I 8.8.62 Lka 63 ACPF Perth'78
LANDERS C b28.2.41 A/I 4.4.62 Ndola 62 Bahrein?
LANDMARK Michael G Cdt 12.5 A/I 3.10.56 Insp 3.10.59 Lstone 60–2
LANE D Gordon b15.4.20 A/I 17.10.46 A/Supt 1.1.52 MU 62
LANE Fred G b13.3.29 PCMet 49 A/I 8.11.51 Insp 8.11.54 A/Supt 1.4.62 SwaziP NZ
LANE John Kenneth UKP A/I Chingola UKP 17.3.53
LATHWOOD R b23.2.40 A/I 28.2.62 Kapiri 63
LAVERY W R b29.8.39 A/I 4.8.60 Kitwe 61
LAW Frank Frederic Const 4.2.32
LAWRENCE Edwd A/I Lshya rsgnd 54 rigger Muf Mne
LAWRENCE John K b13.8.34 A/I 131.55 Insp 8.4.60 PP Lstone 63 R OMan P C/Supt i/c Highway Patrol 83
LAWTON Ray MBE 3.59 WO1 RASC Rtd S/I 3.59 Dvg Instr PTS rgd3.62
LAYNE Gordon H b15.5.22 A/I 28.8.47 A/Supt 30.10.54 Supt 1.7.60 Lshya Dist 63
LEE Denis b17.11.27 PCLancs 48 A/I NRP 19.5.52 Insp 19.5.55 C/I MU 59 A/Supt 1.4.62 L5.5.62
LEE John b24.7.27 BSAP 48 A/I NRP 25.10.51 Insp 21.9.55 rsgnd 24.6.57
LEE Phil W b13.9.30 A/I 13.1.55 Insp 9.10.59 i/c Kabwata 62 C/I Qnsld Abo Welfre 68
LEECH Joan W/A/I 4.6.59 Lshya Tfc 59 Lka L6.6.62 m McFALL
LEGER G Barry S b13.8.26 2Lt WAFF A/I 10.8.50 Insp 13.8.56 S/I PTS 61 AgC/I Monze 62
LEGG A D WPC Bristol 59 W/A/I NRP 8.6.61
LEIGHTON Eric E OBE(62) b.11.5.05 Indian P 24 MI5 46 Malayan P 46–53 ACP SB NRP 26.8.57–62+ d.87
LEMON G L A/I 58 Ndola
LEMON Paul S b15.7.41 A/I 14.9.61 Riverside Kitwe Tfc 63
LENDRUM Peter F b12.2.39 Cdt 28.7.58 A/I 12.2.59 MU 62
LENEY Peter T b11.8.37 A/I 17.5.58 Insp 17.5.61 Ndola CID 62
LENNETT Peter D bLpool 14.4.38 2Lt RA OxfdU A/I 10.12.60 Chinsali CID 9.62 HKP 64 C/I civ FTO 76 rtd Malta d21.9.97
LEONARD F R BSAP 36 A/I NRP 11.3.38 dischge own req 6.12.38
LE ROUX John D b21.1.40 Cdt 24.8.57 A/I 21.1.60 Kitwe Tfc 62 PC Devon & Cornwall Insp
LESTER Wm E 'Tim' b1.12.39 A/I 17.12.59 Chinsali 64
LETCHWORTH Frank H S BSAP 38 A/I NRP 18.8.38 dBlackwater fever Luangwa Bridge Gd 40
LEVERETT David Bernard John bLndn 28.2.41 A/I 27.6.62 NGP rgd 68 SR GSM
LEVERMORE Ray A b31.5.25 NRG6.9.51 A/I 1.6.52 Imm sec'd Fed 1.4.57
LEWIS David N A b2.1.38 RAF A/I 25.10.58 Solwezi 9.62 ZP MU

LEWIS 'Lofty' A/I rgd54
LEWIS Peter R L b5.2.22 A/I 23.7.46 A/Supt'52 Supt 3.1.57 S/Supt 22.10.60 FHQ 24.7.62
LIHOU James Le P b27.5.35 A/I 8.12.55 Insp 9.10.59 Lka CID 63 Guernsey d14.12.96
LILLEY Frank A/I 58 Lshya Tfc 59 Lka CID L61
LINDSAY A/I 39
LINETTE Martin Alan bCheltnhm Cdt 2.11.59 A/I 26.9.60 Kitwe 62
LINNANE Patrick J b19.4.30 DublinMP 53 A/I NRP 11.7.57 D/I 13.4.62
LINMON Quinton Fredk S b11.6.34 A/I 10.6.56 Muf 58
LLOYD Alan A b6.4.34 A/I 10.6.56 Insp 8.4.60 Solwezi L3.63 PC Devon SA 69 Kent JP
LLOYD Richard RAF A/I 21.9.57 Monze Lstone Dist Insp 59
LOCKETT Keith B b2.11.30 PC Leic Cty 50 A/I NRP 12.5.55 A/Supt 16.8.61 DSBO Eastern 63
LODGE Michael W J b1.1.36 A/I 1.5.58 Muf C rsgnd 20.5.61
LOMAX A M b18.7.41 Cdt 17.11.60 A/I 18.7.61 Lstone 62
LOGIE J Const 1.11.26 Sgt to ?Dept 1.4.28 rtd Lusaka
LONG D b16.2.34 A/I 17.12.59 Kalulushi 61
LONG John Edmund b3.4.10 Const 4.2.32 to DA PA, SDO1 1.7.57 DPC Central rtd 29.6.62
LOUSTAU-LALANNE B M bSeychelles 20.6.38 A/I 28.2.62 Bancroft 62
LOVE Glen b17.9.31 RUC'52–3 A/I NRP 10.8.55 Monze 57 rsgnd Dvg Sch Instr Lka by'66
LOVELY Peter AQM 53
LOWES G Ray R b9.6.31 PCLincs 51 A/I NRP 4.12.55 C/I 1.6.62 Lka 63
LOWN Eric E b4.7.37 A/I 25.10.58 Insp 25.10.61 i/c Lshya Tfc 62
LUCAS Steven C b14.4.42 Cdt 17.11.60 A/I 14.4.62 Lshya Tfc 63
LUCHETA J b29.10.20 Const 12.8.42 A/I II 1.4.62 Wusikili 62 A/I I 64
LUCY Richard J H b29.9.34 A/I 11.4.58 Kalulushi 62
LUDBROOKE J V 'Spud' b22.10.33 KenyaP A/I NRP 9.9.57 Chinsali 59 Game Rgr 1.9.60 Kafue
    Nth Pk 62
LUND Piers B H b16.6.26 A/I 15.5.54 Insp 9.10.59 Kitwe 62–3
LUYT A/I Ndola C 60 Wusikili 61
LUSK Mrs J T/W/A/I 1.9.56 Chingola'57
LYALL Crawford b1.6.33 A/I 23.6.56 Lstone L58
LYNAGH John J 'Sean' b4.1.33 BSAP 54 A/I NRP 24.10.57 D/I 24.10.60 Muf 61–2
LYNAGH B L b10.8.36 A/I 18.5.61 Lshya 62
LYON Christopher John b30.4.35 A/I 21.10.56 Insp 21.10.59 PTS 60–resigned 63 H.M. Insp. of
    Taxes

McBRIDE Sally M (Hart) W/A/I 21.2.60 Lka 60–1 d92
McCALLUM A G b4.2.34 A/I 13.10.55 D/A/I Ndola'57
McCALLUM Lindsey A/I Chingola '60?
McCANN Rob b4.2.40 A/I 27.10.60 MU 62
McCOURT T A/I 51 Lshya 53
McCOY Edward Cdt 6.8 A/I 17.10.59 resigned 29.7.62
McCOY Tim C b7.5.39 Cdt 8.1 A/I 7.5.59 rsgnd 24.6.61 2Lt 22.12.63 RSig Maj 31.12.73 rtd94
McCRAE John b20.9.27 A/I 13.3.52 Insp 13.8.56 C/I 1.3.60 i/c Kansenji 10.7.62–63 d92
McCRETON Patrick Kevin BSAP 14.4.38 A/I NRP 18.8.38
McCUE David b3.7.33 A/I 25.10.58 Insp 25.10.61 ZP C/I
MACE Derek G b23.1.26 PC Warwicks 49 A/I NRP 12.8.53 Insp 12.8.56 S/I AgC/I Lka 62 C/I
    Supt CIO Lka 64 West Scy Lka 68 Gen Mgr Securicor rtd 89 dLeeds 31.3.95
McEVOY Noel A/I 63? to Aust
McEWAN T A A/I 63?
McEWEN Brian A/I b15.5.34 A/I 10.3.55 Kansenji 61 rtd62
McFADDEN Denis E b15.1.36 A/I 7.1.61 Ndola CID 62 Sierra Leone Mine Scy
McFALL Jas S OBE 68 b27.2.36 A/I 11.4.58 mJ Leech Insp 13.4.62 Lesotho P
McFARLANE Jas A b7.6.33 A/I 12.5.55 Insp 12.5.58 BH CID 62
MacGILLIVRAY Doug H b6.5.41 A/I 11.1.62 Kashiba 63
McGOVERN Francis O b6.2.36 A/I 17.5.58 Insp 17.5.61 Solwezi 62–3 ZP

McGREGOR A/I Lshya 54
McKENDRICK E W A/I 58 Ndola
McKENNA Peter A/I Chingola rsgnd 53 Nchanga Mine
MacKENZIE D A/I 9.62
McKENZIE Duncan b2.4.31 PCLpool 53 A/I NRP 10.6.56 Insp 14.4.61 S/I Kitwe 62 A/Supt 64
    d94
MacKENZIE John F H b4.10.36 2lt RSx A/I 11.7.57 Insp 1.8.61 Lka 62
MACKEOWN Michael J b24.9.41 A/I 8.8.62
MACKEY M Sheila (Smith) W/A/I 8.8.62 Ndola Tfc 63 Lka 64 WRAF
MACKIE Thos Ian D b25.2.37 A/I 14.2.59 resigned 5.3.62
McKINLEY Harry V b19.10.32 RInnisF Sgt A/I 21.9.57 Insp 13.4.62 Lshya
McINTOSH A J 'Duncan' b15.10.36 A/I 30.6.59 Lka Tfc L15.7.62
MACKINTOSH Iain Ross b12.10.27 HG RN FAA PalP 19.6.47 A/I NRP 27.1.49 A/Supt 15.11.55
    Supt 13.6.62 Chingola Dist 63–rtd64 d00
McKNIGHT J P b22.6.08 PC Warwicks 32 A/Supt NRP 26.10.60 MU 62
MACINTOSH A/I 10.48
McLAUGHLIN Anthony Augustine bShrula4.9.25 RUC 48 A/I NRP 22.2.51 S/I 1.3.57 C/I
    1.4.62 i/c Roan 63 A/Supt
MACLEAN Alistair G b28.7.40 A/I 10.12.60 Muf 62 rgd
McLEAN Donald G b28.7.40 A/I 9.2.61 Chingola Tfc 63
McLEAN Jeffrey Graeme b15.12.32 RAFP A/I NRP 23.6.55 Insp 13.4.62 Dogs ZP WestScy Lka,
    Mgr Lka Club
McLEOD A A/I 10.8.55 Kitwe Lshya 56 Lka rsgnd 57
McLEOD N C Const 1.5.28 A/I 1.1.31 rtd33
McLEOD N E b24.5.41 Cdt 2.11.59 A/I 24.5.61 Lstone 62
McLERNON B L b8.3.36 A/I 23.4.60 L pdg rgn 1.6.62
McMANUS A Gregory b9.2.36 RUC 54 A/I NRP 24.10.57 Insp 13.10.61 Lka Mtd 62
McMENEMY A WPC Renfrew & Bute 60 W/A/I NRP 8.8.62
MACPHERSON Colin J A/I Ndola Tfc 58
MACRITCHIE Donald b1.3.28 PCDumbarton'51 A/I 3.2.55 MU'57 PC Strathclyde C/I'78
McROBERTS Jas Greer b12.5.43 Cdt 8.8.62 A/I 12.5.63 MU HKP 64 Solr Sctld Capt ALS 72–
    5 Procurator Fiscal, Pte Prctce Abdn
McVIE H b8.5.31 A/I 10.6.54 FR L57 BH Mine 58
MADGE Roger J P b23.11.41 Cdt 28.1.60 A/I 23.11.61 Ndola L63
MADGETT David A/I Kitwe 56 rsgnd 2.57
MAER Philip b26.6.36 A/I 17.1.59 BH rsgnd 5.3.62 PC Sx C/I
MAGAI C b1.7.27 Const 7.5.51 A/I II 1.4.62 FJ 62 C/I
MALLAM Tim A/I S Div To RRlys Catering 61
MALONI S b24.6.24 Const 1.7.43 A/I II 1.1.61 Lka 1.9.62
MALTBY Chris Julian bLndn 3.8.41 Cdt 6.8.59 A/I 3.8.61 Choma L1.8.62 Cape Travel Agt &
    SAAFR
MANN Trevor A/I Lshya 54 56
MANSON Alan A/I i/c A'corn L52 Lstone 53
MARAIS Daniel P E b15.2.38 A/I 16.6.59 L pdg rgn 24.6.62
MARCH Michael W b23.8.28 KenyaP 53 A/I NRP 21.10.56 Insp 21.10.59 Kawambwa 61–2 C/I
MARGINSON Alan Wilding b22.1.34 2Lt RAOC A/I NRP 5.5.55 Insp 17.4.59 Maz 5.7.62
    PCLancs Sgt rtd89
MARNHAM David G H b5.3.37 A/I 3.4.58 Nthn Div 64 Papua NGP
MARR Anthony F b25.8.29 A/I 25.7.51 Insp 25.7.54 A/Supt 1.9.59 BH 62
MARRON Michael K b12.1.34 App Chemist, Radiographer Sgt RAMC A/I 24.10.57 Insp 13.4.62
    ZP D/C/I Lka 64–7
MARTIN Alan T b9.2.29 A/I 6.9.51 Insp 6.9.54 S/I to Labour Dept 10.9.60 Lka 62
MARTIN Francis N bSt Helena 13.11.29 Acct Gen's Dept 14.7.49 A/I 23.10.50 A/Supt 15.11.55
    OC Maz D 61–2 Supt, CP St Helena CP Nairu rtd Fiji dQnstn NZ 25.1.97
MARTIN G W b12.5.33 A/I 14.7.55 L27.4.62

MARTIN J A G BSAP 37 A/I NRP 15.9.38
MARUME A/I 63
MASHAWILA J F b23.2.19 Const 19.5.43 A/I III 1.59 II 11.12.60 I 1.12.61 L1.6.62
MASON M E b6.10.40 A/I 10.12.60 Chingola 61–2
MASON Norman b1.5.28 PCMet 52 A/I NRP 19.5.55 Insp 14.4.61 Kitwe 63 Aust Commwlth P
MASSEY-TAYLOR H A/I 27.5.48 Lka
MASTERS D L b12.12.37 Cdt 1.12 A/I 12.12.57 MU 61–2
MATAKA Michael CPM b2.9.21 Const 11.7.41 A/I II 1.59 A/I I 1.4.60 ADC GovGen i/c Chilenje
    61 A/Supt 64 ZP CofP 65 IG, Dist Gov, Advsr to Ambassador Cairo, Angola Lectr PTS
    Lilayi 96 d1.8.00
MATHESON John F CPM 56 bYk 19.3.15 PalP 33 A/Supt Tanganyka 45 Supt NRP 15.1.49 S/
    Supt 2.9.56 CO MU rtd59
MATTHEWS Stephen R b7.6.38 A/I 23.4.60 Chingola 62–3
MAURICE K G b27.11.40 Cdt 18.2 A/I 27.11.60 Muf 62
MAWAWA A b19.3.19 Const 7.1.40 A/I II 1.1.61 Lka 62 A/I I 64
MAWSON J David b16.4.32 A/I 10.3.55 Insp 8.4.60 Kitwe 62–3
MAXWELL John W GM b22.3.37 A/I 9.2.61 Chingola 61–3
MAXWELL Wm P b11.11.29 PCAyrshire'51 A/I NRP 30.12.53 N Div 59
MBANGWETA P b1.7.27 Const 19.10.51 A/I II 1.4.62 Lstone A/Supt 64
MBEWE K b25.12.28 Const 10.3.49 II 1.4.62 Lka
MBEWE Robt M b16.3.22 Const 27.3.43 A/I III 1.59 II 11.12.60 I 1.12.61 PTS 60–2 A/Supt 64
    ZP Supt
MBUMWAE A N b27.7.16 Const 15.1.38 A/I II 1.1.61 Riverside 61–2
MEES David b18.9.40 Cdt 28.1 A/I 18.9.60 Insp 18.9.63 PC B'ham
MELLETT W/A/I Kitwe 56–L57
MELLOY John A b12.2.34 A/I 12.5.55 Insp 12.5.58 Muf 62
MELVIN Jas H b28.11.25 PCWRdg 47 A/I NRP 7.5.53 Insp 30.4.56 C/I 1.1.59 CID HQ 62
MERCER Chas Maurice 'Joe' b4.1.29 PalP'47 BermudaP'48 BSAP'50 A/I NRP 25.5.56 Ndola 58
MICHIE David b19.6.30 BSAP 49 A/I NRP 5.3.53 Insp 5.3.56 S/I 60 Mkushi 62
MIDDLETON-STEWART Alan b9.2.38 A/I 25.10.58 Insp 25.10.61 L27.4.62
MILES Norman J J b13.7.29 A/I 28.4.55 Insp 8.4.60 NW 62 C/I
MILLER James C b1.6.38 A/I 13.10.59 MU 62
MILLER Jeremy John Trevelyan bOngar 21.1.37 A/I 4.4.62 Monze 62
MILLER R J b5.1.44 Cdt 10.1.62 Lka
MILLETT Anthony G b24.4.37 A/I 17.1.59 rsgnd 9.5.61
MILLIGAN R S P b18.5.28 A/I 1.12.53 Insp 1.12.56 Kasama 62
MILLWARD Tom O b21.6.39 SA Cdt 19.3 A/I 21.6.59 Nchanga 60–1
MILNE Alan David RHSM(LS) b20.10.25 IA Capt A/I 48–rsgnd50 A/I 17.9.51 A/Supt 30.10.54
    sec'd Hendon instr'57 Supt 1.7.59 Ch Instr PTS 62 CO MU 64 Civ Instr Swazild P d4.2.00
MILNER Nicholas/Nigel? b18.10.36 A/I 7.1.61 MU 62 d94
MILNER W G Pay Sgt 1.4.31 NRR ACQMS 32 CQMS 1.1.34 RQMS 1.1.37
MILNS Barry E b28.11.40 Cdt 28.10 A/I 28.11.60 Bancroft 62
MINSHULL John L b24.3.36 A/I 19.6.59 L4.7.62 RhodesU to Bulawayo
MINTY Fred F b16.12.38 A/I 19.1.59 Lka Tfc rsgnd 8.62
MITCHELL Brian E b29.12.28 A/I 15.5.52 Insp 15.5.55 Ndola'57 Game Dept
MITCHELL Colin b22.10.34 A/I 16.5.59 Insp 16.5.62 rsgnd
MITCHELL John Henry b15.4.37 Gren Gds A/I 19.7.58 Insp 19.7.61 CDiv Tfc 10.2.62 SwazildP;
    Bar Capt ALS 72 Lt Col 83 rtd 93
MITCHELL Leslie b13.9.11 PalP 33 Const NRP 16.1.36 Supt 20.10.55 Ndola 12.5.62
MITCHELL Mary C W/A/I 12.6.59 Muf 59 Ndola L6.7.62
MITCHELL Owen L CPM 56 bFermanagh 08 edKg Wm's Cllge IoM Const NRP 21.1.32 A/
    Supt 45 Supt 50 S/Supt 12.53 CO Sthn 56 rtd 58
MITCHELL Peter W H b31.12.37 RN A/I 1.11.58 Kasama CID 62
MKANKAULWA David C b15.1.16 Const 6.3.43 A/I III 1.3.59 II 1.1.61 A/I I 1.12.61 Lstone
    A/Supt 64

MOFFATT J B B T/W/A/I 1.8.57 BH
MOLLER Paul J b24.3.35 A/I 19.2.59 Ndola MU 61
MOLLOY Gordon b9.12.32 A/I 14.7.55 C/I 1.4.62 A/Supt PTS 63 ZP
MONTGOMERY Const i/c Bwana Mkubwa 31 rsgnd 32
MONTEITH Robt Stewart b6.8.13 BSAP 38 A/I NRP 18.8.38 A/Supt 1.1.52 Supt 1.6.57 S/Supt
    25.12.60 CO Nthn 6.2.62
MONTILE D E b4.12.37 Probnr 1.2.57 Ndola
MOORE G M Jock b12.6.25 HLI RASC BSAP'49 A/I NRP 27.11.51 Insp 13.8.56 C/I FHQ 59
    rtd 61 SR
MORELY Barry K b12.9.35 A/I 10.6.56 Lstone'57
MORGAN E A CPM 63 bIOW 19.7.13 PalP 21.6.35 UgdaP 41 Insp NRP 14.5.46 A/Supt OC
    EDiv 53 Supt 2.9.56 S/Supt 1.7.60 CO PTS 62 L pdg rtd 31.7.63
MORGAN John R b25.2.19 SwazildP 46 A/I NRP 1.10.52 Insp 1.10.55 A/Supt 11.2.57 Kasama 63
MORLAND J R A/I 63?
MORRIS J E Wm bLpool 6.8.34 King's Regt LF A/I 25.10.58 Insp 25.10.61 BH CID 13.4.62 ZP
    rtd12.64 Guardian RExchnge, Minister URfmd Ch
MORRIS Peter S (Hank) b23.10.28 A/I 6.9.51 Insp 54 Game Dept 1.6.57 rtd 68
MORRISH Peter J b16.4.27 RN PCMet'48 A/I NRP 3.8.50 A/Supt 30.10.54 Lstone C 60 rtd62?
    London Bar
MORRISON Ian b28.1.35 A/I 17.12.59 Muf CID L12.62
MOSS John W P b5.6.28 A/I 26.6.52 Insp 26.6.55 A/Supt 1.12.60 Lka C 61 L16.4.62
MOULDS Arthur b4.1.31 A/I 1.5.57 A/BM mA Corbett rsgnd60
MOWATT Jock A/I 52 rsgnd54
MOY John P C b26.12.32 MalayaP 55–8 A/I NRP 19.6.59 L4.7.62
MUIR Gervase J R b16.9.32 RAF A/I 14.7.55 Insp 14.7.58 SO FHQ 64 Civ WMerciaP
MUIR John D b23.4.29 PCBhm 52 A/I NRP 7.1.54 A/Supt 16.8.61 Luapula SB 62 i/c SB Seych-
    elles 65–8 Estate Agent Salisby SR
MUKAMBA A/I BHC 63
MUKANANI Const A/I Riverside 63
MULCAHY R J Const dischge 7.36
MULELE L Z Fred b1.7.22 Const 1.6.44 A/I III 59 II 11.12.60 A/I I 1.12.61 Chingola 62
    Mkushi 63
MULENGA P O b15.9.19 Const 1.6.43 A/I III 59 II 1.1.61 Mindolo C/I 64
MULLIGAN P Howard b24.6.38 A/I 17.1.59 Insp 17.1.62 L6.2.62
MULLIGAN Andrew A/I MU L62
MULLINS J Anthony MBE(1.1.97) QPM(1.1.94) CPM b28.4.42 Cdt 4.4 A/I 28.4.62 BH Raylton
    63 HKP 64 CSP RHKP ACP i/c NT Sth
MULROONEY Derek P b9.4.39 A/I 28.10.60 Kasama 62
MUMBA J b27.6.20 Const 21.4.44 A/I II 1.4.62 A/I I 64
MUNROE-FAURE Roger b5.10.39 A/I 18.5.61 Chingola C left 22.5.63
MUPOPERI A/I Ndola C 63
MURCH Philip F b6.8.21 MalayaP 25.9.48 KenyaP 54 Supt NRP 28.5.59 S/Supt ᵛ   Div
    62 Dubai
MURPHY D J b26.9.40 A/I 11.1.62 Ndola rsgnd1.64
MURPHY Pat J E b8.4.39 A/I 7.1.61 BH 62 Bermuda P
MURPHY Richard S b31.8.39 PC L'pool57 A/I NRP 18.5.61 MU 61–ˀ
MURRAY Chris A/I 58
MURRAY Ian S b12.9.42 Cdt 10.1 A/I 12.9.62 Kitwe 63
MURRAY John M P bLka 22.4.40 Cdt 8.4.58 A/I 22.4.60 Insᶜ
MUSKET Robt A/I 1954
MUSOLE Anderson b15.12.20 Const 29.8.45 A/I II 1.5ᶜ
MUSONDA C J b23.3.20 Const 12.12.41 A/I III 59
MUYUPI J R b11.10.39 Tech Asst Loc Govt & Sˀ
MWAFULILWA A H K CPM 55 b1.7.13 Coᵣ
MWALA M b1.7.28 Const 7.11.51 A/I II ¹

MWALILINO P S K CPM 59 b30.3.12 Const 2.9.36 A/I III 1.59 II 11.12.60 I 11.12.60 L 1.7.62
MWANAKOMBO L b14.8.24 Const 18.2.43 A/I II 11.12.60 A/I I 1.12.61 Solwezi 63
MWANZA Alfred P b5.8.39 A/I 7.4.62 LkaC 62
MWANZA M b9.9.25 Const 30.12.47 A/I II 11.12.60 Muf 62
MWANZA N b9.11.24 Const 1.10.44 A/I II 1.1.61 Muf rtd62
MWANZA S P b1.7.26 Const 7.6.44 A/I III 59 A/I 11 1.4.60 A/I I 1.11.60 FJ 11.61–2
MWIKISA L W A/I 63
MYHAN Frank J b10.3.31 PCMet 51 A/I 16.5.53 Insp 16.5.56 S/I PP Muf 62 d.87
MYLOD Michael OBE 93 b15.8.37 RN A/I 29.11.57 Insp 13.4.62 PP Ndola 63 ACC Bristol DCC
    Hants 88–DCP Bermuda 95–6

NAISMITH A McL b10.12.37 A/I 15.10.59 Muf 61–2
NAMALONGO B M b1.7.33 Const 19.11.51 Sgt PTS 57 A/I II 1.4.62
NAYLING John T b7.8.30 BSAP'50 A/I NRP 9.4.53 Insp 9.4.56 Choma 57–8
NDHLEW Timothy Augustine CPM 62 bKanchombi 23.9.20 Const 13.11.42 A/I III 59 II 1.4.60
    I 1.11.60 D/I 62 A/Supt 64
NEAL Martin C A/I Ndola 60
NEAL Sidney Albert CPM 55 b4.8.14 PalP 37 A/I NRP 5.12.38 Supt 1.1.54 S/Supt 1.5.58 ACP
    12.62
NEATE Richard C H B30.7.36 A/I 17.12.59 Muf 60–1
NEEDHAM Michael b21.3.42 A/I 8.8.62 Chingola 64 West Scy Muf 68
NELMES L b22.9.35 PCGlam 52 A/I NRP 1.11.58 Insp 1.11.61 D/I Kitwe 62
NELSON H H P b1.10.25 NRG1.1.51 A/I 1.4.52 Imm sec'd Fed 1.4.57
NESBITT R A/I 63 Chingola 64 PCMet
NESS Alex b9.1.26 BSAP 46 PC Met 48 Malaya P 50 A/I NRP 24.2.54 A/Supt 12.4.61 Ndola 62
    Qnsld P d Brisbane 21.5.95
NESS Peter b9.11.32 PC Fife 57 A/I NRP 3.7.58 Insp 3.7.61 BH CID 62 RSSPC Kirkaldy
NETA Samuel CPM 59 b.Kalabo 07 Pte 5.38 CID 40 Sgt 46 S–Maj 51 Sub/Insp 52 D/A/I III
    59 II 11.12.60 Lshya Rtd61
NEVETT H Newton b31.8.29 PCLancs 51 A/I NRP 12.8.53 Insp 12.8.56 A/Supt 1.4.62 Chingola
    64 d92
NEWBY J E A/I 3.7.47
NEWMAN A John b3.10.35 A/I 17.12.59 Lstone 62
NEWTON Bernard Francis b30.7.30 A/I 12.5.55 Insp 15.10.60 Roan 63 Pers Mercedes Benz SA
    rtd90 dELndn 2.9.96
NEWTON P R b8.11.43 Cdt 2.5.62 BH
NGONA J b21.6.21 Const 26.10.40 A/I I 1.12.61 BH Mine 62
NGONA J b1.7.34 Const 29.3.52 Sub Insp 6.6.61 A/I 64
NGULUWE F b1.7.28 Const 10.5.52 Sub Insp 16.10.60 A/I i/c Prospect 11.63
NICHOL Jack J b26.4.35 RUC 53 A/I NRP 19.7.57 mW/A/I Cassell 60 Insp 14.4.61 RTO Muf
    63 PC Grampian? Aust NTP 78
NICHOLAS Ian A b5.5.29 A/I 22.2.51 Insp 22.2.54 Lab Dept 1.3.58 Lka 62 Pers Ford UK 64
    Pers CDC
NISSEN Anthony T b27.9.36 s/o N T A/I 1.9.58 Lka L5.4.62
NISSEN Norris Theodore CPM 52 bEdinburgh 24.4.00 HLI RE BSAP 21–Const NRP 29.8.24–
    26.5.27 Const NRP 28.9.28 A/I 1.4.30 Insp FJ 37 C/I 1.1.38 BH'50 A/Supt rtd f/o A T
NKUNIKA S M H CPM 62 b.Mzimba Ny 4.2.12 NRP 17.11.38 Sgt 45 S/M 47 Sub Insp 2.56
    A/I III 59 II 11.12.60 rtd 64
    ¬S Ernest Robt b22.3.34 A/I 8.12.55 Wdlds 58 Business Maz Turnoff until 69
        ¬ Kenneth L b11.7.21 NRG1.11.46 A/I 23.5.51 Imm sec'd Fed Svce 1.4.57 d89 SA
            ¬n b22.4.23 PCMet 47 A/I NRP 28.2.52 S/I 1.3.57 C/I 1.1.59 Muf Tfc 59

            ¬P 38 Malaya P 48 A/Supt NRP SO PTS 29.6.60 Contract left 63
            ¬ 1.10.59 A/I 3.1.61 rsgnd 30.5.62
            ¬ 62 ZP Lka CID 66 DCI 68 rtd 87

NORTON Cyril Frank CPM 56 b22.4.12 Cdt MN Tpr BSAP 36 A/I NRP 4.8.38 Supt 1.7.55 S/Supt 2.2.59 Ndola 62

NSAKANYA Const A/I Bwacha 63

NUGENT Nick A/I 48 CID Muf 50

NYATI Angelo b24.12.29 Const 2.3.51 Sub/Insp CID HQ 57–8 A/I 111 59 II 11.12.60 A/I I 1.12.61 A/Supt 64 ZP Supt DSO Lka 65 DCP d.RTA 5.69

NYRENDA E T b15.7.20 Const29.12.48 A/I II 1.1.61 Lka 62

NYRENDA W b4.4.18 Const 16.10.42 A/I III 59 Muf II 11.12.60 Luapula 62 A/I I 64

O'BRIEN M L b19.1.44 Cdt 2.5.62 A/I 19.1.64

OCKWELL Robt A b11.11.18 PC City 39–41 A/I NRP 24.5.46 A/Supt 1.1.53 Supt 1.6.59 S/Supt C Div 63

O'CONNELL John 2lt ACC A/I 21.9.57 Resigned 9.60

O'DELL John Fredk 'Ginger' b31.1.39 Hants SomLI 56 A/I 15.10.59 Insp 15.10.62 BH ZP 64–SA 72 Coventry Climax Kalmar 80–d10.95

OLD Brian L b25.2.35 A/I 24.10.57 Insp 13.4.62 Muf Mine 63

OLDACRE Lionel W b9.6.37 A/I 5.10.59 Lka rsgnd 63 Natal Sugar growing

OLDBURY Lionel G Cdt 8.4.58 A/I 5.10.60 A'corn 62

OLDHAM Geo W b25.8.38 A/I 17.4.60 MU 62

O'LEARY Bernard Geo CPM 62 bNaini Tal India 12.2.13 ed Kgs Cllge Londn BSAP 36 A/I NRP 2.5.38 A/Supt 50 Supt 4.1.53 S/Supt 1.7.59 ZP 64 ACP rtd5.67 dSalisby SR

OLIVE Alan W b15.3.38 A/I 11.10.59 Lka 61–2

OLIVE Robt J b27.9.38 A/I 23.4.60 L4.63 rsgnd

OLIVER David I CPM 60 b10.4.22 KOYLI PalP 45 A/I NRP 3.8.50 C/I 1.3.55 A/Supt 64

OLIVER I Neville b10.7.36 KOYLI A/I 11.7.57 Insp 13.4.62 Tchr

OLPIN Peter M b23.2.31 A/I 2.7.53 Insp 12.8.58 Lve 63

O'MAHONEY P T A/I 63?

O'NEILL A A b21.3.39 A/I 24.9.60 Ndola C 61–2

O'REILLY J J Const to Cordon 1.2.29

ORMROD J b3.1.35 A/I 26.8.60 Kitwe 61–2 rsgnd

ORR Robert J RUC A/I 21.9.57 Kalulushi 59

ORR Robert James b26.3.36 RUC 57 A/I NRP 7.1.61 d.11.11.61

OSMOND-JONES Edward J b2.10.38 A/I 25.10.58 Insp 25.10.61 Kafue 63

OSTOCKE H E T b24.8.22 Raj Rif A/I 4.9.47 S/I 15.10.54 i/c Nchanga 55 A/Supt Lka R 59

OTTON Gerry T A/I 54?

OWEN John V b13.11.30 PCLeics Cty 51 A/I NRP 4.7.55 Insp 5.7.58 FR 62

PAGE Harry A/I Kitwe 59 Det to Ny P 60

PALMER E Gerald b8.12.36 A/I 3.7.58 Lstone 60 OC Linda Rgd 62

PALMER Stuart b6.4.32 RASC Animal Tpt A/I 7.9.58 Tsetse Cntrl Sprvsr 1.10.59 Kawambwa 21.4.62

PAMPHILON Edward J b13.9.30 PC Met 52 A/I 21.4.53 Insp 21.4.56 S/I Wusikili 62 Chingola 64 dSA 4.7.83

PARISH David R b31.5.34 A/I 12.5.55 Insp 17.4.59 L15.12.61 C/I

PARKER Robt Norris G b7.1.30 A/I 26.6.52 Insp 26.6.55 S/I L15.3.62 C/I

PARKIN Ida M E SRN W/A/I 22.5.60 BHC 61 CID 62

PARKMAN D John b24.9.33 A/I 9.6.55 Chingola 56–7

PARNABY Kenneth T b15.3.38 A/I 11.4.58 Kafue 62 rsgnd

PARNABY M B b19.3.32 BSAP 54 A/I 28.10.60 BH 62

PARNELL F A A/I 51

PATON M A/I Ndola 39

PATTEN D B M Const Muf 35 resigned 38

PATTERSON George D 'Paddy' CPM 61 b21.10.25 PalP 16.7.45 A/I NRP 9.12.48 D/I 6.52 A/Supt 1.1.53 Ag Supt 28.3.53 Supt 1.7.58 FHQ 14.8.62 S/Supt ZP ACP Pers Courtaulds NI SA

PATTON H RUC MalayaP A/I NRP Lka BH 54 Insp BH 57 rsgnd 5.57
PATTINSON R Wm b6.10.39 Cdt 6.8 A/I 6.10.59 Sigs 61 L21.6.62
PATTULO Jock A/I 51 Lka Chirundu 52 Kitwe 53
PAUTZ Paul? Philip A/I Lka 52 SA d20.1.99
PAUTZ R N 15.9.47
PAYNE W A A/I 50
PEACOCK Stuart C b13.3.40 Cdt 8.1.59 A/I 13.3.60 Kitwe Tfc rsgnd 22.6.61 Ben Line, Shipping HK
PEAKE M W/A/I 8.8.62
PEARCE C W b4.9.36 A/I 14.2.57 Chingola
PEARCE Kenneth A/I 14.5.46 Lshya 46–7 to mng k Muf Mne
PEARCE R P Clyde b21.11.31 PC Cornwall 52 A/I 24.3.55 Insp 8.4.60 Ndola 62
PEARCE W A/I Lshya 54? Roan.58
PEARSON Frank Harding b30.8.36 2Lt Kgs Own A/I 3.7.58 Insp 3.7.61 Lka CID 3.2.62 rtd'64
PEARSON Nigel E b3.10.36 RSx A/I 14.2.57 MU 62 West Scy Ndola 68
PEARSON W/A/I BH 57
PEDLEY Terence W b2.2.36 PC Bmghm 56 A/I 4.8.60 Ndola CID 62
PELLATT R A/I Ndola 61
PELLY Mark N W b23.2.41 A/I 20.4.61 Lka 61 MU 62 HKP 64 SSupt CSO Admn rtd 91 Perth WA d24.12.96
PENNOCK J Keith b31.8.39 A/I 24.9.60 Ndola Tfc 63
PEPLOE H R A/I 46
PERKINS Col Harold B OBE b3.12.05 MN Engrg PragueU, Textile Fcty Poland SIS Brit Mil Msn Poland 15.8.39 i/c SOE ops Poland, Czchoslovakia, Hungary, Rome Stn, Cyprus, i/c Ops Balkans 49–50 ACP(SD) 12.3.59 L15.3.62
PERKINS J C b14.12.41 Cdt 17.11.60 Lstone A/I 14.12.61 Bancroft 62 rsgnd
PETTS Anthony W b11.3.38 A/I 21.5.60 Luwingu 62 i/c Airport Scy Brunei 80
PHAROAH G A 'Bill' A/I 1946 Luanshya Rsgd 49 d.90
PHELPS John F H b19.11.39 A/I 6.8.60 Lka 62 Imm Salisby SR 82
PHILLIPSON James b10.12.36 A/I 10.2.60 Kitwe 62
PHILPOTT Bim F D b2.7.42 Cdt 26.1.61 A/I 2.7.62 Chingola 62
PHILPOTT Horace Bartlett 'Mike' CPM 59 bBwayo 25.8.15 BSAP35 A/I NRP 2.7.38 A/Supt 51 Supt 18.6.56 S/Supt 1.7.59 Ndola Dist 10.62–ZP–rtd65 dSouthbroom Natal 5.10.97
PHILPOTT R Const 13.10.26 A/I by 14.4.28
PHINN Eric J Const 17.3.31 AgA/I 33 A/Supt 46 Supt 48
PHIPPS Geoffrey L b5.5.29 A/I 25.9.52 D/I 13.8.56 S/I Lstone 62 L63
PHIRI D J b7.7.24 Const 3.10.46 A/I II 1.1.61 I 1.12.61 Muf 62
PHIRI Mathew M KPM(G) 48 CPM 64 b15.10.16 D155 25.11.41 DSgt 48 A/I II 1.4.62 Roan CID 1.6.62 A/I I 63
PHIRI P b1.7.34 Const 5.8.53 A/I II 1.4.62 Ndola
PICKUP Andrew CPM 45, BSAP 20 Const NRP 7.7.25 A/Supt 3.10.30 Supt 1.12.30 DCP Aden 40 Lt Col ADInt & Sy NR 2.9.42–Supt NRP 15.8.45 rtd 16.5.46
PICKUP Jack b03 b/o A; BSAP'25 Const NRP 2.9.27 A/I 1.5.30–L1.5.33 PalP'33 A/Supt Nyasald P'40 Eritrea'41 Nyasald P'42 Singapore P'47 rtd'54 Seychelles, Zimbabwe d'95
PIGGOTT R B b4.11.30 PCKent A/I NRP 9.12.54 Kitwe 57 Judcl Dept
PINNEY Keith L b30.5.36 A/I 11.7.57 Kitwe to Lshya 58 Prison Soc UK d3.2.01
PIPE A H Const Lshya 35
PIPER M A/I Info Dept 1.57
PITCHFORD Paddy A/I Lstone 53 RSO L54 Lshya
PITMAN Gary A (Bancroft-P) b7.11.35 2Lt Dorset A/I 6.6.57 Insp 6.6.60 Lka 62–Rtd 10.64 RAF WCdr
PITT Eric Ronald 'Malikopo' b27.1.34 PCMet 54 A/I 11.3.56 Insp 15.10.60 OC Kafue 61–10.62
PLATT Ed A/I FP FHQ Fm Mgr A'corn 56
PLAYER Wm Lawless Dane b23.6.34 ed Harrow RASC 52 Cllge of Aeronautical & Automobile Engrg Chelsea Hons A/I NRP 21.5.60 Chingola 60–2 murdered Zimbabwe 2.99

PLIMMER B H A/I 51
POLLARD I A/I dischge 28.3.38
POLLARD Mark A/I Muf Mine 5
POLLITT Joseph H Cdt 1.7.57 A/I 26.6.59 Kansenji CID 62
POLLOCK W Duncan L b19.9.38 A/I 13.12.58 Insp 13.12.61 Lka Pros 15.7.62
POOLE John b2.8.36 PC Oxfd Cty 56 A/I 10.12.60 Lka Tfc 62
POOLE Malcolm A/I 62 Kitwe CID 63
POPE Henry Ross b24.6.29 A/I 20.5.53 Lstone Polio SDiv Insp 58 Lstone Rly, Dist Insp 59 Accts
    Clk FHQ 13.1.60–64 d10.4.01 SA
PORTER John MM b26.9.19 A/I 19.7.51 Armr AQM 23.8.54 L4.6.62
POTTER E Const 8.9.30 L14.4.33
POTTER Maurice J b8.10.36 A/I 29.11.57 Insp 29.11.60 Monze 62
POTTINGER K A/I.50
POVEY Reuben D b23.2.36 A/I 24.10.56 Insp 24.10.59 Lka62
POWELL Brian D b16.1.29 PalP 47 NRP 29.7.48 A/I Muf 16.1.49 Insp 53 S/I 1.2.57 A/Supt
    14.3.58 Lka 62 Supt
POWELL John L A b21.12.29 NRG20.9.48 A/I 1.4.52 Imm Muf Sec'd Fed Svce 1.4.57
POWER John Richard Ormond b23.1.37 A/I 10.1.58 Insp 10.1.61 Ndola Tfc 62–3 PNGP OC MU
    SA 6.69 SADF Cmdt
PRATT Michael J O b15.8.40 A/I 8.1.61 Mkushi 62 m.d/o ACP Kalomo rsgnd CARS Lka 63
PRATT P K b25.1.40 Cdt 11.10.59 A/I 25.1.60 Ndola 61
PREECE Peter D A/I Chingola 4.51 D/A/I 52
PRENTICE Wm S b22.4.19 A/I 16.10.47 L pdg rtd 1.8.57 d.90
PRICE David R b2.5.31 PCMet 52 A/I 6.1.55 Insp 8.4.60 S/I Muf Pros 62
PRIEST H W Const T&S 1.4.27 Customs 14.12.27 Cox Commssn 46?
PRIOR John A/I Ndola 53 Rtd NRPR Ndola 60
PRIOR W/A/I Chingola 56 left 57
PRITCHARD Raymond H b21.6.28 A/I 22.6.50 Insp 8.8.55 C/I 1.4.62 BH 62 A/Supt
PROTHEROE Michael A/I 58 Kalomo rsgnd60 Fmg Kalomo Exec Liberty Life CT
PROUST Roy E A/I Nkana 40 Insp 1.2.44 A/Supt 28.2.48 Supt to Br Somalild P
PULFORD Arthur W F S b6.3.36 A/I 4.4.62 Lka C rsgnd
PURNELL David J b2.6.40 A/I 10.12.60 Chingola C 61–2
PYRAH Gordon L b21.4.39 NRG 19.7 A/I 9.8.62 ZP MU

RADEMEYER Bernardus Rens b11.11.39 A/I 23.6.60 Lka 61–2
RAMSAY C E Const 18.6.26–30.4.27
RANDELL Roy Jas QPM 60 CPM 53 b14.7.04 articled to Svyr Sandringhm R Estate 23 Rubber
    Pltng Malaya 26 Malay States V Hankow 27 USA UK 30 Const NRP 4.2.32 A/Supt 47
    Supt 53 S/Supt 1.7.54 Lka rtd 3.60 Norfolk
RANDLE J W R b12.2.32 A/I 11.3.56 Insp 8.4.60 Muf Dist 63
RANKIN D A/I Chingola 56
RATCLIFFE Keith CPM bYks 6.5.44 Cdt 8.8.62 Lka A/I 6.5.64 HKP ADist Cmd Adm Central
RAUBENHEIMER Edwd G b.Ft Vic 23.11.00 Const NRP 3.9.26 Sgt Mil Branch 11.28 S&T Dept
    12.1.38 Acct Gen's Dept Rtd to SA d'87
RAY Gerald E b15.5.41 Cdt 2.11.59 A/I 15.5.61 BHC 61–2
READ Robt D Const 13.8.31 D/I 39 to PA?
READ Robt Jeffrey CPM 57 bTwickenhm 11.7.15 PCMet 34 BSAP 38 A/I NRP 9.7.39 A/Supt
    50 Supt 4.7.53 S/Supt 1.7.57 ACP rtd 10.64 d Somerset West SA 11.6.98
REECE P A/I .52 mines 53
REED I A/I Kitwe 62
REED Leonard W H b14.11.23 PC S'ton 47 A/I 6.3.52 S/I 11.4.57 C/I L27.3 A/Supt 1.4.62
REES Geoffrey W L BSAP'23 Const NRP 29.6.28 agA/I i/c Cordon 8.1.30 A/I 1.1.31 Insp i/c
    Muf'35–7, C/I i/c Lka rtd ill–health 21.11.46, Desk Offr SB HQ Lusaka d.10.1.64
REES M N b23.12.39 A/I 7.1.61 BH 62
REID C A A/I 49

REID Douglas J A b30.11.29 PC Meldrum Angus'50 A/I 11.11.54 D/I Riverside CID 60 S/I Kitwe CID 30.12.61–2

REID Ian J b4.11.40 Cdt 2.11.59 A/I 4.11.60 Kitwe 62 2LtUS Army awarded Silver Star Vice President Morgan Stanley d World Trade Centre 11.9.01

REID J C Const 10.6.27–29

REID L A F b7.4.07 PCMet 27 A/Supt NRP 1.10.59 Supt 1.7.60 L23.5.62 rtd 62

REITH E Athol b3.1.37 A/I 17.12.59 FJ 62

RENS Dorothy Mrs A W W/A/I 2.2.59 Chingola 61

RESCORLA Richd b27.5.39 PCMet 60 A/I 20.4.61 Kitwe rsgnd 62 2 Lt US Army awarded Silver Star Vice President Morgan Stanley d. World Trade Centre 11.9.01

REVILL John D b26.9.36 Ches Regt A/I 2.5.62 FJ 63 PNGP

REYNOLDS Adrian Michael Noel bBraintree 19.12.32 BSAP 52–5 RMP 2Lt A/I 7.9.58 Insp 7.9.61 ZP rtd 66 Rgnl Mngr Rd Tpt Trg Bd

REYNOLDS F Martin b21.3.34 A/I 29.11.57 Insp 29.11.60 Mpika 62 SADF Col

RHODES Arnold W CPM 64 SBStJ 59 b22.8.09 PC Bghm 32 A/Supt NRP 13.11.51 Supt 1.7.56 S/Supt 21.3.60

RICHARDSON Vivian A b9.6.26 A/I 19.3.51 Imm Muf 54 sec'd Fed 1.4.57 L5.57

RICE A/I 10.8.55

RICHES R John b28.7.41 Cdt 1.10.59 A/I 28.7.61 Kansenji rgd RN

RIDING M Louise WPCLancs 53 W/A/I NRP 23.4.59 rsgnd 21.6.61

RIGBY Neil H b28.9.35 A/I 7.1.61 Lshya Tfc 63

RILEY Peter E b27.10.36 PCMet 58 A/I 9.3.61 Lka C 63

RITTER M J de K b6.5.34 SAP 53 A/I NRP 16.3.59 Insp 13.4.62 Dogs PTS 63

ROBBINS Terence A b20.3.37 RM A/I 3.7.58 Lka 7.3.62 SwazildP

ROBERTS C H Const 31–2

ROBERTS Fredk Alexdr CPM 53 SBStJ 54 b21.6.14 BSAP 35–7 A/I NRP 29.6.38 S/Supt 3.9.56 ACP(A) 29.12.59 SACP 12.62

ROBERTS J W/A/I Lka Tfc 63

ROBERTS John 2lt Devon A/I 10.57 BHC 1st Mercenary Congo 60

ROBERTS Kenneth b5.2.27 Offr MN A/I 9.11.54 MU'58–61 Offr MN d.Cancer Cape Town 12.69

ROBERTS R V Const Mil 20.11.28 ORC Sgt rtd 33

ROBERTSHAW Barbara WPC WRdg 56 W/A/I NRP 28.1.60 W/Insp 28.1.63

ROBERTSON James b9.9.29 PC Bhm 49 A/I 11.11.54 Rdg Instr PTS'57 Insp 8.4.60 S/I PTS 62

ROBERTSON John E BSAP A/I 55 Lstone CID HQ

ROBERTSON R G b6.5.19 KenyaP 59 C/I NRP 9.8.62 arr Lka 24.8

ROBINSON Brian E b10.4.37 A/I 25.10.58 Roan 60–1

ROBINSON Chas Alex bEd 25.6.40 A/I 20.4.61 Lka kRTA BH 11.12.61

ROBINSON Daniel G CPM b25.2.38 A/I 20.5.60 Ndola CID 62 RHKP SSP 79 rtd94

ROBINSON Elsie Scott W/A/I Lshya Tfc 63

ROBINSON Ian A/I Lka C 58 Tfc 59 Kabwata rsgnd Aust

ROBINSON John L b9.3.37 A/I 26.9.60 MU 61–rsgnd 9.63 RhodesU 2.64 Civ Trg Offr ZP PTS 2.68 RAF WCdr rtd 89 Edn Offr KentCC 90

ROBINSON Laurence Hector b23.3.98 War Svce 5.15–3.19 BSAP 11.6.19–Const NRP 15.9.24 3/ D/Sgt 1.4.26 D/A/I Lka 18.4.28

ROBINSON R Wm b28.11.39 PC Nthhmbld A/I 9.3.61 Instr PTS rsgnd 63 Instr Otwd Bd N Wales

ROBSON D A/I Monze CID 58

ROBSON Michael G b2.10.31 A/I 28.4.55 Insp 28.4.58 S/I AgC/I Lka 8.6.62 C/I

ROEBUCK Roy A/I Chingola 63–4

ROEDER V G 'Bert' b25.6.38 A/I 12.1.60 Ndola C rsgnd 63

ROETS Jo A/I 59 Ft J 13.10.59

ROGERS A E b2.6.36 A/I 18.5.61 MU 62

ROGERS J C Bryan b17.2.41 Cdt 17.8.60 A/I 17.2.61 Chingola 61–L63

ROGERS Guy A/I 61 Ndola

ROGERS Pat b14.1.35 Home Svce 22.11.51 A/I 14.2.57 MU 62
ROGERS Peter G b25.8.25 A/I 21.7.49 CIDHQ D/I 12.53 S/I 4.8.57 A/Supt 1.1.58 DSBO
    Lstone L20.7.62
ROSE David St John A/I Lka 52 Chirundu 52
ROSE Ken A/I Kitwe left 57
ROSEGOLD Christopher b14.12.35 RN A/I 24.10.57 Insp 13.4.62 Namwala 63 Joburg
ROSS M David R M b28.1.43s/o M Cdt 1.10.61 A/I 28.1.63 k.RTA63
ROSS Ian C b7.7.35 A/I 6.6.57 Insp 29.9.61 Lstone 62
ROSS John W E CPM 58 bMaritzburg 22.3.11 BSAP 31 Const NRP 5.12.35 A/Supt 1.1.50 Supt
    1.1.53 S/Supt Sthrn 6.58 rtd3.61 d87
ROSS Michael b24.4.18 to SR RRR KRRC A/I 19.2.46 Civ Clk FHQ 14.5.53 Offce Supt 1.7.59–62
ROSS-CLUNIES R C b'05 ed SA & Westmnstr 2Lt NRP 31.1.31 NRR Lt 12.7.33 Cyprus P 1st
    Cl Local Supt 17.7.34
ROTHERY Joseph A/I 11.7.57 Muf Mine rsgnd 60 PCManch
ROUNDTREE R J A b10.6.38 RUC 59 A/I NRP 8.8.62
ROUTLEDGE D Brian b6.1.34 A/I 10.3.55 Kitwe CID 59
ROWAN J Denis b29.7.23 A/I 26.2.48 A/Supt 27.5.54 Supt 1.7.59 Lka 62 S/Supt
ROWBOTTOM Ron A/I Muf 54 Serenje 54 Kitwe rsgnd2.56 Kitwe
ROWE G E b14.8.38 A/I 13.12.58 BH 21.7.62
ROWLAND C W b6.1.32 A/I 3.5.55 Insp 17.4.59 Choma 1.8.62 C/I
ROWLAND J b13.9.40 RUC 59 A/I 9.2.61 Choma PTS 62
RUDGE V T R b12.5.25 RN Malaya P 48–51 PCMet 53 A/I NRP 30.12.54 Insp 14.4.61 S/I RTO
    Kitwe 11.3.62
RUFUS Angus H E b16.3.40 A/I 27.10.60 Lka CID 63
RUGMAN Nigel M A Cdt Chilanga 62 A/I 63
RULE Francis A/I 28.8.47
RUNDLE Henry Leonard CPM 50 b5.12.16 BSAP 34 A/I NRP 7.3.38 A/Supt 47 S/Supt 1.7.54
    Fed Int Bureau 15.10.57
RUSHBROOKE W Michael b10.5.37 A/I 3.7.58 Insp 3.7.61 Mongu 62
RUSSELL G Joseph b16.3.35 RUC'54 A/I 11.3.56 Insp 14.4.61 Kitwe CID 61–2 Chingola 64
RUSSELL Ian J S b13.10.33 A/I 11.3.56 FR'60
RUSSELL Paul OBE 96 ZP C/I Para Mil 68–6.69 Anti Corruptn Commr Zambia
RYAN Patrick b20.11.34 Garda Siochana 55 A/I NRP 24.10.57 Insp 24.10.60 Pros Lka 25.5.61–2
RYNO Vera D A WPC Hants 51 W/A/I NRP 23.4.59 rsgnd 12.5.62

SADOKI Donald D/Const Ft J 62 A/I Solwezi 63 Hendon 63
SADLER John C b12.6.34 A/I 10.3.55 Insp 17.4.59 CIDHQ 60–2
SAFFIN Peter Fredk b10.5.34 CdtMet RMP PCMet 56 A/I NRP 25.10.58 Insp 25.10.61 ZP A/
    Supt Lka C 65 Scy Salisby Airpt
SANDCRAFT David J b16.8.33 PC Ptsmth Cty 57 A/I NRP 18.7.57 Insp 14.4.61 Dist Insp Maz
    61–2
SANDERS M A A/I 63
SANDILANDS G V b4.10.24 A/I 15.6.50 Insp 10.8.54 A/Supt 1.7.57 AgSupt sec'd Fed Int
    Bureau 62
SANDUKYA B K b11.11.24 Const 19.11.47 A/I III 59 II 1.1.61 PTS 62
SASHILA M b20.8.22 Const 22.1.48 A/I III 59 II 1.1.61 FR 62
SAUL Eric BSAP A/I NRP 58 Matero BSAP Insp?
SAUNDERS Jack E T b22.11.27 A/I 13.8.53 Insp 26.8.57 S/I Muf CID 61–2 West Scy Kitwe 68
    MD Securicor Malaga 79
SAWTELL R F b20.3.33 BSAP'52 A/I NRP 1.7.55 resigned 1.7.57
SCARD L H D Const 16.5.29 A/I 1.7.31 Luanshya 33
SCHEEPERS Marjory Mrs K F NRG10.5.54 T/W/A/I 1.7.55 Ndola IB L9.5.57
SCHIERHOUT P A M b18.11.35 BSAP 56 A/I NRP 7.1.61 Ndola 62
SCHNEEMANN Harry bTanganyika 31.5.38 WelchR A/I 14.2.59 Insp 14.2.62 Lka 24.8.62

SCHOFIELD A Victor b11.5.35 A/I 13.8.55 Insp 9.10.59 D/C/I CIO Lshya 63 RAF P&SS Wg Cdr rtd 90
SCHULTZ E F Const 6.1.28 Mil Depot 31.3.28 Sgt to ?Dept 21.11.28
SCOTT Donald B b26.3.33 PC Glasgow 54 A/I NRP 13.12.58 Insp 13.12.61 Ndola 21.8.62
SCOTT P C b5.10.41 A/I 28.2.62 Lstone
SCOTT-KNIGHT Hamish G b30.4.28 PalP 46–8 A/I NRP 20.5.53 Insp 20.5.56 C/I 1.12.60 Lka 62 USA
SCOTT-TAYLOR Derek A/I 53 Luanshya 55 Nakonde 55–rsgnd 11.56
SCULLY Patrick Francis Joseph BSAP 12.4.38 A/I NRP 12.9.38
SEAL B W WPC Glam 59 W/A/I NRP 27.9.60 Muf 62
SEARLE Victor Albt Wm b11.5.27 PC Met 48 A/I NRP 19.5.52 Insp 19.5.55 C/I 1.3.60 L10.4.62
SEED Jack Baron b5.9.17 BSAP 4.38 A/I NRP 12.9.38 A/Supt 52 Supt 26.7.56 S/Supt 1.7.60 CO Sthn 62
SEMPLE J K b16.9.26 A/I 15.2.54 Imm Offr sec'd Fed 1.4.57
SETTERFIELD Peter H b9.8.27 A/I 9.11.50 Insp 9.11.53 A/Supt 12.1.59 CIO Ndola 62 Legal Executive Brighton
SEWARD J L A b21.7.09 A/I 30.7.36 Forestry Dept 15.6.38 Mongu 62
SHACKLETON Alec b18.1.30 A/I 13.1.55 Insp 13.1.58 S/I i/c Kawambwa 62 Salisby SR
SHAMBONO D F b1.1.16 Const 22.2.42 A/I III 59 II 1.1.61 Lstone 23.7.62 rtd64
SHANKS S M b7.9.21 PCGlasgow 41 MalayaP 50 A/Supt NRP 29.6.60 WDiv 62
SHARP Geo A/I Sept 58 Lka resigned 9.60
SHARP Vaughan b.Maritzburg 22.1.03 SAP 24 A/I NRP CID HQ 18.11.55 Insp 9.7.56 S/I rtd 12.5.62
SHARROD Ed H b9.3.36 A/I 28.10.60 Chirundu 63 Met Supt rtd96
SHAW John Wm b.Ft J 9.10.23 ed Chaplin HS Gwelo 51 Rhod Sqn RAF Italy A/I NRP 9.2.46 A/Supt 30.10.54 Supt 1.7.59 Lshya 62 S/Supt rtd Umtali FLt RRAF ELondon SA d29.9.98
SHAW Trevor b29.1.31 A/I 15.9.54 Insp 9.10.59 S/I PTS 60–2 C/I
SHAW Mrs T T/W/I 13.8.62 PTS
SHEAHAN Erroll W b13.11.38 A/I 18.4.61 Lshya 61–2
SHEARD John R b22.9.41 Cdt 4.5.59 A/I 22.9.61 L7.5.62
SHELLEY David R b25.4.33 A/I 11.7.57 Insp 11.7.60 Mongu 62
SHEPPARD Gordon A b18.8.40 A/I 7.1.61 Chingola C 62
SHIMULOPWE P b23.2.21 Const 1.11.41 A/I III 59 II 1.1.61 Chinsali 64
SHORT Frank A/I 62 Swazi P HKP 68 Bophuthatswana P SAP 95 CofP Solomons 97
SHORT Fred A/I 62 Ndola Loc
SHORTT Peter b30.7.36 A/I 6.6.57 Insp 6.6.60 MU 62
SHUTT Ken PC Hants A/I NRP 62 Muf PC Hants 65 Met C/I
SILOKA Maxwell Felix b24.2.14 pte 6.4.35 A/I III Lka C 59 II 1.1.61 Matero 62
SIMATAA Aggrey b15.7.29 Const 12.3.52 A/I II 1.4.62 Muf Mine A/I 1.63
SIMMONDS Alan Maurice b1.9.29 UKCS A/I 15.9.54 A/Supt 1.7.61 Lka R 3.62–4 Solr GPO London
SIMONDA L Michael b15.6.21 Const 4.6.40 A/I III.59 II 11.12.60 Lka 62
SIMONS A P b14.7.38 A/I 18.7.59 Insp 18.7.62 L21.7.62
SIMPSON A A A b3.1.39 A/I 17.12.59 Kitwe 61 L25.6.62 rsgnd
SIMPSON Jack b26.1.38 PC WRdg 55 A/I NRP 19.3.59 Insp 19.3.62 L1.4.62
SIMPSON Wm Marmaduke BSAP 9.4.36 A/I NRP 11.8.38
SINCLAIR G H A/I.47
SINGOGO D b1.7.26 Const 1.9.44 A/I II 1.4.62 Ndola 62
SITALI O b1.7.26 Const 10.6.49 A/I II 1.4.62 Mongu 62
SKINNER Charlie H b1.5.28 A/I 13.5.54 Insp 13.5.57 S/I Chingola 62
SLATER Doreen A WPCLancs 52 W/A/I NRP 4.6.59 Muf 59–61
SLATER Geoff A/I 51 Kitwe 52 L54
SLEIGH Daniel B b3.10.42 Cdt 1.3.61 Ndola 62
SLOANE John Philip b22.6.30 A/I 24.9.53 Insp 24.9.56 A/Supt 1.7.61 Kitwe 62 Kloof Natal

SMALLWOOD Harry Kedwards LLB(Hons) Lon b19.11.08 Const 4.7.35 Insp, Workmen's Compensatn Commr 29.11.45 rtd 1.8.61

SMART C R A/I.52

SMIT Heine P b25.8.41 Cdt 11.3.60 A/I 25.8.61 Lka Mtd 62

SMITH A A/I 48

SMITH A A/I 62

SMITH Brian P b9.4.32 A/I 8.12.55 Insp 9.10.59 L24.6.62 A/Supt

SMITH D A/I 57 Muf

SMITH Derek P b20.1.42 Cdt 28.7.60 A/I 20.1.62 MU kia25.6.64

SMITH Frank J b11.3.34 A/I 14.2.57 Kitwe CID 59

SMITH Geo CARR- CPM 50 'Bwana Ngungu' = dignified b.Scotland 4.6.96 ed CentralHS Aberdn to SA; Pte DurbanLI'14 4SAI 15–19 SAP'24 Const NRP 14.1.27 A/I 1.7.29 Insp'33 C/I 1.1.38 A/Supt'41 S/A/Supt 1.4.46 Supt 1.1.48 S/Supt'50 ACP 1.1.51 DCP 4.9.51 Rtd 5.12.53 R/Supt Div Cmdt NRPR Lusaka, Sgt at Arms LegCo, Town Cncllr & Chmn Lka Race Relations Cttee d.28.8.59

SMITH G Les b29.5.28 A/I 10.6.54 Insp 9.10.59 Kitwe Dist 63

SMITH L A b6.3.41 A/I 2.5.62

SMITH Malcom Andrew FLOWER b12.7.38 RN 57 A/I 19.3.59 Insp 19.3.62 BEd 2Lt RAEC 26.2.67 MSC Maj 28.8.78 rtd 93

SMITH Robt K D b13.4.36 A/I 1.6.57 Muf 58

SMITH Shirley WPC Nottghm City W/A/I NRP 28.1.60 mJ M Woodward Lka 61

SMYTH M S b1.10.33 Garda Siochana 53 A/I NRP17.12.59 Ndola 61–2

SOKO E D L b6.7.20 Const 14.1.44 A/I III.59 II 11.12.60 A/I I 1.12.61 Lshya A/Supt 64

SONDERHEN Geo A/I Sthn SB 54

SOULSBY G Brian b22.7.30 RN PCNotts 51 A/I NRP 27.3.54 Insp 27.3.57 S/I i/c Lstone Tfc 62

SPEEDY A Martin b27.1.35 A/I 23.6.55 Insp 15.10.60 Maz 4.8.62

SPEICH Paul R B b1.7.31 A/I 2.7.53 Insp 2.7.56 S/I FHQ 62 A/Supt 63 Supt

SPENCER S F A/I 46

SPILLETT Edwin Darell bSheerness 23.6.23 PalP 21.3.46 A/I NRP 4.11.48 S/I 1.10.55 A/Supt 1.8.56 Lstone Dist Supt 10.62 Caterham d.86

SPOFFORTH John S b29.3.40 A/I 23.4.60 mKennedy Ndola 62

SPOONER Peter A/I Chingola 53 Prop Woodpecker Inn Lka 58

SPRING Peter b22.8.33 A/I 10.1.58 Insp 10.1.60 Mkushi 61–2 Ag S/I 62

STACEY J St G b30.3.38 A/I 3.4.58 resigned 12.3.61

STACPOOLE Richard B b11.4.42 s/oSupt CyprusP Cdt 27.10.60 A/I 11.4.62 Lka C 62 ZP Lka CID

STAMP Barry W b12.7.25 Durban CtyP 46 BSAP 50 NRP A/I 2.11.53 Insp 2.11.56 S/I Kitwe 62

STANDALOFT Peter A/I 62 Kansenji 63 MU 6.64

STAPLEY E G b21.3.40 A/I 9.3.61 Kitwe 62

STARR Eric D b15.11.30 BPP 57 A/I NRP 13.1.60 SB Kashiba 62

STEEL David R b5.4.42 Cdt 12.5.60 A/I 5.4.62 Ndola Tfc 63

STEEL James A b29.7.38 A/I 16.6.59 Ndola 59–61

STEELE W K A/I 2.11.47

STEER Kenneth G b2.8.36 RAF A/I 10.1.58 Insp 13.10.61 Chinsali 4.62

STEPHENS E J b25.5.21 A/I 3.7.47 A/Supt 1.11.56 MU 62 ZP Supt

STEPHENS R Bernard A/I 51

STEPHENSON Arthur CBE 39 CMG 19 DSO 18 MC 11.3.16, GPO UK, Cape, SA War, P&T SR'02 PostMr Lstone 12.6.04 Ag Controller P&T NWR 1.5.07 Ch Postmr to RNLB'11; 2Lt 9KOYLI BEF 9.15 T/Capt by 16.1.16 2i/c 25.4.16 A/Lt Col 16RScots 11.16 sick gas 11.17–13.4.18 Cdg 1O1 Bde to 23.4.18 CO 9RScots 3.8.18 Fmr Ry Fm 27a Monze & Cmdt NRRifles 19.8.19 & Ch Int Offr NR 14.5.20 Att'd NRP 7.24 Cmdt 31.3.25 L1.3–Rtd 19.4.30 Mngr Native Lab Asscn, MLC Ndola'35, Col Cdg NR Sub-Area'39–Mgr Chamber of Mines Kitwe'42 NR Labour Offr Salisbury SR'45 d'50

STEPHENSON Donald b18.7.36 A/I 16.5.59 Ndola rsgnd 1.6.61

STEPHENSON R J b22.2.42 Cdt 8.11.61 A/I 22.2.62 Kitwe

STEVENS Jack W b22.11.32 BSAP 52 Insp NRP Farrier 16.12.60–62
STEVENS Peter M C b3.9.36 A/I 7.1.61 Lstone 62
STEVENSON Edwd J CPM(G)68 CPM b1.4.38 A/I 28.2.62 RHKP rtd 94 HK
STEWART Douglas A/I FHQ 52 D/Insp Luanshya rsgnd Roan Mine 54
STEWART D A D/I 31.5.46 svg 53
STEWART D A BSAP 50 A/I NRP 55
STEWART Gordon R b24.8.28 BSAP'49 A/I NRP 12.12.54 Kitwe 57
STEWART J A Const 1.11.27
STEWART J Douglas A/I 21.5.59 rsgnd by 62 Lka d94?
STEWART J Lindsay Cdt 12.5.60 A/I 14.6.61 Kitwe 62–rsgnd 63
STEWART M b5.3.40 A/I 11.1.62 Ndola Loc 62
STEWART Stair Johnson BSAP 9.4.36 A/I NRP 25.8.38
STILLWELL J Alan b19.7.37 A/I 13.12.58 Kitwe 59–61
STOCK Brian W A/I 57
STOCKDALE Timothy E b6.12.39 Cdt 4.12.58 A/I 6.12.59 PTS MT 62
STOCKER John S b13.7.40 A/I 10.12.60 Lka 61
STONE Frank A b1.12.34 KenyaP 55 A/I NRP 18.7.57 Insp 14.4.61 Petauke 2.62 ZP rtd66
STONE John b15.4.35 A/I 7.9.58 Insp 7.9.61 PTS 62 DSupt Seychelles 68
STOREY Eric b24.8.37 A/I 18.7.59 Insp 18.7.62 MU 63 ZP A/Supt 68 d90
STOTT Vic R b7.8.39 A/I 20.2.60 resigned 18.8.62
STRAW A K b26.4.43 Cdt 4.4.62 Lka A/I 26.4.63 resigned 64
STUART Donald D Cdt 28.3.60 A/I 27.7.61 Ndola 62 Bermuda P 64
STUBBS William Frederick CMG CBE, b.India 19.6.02 s/o L M S CSI CIE ICS, ed Winchester,
    Tpr BSAP 11.21–Const NRP 18.4.24 FJ 25 PA 4.7.26 DC Kawambwa'35 Labour Dept'41
    Lab Cmmr 44 PC'49 Sec Native Affairs MLC'52 Rtd'57 Spkr Leg Assembly & Ch Public
    Svce Comm Somaliland'60 d.22.9.87
STURGEON D E Const 13.7–16.11.27
SUGG Aldhelm St John CMG b21.10.09 ed ColchstrRGS; Pal P'30 Const NRP 1.2.32 Lshya'41
    to PA DO'43 DC Petauke'50 PC Southern 1.12.58–63 Pearce Commission Rhodesia'71
SUNDERLAND Gilbert R bYks 7.9.27 ARPw RScots 44–8 A/I 23.3.51 Insp 13.8.56 S/I Lstone
    Tfc rtd 62 RAF FLt rtd 82 d12.9.95
SUTCLIFFE J Peter b28.4.40 Cdt 8.1.59 A/I 28.4.60 Samfya 63
SUTTILL Brian b18.5.38 A/I 2.5.62 Bwacha 62 MU LC A/Supt ZP DRegistrar HK rtd 94 Ch
    Reg & Commr High Ct Kiribati; Jersey
SUTTON M John b11.4.41 Cdt 17.11.60 A/I 11.4.61 Kitwe 62–3
SUTTON Leonard J MC MBE b27.10.19 A/I 21.8.47 A/Supt 30.10.54 Supt 1.6.59 AgSSupt Lka
    62 S/Supt to Aden i/c SB Seychelles, Belize
SWAIN Bruce W b10.11.39 A/I 24.9.60 PTS 62 Vancouver
SWARBRICK Eric J b19.9.31 A/I 13.8.53 Insp 13.8.56 A/Supt 1.3.60 Ndola 62
SWAYNE J C R b25.7.40 Cdt 2.11.59 A/I 25.7.60 Kasempa 63
SWEENEY A/I 63
SWEETMAN M Anthony b18.5.36 A/I 25.10.58 Lka MU L19.7.61

TAAFE Paddy A/I.49 dschge Warden Blue Lagoon, Muf Mne drnd hntg Mozambique 53?
TANNER P N Mark b17.11.39 A/I 4.10.61 Choma 62–4
TAPER Roger J H b31.5.36 RAF A/I 21.9.57 i/c Linda 62
TAPSON E H Const 1.11.26
TARLING John A/I Kitwe 53 BH 54
TARR Michael J b27.6.35 A/I 11.3.56 Insp 14.4.61 Choma 62
TARR Joan W/A/I 11.6.56 Bancroft 58
TAUNTON Peter J b2.10.23 A/I 7.11.49 SImmOffr 1.7.55 sec'd Fed Svce 1.4.57
TAYLOR Derek E W? A/I Ndola 53–4
TAYLOR Harry b15.6.25 A/I 9.8.51 Insp 9.8.54 A/Supt 5.12.56 AgSupt CO Eastn 62
TAYLOR Mrs J A C T/W/A/I 24.2.56 Kitwe'57
TAYLOR Jock A/I Lka C 61

TAYLOR L J A/I 38? resigned 26.5.46
TAYLOR M b2.11.41 A/I 2.5.62 rsgnd 64
TAYLOR Peter D b21.4.32 RM A/I 14.2.57 mL.Derby 58 Insp 14.2.60 Chingola Tfc 22.9.60–62
TAYLOR Robert S b4.10.24 RN A/I 3.7.47 A/Supt 1.1.52 S/Supt 4.3 61 CO MU 62
TAYLOR Roy b13.12.39 A/I 10.12.60 Ndola 62 HKP 68–79 FTrg Offr 79–
TAYLOR S C E W/A/I 28.8.60 Ndola 62
TEALE Wm Robt b8.6.35 BSAP 53 A/I NRP 22.6.58 L28.6.61
TEDFORD John D b16.4.37 A/I 17.1.61 Lka 61–2
TEMBO K J B b17.7.25 Const 26.11.45 A/I III 59 II 11.12.60 A/I 1.12.61 Chingola 63 C/I 64
TEMBO L C b15.6.21 Const 21.8.43 A/I II 1.1.61 Lshya 62
TEMBO M b15.4.23 Const 16.6.43 A/I III 60 II 1.4.62 Muf 62
TENNANT Adam G b10.5.35 RAC 2Lt A/I 13.12.58 Insp 13.12.61 BH 15.6.62
TERRY Brian W b6.7.41 Cdt 28.1.60 A/I 6.7.61 Lka 62 L63
TERRY H N Const 2.11.26
TERRY Ian N b6.1.36 A/I 24.9.60 Balovale CID 62
THACKERAY David T b28.11.34 PC Norwich 55 A/I NRP 18.5.61 Kashiba 63 Bermuda P S/I
    PNGP 66
THOMAS Arthur A/I 58 Lshya
THOMAS Brian B (s/o B J) b28.6.27 A/I 21.7.49 Insp 10.8.54 C/I 1.12.60 i/c Chiwempala L3.8.62
THOMAS D A b29.4.41 Cdt 1.10.59 A/I 29.4.61 Chingola L5.8.62
THOMAS F A (s/o B J) b30.8.29 A/I 54? Accts Clk Lands & Nat Rsces 2.2.59 Lka 21.6.62
THOMAS M R b27.11.40 A/I 10.12.60 Maz 62
THOMAS Steven Humphrey b23.8.38 A/I 16.5.59 BH resigned 8.6.61
THOMPSON David A/I.52 Chairman Rank Xerox UK 90
THOMPSON Ken W b23.8.38 A/I 2.5.62 Raylton 63
THOMPSON R G Const by 36 Insp Lstone 46–7
THOMPSON W David b20.8.36 A/I 15.10.59 Kitwe 63
THOMS Peter K A/I Mindolo 63
THOMSON James Crawford b16.12.26 A/I 13.3.52 Insp 13.3.55 C/I 16.8.61 Matero 63 A/Supt
    Estate Agt Salisby SR
THOMSON Mac G B b6.4.37 A/I 8.9.58 Insp 8.9.61 Kafue 62 C/I d.Zambia 85
THOMSON N A b29.11.35 A/I 17.1.59 Kitwe 61
THORNE Christopher John b12.4.27 2Lt 7GR PWD NR 28.2.51 A/I 13.11.52 A/Supt 1.4.56 SO
    Lka D AgSupt 62 Solr 67 to SA
THORNEYCROFT Gordon A b28.3.34 A/I 17.5.58 Insp 17.5.61 Lstone 19.1.62
TILSLEY John C H b29.3.38 A/I 19.2.59 Lka Ru resigned 1.7.61
TILSON J 'Paddy' A/I 55 Chingola rsgnd 57
TIMM O David G b26.6.38 Prob 25.3.57 A/I 26.6.58 Insp 13.10.61 Lka C 63
TOBIN Paul T G b6.10.30 PCMet 51 A/I NRP 27.3.54 Insp 27.3.57 S/I Kitwe Tfc 61–62
TOBIN J S 'Paddy' b14.8.33 A/I 10.1.58 A'corn 62
TOBIN Russell M b19.10.34 PCWRdg 55 A/I NRP 29.11.57 Insp 29.11.60 i/c Muf Mine 63 C/I
TOMLINSON Michael L b16.7.41 Cdt 2.11.59 A/I 16.7.61 L11.62
TOMLINSON Robin M b11.10.41 Cdt 2.11.59 A/I 11.10.61 BH L2.63
TOMS Peter K b28.10.37 A/I 11.1.62 Kitwe 62 ZP Stn Insp Kitwe 66 to Rhod
TONKIN John A/I Lka 60
TOOZE Wm Alan b.Monmouth 17.10.35 Para A/I 17.2.57 MU 58–rsgnd 60 d.Sx 86
TOPLEY Wm O'N b18.3.31 A/I 10.6.54 Insp 1.4.59 S/I Lstone 62
TOSH Archibald J b27.2.37 A/I 18.6.59 Lka Tfc 1.63
TOTMAN Lt Col Walter 'Ginger' MBE(Mil'42) Const NRP 14.3.27 D/I 1.8.31 A/Supt 23.8.37
    sec'd Mil Svce–Supt CID 8.8.46 lve29.4.47–Rtd'48
TOWLSON G Eric b16.6.40 A/I 26.8.60 Muf Mine CID L63
TOWNLEY M 'Bill' b10.5.20 A/I 26.2.48 S/I 8.8.55 A/Supt 1.10.56 AgSupt Ndola Dist 63
TOZER William H Const 3.11.31 A/Supt'47 Supt'54 Central Div rtd 24.4.55
TRICKETT Garth b1.11.43 Cdt 8.11.61 Kalomo A/I 1.11.63
TRINCKLE N Geo b22.6.35 A/I 18.4.58 Namwala resigned 8.5.61

TRINDER P H b27.11.24 A/I 1.7.52 Imm 54 sec'd Fed Svce 1.4.57
TRISTRAM P A D b24.3.39 A/I 9.3.61 Lshya 62
TRURAN Brian J A/I Wdlds 59 resigned 10.60 Insce Salesman
TROUTEAUD Max J b7.12.40 Cdt 28.1 A/I 7.12.60 Muf L63
TUCKER Alan Fredk b3.8.26 A/I 15.5.52 Insp 13.8.56 S/I L6.3.62 Kansenji 63 C/I d93
TUDOR-JONES D Garry b2.2.37 A/I 11.1.62 Kitwe 62 NGP rsgnd 69
TUKE Jas S b16.1.39 A/I 4.8.60 Chingola 62 L8.63
TUNNOCK F Stuart K b10.2.38 2Lt RWF A/I 13.12.58 Kafue 60–1 Lt RCT
TURNER David R b2.8.30 A/I 20.4.54 Insp 20.4.57 Kitwe 59
TURNER J Glyn J b25.2.25 PCSom 50 A/I 12.8.53 Insp 5.8.56 FHQ 61 S/I 62
TURNER Mrs S E T/W/A/I 18.1.57 Muf
TURRAL Richard R b29.6.38 RA A/I 15.10.59 PTS 62 resigned 63
TWIGGS Karl E A/I 58 Lka
TWISS Gordon A b7.10.26 PC Manch 47 A/I NRP 53 rsgnd 56 A/I 27.6.57 Insp 27.6.60 S/I L63 C/I d11.79 Durban
TYRER Derek J 'Charlie' b27.5.30 Mx Rgt PCMet 50 A/I NRP 19.6.52 Insp 19.6.55 C/I 1.3.60 i/c Lka CID 63 A/Supt
TYRRELL Geo b.NR A/I FJ 58

UPTON Maureen d/o G R E T/W/A/I 18.11.56 mT R Williamson 58
USHER Derek G b1.7.30 PCMet'50 A/I 21.4.55 Lka C Ft J L58

VAN OPPEN Hugh E b26.8.31 RTR Korea Sgt A/I NRP 10.6.56 MU 58 Rsgnd 59 Sgt RRR Nyasald BEM 59 Lt RNSC TF Zaire 2i/c 5 Cdo k.13.5.66
VAN OUDTSHORN W Larry van R b27.12.39 Cdt 13.6 A/I 27.12.59 Riverside 63
VAN RENSBURG David J b11.4.40 A/I 23.6.60 Lka rsgnd63
VAN WYK Marius U b12.1.39 A/I 13.1.60 Bwacha 63
VAN ZYL J Michael b22.5.42 Cdt 13.8.60 A/I 22.5.62 Muf
VAUGHAN Cecil A 'Paddy' b20.11.19 PCMet 39 A/I NRP 2.4.48 S/I 11.4.57 A/Supt 1.1.58 L6.5.62 Supt
VAUGHAN N J b12.4.41 Cdt 28.7.60 A/I 12.4.61 Muf C 61–2 rgd 63
VAUGHAN-JOHNSON Chas P T b20.2.34 A/I 24.3.55 rsgnd 31.5.57 Bank of Bermuda Pres & Ch Exec 94
VAUGHAN-JOHNSON Robin Campbell bChertsey 12.8.28 A/I 26.6.52 Insp 27.6.55 C/I 1.3.60 rsgnd 5.6.62 Helicopter Pilot Bristows Abu Dhabi, WAust
VENING David J b9.5.37 A/I 19.7.58 Insp 13.10.61 Muf 26.4.62 PC Kent C/I Crime Prevn 79 Supt
VERMEULEN Christie Francois b27.1.37 Bank Lstone A/I 13.5.57 Insp 13.5.60 i/c Wdlds 10.62
VERNON Jas PC WRdg A/I NRP Chingola 6.53
VERRALL Maj Robert John Wyndham MVO 47 CPM 50 b.96 ed Cologne Cllge, Army Svce 16–19 BSAP 26.9.20 Cpl 10.11.21 dschge 26.2.28 Const NRP 29.6.28 Lt BH A/Supt'29 Supt 1.4.31 DCP 23.8.37 CofP Bahamas'51 Mgr Mine Police Dept Rand Mines Ltd 195? Rtd to Isle of Man'63
VIGORS R H b4.9.28 Insp 21.4.60 C/I 12.4.61 Lka 62 A/Supt 64
VOSS John E b24.8.33 A/I 18.4.57

WADE Robt T Insp 16.10.45 A/Supt Nigeria 46
WAIDE M A/I 49
WAIT Anthony R b27.12.37 A/I 25.10.58 Mindolo 59 Wusikili 61
WALDEN Norman D b14.5.33 KenyaP'54 A/I NRP 14.2.57 Kitwe C
WALDRON Gerald R b18.12.35 RF A/I 29.11.57 Insp 29.11.60 i/c BH Mine 1.62 SB 62 RCAFP PC Sx Insp Leics
WALFORD G I 'Taff' b31.3.33 Welsh Gds A/I 11.3.56 MU drnd Chavuma 29.8.61
WALKER Alan R b23.1.39 A/I 28.10.60 Kitwe 61–2 Sc Prsns, Op Dir Prisons Eng & Wales 3.96
WALKER A/I Kitwe 56

WALKER Ryrie W/A/I 59 m.Bestic 60 Lshya
WALKER Victor A/I 58 Kitwe C Bancroft Army of Rhod & Ny 61
WALL Alan b/o H S A/I 48?
WALL Hedley Saml 'Jack' bBristol 8.5.19 A/I 14.8.46 A/Supt 15.11.55 Supt 18.5.62 NZ
WALLACE Arthur 'Chick' CPM 54 b07 ed Marylebone LCC Sch, BSAP 28 Const NRP 27.1.31
    A/Supt 1.1.45 Supt CO Southern 8.50 S/Supt'54 rtd 27.7.56
WALLACE Mervyn A Cdt 8.1 A/I 9.5.59 Insp 9.5.62 Kasama 62
WALLACE Michael A b30.4.35 A/I 4.8.55 Kitwe 56 Lka 57
WALLER Jan L b1.7.13 BSAP 37 A/I NRP 11.8.38 A/Supt 51 Supt 1.7.56 DCIO Sthn L4.63
    d5.88
WALLING R Norman A/I 50 Chingola 52 NRCS EO 25.2.57 Sec FHQ 60 svg9.62
WALLIS O J Const 3.9.31 D/A/I 1.4.32 Passport Offr dLstone 7.5.37 heart
WALMSLEY T J K b4.5.35 RUC 53 A/I NRP 19.7.58 Muf rsgnd 12.3.61
WALSH H b18.2.35 A/I 2.5.62
WALSH Ian Lambert b9.3.33 A/I 13.8.55 CID 3.57 Kansenji 63?
WALSH Nicola W/A/I.59 BH 11.59 m.D Crowther
WALTERS F A/I 55 Lshya rsgnd57
WALTERS Clifford V b4.12.36 A/I 16.5.59 Lka L7.6.62 Emmasdale
WAPAMESA Louis b19.4.20 Const 12.7.39 A/I II 1.59 A/I I 1.11.60 Lka C 62 ASupt 64 ZP Supt
    Lka Div 65
WARD David Jas bWLavingtn 10.10.30 PCWilts 50 A/I NRP 12.8.53 Insp 12.8.56 A/Supt 1.4.62
    Muf C L63
WARD D J b24.10.38 A/I 17.12.59 Choma 61
WARD Ivor Osman b11.4.10 Tpr Sx Yeo; Const NRP 21.1.32 Pal P.33 A/I NRP 21.1.35 A/Supt
    1.1.50 RSO Lstone rtd.63
WARD J Robt b27.11.41 Cdt 26.9.60 A/I 27.11.61 Kitwe 62 rsgnd63
WARD M D b30.3.40 A/I 20.4.61 Kitwe 61–2
WARDLE Ralph b13.3.32 RAOC Lt A/I NRP 6.6.57 Insp 13.4.62 Luwingu 62
WARRINGTON Eric H N b24.1.28 PalP 46–8 A/I NRP 3.8.50 Insp 10.8.54 S/I MU 58 i/c FJ
    61–2 Chingola 64
WARR A Terence M b18.1.25 BSAP 49 A/I NRP 19.2.53 Insp 26.8.57 S/I Pros BH 62 C/I
WATERS Douglas W b22.10.20 A/I 27.5.48 A/Supt 15.11.55 Supt 15.5.60 DCIO Lka 2.1.62
WATERS Harry L b4.2.19 A/I 6.6.46 A/Supt 15.11.55 Supt 1.7.60 L9.6.62
WATSON Ed A/I 58 Lka C Kitwe C
WATSON N 2Lt 30.7.25–18.12.25
WATT John A/I Lstone Lka 52
WATTERS Nighean WPC Dumfries & Galloway 58 W/A/I NRP 9.2.61 Kitwe mDarlaston, rsgnd
    12.63 JP Kent
WATTS Anthony D b2.2.41 Cdt 28.1.60 A/I 2.2.61 Lshya Rsgnd 63
WAUGH A D Michael b21.1.27 Assam Regt NRG 12.1.50 A/I 26.5.51 Imm 54 sec'd Fed 1.4.57
WEBB C A MBE CPM Const'30 Sgt 1.4.31 QM's Dept Mil 32–33 Bechuanaland Police'33
WEBB Edwd A/I 58
WEBSTER John G b27.3.27 A/I 21.7.49 Insp 10.8.54 A/Supt 12.4.61 L7.4.62 Pilot Zambia Elec
    Supply Corp 78
WEBSTER Potifer A/I Ndola Muf IB 53
WEITCZ S C b24.6.40 Cdt 19.5 A/I 24.6.60 MU 62 rsgnd63
WELLER D B E A/I MU 52
WELLER F E Const 19.6.31 L'stone 33
WENHAM A John b11.9.39 A/I 4.8.60 Muf 61 rsgnd 20.8.62
WENMAN T A b13.3.36 A/I 28.2.62 Lshya
WESSON L S b15.2.40 A/I 21.6.60 Muf 61
WEST Ken H b19.11.34 A/I 15.5.55 C/I 1.4.62 Bancroft 15.7.62 fdr West Scy
WEST John A/I Chingola 52 rsgnd mnes 6.53
WEST Michael G b15.9.36 A/I 3.4.58 Insp 3.4.61 Kasama 62
WEST Robt C b/oK H Cdt 5.12.60 A/I 5.11.61 BHC 62 rsgnd 63

WHATLEY A Russell b15.3.42 A/I 8.8.62 Mwensi(Kashiba) 63
WHEELER Paul bLyndhurst 2.2.28 A/I 28.7.50 A/Supt 15.11.55 FHQ AgSupt 62 Supt ZP ACP rtd 68 Solr 72
WHITE Brian L b2.5.41 Cdt 28.1.60 A/I 2.5.61 Chingola 61–2
WHITE David Henry bMargate 5.3.33 A/I 10.6.56 Insp 14.4.61 Lka CID 62
WHITE Richard Wm b31.12.33 A/I 8.12.55 LkaC 57 A'corn 58
WHITE Ronald Boyd bLargs 24.7.33 PCMet 54 A/I NRP 24.3.55 Insp 24.3.58 Lka 18.5.62 C/I A/Supt 64 dAust 93
WHITTAKER A W J A/I 48
WHITEHEAD Wm R b17.7.31 A/I 12.5.55 Lshya L 58
WHITEHOUSE Michael J b16.2.37 A/I 29.11.57 Insp 29.11.60 Kawambwa 61–2
WHITELEY Tom b22.3.37 A/I 18.4.58 Insp 6.11.61 Mongu 62
WHITTAKER-WOOD C H b27.5.41 A/I 11.1.61 BH dschge 63
WHYMAN Alan G b11.1.38 A/I 25.10.58 Kariba 59 MU 61
WICKERSON Paddy A/I 1.62 Sub Insp HKP 63 C/I DSgt NZP ACPF 80
WICKS Anthony A/I Monze 53 Imm
WICKS Fredk L DSM b4.12.20 A/I 29.11.46 Judcl Dept 30.4.55 A/Sherriff NR 1.12.60
WIDD P Brian b10.8.32 A/I 3.3.55 Insp 3.3.58 Chingola 4.6.62–4 d.91
WIGHTMAN Nurse W/A/I Raylton 59
WILKINS John S b8.1.34 BSAP'53 A/I NRP 2.8.55 Insp 15.10.60 L29.6.62
WILKINSON E G P Const 16.4.26 Sgt S&T lve 17.10.28
WILKINSON Henry Michael Lawler CPM(G) 40 Const 26.7.29 A/I 1.7.31 Insp Ag/Supt 23.12.37 Supt 39 rtmnt L26.2.47
WILKINSON James Ronald A/I 9.9.58 i/c Prospect 2.60 rsgnd 61
WILKINSON W R b30.6.27 A/I 12.8.55 Imm sec'd Fed 1.4.57
WILKS John T b2.10.30 MalayaP 55 A/I NRP 20.6.59 rsgnd 26.7.61 SwazildP MU
WILLETT J Stewart b11.6.30 A/I 13.9.51 Judcl Dept 1.5.53 A/I 1.6.56 Insp 1.6.59 S/I i/c Kalomo 60 L5.4.62 A/Supt 63
WILLIAMS E L A/I 46
WILLIAMS D b28.7.39 A/I 10.12.60 Lka 62
WILLIAMS David John bSale 8.12.36 A/I 17.1.59 Insp 17.1.62 DivI Luapula 4.64 rtd 10.64
WILLIAMS D H b18.10.38 BSAP 57 A/I NRP 10.12.60 Kalomo 62
WILLIAMS Gavin R P b5.10.40 A/I 10.12.60 Ndola 61 rsgnd 63 BermudaP to Aust
WILLIAMS Graham E b24.7.41 Cdt6.8.59 A/I 24.7.61 Wdlds 63
WILLIAMS Harry A/I Chingola 59 car salesman 59
WILLIAMS J David CPM b23.2.27 BSAP 47 A/I NRP 27.6.50 Insp 14.4.54 A/Supt 1.7.57 NDiv 61–2
WILLIAMS J T b15.2.42 Cdt 17.11.60 A/I 15.2.62 PTS 62
WILLIAMS J W b18.1.39 A/I 23.4.60 Chingola 61
WILLIAMS Ken J b19.7.39 A/I 10.12.60 Bancroft 62
WILLIAMS Peter R CPM 62 b17.3.31 BSAP 49 A/I NRP 20.5.53 Insp 20.5.56 A/Supt 12.4.61 L2.8.62 Lka 63 Rhod DC Mt Darwin 78
WILLIAMS Warwick A/I Chingola 60
WILLIAMSON John A/I d.SA 89
WILLIAMSON P T C A/I Lstone C 60
WILLIAMSON P S b23.3.39 A/I 10.5.60 Lstone Rly 62
WILLIAMSON Tom R b18.5.35 A/I 14.12.55 m.M Upton Insp 4.12.58 Div Insp Northern 63 C/I
WILLING Nicholas R J b27.11.32 A/I 10.6.56 Insp 8.4.60 MufC 63 d.86
WILLIS Philip Para A/I Kitwe 53 BH 54
WILLIS Trevor C RAFP A/I 21.9.57 Chingola rsgnd 60
WILLOWS Tom H b12.4.36 A/I 6.6.57 d.88
WILSON Geoffrey W b7.2.39 Coldm Gds A/I 2.5.62 Raylton 12.62
WILSON J A Clk Tpt Dept 10.7.16 Sgt S&T by 30.1.27 rsgnd 14.4.28
WILSON J L BOYD Lt TA 2Lt NRP 28 Lt NRR Adjt 9.5.34 PA 1.10.37
WILSON J WPC Middlesboro 59 W/A/I NRP 8.8.62 Ndola Loc 63

OFFICERS OF THE NORTHERN RHODESIA POLICE APPOINTED 1.4.24–23.10.64

WILSON Michael A/I Kitwe 53 Mindolo 54
WILSON Mostyn P bTalgarth 8.9.34 A/I 10.8.55 L26.3.62 BH CID
WILSON Richard A/I Choma 60
WILSON Stewart A/I 62 Chingola 63
WILSON-JOHNSON John F A/I.50
WILTSHIRE H Gerald bHemswth Yks 10 Tpr 4H 13/18H BSAP 35 A/I NRP 9.3.38 Insp 46 A/
    Supt 1.1.52 rtd10.62 SA d89
WINNEY Robert Vivien KPM(G) b.20.12.33 Handleton Wales Clk N Scotld Yd RMP PC Met 54
    A/I NRP 20.7.58 Kitwe Tfc d.1.11.59
WINTLE C D S
WISEMAN Edward J W b24.10.24 A/I 24.4.52 Insp 24.4.55 A/Supt 1.4.62
WITHAM C 'Vic' A/I Lshya 47
WITHERSPOON Phil C b23.7.36 RUC 55 A/I NRP 29.11.57 Insp 29.11.60 Chingola 62 Solr
WITHINGTON D Harry b23.9.24 PCMet 49 A/I 12.7.52 Insp 11.7.55 C/I 1.1.59 Div I Southern
    L19.7.62 back d.86
WOOD John R b17.1.33 A/I 10.6.56 Insp 8.4.60 Lka CID 61–2
WOOD S Const 35
WOODING Vic G b10.5.35 RN A/I 24.9.60 Ndola Tfc 62–3
WOODS Fredk Lewis b'86 4KRRC 27.11.06 BM 1RF 30.5.14–23.2.26 BM NRP 5.29 NRR d acute
    nephritis 6.2.33
WOODWARD J Michael b13.3.34 PCMet 55 A/I NRP 10.6.56 Insp 10.6.59 Pros Lka 4.1.60–2
    mW/A/I Shirley Smith
WOOLCOTT A/I Chingola 53
WOOLFORD M W/A/I 8.6.61 Lstone 62
WORKMAN Col John Edwd 'Shamilimo' b97 pte Glos 15 2Lt Kgs RFC RAF Dist Insp RIC Pl
    Cmd USC 22 ACP Gold Coast 1.25 CP 1.33 CP Fiji.37 NR 6.47 Rtd 8.51 d.13.9.75
WORSLEY David R b9.7.38 A/I 9.2.61 Kitwe 62
WRAY Malcolm C Cdt 28.1.60 A/I 23.5.61 Maz 61–2 BermudaP 64
WRIGHT Alan J K b30.3.40 s/o S A Cdt 17.1 A/I 30.3.60 m.B Hayward; Insp 63 ZP LkaU Dist
    Insp
WRIGHT Byron A b22.11.40 A/I 11.1.62 FJ
WRIGHT D b8.10.39 A/I 23.4.60 resigned 25.4.62
WRIGHT David Tolliday b29.4.43 Cdt 28.2.62 A/I 29.4.63 RN FAA 4.63 Bar HK
WRIGHT Hilary E Typist 9.6.58 W/A/I 6.4.62 Ndola CID 63
WRIGHT J S b23.12.39 A/I 4.8.60 Muf 62
WRIGHT Michael W s/o T A Cdt 1.7.57 A/I 4.6.58 Insp 29.9.61 Ndola 62
WRIGHT Roy Malcolm bPembroke 27.5.37 RUC 57 A/I NRP 24.10.57 Insp 13.4.62 Kalulushi 62
WALLIS O J Const 3.9.31 D/A/I 1.4.32 Passport Offr dLstone 7.5.37 heart
WRIGHT Sidney A LSM(St J) 46 Const NRP 10.9.31 A/Supt f/o A J K
WRIGHT Timothy Blake bHove 18.6.36 RSx A/I 21.9.57 Insp 21.9.60 C/I 7.64 ZP rtd 22.9.66
    Solr 70 Capt ALS 1.4.70 Col rtd 30.9.96
WRIGHT Trevor Alfred CPM 51 'Bwana Siachitema' Const 29.9.30 A/I 1.1.35 Insp Choma'51
    A/Supt Rtd to Choma to SA d'85 f/o M W
WRIGHT Trevor Ernest Arthur b.Watford 14.4.30 2lt RA A/I 20.5.53 Insp 20.5.56 C/I 1.4.62 A/
    Supt 63 Supt 64 Factory Adm Offr Africn Explosives & Chem I Witbank 69 d.23.5.85
WYETH John H b5.5.26 PCMet 47 A/I NRP 22.2.51 Insp 8.8.55 S/I Kitwe 1.1.62 ACPF Curator
    Bare Isld Botany Bay 69
WYLDE A/I Ndola 53
WYLLIE John A/I FJ 59
WYNN Barry C b29.8.42 Cdt 26.1.61 A/I 29.8.62 Lka C 62 PCMet Insp 78

YEARSLEY J Andrew b14.3.41 A/I 28.2.62 Kitwe Riverside 62
YENDOLE D R b26.12.39 A/I 10.12.60 Choma 62
YOUNG Alan b9.8.40 PCMet 59 A/I 28.10.60 Lshya 61 rsgnd 31.8.62
YOUNG Andrew A/I 63

YOUNG Brian PCMet A/I NRP 58 Choma Monze 58
YOUNG E B b15.6.34 MalayaP 55 A/I NRP 11.4.58 rsgnd 15.4.61
YOUNG Leonard Keith bNewcastle 3.1.32 PCMet 54 A/I NRP 1.5.58 Insp 1.5.61 FR 7.2.62 Law
    Lectr UPNG 68 Pte Pctce 71 DLegal Trg UPNG 78–84 Melbourne DDist Reg Vic 90
YOUNG Stanley b3.1.31 A/I Chingola 6.53 Mpika 54 L12.3.56 Pers Bancroft Mine, NRG Info
    Dept 1.10.58 SEO 1.5.59 BH 31.12.61 d.7.10.84
YOUNG Tom A b2.12.34 A/I 6.6.57 Insp 6.6.60 D/I Lshya 62–3
YOUNGE A R b28.6.41 Cdt 20.4 A/I 28.6.61 Lshya 62 rsgnd
YOUNGE Richard Hugh CPM bMansfld Cdt 3.3.60 A/I 22.6.60 Lka 62 Sub Insp HKP 64 Supt
    79 SSupt SOHQ 15.8.86 i/c MTRDist rtd97

ZIMBA Albert Chesterfield Kitwe A/I 63 Ndola CID 63

Select Bibliography

ADAM Hargrave L – *The Police Encyclopaedia*, The Blackfriars Publishing Co, London.

ALLEN Chas (ed) – *Tales from the Dark Continent*, Andre Deutsch Ltd 1979.

BERGER Elena L – *Labour, Race and Colonial Rule, The Copperbelt from 1924 to Independence*, Oxford Studies in African Affairs, Clarendon Press 1974 ISBN 0 19 821690 4.

BRADLEY Kenneth – *Once a District Officer*, MacMillan 1966.

BRELSFORD W V (ed) – *The Story of the Northern Rhodesia Regiment*, Government Printer, Lusaka 1954 reprinted Galago Publishing Ltd Bromley 1990 ISBN 0.946995 83 4.

BRELSFORD W V – *A Generation of Men*.

BRELSFORD W V – *Lusaka, Capital City of Northern Rhodesia*, Astonian Press, Lusaka 1963.

CARTER Terence D MM – *The Northern Rhodesian Record*, Privately published by David Bell, Worthing 1992.

COLVIN Ian – *The Rise and Fall of Tshombe*, Leslie Frewin, London 1968.

CRAMER James – *The World's Police*, Cassell & Co Ltd 1964.

CROWE Br Gen J H V CB – *General Smuts' Campaign in East Africa*, John Murray 1918.

DAYAL Rajeshwar – *Mission for Hammarskold, the Congo Crisis*, Oxford University Press.

FAGAN Brian M PhD MA (ed) – *The Victoria Falls – A Handbook to the Victoria Falls, the Batoka Gorge and part of the Upper Zambezi River* (Second Edition), Commission for the Preservation of Natural and Historical Monuments and Relics, Northern Rhodesia 1964.

FRANKLYN Harry – *The Flag Wagger*, Shepheard Walwyn (Publishers) Ltd 1974.

GANN L H – *The Birth of a Plural Society, The development of Northern Rhodesia under the British South Africa Company*, Manchester University Press 1958.

GELFAND Michael – *Northern Rhodesia in the days of the Charter* Oxford 1961.

GOULDSBURY C & SHEANE H – *The Great Plateau of Northern Rhodesia*, E Arnold, London 1911.

GREEN Lawrence G – *Old Africa's Last Secrets*, Putnam & Co 1961.

GROLPETER John J – *Historical Dictionary of Zambia*, African Historical Dictionaries No.19 The Scarecross Press 1979.

HARDING Col Colin CMG – *In Remotest Barotseland*, Hurst & Blackett, London 1905.

HARDING Col Colin CMG DSO – *Far Bugles*, Simpkin Marshall, London 1933.

HARDING Col Colin CMG DSO – *Frontier Patrols, a History of the BSA Police and other Rhodesian Forces*, G Bell & son, London 1937.

HOBSON Dick – *Tales of Zambia*, The Zambia Society Trust 1996 ISBN 0 9527092 0 1.

HOLE Hugh Marshall CMG – *The Making of Rhodesia*, MacMillan 1926.

HORDERN Lt Col C – *History of the Great War based on Official Documents, Military Operations in East Africa Vol.1 August 1914–September 1916*, 1941.

HUDSON John – *A Time to Mourn, a Personal Account of the1964 Lumpa Church Revolt in Zambia* Bookworld Publishers, Lusaka ISBN 9982-24-012-9.

INGLETON Roy D – *Police of the World*, Ian Allen Ltd, London 1979.

JOHNSTON Sir Harry H KCB – *British Central Africa* Methuen 1897.

LEWIS Roy & FOY Yvonne – *The British in Africa (Social History of the British Overseas)*, Weidenfeld & Nicholson 1971.

LOCKHART J G & WOODHOUSE the Hon C M – *Rhodes*, Hodder & Stoughton 1963.

LUCAS Sir Charles KCB KCMG – *The Empire at War Vol.IV*, Oxford University Press.

MOYSE-BARTLETT Lt Col H – *The King's African Rifles; a study in the military history of East and Central Africa*, Gale and Polden 1956.

MULFORD David C – *Zambia The Politics of Independance 1957–1964*, Oxford University Press 1967.

O'BRIEN Connor Cruise – *To Katanga and Back*.

SAMPSON Richard – *So this was Lusaaka's*.

SHANKLAND Peter – *Phantom Flotilla*, Collins 1968.

SHORT Robin – *African Sunset*, Johnson, London 1973.

SILLITOE Sir Percy – *Cloak without Dagger*, Cassell 1955.

SMITH John ed Tony Bagnall Smith – *Vet in Africa, Life on the Zambezi 1913–1933*, The Radcliffe Press, London ISBN 1 86064 132 6.

STEVENSON J E *Chirupula's Tale* London 1937.

STRAGE Mark – *Cape to Cairo*.

ZAMBIA NATIONAL TOURIST BUREAU – *Zambia Travel Guide*, September 1970.

Newspapers & Periodicals:

Bulawayo Chronicle, 15 June 1935.
Northern News, Ndola 31 July 1963.
Central African Post, Lusaka 31 July & 9 October 1963.
African Life, Nairobi, January 1959.
Inside the New Africa, Portrait of the Federation of Rhodesia and Nyasaland, Voice & Vision Ltd, London.

Nkhwazi, The Magazine of the Northern Rhodesia Police, 1952–1964.

Northern Rhodesia Journal Vols I–VI, Government Printer Lusaka 1951–1963.

Nshila Government Printer Lusaka, 16 January 1962.

The Northern Rhodesia Police Association Newsletter 1967–1998.

The Police Journal, Vol.III, 1930, articles by Lt Col A Stephenson CMG DSO MC, 'Mwanalesa' p.111, 'Crime in Northern Rhodesia' p519: Feb 1965 article by D M Brockwell 'The Burton Atrocity'.

The Orders and Medals Research Society *The Miscellany of Honours* No.8 1987 article 'The BSA Police Issue of the "1914–1915 Star"' Bruce C Cazel.

The Rhodesian (and Central African) Annual 1958.

LUSAKA GOLDEN JUBILEE SOUVENIR PROGRAMME, Lusaka 1963.

Unpublished papers:

FFORDE J P I CBE KPM CPM KStJ – 'Eleven Years in Northern Rhodesia'

MESSUM Capt A L – Transcript of interview re the East African Campaign 1916–18 with W V Brelsford and copy Br Gen Northey's report 21 Nov 1916, The Liddle Collection Leeds University

NORTHEY Maj Gen Sir Edward – papers relating to the Nyasaland Rhodesia Field Force 1916–1918 in the IWM

PHILIPS Col G F CBE DSO – Diary as General Staff Officer, HQ East Africa Force 1916–18, Liddle Collection

Official Documents:

Africa South PRO CO417/276-705 Vols relating to N&SR & BSACo

'History of the Great War based on Official Documents' – Draft Chapters for unpublished Vol II – PRO CAB44/4-9 Contributions – NRP CAB45/9 Occupied Territory CAB45/18, G Parson 45/20, A J Tomlinson 45/26, diaries R E Murray 45/49–56, B K Castor 45/70

North-Eastern Rhodesia Government Gazette PRO CO 669/1

Northern Rhodesia Colonial Office Despatches 1924 PRO CO795/1–11

PRO CO/795/45002 Dress NRP

PRO CO/795/45083 Copperbelt Riots 1935

PRO CO/795/111/45237 Precautionary measures 1939

PRO CO/795/116/45109/7F Copperbelt unrest 1940

PRO CO/795/133/45369 Internment camps World War II

Northern Rhodesia Government Gazette, 1911–1928 British Library

Northern Rhodesia Annual Reports 1925–1963 PRO CO799/1–21

Northern Rhodesia Police Annual Reports 1928 and 1933–39, 1947-63 Rhodes House Library Oxford

Northern Rhodesia Report 1940–1946 IWM

Northern Rhodesia Police Handbook, Govt Printer Lusaka

'Note on the Barotse Witchcraft Murders', Criminal Investigation Department, Lusaka 18 March 1957

'Report of the Commission of Inquiry into the Lumpa Disturbances', Lusaka 1964

Report Cox 1947 National Police College Library, Bramshill
Report Dowbiggin National Police College Library
Report IG KAR 18.12.26 PRO CO795/14/18020
'Scheme of Retirement Benefits for Members of H.M.O.C.S. and for Officers Designated under the Overseas Service (Northern Rhodesia) Agreement 1961', NR Establishment Circular No.B166 dated 6 January 1964
CO 1037/28 Pol 94/3/02 1956
War Diaries East African Campaign 1914–18 PRO WO95
EAST AFRICA HQ 5289–5313
IRINGA Force
MURRAY's Column 15.4.16–29.6.16
NORFORCE 5229, 5330, 5331, 5334
NYASA-RHODESIA Frontier Force
SONGEA Force 5334
1/1 KAR 1.17
1/4 KAR 1918

Index of Persons

LANGHAM R W M NRP 120, 123, 133, 140, 148, 161
LANSDOWNE Lord 326
LAPRAIK J SRC att NRP 149
LATHAM G C NC NRP 113, 128, 135, 152
LATIMER R D N NRP 129, 136, 138, 148
LAUDER Sir Harry 14
LAW Andrew NC 20
LAW F F 195
LAWLEY Hon Arthur 40, 69n7
LAWRENCE John NRP 320
LAYNE G H NRP 252, 254, 283, 320
LEAKE R Tpr BSAP 33, 36n5
LEANEY H NRP 88
LEE Denis NRP 275
LEGGE Sgt Bechuanald P 95
LEIGHTON Eric NRP 274, 337
LELEUX Lt Belgian forces 100
LENDRUM Peter NRP 331
LENSHINA Alice, priestess 293, 339–45
LENTON E Pilot 255
LEOPOLD King of the Belgians 1, 9n4
LESLIE E J BSAP 143, 153n68
LESTER W E 'Tim' 340
LETCHWORTH F H NRP 228
LETHBRIDGE J A M Sgt BNP 52, 67
LETIA son of Lewanika 34, 38, 40
LEVERSEDGE L F DO 238
LEWANIKA 3, 6, 9n8, 33–6, 38–44, 50–6, 58–9, 7, 93, 96
LEWIS Frank R Northern Copper Co 51, 69
LINDSAY A/Insp NRP 230–1
LIVINGSTONE Charles 4
LIVINGSTONE Capt C T 14, 30n13
LIVINGSTONE David 4–6, 9n14
LOBENGULA Matabele Chief 1, 9n3, 33
LOCHNER F E 33, 36n1
LOCHNER J BSAP 128, 151n21
LOGAN Sir E R, Judge 191, 197n30
LONG J E NRP 105, 217
LOWES G R R NRP 327
LUCAS Tpr BNP 35, 42–4, 46, 48, 65
LUCHEMBE SM NRP 321–4, 326
LUGARD F D ltr Lord 1, 7, 9n21
LUMUMBA Patrice 316, 335n6
LUNAN Dr W S BSAP 35, 36–7n9
LUNGU Const NRP 324
LUNGU Jacobi, Lumpa rebel 346
LUPASHYA Sgt NRP 257
LYONS G G P NC 110, 114n28

MAAKOYI Lice murderer 272
MABUMBA Chief Ft Rosebery Dist 271
MACAULAY F C BNP 33, 38, 40–8, 65
MacDONNELL P J Judge 154, 168n1
MacGREGOR G A 'One Eye' NC 55–6, 59, 61–2, 70n44, 99
MACHISA Detective NRP 217
MacKENZIE-KENNEDY H C D C ltr Sir, NRG att NRP 150
MacKINNON Chas 15, 19–20, 31n21

MacLEOD Ian, Colonial Secretary 312–3, 321, 335n3
MacMILLAN Harold PM UK 312, 335n3
MADI Pte NRP 99
MAFULO 4109 Dvr Const NRP 331
MAGODI Chief, Lundazi Dist 332–3
MAGUIRE Capt C M Hyderabad Lancers 11, 29n3
MAHANGO Const NRP 324
MAHER T L MM SRC att NRP 149
MAKANJIRA slaver 11
MALALO Pte NRP 91 Sgt 235
MALAZANI 1185 Pte NRP 109
MALINGUKA 126 Pte NRP 110
MALIPENGA SM NRP 222
MALONI Belina GM 328–9
MAMBO 575 Cpl NRP 134, 152n45
MANAWIRI see Verrissimo
MANNING Sir W H 12, 18, 24, 29n4
MAPANZA Chief 284
MARGESSON Capt E C SWB 20, 31n31
MARIE-LOUISE Princess 186
MARITZ Gen S G SA rebel 91, 96, 113n3
MARNHAM David G H NRP 342
MARRAPODI J 83
MARRIOTT Capt T 2SAR 126, 151n26
MARSHALL H C 12–13, 30n7, 161
MARSTON L J Hotelier 84
MARTIN BNP 35, 65
MARTIN H F BSAP att NRP 113, 120
MASEA Sgt NERC 22
MASHAWILA J NRP A/Insp 83
MASHAWILA P W pte NRP ltr Detective D6 83, 190
MATAKA Michael Insp NRP 256–7, 330 ltr CofP Zambia
MATAKENYA 8
MATE Const NRP 294–5
MATLICK Col Ben USAF 327
MATHESON J F NRP 274, 292
MAUSER N German POW 145n7
MAXWELL John NRP 172, 186, 204, 212–15, 222
MAXWELL A/Insp John W GM NRP 328–9
MAY Dr Alston J W Bishop of NR 161, 19n18
MAY Dr Aylmer PMO 86
MAYBANK Frank EMWU 233–4
MAYENGO 2007 Const NRP 324
MBAU cousin of Lewanika 77
MBENJERE 623 Pte ltr Cpl NRP 77, 105
MBURUMA Nsenga chief 4, 174
McADAMS L B J SRC att NRP 149
McBRIDE E K NRP 168, 171
McCARTHY J J NRP 67, 77–9, 99, 104–5, 120, 130, 137, 158
McEWEN Brian NRP 291
McLEAN J G NRP 332
McNAMARA C J NC 59, 70n54
M'DALA Cpl 544 BNP 61
MELLAND Frank H 21, 34 n30
MERRY Jack, Volunteer NRP 105, 153n72
MESSUM A L NRP 123, 129, 148, 165, 171
MGALA Chief 35, 44

Geographical Index

Index of Organisations

INDEX OF ORGANISATIONS